THE SCHOLARSHIP OF TEACHING AND LEARNING IN HIGHER EDUCATION: AN EVIDENCE-BASED PERSPECTIVE

Part of this work has been previously published.

THE SCHOLARSHIP OF TEACHING AND LEARNING IN HIGHER EDUCATION: AN EVIDENCE-BASED PERSPECTIVE

Edited by

Raymond P. Perry
University of Manitoba, Winnipeg, Canada

John C. Smart
University of Memphis, Memphis, USA

 Springer

A C.I.P. Catalogue record for this book is available from the Library of Congress.

ISBN 978-1-4020-4944-6 (HB)
ISBN 978-1-4020-5742-7 (e-book)

Published by Springer,
P.O. Box 17, 3300 AA Dordrecht, The Netherlands.

www.springer.com

Printed on acid-free paper

We are deeply appreciative of the support received from our families and close friends who remind us that achieving important goals is best done within a framework that balances personal and professional life. I (Ray) am indebted to my wife, Judy G. Chipperfield, for fostering a creative environment for consultation and reflection, and to my son, Jason P. Perry, for reminding me of the important things in life. I (John) would like to thank my mentor, Charles F. Elton, my wife, Bunty Ethington, and my children, Dawn Farrar and David Smart.

TABLE OF CONTENTS

ACKNOWLEDGEMENTS

No undertaking such as this progresses without the support of a number of dedicated individuals. The authors of the chapters/commentaries were essential to the initiative in their enthusiastic backing in spirit and commitment. Their assiduous attention to quality work and to deadlines enabled the book to move forward with dispatch. As editor of Springer Publishers' higher education office, Tamara Welschot initiated the project, and Cathelijne van Herwaarden and Maria Jonckheere brought it to fruition. From the very beginning, Astrid Noordermeer provided invaluable assistance in guiding the project to a successful completion.

Harvey Keselman, as Head of the Department of Psychology at the University of Manitoba, was instrumental in organizing an international conference based on the book. Invited addresses by chapter authors brought state-of-the-art research on teaching and learning to the attention of over 200 researchers, classroom practitioners, academic administrators, and other policy-developers, from North America, Australia, New Zealand, Asia, Europe, and Africa, to foster the primary objective of the book, knowledge dissemination, even before the book was published.

Several others played key roles along the way, notably Robert Stupnisky and Lia Daniels, research associates at the University of Manitoba. Robert's meticulous organizational skills ensured that the editing and publishing phases moved forward successfully, and Lia's diligent attention to detail was instrumental to the success of the conference. Tara Haynes, Steve Hladkyj, Joelle Ruthig, Nancy Newall, and Audrey Swift provided able assistance along the way.

CONTRIBUTORS

PHILIP C. ABRAMI is professor, director, and research chair at the Centre for the Study of Learning and Performance, Concordia University. He is also a founding member of CanKnow: The Canadian Network for Knowledge Utilization and both the Co-Chair of the Education Coordinating Group and Steering Committee member of the International Campbell Collaboration. Phil's expertise is in educational psychology, quantitative methods, and the integration of technology into teaching. He is also interested in the use of evidence for policy and practice and the role of systematic reviews in improving education and other facets of the human sciences. He welcomes visitors to the CSLP website to learn more about his work in the area. See: http://doe.concordia.ca/cslp

ANN E. AUSTIN holds the Dr. Mildred B. Erickson Distinguished Chair in Higher, Adult, and Lifelong Education (HALE) at Michigan State University. Her research focuses on faculty careers, doctoral education, teaching and learning, and organizational change in higher education. She is a past President of the Association for the Study of Higher Education (ASHE) and is currently Co-P.I. of the Center for the Integration of Research, Teaching, and Learning (CIRTL), a National Science Foundation project to prepare future faculty in science fields.

ELISHA BABAD is Anna Lazarus Professor of Educational and Social Psychology and former Dean of the School of Education at the Hebrew University of Jerusalem. He investigated self-fulfilling Pygmalion and Golem effects in the classroom, teachers' susceptibility to bias and their differential classroom behavior, and the teachers' pet phenomenon. Recent research examines thin slices of teachers' nonverbal behavior in higher education, students' perceptions and judgments of teachers, students' decision making processes in selecting and dropping courses, and the psychological price of media bias.

CHRISTINA RHEE BONNEY recently completed her doctorate at the University of Michigan, in the Combined Program in Education and Psychology, specializing in motivation research. Specifically, her graduate work was primarily focused on the influence of achievement goals on students' and athletes' subsequent motivation and performance. Christina is currently a research associate in the Evaluation and Policy Research group at Learning Point Associates in Naperville, IL where she is involved in the development, implementation, and assessment of evaluation programs aimed at school and curricular reform, and increasing student achievement-related outcomes.

MARTIN V. COVINGTON is professor of psychology at the University of California at Berkeley. He holds the Berkeley Presidential Chair in Undergraduate Education and is a recipient of the Berkeley Distinguished Teaching Award as well as recipient of the Phi Beta Kappa Award (California district): Outstanding College Instructor of the

Year. He is a past-president of the International Society for Test Anxiety Research. His research interests include human motivation, creativity, problem solving, the fear of failure, and self-worth dynamics.

SYLVIA D'APOLLONIA is an adjunct professor at the Centre for the Study of Classroom Processes and instructor at Dawson College in Montreal, Quebec. Her research interests include postsecondary instruction (especially science education) and meta-analysis.

HELENA DEDIC is a professor in the Department of Physics at Vanier College, St. Laurent, Quebec, adjunct professor in the Department of Education and Educational Technology at Concordia University and an associate member of Centre for the Study of Learning and Performance at Concordia University. For the last fourteen years Helena's research focus has been on mathematics/science education, in particular the integration of technology into post-secondary mathematics/science classes. She is also interested in factors affecting student achievement and perseverance in mathematics/science classes, in particular the effect of student perceptions of the learning environment on motivation.

KENNETH A. FELDMAN is professor of sociology at Stony Brook University. Along with authoring a wide array of articles, he has written or edited several books, the best known of which are *The Impact of College on Students* (with Theodore Newcomb), *Teaching and Learning in the College Classroom* (with Michael Paulsen), and *Academic Disciplines* (with John Smart and Corinna Ethington). He was a consulting editor for *Journal of Higher Education* from 1974 to 1994, and has long been a consulting editor for *Research in Higher Education* (since 1982). Among his awards are two from the American Educational Research Association (Wilbert J. McKeachie Career Achievement Award of the Special Interest Group for Faculty Teaching, Evaluation and Development; Distinguished Research Award of the Postsecondary Education Division) and one from the Association for the Study of Higher Education (Research Achievement Award).

NATHAN C. HALL is a post-doctoral scholar in the Department of Psychology and Social Behavior at the University of California at Irvine. He received his B.A. degree in psychology (1999), M.A. degree in social psychology (2002), and Ph.D. in social psychology (2006) from the University of Manitoba. His research concerns the theoretical implications and real-world applications of socio-cognitive paradigms, with a specific focus on the influence of control perceptions and strategies, attributions, and metacognition in the achievement and health domains, and the development and administration of psychotherapeutic interventions for at-risk individuals.

STUART A. KARABENICK is a senior research scientist in the Combined Program in Education and Psychology at the University of Michigan and a professor of psychology at Eastern Michigan University. His research interests focus on the social and cultural aspects of motivation and self-regulation. These include achievement goal theory, help seeking, delay of gratification, and personal epistemology. Karabenick is currently Associate Editor of *Learning and Instruction*, co-editor of the *Advances in Motivation and*

Achievement series (Elsevier), and coordinator of the Motivation and Emotion special interest group of the European Association of Research on Learning and Instruction.

MICHELE MARINCOVICH, Ph.D., is Associate Vice Provost for Undergraduate Education and Director of the Center for Teaching and Learning at Stanford. At the Center since 1977, her work with faculty and TAs brought her the University's prestigious Dinkelspiel Award for Outstanding Service to Undergraduate Education in 1988. A past president of the Professional and Organizational Development (POD) Network in Higher Education, she is a frequent speaker at campuses and conferences in the U.S. and abroad. Her major publications include (with Nira Hativa) *Disciplinary Differences in Teaching and Learning: Implications for Practice* (Jossey-Bass, 1995) and *The Professional Development of Graduate Teaching Assistants* (with Jack Prostko and Fred Stout) (Anker, 1998).

HERBERT W. MARSH (PhD, DSc, Aust Acad of Soc *Sci*): Herb Marsh accepted a professorship at Oxford University in 2006 after serving as Research Professor, Dean of Graduate Research Studies, and Pro-Vice-Chancellor of Research at the University of Western Sydney. He has published more than 300 articles in 70 different journals, served on the editorial boards of 14 international journals, is one of the most productive educational psychologists, and on ISI's list of the *"world's most cited and influential scientific authors over a sustained period according to a common standard that covers all countries and all scientific disciplines"* Other international awards include the AERA McKeachie Career Achievement Award for his research in students' evaluation of university teaching.

MELISSA MCDANIELS is a doctoral candidate in higher, adult, and lifelong education (HALE) at Michigan State University. She is also a research associate in the Center for the Scholarship of Teaching in the Michigan State College of Education. Her research focuses on the professional development of faculty and scholars, assessment of teaching and learning, and the uses of multimedia to improve teaching and learning in higher education.

BILL McKEACHIE graduated from Michigan State Normal College in 1942 and served the next 3 years as a destroyer radar officer in the Pacific. He wrote his wife that if he survived (every ship in his squadron was hit by a suicide plane and his was the only one that was not sunk), he would like to go into psychology. Bill became a Teaching Fellow at the University of Michigan in 1946 and continued to teach until 2004, retiring only after a it and showed a replacement, the result of pitching fast-pitch softball for 50 years. Bill chaired the Department of Psychology at the University of Michigan in the 1960s, and later served as Director of the Center for Research on Teaching and Learning. He has written many books and articles, the best-known of which is *Teaching Tips: Strategies, Research, and Theory for College and University Teachers*, now in its 12th edition. He is Past-President of the American Association for Higher Education, the American Psychological Association, and the American Psychological Foundation. Bill received the American Psychological Foundation Gold Metal for Lifetime Contributions to Psychology in the Public Interest and the Distinguished Lifetime Contributions to Teaching and Learning in Higher Education Award from the Professional and Organizational Development Network in Higher Education.

HARRY G. MURRAY, Ph.D. 1968, University of Illinois, is Professor Emeritus in the Department of Psychology, University of Western Ontario, London, Canada. He has conducted research over the past 30 years on teacher characteristics that contribute to effectiveness in university teaching, including personality traits and classroom teaching behaviours; and on methods of evaluating and improving university teaching, including summative and formative student instructional ratings. Professor Murray has authored approximately 100 published papers on university teaching, and has won national awards for excellence in both teaching and research, including the 3M Canada Teaching Fellowship, the W. J. McKeachie career achievement award from the American Educational Research Association.

Dr. REINHARD PEKRUN is a professor of educational psychology at the Department of Psychology, University of Munich, Germany. His research interests pertain to achievement emotion and motivation, educational assessment, and the evaluation of educational systems. He has written books and edited volumes on students' personality development, and contributed actively to journals like the Journal of Educational Psychology, Learning and Instruction, and Cognition and Emotion. He is past-president of the Stress and Anxiety Research Society and has been co-editor of the German Journal of Developmental and Educational Psychology. Currently, he serves as co-editor of Anxiety, Stress and Coping: An International Journal. Being involved in the OECD's Programme for International Student Assessment, he is active in policy development and implementation, and serves on a number of committees on educational reform.

RAYMOND P. PERRY received his Ph.D. in social psychology from the University of Calgary (1971) and is professor of social psychology at the University of Manitoba. He has spent research leaves at UCLA, Stanford University, the University of British Columbia, the University of Munich, the Max Planck Institute, and the UNESCO Institute of Education (Hamburg), among others. His primary research interests include teaching and learning in higher education, academic success in college students, and faculty development. Since 1989, Perry has been an associate editor of *Higher Education: Handbook of Theory and Research*, and has served on the editorial boards of *Research in Higher Education* and the *Journal of Educational Psychology* for more than 15 years. He has received career research awards from the American Educational Research Association, the American Psychological Association, the Canadian Psychological Association, and the Canadian Society for the Study of Higher Education.

PAUL R. PINTRICH (1953–2003) was professor of education and psychology and Chair of the Combined Program in Education and Psychology at the University of Michigan, Ann Arbor. His research focused on the development of motivation and self-regulated learning in adolescence and how the classroom context shapes the trajectory of motivation and self-regulation development. He published over 100 articles and book chapters and was co-author or co-editor of eight books including a graduate level text on motivation, entitled *Motivation in Education: Theory, Research and Applications*.

R. EUGENE RICE is Senior Scholar at the Association of American Colleges and Universities and professor at Antioch University. He received his Ph.D. from Harvard University and, for much of his career, was professor of sociology and religion at the

University of the Pacific and served as Chairperson of the Department of Sociology. He also had administrative roles with the American Association for Higher Education and the Carnegie Foundation. With Ernest Boyer, Rice carried out the national study of the American professoriate, *Scholarship Reconsidered*, and is current consulting editor for the New Directions in Teaching and Learning Series published by Jossey-Bass. In *Change* magazine's survey of leadership in American higher education, he is recognized as one of a small group of "idea leaders" whose work has made a difference. Rice has also been awarded the Danforth Fellowship, the National Endowment of the Humanities Research Fellowship, the Mina Schaughnessy Scholar's Award, the Academic Leadership Award ("for exemplary contribution to American higher education") from the Council of Independent Colleges, and an honorary doctorate in humane letters from Marietta College.

STEVEN ROSENFIELD is a professor in the Department of Mathematics at Vanier College, St. Laurent, Quebec, adjunct professor in the Department of Education and Educational Technology at Concordia University and an associate member of Centre for the Study of Learning and Performance at Concordia University. For the last eighteen years Steven's research focus has been on mathematics/science education, in particular the integration of technology into post-secondary mathematics/science classes. Latterly he has also been interested in factors affecting student achievement and perseverance in mathematics/science classes, in particular the effect of student perceptions of the learning environment on motivation.

JOELLE C. RUTHIG is assistant professor of psychology at the University of North Dakota. She received her B.A. degree in psychology (1997) and M.A. (2001) and Ph.D. degrees (2004) in social psychology from the University of Manitoba. Her research mainly focuses on social cognition within the academic and health domains with a particular focus on the roles of psychosocial factors such as perceived control and optimism in achievement motivation, physical health, and psychological well-being.

BRIAN C. SIMS is an assistant professor in the psychology department at North Carolina A&T University. A graduate of Florida A&M University, He earned a Master's degree in social psychology and a doctorate in education & psychology from the University of Michigan. His research examines college student learning and motivation, as well as links between racial identity and strategy use among African American students. Sims is co-founder of THREADS, a national mentoring program for middle-school boys, and executive director of the Hip Hop Journalism Association.

JOHN C. SMART received his Ph.D. in higher education from the University of Kentucky in 1971. He is currently professor of higher education and educational research at the University of Memphis, having previously served on the faculties of Virginia Tech, University of Kentucky, and the University of Illinois at Chicago. His primary research interests are academic discipline differences in the professional attitudes and behaviors of faculty members and differential patterns of learning by college students. Smart has been Editor of the annual volumes of *Higher Education: Handbook of Theory and Research* since 1985 and *Research in Higher Education* since

1990. He is the recipient of distinguished career research awards from the American Educational Research Association (Division J, 1997), Association for Institutional Research (1998), and Association for the Study of Higher Education (2001).

MARY DEANE SORCINELLI is Associate Provost for Faculty Development and associate professor in the Department of Educational Policy, Research, and Administration at the University of Massachusetts Amherst. Her research focuses on faculty career development, teaching and learning, and faculty development in higher education. She is a past President of the Professional and Organizational Development Network (POD) in Higher Education and is currently Co-PI of a Mutual Mentoring Initiative funded by the Andrew W. Mellon Foundation.

MICHAEL THEALL received his Ph.D. from Syracuse University (1980) in instructional design, development, and evaluation, and is currently Director, Center for the Advancement of Teaching and Learning, and associate professor of education at Youngstown State University, USA. Theall has served as the director of teaching and learning centers at several universities in the U.S. His research interests include college teaching and learning, faculty evaluation and development, student ratings of teaching, the professoriate, and higher education organizational development. He has edited and/or published over 70 books, monographs, papers, and reviews and made over 100 presentations and/or conducted workshops on college teaching, faculty evaluation, teaching improvement and educational technology. In recognition of his work, Theall received the W. J. McKeachie Career Achievement Award and the Relating Research to Practice: Integrative Scholarship Award from the American Educational Research Association.

PAUL D. UMBACH is an assistant professor of higher education in the Department of Educational Policy and Leadership Studies at the University of Iowa. His research explores the effects that the organizational contexts of colleges and universities have on college students and faculty. He also studies survey research methods, particularly as they apply to college settings. His work has appeared in *Research in Higher Education, The Journal of Higher Education, The Review of Higher Education,* and the *Journal of College Student Development.*

AKANE ZUSHO is currently an assistant professor of educational psychology in the Graduate School of Education at Fordham University. She received her B.A. and M.A in psychology as well as her Ph.D. in education and psychology all from the University of Michigan, Ann Arbor. Her research focuses on examining the intersection of culture, achievement motivation, and self-regulation. The overarching goal of her research is to develop informed, less prescriptive, culturally sensitive theories of motivation and self-regulated learning that take into consideration the academic and motivational processes of urban youth from culturally-diverse backgrounds.

1. Introduction to the Scholarship of Teaching and Learning in Higher Education: An Evidence-Based Perspective

Raymond P. Perry* and John C. Smart†

*The University of Manitoba
rperry@cc.umanitoba.ca
†The University of Memphis
jsmart@memphis.edu

Abstract

This Introduction provides an overview of the book in terms of an historical framework underpinning the content of the book, the relevance of the content to stakeholders, and the structure of the chapters

Key Words: Post-secondary and Higher Education, Teaching and Learning in College Classrooms, Scholarship of teaching and learning, evaluation of college teaching, Carnegie Foundation, faculty development, faculty careers

Transformation is the lexicon of the 21st Century – from politics and economics, to travel and technology, accepted ways of doing things are undergoing momentous change. The dominant fascist régimes of the 20th Century in Germany, Italy, Japan, and more recently Russia, have acceded to democratic rule, and new totalitarian states have emerged – portending ominous and unanticipated global tensions. The economies of single countries are being superseded by international trading partnerships encompassing hundreds of millions of people and multinational businesses now have budgets larger than many developing nations. And the average traveler no longer plans a single annual vacation in the local vicinity, but looks forward to many holiday trips each year in search of exotic settings.

Nowhere is transformation more evident than the information revolution spawned by the computer and the Internet. Together, they give substance to Marshall McLuhan's "global village" in which politics, economics, travel, and other forms of international discourse

R.P. Perry and J.C. Smart (eds.), The Scholarship of Teaching and Learning in Higher Education: An Evidence-Based Perspective, 1–8.
© 2007 Springer.

unfold in the communal ambience of a village neighborhood. Social exchange no longer requires face-to-face contact; instead a cup of coffee and a computer are the requisite tools for conversing with someone thousands of miles away in a distant country. Not even McLuhan anticipated such profound changes to human discourse when beginning his career at the University of Manitoba many decades ago.

Transformation is inherent to postsecondary institutions whose basic mission is to inculcate critical thinking and advanced knowledge, implicitly linking education and change. But these institutions in themselves are undergoing radical shifts in structure and substance in organizational diversity and in the nature of academic work. At the beginning of the 20th Century, post-secondary institutions were primarily teaching and service oriented, with little in the way of a research focus. The increasing emphasis on research as a primary mission of universities, to complement teaching, was just emerging in response to the leadership of Humboldt University in Berlin. Today in the USA, over 3000 postsecondary institutions, having a multitude of organizational structures, reflect a profound transformation of both structure and substance.

In trying to account for this institutional diversity, the Carnegie Foundation developed a classification system which sorts postsecondary institutions in the USA according to mission, research funds, degree granting status, student attributes, and so on (Boyer, 1990; Rice, 1986). In Canada, Maclean's Magazine has provoked vociferous debate in response to its classification system and Statistics Canada is creating its own framework to guide government funding policies. In Germany, Der Spiegel has generated widespread public interest in its classification of specific disciplines within the institutions, rather than on the institutions in general.

Coincidental with these institutional transformations, the nature of academic work has undergone pronounced changes. Early in the 20th Century, academic work was primarily centered on teaching, with some emphasis on student advising and community involvement. By comparison, academic work in the 21st Century has greater complexity in job demands and responsibilities, mirroring parallel developments in the organizational structure of postsecondary institutions. The Carnegie Foundation describes this evolution of academic work as a transformation from the traditional model distinguishing between teaching and research that dominated much of the 20th Century to a multifaceted model of scholarship having four distinctions: the scholarship of discovery, integration, application, and teaching and learning

(Rice, 1996). This model of academic work highlights the creation, synthesis, application, and dissemination of knowledge.

This book focuses on teaching and learning with such propitious transformations in organizational structure and in academic work as a backdrop. By providing a comprehensive analysis of the underpinning theoretical and empirical literatures (synthesis), it seeks to foster the utilization of this knowledge by educational researchers, classroom instructors, academic administrators, faculty developers, and policymakers (application). Whereas the 20th Century was an era devoted to knowledge creation through research, the 21st Century is fast becoming an era dedicated to knowledge dissemination (teaching and learning). Dissemination, in turn, should greatly enhance new knowledge creation (discovery; integration) in a symbiotic process. The challenge for postsecondary institutions is to ensure that the computer and the Internet do not make them obsolete in their historical role as purveyors of knowledge.

THE SCHOLARSHIP OF TEACHING AND LEARNING

Due to greater scrutiny from stakeholders, concerns about financial solvency, and the evolution of academic work, pedagogy will be central to transforming postsecondary institutions in the 21st Century. With these momentous transformations unfolding, it becomes paramount to foster the linkage between the traditional research literature on teaching and learning processes and the Carnegie model of academic work underscoring the scholarship of teaching and learning. This book advances this linkage of these two solitudes by systematically examining the scientific evidence underpinning the scholarship of teaching and learning in terms of: the nature of effective teaching in college classrooms; the psychometric integrity of measures designed to assess teaching effectiveness (e.g., student ratings); the use of such measures for tenure, promotion, and salary decisions; and, the impact of instruction on the academic development of college students.

The necessity of making advanced research available to end-users and policymakers is paramount in view of the dramatic expansion of the postsecondary education system in the last 50 years. In Canada, for example, the number of undergraduate students has increased almost 8-fold from 1960 to 2000, from approximately 115,000 to almost 850,000 students, while Canada's population grew by less than 2-fold (Canadian Association of University Teachers, 2003; Clifton, 2000; Sokoloff, 2004). Participation rates in the U.S. postsecondary education

3

system are comparable (National Center for Educational Statistics, 2004). Similar trends are manifest in European and other developed countries. In short, there is an increasing urgency for evidence-based decision-making on practical issues related to teaching and learning to replace the experiential, anecdotal, "common sense" evidence used for decision-making in the past.

A case in point is the rising number of undergraduates leaving college prematurely and of new graduates deficient in basic numeracy and literacy skills. Participation rates in U.S. postsecondary institutions show that approximately 50% of graduating high school students enroll in college, but of these, 27% leave at the end of their first year, and fewer than 55% of those remaining graduate after five years (Desruisseaux, 1998; Geraghty, 1996). Of every 100 high school students in Grade 11, no more than 14 will graduate from college after five years. Figures for Canadian postsecondary institutions are equally disconcerting, in which typically only 55% of first-year students graduate within six years after entering their undergraduate programs.

Exacerbating these problems is that postsecondary institutions in Canada, the US, and elsewhere will replace the majority of their faculty members in the next decade due to the retirements. The departure of large numbers of faculty members will place severe strains on postsecondary institutions in recruiting and retaining new faculty members whose survival depends on mastering the complexities surrounding teaching and learning in their classrooms. Accordingly, the dissemination of research on teaching and learning to end-users and stakeholders will help new faculty members succeed in this adjustment process (Perry, 2003; Smart & Ethington, 1995).

STRUCTURE OF BOOK

The book comprises chapters by pre-eminent scholars from Australia, Canada, Europe, the Middle East, and the USA who critically assess teaching and learning issues that cut across most disciplines. In so doing, the book addresses the nexus between knowledge production by researchers and knowledge utility for end-users made up of classroom instructors, department heads, deans, directors, and policymakers. The book combines eight new chapters and seven chapters originally published in *Higher Education: A Handbook of Theory and Research* edited by John Smart (1985-present). Each chapter originally published in the Higher Education Handbook series is followed by a Commentary that provides an update of the original chapter, unless the original chapter is recent (Perry et al.; Pintrich & Zusho). The 15 chapters are divided into three sections, the *Overview* focusing on teaching and learning in the broader context of postsecondary institutions, the *Teaching* and the *Learning* sections dealing with more specific issues in turn.

In the *Overview* Section, the first three chapters of the book provide a contextual framework within which to consider teaching and learning in the evolution of academic work. In his chapter, Rice describes the evolution of academic work through the 20th Century, in which the early focus was primarily on teaching, to 21st Century Carnegie Foundation multifaceted model of academic work involving the scholarship of discovery, integration, application, and teaching and learning. Academic work is seen as transforming from a unitary model with its singular focus on pedagogy, to a dual model in which pedagogy serves a secondary role, to a multifaceted model in which pedagogy is an equal partner in scholarship. Marincovich recounts how this evolution of academic work has affected the relationship between teaching and learning in the context of a research-intensive university and the role of faculty developers and educational researchers in such a setting. Understanding these developments within the context of a research-intensive university provides unique insights into the broader nature of academic work in the future. Austin et al. present a longitudinal perspective on the scholarship teaching and learning by exploring academic work in the context of career development in junior faculty members.

In the next section on *Teaching*, seven chapters are devoted to the characteristics of effective college teaching, the assessment of teaching effectiveness, and disciplinary differences in instruction. Chapters/Commentaries by Feldman, Feldman and Theall, McKeachie, and Umbach focus on the nature of effective college instruction in terms of ubiquitous teaching methods, such as lecturing and discussion, and the implications of disciplinary differences in specifying effective instruction. Chapters/Commentaries by Abrami et al., Marsh, and Murray provide extensive empirical support for understanding what constitutes effective college teaching. Their state-of-the-art analyses systematically document the extensive psychometric evidence underpinning measures for assessing teaching effectiveness in college classrooms and how this evidence can be used in making administrative decisions concerning promotion and tenure. Finally, Babad argues that the analysis of effective college teaching is incomplete without considering the role of discrete, nonverbal teaching behaviors. He demonstrates how these subtle teaching behaviors contribute directly to effective instruction and significantly impact students' academic performance.

In the last section on *Learning*, five chapters document the role of motivation in the academic development of college students. Both Covington and Perry et al. provide an attributional analysis of motivation in which self-worth and perceived control are seen as significant motivational determinants. They argue that students' explanations for their successes and failures are primarily responsible for their self-worth and perceived control which, in turn, shape subsequent academic motivation and achievement striving. Pintrich and Zusho and Zusho et al. portray motivation in terms of goal theory wherein students' goal orientations determine achievement motivation, and subsequently, both academic help seeking and performance. In arguing that learning related emotions are fundamental to achievement settings, Pekrun provides a theoretical account of how such emotions drive motivational states, and as a consequence, are instrumental to academic performance.

INTENDED AUDIENCE

Because the research literature on postsecondary teaching and learning is voluminous and appears in a multitude of sources, it is virtually impossible for stakeholders to keep up with recent developments. The research on the evaluation of college teaching, for example, spans 80+ years and comprises thousands of studies. One key group of stakeholders, educational researchers, graduate-level instructors, and graduate students, will be interested in the comprehensive, state-of-the-art literature reviews of pivotal research topics on teaching and learning in college classrooms.

The book will also interest faculty members developing evidence-based pedagogical practices and wish to apply the material in this book to job-related teaching responsibilities. Pedagogical activities constitute the primary job responsibility for faculty members in two-year, four-year, and technological colleges, resulting in much of their academic careers being devoted to teaching and learning issues. Even in Research-intensive and Comprehensive universities, teaching is a major job responsibility for faculty members in their academic work. In short, most faculty members spend the bulk of their careers engaged in pedagogical activities that are common to most disciplines involving student learning, memory, motivation, performance, and so on. The chapters on the nature of effective teaching and the evaluation of instruction, for example, will help classroom instructors in all disciplines to use student ratings of instruction to improve their teaching effectiveness.

Another group of our users can benefit from the material in this book are academic administrators, including vice presidents, deans, directors, department heads and other policymakers responsible for instituting teaching and learning protocols. Invariably, a major part of their job duties involves policy development and implementation related to pedagogical issues, such as the evaluation of teaching, the assignment of teaching responsibilities, promotion and tenure decisions, etc. Knowledge about recent developments in effective instruction, for example, will help department heads fine-tune yearly teaching assignments by underscoring the importance of matching certain types of instructors with certain types of students and classroom settings.

Finally, faculty development officers are another constituency of practical users who can benefit from the material in this book. There job responsibility is to advise and to assist faculty members in their academic work, a major aspect being focused on teaching and learning issues. The book provides critical knowledge on teaching and learning to faculty developers that will be instrumental to advising and assisting faculty members in their job responsibilities.

REFERENCES

Boyer, E.L. (1990). *Scholarship Reconsidered: Priorities of the Professoriate.* Princeton, NJ: Carnegie Foundation for the Advancement of Teaching.

Canadian Association of University Teachers. (2003). *CAUT Almanac of post-secondary education in Canada.* Ottawa, ON: Author.

Clifton, R.A. (2000, May). *Post-secondary education in Canada: 1960 to 2000: The best years we have ever had.* Paper presented at the annual meeting of the Canadian Society for the Study of Higher Education, Edmonton, AB.

Desruisseaux, P. (1998). US trails 22 nations in high school completion. *The Chronicle of Higher Education,* December 4, A45.

Geraghty, M. (1996, July 19). More students quitting college before sophomore year, data show. *The Chronicle of Higher Education,* pp. A35–A36.

National Center for Educational Statistics. (2004, August 22). *Enrollment in Degree-granting Institutions* [On-line]. Available: http://nces.ed.gov/pubs2002/proj2012/ch_2.asp

Perry, R.P. (2003). Perceived (academic) control and causal thinking in achievement settings. *Canadian Psychologist* 44(4): 312–331.

Rice, R.E. (1986). The academic profession in transition: Toward an new social fiction. *Teaching Sociology* 14 (1)m: 12–23.

Rice, R.E. (1996). *Making A Place for the New American Scholar.* Washington, DC: American Association for Higher Education.

Rice, R.E., Sorcinelli, M.D., and Austin, A.E. (2000). Heeding new voices: Academic careers for a new generation. *New Pathways Inquiry No. 7.* Washington, DC: American Association for Higher Education.

Smart, J.C., and Ethington, C.A. (1995), Disciplinary and institutional differences in institutional goals. In N. Hativa and M. Marincovich (eds.), *Disciplinary Differences in Teaching and Learning: Implications for Practice* (New Directions for Teaching and Learning, Number 64, pp. 49–57). San Francisco: Jossey-Bass.

Sokoloff, H. (2004, March 6). Why aren't men going to university? *National Post,* p. RB1, RB2.

SECTION I: AN INTRODUCTION TO THE SCHOLARSHIP TEACHING AND LEARNING IN HIGHER EDUCATION

2. FROM ATHENS AND BERLIN TO LA: FACULTY SCHOLARSHIP AND THE CHANGING ACADEMY

R. Eugene Rice

Senior Scholar Association of American Colleges & Universities
grice@phd.antioch.edu

Abstract

This chapter traces the history of the scholarly work of faculty with special attention given to my work on the Carnegie Report *Scholarship Reconsidered: Priorities of the Professoriate* and the advances that have been made (and not) since its publication in 1990. Topics considered include the scholarship of engagement, tensions between the collegial culture and the managerial culture, and the need to develop a change strategy that is transformative and not just a continuation of the incremental approach. How we build on the scholarly strengths of our pasts, symbolically represented by Athens and Berlin, while organizing in new ways for a diverse, growing, transnational world represented in the challenges of LA is at the heart of this analysis

Key Words: Scholarly Work; Carnegie Foundation Report; Scholarship of Teaching and Learning; Scholarship of Engagement

In searching for an image that would best catch the future role of faculty in a changing, vibrant democracy, I—following the lead of Ralph Waldo Emerson—have often referred to "the new American scholar." (1996) That vision now has lost its resonance; the image has been seriously tarnished in the new global environment and become restricting. In probing for an alterative I have turned to Los Angeles, not because LA is an American city, but because it is an international— a transnational—city. LA is, as the University of Southern California boasts on its Web page, a "global city, the city of the future of the planet." One visit and you are struck by the rich, pulsating diversity— a stimulating cultural mosaic. But LA is also the template for unplanned, sprawling, privatized growth; it is denigrated as the city with the largest number of backyard swimming pools and the smallest

R.P. Perry and J.C. Smart (eds.), The Scholarship of Teaching and Learning in Higher Education: An Evidence-Based Perspective, 11–21.
© 2007 *Springer.*

11

number of public parks. A city on the verge of gridlock, the City of Angels is the place to encounter examples of the world's best music, art, and architecture. LA represents the kind of dramatic change and promise the academy of the future will be called upon to address and serve.

In examining the role of faculty in the new academy, I want to underscore the significance of the changes taking place. Faculty, particularly, are prone to dismiss the changes they see coming as cyclical—"we've seen that before"—and minimize their impact. I then want to address our approach to change. The additive or incremental approach to reform will no longer suffice; a more transformative way of thinking about faculty work is required. It is important to build on the strengths of our past—symbolized here by references to the contributions of Athens and Berlin—while simultaneously exploring new ways to organize faculty work for the future—symbolized by LA.

APPROACHES TO CHANGE

Following World War II, and particularly during the expansionist years of the 1960s, the major changes made in higher education in the United States were genuinely transformative. The California Master Plan under the leadership of Clark Kerr is one example of such comprehensive, holistic change. The explosive growth in community colleges across the country is another.

In my own experience, I went directly from graduate work at Harvard in 1964 to participate in the founding of Raymond College, an experimental college at the University of the Pacific. Those were exciting, heady times. Cluster colleges, as they were called, were erected from the ground up. They were living–learning communities in the fullest sense. Raymond College was intentionally patterned after Oxford and Cambridge: students graduated in three years; a complete liberal arts curriculum was required (one-third humanities, one-third social sciences, one-third math and natural sciences); there were no majors; and narrative evaluations were used instead of letter grades.

While approaching change in a transformative way, the experimental colleges of the 1960s were, by and large, counterrevolutionary. They came into being in opposition to the dominance of the large research-oriented universities. What they were opposed to was the rise of an academic hegemony dominated by an increasingly professionalized, research-oriented, discipline-driven, specialized faculty. The counter-vision was a more intimate, democratic, student-oriented learning community. These institutions—365 by one count—were decidedly utopian and often naive in their assumptions. They took on an academic juggernaut of enormous proportions and, in doing so, often met with defeat. Nonetheless, these experimental institutions launched the movement from teaching to learning that continues to have an impact on the academic environment and, particularly, the role of faculty.

The faculty who participated in the launching of the experimental colleges in the 1960s were part of a much larger cohort—a group of early-career faculty who shared a vision for higher education. They saw themselves not as independent scholars bent on hustling a burgeoning academic market—and there were jobs and opportunities aplenty—but as contributors to the building of institutions that would shape the future of higher education in the society. For their associational life, these faculty were attracted not as much to their disciplinary associations as to what was then the Association of American Colleges and the American Association for Higher Education. Many of these same people provided the leadership, ideas, and energy that drove the undergraduate education reform movements of subsequent decades.

In the 1970s, the approach to change shifted from building whole new institutions to reforming what was already in place. The movements to reform undergraduate education that were launched in the last three decades of the twentieth century were creative, energetic, and initiated in response to serious needs. They were, however, added on at the margins and, in most places, conceptualized and organized to be institutionally peripheral. Every one of these initiatives was important and contributed something significant, beginning with faculty development and followed by the assessment movement, service learning, learning communities, technologically enhanced instruction, problem-based learning, diversity programs, and community-based research. In each case, the reform effort was usually sustained at the margins of the institution and, therefore, created serious problems for faculty—especially the junior faculty most excited about participating in the change initiative.

In only a few places have these important reforms been integrated into the central mission of the institution, structured into the reward system, and built into the life of the departments regarded by most faculty as their institutional home. The additive approach has been utilized so often that, for some faculty, the term "reform" has been sullied; it is viewed as another task being imposed by the provost or dean. For that cohort of faculty involved in the experimental colleges of the 1960s, being involved in more holistic changes provided the excitement and the challenge of being in higher education. The more recent approach to change has made innovative reform initiatives distractions from what is perceived as central and genuinely valued in a professional career.

ATHENS

Mihaly Csiksentmihalyi recently asked students from six leading liberal arts colleges to rank, first, their own educational goals and, second, their perceptions of the goals of their institutions. The students reported that their primary goal in attending college was "learning to find happiness." Of seventeen items, the goal ranked at the bottom was "a broad liberal arts education." At the same time, when asked about their perceptions of the goals of their institutions, the students put "a broad liberal arts education" at or near the top. What is striking is that these students saw no connection between "learning to find happiness" and a "broad liberal arts education."

For the ancient Athenian philosophers to whom we look for much of our understanding of what we regard as quality education, the connection between liberal education and "learning to find happiness" was central. This was particularly true for Aristotle. For Aristotle—and later for Thomas Jefferson who used Aristotle's phrase "the pursuit of happiness" in this nation's Declaration of independence—happiness had a much broader meaning than it has now. In fairness to the students interviewed as part of Csiksentmihalyi's study, we need to acknowledge that the meaning of the term happiness has been allowed to degenerate into a subjective feeling of momentary pleasure. Happiness was, for the ancient Athenian philosophers, the highest good (*eudaimonia*); it was the deep sense of satisfaction that comes with the development of our uniquely human capacities. Happiness, for Aristotle, meant "a complete life led in accordance with virtue"; "the highest of all goods achievable by action"; "the supreme end to which we aspire." All of these meanings are congruent with the most fundamental purposes of a liberal education, yet as Csikszentmihalyi's student interviews indicate, we obviously have failed to make the connection.

In *Orators and Philosophers: A History of the Idea of Liberal Education* (1986), Bruce Kimball argues that out of ancient Athens came two traditions that shape the work of faculty in liberal education. The first is the tradition of the philosophers, which holds that the pursuit of knowledge is the highest good (Socrates and Plato). The

14

second focuses on the development of character and the building of community through the cultivation of leadership (Cicero). These two traditions persist today and, presently, divide faculty committed to taking the liberal arts seriously.

I recently participated in a Wingspread conference on "Religion and Public Life: Engaging Higher Education." We began with research from the Higher Education Research Institute at the University of California–Los Angeles, which shows that a large percentage of students want to address questions of meaning and purpose, but also that students perceive that faculty are hesitant to engage larger religious and spiritual questions. In the subsequent discussion, the classical division between the philosophers and orators surfaced.

Thoughtful religious studies faculty argued that the key function of the professor is the pursuit of knowledge, and the cultivation of the skills that requires, unencumbered with responsibilities for character development and civic engagement. They argued persuasively that the new breed of "change agents" ought to leave them free to pursue their subject matter, that the open discussion of carefully chosen texts will raise the larger questions of meaning. As examples, they cited Saul Bellow's *Seize the Day*, Augustine's *Confessions*, and Toni Morrison's *Beloved*. As one professor put it, "we don't want to be therapists or community organizers."

On the other side, equally persuasive faculty contended that the professoriate needs to be attentive to what we are learning about learning, student development, and the power of actively engaged learning. They invoked the responsibilities of higher education in a diverse democracy. The two major thrusts of faculty work in liberal education—and their conflicts—were fully evident in this recent discussion. Much of our understanding of liberal education and the role of faculty continues to be solidly rooted in the scholarly traditions of ancient Athens.

BERLIN

The second city that fundamentally shaped our understanding of faculty work is Berlin. Toward the latter part of the nineteenth century, a radically new approach to scholarship was imported from Germany and profoundly influenced the conception of the faculty role in the new American university. The understanding of what was to be regarded as scholarly work narrowed and began to be defined as specialized, discipline-based research. With the conceptual shift came a new organizational structure of graduate education with its research laboratories and specialized seminars. Newly organized disciplines and departments began to assume a dominant place in the new research universities. A powerful vision of the priorities of the professoriate began to take hold, one that has gathered strength and demonstrated enormous resilience over the years.

This vision was articulated best by Max Weber in a lecture entitled "Science as a Vocation," which he delivered in 1918 at the University of Munich. Weber spoke of the "inner desire" that drives the scholar to the cutting edge of a field, and talked eloquently about the "ecstasy" that comes only to the specialist on the frontiers of knowledge engaging in advanced research. The assumption was that if the passion for research were pursued wholeheartedly, the quality of teaching and what we now call service would fall into place. The moral obligation of the teacher was, for Weber, "to ask inconvenient questions."

After the Soviet Union launched Sputnik in 1957 and the Cold War began to heat up, the infusion of federal funding for scientific research further constricted the dominant understanding of scholarly work. With the rapid expansion and affluence of colleges and universities during what is often referred to as the heyday of American higher education, a consensus emerged to form what I have described elsewhere as "the assumptive world of the academic professional" (1986). The central tenets of that dominant professional image were the focus on research; the preservation of quality through peer review and the maintenance of professional autonomy; the pursuit of knowledge through the discipline; establishing reputations through international professional associations; and the accentuation of one's specialization.

The consensus that formed around this set of values and commitments is still solidly engrained in graduate education and continues to shape the socialization of the new generations of faculty. At tenure and promotion time in much of higher education—and particularly in the most prestigious institutions—this assumptive world continues to be normative. It becomes particularly dominant when professional mobility emerges as a possibility, as is happening now in many fields. During the last three decades of the twentieth century, tremendous energy and extensive resources were poured into cultivating new priorities for faculty, and imaginative reform initiatives were launched across higher education. But the new efforts to reform undergraduate education were introduced on the margins of institutions—to be added onto what faculty were already doing.

16

A major study of faculty just launching their careers found that many are overwhelmed (2000). These early-career faculty are caught between the times; they have to meet the demands of the research-oriented "assumptive world," while also responding to the attractions and demands of the new reform agenda. Junior faculty consistently reported having to cope with what they regarded as "over-flowing plates." As higher education begins to take seriously the demands for change in undergraduate education, early-career faculty are feeling extraordinary pressure and are beginning to question whether the career that has evolved is even viable. Questions are being raised about whether the best of a new generation can be attracted into the profession. We can no longer pursue an add-on approach to the changing faculty role; something more comprehensive is required.

LOS ANGELES

While these changes in the academic profession and on campuses are taking place, the larger context within which faculty conduct their work is undergoing a major transformation. This brings us to the third city, Los Angeles. Kingsley Davis (1973) made a career of reminding us that "demography is destiny." LA represents in a dramatic way the size and the complexity of the changes with which we have to grapple.

The sheer demographic pressures on higher education are startling—new students, new immigrant communities, new demands. The rich diversity found in places like the LA basin is emerging not only as a difficult challenge, but also as an opportunity. It is an educational value and a catalyst. Moreover, the majority of the nation's students are first-generation learners. How do we prepare faculty to build on the vision of academic excellence? How do faculty prepare students for life in an inclusive democracy?

At the same time, we have moved into a global century. We are interdependent, whether we like it or not. To succeed in the twenty-first-century environment, graduates will need to be intellectually resilient, cross-culturally literate, technologically adept, and fully prepared for a future of continuous and cross-disciplinary learning. And yet, as Cliff Adelman has demonstrated (1999), less than 10 percent of today's four-year graduates leave college globally prepared. What does all of this mean for faculty preparation?

The new context requires a rethinking of faculty work. The growth of non-tenured, full-time positions, the uses of adjunct faculty, and the demographic shifts in non-tenured faculty—more female, diverse, and older—are the result of arbitrary, expedient, short-term decisions rather than thoughtful planning for a radically different future. The current generational change in the make-up of the American professoriate provides an extraordinary opportunity. We need to make sure that the changes are carefully planned and make for a coherent whole.

We already have shifted the focus from faculty to learning. Shaping an academic staff to prepare students for participation in an interdependent global community where innovation is vital for success presents a different kind of challenge.

Getting faculty to change the way they think about their work—moving from an individualistic approach ("my work") to a more collaborative approach ("our work")—is a critical transition that challenges deeply rooted professional assumptions. Related to this is the call for "unbundling" the faculty role. I've resisted this development in the interest of the "complete scholar," a concept that values continuity and coherence, but I am losing the argument. What is already being called for are new "networks for learning" that will reach across academic staff and into the larger community. New forms of reintegrating what we have known in the past as faculty work will need to be developed.

Over the past several years, a tension has emerged between the established "collegial culture" among faculty and a growing "managerial culture" in our colleges and universities. Each culture is driven by an economy that exerts enormous power; on the collegial side is the prestige economy, and on the managerial side is the market economy. Rethinking faculty work and structuring academic work in a way that best serves a dynamic and responsive new academy will require addressing this tension and moving toward a more collaborative culture. The overpowering influences of both the prestige economy and the market economy must be superceded by a primary commitment to the kind of learning required for a knowledge-driven, interdependent, global world.

THE FUTURE OF SCHOLARSHIP

As it is evolving, the broader conception of scholarship provides an opportunity to rethink the scholarly work of faculty in a way that is genuinely transformative and begins to address the scholarly needs of the LAs of the world. AAC&U's "Principles of Excellence for Student Learning in College" contends "narrow learning is not enough." I want to agree and add a necessary corollary: narrow scholarship is not enough. The scholarship of discovery is essential for a diverse and inter-dependent global community, but it is not enough. The scholarship of integration is required to sustain liberal learning. Thanks to the energetic leadership of the Carnegie Foundation for the Advancement of Teaching, the scholarship of teaching and learning is now well established and is receiving widespread international attention.

The scholarship of engagement, which is only beginning to attract the attention it deserves, will require the greatest change in our thinking about what counts as scholarship. In the future, the walls of the academy will become increasingly permeable. Academics on the inside will be moving out into the larger world, and many on the outside will be moving in. There is serious concern about college and university faculty becoming disengaged, particularly at a time when knowledge creation is at the heart of economic development. Civic engagement and social responsibility can hardly be expected of the students of the future if faculty are not themselves engaged and responsible in their scholarly work.

In order for this form of scholarship to be taken seriously, the role of the scholar must change significantly. This will require a shift in our basic epistemological assumptions. No longer can we speak of the application of knowledge and assume that faculty in the university will generate new knowledge and apply it to the external world. Our under-standing of who constitute peers for the peer review process will have to be reevaluated. The relationship between cosmopolitan knowledge and local knowledge will have to be reconsidered. Community-based research and the role of the public scholar will have to be viewed in a new light. We can no longer avoid honoring the wisdom of practice.

Ironically, in thinking about the scholarly work of faculty in this very programmatic, instrumental society, practice has been widely ignored, if not denigrated. Only recently, in reading the reflections of the Beat poet Gary Snyder (1990) on the power of meditative practice in the Buddhist tradition have I come to a fuller appreciation of practice. He writes: "Practice is the path.... Practice puts you out there where the unknown happens, where you encounter surprise." As colleges and universities struggle to take seriously the intellectual and social needs of the LA's of this world we must be more open to the "surprise" that comes with practical engagement in this new global, diverse, interdependent context.

The argument I have set forth about the future of faculty work is strengthened significantly by the empirical research on teaching and learning in higher education described in the chapters of this book.

The conceptual framework for which I have tried to make a case and the empirical evidence being advanced by the research found in what follows here—examples of some of the best work being done in the scholarship of teaching and learning—build on one another in setting forth the beginnings of a coherent approach to change in higher education that is evidence-based.

Reprinted with permission from Liberal Education, Fall 2006. Copyright 2006 by the Association of American Colleges and Universities.

REFERENCES

Adelman, C. (1999). *Answers in the Tool Box: Academic Intensity, Attendance Patterns, and Bachelor's Degree Attainment.* Washington, DC: U.S. Department of Education.

Aristotle. (1925). In W.D. Ross (ed.), *Aristotle's Nicomachean Ethics* from J. O'Toole, *Creating the Good Life.* New York: Holtzbrinck Publishers (2005).

Astin, A. (2004).Why Spirituality Deserves a Central Place in Liberal Education. Liberal Education, Vol. 90.

Csiksentmihalyi, M. (2005). Presentation at the annual meeting of the New England Association of Schools and Colleges, Boston.

Davis, K. (1973). *Cities: Their Origin, Growth and Human Impact.* New York: W.H. Freeman

Kimball, B. (1986). *Orators and Philosophers: A History of the Idea of Liberal Education.* New York: Columbia University Press.

Rice, R.E. (1986). The academic profession in transition: Toward an new social fiction. *Teaching Sociology* 14 (1)m: 12–23.

Rice, R.E. (1991). "The new American scholar: Scholarship and the purposes of the university", in *Metropolitan Universities* 1: 7–18.

Rice, R.E., Sorcinelli, M., and Austin, A. (2000). *Heeding New Voices: Academic Careers for A New Generation.* Washington, DC: American Association for Higher Education.

Snyder, G. (1990). *The Practice of the Wild.* San Francisco, CA: North Point Press.

Weber, M. (1918). Science as a vocation. In H.H. Gerth and C. Wright Mills (Translated and edited), *From Max Weber: Essays in Sociology* (pp. 129–156). New York: Oxford University Press, 1946.

3. Teaching and Learning in a Research-Intensive University

Michele Marincovich

Stanford University
marin@stanford.edu

Abstract

My perspective in this chapter is that of a practitioner, the director of a teaching and learning center for twenty-five plus years, who has been using the insights of educational researchers to enrich teaching and learning on my own research-intensive campus, Stanford, and at other universities. I assert that teaching—and therefore the relationship between teaching and research—has been redefined on my campus and that teaching is being taken seriously as never before. As a result, educational researchers have extraordinary opportunities for practical implementation of their work, especially if such researchers and we practitioners collaborate, and we all remain fully sensitive to the special culture of faculty at research universities

Key Words: Commission on Undergraduate Education; Educational research/ers; Faculty Development; Interdisciplinarity; Research-intensive universities; Scholarship of teaching and learning; Stanford University; TA development; TA training; Teaching and learning centers; Teaching and research; Undergraduate education; Undergraduate research

This chapter will be rather different from most others in this volume because it is written by a practitioner, the director of a teaching and learning center for twenty-five plus years. What I hope to offer is the experience of someone who has been trying to use the insights of educational researchers to enrich teaching and learning on my own research-intensive campus, Stanford, and at other universities where I have spoken or consulted. To anticipate my argument, I will be asserting that teaching—and therefore the relationship between teaching and research—has been redefined at many research-intensive universities, including Stanford, and that teaching is being taken seriously as never

R.P. Perry and J.C. Smart (eds.), The Scholarship of Teaching and Learning in Higher Education: An Evidence-Based Perspective, 23–37.
© 2007 *Springer.*

before. As a result, educational researchers have extraordinary opportunities for practical implementation of their work, especially if such researchers and we practitioners collaborate, and we all remain fully sensitive to the special culture of faculty at research universities.

My credentials for these thoughts are in part simply those of a survivor—when I started at Stanford's Center for Teaching and Learning in 1977, on a 10-month appointment, there were three of us working half-time, with little real confidence that we would ever work directly with our research-driven faculty on teaching. In 2006 there are now 14 of us full-time at the Center, and each year we come in contact with 200 or more of our still research-driven faculty who are nonetheless showing a deep and impressive commitment to their teaching responsibilities. (As I wrote that last sentence, I realized that it had been many years since I'd heard a faculty member at Stanford refer to their classes as their "teaching load.") But these thoughts also reflect not only my own ideas but also the wisdom of my colleagues at the Center for Teaching and Learning, especially our three associate directors, Robyn Wright Dunbar, Marcelo Clerici-Arias, and Mariatte Denman.

GROWING EMPHASIS ON TEACHING AT STANFORD AND OTHER RESEARCH UNIVERSITIES

Let me start with a little historical background on the teaching/research relationship—since I was originally trained as an historian and still believe in the absolute necessity of an historical perspective on almost every issue—the year 1990, to be exact. At that time, our Center was 15 years old and had a small stream of faculty, perhaps 25–50/year, with whom we worked. That April, Stanford's then president, Donald Kennedy, a biologist and an outstanding teacher in his own right, gave a particularly stirring presentation to the faculty Academic Council. As he explained (1997) later in his thoughtful and insightful book, *Academic Duty*, he had felt that it was time to send clear institutional signals regarding the teaching expectations Stanford had of the faculty. In his profoundly moral view of the university's purpose, "responsibility to students is at the very core of the university's mission and of the faculty's academic duty" (p. 59). His speech vividly and passionately made a case for the importance of faculty teaching:

> I believe we can have superb research and superb teaching too; and
> in support of that proposition I offer the example of departments,

programs, and countless individual colleagues who have excelled at both. We need to talk about teaching more, respect and reward those who do it well, and make it first among our labors. It should be our labor of love, and the *personal* [his emphasis] responsibility of each one of us. (1990, p. 11)

The talk drew national attention—even more, apparently, than Kennedy (1997) himself had anticipated—and was followed a year later by the announcement of significant funds—$7,000,000 from Stanford Trustee Peter Bing and his wife, Helen, as well as smaller gifts from several different sources—that had been successfully raised to reward teaching and support pedagogical innovation (*Campus Report*, 1991). The initiatives included: the Bing Professorships and Fellowships (now exhausted), which conferred a considerable monetary award as well as prestige on faculty chosen annually on the basis of outstanding teaching; other faculty raises granted on the basis of teaching excellence; competitive grants of up to several thousand dollars for faculty who proposed promising teaching innovations and improvements; expanded opportunities for undergraduates to pursue independent research under faculty guidance; $3,500 salary supplements for faculty teaching Peters Seminars (now called the Freshmen and Sophomore Seminars) or small classes of eight to ten sophomores on a topic of the faculty member's research; and $1,000 salary supplements to faculty who taught dialogue tutorials (no longer offered), courses with just two to four sophomores on topics related to the faculty member's research. Although Kennedy left the presidency in 1992, just a year after these initiatives were announced, his successor, President Gerhard Casper, continued the emphasis on teaching and, as we shall see, set in motion a renaissance in undergraduate education.

I was thrilled with the new vision President Kennedy had proposed for faculty work at Stanford—that successful faculty would be those who could do both research and teaching at the highest levels. I was even more thrilled when I realized that not only on my campus but at a whole series of research-intensive universities, developments very favorable to teaching were taking place. I gave a series of talks in the early 1990s (Marincovich, 1990, 1991, 1992a, 1992b), both in the U.S. and abroad, on this theme mentioning such developments as:

At the University of Michigan: "In August of 1990 a faculty committee issued a 123-page plan for changes in undergraduate teaching, including an undergraduate college for freshmen and sophomores where courses would be taught by senior faculty members" (Grassmuck, 1990, p. A31).

25

At the University of California, Berkeley: Berkeley's Board of Regents was reported to have "...revamped the faculty reward system to require that teaching and service be given greater consideration in evaluating and promoting professors" ("U. of California to stress teaching and service," 1992, p. A5). The same article went on to report "The standards used for promoting faculty members to higher salary levels within the rank of full professor also have been modified. In the past promotion to the higher levels required national or international distinction in research. Now such distinction can be in teaching or research."

At Harvard, Professor Richard Light of the Graduate School of Education and the Kennedy School of Government led a major effort, the Harvard Assessment Seminars, to study ways to improve teaching and student learning at Harvard and elsewhere. A hundred faculty members, as well as many administrators, were involved (Light, 1990, 1992).

At Syracuse University: In 1990–91 researchers there surveyed faculty and administrators at 47 research universities all over the United States. The survey indicated that even in research institutions of the first rank, where faculty believed research should hold an upper hand over teaching, faculty still felt that the emphasis on research was currently too great and needed to be modified. The Syracuse researchers summarized their findings thus: "Perhaps one of the best kept secrets in higher education is that most faculty *and* administrators at research universities disagree with the present emphasis on research as opposed to teaching" (Gray, Froh, & Diamand, 1991, p. 2).

RHETORIC OR SUBSTANCE?

Did all these efforts at Stanford, and elsewhere, have an effect? Or, as some of my colleagues at other research universities less kindly put it at the time—was the talk of more emphasis on teaching just rhetoric, or would it lead to real changes? At Stanford the answer was a definite yes. Judging by the use of the services of my office, more faculty were aware of and concerned about their teaching responsibilities. Demand for teaching consultations went up enough that in 1999 our Center was able to add an associate director and, for the first time, hire someone with a science Ph.D. and research university science teaching experience for this new position. Just two years later we were funded to add a third associate director, with a background in economics, to work with faculty and TAs in the social sciences and technology. There was also enthusiastic participation in the teaching awards, teaching grants, and the new small seminar programs that followed in the years after President Kennedy's remarks.

As far as the situation on other campuses was concerned, some of the most encouraging data came from a 1996 resurvey by Syracuse University of 11 of the institutions reported on in the 1990–91 report.

"In the 1991 survey, when asked whether their institutions favored research, teaching, or a balance between the two, 73 per cent of the faculty respondents reported that the emphasis was on scholarship. In the follow-up study, conducted in 1996, that proportion fell to 49 per cent. Similar shifts were apparent when the same question was posed to department heads, academic deans, and other administrators" (Magner, 1998, p. A16).

Let me continue by quoting a particularly important passage: "The 'most pronounced' shift in attitudes toward teaching came from academic deans... In 1991, 45 per cent of them said their institutions should emphasize research, 20 per cent preferred teaching, and 35 per cent favored a balance between the two. In the new survey, only 17 per cent felt that their institutions should emphasize research, 34 per cent said teaching, and 50 per cent said the two duties should be balanced" (Magner, 1998, p. A16).

In Stanford's case not only did President Kennedy's successor, Gerhard Casper, keep up the emphasis on the importance of teaching, he also implemented a comprehensive program to reinvigorate under-graduate education that would depend for its success on the faculty's serious commitment to teaching. In 1993 he started this process with the appointment of a Commission on Undergraduate Education, composed mostly of faculty. A year later, the Commission had produced a highly influential report (1994). Although Kennedy and Casper were in many ways very different men, they shared a broad view of the role of universities in American society, a sensitivity to public critiques that universities neglected undergraduate students, and a strong commitment to faculty's duty to students. In some sense, under Casper, the university staked its reputation on institutionalizing a first-rate course of study for undergraduates delivered predominantly by faculty who would also be expected to continue to produce world-class research.

In 1997, just three years after receiving the Commission's report, Casper proudly noted that it took less than a year to line up 50 seminars in a new program (Stanford Introductory Studies) that would allow at least half of the freshman class entering Stanford that year to have a small class experience with a faculty member (1997). Since the administration realized that it would take numerous carrots for the faculty and significant funding to fully implement and institutionalize the reinvigoration of undergraduate education, President Casper's successor, John Hennessy, launched the first American billion-dollar campaign for undergraduate education. Between 2000–2005, he supervised a fund-raising effort that exceeded the official goal of $1 billion.

TEACHING REDEFINED

What came out of those years—a change I would argue was more important than the amount of money raised—was, as I foreshadowed, a redefinition of teaching and its relationship with research. Research and teaching were no longer two distinct and often competing responsibilities that professors had to find a way to balance. Instead, they were coming together synergistically. President Casper called them two sides of the same coin, not existing in opposition but in completion of one another. ("Casper: On Teaching, research, finances, multiculturalism," 1992, p. 13.) It wasn't that our faculty had signed onto Ernie Boyer's (1990) vision of the different kinds of scholarship, one of which is the scholarship of teaching. We still rare usely the words "scholarship of teaching and learning" on our campus. But in their everyday working lives, our faculty now experienced their teaching and research responsibilities as increasingly seamless.

Let me give some examples. One of many significant changes in undergraduate education that Stanford made in the mid- to late 1990s was to enormously increase the opportunities for our undergraduates to do research, usually starting by helping faculty with their research and then moving on to research of the undergraduates' own design. We went from roughly 350 undergraduates doing university-funded research per year before the changes to 1,350 doing research currently (S. Brubaker-Cole, personal communication, March 29, 2006)—almost a four-fold increase. Faculty discovered that these student researchers could be enormously helpful to them in the present as well as potentially wonderful future colleagues. But when a faculty member is directing these young researchers, is that teaching or research? And if a professor's teaching ability attracts young researchers to work with her, is that not a further example of teaching and research productively reinforcing each other? And if a professor is in the sciences and has a well-functioning team of postdocs, graduate students, and undergraduates working for her, and if some of the graduate students also TA for

28

her and if colleagues on other campuses who used to be her graduate students or TAs send her wonderful students, is that all a result of her research or her teaching? As you can see, it's become very difficult to tell them apart. Many of our faculty don't even try any more. Their research and their teaching have become indistinguishable.

In addition, we are finding that the new, incoming faculty both expect and seem to welcome that teaching will be a large and important part of their career success. Although we have reached out to new faculty for years, many more of them now attend our workshops, use our midterm evaluation services, or ask for other consulting resources from us. Our largest School, the School of Humanities and Sciences, even asked us if they could *require* all new faculty to use us. Happy as we were with this vote of confidence, we asked that the School instead *recommend* us as one item in a menu of support for new faculty, so that if new professors do choose to work with us, they will have the mind set of having chosen our help, rather than of having had it thrust upon them.

And even if we still aren't using the vocabulary of the scholarship of teaching and learning on our campus, we are beginning to see at Stanford and other research universities examples of faculty who are forging successful careers based on their commitment to teaching in its new, broader definition. In our Mechanical Engineering Department, for example, Professor Sheri Sheppard was promoted to full professor in 2005 on the basis of her national and international leadership in engineering education. Originally a specialist in weld fatigue and impact failures, she made her promotion case on the basis of her careful and extensive studies on how engineering students learn to be effective engineers. At the University of Michigan Chemistry Department, we see Professor Brian Coppola—who was recently invited to speak to Stanford's Chemistry faculty and graduate students by the department—making a successful career out of his work on chemistry education. (For more on Professors Sheppard and Coppola and others, see Huber, 2004). I predict that we will see more and more faculty at leading research universities choosing this path to their professional success.

Even faculty at Stanford who don't stake their professional reputation on their "educational" role find that teaching and the documentation of their teaching ability at the time of consideration for tenure or promotion have grown hugely more important. The papers on any candidate up for appointment or promotion have grown much more elaborate in general but especially in the area of teaching. It used to be that one had to have world-class research credentials and good teaching. The actual language in the appointment papers now specifies:

> "Teaching is an important component of professorial appointments at Stanford, and the University is dedicated to outstanding achievement in this area. The teaching record must clearly reveal that a candidate is capable of sustaining a first-rate teaching program during his or her career at Stanford. Teaching is broadly defined to include the classroom, studio, laboratory, or clinical setting, advising, mentoring, program building, and curricular innovation. The teaching record should include, as appropriate, undergraduate, graduate, and postdoctoral instruction, of all types." (*Stanford University Faculty Handbook*, 2001, p. 13)

In February of 2006, the University of Michigan Center for Research on Teaching and Learning surveyed 26 leading research universities (largely Big 10 and Ivy Plus institutions) on the question of whether one of 10 different teaching evaluation methods was mandated by the provost for university-wide use in tenure and promotion decisions. All but two of the universities reported the required use of some teaching evaluation method at the high-stakes decision-making time of tenure and promotion. (For more details on this survey, contact Constance "Connie" Cook, director of the Michigan Center for Research on Teaching and Learning at cecook@umich.edu.)

FUTURE DEVELOPMENTS

Now I hope I've made a case for a new definition of teaching at Stanford and other American research universities and of its greater professional importance. Let me turn next to the implications these changes have for educational researchers and for teaching and learning centers.

The first argument I would offer is that these changes present unprecedented opportunities for both these groups and that we should collaborate in taking advantage of them. Educational researchers who do not have working relationships with teaching centers should develop them and vice versa. Before their retirements from Stanford's School of Education, both N. L. Gage (1978; Gage & Berliner, 1998) and Lee Shulman (1986, 1987, 1989), authors of pivotal works in the improvement and evaluation of teaching, generously provided informal consulting and advice to our Center for Teaching and Learning; we in turn sought their wisdom on difficult faculty cases and on "white papers" or other memos we were asked to produce for deans or chairs. When Gage and Shulman each chaired university committees on teaching, they both invited my participation as a committee member and were attentive to roles the Center could play in the implementation of the committee's recommendations. Other centers have benefited from the appointment of educational researchers to their staff, such as the role Dr. Raymond Perry played for several years at the University of Manitoba's teaching center.

Secondly, although interdisciplinarity has also become extremely important on our campus, I would argue that the way to faculty hearts and minds is still through their disciplines. For teaching centers, this means that our very organization should, ideally, reflect an appreciation of the disciplines (Hativa and Marincovich, 1995). At our Stanford Center, as soon as we could secure the necessary funding, we put in place three associate directors—one for science and engineering, one for the social sciences, and one for humanities—who do the bulk of our faculty consulting and TA development work. The response from our faculty has been enormously positive. Within three years of hiring someone for the sciences and engineering, for example, our requests from those areas had more than doubled, we had a monthly teaching discussion group for junior faculty in science and engineering, and there were TA programs in almost every department.

One of the responsibilities of these associate directors is to stay in touch with research on the teaching of disciplines in her/his area and to share that with faculty. Our senior associate director for science and engineering has found ready audiences for such works as the National Research Council's *Science Teaching Reconsidered* (1997) and Eric Mazur's *Peer Instruction* (1996). At the beginning of academic year 2006–07, we plan to give each new faculty member not only a copy of our own teaching handbook (Marincovich, 2004) but also a book on teaching that the associate director for that disciplinary cluster has picked out as particularly appropriate—whether it's Wilbert (Bill) McKeachie's *Teaching Tips* (2001) for social scientists, Elaine Showalter's *Teaching Literature* (2002) for humanists, or Davidson and Ambrose's *The New Professor's Handbook* (1994) and Rick Reis's *Tomorrow's Professor* (1997) for faculty in science and engineering.

Thirdly, we should be working at the level not just of individual faculty and/or fields, but at the level of institutional change, to make sure that the trends we are seeing become institutionalized and strengthened. To this end, Stanford is a member of the Oxford Network for Developing Teaching and Learning in Research-Intensive Environments ("Developing teaching in research-intensive environments,"

31

n.d.). The Network was developed and is led by Professor Graham Gibbs of Oxford University's Learning Institute, himself a model of a faculty developer who presents extensive and persuasive insights from educational research in enlarging and enriching the teaching of his colleagues. Proposed in 2004 and convened for the first time in 2005, Gibbs's network is a result of his strategic view of change in higher education and of his ability both to secure grants and to put together coalitions. Consisting of 13 internationally prominent research universities that all take teaching seriously, the network rather unusually brings together on an annual basis a senior administrator from each of the member institutions (generally a rector, pro-vice chancellor, vice rector, vice principal, or vice provost) and the director of the same institution's teaching and learning center for a meeting on organizational strategies that support effective teaching. The meetings are part information sharing, part brainstorming, part morale-building, and part team-building. A parallel project, also funded by Oxford, has sent two educational researchers to most of the campuses to study two departments known for their effective support of teaching. These efforts resulted in case studies of departmental leadership for teaching that formed the basis of rich discussions and new ideas at the most recent set of meetings.

As a result of Stanford's participation, our Vice Provost for Undergraduate Education has already held two brainstorming sessions with prominent scholar/teachers on campus and with their help has identified some of the obstacles to teaching effectiveness that still exist. For example, most of our faculty see team-teaching as a big help to their development as teachers and highly complementary to their interdisciplinary research and yet team teaching can be as time-consuming, if not more so, than teaching a class alone. Only some departments, however, give faculty full credit for teaching a team-taught course. Faculty also pointed out that although there were numerous pots of internal money for them to apply to for research help, very few pots existed to help with teaching. They wanted such pots to exist and to exist only for teaching purposes.

What else should educational researchers and faculty developers do? It's been our Center's custom to constantly look for and make common cause with faculty who show a particular interest in teaching and curricular issues. And we've had some good mechanisms for doing that. Our "Award-Winning Teachers on Teaching" series ("CTL Events – Award-Winning Teachers on Teaching," n.d.), for example, lets us reach out to pedagogically accomplished and committed faculty whom we don't know (as well as inviting a lot that we do know). If they accept our invitation to speak—and almost all do unless they are on sabbatical—we get to know them while they, in many cases for the first time, have an opportunity for structured reflection on their teaching. Not only does the resulting talk highlight excellent teaching on campus and disseminate general teaching wisdom along with discipline-specific pedagogical content knowledge, but some faculty who speak in the series begin to think of themselves differently after such an experience. One of our prominent economists, for example, who served on both President Ford's and the first President Bush's Council of Economic Advisers, decided to hold a conference on teaching Economics 1 after he had spoken in our series and realized he had wisdom to share about teaching that very challenging kind of course.

The Vice Provost for Undergraduate Education, to whom the Stanford Center reports, came up with another very effective strategy for stimulating as well as identifying faculty pedagogical/curricular innovators. He offered substantial sums of money to departments that had faculty willing to redesign their large, introductory courses to be more effective for their undergraduate students. Our office was recommended as a major resource for the departments that won such grants. In this way, we have worked extensively with Mathematics, Psychology, and Chemistry, three of the largest departments to receive funding. One aspect of the reforms in all these fields has been more elaborate and sustained TA training, a natural way for us to lend our expertise (Marincovich, Prostko, Stout, 1995).

But I realized in a March, 2006 discussion with Michele Scoufis, Director of the Learning and Teaching Unit at the University of New South Wales in Australia, that in some sense I have been waiting for faculty leaders on teaching issues to emerge and then we have been reaching out to collaborate with them. Michele suggested that, instead, we may want to groom such leaders ourselves. This production of leaders, instead of identification of them, will take a much more proactive and strategic approach than our Center has engaged in thus far, but it does seem the appropriate step at this point. Certainly the President's Teaching Scholars Program ("President's Teaching Scholars Program," n.d.) conducted by Mary Ann Shea of the Faculty Teaching Excellence Program at the University of Colorado at Boulder, has already been doing this, with some wonderful results. As noted above, under Graham Gibb's guidance and drawing on the work of Paul Ramsden (1998), the Oxford Network also has a project focusing on the role of departmental leadership in supporting teaching. Once we know the critical factors chairs can bring to bear in encouraging and developing a culture of teaching in their departments, teaching centers can work more effectively to develop chairs as strong links in the teaching support infrastructure.

What else have we learned that could be helpful to educational researchers, faculty developers, and administrators? Our work with the introductory course initiative faculty has shown that faculty innovators want materials relevant to their discipline AND a holistic approach. That is, they don't want to have to inform themselves one by one about such topics as small group work, personal response systems, or online discussion forums; they want to know, *overall*, what do you do to make a large introductory course effective. They want someone to put the whole package together for them, even though most researchers, of course, have to break down problems to work on them.

I would also draw your attention to the extraordinary generation of new faculty—though you are probably aware of it already—that's been coming to our campuses for a few years now and will be coming in even greater numbers as Baby Boomer retirements open up more and more faculty billets. Through Preparing Future Faculty (for more information on PFF see Tice, Gaff, & Pruitt-Logan, 1998) or other programs, many of these faculty have had considerable pedagogical and professional training for their professorial role during their graduate student years. The campuses they studied on may have had a teaching and learning center and that center may have acquainted them with the value of educational research. We have found them interested in what we have to say and anxious to excel in the classroom. Educational researchers can expect them to be a good potential audience for their work, particularly if there is a teaching center acting as a friendly interface.

Let me make one other suggestion, especially for those of you who work in Schools or Departments of Education. If the faculty of such Schools were themselves actively engaged in teaching improvement efforts of their own, I think the moral authority and the research influence of Schools of Education would go way up. In Stanford's School of Education several years ago, a tenured, senior member of the faculty insisted on an evaluation of his teaching as part of what had become a mechanical review process. He hoped to establish a tradition of taking teaching seriously and learning from each other that his senior colleagues would emulate. And he produced very thoughtful pedagogical materials for his own review process. Sadly, however, even with his shining example, other members of his School did not follow in his footsteps. Although the School has been involved in all kinds of educational reforms for primary and secondary school teachers, it has not had a similar tradition in terms of its own teaching programs.

Let me finally say, in summary, that I think the next decade is going to be an extraordinary time for both educational researchers and teaching and learning centers. Global competition in higher education has heated up and both European and Asian universities are reconsidering their approaches and structures as never before. At American universities, even the research-intensive ones, we can expect more faculty than ever to want to work with teaching and learning centers and to know about the work of educational researchers. I hope that those in the research field and those of us in faculty development can effectively collaborate to take advantage of this opportunity for real advancement in teaching and learning on our campuses!

REFERENCES

Boyer, E.L. (1990). *Scholarship Reconsidered: Priorities of the Professoriate*. Princeton, NJ: Carnegie Foundation for the Advancement of Teaching.

Campus Report. (1991, March 6). [Kennedy announces new teaching resources], p. 1, 13.

Casper: On Teaching, Research, Finances, Multiculturalism. (1992, April 1). *Campus Report*, p. 13.

CTL Events – Award-Winning Teachers on Teaching. (n.d.). Retrieved August 17, 2006, from http://ctl.stanford.edu/AWT/

Commission on Undergraduate Education. (1994). *Report of the Commission on Undergraduate Education*. Stanford: Stanford University.

A Conversation with Gerhard Casper. (1997, June 25). *Palo Alto Weekly*. Retrieved August 17, 2006, from http://www.paloaltoonline.com/weekly/morgue/cover/1997_Jun_25.COVER25.html

Davidson, C.I., and Ambrose, S.A. (1994). *The New Professor's Handbook*. Bolton, MA: Anker Publishing Company.

Developing Teaching in Research-Intensive Environments. (n.d.). Retrieved August 17, 2006, from http://www.learning.ox.ac.uk/oli.php?page=39

Gage, N.L. (1978). *The Scientific Basis of the Art of Teaching*. New York: Teachers College Press.

Gage, N.L., and Berliner, D.C. (1998). *Educational Psychology* (6th edition). Boston: Houghton Mifflin.

Grassmuck, K. (1990, September 12). Some Research Universities Contemplate Sweeping Changes, Ranging from Management and Tenure to Teaching Methods. *The Chronicle of Higher Education*, p. A1, 29–31.

Gray, P.J., Froh, R.C., and Diamond, R.M. (1991). Myths and Realities: First data from a national study on the balance between research and teaching at research universities. *AAHE Bulletin* 44: 4–5.

Hativa, N., and Marincovich, M. (1995). *Disciplinary Differences in Teaching and Learning. New Directions for Teaching and Learning*, 65. San Francisco: Jossey-Bass.

Huber, M.T. (2004). *Balancing Acts: The Scholarship of Teaching and Learning in Academic Careers*. Washington, DC: American Association for Higher Education and the Carnegie Foundation for the Advancement of Teaching.

Kennedy, D. (1990, April 5). *Stanford In Its Second Century, An Address to the Stanford Community*. Meeting of the Academic Council. Stanford, California.

Kennedy, D. (1997). *Academic Duty*. Cambridge: Harvard University Press.

Light, R.J. (1990). *The Harvard Assessment Seminars: Explorations with Students and Faculty about Teaching, Learning, and Student Life*. First Report. Cambridge: Harvard University.

Light, R.J. (1992). *The Harvard Assessment Seminars: Explorations with Students and Faculty about Teaching, Learning, and Student Life*. Second Report. Cambridge: Harvard University.

Magner, D.K. (1998, January 9). Survey Suggests Teaching May Be Getting More Emphasis at Research Universities. *The Chronicle of Higher Education*, p. A16.

Marincovich, M. (1990, November 2). *Teaching at Research Universities: The Possibility of a Renaissance?* Professional and Organizational Development Network in Higher Education Annual Conference. Lake Tahoe, California.

Marincovich, M. (1991, January 25). *Acceptable Tradeoffs Between Teaching and Research for the Professional Academic*. Symposium on the Prospects for Improvement in Pedagogical Skills at Swedish Högskolor and Universities. Stockholm, Sweden.

Marincovich, M. (1992a, October 20). *The Teaching/Research Relationship at Stanford: A New Balance*. 75th Jubilee of the Royal Institute of Technology. Stockholm, Sweden.

Marincovich, M. (1992b, October 21). *Faculty Development within University Departments – The Case of Stanford*. University of Stockholm. Stockholm, Sweden.

Marincovich, M. (2004). *Teaching at Stanford: An Introductory Handbook for Faculty, Academic Staff, and Teaching Assistants*. Stanford, CA: Center for Teaching and Learning.

Marincovich, M., Prostko, J., and Stout, F. (1998). *The Professional Development of Graduate Teaching Assistants*. Bolton: Anker Publishing.

Mazur, E. (1996). *Peer Instruction*. Upper Saddle River, NJ: Prentice Hall.

McKeachie, W. (2001). *Teaching Tips* (11th edition). Boston: Houghton Mifflin.

National Research Council. (1997). *Science Teaching Reconsidered*. Washington, DC: National Academy Press.

President's Teaching Scholars Program. (n.d.). Retrieved August 17, 2006, from http://www.colorado.edu/ptsp/

Ramsden, P. (1998). *Learning to Lead in Higher Education*. London: Routledge.

Reis, R.M. (1997). *Tomorrow's Professor*. New York: IEEE Press.

Showalter, E. (2002). *Teaching Literature*. Malden, MA: Blackwell Publishers.

Shulman, L.S. (1986). Those Who Understand: Knowledge Growth in Teaching. *Educational Researcher* 15: 1–11.

Shulman, L.S. (1987). Knowledge and Teaching: Foundations of the New Reform. *Harvard Educational Review* 57: 1–22.

Shulman, L.S. (1989). Toward a Pedagogy of Substance. *AAHE Bulletin* 41(10): 8–13.

Stanford University Faculty Handbook. (2001). Stanford: Provost's Office. Retrieved August 17, 2006, from (http://facultyhandbook.stanford.edu/pdf/B3.pdf)

Tice, S.L., Gaff, J.G., and Pruitt-Logan, A.S. (1998). Preparing Future Faculty Programs: Beyond TA Development. In M. Marincovich, J. Prostko and F. Stout (eds.), *The Professional Development of Graduate Teaching Assistants* (pp. 275–292). Bolton: Anker Publishing.

U. of California to stress teaching and service. (1992, July 29). *The Chronicle of Higher Education*, p. A5.

4. Understanding New Faculty: Background, Aspirations, Challenges, and Growth

Ann E. Austin*, Mary Deane Sorcinelli†, and Melissa McDaniels‡

*Michigan State University
aaustin@msu.edu
†University of Massachusetts, Amherst
‡Michigan State University

Abstract

Early career faculty, defined as those within the first seven years of appointment to a faculty position or those who have not yet received tenure, contribute to the present and create the future of universities and colleges. This chapter contributes to deeper understanding of new faculty by addressing these issues: 1) the demographics of early career faculty; 2) the preparation they receive and the gaps in their graduate and post-doctoral backgrounds; 3) the abilities and skills early career faculty need to succeed in higher education; 4) the expectations early career faculty have for their careers and the challenges they experience in their new roles; 5) the strategies individual early career faculty and institutions can employ to enhance their professional growth; and 6) directions for future research

Key Words: Early career faculty; New faculty; Demographics; Socialization; Preparation; Expectations; Motivations; Tenure process; Colleagueship; Community; Mentoring; Balance; Flexibility; Non-majority faculty; Strategies

Early career faculty contribute to the present and create the future of universities and colleges. When a higher education institution recruits, selects, and hires a new faculty member, it is making a major investment of resources and trust. Ideally, the faculty member will thrive at the institution, finding intellectual excitement and professional and personal satisfaction as well as contributing his or her talents to achieving institutional missions and enhancing organizational excellence. Yet the success of new faculty members usually requires more than simply good hiring decisions. Institutional leaders and estab-

R.P. Perry and J.C. Smart (eds.), The Scholarship of Teaching and Learning in Higher Education: An Evidence-Based Perspective, 39–89.
© 2007 Springer.

lished professors need to understand what new faculty need and what strategies support their growth and success.

This chapter contributes to deeper understanding of new faculty, with particular attention to five key issues: 1) What are the demographics of early career faculty today? 2) What preparation do they receive and what are the gaps in their graduate and post-doctoral backgrounds? 3) What abilities and skills must early career faculty have to succeed in higher education? 4) What expectations do early career faculty have for their careers and what are the challenges they experience in their new roles? 5) What strategies can individual early career faculty and institutions that employ them use to enhance their professional growth? This chapter highlights, synthesizes, and analyzes key findings from research that enhance knowledge and understanding of new faculty. It also provides suggestions for institutional leaders, established faculty members, and new faculty members themselves about specific strategies to help early career faculty succeed.

Several points need to be clarified at the beginning of this chapter. The term "new faculty" is not precisely defined in the literature. Here we are defining new faculty as those within the first seven years of appointment to a faculty position or those who have not yet been awarded tenure (in institutional contexts where tenure is a possibility), acknowledging that, in some cases, faculty members are awarded tenure prior to the seventh year. We note also that new faculty may be individuals in their 20s or individuals who are older in age, having had other professional posts prior to moving into the professoriate. Furthermore, new faculty may work either full-time or part-time. We sometimes use the term "early career faculty member" in place of "new faculty member."

The literature concerning new faculty has some limitations. Much of the literature is based on research that specifically concerns new faculty in tenure-track positions and has focused less on the experiences of a growing number of new faculty in part-time, fixed-term, or non-tenure-track positions. Another limitation of the literature is that faculty in four-year institutions are more likely to have been included in studies than faculty working in two-year colleges.

Current shifts in the academic workforce make studying new faculty particularly important at the present time. Over the past fifty years, the need for new faculty has waxed and waned. Currently, the demand for new faculty members is expected to increase: between 2000 and 2010, the number of faculty is expected to grow overall by 24% (Jones, 2002). The University of North Carolina system, for example, has projected the need to hire 10,000 new faculty members between 2001 and 2010. The cost to achieve this goal is high, estimated at about 32 million dollars annually in the early part of the decade and increasing to 61 million per year by 2010 (Brown, cited in Gappa, Austin, and Trice, 2007).

What factors require the hiring of so many new faculty? First, enrollment figures of both traditional age and older students are increasing—in some states, dramatically. Second, even as student numbers are growing, faculty retirements are projected to increase also in the next ten years. At present, 37% of all full-time faculty are 55 or older, as compared to 24% in 1989 (Lindholm, Astin, Sax, & Korn, 2002; Lindholm, J. A., Szelenyi, K., Hurtado, S., & Korn, W.S., 2005). Among tenured faculty, 50.5% are 55 or older (U.S. Department of Education, NCES, 2004). Third, some faculty not yet at retirement age may choose to leave higher education. In the Higher Education Research Institute Survey of Faculty, one-third of the respondents indicated they had considered departing from academe for another job, and 28% had received at least one firm offer (Lindholm et al., 2005). Furthermore, in the recruitment process, higher education is facing more competition from other fields. While scholars completing graduate work in science and engineering have long been attracted to industry and other non-academic careers, the number of doctoral graduates in the humanities considering non-academic options is also expanding (Gappa, Austin, & Trice, 2007; Jones, 2002).

DEMOGRAPHICS: WHO ARE THE NEW FACULTY?

Overall, full or part-time faculty members with seven or fewer years in academic appointments constitute 41.3% of the faculty in the United States (U.S. Department of Education, NCES, 2004). More specifically, they constitute 36.7% of the faculty within research universities, 37.3% within doctoral-granting institutions, 40.4 % in comprehensives, 40.8 % in private liberal arts institutions, and 46.8 % in public two-year colleges. When considering only full-time faculty members, the early cohort (seven or fewer years) comprises 32.4% (U.S. Department of Education, NCES, 2004).

Across institutional types, the new faculty group is becoming somewhat more diverse in terms of gender, race, ethnicity, and appointment type. For example, the group includes a greater proportion of women than in previous years. Forty-four percent of new faculty in their first six years of full-time employment were women in 2003, compared to 20% in 1969 (Finkelstein & Schuster, 2001; U.S. Department of Education, NCES, 2004). Furthermore, the percentage of women in the new faculty ranks is likely to increase, since an increasing number of women are earning doctorates. In 2003, women scholars received 51% of all doctorates awarded to U.S. citizens and 45% of all doctorates awarded (Hoeffer, Welch, Williams, Webber, Lisek, Lowe, & Guzman-Barron, 2005).With regard to race and ethnicity, across institutional types, the early career faculty group is more diverse than their senior cohort of colleagues. Among full-time early career faculty, about one quarter are from non-majority ethnic groups, compared to approximately 17% of those who have been academics for more than seven years (see Table 1).

One of the most significant shifts occurring within the American professoriate concerns the pattern of appointment types, particularly the shift from tenure-track to non-tenure track positions (often called contract or fixed-term) appointments. Tenure-track appointments were the norm for many years in American academe. Of the full-time early career faculty group (seven years or less), 46.1% hold non-tenure track positions, compared to the senior cohort (over 7 years) in which 25.1% are in non-tenure track positions (U.S. Department of Education,

Table 1: Early and Established Faculty (Full-Time) Cohorts Compared on Race/Ethnicity (2003)

Race/Ethnicity	Early Career Faculty	Established Faculty
AmericanIndian/NativeAlaskan	0.4%	0.3%
Asian/Pacific Islander	12.5%	6.8%
Black/African American	6.3%	5.0%
Hispanic White/Hispanic Black	4.0%	2.7%
White/non-Hispanic	74.5%	83.1%
More than one race	2.3%	2.1%

Note: Early career faculty members include those individuals who have been faculty members for 7 years or less. Established faculty members include individuals who have been faculty members for over 7 years.
Source: U.S. Department of Education, National Center for Education Statistics. (2004). *National Study of Postsecondary Faculty, 2004* [Data file].

NCES, 2004). While the proportion of women taking faculty positions is increasing, women are more likely than men to hold non-tenure track positions (Gappa, Austin, & Trice, 2007).

BACKGROUND OF NEW FACULTY: THE DOCTORAL EXPERIENCE

When individuals begin their first faculty appointment, they assume new roles and responsibilities and typically experience a period of adjustment. For those considering faculty careers, however, the first stage of the academic career begins during graduate education (Austin, 2002b). Socialization theory helps to explain the important role of graduate education in preparing new faculty. Overall, graduate education functions as a period of anticipatory socialization during which future faculty members develop values and perspectives as well as specific skills that they need to become faculty members. In this section, we examine how and to what extent new faculty are prepared (or not prepared) through their doctoral experiences. First, we discuss how socialization to new faculty roles occurs in doctoral education. Second, we present concerns pertaining to how graduate school socializes doctoral students for faculty roles.

HOW SOCIALIZATION TO FACULTY ROLES OCCURS IN DOCTORAL EDUCATION

Socialization is a process through which individuals become part of a society as they internalize standards, expectations, and norms (Bragg, 1976; Brim, 1966; Bullis & Bach, 1989; Merton, 1957; Merton, Reader, & Kendall, 1957). More specifically, socialization consists of "the processes through which [a person] develops [a sense of] professional self, with its characteristic values, attitudes, knowledge, and skills...which govern [his or her] behavior in a wide variety of professional (and extraprofessional) situations" (Merton, Reader, & Kendall, 1957, p. 287).

Austin and McDaniels (2006) examined in detail how graduate education functions as a socialization process for faculty roles, and noted important earlier work in this area. For example, Clark and Corcoran (1986) offered a stage model that highlights the place of graduate education in preparing future faculty. In the first stage, they asserted, individuals (such as undergraduates) are recruited to be graduate students in a field and begin to experience anticipatory social-ization. The second stage of occupational entry and induction occurs as they pursue their graduate education, participating in classes and internships, working with and being mentored by advisors, taking exams and writing dissertations, beginning to publish and attending conferences, and seeking jobs. The third stage of socialization begins, in this model, when scholars assume faculty positions. Kirk and Todd-Macillas (1991) highlighted "turning points" in academic life, and Braxton and Baird (2001) offered a stage-based theory of graduate student careers. Offering a stage model of teaching assistants' learning that acknowledges the non-linearity of the graduate student devel-opment process, Sprague and Nyquist (1989, 1991) hypothesized three stages to their development: "senior learner" early in their graduate experience, "colleague in training" as they become more comfortable as teaching assistants, and "junior colleague" as they become more secure in their new professional identities.

While acknowledging the contributions of Merton and others in defining socialization, some theorists have been concerned about taking an approach that assumes socialization to be a one-way process through which individuals gain necessary knowledge and are assimi-lated into the organization (Antony, 2002; Tierney, 1997). Responding to such concerns, some theorists prefer to conceptualize socialization as more dialectical and culturally based (Staton, 1990; Tierney, 1997; Tierney & Bensimon, 1996; Tierney & Rhoads, 1994). More culturally-based dialectical approaches emphasize that culture is "contestable" (Tierney, 1997, p. 6), and that individuals bring their own experi-ences, perspectives, and ideas that interact with the expectations they find in the organization (Staton, 1990). Such a postmodern view recognizes that organizations can help newcomers understand expectations, while simultaneously welcoming them for the oppor-tunity they offer for the organization to "re-create" its culture rather than simply to replicate it (Tierney, 1997, p. 16). In other words, newcomers learn about the organization while at the same time they change it.

Austin, Nyquist, Sprague, and Wulff led a team that conducted longitudinal research to study how doctoral students develop as aspiring faculty (Austin, 2002b; Nyquist et al., 1999; Wulff, Austin, Nyquist, & Sprague, 2004). They too concluded that socializing prospective faculty during graduate education is not a simple linear process that can easily be categorized in distinct steps or defined by specific events. Rather, throughout their graduate experiences, prospective faculty seek to make sense of what a faculty career might be like. Their development and commitment to a future career as a faculty member is influenced by their observations of faculty members, their interactions with faculty, peers, family, and friends, the experiences they have as developing professionals, and their interpretation of implicit and explicit messages about what is expected and valued in academic life.

A postmodern, bidirectional approach to socialization (Staton & Darling, 1989; Staton-Spicer & Darling, 1986, 1987; Tierney & Bensimon, 1996) may be particularly helpful in considering how to attract more women and people of color to faculty careers. These individuals sometimes feel unwelcome within academe and, as graduate students, sometimes encounter difficulty finding and establishing mentoring relationships (Clark & Corcoran, 1986; Tierney & Bensimon, 1996; Tierney & Rhoads, 1994; Turner & Thompson, 1993). Antony (2002) has been especially concerned that equating socialization to a faculty career with assimilation to particular values and standards may be a significant barrier for attracting individuals of color as well as women. He urged socialization during graduate education that is "more unique, individualistic, and reflective of the nature of recent incumbents to academic and professional roles" (p. 350). In their research on the doctoral experiences of successful African-American faculty members, Antony and Taylor (Antony & Taylor, 2004; Taylor & Antony, 2001) found these individuals understood the normative expectations in their workplaces, while also maintaining their own values. In contrast, those who relinquished some of their own values in favor of more fully assuming specific values within the profession felt less satisfied or left the profession. Seeing socialization processes as moving in two directions—the individual learning about organizational expectations and values, and the organization benefiting and changing based on the contributions brought by newcomers—presents a promising framework for conceptualizing ways to diversify the ranks of graduate students and ultimately the faculty.

Building on the contributions of both the traditional research on socialization and the newer work that takes a more cultural perspective, Weidman, Twale, and Stein (2001) offered a comprehensive framework for understanding graduate and professional socialization. While their framework pertains to all graduate students (not only those considering faculty careers), it helps explain the background experiences that prepare individuals who will become new faculty members. Their framework acknowledges that graduate students learn required roles, while simultaneously influencing the nature of their experiences and the norms of the organization. Additionally, they assert that socialization occurs in a cultural context, which includes the culture of the organization and the climate created by peers. Their framework emphasizes that socialization occurs as graduate students interact with faculty and peers, learn the skills and language needed for professional practice, and integrate into the activities of their fields. Weidman, Twale, and Stein's model (2001) also highlights four influences on graduate student socialization. First, students are influenced by their own backgrounds, education, race and ethnicity, values and beliefs, and aspirations. Second, their socialization is influenced by the various communities of which they are a part, including their families, friends, and employers, influences also confirmed by other researchers (Austin, 2002b; Nyquist et al., 1999). Third, professional communities affect the socialization of graduate students. They hold standards and sometimes licensing requirements for admission to the field and, through conferences or internships, they provide opportunities for graduate students to interact with experienced members of the profession. Weidman, Twale, and Stein (2001) also indicated that novice professional practitioners are an influence on graduate students, but did not fully explain the nature of this impact.

Overall, Weidman, Twale, and Stein (2001) presented a model that acknowledges that the development of professional identity is "dynamic" and "interactive." Socialization to future professional work—faculty work or other work—begins in graduate school, and is affected by multiple influences and experiences. At the same time, as the individual enters his or her initial professional appointment, the socialization that occurs during graduate study is only the groundwork for ongoing professional development:

> Professional identity and commitment are not achieved at some finite level but continue to evolve. Socialization is dynamic and ongoing, without a definite beginning or end. (Weidman, Twale, & Stein, 2001, p. 40)

CHALLENGES IN DOCTORAL EDUCATION AS PREPARATION FOR FACULTY CAREERS

Recent research on graduate education provides important insights into the background and preparation that new faculty bring into first appointments. Wulff and Austin's recent book entitled *Paths to the*

Professoriate (2004) as well as a recent chapter on "Preparing the Professoriate of the Future" in *Higher Education: Handbook of Research and Theory* (Austin & McDaniels, 2006) highlight several concerns that have emerged in the research on graduate education concerning the socialization processes experienced by future faculty.

Limited preparation for academic work. First, doctoral education provides only limited preparation for academic work. The findings from several major studies provide consistent indications that the doctoral experience is neither preparing aspiring faculty systematically nor comprehensively for faculty positions (Austin, 2002a, b; Golde & Dore, 2001; Nerad, Aanerud, & Cerby, 2004; Nyquist et al., 1999; Wulff et al., 2004). Golde and Dore (2001) are often cited for their compelling conclusion about the limits of doctoral preparation for academic as well as non-academic careers, based on their research with more than 4000 doctoral students in 11 disciplines at 28 research universities. They concluded that "the training doctoral students receive is not what they want, nor does it prepare them for the jobs they take" (p. 3). Similarly, Davis and Fiske (2000) reported that 37% of the doctoral student respondents in their study reported that they received little guidance about entering and succeeding within an academic career.

The research also highlights specific areas of faculty work for which there is modest or weak preparation. It is noteworthy that a longitudinal qualitative study of approximately 100 doctoral students at 3 universities concluded that aspiring faculty did not understand the full range of faculty work. Particular areas in which prospective faculty exhibited minimal knowledge included the following: the range of higher education institutional types and the cultures, missions, and nature of faculty work at these institutions; the history of higher education and the academic profession; the kind of responsibilities professors have to society, including public service and outreach; the nature of faculty responsibilities in governance; advising; curriculum development; institutional citizenship; grant writing; and ethical issues relevant to the profession (Austin, 2002a, b; Wulff et al., 2004).

One might expect that the areas in which doctoral students would receive the greatest preparation for faculty careers would be research and teaching. Indeed, Golde's pilot study (1998) involving 187 doctoral students at 6 universities showed that 90% felt prepared to do research. In contrast, only 63% reported that they felt prepared to teach undergraduates, 33% to teach graduate students, 30% to advise undergraduates, 26% to advise graduate students, and 19%

to participate in governance and service roles. And despite the high percentage reporting that they felt prepared to do research, only 38% felt prepared to find research funding. The data from a web-based survey conducted by the National Association of Graduate and Professional Students (NAGPS, 2001) to which more than 32,000 students responded indicated similar concerns by doctoral students about their grounding in teaching. While 80% said they were satisfied with their preparation for their academic careers, far fewer indicated sufficient preparation for teaching specifically, although there were differences across disciplinary areas (43% in the life sciences, and 72% in the humanities).

Furthermore, the preparation for faculty work that does occur in graduate school typically is not organized in a developmental way nor is it necessarily systematic in addressing specific competencies (Austin, 2002a, b; Austin & McDaniels, 2006; Nyquist et al., 1999). Doctoral students learn a great deal about faculty work through observation and apprenticeship, as they interact with graduate and undergraduate faculty. Prospective faculty observe how current faculty allocate their time, what work they do, what they value, and what tasks they enjoy. However, the research indicates that doctoral students typically perceive "mixed messages" about what they should emphasize in academic careers, with the messages about the relative importance of teaching often contradictory. While some doctoral students have the experience of serving as teaching assistants, their responsibilities are not necessarily organized to ensure their progressive professional development nor do they always experience explicit and regular guidance (Austin & McDaniels, 2006; Austin, 2002b; Nyquist et al., 1999; Wulff et al., 2004).

Worrisome perceptions of academic life developed during graduate education. The research on doctoral students preparing for careers in the professoriate indicates that they express significant concerns about academic careers. They observe that faculty members appear to live particularly hectic lives, an observation leading many doctoral students to wonder whether academic careers allow one to live what some call "integrated" or "balanced" lives that embrace both personal and professional responsibilities (Austin, 2002a, b; Golde, 1998; Golde & Dore, 2001; Rice, Sorcinelli, & Austin, 2000; Wulff et al., 2004). Those committed to or interested in having meaningful personal relationships wonder how to manage dual career situations. Another frequently articulated worry is that professorial life may be characterized more by competition and isolation than by collegiality and community (Austin,

2002 a, b; Nyquist et al., 1999; Rice, Sorcinelli, & Austin, 2000; Wulff et al., 2004).

Some doctoral students feel sufficient concern about the nature of academic life to consider other career options that seem more attractive. Even those aspiring to the professoriate, however, often finish graduate school with some uncertainty about how they will manage the multiple responsibilities and daily pace that they perceive is required of faculty members. Some women and individuals of color feel particularly worried whether their vision for their lives—particularly if that vision includes balance and connection—can come to fruition in an academic career (Lovitts, 2004).

Few opportunities for guided reflection. On the one hand, the doctoral experience presents challenges and raises questions about values, life choices, and career goals for prospective faculty. On the other hand, despite having many occasions to observe faculty members, doctoral students report experiencing few explicit conversations with their faculty advisors about life as an academic and how to best prepare for this work. Students of color and female students often experience even less mentoring and guidance from faculty than do other students (Taylor & Antony, 2001; Turner & Thompson, 1993).

Overall, aspiring faculty members (as well as other doctoral students) are left on their own to make sense of the socialization they experience in their doctoral education, to envision their future work as faculty members, and to make important decisions about their careers. Information and support are often provided primarily from peers in the doctoral program, family, and friends (Anderson & Swazey, 1998; Austin, 2002b; Austin & McDaniels, 2006).

Students in a longitudinal, multi-year interview study expressed appreciation for the occasions for reflection afforded by the study interviews (Austin, 2002b; Nyquist et al., 1999; Wulff et al., 2004), suggesting that more opportunities to interact with faculty members about the nature of the academic career would likely help young scholars feel more prepared when they enter the ranks of new faculty members.

STRENGTHENING THE PREPARATION OF NEW FACULTY

Scholars who study doctoral education (Austin, 2002b; Austin & McDaniels, 2006; Wulff & Austin, 2004; Wulff et al., 2004) have argued that the graduate experience should provide future faculty with opportunities to gain the knowledge they will need to be faculty members, to interact with faculty and experience faculty work, and to invest time and energy into the profession, even as doctoral students. In other words, new faculty members should not be surprised by what faculty members do or the kinds of lives they live. An interesting paradox is at work, however. Virtually all doctoral students study in research universities, where research is particularly emphasized—but many will be new faculty at different institutional types. Thus, even in situations where advisors strive to discuss their work as faculty members with their doctoral students who aspire to the professoriate, much of the preparation is likely to be most pertinent to work in research universities.

The anticipatory socialization experience provided through doctoral education is complex, necessarily involving many experiences. As aspiring faculty gain knowledge and develop a professional identity, they are influenced by faculty members, peers, family and friends, and professional groups (Austin, 2002b; Nyquist et al., 1999; Wulff, Austin, Nyquist, & Sprague, 2004). Future faculty experience significant learning individually and in groups, through formal parts of their programs and more informal interactions, through structured, sequential experiences and through more randomly organized experiences. The complex nature of the learning process at the doctoral level means that responsibility for preparing new faculty during the doctoral experience rests with various people— doctoral students themselves, as well as individual faculty members, department chairs, and graduate deans. More purposeful attention by all stakeholders to helping doctoral students reflect upon their values and make sense of their experiences would enhance the effectiveness of the socialization experience as preparation for faculty careers.

BACKGROUND OF NEW FACULTY: POST-DOCTORAL EXPERIENCES

In addition to doctoral education, post-doctoral experiences contribute to the background preparation of new faculty. The number of postdoctoral scholars in the United States has grown since the mid-1980s due to increasing requirements for faculty (and other) jobs, graduate schools not being able to provide all training scientists need for a career in research, and an employment market in which the number of graduate students exceeds appropriate and available jobs (in academia and other industries) (Committee on Science, Engineering, and Public Policy [COSEPUP], (2000)).

In many fields, a postdoctoral research fellowship, hereafter referred to as a "postdoc", is a short-term apprenticeship during which individuals can develop their research skills (Davis, 2005). Especially in the sciences, a one- to three-year postdoctoral research fellowship is either highly desirable or required before an individual is considered for a tenure-track faculty position. In the 2004 Survey of Earned Doctorates, 45% of science and engineering respondents who had definite plans after graduation stated that they were going to undertake postdoctoral study, with precise figures varying by field (Hoffer, Welch, Williams, Hess, Webber, Lisek, Lowew, & Guzman-Barron, 2005).

Rather than focusing on research, some doctoral graduates, particularly those in the humanities and social sciences, use post-doctoral experiences to focus on teaching skills. An increasing number of colleges and universities are offering such opportunities. For example, the University of Georgia's Franklin College of Arts and Sciences, in cooperation with their Institute of Higher Education, conducts a postdoctoral teaching fellowship program for recent Ph.D. graduates from leading universities across the United States. Fellows teach undergraduate students; in return, the University offers a salary, travel funds, a new computer, and a set of professional development opportunities such as mentoring by senior faculty, seminars, classes, and workshops that provide opportunities for development as teachers and scholars (University of Georgia, 2006). Some aspiring faculty, especially those in the basic sciences, who aspire to faculty roles in research institutions, may find such time focused on teaching must be negotiated in light of their advisors' expectations and their own interests in their research development; others who aspire to institutions with a heavy teaching mission may seek out such teaching-oriented postdoctoral experiences.

Postdoctoral fellowships, like doctoral education, also are the focus of concerns and critique (AAU Graduate and Postdoctoral Education Committee, 2005; COSEPUP, 2000; Davis, 2005). Some of the issues highlighted in the reports on post-doctoral education parallel those occurring in doctoral education, such as concerns about the quality of mentoring and, for those in the sciences, the availability of career preparation beyond laboratory and research work. Other issues pertain to the nature of employment conditions, salaries and benefits provided to postdoctoral fellows, visa challenges experienced by international fellows, and indefinite lengths of time for postdoctoral work, particularly in the sciences. As with doctoral students, the preparation of postdocs for faculty roles is not very systematic or comprehensive, and researchers have theorized about and studied the post-doctoral experience (as preparation for an academic career) less than the doctoral experience.

NEW FACULTY IN THE 21ST CENTURY: EXPECTED COMPETENCIES AND SKILLS

In addition to studying doctoral and post-doctoral experiences as preparation for the professoriate, some higher education scholars have considered the question of what abilities and skills future faculty should develop. In a recently published chapter in *Higher Education: Handbook of Theory and Research*, Austin and McDaniels (2006) analyzed critical forces affecting faculty work and academic workplaces and proposed general competencies and abilities that faculty today must have to negotiate these multiple demands. They asserted that, while faculty need to continually refine and adapt critical competencies over the course of their academic careers, aspiring and new faculty would benefit from explicit attention to developing these skills and abilities. Their proposed competencies included: knowledge and skills, professional attitudes, interpersonal skills, and conceptual understandings. Future research might explore such questions as the extent to which new faculty begin their careers with these abilities and skills, whether the depth of graduate preparation for these competencies varies across disciplines, and new and established faculty members' views of the importance of these competencies in their work. Short descriptions of Austin and McDaniels' proposed competencies (2006) are provided here:

Knowledge and Skills in the Core Areas of Faculty Work: As teachers, early career faculty should understand various strategies for engaging in course design, teaching diverse learners, supporting active learning, using technology to facilitate learning, assessing student learning, and managing their own professional growth. As researchers, new faculty must be able to engage in all parts of the research process, including framing appropriate questions, designing projects, analyzing results, and communicating findings to stakeholders as diverse as fellow scholars, community members and policy makers. Grant writing and the ability to give and receive critical feedback are also very important skills. In order to fulfill their service roles to their disciplines and communities, faculty must be able to connect theory and practice. Other important skills include strategic planning, conflict resolution, time management, creativity, and entrepreneurialism.

Professional Attitudes and Habits: Several important professional habits and attitudes are also integral to successful faculty work and important to begin developing in graduate school. Such habits include commitment to integrity and ethical behavior in all aspects of work and eagerness to engage in life-long learning and reflection through attending conferences, reading research and teaching publications, and participating in faculty development workshops on campus. Aspiring and new faculty members also are well-served to learn how to develop professional networks as well as strategies for maintaining balance in their work and lives.

Interpersonal Skills: New faculty also should be able to communicate effectively both orally and in writing to a variety of audiences, including students, government and industry leaders, and policy-makers. In addition, of increasing importance is the ability of faculty members to work with colleagues different from them in terms of gender, race and ethnicity, sexual orientation, religious commitment, and disciplinary home.

Conceptual Understandings: In addition to thorough knowledge of their disciplines and disciplinary-based research norms, new faculty need some sense of their professional identities as scholars. They should understand the history of higher education, the variety of institutional types and missions, and the diverse work-related expectations encountered by faculty based on institutional type. Furthermore, with the increasing proportion of non-tenure-track and part-time faculty positions, aspiring and new faculty should be familiar with the particular expectations associated with these appointment types.

THE NEW FACULTY EXPERIENCE

Following doctoral and sometimes postdoctoral experiences, both of which serve as periods of anticipatory socialization, new faculty assume their roles and experience on-the-job sense-making. These early years constitute a developmental period in which faculty strive to develop their personal abilities and skills as well as to decipher expectations for performance in a new institutional context. In his interviews with new faculty, which resulted in *Faculty in New Jobs* (1999), Menges and his colleagues found that as prospective faculty moved into their first appointments, their anxieties "shifted from anxiety about getting a job to anxiety about surviving on the job" (p. 20). Indeed, faculty development literature shows that the early years of a faculty appointment are a period of intense socialization—a time of high stress but also of satisfaction (Olsen, 1993; Olsen & Sorcinelli, 1992; Rice, Sorcinelli, & Austin, 2000; Trower, 2005). What attracts the best graduate students to the professoriate and encourages their early career development? What factors are important to and positively affect new faculty productivity and success? Conversely, what do newcomers identify as troublesome aspects of the early academic career, meriting serious attention? What aspects are most likely to cause a decline in satisfaction over time if unaddressed?

Through studies of new faculty, conducted since the mid-1980s, we know a fair amount about the specific kinds of satisfactions, dissatisfactions, and stresses, both professional and personal, that faculty experience in their early career. The literature includes, for example, discipline-specific research on new geography faculty (Fink, 1984; Solem & Foote, 2004), planning faculty (Hamlin, Marcucci & Wenning, 2000), dental educators (Schenkein & Best, 2001), and nursing educators (Luce & Murray, 1998; Nugent, Bradshaw & Kito, 1999). Work includes studies of early career faculty in single institutions (Luce & Murray, 1998; Sorcinelli, 1988, 1992), multiple campuses in one university system (Trotman & Brown, 2005), and multiple institutions (Finkelstein, Seal & Schuster, 1998; Rice, Sorcinelli, & Austin, 2000; Tierney & Bensimon, 1996; Trower, 2005). Finally, there are qualitative case studies of junior faculty (Reynolds, 1992; Whitt, 1991), and longitudinal studies that have tracked new faculty over several years using both interviews and surveys (Boice, 1992; Menges, 1999; Olsen, 1993; Olsen & Crawford, 1998; Olsen & Sorcinelli, 1992).

In reviewing these studies, one is struck by the extensive congruence in the findings emerging from widely varying research approaches. Many of the overarching themes emerging from recent studies (Rice, Sorcinelli, & Austin, 2000; Trotman & Brown, 2005; Trower, 2005) echo themes identified some twenty years ago (Fink, 1984; Sorcinelli, 1985). In presenting the sources of satisfaction and concern that shape new faculty careers, we chose to draw on a framework developed in *Heeding New Voices* (Rice, Sorcinelli, & Austin, 2000). This multi-institutional study looked carefully at the rewards and challenges facing prospective and early career faculty, and made a special effort to interview representative groups of prospective and early career faculty across the various sectors of higher education and across disciplines, race, ethnicity, gender and region. What then are the experiences and factors that impact new faculty positively or negatively as they enter, navigate, and integrate into the fabric of a faculty career, department, and institution?

ASPIRATIONS, EXPECTATIONS, AND MOTIVATIONS

New faculty entering the professoriate have been consistent in highlighting the appeal of what has been called the "intrinsic" rewards of an academic career (i.e., factors intrinsic to academic work itself and not dependent on external circumstances). Thus, for example, newcomers report high levels of satisfaction with the nature of academic work and the relative autonomy with which it is pursued. They value the opportunity to pursue issues that they believe are important and to frame their own research agendas. They also are excited by the flexibility in time promised by an academic appointment and the opportunity to determine how they will organize their work (Olsen, 1993; Sorcinelli, 1988).

Opportunities for intellectual growth and discovery and the wise use of skills and abilities also seem essential to new faculty well-being. New faculty frequently mention a love of learning and a desire to share their passion for their disciplines and fields with new students and others. They look forward to the intellectual challenge that is part of academic work; they are eager to participate in opportunities to continue their own intellectual development through interaction with stimulating colleagues. For example, as they entered their first appointments, new faculty in *Heeding New Voices* (Rice, Sorcinelli, & Austin, 2000) were eloquent as they expressed passion for the academic work itself—the teaching and research. In describing both their classrooms and research projects or labs, a number of new faculty enumerated why: the cognitive stimulation, the personal contact with students, the discovery-oriented environment, and the opportunity to stretch their minds (Boice, 1992; Rice, Sorcinelli, & Austin, 2000; Sorcinelli & Austin, 1992).

A related theme that has been articulated in recent research on early career and aspiring faculty is the notion of "meaningful work" (Austin, 2002b; Rice, Sorcinelli, & Austin, 2000). There is a willingness to work hard, especially if the work is of consequence. Some newcomers are explicit in wanting to find ways to connect their scholarly interests with the needs of students and the broader society. Some specifically mention a desire to work in a community of people who are diverse. A graduate student quoted in the *Heeding New Voices* study (Rice, Sorcinelli, & Austin, 2000) echoed the hopes of other aspiring faculty: "What I want most in a faculty career is a profession that makes me feel connected to my students, to my colleagues, to the larger community, and to myself" (p. 16). Some aspiring and new faculty—particularly women and people of color—are explicit about seeing their work as part of a life mission to contribute in substantive ways that better their communities and society and as a way to serve as role models for others (Rice, Sorcinelli, & Austin, 2000).

Two decades of research on new and early career faculty, then, confirm that the strongest effects on early career satisfaction have remained essentially the same, and they spring from a rich internal source. Newcomers demonstrate a high level of idealism about the profession and the quality of life that promises to go with it. As a group, new faculty are enthusiastic, committed, and willing to work hard. They are highly motivated and poised to make significant impacts on their institutions, disciplines, communities, and society (Boice, 1992; Olsen, 1993; Rice, Sorcinelli, & Austin, 2000; Trower, 2005). Unfortunately, research also confirms that what early career faculty hope for and need from their work life, and what they actually experience over time, do not fully match. As Rice, Sorcinelli, and Austin (2000) asserted, a disquieting gap exists between the vision and the reality of the early academic career.

REALITIES AND NEED FOR IMPROVEMENT

Even as new faculty speak passionately about their vision for academic work, they also reveal deep concerns about the reality of that work. Such worries begin in graduate school and then are further accentuated as individuals move into new jobs (Menges, 1999; Nyquist, Manning, Wulff, Austin, Sprague, Fraser, Calcagno, & Woodford, 1999; Rice, Sorcinelli, & Austin, 2000). In the face of these concerns, however, many continue to expect that they can find the kind of faculty situations that enable them to live the lives of commitment and connection that they envision. Again and again, graduate students hoping to find faculty positions hold to their vision, in which they find colleagues who are active and engaging, students who are talented and enthusiastic, and resources that allow them to do their best and important work.

When aspiring faculty do become new faculty, however, the tension between expectations and reality intensifies. As detailed earlier, young faculty indeed report real satisfactions with their careers. At the same time, virtually all studies of new faculty find that respondents rate their work as stressful, particularly as they struggle to define their roles as professionals and understand their departmental and institutional contexts. Descriptors like "pressure," "anxiety," and "worry" crop up in nearly every interview, focus group or survey (Rice, Sorcinelli, & Austin, 2000; Trotman & Brown, 2005). And, unfortunately, the tensions of these faculty members' first years do not appear to be offset by experience. A study of new hires over a three-year period found "a trend toward greater stress from work" from years one to three (Menges, 1999, p. 26). Also, a longitudinal study found that the proportion of newcomers reporting their work life as very stressful rose dramatically during the first five years of appointment, and even among highly satisfied individuals, work stress steadily eroded satisfaction (Olsen, 1993; Olsen & Sorcinelli, 1992).

One research study identified fifteen distinct career issues that are cause for concern among early-career faculty (Solem & Foote, 2004). We have categorized many discrete issues under three overarching and interwoven themes. These three core issues, which can negatively affect the productivity and success of early career faculty include: expectations for performance, particularly the tenure process; collegiality and community; and balance among professional roles and between personal and professional life. It should be noted that these concerns closely parallel those that aspiring faculty worry about when they observe the faculty with whom they work. In the following sections, we elaborate on each of these topics.

EVALUATION AND TENURE PROCESSES

Rice (1996) noted that almost a decade ago, new faculty from a distinguished Presidential Young Investigator Colloquium identified the current tenure and promotion system as "our greatest barrier to a better future." Nearly a decade later, similar concerns about feedback, evaluation, and lack of clarity and guidance through the tenure process have been expressed consistently in studies on new faculty (Austin & Rice, 1998; Rice, Sorcinelli, & Austin, 2000; Tierney & Bensimon, 1996; Trotman & Brown, 2005; Trower, 2005). Mixed reviews of the tenure system also have been identified in data from the 1989 Carnegie Survey of Faculty (Carnegie Foundation for the Advancement of Teaching,

1989) and the 1995 faculty survey conducted by the Higher Education Research Institute at the University of California-Los Angeles (Sax, Astin, Arredondo, and Korn, 1996).

On the whole, both pretenure and tenured faculty support academic tenure, but many favor some modification of the system. While early career faculty express reservations about the tenure system as a whole, most identify the *process* of contending for tenure as their greatest concern (Austin & Rice, 1998; Chait, 2002). We highlight here four common problems identified by early career faculty.

Expectations for performance. Paralleling the concerns of doctoral students, new faculty fret about vague and unclear expectations for performance. They want to do good work, but they find that expectations are not stated openly or explicitly. New faculty want clear tenure and promotion criteria—spelled out in writing—for research, teaching, service, advising and administrative duties (Austin & Rice, 1998; Rice & Sorcinelli, 2002; Trower, 2005). Some recommend that a statement of expectations be included in the letter of appointment. Others ask that chairs and departments review tenure and promotion criteria to make sure that they are up-to-date, clear, and matched to the particular mission and resources of the department.

New faculty also want departmental and institutional expectations that match, to avoid the confusion that comes from mixed messages. When they hear more senior colleagues speak about what one must do to be successful, the messages often conflict. Furthermore, as institutions themselves shift their emphases (perhaps, for example, a university clarifying its commitment to high-quality teaching and outreach work as well as to research, or a liberal arts college reconceptualizing itself as "research-oriented"), early career faculty are especially uncertain about where to put the emphasis of their own work. One study found that concerns about lack of clear expectations were particularly true for faculty of color, and faculty of color also were more likely to report worries about fitting the expectations that their institutions held for them (Alexander-Snow & Johnson, 1999). As noted earlier, many new faculty have called for their chairs, departments, and institutions to spell out the standards by which they will be judged and to arrive at some "hard and fast" criteria for tenure. At the same time, some argue that criteria and standards should be flexible, acknowledging disciplinary and individual differences (Rice, Sorcinelli, & Austin, 2000).

New faculty also look for expectations that are reasonable and fair. Many perceive that the tenure bar has been raised far above the achievements that had been required of the same senior colleagues who decide their fate. Ironically, in calling for renewed attention to multiple aspects of faculty work, national forums and associations may be contributing to the problem of more and ever escalating expectations (O'Meara & Rice, 2005). For many campuses, the approach driving academic reform has been what one might call the "additive strategy of change" in which more and more is added to the list of faculty responsibilities. For example, demands for greater productivity and quality in research, teaching, and service, especially in public institutions, may make matters worse by creating even greater tensions and even more unreasonable performance expectations for new faculty (Rice & Sorcinelli, 2002).

Feedback on progress. Insufficient, unfocused, and unclear feedback on performance from senior colleagues, chairs, deans, and members of promotion and tenure committees only serves to exacerbate lack of clarity around expectations. Early career faculty are looking both for guidance about what expectations they should meet and for periodic reviews in which they receive specific feedback on the extent to which they are meeting expectations. According to Boice (1992), academic life is marked by a conspiracy of silence; essential knowledge that one needs to succeed is often unspoken. Several other studies have similarly concluded that explicit and focused conversations are not occurring regularly or systematically (Menges, 1999; Olsen & Sorcinelli, 1992; Rice & Sorcinelli, 2002; Trower, 2005). Menges (1999) found that new faculty want three types of feedback: affirming feedback, which many received; corrective feedback to help them make improvements; and clarifying feedback on expectations. As well, new faculty concur that feedback might better serve them, particularly in their first year, if such appraisals were oriented more to development than evaluation (Rice & Sorcinelli, 2002).

Furthermore, early career faculty worry that senior colleagues who have the responsibilities to provide feedback and evaluation may not be sufficiently knowledgeable in new research areas to judge the work of their newer colleagues fairly and appropriately. There are complaints that what counts as serious scholarship is too narrowly circumscribed and that "...feedback and evaluation processes have not kept pace with the increasing level of interdisciplinary activities" (Rice, Sorcinelli & Austin, p. 11). These perceived worries can create distance between early and senior colleagues, as well as undermine the confidence that new faculty have in the evaluation process.

Collegial review structure. Early career faculty seek more transparency in the review process and believe the problem with feedback and evaluation is exacerbated by several flawed aspects of the review process. These include frequently rotating chairs, turnover in the membership of personnel committees, and closed committee meetings, which surround tenure deliberations and the values that inform them with uncertainty and often secrecy (Austin & Rice, 1998; Chait, 2002; Rice & Sorcinelli, 2002). Some suggest that tenure review committees could routinely share with probationary faculty information on their composition, charge, and review process in order to make the process less mysterious and the senior faculty and committee structure appear less insular and protective.

Several studies noted that new faculty identify their chairpersons as advocates and, in many cases, the most important individuals during their first year (Boice, 1992; Sorcinelli, 1988). But while a dean or chair may have given positive and encouraging feedback during the first few years of a new faculty member's career, someone new—perhaps with different priorities and values—may be in the role of chair, dean, or head of a personnel committee when the time comes for formal evaluation for reappointment or tenure. Here again, agreed-upon departmental criteria for tenure and systematic reviews may ameliorate the impact of a change in chairs during the tenure process. In addition, Moody (2001) noted that new faculty themselves would be well served if they kept careful records of their activities and accomplishments.

Timeline. For some early career faculty, the tenure timeline is a major concern. In some departments and disciplines, as mentioned earlier, the amount of work which early career faculty are expected to accomplish in the pretenure years seems to have increased over the last decade. Yet, though expectations for performance are high, funding opportunities are decreasing and backlogs in journal publication schedules often result in long delays before accepted manuscripts appear in print. (Rice, Sorcinelli, & Austin, 2000). Early career faculty in science-related fields face particular problems associated with the tenure timeline when their institutions do not ensure that they have the laboratories, equipment, and technology needed to do their research in a timely way. Finally, the tenure timeline can be particularly unkind to women, and sometimes men, who struggle with the conflicts that arise when heavy family responsibilities, especially childbirth and raising young children, coincide with the timeframe for tenure. In several studies, new faculty would like to see more flexibility in the timeline for tenure, such as stopping the clock and being assured that it will not negatively impact the tenure decision (Rice, Sorcinelli, & Austin, 2000; Trower, 2005)

As new faculty reflect on their work and hopes for their futures, then, a key concern revolves around expectations, feedback, evaluation, and the tenure process. Many early career faculty value the tenure system for its promise to protect academic freedom, to provide some degree of employment security, and to systematize peer collegial evaluation. Yet the current evaluation and tenure systems do not seem to be living up to their potential and promise. From annual review, to mini-tenure reviews after three years, to the tenure process, new faculty seek explicit criteria for performance, focused feedback, transparent review processes, and a flexible time frame for pursuing and completing significant work.

COLLEAGUESHIP AND COMMUNITY

Many early career faculty hold a vision of a "culture of collegiality" in which they wish to work; evidence supporting this is consistent across studies (Boice, 1992; Fink, 1984; Menges, 1999; Rice, Sorcinelli, & Austin, 2000; Sorcinelli, 1988; Tierney & Bensimon, 1996; Trower, 2005; Whitt, 1991). They want to pursue their work in a community where collaboration is respected and encouraged, where colleagues serve as mentors and role models, where friendships develop between colleagues within and across departments, and where there is time and opportunity for interaction and talk about ideas, one's work, and the institution.

The importance of collegiality in the development of early career faculty cannot be understated. "The colleagues in my department" and "good relations with colleagues" have been cited in several studies as key reasons for accepting, thriving, and remaining in an academic position (Luce & Murray, 1998; Trotman & Brown, 2005; Trower, 2005). First-year faculty often point to a supportive department chair, in particular, as having a positive effect on their performance and early career success (Boice, 1992; Sorcinelli, 2000).

In contrast to the above examples of collegiality, too many early career faculty report experiencing isolation, separation, fragmentation, loneliness, and competition (Luce & Murray, 1998; Solem & Foote, 2004). Bode (1999) and Olsen (1993) found that satisfaction with mentoring and collegiality, as well as perceptions of collegial support, diminished over the early years. Furthermore, according to Bode

(1999), women were even less satisfied than men with the collegiality they found at their institutions. New faculty describe turning outside of the campus for support and becoming less fulfilled as they seek, but do not find, the enrichment of a community of scholars in their home departments or institutions. Notable exceptions tend to occur either in elite private universities where colleagues are described as "brilliant," or in small colleges where a sense of institutional community—among colleagues and students—is nurtured as an identifying organizational feature. In general, however, studies of early career faculty report a need for more effective connections among faculty (Rice, Sorcinelli, & Austin, 2000; Trower, 2005).

Time. Early career faculty report that time is a major factor contributing to the lack of a community of peers. In fact, in several studies, the most significant issue for new faculty was time management; it was identified as a fundamental problem that affects faculty performance in teaching and research (about which more will be said later) as well as in establishing collegial relations. A sense of social isolation or disconnection from colleagues also was reported to come from personal and family issues that compete for time with attention to collegial interaction and engagement in departmental activities (Hamlin, Marcucci & Wenning, 2000; Olsen, 1993; Olsen & Sorcinelli, 1992; Solem & Foote, 2004). Overall, with the pressure to meet multiple demands, both on the work and home front, early career faculty often reported that they have little time for informal collegial interaction or for structured discussion groups. Feelings of isolation from peers and struggles with time pressures and management seemed particularly acute for women faculty (Bode, 1999).

Mentoring and Networks. Lack of mentoring and networking opportunities is another related aspect of the academic workplace that early career faculty perceive to diminish their sense of community. They feel the need for more established colleagues to help them "put a context" around institutional issues, priorities, and even rumors; to provide insights that assist them in understanding their students; and to identify useful institutional resources—all of which imply the importance of their colleagues' investment in helping them to succeed.

Yet, according to early career faculty, such mentoring or guidance is not easy to find. In *Heeding New Voices* (Rice, Sorcinelli, & Austin, 2000), participants perceived a generational gap between faculty early in their academic careers and their senior colleagues. As mentioned earlier in this chapter, academic appointment patterns in recent decades have created a bimodal faculty distribution, with a large senior group who entered and established themselves in an academic world that is very different in significant ways from the academic arena that new colleagues must negotiate.

In fact, early career faculty often report significant differences between themselves and their senior colleagues. Newcomers perceive themselves as more interested in forming connections across disciplines and faculty cohorts. At the same time, some early career faculty express doubts about their own ability to support such an interactive and collegial culture. The advent of the computer and the capacity to work at home, the press of two-career family responsibilities, the span of work responsibilities, the absence of new faculty appointments over a long period of time, and the concomitant decline of social connections in departments are all factors and conditions that work against creating and sustaining a sense of community (Rice, Sorcinelli, & Austin, 2000).

When effective mentoring and networking do occur, however, they have been found to enhance the satisfaction and success of early career faculty (Cawyer, Simonds & Davis, 2002; DeJong, Hartman & Fisher-Hoult, 1994; Hardwick, 2005; de Janasz & Sullivan, 2003; Schrodt, Cawyer & Sanders, 2003; Smith, Whitman, Grant, Stanutz, Russett, & Rankin, 2001). It is important to note, however, that most of the mentoring research and programming has been based on traditional, hierarchical mentor/mentee relationships. The short- and long-term outcomes of these relationships are difficult to measure, as is the quality and quantity of information shared. Further complicating this problem is the fact that unsuccessful mentoring relationships are rarely reported or remedied, in large part because traditional mentoring is a top-down, "deficiency-driven" process in which senior colleagues are expected to share knowledge, and new faculty members are expected to receive it (de Janasz & Sullivan, 2003; Sorcinelli & Jung, 2006).

Much like the dynamic, bi-directional models of the faculty socialization process (Tierney & Bensimon, 1996), new mentoring models are emerging that call for non-hierarchical and collaborative mentoring that supports the needs of new faculty through a network of mentors (de Janasz & Sullivan, 2003). This network or web of mentors is built upon the idea that all members of a community have something to teach and learn. For example, one-to-one mentoring might include a peer, "near-peer" (such as a recently tenured faculty member), senior faculty member, or department chair. Group mentoring might include peers or near-peers, or a group facilitated by a senior faculty member.

A newer form of mentoring, distance mentoring, can occur via e-mail, video conference, discussion boards, listservs, and/or chat/IM, encouraging an even wider web of networking and mentoring relationships with professional communities within and beyond the institution (Sorcinelli & Jung, 2006).

Regardless of the model, research on successful mentoring pairs suggests the importance of setting specific goals for the relationship, being proactive in seeking and providing support, meeting regularly, and recognizing that the relationship is reciprocal rather than hierarchical. Lessons learned from successful programs suggest the importance of integrating academic tasks with networking and social opportunities (food/meals), considering the benefits not only of departmental mentoring but also interdisciplinary/college-level pairs and groups, and integrating mentoring in the department with campus-wide faculty development initiatives (Sorcinelli, 1995).

A BALANCED LIFE

Issues of tenure, mentoring and collegiality need to be placed within a larger context that relates to the kind of lives individuals who choose academic careers are able to live. It has been argued that the threads of time and balance weave through every other category of concern described by new faculty. They contribute to the pressures of work, to the imbalance between work and personal life, to fundamental problems with the tenure process, and to difficulties in building collegiality and community. They are also linked to the special career issues with which women and minority faculty struggle (Rice, Sorcinelli, & Austin, 2000).

Balancing professional roles. "Finding enough time to do my work" emanates as one of the predominant sources of stress reported in nearly all studies of early career faculty (Boice, 1992; Fink, 1984; Luce & Murray, 1998; Sorcinelli, 1988; Whitt, 1991). Many newcomers describe their semesters as fragmented by too many tasks and too little time to complete them. Faculty worry about managing new teaching responsibilities, establishing research agendas that will meet their institutions' publication expectations, fulfilling committee responsibilities, and simply keeping up with the discipline. While faculty members have probably always felt pressed for time, the range of tasks they are now expected to do has arguably increased in recent decades. For example, higher education institutions today are asking faculty to engage with the broader community in new ways, the increasing diversity of students is necessitating more faculty attention to addressing individuals' learning needs, and the increase in technology requires faculty to learn and implement new technology-related skills to facilitate their teaching and to respond to the constant press of email messages. Additionally, changes in societal expectations about gender roles in recent decades mean that many faculty members—men as well as women—are in households where each adult is expected to balance both work and domestic responsibilities (Gappa, Austin, & Trice, 2007).

A recent study of new faculty in the discipline of geography, for example, found that time management was a core, fundamental problem that negatively affected faculty performance. Interestingly, new faculty who performed well in research were significantly better at practicing time management. It was time management difficulties related to teaching that detracted most from faculty performance (Solem & Foote, 2004).

In fact, several recent studies have concluded that teaching is a primary source of anxiety among new professors, many of who begin their first academic positions with little or no preparation in teaching. While many early career faculty are deeply committed to teaching, issues such as their own insufficient preparation, heavy teaching loads, a more diverse student body (e.g., academic preparation, race, class), disparity between student and faculty goals (e.g., consumer versus learning orientation), distrust of student evaluations, and the lack of a teaching community all serve to fray the connections between teachers and learners (Hamlin et al., 2000; Luce & Murray, 1998; Menges, 1999; Solem & Foote, 2004).

In fact, a perceived sense of personal control over teaching demands may be crucial to new faculty adjustment, according to Perry, Menec and Struthers (1999). From their study of new hires over three-year period, perceived control (a function of skill acquisition, motivational beliefs, innate ability, and prior success) was central to adjustment, shaping new hires' perceptions of teaching, specifically, and of their careers more generally. New hires who reported feeling little control over their teaching (e.g., load, schedule, demands) experienced lower job satisfaction, higher stress, and more negative emotions related to their careers. In addition, the tenure process—particularly the ways in which teaching is measured and valued—appears to have altered the way in which early career faculty view students and the instructional role. In several studies, early career faculty described their students as having too much power, particularly since student ratings were often the only judge of teaching effectiveness. Student

65

evaluations, in particular, were distrusted and, for some women and faculty of color, questioning of their intellectual authority only complicated their interactions with students (Luce & Murray, 1998; Rice, Sorcinelli, & Austin, 2000). Adding to the problem, teaching often did not engender the respect reserved for research at the tenure decision. Thus, striving for quality teaching and learning, which necessitates personal contact with students in and out of class, may be problematic or challenging to early career faculty pursuing the track to tenure.

Another central concern of new faculty related to time is the incongruity between work roles and responsibilities and the structure of rewards. Many early career faculty spend a great deal of time worrying about what to teach, how best to teach, and how to motivate students. Departmental expectations for teaching can vary, ranging from updating the curriculum with new course offerings, teaching large lecture courses, infusing technology into teaching, and dealing with a more diverse student body. Despite eagerness to expand their pedagogical repertoire, many newcomers have little prior training to prepare them for such teaching and already suspect that they devote more time to teaching than their institution will reward. In some cases, they also feel that their senior colleagues and departments offer them little help in maintaining balance (Luce & Murray, 1998; Rice, Sorcinelli, & Austin, 2000; Solem & Foote, 2004).

The complicated tensions between teaching and research, and the rewards for each, may be most predominant in universities with complex missions. For example, Perry, Menec & Struthers (1999) found that, like perceived control, institution type had a major impact on the adjustment of new hires. Their study of new hires, mentioned earlier, also observed that institutions with more focused (i.e. teaching or research) than diffuse missions may put less pressure on early career faculty. They concluded that adjustment to work roles for new hires was far more difficult in the liberal arts and comprehensive institution than in either the community college or research university.

In addition, the concern of new faculty about lack of time and inability to successfully balance work roles is the most consistent source of stress over time. One study found that by the fifth year junior faculty members described an increased personal comfort with teaching as well as greater clarity and direction in their research agenda. At the same time, however, satisfaction with the ability to find enough time to do work and to balance the conflicting demands of research, teaching, and service continued to decline (Olsen, 1993; Olsen & Crawford, 1998; Olsen & Sorcinelli, 1992).

Balancing professional and personal life. Research on new and early career faculty reveals that efforts to balance the demands of professional work and personal life—which can include being a spouse, a parent, a child of aging parents, an involved citizen—compound new faculty stress. In studies across career stages (Sorcinelli, 1985; Sorcinelli & Near, 1989), researchers found that approximately half of the faculty members they interviewed or surveyed reported considerable stress in trying to balance personal and family life and the requirements of professional success. Surveys by the Carnegie Foundation for the Advancement of Teaching (1989) also indicated that the extent to which work intruded into personal life was a primary factor in influencing overall dissatisfaction among faculty members.

One study found, in particular, that balancing work and family seems to be more difficult for early career faculty members who struggle with time management (Solem & Foote, 2004). Another study found that junior faculty reported significantly more of what is called negative spillover (their work life negatively "spilled over" into their personal life) than did associate or full professors (Sorcinelli & Near, 1989). Data also indicated that faculty were less satisfied with the balance between their work and non-work lives after being faculty members for several years. In particular, there was an increase in the percentage of early career faculty indicating that their work lives exercised a great deal of negative impact on their non-work lives. The conflict stemmed largely from "an erosion of leisure time and social relations under the press of institutional and self-imposed work commitments" (Olsen, 1993, p. 8).

In *Work, Family, and the Faculty Career*, Gappa and MacDermid (1997) considered work-family issues as they affect faculty recruitment, retention and productivity. They drew several conclusions. First, pretenure faculty workloads are exacerbated in dual-career relationships. Academic career patterns originally were established by and for male faculty who had the support of a spouse at home, and that prevailing conception remains. Second, concerns about time and balance are greater for pretenure faculty who try to balance career demands and "the tenure rat race" versus family and personal time. Women faculty, in particular, speak of having to juggle (and sometimes hide) other roles and responsibilities. Third, senior faculty do not seem to understand the stresses and demands of work and family life on younger colleagues, particularly during the tenure process.

Finally, academe's decentralized structure, resources, and policies further hamper the creation of an environment sensitive to work-family conflicts because communication and cooperation across decentralized structures are so difficult (Gappa & MacDermid, 1997).

Throughout the years before tenure, then, early career faculty continue to experience difficulties balancing time for family or other responsibilities outside work with career aspirations. Striking a balance between the two significant domains of their lives may take considerable time to achieve.

SPECIAL ISSUES FACED BY NON-MAJORITY FACULTY

Certainly, in some departments, early career faculty can find exceptions to the intense experiences reported in this section about tenure, community, and a balanced life. Yet a number of studies (Gappa & Leslie, 1993, 1997; Rice, Sorcinelli, & Austin, 2000; Tierney & Bensimon, 1996; Trower, 2005) indicate that such experiences are both commonplace and especially keen for specific groups within the professoriate. The overall numbers of non-majority faculty represented in new faculty studies is small; however, the voices of women and faculty of color strongly accentuate the three themes that figure so prominently in other research. We have noted the research on women and faculty of color when possible throughout this chapter; here we summarize key themes related to their particular experiences.

Early career women faculty reported unusual difficulty in finding advisors or mentors among those more senior, and they described environments where subtle discrimination causes them to struggle with being taken seriously and as equals of their male colleagues. Women reported a sense of isolation, because they felt they could not openly discuss the multiple professional and personal responsibilities that comprise their daily lives for fear that colleagues would perceive them as trying to make excuses or not being serious about their work (Rice, Sorcinelli, & Austin, 2000; Solem & Foote, 2004). From their departments, especially, women faculty expressed a desire for more equitable treatment in terms of work (e.g., teaching loads, lab facilities, committee assignments), for inclusion in professional and social networks, and for more sensitivity to their personal lives.

Faculty of color also noted concerns that arise from the interplay of tenure, community, work, and life outside of work. Moody (2001) has enumerated a number of cultural, racial, gender or class "taxes" that are extracted from underrepresented faculty. These include: encountering a chilly climate in the department or institution; standing out from colleagues, most of whom are majority group members; having excessive committee assignments and student advising duties; and being undervalued in terms of scholarship or as an affirmative action hire. Isolation especially stands out as a core issue for faculty of color as they attempt to handle the day-to-day stress when one is a member of a minority group in a department or institution. Collegiality becomes even more of a challenge with the added stresses of differences among faculty in age, gender, cultural background, and intellectual and research interests. In these circumstances, special effort and time are required to find or create a sense of community, even as one may be asked to fulfill an unusually heavy load of institutional requirements as a representative of the minority group.

Faculty of color, in particular, have called for a stronger ethos of collegiality and mentorship in the academy (Moody, 2001; Rice, Sorcinelli, & Austin, 2000; Tierney & Bensimon, 1996). In this way, a range of their concerns—such as how to find support for controversial research, deal with problems and prejudices encountered in the classroom, ascribe value to service, approach tenure, figure out how the institution works, move inside traditional professional and campus networks, and attend to the family unit (e.g., childcare, spousal situations)—might be areas for particular institutional attention.

STRATEGIES FOR SUPPORTING EARLY CAREER FACULTY

The experiences and concerns that appear in the research concerning new faculty have led researchers, faculty developers, and institutional leaders to consider and develop strategies for supporting new faculty in their roles. One strategy, however, is not sufficient to ensure success. Rather, multiple players and a variety of efforts are necessary to ensure that new faculty embark on successful and rewarding careers. Department chairs and senior colleagues play a critically important role in ensuring resources are available, creating a supportive climate, and providing guidance. Institutional leaders, including provosts, deans, and faculty developers, help set an institutional tone of interest in the well-being of faculty and can allocate resources for useful institution-wide initiatives. In a recent study of faculty developers, respondents indicated that providing programs for new and early career faculty was one of the top priorities of their institutions (Sorcinelli, Austin, Eddy, & Beach, 2006). New faculty themselves also can take specific steps to structure their work in ways that enhance their likelihood of success and satisfaction.

In this section, we discuss specific strategies for helping new faculty get started and progress successfully. The first part of this section focuses on strategies that new faculty members can use to help themselves. The rest of the section suggests strategies for senior institutional leaders, department chairs, and senior colleagues to consider, all based in recommendations from major studies from the past two decades, including, for example, such studies as those of Boice (1992), Menges (1999), Sorcinelli & Austin (1992), Rice, Sorcinelli, and Austin (2000), and Tierney & Bensimon (1996). In 2000, when the American Association of Higher Education published results from its study of aspiring and new faculty in *Heeding New Voices* (Rice, Sorcinelli, & Austin, 2000), it also published a companion piece *Principles of Good Practice for Supporting Faculty on the Tenure Track* (Sorcinelli, 2000). This monograph presented ten "principles of good practice," and, for each, included specific actions as well as institutional examples. This monograph is now out-of-print, but we follow much of its pattern for organizing strategies and highlight many of its suggestions in this section.

EFFECTIVE STRATEGIES USED BY SUCCESSFUL NEW FACULTY MEMBERS

An individual faculty member can significantly increase the chances of successful performance in the earliest stages of his or her faculty career. Boice (1991) identified what he refers to as "Quick Starters"—those faculty who scored in the top 25% along three dimensions of faculty teaching activity—classroom observations, student ratings, self-ratings. These "quick starters" demonstrated what Boice (2000) later referred to as an ability to teach, write, or engage in service activity "with moderation".

These individuals share several characteristics. First, in the classroom, they lecture in such a way that allows for student involvement. Second, they express "uncritical, accepting, and optimistic attitudes" (p. 113) about undergraduates at their institutions, and do not express high levels of criticism about colleagues and the campus. Third, these individuals seek advice from others about

70

scholarship and teaching. Fourth, they are efficient in their class preparation and writing activity. Fifth, they are able to balance expenditure of time across their faculty responsibilities. Sixth, they integrate their research/scholarly interests into their classroom teaching. Seventh, they demonstrate evidence of high energy, wide array of interests, humor and consciousness about self-presentation.

Based on his research on effective new faculty, Boice set out what he called "First Order Principles" (1991, 2000), normative behaviors that his research demonstrated to be characteristic of early career faculty who thrive in their positions. Boice saw these principles as forming the foundation for "comfortable and efficient practice" (Boice, p. 116, 1991). They include what he called "patience and waiting"— taking the time to ensure student learning in a lecture or to prepare and arrange relevant materials before beginning a writing project. He also admonished new faculty to "begin before you are ready" and to avoid postponing or procrastinating in handling writing or teaching tasks. This approach enables one to get work accomplished before it feels burdensome. Third, he suggested that new faculty work in brief but regular sessions. Fourth, effective new faculty need to know when to stop their writing or class preparation in order that their efforts do not result in diminishing returns. Additionally, new faculty should "avoid negative self-talk," strive to manage their reactions to criticisms, and learn from criticism. Collaborating and sharing work with others is another "first order principle" (Boice, 1991, 2000).

Other writers offer strategies for junior faculty interested in participating in specific activities such as curriculum change. For example, recognizing the limited influence of junior faculty and the potential political "landmines" involved in this work, Hetrick (2005) suggested new faculty might find a useful role in managing communication and information gathering on a curricular change project.

New faculty members can be particularly wise in their approach to the tenure process. Whicker, Kroenfeld, and Strickland (1993) suggested that a pre-tenure faculty member: (1) polish his or her political abilities and build a supportive coalition; (2) manage his or her professional image, deciding with whom, when and how to share his or her successes; (3) identify people with whom he or she shares similar backgrounds, and use this similarity to begin effective communications; and (4) try to secure grant funds, no matter how small and distribute funds to the department. In an issue of the *National Teaching and Learning Forum* in which Sorcinelli (2004) provided a concise list of tips for new faculty members and the institutional leaders supporting them, she recommended that early career faculty ask newly tenured faculty members about what does and what does not count in relation to tenure and promotion review.

In sum, while institutional leaders and established faculty have a serious responsibility to support new faculty members as they become acquainted with the institution and learn their roles, individual faculty members must take responsibility also. Through how they approach their daily responsibilities and interactions with colleagues, new faculty members can do much to pave the way for their own success.

EFFECTIVE STRATEGIES FOR USE BY CHAIRS, SENIOR FACULTY, AND INSTITUTIONAL LEADERS

This section highlights four sets of strategies that provosts and deans, department chairs, and senior faculty can use to help new faculty get started and progress with success: strategies that get new faculty started and connect them with resources, strategies that encourage collegial connections, strategies that address time, balance, and flexibility issues, and strategies that pertain to tenure. Various books and articles have explored the roles and responsibilities of department chairs, in particular, and offer guidance about their important role in helping new faculty become established in the early years of their careers (Bensimon, Ward, & Sanders, 2000; Leaming, 1998; Moody, 2001; Sorcinelli, 1989).

Strategies that connect faculty with resources. New faculty members need some resources right from the start. Appropriate office space and equipment to do their work are necessities. One of the understandable concerns expressed by early career faculty, particularly in science and engineering, when they discuss the tenure process is the anxiety and pressure created when the equipment or laboratory resources they have been promised are not available in a timely way.

Chairs, deans, and senior institutional leaders should also encourage new faculty to participate in orientations to their departments and institutions. At the department level, they need to become acquainted with their immediate colleagues, and they need information about the unit's culture, overall expectations, and resources to support their work. At the institution level, they need to learn about the culture and values of the institution, an overview of general expectations for promotion and tenure (when applicable), an introduction to the breadth of resources available for them to use, including teaching centers, research units that often help with grant devel-opment, and networks that bring together faculty with similar interests (e.g., first-year faculty, women faculty, faculty interested in exploring technology resources). Orientations also should convey a strong sense of welcome to the institution and the message that the unique contri-butions that the new faculty will make are invited and valued. Faculty development professionals often see one of their primary responsi-bilities as helping new faculty become oriented and settled into the institution, and they are resources that deans and chairs can use (Sorcinelli, Austin, Eddy, & Beach, 2006). At a number of institu-tions, orientations go beyond one-time events at the start of the academic year, and instead include a variety of seminars, gatherings, and programs across the first year. Such extended programs give faculty members opportunities to develop meaningful relationships with colleagues from across campus (Welch, 2002). A new and creative option being piloted on some campuses is flexible, accessible web-based orientations for new faculty.

Many universities and colleges have active faculty development or teaching and learning centers that provide opportunities for faculty members to develop their professional abilities. New faculty members sometimes feel hesitant about taking time to participate in such opportunities. Yet, research shows that the time spent strength-ening their teaching abilities enhances their confidence and skills. Furthermore, participating in seminars, programs, and events provides another opportunity to meet colleagues and learn about the insti-tution (Austin, 1992). As new faculty members become more diverse in their appointment types, with institutions having some faculty holding part-time and contract appointments as well as others in traditional full-time, tenure-track appointments, faculty development professionals should help their institutions find innovative ways to provide professional development opportunities that accommodate the time constraints that many faculty feel. More use of the web and on-line resources and interactions are interesting avenues for institutions to explore (Gappa, Austin, & Trice, 2007).

One concern that is often on the minds of new faculty pertains to institutional citizenship. They sometimes are unsure about the kinds of committees on which they should serve and the appropriate allocation of their time in such institutional work. Department chairs can provide helpful guidance concerning the role of citizenship in the institution's culture, the expectations that the department, college, or university has for new faculty involved in governance and other aspects of institutional life, and the range of ways in which a new faculty member might fulfill institutional responsibilities while also devoting reasonable time to research and teaching responsibilities. Faculty of color and female faculty sometimes find they are called on to a greater extent than their white, male colleagues to serve on department or institutional committees. Department chairs need to be especially alert to helping faculty negotiate this situation in order to ensure that the new faculty members develop balanced portfolios appropriate for progress toward tenure within the institutional context (Rice, Sorcinelli, & Austin, 2000; Tierney & Bensimon, 1996).

Strategies that encourage collegial connections. Establishing strong collegial connections is critical for new faculty success. Deans, chairs, and senior faculty can play an important role in helping their new colleagues make such connections. Collegial connections help new faculty feel welcome, they can lead to interesting research and teaching collaborations, and they expose new faculty to a broader view of the institution. Early career faculty understandably interpret faculty life from the perspective of their own departments and sometimes are unsure of what constitutes typical or unusual expectations or circumstances; interactions with colleagues who are more senior or are from other parts of the university provide them with broader perspective from which to interpret their own experiences (Austin, 1992).

One strategy to help new faculty establish collegial relationships is for department chairs and deans to encourage senior faculty to serve in mentoring roles. As noted earlier, various models have been used, with each having its advantages. Some departments assign each new faculty member a senior faculty mentor, while others ask the new colleague to choose a mentor. Departments often find mentoring committees work well, with several faculty members agreeing to work as a team to provide the new colleague with guidance, support, and an available sounding board. Emeritus faculty can be wise participants in such a team. Some new faculty also value mentors from outside the department, since they may be concerned about revealing their weaknesses or uncertainties to departmental colleagues who ultimately have responsibility to render decisions about their tenure or future employment. One university's professional development center provides each new faculty member a one course reduction in teaching during the first semester; in exchange, the new colleagues are expected to participate in a mentoring program in which senior colleagues, appointed as special Teaching Scholars for a three-year term, provide support (Sorcinelli, 2000).

In addition to establishing explicit mentoring arrangements, department chairs can encourage senior faculty to be welcoming to new colleagues, perhaps by inviting them to lunch, inviting them to teach-team, offering to read their papers, or discussing co-authoring a paper or grant. All faculty members have heavy loads and find their days very busy. While most faculty probably want to support new faculty, time demands may thwart their intentions. Deans and chairs can encourage the efforts of senior faculty to be supportive colleagues by building mentoring of new faculty into evaluation processes for established faculty. They can also provide rewards or recognition for efforts to help new faculty succeed.

As interdisciplinary research expands and as universities and colleges develop interdisciplinary programs and courses, new faculty may be interested in participating in interdisciplinary or collaborative research teams or teaching assignments. If their departments support work of this kind, chairs can help them meet colleagues who are possible collaborators. Such interdisciplinary collaborations can be especially supportive for new faculty whose specialties are not shared with other faculty in their own departments but relate to areas that faculty elsewhere in the institution study.

Finally, deans and department chairs can explicitly encourage new faculty to ask questions and to be proactive in seeking collegial relationships. For example, deans can consider providing funds for faculty members to invite colleagues to lunch during the first year.

Strategies that address time, balance, and flexibility issues. One of the greatest sources of stress and concern for new faculty is the issue of time. New faculty feel pulled in all directions and sometimes express uncertainty about where to put their priorities (Rice, Sorcinelli, & Austin, 2000; Sorcinelli, Austin, & Trower, 2001; Trower Austin, & Sorcinelli, 2001). One specific concern is that they want to do well in their new responsibilities, but they sometimes are not sure what specific steps they can take to ensure success. Resources that are available often seem to require too much time to use. In addition to getting established with their new professional responsibilities, they often also have personal responsibilities that require their attention. This collage of issues comes down to concerns about time, balance, and flexibility for many faculty. Deans, department chairs, and senior faculty members can enlist specific strategies and interventions that address these concerns (Sorcinelli, 2000).

First, department chairs can help new faculty get a good start with their teaching responsibilities. They can begin by assigning newcomers courses whose content they know or that are related to their areas of interest and expertise. Many deans and chairs provide first-year faculty with reduced teaching loads or at least keep an eye on the number of course preparations involved. Chairs can also provide an array of resources to support new faculty members' teaching efforts. They can provide information on expected or typical office hour arrangements and on the characteristics of the students who typically take the courses, and they can provide sample syllabi. Chairs can also encourage established faculty members to invite newcomers to observe their courses or, if the newcomer is willing, suggest that senior colleagues could visit the new colleague's courses to provide informal feedback. Some departments also organize informal discussions among all colleagues about teaching-related issues, such as motivating students, grading, and using peer writing strategies.

Department chairs also have an important role in encouraging new faculty to take advantage of the institutional teaching and learning or professional development center. Such centers typically offer one-time programs on teaching topics as well as programs that bring faculty together over an extended time period—such as teaching fellows programs that create learning communities among early career faculty interested in enhancing their thinking and practice as teachers (Austin, 1992). Teaching and learning centers often offer informal feedback involving visits to classes by unbiased evaluators (Sorcinelli, 2000; Sorcinelli, Austin, Eddy, & Beach, 2006). New faculty may be uncertain whether using the resources of the teaching and learning center is a productive use of their time, and may also be concerned whether use of such resources signals weakness in their credentials. The encouragement and assurance by a chair that efforts to improve one's teaching are valued and viewed as signals of professional commitment can encourage new faculty to use available resources. Chairs also can maintain a budget to support faculty interested in purchasing books that provide guidance on teaching and who wish to attend teaching-related workshops for which there are fees.

Second, institutional leaders, deans, and department chairs have a responsibility to support new faculty in their development as researchers. As with teaching, new faculty need basic resources upon their arrival. They should be able to count on adequate laboratory, office, or studio space, as well as a computer. Faculty in science, engineering, or computer science fields may have specific equipment needs that are discussed during the hiring negotiations. Chairs should monitor whether these agreements are fulfilled appropriately. New faculty also need support in the form of graduate assistants, clerical staff, and technical help, as appropriate for the institutional context. Deans and chairs should also consider what travel support is available to new faculty, who need to attend conferences to deliver papers and make professional contacts necessary for the development of their scholarly progress and reputations, but who are likely to be least able to fund their own travel.

Chairs can also help faculty locate institutional resources that will support their research, including grant development help and special institutional research competitions for early career faculty. Within the department, a chair might encourage informal discussion (e.g., brown bags) where new and senior faculty can discuss their work in progress or ideas in incubation or explore possible collaborative ventures. Chairs can also guide new faculty to understand the range of research products that are acceptable within the institution, college, and department context. With the increasing interest in interdisciplinary research, the scholarship of teaching, and the scholarship of engagement, new faculty need advice about what kinds of scholarship are valued in the contexts they have entered, and how their scholarly work can be pursued in ways that are favorable for their long-term success. Some departments also offer "internal sabbaticals" through which colleagues organize teaching responsibilities so that individuals can have lighter teaching loads some semesters to pursue research projects (Gappa, Austin, & Trice, 2007). The logic behind providing the kind of support for research suggested here is that new faculty can be more successful if their time can be used most productively. When they have opportunities to gain information, connect with resources, and make connections with junior or senior colleagues with whom they might work or who have ideas or information that help them in their work, they are likely to save time in the long-run.

Third, institutional leaders, deans, and department chairs can help new faculty manage their personal and professional lives. A first step is to be sure new faculty perceive the department and institutional contexts they are entering as welcoming and supportive. Department chairs do much to influence and convey the nature of the culture in which the new colleague will work. Chairs should be sure that new faculty automatically receive information about policies that relate to their professional and personal lives, including, for example, policies concerning health-related, parental or family leave, guidelines for shifting status from full-time to part-time under particular circumstances, and flexibility available under tenure policies. Additionally, new faculty should be given information about the array of institutional resources that may help with their personal responsibilities: health care options, childcare opportunities, any support provided for emergency sick children situations, and recreation opportunities on campus of interest to adults and children.

Interest in institutional policies that help faculty manage their professional and personal responsibilities has increased greatly in recent years, particularly as the professoriate has become more diverse. Several useful resources that suggest specific institutional strategies for addressing flexibility in the faculty career, many of which are directly relevant to new faculty, are recently available. These include the American Council on Education report on *An Agenda for Excellence: Creating Flexibility in Tenure-Track Faculty Careers* (2005), a report from the University of Michigan on policies to support career flexibility (Weiss & McDonald, 2005), and Gappa, Austin, and Trice's recently completed book entitled *Rethinking Faculty Work: Higher Education's Strategic Imperative* (2007).

Strategies pertaining to tenure. For those new faculty in tenure-track positions, the process through which they must progress to attain tenure is probably the most stressful aspect of the early career. Over the past decade, several very comprehensive and useful publications have addressed both the issues concerning tenure and ways to address these concerns (including, for example, American Council on Education, 2005; Austin, 1992; Austin & Rice, 1998; Chait, 2002; Gappa Austin, & Trice, 2007; Rice, Sorcinelli, & Austin, 2000; Sorcinelli, 2000). The research is quite consistent in the recommendations for ways to help new faculty manage the tenure process with less stress and with more success.

First, senior institutional leaders, deans, and department chairs need to communicate expectations about tenure criteria and information about the tenure process as clearly as possible. New faculty need clear statements at the time of their appointments concerning the specific expectations associated with the position. They also need clear and specific information about how the tenure process works at their institutions: What is the time schedule, who is involved at each step of the process, what information must they compile and when, and what overall criteria does the institution, college, and department utilize to evaluate tenure dossiers. In addition to specific information about the expectations associated with one's position that is provided at the time of appointment, many institutions address basic tenure processes and criteria during institutional orientation sessions. Recognizing that new faculty have much on their minds (such as getting their homes and offices organized, preparing initial syllabi, and setting up their research labs), some institutions offer annual seminars for early career faculty, scheduled later in the academic year, that go into much more detail about the tenure process. At such seminars, new faculty can be provided with copies of the institution's tenure policies and guidelines and examples of successful tenure dossiers (with names deleted). Ample time can be provided for questions so that faculty leave feeling that what is often perceived as mystery around the tenure process has been lifted. New faculty also often report receiving "mixed messages" from faculty colleagues about how the tenure process works, so in-depth institutional seminars can help them sort through some of the conflicting messages they hear (Rice, Sorcinelli, & Austin, 2000).

Provosts, deans, and department chairs should also ensure that complete information about flexibility in tenure policies is available to all faculty members. Such policies include, for example, "stopping the tenure clock," personal and parental leaves, modified duties and reduced load options, and shared appointments (American Council on Education, 2005; Gappa, Austin, & Trice, 2007). New faculty, particularly women, are often reluctant to ask about such policies, not wishing to set themselves apart from the norm or to appear uncommitted to their work. As universities and colleges seek to support diverse and talented faculty members, they are wise to ensure that policies are widely understood and that all faculty feel welcome to use them without penalty.

A third strategy to help new faculty with the tenure process involves systematic, specific, and clear feedback. Department chairs should provide new faculty members with annual reviews to discuss their progress. These reviews should highlight what is positive and commendable in the new faculty member's work, what issues need attention, and specific suggestions for how the faculty member can continue to progress and enhance the strength of his or her case for tenure. Chairs can also encourage new faculty to manage and monitor their own progress by setting realistic and appropriate goals, and maintaining complete records of their accomplishments and efforts. Chairs should also encourage new faculty to stay in contact through on-going, informal conversations in addition to the annual review, so that the new faculty member can ask questions as they arise and the chair is well-informed about the choices the faculty member is making in regard to his or her work. Such conversations provide opportunities for the new faculty member to receive on-going, formative feedback.

Another strategy deans and chairs can use to help support a fair and equitable tenure process is to ensure that all faculty members, senior as well as junior, understand expectations and criteria. Typically, faculty members who serve on department, college, or institution-level tenure and promotion committees rotate over time. Ensuring that criteria and policies are interpreted and implemented consistently requires wide understanding of institutional expectations, procedures, and policies. In addition to the orientation sessions mentioned above, college-level tenure and promotion committees can hold meetings with early career faculty to provide information about the process, to offer an avenue for questions to be raised, and to contribute to broader understanding among all colleagues about how the process works and what is expected.

DIRECTIONS FOR FUTURE RESEARCH

Over the past two decades, the research on new faculty as well as on graduate students aspiring to the faculty has been steadily increasing. This solid body of work is fairly consistent in its findings regarding the preparation, experiences, and concerns of new faculty. Five key issues consistently emerge as particularly important to early career faculty: getting started, excelling in both teaching and research, navigating the tenure track, building collegial and professional networks, and balancing work and life outside work. Department chairs, deans, provosts, and new faculty themselves all have roles to play in helping early career faculty manage these issues and succeed in their careers. The consistency of the research findings about new faculty should provide institutional leaders some confidence as they consider strategies to support the work of these important members of the academic community. Some questions remain unanswered, however, and some are emerging as the faculty becomes more diverse and as the patterns of appointment types into which new faculty are hired are shifting. Here we suggest several areas in which further research is needed.

Faculty in different institutional types. Much of the research to date has focused predominantly on faculty members in research universities. While the faculty experience has many similar aspects across institutional types, important differences are at work also. For example, the relative balance of emphasis that faculty members are expected to devote to teaching and research varies across institutional type, with different expectations at liberal arts colleges, community colleges, comprehensive master's-granting institutions, and research institutions. In addition, the experiences of new faculty at fully on-line universities to our knowledge have not been studied at all. Future research that focuses specifically on the experiences and issues for faculty at institutions other than research universities will broaden and deepen what is known about new faculty.

Faculty in various appointment types. Just as most of the research has focused more heavily on new faculty in research universities, so too has the emphasis been mostly on tenure-track faculty. With more than the majority of new appointments now being off the tenure-track, research studies should explore the experience of new faculty in fixed term and part-time appointments. These faculty members do not face the challenges of negotiating tenure expectations, but they have to deal with an array of other significant challenges. Research that examines their experiences should provide useful information to institutions trying to welcome and support these new colleagues.

Women faculty and faculty of color. As discussed earlier in this chapter, some of the research in recent years has concerned specifically the experiences of new faculty of color and female faculty. The methodology of that research has often involved qualitative studies of relatively small numbers of faculty. As important as the existing research has been in highlighting the particular issues confronting women and faculty of color, more extensive research involving larger numbers of faculty would expand what is known and provide findings that can inform institutional efforts to diversity the faculty.

The impact of policies to expand career flexibility. As higher education institutions develop policies designed to support a diverse professoriate, including policies to bring more flexibility into the tenure track, individual faculty members are choosing ways to construct faculty careers that differ from traditional patterns in the past. For example, some early career faculty choose to use policies that enable them to handle professional and personal responsibilities through modified duties or extended tenure clocks. An important research direction would include studies that examine the impact of faculty use of policies designed to provide flexibility on the work experience and satisfaction of new faculty and on the quality and extent of their institutional contributions.

Integrated faculty development. Closely related to the previous suggestion is a recommendation to study integrated faculty devel-

81

opment efforts. Some universities and colleges are putting into place comprehensive, integrated plans to recruit and support new faculty. Such plans might include, for example, mentoring, professional development workshops, leadership development, collegial networks, professional development plans, guidance to chairs who are working with new faculty, and work-family supports for dual career families with young children. Systematic research on the impact of comprehensive institutional plans on faculty members and on institutional variables is necessary to indicate whether such efforts have useful and cost-effective outcomes.

The faculty portrait is changing as senior faculty who have served their institutions and disciplines for many years retire and new colleagues take their place, and as patterns of academic appointments change (Schuster & Finkelstein, 2006). Universities and colleges need to welcome and support the new faculty who will become the backbone of the academic endeavor in the coming decades. We must use what we know about supporting new faculty as they strive to do excellent work and find satisfying homes in the academy—and we must ensure that our knowledge stays apace of the changing experiences and challenges of the new faculty.

REFERENCES

Alexander-Snow, M., and Johnson, B. (1999). Perspectives from faculty of color. In R. J. Menges and Associates (eds.), *Faculty in New Jobs: A Guide to Settling in, Becoming Established, and Building Institutional Support* (pp. 88–117). San Francisco: Jossey-Bass.

American Council on Education. (2005). *Creating an Agenda for Excellence: Creating Flexibility in Tenure-Track Faculty Careers*. Washington, DC: Author.

Association of American Universities. (2005). *Postdoctoral Education Survey: Summary of Results*. Washington, DC: Author. Retrieved on April 30, 2006 from http://www.aau.edu/education/postdoct.cfm.

Anderson, M.S., and Swazey, J.P. (1998). Reflections on the graduate student experience: An overview. In M.S. Anderson (ed.), *The Experience of being in Graduate School: An Exploration. New Directions for Teaching and Learning*, 101. San Francisco: Jossey-Bass.

Antony, J.S. (2002). Reexamining doctoral student socialization and professional development: Moving beyond the congruence and assimilation orientation. In J.C. Smart (ed.), *Higher Education: Handbook of Theory and Research* (Vol. 17, pp. 349–380). New York: Agathon Press.

Antony, J.S., and Taylor, E. (2004). Theories and strategies of academic career socialization: Improving paths to the professoriate for black graduate students. In D.H. Wulff and A.E. Austin (eds.), *Paths to the professoriate: Strategies for enriching the preparation of future faculty* (pp. 92–114). San Francisco: Jossey-Bass.

Austin, A.E. (1992). Supporting the professor as teacher: The Lilly teaching fellows program. *The Review of Higher Education* 16 (1): 85–106.

Austin, A.E. (2002a). Creating a bridge to the future: Preparing new faculty to face changing expectations in a shifting context. *Review of Higher Education* 26(2): 119–144.

Austin, A.E. (2002b). Preparing the next generation of faculty: Graduate school as socialization to the academic career. *Journal of Higher Education* 73(1): 94–122.

Austin, A.E., and McDaniels, M. (2006). Preparing the professoriate of the future: Graduate student socialization for faculty roles. In J.C. Smart (ed.), *Higher Education: Handbook of Theory and Research* (Vol. 21, pp. 397–456). The Netherlands: Kluwer Academic Publishers.

Austin, A.E., and Rice, R.E. (1998). Making tenure viable: Listening to early career faculty. *American Behavioral Scientist* 41(5): 736–754.

Bensimon, E.M., Ward, K., and Sanders, K. (2000). *The department chair's role in developing new faculty into teachers and scholars*. Bolton, MA: Anker Publishing.

Bode, R.K. (1999). Mentoring and collegiality. In R.J. Menges and Associates (eds.), *Faculty in New Jobs: A Guide to Setting in, Becoming Established, and Building Institutional Support* (pp. 118–144). San Francisco: Jossey-Bass.

Boice, R. (1991). Quick starters: New faculty who succeed. In M. Theall and J. Franklin (eds.), *Effective Practices for Improving Teaching* (pp.111–121). *New Directions for Teaching and Learning*, 48. San Francisco: Jossey-Bass.

Boice, R. (1992). *The New Faculty Member: Supporting and Fostering Professional Development*. San Francisco: Jossey-Bass.

Boice, R. (2000). *Advice for New Faculty Members: Nihil Nimus*. Boston, MA: Allyn and Bacon.

Bragg, A.K. (1976). *The Socialization Process in Higher Education*. Washington, DC: The American Association of Higher Education.

Braxton, J.M., and Baird, L.L. (2001). Preparation for professional self-regulation. *Science and Engineering Ethics* 7: 593–610.

Brim, O.G., Jr. (1966). Socialization through the life cycle. In O.G. Brim, Jr. and S. Wheelter (eds.), *Socialization after childhood: Two essays* (pp. 1–49). New York: Wiley.

Brown, B.E. (2005). Personal communication on March 16, 2005. In J. Gappa, A. Austin and A. Trice (2007), *Rethinking Faculty Work: Higher Education's Strategic Imperative*. San Francisco: Jossey-Bass.

Bullis, C., and Bach, B. (1989). Socialization turning points: An examination of change in organizational identification. Paper presented at the annual meeting of the Western Speech Communication Association, Spokane, WA (ED 306 607).

Carnegie Foundation for the Advancement of Teaching. (1989). *Condition of the Professoriate: Attitudes and Trends*. Princeton, NJ: The Carnegie Foundation for the Advancement of Teaching.

Cawyer, C.S., Simonds, C., and Davis, S. (2002). Mentoring to facilitate socialization: The case of the new faculty member. *Qualitative Studies in Education* 15(2): 225–242.

Chait, R.P. (ed.). (2002). *The Question of Tenure*. Cambridge, MA: Harvard University Press.

Clark, S.M., and Corcoran, M. (1986). Perspectives on the professional socialization of women faculty. *Journal of Higher Education* 57(1): 20–43.

Committee on Science, Engineering, and Public Policy (COSEPUP) (2000). *Enhancing the postdoctoral experience for scientists and engineers: A guide for postdoctoral scholars, advisers, institutions, funding organizations, and disciplinary societies*. Washington, D.C.: National Academies Press. Retrieved on April 30, 2006 from http://books.nap.edu/catalog/9831.html.

Davis, G. (2005). Doctors without orders. *American Scientist*, 93 (3, supplement). Retrieved on April 30, 2006 from http://www.postdoc.sigmaxi.org/results.

Davis, G., and Fiske (2000). Results of the 1999 PhDs.org graduate school survey. A paper presented at the Re-envisioning the PhD Conference, Seattle.

de Janasz, S.C., and Sullivan, S.E. (2003). Multiple mentoring in academe: Developing the professorial network. *Journal of Vocational Behavior* 64: 263–283.

De Jong, C., Hartman, M., and Fisher-Hoult, J. (1994). Mentoring new faculty. *Journal of Staff, Program, & Organization Development* 12(1): 41–49.

Fink, L.D. (1984). *The first year of college teaching*. New Directions for Teaching and Learning, 17. San Francisco: Jossey-Bass.

Finkelstein, M.J., and Schuster, J.H. (2001). Assessing the silent revolution: How changing demographics are reshaping the academic profession. *AAHE Bulletin* 54(2): 3–7.

Finkelstein, M.J., Seal, R.J., and Schuster, J.H. (1998). *The New Academic Generation: A Profession in Transformation*. Baltimore, MD: The Johns Hopkins University Press.

Gappa, J.M., Austin, A.E., and Trice, A.G. (2007). *Rethinking Faculty Work: Higher Education's Strategic Imperative*. San Francisco: Jossey-Bass.

Gappa, J.M., and Leslie, D.W. (1993). *The Invisible Faculty: Improving the Status of Part-timers in Higher Education*. San Francisco, CA: Jossey-Bass.

Gappa, J.M., and Leslie, D.W. (1997). Two faculties or one? The conundrum of part-timers in a bifurcated work force. *New Pathways Inquiry No. 6.* Washington, DC: American Association for Higher Education.

Gappa, J.M., and MacDermid, S.M. (1997). Work, family, and the faculty career. *New Pathways Working Paper Series #8.* Washington, DC: American Association for Higher Education.

Golde, C.M. (1998). Beginning graduate school: Explaining first-year doctoral attrition. In M.S. Anderson (ed.), *The Experience of being in Graduate School: An Exploration. New Directions for Higher Education,* No. 101. San Francisco: Jossey-Bass.

Golde, C.M., and Dore, T.M. (2001). *At Cross Purposes: What the Experiences of Today's Doctoral Students Reveal about Doctoral Education.* Philadelphia: Pew Charitable Trusts.

Hamlin, E., Marcucci, D.J., and Wenning, M.V. (2000). The experience of new planning faculty. *Journal of Planning Education and Research* 20(1): 88–99.

Hardwick, S.W. (2005). Mentoring early career faculty in geography: Issues and strategies. *The Professional Geographer* 57(1): 21–27.

Hetrick, J. (2005). Junior faculty participation in curricular change. In S. Chadwick-Blossey and D. Reimondo Robertson (eds.), *To Improve the Academy,* 23, 254–266.

Hoffer, T.B., Welch, V., Jr., Williams, K., Hess, M., Webber, K., Lisek, B., Lowew, D., and Guzman-Barron, I. (2005). *Doctorate recipients from United States universities: Summary report 2004.* Chicago: National Opinion Research Center. Retrieved December 6, 2005, from http://www.norc.uchicago.edu/issues/docdata.htm

Jones, E. (2002–2003). Beyond supply and demand: Assessing the Ph.D. job market. *Occupational Outlook Quarterly.* Winter 2002–2003, 22–33.

Kirk, D., and Todd-Macillas, W.R. (1991). Turning points in graduate student socialization: Implications for recruiting future faculty. *Review of Higher Education* 14(3): 407–422.

Leaming, D.R. (1998). *Academic Leadership: A Practical Guide to Chairing the Department.* Bolton, MA: Anker.

Lindholm, J.A., Astin, A.W., Sax, L.J., and Korn, W.S. (2002). *The American collegeteacher: National norms for the 2001–02 HERI faculty survey.* Los Angeles: Higher Education Research Institute, UCLA.

Lindholm, J.A., Szelenyi, K., Hurtado, S., and Korn, W.S. (2005). *The American College Teacher: National Norms for the 2004–2005 HERI Faculty Survey.* Los Angeles: Higher Education Research Institute, UCLA.

Lovitts, B.E. (2004). Research on the structure and process of graduate education: Retaining students. In D.H. Wulff and A.E. Austin (eds.), *Paths to the professoriate: Strategies for enriching the preparation of future faculty* (pp. 115–136). San Francisco: Jossey-Bass.

Luce, J.A., and Murray, J.P. (1998). New faculty's perception of the academic work life. *Journal of Staff, Program, and Organization Development* 15(3): 103–110.

Menges, R.J. (1999). *Faculty in New Jobs.* San Francisco: Jossey-Bass.

Merton, R.K. (1957). *Social Theory and Social Structure.* Glencoe, Ill: The Free Press.

Merton, R., Reader, G., and Kendall, P. (1957). *The Student Physician.* Cambridge, MA: Harvard University Press.

Moody, J. (2001). *Demystifying the Profession: Helping Junior Faculty Succeed.* New Haven, CT: University of New Haven Press.

National Association of Graduate-Professional Students. (2001). *The National Doctoral Program Survey: Executive Summary*. National Association of Graduate-Professional Students.

Nerad, M., Aanerud, R., and Cerny, J. (2004). "So you want to become a professor!": Lessons from the PhDs-Ten Years Later study. In D.H. Wulff and A.E. Austin (eds.), *Paths to the Professoriate: strategies for enriching the preparation of future faculty* (pp. 137–158). San Francisco: Jossey-Bass.

Nugent, K., Bradshaw, M., and Kito, N. (July/August 1999). Teacher self-efficacy in new nurse educators. *Journal of Professional Nursing* 15(4): 229–237.

Nyquist, J.D., Manning, L., Wulff, D.H., Austin, A.E., Sprague, J., Fraser, P.K., Calcagno, C., and Woodford, B. (1999). On the road to becoming a professor: The graduate student experience, *Change* 31(3): 18–27.

Olsen, D. (1993). Work satisfaction and stress in the first and third year of academic-appointment. *Journal of Higher Education* 64(4): 453–471.

Olsen, D., and Crawford, L. (1998). A five-year study of junior faculty expectations about their work. *Review of Higher Education* 22(1): 39–54.

Olsen, D., and Sorcinelli, M.D. (1992). The pretenure years: A longitudinal perspective. In M.D. Sorcinelli and A.E. Austin (eds.), *Developing New and Junior Faculty*. New Directions for Teaching and Learning, 48. San Francisco: Jossey-Bass.

O'Meara, K., and Rice, E.R. (2005). *Faculty Priorities Reconsidered: Rewarding Multiple forms of Scholarship*. San Francisco: Jossey-Bass.

Perry, R.P., Menec, V.H., and Struthers, C.W. (1999). The role of perceived control in the adjustment of new faculty. In R. Menges and Associates (eds.), *Faculty in New Jobs* (pp. 186–215). San Francisco, CA: Jossey-Bass.

Reynolds, A. (1992). Charting the changes in junior faculty: Relationships among socialization, acculturation, and gender. *Journal of Higher Education* 63: 637–652.

Rice, R.E. (1996). *Making a Place for the New American Scholar*. Washington, DC: American Association for Higher Education.

Rice, R.E., and Sorcinelli, M.D. (2002). Can the tenure process be improved? In R. P. Chait (ed.), *The Questions of Tenure* (pp. 101–124). Cambridge, MA: Harvard University Press.

Rice, R.E., Sorcinelli, M.D., and Austin, A.E. (2000). *Heeding New Voices: Academic Careers for a New Generation*. New Pathways Inquiry No. 7. Washington, DC: American Association for Higher Education.

Sax, L.J., Astin, A.W., Arredondo, M., and Korn, W.S. (1996). *The American College Teacher: National Norms for the 1995–96 HERI Faculty Survey*. Los Angeles: Higher Education Research Institute, UCLA.

Schenkein, H.A., and Best, A.M. (2001). Factors considered by new faculty in their decision to choose careers in academic dentistry. *Journal of Dental Education* 65(9): 832–840.

Schrodt, P., Cawyer, C.S., and Sanders, R. (2003). An examination of academic mentoring behaviors and new faculty members' satisfaction with socialization and tenure and promotion processes. *Communication Education* 52: 17–29.

Schuster, J., and Finkelstein, M. (2006). *The American Faculty*. Baltimore, MD: Johns Hopkins University Press.

Smith, J.O., Whitman, J.S., Grant, P.A., Stanutz, A., Russett, J.A., and Rankin, K. (2001). Peer networking as a dynamic approach to supporting new faculty. *Innovative Higher Education* 25(3): 197–207.

Solem, M.N., and Foote, K.E. (2004). Concerns, attitudes, and abilities of early career geography faculty. *Annals of the Association of American Geographers* I (4), 889–912.

Sorcinelli, M.D. (1985). Faculty careers: Satisfactions and discontents. In G.R. Erickson and J.R. Jeffery (eds.), *To Improve the Academy*. Stillwater: New Forums Press, 44–61.

Sorcinelli, M.D. (1988). Satisfactions and concerns of new university teachers, *To Improve the Academy* 7: 121–133.

Sorcinelli, M.D. (1989). Chairs and the development of new faculty. *The Department Advisor* 5(20): 1–5.

Sorcinelli, M.D. (1992). New and junior faculty stress: Research and responses. In M.D. Sorcinelli and A.E. Austin (eds.), *Developing New and Junior Faculty* (pp. 27–37). *New Directions for Teaching & Learning*, 50.

Sorcinelli, M.D. (1995). How mentoring programs can improve teaching. In P. Seldin and Associates (eds.), *Improving College Teaching* (pp. 125–136). Bolton, MA: Anker Publishing Company.

Sorcinelli, M.D. (2000). Principles of good practice: Supporting early-career faculty. Guidance for deans, department chairs, and other academic leaders. Washington, DC: American Association for Higher Education.

Sorcinelli, M.D. (2004). The top ten things new faculty would like to hear from colleagues. *The National Teaching and Learning Forum* 13(3): 1–4.

Sorcinelli, M.D., and Austin, A.E. (eds.). (1992). *Developing New and Junior Faculty. New Directions for Teaching and Learning. No. 50*. San Francisco: Jossey-Bass.

Sorcinelli, M.D., Austin, A.E., Eddy, P.L., and Beach, A.L. (2006). *Creating the Future of Faculty Development: Learning from the Past, Understanding the Present*. Bolton, MA: Anker.

Sorcinelli, M.D., Austin, A.E., and Trower, C.A. (Summer, 2001). Paradise lost. *The Department Chair* 12(1): 1–3, 6–7.

Sorcinelli, M.D., and Jung, Y. (2006). Mutual mentoring initiative: Envisioning a new culture of mentoring. Poster presentation at the 4th annual International Conference on Teaching & Learning in Higher Education, June 8–9, Gallway, Ireland.

Sorcinelli, M.D., and Near, J. (1989). Relations between work and life away from work among university faculty. *Journal of Higher Education* 60(1): 59–81.

Sprague, J., and Nyquist, J.D. (1989). TA supervision. In J.D. Nyquist, R.D. Abbott and D.H. Wulff (eds.), *Teaching Assistant Training in the 1990s. New Directions for Teaching and Learning*, No. 39 (pp. 37–53). San Francisco: Jossey-Bass.

Sprague, J., and Nyquist, J.D. (1991). A development perspective on the TA role. In J.D. Nyquist, R. Abbott, D. Wulff and J. Sprague (eds.), *Preparing the Professoriate of Tomorrow to Teach: Selected readings in TA training*. Dubuque, IA: Kendall/Hunt.

Staton, A.Q. (1990). *Communication and Student Socialization*. Norwood, NJ: Ablex.

Staton, A.Q., and Darling, A.L. (1989). Socialization of teaching assistants. In J. D. Nyquist, R.D. Abbott and D.H. Wulff (eds.), *Teaching assistant training in the 1990s* (pp.15–22). San Francisco: Jossey-Bass.

Staton-Spicer, A.Q., and Darling, A.L. (1987). A communication perspective on teacher socialization. *Journal of Thought* 22(4):12–19.

Staton-Spicer, A.Q., and Darling, A.L. (1986). Communication in the socialization of pre-service teachers. *Communication Education* 35(3): 215–230.

Taylor, E., and Antony, J. S.(2001). Stereotype threat reduction and wise schooling: Towards successful socialization of African American doctoral students in education. *Journal of Negro Education* 69(3): 184–198.

Tierney, W. G. (1997). Organizational socialization in higher education. *Journal of Higher Education* 68(1): 1–16.

Tierney, W.G., and Bensimon, E.M. (1996). *Promotion and Tenure: Community and Socialization in Academe*. Albany, NY: State University of New York Press.

Tierney, W.G., and Rhoads, R.A. (1994). *Enhancing Promotion, Tenure and Beyond: Faculty Socialization as a Cultural Process. ASHE-ERIC Higher Education Report No. 6*. Washington, DC: The George Washington University, School of Education and Human Development.

Trotman, C.A., and Brown, B.E. (2005). Faculty recruitment and retention: Concerns of early and mid-career faculty. *Research dialogue: TIAA-CREF Institute* 86: 1–5.

Trower, C. (2005). How do junior faculty feel about your campus as a work place? *Harvard Institutes for Higher Education: Alumni Bulletin*. Cambridge, MA: Harvard University.

Trower, C.A., Austin, A.E., and Sorcinelli, M.D. (May, 2001). Paradise lost: How the academy converts enthusiastic recruits into early career doubters. *American Association of Higher Education (AAHE) Bulletin* 53(9): 3–6.

Turner, C.S.V., and Thompson, J.R. (1993). Socializing women doctoral students: Minority and majority experiences. *Review of Higher Education* 16(3): 355–370.

U.S. Department of Education. (2004). *Digest of Educational Statistics, 2004* (NCES Publication No. 2004-331). Washington, DC: Author.

U.S. Department of Education, National Center for Education Statistics. (2004). *National Study of Postsecondary Faculty, 2004* [Data file].Washington, DC: Author. Retrieved April 2, 2006, from http://www.nces.ed.gov/das.

University of Georgia. (2006). *Postdoctoral Teaching Fellows*. Retrieved on June 22, 2006 from http://www.uga.edu/ihe/ptf.html.

Weidman, J.C., Twale, D.J., and Stein, E.L. (2001). *Socialization of Graduate and Professional Students in Higher Education – A Perilous Passage? ASHE-ERIC Higher Education Report*, 28(3). Washington, DC: The George Washington University, School of Education and Human Development.

Weiss, J.A., and McDonald, T.J. (June 30, 2005). Report of the Committee to Consider a More Flexible Tenure Probationary Period. Ann Arbor, MI: University of Michigan. Retrieved on June 23, 2006 from http://www.provost.umich.edu/reports/flexible_tenure/contents.html.

Welch, G.F. (2002). A new faculty orientation program: Building a core of new faculty to shape the future of the college. In G.E. Watts (ed.), *Enhancing community colleges through professional development. New Directions for Community Colleges*, 120, (pp. 11–16).

Whicker, M.L., Kroenfeld, J., and Strickland, R.A. (1993). *Getting Tenure*. Newbury Park, CA: Sage Publications.

Whitt, E. (1991). Hit the ground running: Experiences of new faculty in a school of education. *Review of Higher Education* 14(2): 177–197.

Wulff, D.H., and Austin, A.E. (2004). *Paths to the Professoriate: Strategies for Enriching the Preparation of Future Faculty*. San Francisco: Jossey-Bass.

Wulff, D.H., Austin, A.E., Nyquist, J.D., and Sprague, J. (2004). The development of graduate students as teaching scholars: A four-year longitudinal study. In D.H. Wulff and A.E. Austin (eds.), *Paths to the Professoriate: Strategies for Enriching the Preparation of Future Faculty* (pp. 46–73). San Francisco: Jossey-Bass.

SECTION II: RESEARCH ON TEACHING IN HIGHER EDUCATION

5. IDENTIFYING EXEMPLARY TEACHERS AND TEACHING: EVIDENCE FROM STUDENT RATINGS[1]

Kenneth A. Feldman

SUNY-Stony Brook University
Kenneth.Feldman.1@sunysb.edu

Key Words: College teaching; dimensions of teaching; exemplary teaching; student ratings of instruction; reliability and validity; teaching myths vs. research evidence; faculty evaluation; faculty development

Formal or systematic evaluation by college students of their teachers has long been used to help students in their selection of courses, to provide feedback to faculty about their teaching, and to supply information for administrators and personnel committees in their deliberations on the promotion and tenure of individual faculty members. Moreover, with the increasing emphasis that many colleges and universities are currently putting on good teaching and on designating, honoring, and rewarding good teachers, the use of student ratings is, if anything, likely to increase. Yet, for all their use, student ratings of instructors and instruction are hardly universally accepted. It is no secret, for example, that some college teachers have little regard for them. For these faculty, student evaluations of teachers (or courses)—whether sponsored by the university administration, faculty-development institutes, individual academic departments, or student-run organizations—are not reliable, valid, or useful, and may even be

[1] This paper is based on an earlier one (Feldman, 1994) commissioned by the National Center on Post-secondary Teaching, Learning, and Assessment for presentation at the Second AAHE Conference on Faculty Roles & Rewards held in New Orleans (January 28–30, 1994). The earlier paper benefited by the thoughtful suggestions of Robert Menges and Maryellen Weimer. As for the present paper, I am grateful to Herbert Marsh, Harry Murray, and Raymond Perry for their helpful comments. A brief version of this paper is to appear in an issue of *New Directions for Teaching and Learning*, edited by Marill Svinicki and Robert Menges (Feldman, forthcoming).

R.P. Perry and J.C. Smart (eds.), The Scholarship of Teaching and Learning in Higher Education: An Evidence-Based Perspective, 93–143.
© 2007 *Springer.*

harmful. Others, of course, believe more or less the opposite; and still others fall somewhere in between these two poles of opinion.

If the credibility of teacher evaluations is to be based on more than mere opinion, one asks what the research on their use shows. This question turns out to be more difficult to answer than might be thought because, even apart from the substance of the pertinent research, the number of relevant studies is voluminous. A few years ago, in a letter to the editor in *The Chronicle of Higher Education* (Sept. 5, 1990), William Cashin pointed out that 1,300 citations could be found in the Educational Resources Information Center on "student evaluation of teacher performance" at the postsecondary level. This same year, my own collection of books and articles on instructional evaluation numbered about 2,000 items (Feldman, 1990b). This collection has grown still larger since then, of course. It is true that, at a guess, well over one-half of the items in this collection are opinion pieces (filled with insightful observations at best and uninformed polemics at worst). Even so, this still leaves a large number of research pieces.

Luckily, this research—either as a whole or subportions of it— has been reviewed relatively often (see, among others, Aubrect, 1981; Braskamp, Brandenburg and Ory, 1984; Braskamp and Ory, 1994; Centra, 1979, 1989, 1993; Costin, Greenough and Menges, 1971; Doyle, 1975, 1983; Kulik and McKeachie, 1975; Marsh, 1984, 1987; Marsh and Dunkin, 1992; McKeachie, 1979, Miller, 1972, 1974; and Murray, 1980). Cashin (1988, 1995) has even supplied particularly useful reviews of the major reviews. My own series of reviews started in the mid-1970s and has continued to the present. (See Feldman, 1976a, 1976b, 1977, 1978, 1979, 1983, 1984, 1986, 1987, 1989a, 1989b, 1990a, 1993; two other analyses—Feldman, 1988, 1992—are indirectly relevant.)

One of the best overviews in the area is that by Marsh (1987), which is an update and elaboration of an earlier review of his (Marsh, 1984). In this review, after 100 pages or so of careful, critical, and reflective analysis of the existing research and major reviews of student ratings of instruction, Marsh (1987) sums up his findings and observations, as follows:

> Research described in this article demonstrates that student ratings are clearly multidimensional, quite reliable, reasonably valid, relatively uncontaminated by many variables often seen as sources of potential bias, and are seen to be useful by students, faculty, and administrators. However, the same findings also demonstrate that student ratings may have some halo effect, have at least some unreliability, have only modest agreement with some criteria

of effective teaching, are probably affected by some potential sources of bias and are viewed with some skepticism by faculty as a basis for personnel decisions. It should be noted that this level of uncertainty probably also exists in every area of applied psychology and for all personnel evaluation systems. Nevertheless, the reported results clearly demonstrate that a considerable amount of useful information can be obtained from student ratings; useful for feedback to faculty, useful for personnel decision, useful to students in the selection of courses, and useful for the study of teaching. Probably, students' evaluations of teaching effectiveness are the most thoroughly studied of all forms of personnel evaluation, and one of the best in terms of being supported by empirical research (p. 369).

Marsh's tempered conclusions set the stage for the present comments. This discussion first explores various interpretations that can be made of information gathered from students about their teachers (which includes a consideration of the possible half-truths and myths that continue to circulate about teacher and course evaluations). It then analyzes the differential importance of the individual items that constitute the rating forms used to evaluate teachers. The primary aim of this discussion is to see how student evaluations can be used to help identify exemplary teachers and instruction.

TRUTHS, HALF-TRUTHS, AND MYTHS: INTERPRETING STUDENT RATINGS

The unease felt by some faculty, and perhaps by some administrators and students as well, in using teacher and course evaluations to help identify exemplary teachers and instruction may in part be due to the half-truths if not outright myths that have cropped up about these evaluations. Some of the myths can be laid to rest; and the half-truths can be more fully analyzed to separate the real from the imagined. To do so requires a consideration of certain factors or influences that have been said to "bias" ratings. At the moment there is no clear consensus on the definition of bias in the area of student ratings (see Marsh, 1984, 1987; and Marsh and Dunkin, 1992). I take bias to mean something other than (or more than) the fact that student ratings may be influenced by conditions not under the teacher's control or that conditions may somehow be "unfair" to the instructor (making it harder for him or her to teach well and thus to get high ratings compared to teachers in "easier" situations). Rather, bias here refers to one or more factors directly and somehow inappropriately influencing students' judgments about and evaluation of teachers or courses. In essence, the question is whether a condition or influence actually affects teachers and their instruction, which is then accurately reflected in students' evaluations (a case of *non*bias), or whether in some way this condition or influence only affects students' attitudes toward the course and students' perceptions of instructors (and their teaching) such that evaluations do not accurately reflect the instruction that students receive (a case of bias). (For a more extensive discussion of the meaning of bias as it pertains to student ratings, see Feldman, 1984, 1993; Marsh, 1987, and Marsh and Dunkin, 1992.) Implications and examples of this conceptualization of bias will be given as the discussion proceeds.

MYTHS

Aleamoni (1987) has listed a number of speculations, propositions, and generalizations about students' ratings of instructors and instruction that he declares "are (on the whole) myths." Although I would not go so far as to call each of the generalizations on his list a myth, some of them indeed are—at least as far as current research shows—as follows: students cannot make consistent judgments about the instructor and instruction because of their immaturity, lack of experience, and capriciousness (untrue); only colleagues with excellent publication records and expertise are qualified to teach and to evaluate their peers' instruction—good instruction and good research being so closely allied that it is unnecessary to evaluate them separately (untrue); most student rating schemes are nothing more than a popularity contest, with the warm, friendly, humorous instructor emerging as the winner every time (untrue); students are not able to make accurate judgments until they have been away from the course, and possibly away from the university for several years (untrue); student ratings are both unreliable and invalid (untrue); the time and day the course is offered affect student ratings (untrue); students cannot meaningfully be used to improve instruction (untrue). I call these statements untrue because supporting evidence was not found for them in one or another of the following research reviews: Abrami, Leventhal, and Perry (1982); Cohen (1980b); Feldman (1977, 1978, 1987, 1989a, 1989b); Levinson-Rose and Menges (1981); L'Hommedieu, Menges and Brinko (1988, 1990); Marsh (1984, 1987); and Marsh and Dunkin (1992).

For the most part, Aleamoni (1987) also seems correct in calling the following statement a myth: "Gender of the student and the instructor affects student ratings." Consistent evidence cannot be found that either male or female college students routinely give higher ratings to teachers (Feldman, 1977). As for the gender of the teacher, a recent review (Feldman, 1993) of three dozen or so studies showed that a majority of these studies found male and female college teachers not to differ in the global ratings they receive from their students. In those studies in which statistically significant differences were found, more of them favored women than men. However, across all studies, the average association between gender and overall evaluation of the teacher, while favoring women, is so small (average $r = +.02$) as to be insignificant in practical terms. This would seem to show that the gender of the teacher does not bias students' ratings (unless, of course, it can be shown by *other* indicators of teachers' effectiveness that the ratings of one gender "should" be higher than the other to indicate the reality of this group's better teaching).

This said, it should also be noted that there is some indication of an interaction effect between the gender of the student and the gender of the teacher: across studies, there is some evidence to suggest that students may rate same-gendered teachers a little more highly they than do opposite-gendered teachers. What is unknown from the existing studies, however, is what part of this tendency is due to male and female students taking different classes (and thus having different teachers) and what part is due to differences in preferences of male and female students within classes (thus possibly indicating a bias in their ratings).

HALF-TRUTHS AND THE QUESTION OF BIAS IN RATINGS

Aleamoni (1987) also presents the following statements as candidates for the status of myth: the size of the class affects student ratings; the level of the course affects student ratings; the rank of the instructor affects student ratings; whether students take the course as a requirement or as an elective affects their ratings; whether students are majors or nonmajors affects their ratings. That these are myths is not clear-cut. Each of these course, instructor or student factors is, in fact, related to student evaluation. The real question is: "Why?"

Although the results of pertinent studies are somewhat mixed, some weak trends can be discerned: *slightly* higher ratings are given (a) to teachers of smaller rather than larger courses (Feldman, 1984; Marsh, 1987); (b) to teachers of upper-level rather than lower-level courses (Feldman, 1978); (c) to teachers of higher rather than lower academic ranks (Feldman, 1983; Marsh, 1987); (d) by students taking a course as an elective rather than as a requirement (Feldman, 1978; Marsh, 1987); and (e) by students taking a course that is in their major rather than one that is not (Feldman, 1978; Marsh, 1987). These associations do not prove causation, of course; each of these factors may not actually and directly "affect" ratings, but may simply be associated with the ratings due to their association with other factors affecting ratings.

Even if it can be shown that one or more of these factors actually and directly "affect" students' ratings, the ratings are not necessarily biased by these factors, as is often inferred when such associations are found (probably an important underlying worry of those prone to discount teacher or course evaluations). To give an example, at certain colleges and universities teachers of higher rank may in fact typically be somewhat better teachers, and thus "deserve" the slightly higher ratings they receive. To give another example, teachers in large classes may receive slightly lower ratings because they indeed are somewhat less effective in larger classes than they are in smaller classes, not because students take out their dislike of large classes by rating them a little lower than they otherwise would. So, while it may be somewhat "unfair" to compare teachers in classes of widely different sizes, the unfairness lies in the difference in teaching conditions, not in a rating bias as defined here.[1]

To put the matter in general terms, certain course characteristics and situational contexts—conditions that may not necessarily be under full control of the teachers—may indeed affect teaching effectiveness; and student ratings may then accurately reflect differences in teaching effectiveness. Although rating bias may not necessarily be involved, those interested in using teaching evaluations to help in decisions about promotions and teaching awards may well want to take into account the fact that it may be somewhat harder to be effective in some courses than in others. Along these lines, note that student ratings gathered from the Instructional Development and Effectiveness Assessment (IDEA) system are reported *separately* for four categories of class size—small (1–14 students), medium (15–34), large (35–99) and very large (100 or more)—as well as for five levels of student motivation for the class as a whole (determined by the average of the students' responses to the background question, "I have a strong desire to take this course"). The reason for this procedure is made clear to users of the evaluation instrument, as follows:

---

[1] Using a different definition of bias, Cashin (1988) would consider the size of class a source of bias if its correlation with student ratings of teachers were sufficiently large (but see Cashin, 1995).

In addition to using flexible criteria, the IDEA system also controls for *level of student motivation* or the students' desire to take the course...and the *size of the class*—two variables which the research has shown are correlated with student rating....The IDEA system assumes that it is harder to teach large groups of students who do not want to take a course than it is to teach small groups of students who do want to take a course. IDEA controls for this by comparing an instructor's ratings, not only with "All" courses in the comparative data pool, but with "Similar" courses [same level of student motivation and same class size] as well (Cashin and Sixbury, 1993, pp. 1–2, emphasis in original).

Another candidate for the status of myth concerns students' grades. As Aleamoni (1987) words it, "the grades or marks students receive in the course are highly correlated with their ratings of the course and instructor." On the one hand, the word "highly" indeed makes the statement mythical; grades are not *highly* correlated with students' ratings. On the other hand, almost all of the available research does show a small or even modest positive association between grades and evaluation (usually a correlation somewhere between $+.10$ and $+.30$), whether the unit of analysis is the individual student or the class itself (see Feldman, 1976a, 1977; Stumpf and Freedman, 1979).

Research has shown that some part of the positive correlation between students' grades (usually expected grades) and students' evaluation of teachers is due to "legitimate" reasons and therefore is unbiased: students who learn more earn higher grades and thus legitimately give higher evaluations. This has been called the "validity hypothesis" or "validity effect" (see Marsh, 1987, and Marsh and Dunkin, 1992). Moreover, some part of the association may be spurious, attributable to some third factor—for example, students' interest in the subject matter of the course—which has been referred to as the "student characteristics hypothesis" or "student characteristics effect" (see Marsh, 1989, and Marsh and Dunkin, 1992). Yet another part of the positive correlation may indeed be due to a rater bias in the ratings, although the bias might not be large. Researchers currently are trying to determine the degree to which an attributional bias (students' tendency to take credit for successes and avoid blame for failure) and a retributional bias (students "rewarding" teachers who give them higher grades by giving them higher evaluations, and "punishing" teachers who give them lower grades by giving them lower evaluations) are at work (see Gigliotti and Buchtel, 1990; Theall, Franklin, and Ludlow, 1990a, 1990b). The second of these two biases has been called a "grading leniency hypothesis" or "grading leniency effect" (Marsh, 1987; Marsh and Dunkin, 1992). In their review of research relating grades and teacher evaluations, Marsh and Dunkin (1992) conclude as follows:

> Evidence from a variety of different types of research clearly supports the validity hypothesis and the student characteristics hypothesis, but does not rule out the possibility that a grading leniency effect operates simultaneously. Support for the grading leniency effect was found with some experimental studies, but these effects were typically weak and inconsistent, may not generalize to nonexperimental settings where SETs [students' evaluations of teaching effectiveness] are actually used, and in some instances may be due to the violation of grade expectations that students had falsely been led to expect or that were applied to other students in the same course. Consequently, while it is possible that a grading leniency effect may produce some bias in SETs, support for this suggestion is weak and the size of such an effect is likely to be insubstantial in the actual use of SETs (p. 202).

Yet another correlate of—and, therefore, a possible influence on—teacher evaluations is not mentioned by Aleamoni (1987): academic discipline of the course. Reviewing eleven studies available at the time (Feldman, 1978), I found that teachers in different academic fields tend to be rated somewhat differently. Teachers in English, humanities, arts, and language courses tend to receive somewhat higher student ratings than those in social science courses (especially political sciences, sociology, psychology and economic courses); this latter group of teachers in turn receive somewhat higher ratings than teachers in the sciences (excepting certain subareas of biological sciences), mathematics and engineering courses. Recently, based on data from tens of thousands of classes either from the IDEA system only (Cashin and Clegg, 1987; Cashin and Sixbury, 1993) or from this system and the Student Instructional Report (SIR) of the Educational Testing Service combined (Cashin, 1990), differences among major fields similar to those in my review have been reported.

Cashin and his associates have suggested several possible causes that could be operating to produce these differences in ratings of teachers in different academic disciplines, including the following: some courses are harder to teach than others; some fields have better teachers than others; and students in different major fields rate differently because of possible differences in their attitudes, academic skills, goals, motivation, learning styles, and perceptions of the constituents of good teaching. The following practical advice given by Cashin and Sixbury (1993) is informative:

> There is increasing evidence that different academic fields are rated differently. What is not clear is why. Each institution should examine its own data to determine to what extent the differences found in the general research hold true at that particular institution. If an institution concludes that the differences found at that institution are *due to something other than the teaching effectiveness of the instructors*, e.g., because low rated courses are more difficult to teach, or reflect a stricter rating response set on the part of the students taking those courses, then some control for those differences should be instituted. Using the comparative data in this technical report is one possibility. If however, it is decided that the *differences in ratings primarily reflect differences in teaching effectiveness*, that is, that the low rated courses are so rated because they are *not* as well taught, then of course no adjustments should be made (pp. 2–3, emphases in original).

IDENTIFYING INSTRUCTIONAL DIMENSIONS IMPORTANT TO EFFECTIVE TEACHING

Thus far, I have explored how student ratings can be used to identify those persons who are seen by students as exemplary teachers (as well as those who are not), noting certain precautions in doing so. Now, I turn to the related topic of how exemplary teaching itself can be identified through the use of student ratings of specific pedagogical dispositions, behaviors and practices of teachers.[2] Teaching comprises many different elements—a multidimensionality that instruments of teacher evaluation usually attempt to capture. The construction of most of these instruments, as Marsh and Dunkin (1992) point out, is based on "a logical analysis of the content of effective teaching and the purposes the ratings are intended to serve, supplemented by reviews of previous research and feedback" (p. 146). Less often used is an

---

[2] As with overall evaluation of teachers, the characteristics of courses, of teachers themselves, and of situational contexts have all been found to correlate with specific evaluations. Those characteristics most frequently studied have been class size, teacher rank/experience and the gender of the teacher. Class size and the rank/experience of the teacher each correlate more highly with some specific evaluations than with others (for details, see Feldman, 1983, 1984). (The degree to which these factors actually affect teaching rather than "biasing" students in their ratings has yet to be determined.) With the possible exception of their sensitivity to and concern with class level and progress, male and female teachers do not consistently differ in the specific evaluations they receive across studies (Feldman, 1993).

empirical approach that emphasizes statistical techniques such as factor analysis or multitrait-multimethod analysis.

Marsh and Dunkin (1992) also note that "for feedback to teachers, for use in student course selection, and for use in research in teaching ... there appears to be general agreement that a profile of distinct components of SETs [students' evaluations of teaching effectiveness] based on an appropriately constructed multidimensional instrument is more useful than a single summary score" (p. 146). However, whether a multidimensional profile score is more useful than a single summary score for personnel decisions has turned out to be more controversial (see Abrami, 1985, 1988, 1989a, 1989b; Abrami and d'Apollonia, 1991; Abrami, d'Apollonia, and Rosenfield, 1993, 1996; Cashin and Downey, 1992; Cashin, Downey, and Sixbury, 1994; Hativa and Raviv, 1993; and Marsh, 1987, 1991a, 1991b, 1994).

In earlier reviews (Feldman, 1976b, 1983, 1984, 1987, 1989a), I used a set of roughly 20 instructional dimensions into which the teaching components of relevant studies could be categorized. In recent years, I extended this set in one way or another to include more dimensions (see Feldman, 1988, 1989b, 1993). The fullest set—28 dimensions—is given in the Appendix, along with specific examples of evaluation items that would be categorized in each dimension. Unlike studies using factor analyses or similar techniques to arrive at instructional dimensions, the categories are based on a logical analysis of the single items and multiple-item scales found in the research literature on students' views of effective teaching and on their evaluations of actual teachers. Over the years, I have found the system of categorization to be useful in classifying the characteristics of instruction analyzed in various empirical studies even though it may differ from the definitions and categories found in any one of these studies.[3]

TEACHING THAT IS ASSOCIATED WITH STUDENT LEARNING

Although all 28 dimensions of instruction found in the Appendix would seem to be important to effective teaching, one would assume that some of them are more important than others. One way of establishing this differential importance is to see how various teaching

[3] Abrami and d'Apollonia (1990) adapted these categories for use in their own work (also see d'Apollonia and Abrami, 1988). More recently, they have made more extensive refinements and modifications to the dimensions and concomitant coding scheme (Abrami, d'Apollonia, and Rosenfield, 1993, 1996).

dimensions relate to student learning, which Cohen (1980a, 1981, 1987) did in his well-known meta-analytic study of the relationships of student achievement with eight different instructional dimensions.[4] Based in large part on work by d'Apollonia and Abrami (1987, 1988) and Abrami, Cohen, and d'Apollonia, 1988), I extended Cohen's meta-analysis a few years ago by using less heterogeneous categories for coding the evaluation items and scales in the studies under review, widening the range of instructional dimensions under consideration, and preserving more of the information in the studies Cohen used in his meta-analysis (see Feldman, 1989b, 1990a). To be included in Cohen's meta-analysis or my own, a study had to provide data from actual college classes rather than from experimental analogues of teaching. The unit of analysis in the study had to be the class or instructor and not the individual student. Its data had to be based on a multisection course with a common achievement measure used for all sections of the course (usually an end-of the course examination as it turned out). Finally, the study had to provide data from which a rating/achievement correlation could be calculated (if one was not given).

The correlations between specific evaluations and student achievement from the studies under review were distributed among 28 instructional dimensions (given in the present Appendix), with weighting procedures used to take into account evaluational items or scales that were coded in more than one dimension. Average correlations were calculated for each of the instructional dimensions having information from at least three studies. These average correlations are given in Table 1,T1 along with the percent of variance explained (r^2).[5]

Note that average r's for the instructional dimensions range from +.57 to −.11. All but one (Dimension No. 11) are positive, and all but three (Dimensions No. 11, No. 23, No. 24) are statistically significant. The two highest correlations of .57 and .56—explained variance of over 30%—are for Dimensions No. 5 (teacher's preparation and course organization) and No. 6 (teacher's clarity and understandableness). The teacher's pursuit and/or meeting of course objectives and the student-perceived outcome or impact of the course (Dimensions No. 28 and No. 12) are the next most highly related dimensions with achievement (r = +.49 and +.46). Somewhat more moderately-sized correlations—indicating between roughly 10% and 15% of explained

---

[4] These dimensions are labeled: Skill; Rapport; Structure; Difficulty; Interaction; Feedback; Evaluation; and Interest/Motivation.

[5] The results given in Table 1 are similar to those shown in an analysis in d'Apollonia and Abrami (1988), although there are some differences (see Abrami, d'Apollonia, and Rosenfield, 1996).

Table 1: Average Correlations of Specific Evaluations of Teachers with Student Achievement

Percent Variance Explained		Instructional Dimension	Average r
30.0%-34.9%	No. 5	Teacher's Preparation; Organization of the Course	.57
	No. 6	Clarity and Understandableness	.56
25.0%-29.9%			
20.0%-24.9%	No. 28	Teacher Pursued and/or Met Course Objectives	.49
	No. 12	Perceived Outcome or Impact of Instruction	.46
15.0%-19.9%			
10.0%-14.9%	No. 1	Teacher's Stimulation of Interest in the Course and Its Subject Matter	.38
	No. 20	Teacher Motivates Students to Do Their Best; High Standard of Performance Required	.38
	No. 16	Teacher's Encouragement of Questions, and Openness to Opinions of Others	.36
	No. 19	Teacher's Availability and Helpfulness	.36
	No. 7	Teacher's Elocutionary Skills	.35
	No. 9	Clarity of Course Objectives and Requirements	.35
	No. 3	Teacher's Knowledge of the Subject	.34
5.0%-9.9%	No.8	Teacher's Sensitivity to, and Concern with, Class Level and Progress	.30
	No. 2	Teacher's Enthusiasm (for Subject or for Teaching)	.27
	No. 13	Teacher's Fairness; Impartiality of Evaluation of Students; Quality of Examinations	.26
	No. 25	Classroom Management	.26
	No. 17	Intellectual Challenge and Encouragement of Independent Thought (by the Teacher and the Course)	.25
	No. 14	Personality Characteristics ("Personality") of the Teacher	.24
	No. 18	Teacher's Concern and Respect for Students; Friendliness of the Teacher	.23
	No. 15	Nature, Quality, and Frequency of Feedback from the Teacher to the Students	.23
	No. 26	Pleasantness of Classroom Atmosphere	.23

Table 1: *(Continued)*

0.0%-4.9%	No. 10	Nature and Value of the Course (Including Its Usefulness and Relevance)	.17
	No. 23	Difficulty of the Course (and Workload)—Description	.09
	No. 24	Difficulty of the Course (and Workload)—Evaluation	.07
	No. 11	Nature and Usefulness of Supplementary Materials and Teaching Aids	−.11

Note: This table has been constructed from data given in Table 1 in Feldman (1989b), which itself was based on information in the following studies: Benton and Scott (1976); Bolton and Marr (1979); Braskamp, Caulley, and Costin (1979); Bryson (1974); Centra (1977); Chase and Keene (1979); Cohen and Berger (1970); Costin (1978); Doyle and Crichton (1978); Doyle and Whitely (1974); Elliott (1950); Ellis and Rickard (1977); Endo and Della-Piana (1976); Frey (1973); Frey (1976); Frey, Leonard, and Beatty (1975); Greenwood, Hazelton, Smith, and Ware (1976); Grush and Costin (1975); Hoffman (L978); Marsh, Fleiner, and Thomas (1975); Marsh and Overall (1980); McKeachie, Lin and Mann (1971); Mintzes (1976–77); Morgan and Vasché (1978); Morsh, Burgess, and Smith (1956); Murray (1983); Orpen (1980); Rankin, Greenmun, and Tracy (1965); Remmers, Martin, and Elliott (1949); Rubinstein and Mitchell (1970); Solomon, Rosenberg, and Bezdek (1964); and Turner and Thompson (1974). Each r given in (or derived from information in) individual studies was converted to a Fisher's Z transformation (z_r) and weighted by the inverse of the number of instructional dimensions in which it was coded. For each instructional dimension, the weighted z_r's were averaged and then backtransformed to produce the weighted average r's given in this table. These r's are shown only for those instructional dimensions having information from at least three studies; thus there are no entries for Dimensions 4, 21, 22 and 27. All correlations in this table are statistically significant except those for Dimensions 11, 23, and 24.

variance—were found for several instructional dimensions: teacher's stimulation of students' interest in the course and its subject (Instructional Dimension No. 1, average $r = +.38$); teacher's motivation of students to do their best (No. 20, +.38); teacher's encouragement of questions and discussion, and openness to the opinions of others (No. 16, +.36); teacher's availability and helpfulness (No. 19, +.36); teacher's elocutionary skills (No. 7, +.35); clarity of course objectives and requirements (No. 9, +.35); and teacher's knowledge of subject (No. 3, +.34).

Less strongly associated with student achievement are: the teacher's sensitivity to, and concern with, class level and progress (No. 8); teacher's enthusiasm (No. 2); teacher's fairness and impartiality of evaluation (No. 13); classroom management (No. 25); intellectual challenge and encouragement of students' independent thought (No. 17); teacher's "personality" (No. 14); teacher's friendliness and respect or concern for students (No. 18); the quality and frequency of teacher's feedback to students (No. 15); the pleasantness of the classroom atmosphere (No. 26); and the nature and value of the course material (No. 10). The nature and usefulness of supplementary materials and teaching aids as well as the difficulty and workload of the course (either as a description or as an evaluation by students) are not related to student achievement. Because of insufficient data in the set of studies under consideration, the relationship of the following dimensions to student achievement is not clear from these studies: No. 4 (teacher's intellectual expansiveness); No. 21 (teacher's encouragement of self-initiated learning); No. 22 (teacher's productivity in research); and No. 27 (individualization of teaching).

DO CERTAIN KINDS OF TEACHING ACTUALLY PRODUCE STUDENT ACHIEVEMENT?

It is important to recognize that the associations between specific evaluations of teachers and student achievement by themselves do not establish the causal connections between the instructional character-istics under investigation and student achievement. For example, it is possible that the correlations that have been found in some proportion of the studies (whose results were used to create Table 1) do not necessarily indicate that the instructional characteristics were causal in producing the students' achievement. Rather, as Leventhal (1975) was one of the first to point out, some third variable such as student motivation, ability or aptitude of the class might independently affect both teacher performance and student learning, which would account for the correlations between instructional characteristics and student achievement even if there were no direct causal connection.

Leventhal (1975) has suggested that causality can be more clearly established in studies in which students are randomly assigned to sections of a multisection course rather than self-selected into them, for the "random assignment of students...promotes equivalence of the groups of students by disrupting the causal processes which ordinarily control student assignment" (p. 272). It is not always possible, however, to assign students randomly to class sections. In some of the studies reviewed by Cohen (and by Feldman, 1989b), students were randomly assigned to class sections, whereas in other studies they were not. Interestingly, in his meta-analysis, Cohen (1980a) found that, for each of the four instructional dimensions that he checked, studies in which students were randomly assigned to sections gave about the same results as did studies where students picked their own class sections. Cohen (1980a) also compared studies where the ability of students in class sections was statistically controlled with studies where it was not. Again, for each of the four instructional dimensions that he checked, the correlations for the two sets of studies did not differ. Results such as these increase the likelihood that the instructional characteristics and student achievement are causally connected, although the possibility of spurious elements has not been altogether ruled out. Even with random assignment, the results of multisection validation studies may still permit certain elements of ambiguity in interpretation and generalization (Marsh, 1987; and Marsh and Dunkin, 1992; but see Abrami, d'Apollonia, and Rosenfield, 1993, 1996).

The results of experimental studies—whether field experiments or laboratory experiments–are obviously useful here, for they can help clarify cause-effect relationships in ways that the correlational studies just reviewed cannot. Relevant research has been reviewed (selectively) by Murray (1991), who notes in his analysis of pertinent studies that either teacher's enthusiasm/expressiveness or teacher clarity (or both) has been a concern in nearly all relevant experimental research, and that these studies usually include measures of amount learned by students. In his overview of this research, Murray (1991) reports that "classroom teaching behaviors, at least in the enthusiasm and clarity domains, appear to be *causal antecedents* (rather than mere correlates) of various instructional outcome measures" (p. 161, emphasis added).

Although Murray's (1991) definitions of these domains are not completely identical with the definitions of pertinent dimensions of the present analysis, it is still of interest to compare his conclusions and the findings given here. Thus, in the present discussion, teacher clarity has also been shown to be of high importance to teaching, whether indicated by the correlation of teacher clarity with student achievement in the multisection correlational studies or, as will be seen in a later section of this paper, by the association of teacher clarity with the global evaluation of the teacher. As for the enthusiastic/expressive attitudes and behaviors of teachers, highlighted in Murray's (1991) analysis, the instructional dimensions of "teachers enthusiasm (for subject or for teaching)" referred to in the present discussion is, in fact, associated with achievement in the multisection correlational studies, but only moderately so compared to some of the other instructional dimensions. However, the instructional dimension of "teacher's elocutionary skills," which assumedly is an aspect of enthusiasm/expressiveness is more strongly associated with achievement in the multisectional-correlational studies. Furthermore, note that Murray writes that "behaviors loading on the Enthusiasm [Expressive] factor share elements of spontaneity and stimulus variation, and thus are perhaps best interpreted as serving to elicit and maintain student attention to material presented in class" (p. 146). Given this interpretation, it is of relevance that the instructional dimension of "teacher's stimulation of interest in the course and its subject matter" has been found to be rather highly correlated (albeit less so than the top four dimensions) with students' achievement in multisectional correlational studies; moreover, this particular dimension is highly associated, as well, with global evaluation of instruction relative to the other instructional dimensions (to be discussed in a later section of this paper).

Underlying Mechanisms and Other Considerations

Whether the associations between student learning and teacher's attitudes, behaviors, and practices are established by correlational studies or by experimental studies, the exact psychological and social psychological mechanisms by which these instructional characteristics influence student learning need to be more fully and systematically detailed than they have been. When a large association between an instructional characteristic and student achievement is found, the tendency is to see the finding as obvious—that is, as being a self-explanatory result. For example, given the size of the correlation involved, it would seem obvious that a teacher who is clear and understandable naturally facilitates students' achievement; little more needs to be said or explained, it might be thought. But, in a very real sense, the "obviousness" or "naturalness" of the connection appears only after the fact (of a substantial association). Were the correlation between dimension of "feedback" and student achievement a great deal larger than was found, then this instructional characteristic, too, would be seen by some as obviously facilitative of student achievement: naturally, teachers who give frequent and good feedback effect high cognitive achievement in their students. But, as previously noted, frequency and quality of feedback has not been found to correlate particularly highly with student achievement, and there is nothing natural or obvious about either a high or low association between feedback and students' achievement; and, in fact, to see either as natural or obvious ignores the specific psychological and social psychological mechanisms that may be involved in either a high or low correlation.

In short, although a case can be made that many of the different instructional characteristics could be expected to facilitate student learning (see, for example, Marsh and Dunkin, 1992, pp. 154–156), what is needed are specific articulations about which particular dimensions of instruction theoretically and empirically are more likely and which less likely to produce achievement. A crucial aspect of this interest is specifying exactly how those dimensions that affect achievement do so—even when, at first glance, the mechanisms involved would seem to be obvious. Indeed, conceptually and empirically specifying such mechanisms in perhaps the most "obvious" connection of them all in this area—that between student achievement and the clarity and understandableness of instructors—has turned out to be particularly complex, not at all simple or obvious (see, for example, Land, 1979, 1981; Land and Combs, 1981, 1982, Land and Smith, 1979, 1981; and Smith and Land, 1980). Likewise, the mechanisms underlying the correlation between teacher's organization and student achievement have yet to be specifically and fully determined, although Perry (1991) has recently started the attempt by offering the following hypothetical linkages:

> Instructor organization...involves teaching activities intended to structure course material into units more readily accessible from students' long-term memory. An outline for the lecture provides encoding schemata and advanced organizers which enable students to incorporate new, incoming material into existing structures. Presenting linkages between content topics serves to increase the cognitive integration of the new material and to make it more meaningful, both of which should facilitate retrieval. (p. 26)

One other consideration may be mentioned at this point. McKeachie (1987) has recently reminded educational researchers and practitioners that the achievement tests assessing student learning in the sorts of studies being considered here typically measure lower-level educational objectives such as memory of facts and definitions rather than the higher-level outcomes such as critical thinking and problem solving that are usually taken as important in higher education. He points out that "today cognitive and instructional psychologists are placing more and more emphasis upon the importance of the way in which knowledge is structured as well as upon skills and strategies for learning and problem solving" (p. 345). Moreover, although not a consideration of this paper, there are still other cognitive skills and intellectual dispositions as well as a variety of affective and behavioral outcomes of students that my be influenced in the college classroom (see, for example, discussions in Baxter Magolda, 1992; Bowen, 1977; Chickering and Reisser, 1993; Doyle, 1972; Ellner and Barnes, 1983; Feldman and Newcomb, 1969; Feldman and Paulsen, 1994; Hoyt, 1973; King and Kitchener, 1994; Marsh, 1987; Pascarella and Terenzini, 1991; Sanders and Wiseman, 1990; Sockloff, 1973; and Turner, 1970).

SPECIFIC ASPECTS OF TEACHING AS RELATED TO OVERALL EVALUATION OF THE TEACHER

There is another way of determining the differential importance of various instructional dimensions, one that uses information internal to the evaluation form itself. If it is assumed that each student's overall evaluation of an instructor is an additive combination of the student's evaluation of specific aspects of the teacher and his or her instruction, weighted by the student's estimation of the relative importance of these aspects to good teaching, then it would be expected that students' overall assessment of teachers would be more highly associated with instructional characteristics that students generally consider to be more important to good teaching than with those they consider to be less important (cf. Crittenden and Norr, 1973). Thus, one way to establish the differential importance of various instructional characteristics is to compare the magnitudes of the correlations between the actual overall evaluations by students of their teachers and their ratings of each of the specific attitudinal and behavioral characteristics of these teachers. Otherwise put, the importance of an instructional dimension is indicated by its ability to discriminate among students' global assessment of teachers.[6]

In an analysis (Feldman, 1976b) done a while ago now, though one still of full relevance here, I located some 23 studies containing correlations (or comparable information showing the extent of the associations) between students' overall evaluations of their teachers and their ratings of specific attitudinal and behavioral characteristics of these teachers.

---

[6] Limitations of this approach to determining the importance of instructional dimensions are discussed in Feldman (1976b, 1988; also see Abrami, d'Apollonia and Rosenfield, 1993, 1996).

This information in each study was used to rank order the importance of these characteristics (in terms of size of its association with overall evaluation) and then to calculate for each study standardized ranks (rank of each item divided by the number of items ranked) for the specific evaluations in the study. Finally, for each of the instructional dimensions under consideration (see Feldman, 1976, Table 1 and note 5), standardized ranks were averaged across the pertinent studies.

These average standardized ranks are given in Column 2 of Table 2.T2 Column 1 of this same table repeats those data previously given in Table 1 on the associations between instructional dimensions and student achievement for just those instructional dimensions considered in both analyses. The two analyses, each determining the importance of instructional dimensions in its own way, have eighteen instructional dimensions in common, although data for only seventeen of them are given in the table. Instructional Dimension No. 4 (teacher's intellectual expansiveness) has been left out, as it was in Table 1, because of insufficient data about the correlation between it and student achievement. Table 2T2 also shows (in parentheses) the rank in importance of each of the instructional dimensions that is produced by each of the two different methods of gauging importance of the dimensions.

There is no overlap in the studies on which the data in Columns 1 and 2 of Table 2 are based. Furthermore, because the studies considered in the student achievement analyses (Col. 1) are mostly of students in multisection courses of an introductory nature, these students and courses are less representative of college students and courses in general than are the students and courses in the second set of studies (Col. 2). Despite these circumstances, the rank-order correlation (rho) between the ranks shown in the two columns is +.61. Those specific instructional dimensions that are the most highly associated with student achievement tend to be the same ones that best discriminate among teachers with respect to the overall evaluation they receive from students. The correlation is not a perfect one, however. The largest discrepancies are for teacher's availability and helpfulness (relatively high importance in terms of its association with achievement and relatively low importance in terms of its association student's global evaluations) and for intellectual challenge and encouragement of students' independent thought (relatively low importance by the first indicator and relatively high importance by the second indicator). The other large "shifts" between the two indicators of importance are less dramatic: teacher's preparation and course organization (from Rank 1

Table 2: Comparison of Instructional Dimensions on Two Different Indicators of Importance

	Instructional Dimension	Importance Shown by Correlation with Student Achievement (1)	Importance Shown by Correlation with Overall Evaluations (2)
No. 5	Teacher's Preparation; Organization of the Course	.57 (1)	.41 (6)
No. 6	Clarity and Understandableness	.56 (2)	.25 (2)
No. 12	Perceived Outcome or Impact of Instruction	.46 (3)	.28 (3)
No. 1	Teacher's Stimulation of Interest in the Course and Its Subject Matter	.38 (4)	.20 (1)
No. 16	Teacher's Encouragement of Questions and Discussion, and Openness to Opinions of Others	.36 (5.5)	.60 (11)
No. 19	Teacher's Availability and Helpfulness	.36 (5.5)	.74 (16)
No. 7	Teacher's Elocutionary Skills	.35 (7.5)	.49 (10)
No. 9	Clarity of Course Objectives and Requirements	.35 (7.5)	.45 (7)
No. 3	Teacher's Knowledge of the Subject	.34 (9)	.48 (9)
No. 8	Teacher's Sensitivity to, and Concern with, Class Level and Progress	.30 (10)	.40 (5)
No. 2	Teacher's Enthusiasm (for Subject or for Teaching)	.27 (11)	.46 (8)
No. 13	Teacher's Fairness; Impartiality of Evaluation of Students; Quality of Examinations	.26 (12)	.72 (14.5)
No. 17	Intellectual Challenge and Encouragement of Independent Thought (by the Teacher and the Course)	.25 (13)	.33 (4)
No. 18	Teacher's Concern and Respect for Students; Friendliness of the Teacher	.23 (14.5)	.65 (12)
No. 15	Nature, Quality, and Frequency of Feedback from the Teacher to Students	.23 (14.5)	.87 (17)

Table 2: *(Continued)*

	Instructional Dimension	Importance Shown by Correlation with Student Achievement (1)	Importance Shown by Correlation with Overall Evaluations (2)
No. 10	Nature and Value of the Course Material (Including Its Usefulness and Relevance)	.17 (16)	.70 (13)
No. 11	Nature and Usefulness of Supplementary Materials and Teaching Aids	−.11 (17)	.72 (14.5)

Note: This table is adapted from Table 3 in Feldman (1989b). The correlations shown in Column 1 are the same as those in Table 1 of the present analysis. The higher the correlation, the more important the instructional dimension. The correlations have been ranked from 1 to 17 (with the ranks shown in parentheses). The average standardized ranks given in Column 2 originally were given in Feldman (1976b, see Table 2 and footnote 5), and are based on information in the following studies: Brooks, Tarver, Kelley, Liberty, and Dickerson (1971); Centra (1975); Cobb (1956); French-Lazovik (1974, two studies); Garber (1964); Good (1971); Harry and Goldner (1972); Harvey and Barker (1970); Jioubu and Pollis (1974); Leftwich and Remmers (1962); Maas and Owen (1973); Owen (1967); Plant and Sawrey (1970); Remmers (1929); Remmers and Weisbrodt (1964); Rosenshine, Cohen, and Furst (1973); Sagen (1974); Spencer (1967); Van Horn (1968); Walker (1968); Widlak, McDaniel, and Feldhusen (1973); and Williams (1965). The lower the average standardized rank (that is, the smaller the fraction), the more important the dimension. The average standardized ranks in Column 2 have been ranked from 1 to 17 (with the ranks shown in parentheses). This table includes only those dimensions considered in both Feldman (1976b) and Feldman (1989b), and thus there are fewer dimensions in this table than there are in Table 1.

to Rank 6, the latter still relatively high in importance), and teacher's encouragement of questions and openness to others' opinion (from rank 5.5 to rank 11).

If ranks 1 through 6 are thought of as indicating high importance (relative to the other dimensions), rank 7–12 as indicating moderate importance, and ranks 13–17 as indicating low importance (low, that is, relative to the other dimensions, not necessarily unimportant), then the two methods determining the importance of instructional dimensions show the following pattern. Both methods indicate that the teacher's preparation and course organization, the teacher's clarity and understandableness, the teacher's stimulation of students' interest and the students' perceived outcome or impact of the course are of high importance (relative to the other dimensions). Although the teacher's encouragement of questions and openness to others' opinion as well as his or her availability and helpfulness are also of high importance in terms of the association of each with achievement, the first is only of moderate importance and the second of low importance in terms of its association with global evaluation of teachers.

Both methods of determining the importance of the instructional dimensions show the following to be of moderate importance relative to other dimensions: teacher's elocutionary skill, clarity of course objective and requirements, teacher's knowledge of subject, and teacher's enthusiasm. The importance of the teacher's sensitivity to class level and progress is also moderate by the first indicator (association with student learning) but high by the second (association with overall evaluation of the teacher), whereas the teacher's fairness and impartiality of evaluation is moderate by the first and low by the second. Each of the following five dimensions is of low relative importance in terms of its association with student achievement, although only the first three are also relatively low in importance in terms of their association with global evaluation: nature, quality and frequency of feedback to students; nature and value of course material; nature and usefulness of supplementary materials and teaching aids; intellectual challenge and encouragement of independent thought (which is of relatively high importance in the strength of its association with the global evaluation of teachers); and teacher's friendliness and concern/respect for student (of moderate importance in its association with global evaluation).

Table 3T3 offers a summary of the results of using the two different ways considered here of determining the importance of various instructional dimensions from student ratings of teachers. By averaging (when possible) the rank order of the dimensions produced by the two methods, information in Table 2 (and, in some cases, Table 1 as well) has been used to classify roughly the instructional dimensions into four categories of importance: high importance; moderate importance; moderate-to-low importance; and low (or no) importance. For most of the instructional dimensions, placement into the categories depended on information from both indicators of importance (association with achievement and association with global rating); in the other cases, classification was based on information from only one indicator (association with achievement).

Table 3: Summary of the Importance of Various Instructional Dimensions Based on Student Ratings

		High Importance
(Two Sources)	No. 6	Clarity and Understandableness
(Two Sources)	No. 1	Teacher's Stimulation of Interest in the Course and Its Perceived Subject Matter
(Two Sources)	No. 12	Perceived Outcome of Impact of Instruction
(Two Sources)	No. 5	Teacher's Preparation; Organization of the Course
(One Source)	No. 28	Teacher Pursued and/or Met Course Objectives
(One Source)	No. 20	Teacher Motivates Students to Do Their Best; High Standard of Performance Required
		Moderate Importance
(Two Sources)	No. 9	Clarity of Course Objectives and Requirements
(Two Sources)	No. 8	Teacher's Sensitivity to, and Concern with, Class Level and Progress
(Two Sources)	No. 16	Teacher's Encouragement of Questions and Discussion, and Openness to Opinions of Others
(Two Sources)	No. 17	Intellectual Challenge and Encouragement of Independent Thought
(Two Sources)	No. 7	Teacher's Elocutionary Skills
(Two Sources)	No. 3	Teacher's Knowledge of the Subject
(Two Sources)	No. 2	Teacher's Enthusiasm for the Subject
(Two Sources)	No. 19	Teacher's Availability and Helpfulness
		Moderate-to-Low Importance
(Two Sources)	No. 13	Teacher's Fairness; Impartiality of Evaluation of Students; Quality of Examinations
(Two Sources)	No. 18	Teacher's Concern and Respect for Students; Friendliness of the Teacher
(One Source)	No. 25	Classroom Management
(One Source)	No. 14	Personality Characteristics ("Personality") of the Teacher
(One Source)	No. 26	Pleasantness of Classroom Atmosphere
		Low Importance or No Importance
(Two Sources)	No. 10	Nature and Value of the Course (Including its Usefulness and Relevance)
(Two Sources)	No. 15	Nature, Quality, and Frequency of Feedback from the Teacher to the Student

(*cont.*)

115

Table 3: *(Continued)*

(Two Sources)	No. 11	Nature and Usefulness of Supplementary Materials and Teaching Aids
(One Source)	No. 23	Difficulty of the Course (and Workload)—Description
(One Source)	No. 24	Difficulty of the Course (and Workload)—Evaluation

Note: By averaging (when possible) the rank ordering of dimensions produced by two different methods of determining importance of various instructional dimensions, information in Table 2 (and, in some cases, Table 1) has been used to classify instructional dimensions into one of the four categories shown in this table. As indicated in the table, for some instructional dimensions two sources of information were available (association of the instructional dimension with achievement and with global evaluations, as given in Table 2); for other instructional dimensions, only one source of information was available (association of the instructional dimension with achievement, as given in Table 1.)

Although the present paper has concentrated on data derived from student ratings of actual teachers, I want to note briefly another way of determining the importance of various instructional dimensions using different information: Those most involved with teaching and learning can be asked directly about the importance of various components of instruction. In one analysis (Feldman, 1988), I collected thirty-one studies in which both students and faculty (separately) specified the instructional characteristics they considered particularly important to good teaching and effective instruction. Students and faculty were generally similar, though not identical, in their views, as indicated by an average correlation of +.71 between them in their valuation of various aspects of teaching. However, the ordering of the instructional dimensions by either of these groups shows differences (as well as some similarities) with that based on the two indicators of importance using student ratings of actual teachers.

A few examples may be given. Similar to the results shown in Table 3, Instructional Dimensions No. 5 (teacher's preparation and organization of the course) and No. 6 (clarity and understandableness) are of high importance to students and to faculty when these groups are asked directly about what is important to good teaching and effective instruction. Further, when asked directly, students again place high importance on Dimension No. 1 (teacher's stimulation of interest), but in this case faculty (when asked directly) see this aspect of teaching as less important than do the students (when asked directly) or by the two indicators of importance derived from student evaluations (summarized in Table 3). Moreover, compared to the importance determined

116

by the analysis of data from student evaluations, students and faculty, when asked directly, place less importance on Instructional Dimension No. 12 (perceived outcome or impact of instruction) but more importance on Dimensions No. 8 (teacher's sensitivity to, and concern with, class level and progress), No. 3 (teacher's knowledge of subject matter), and No. 2 (teacher's enthusiasm).[7]

CONCLUDING COMMENTS

This paper was not intended as a comprehensive review of the research literature on evaluation of college students of their teachers or on the correlates of effective teaching in college. Indeed, several topics or areas usually explored in such reviews have not been considered in this paper. To take two instances, I have ignored an analysis of whether there is a connection between research productivity and teaching effectiveness as well as a discussion of the usefulness of student ratings as feedback to faculty to improve their teaching (other than to label as myths the statements that good instruction and good research are so closely allied as to make it unnecessary to evaluate them separately and that student ratings cannot meaningfully be used to improve teaching). Rather, I have somewhat single-mindedly focused on the use of student ratings to identify exemplary teachers and teaching. In doing so, I have drawn together relevant parts of my own work over the years in addition to incorporating findings and conclusions from selected others.

Nothing I have written in this paper is meant to imply that the use of teacher evaluations is the only means of identifying exemplary teachers and teaching at the college level. The recent discussion of the multitude of items that would be appropriate for "teaching portfolios" by itself suggests otherwise (see, among others, Centra, 1993, Edgerton, Hutchings and Quinlan, 1991, and Seldin, 1991). For instance, in a project sponsored by the Canadian Association of University Teachers to identify the kinds of information a faculty member might use as evidence of teaching effectiveness, some forty-nine specific items were suggested as possible items for inclusion in a dossier (Shore and associates, 1986); only one of these items

---

[7] Other similarities and differences can be found in Feldman, 1989b (Table 3), where data for all four indicators of the importance of various instructional dimensions—association with achievement, association with global ratings, direct report of students, and direct report of faculty—are given.

referred to student ratings (listed as "student course and teaching evaluation data...."). Given the diverse ways noted in these dossiers of "capturing the scholarship of teaching," as Edgerton, Hutchings and Quinlan (1991) put it, gathering teacher evaluations may or may not be the one best way to identify excellence in teaching. But it is an important way; and current research evidence does show that when teacher evaluation forms are properly constructed and administered (Feldman, 1979), the global and specific ratings contained in them, as interpreted with appropriate caution, are undeniably helpful in identifying exemplary teachers and teaching.

Reprinted by permission of Agathon Press, New York.

REFERENCES

Abrami, P.C. (1985). Dimensions of effective college instruction. *Review of Higher Education* 8: 211–228.

Abrami, P.C. (1988), SEEQ and ye shall find: A review of Marsh's "Students' evaluation of university teaching." *Instructional Evaluation* 9: 19–27.

Abrami, P.C. (1989a). How should we use student ratings to evaluate teaching? *Research in Higher Education* 30: 221–227.

Abrami, P.C. (1989b). SEEQing the truth about student ratings of instruction. *Educational Researcher* 43: 43–45.

Abrami, P.C., Cohen, P.A., and d'Apollonia, S. (1988). Implementation problems in meta-analysis. *Review of Educational Research* 58: 151–179.

Abrami, P.C., and d'Apollonia, S. (1990). The dimensionality of ratings and their use in personnel decisions. In M. Theall and J. Franklin (eds.), *Student Ratings of Instruction: Issues for Improving Practice* (New Directions for Teaching and Learning No. 43). San Francisco: Jossey-Bass.

Abrami, P.C., and d'Apollonia, S. (1991). Multidimensional students' evaluations of teaching effectiveness—generalizability of "N = 1" research: Comments on Marsh. *Journal of Educational Psychology* 83: 411–415.

Abrami, P.C., d'Apollonia, S., and Rosenfield, S. (1993). *The Dimensionality of Student Ratings of Instruction: Introductory Remarks*. Paper presented at the annual meeting of the American Educational Research Association.

Abrami, P.C., d'Apollonia, S., and Rosenfield, S. (1996). The dimensionality of student ratings of instruction: What we know and what we do not. In J.C. Smart (ed.) *Higher Education: Handbook of Theory and Research* (Vol. 11). New York: Agathon Press.

Abrami, P.C., Leventhal, L., and Perry R.P. (1982). Educational seduction. *Review of Educational Research* 52: 446–464.

Aleamoni, L. (1987). Student rating myths versus research facts. *Journal of Personnel Evaluation in Education* 1: 111–119.

Aubrecht, J.D. (1981). Reliability, validity and generalizability of student ratings of instruction. (IDEA Paper No. 6). Manhattan, KS: Kansas State University, Center for Faculty Evaluation and Development. (ERIC Document Reproduction Service No. ED 213 296)

Baxter Magolda, M.B. (1992). *Knowing and Reasoning in College: Gender-Related Patterns in Students' Intellectual Development*. San Francisco: Jossey-Bass.

Benton, S.E., and Scott, O. (1976). *A Comparison of the Criterion Validity of Two Types of Student Response Inventories for Appraising Instruction*. Paper presented at the annual meeting of the National Council on Measurement in Education.

Bolton, B., Bonge, D., and Marr, J. (1979). Ratings of instruction, examination performance, and subsequent enrollment in psychology courses. *Teaching of Psychology* 6: 82–85.

Bowen, H.R. (1977). *Investment in Learning: The Individual and Social Value of American Higher Education*. San Francisco: Jossey-Bass.

Braskamp, L.A., Brandenburg, D.C., and Ory, J.C. (1984). *Evaluating Teaching Effectiveness: A Practical Guide*. Beverly Hills, Calif.: Sage.

Braskamp, L.A., Caulley, D., and Costin, F. (1979). Student ratings and instructor self-ratings and their relationship to student achievement. *American Educational Research Journal* 16: 295–306.

119

Braskamp, L.A., and Ory, J.C. (1994). *Assessing Faculty Work: Enhancing Individual and Institutional Performance.* San Francisco: Jossey-Bass.

Brooks, T.E., Tarver, D.A., Kelley, H.P., Liberty, P.G., Jr., and Dickerson, A.D. (1971). Dimensions underlying student ratings of courses and instructors at the University of Texas at Austin: Instructor Evaluation Form 2. (Research Bulletin RB-71-4). Austin, Texas: University of Texas at Austin, Measurement and Evaluation Center.

Bryson, R. (1974). Teacher evaluations and student learning: A reexamination. *Journal of Educational Research* 68: 11–14.

Cashin, W.E. (1988). *Student Ratings of Teaching: A Summary of the Research.* (IDEA Paper No. 20). Manhattan, KS: Kansas State University, Center for Faculty Evaluation and Development.

Cashin, W.E. (1990). Students do rate different academic fields differently. In M. Theall and J. Franklin (eds.), *Student Ratings of Instruction: Issues for Improving Practice* (New Directions for Teaching and Learning No. 43). San Francisco: Jossey-Bass.

Cashin, W.E. (1995). *Student Ratings of Teaching: The Research Revisited.* (IDEA Paper No. 32). Manhattan, KS: Kansas State University, Center for Faculty Evaluation and Development.

Cashin, W.E., and Clegg, V.L. (1987). *Are Student Ratings of Different Academic Fields Different?* Paper presented at the annual meeting of the American Educational Research Association. (ERIC Document Reproduction Service No. ED 286 935)

Cashin, W.E., and Downey, R.G. (1992). Using global student rating items for summative evaluation. *Journal of Educational Psychology* 84: 563–572.

Cashin, W.E., Downey, R.G., and Sixbury, G.R. (1994). Global and specific ratings of teaching effectiveness and their relation to course objectives: Reply to Marsh. *Journal of Educational Psychology* 86: 649–657.

Cashin, W.E., and Sixbury, G.R. (1993). *Comparative Data by Academic Field.* (IDEA Technical Report No. 8). Manhattan, KS: Kansas State University, Center for Faculty Evaluation and Development.

Centra, J.A. (1975). Colleagues as raters of classroom instruction. *Journal of Higher Education* 46: 327–337.

Centra, J.A. (1977). Student ratings of instruction and their relationship to student learning. *American Educational Research Journal* 14: 17–24.

Centra, J.A. (1979). *Determining Faculty Effectiveness: Assessing Teaching, Research, and Service for Personnel Decisions and Improvement.* San Francisco: Jossey-Bass.

Centra, J.A. (1989). Faculty evaluation and faculty development in higher education. In J.C. Smart (ed.), *Higher Education: Handbook of Theory and Research* (Vol. 5). New York: Agathon Press.

Centra, J.A. (1993). *Reflective Faculty Evaluation: Enhancing Teaching and Determining Faculty Effectiveness.* San Francisco: Jossey-Bass.

Chase, C.I., and Keene, J.M., Jr. (1979). Validity of student ratings of faculty. (Indiana Studies in Higher Education No. 40). Bloomington, Ind.: Indiana University, Bureau of Evaluation Studies and Testing, Division of Research and Development. (ERIC Document Reproduction Service No. ED 169 870).

Chickering, A.W., and Reisser, L. (1993). *Education and Identity* (2nd edition). San Francisco: Jossey-Bass.

Cobb, E.B. (1956). *Construction of a Forced-choice University Instructor Rating Scale.* Unpublished doctoral dissertation, University of Tennessee, Knoxville.

120

Cohen, P.A. (1980a). *A Meta-analysis of the Relationship between Student Ratings of Instruction and Student Achievement.* Unpublished doctoral dissertation, University of Michigan, Ann Arbor.

Cohen, P.A. (1980b). Effectiveness of student-rating feedback for improving college instruction: A meta-analysis of findings. *Research in Higher Education* 13: 321–341.

Cohen, P.A. (1981). Student ratings of instruction and student achievement. *Review of Educational Research* 51: 281–309.

Cohen, P.A. (1987). *A Critical Analysis and Reanalysis of the Multisection Validity Meta-analysis.* Paper presented at the annual meeting of the American Educational Research Association. (ERIC Document Reproduction Service No. ED 283 876)

Cohen, S.H., and Berger, W.G. (1970). Dimensions of students' ratings of college instructors underlying subsequent achievement on course examinations. *Proceedings of the 78th Annual Convention of the American Psychological Association* 5: 605–606.

Costin, F. (1978). Do student ratings of college teachers predict student achievement? *Teaching of Psychology* 5: 86–88.

Costin, F., Greenough, W.T., and Menges, R. J. (1971). Student ratings of college teaching: Reliability, validity and usefulness. *Review of Educational Research* 41: 511–535.

Crittenden, K.S., and Norr, J.L. (1973). Student values and teacher evaluation: A problem in person perception. *Sociometry* 36: 143–151.

d'Apollonia, S., and Abrami, P.C. (1987). *An Empirical Critique of Metaanalysis: The Literature on Student Ratings of Instruction.* Paper presented at the annual meeting of the American Educational Research Association.

d'Apollonia, S., and Abrami, P.C. (1988). *The Literature on Student Ratings of Instruction: Yet Another Meta-analysis.* Paper presented at the annual meeting of the American Educational Research Association.

d'Apollonia, S., Abrami, P.C., and Rosenfield, S. (1993). *The Dimensionality of Student Ratings of Instruction: A Meta-Analysis of the Factor Studies.* Paper presented at the annual meeting of the American Educational Research Association.

Doyle, K.O., Jr. (1972). *Construction and Evaluation of Scale for Rating College Instructors.* Unpublished doctoral dissertation, University of Minnesota, Minneapolis.

Doyle, K.O., Jr. (1975). *Student Evaluation of Instruction.* Lexington, MA: D. C. Heath.

Doyle, K.O., Jr. (1983). *Evaluating Teaching.* Lexington, MA: D. C. Health.

Doyle, K.O., Jr., and Crichton, L.I. (1978). Student, peer, and self evaluation of college instruction. *Journal of Educational Psychology* 70: 815–826.

Doyle, K.O., Jr., and Whitely, S.E. (1974). Student ratings as criteria for effective teaching. *American Educational Research Journal* 11: 259–274.

Edgerton, R., Hutchings, P., and Quinlan, K. (1991). *The Teaching Portfolio: Capturing the Scholarship in Teaching.* Washington, DC: American Association for Higher Education.

Elliott, D.N. (1950). Characteristics and relationship of various criteria of college and university teaching. *Purdue University Studies in Higher Education* 70: 5–61.

Ellis, N.R., and Rickard, H.C. (1977). Evaluating the teaching of introductory psychology. *Teaching of Psychology* 4: 128–132.

Ellner, C.L., and Barnes, C.P. (1983). *Studies of College Teaching: Experimental Results, Theoretical Interpretations, and New Perspectives.* Lexington, MA: D. C. Heath.

Endo, G.T., and Della-Piana, G. (1976). A validation study of course evaluation ratings. *Improving College and University Teaching* 24: 84–86.

121

Feldman, K.A. (1976a). Grades and college students' evaluation of their courses and teachers. *Research in Higher Education* 4: 69–111.

Feldman, K.A. (1976b). The superior college teacher from the students' view. *Research in Higher Education* 5: 243–288.

Feldman, K.A. (1977). Consistency and variability among college students in rating their teachers and courses: A review and analysis. *Research in Higher Education* 6: 223–274.

Feldman, K.A. (1978). Course characteristics and college students' ratings of their teachers: What we know and what we don't. *Research in Higher Education* 9: 199–242.

Feldman, K.A. (1979). The significance of circumstances for college students' ratings of their teachers and courses. *Research in Higher Education* 10: 149–172.

Feldman, K.A. (1983). Seniority and experience of college teachers as related to evaluation they receive from students. *Research in Higher Education* 18: 3–124.

Feldman, K.A. (1984). Class size and college students' evaluations of teachers and courses: A closer look. *Research in Higher Education* 21: 45–116.

Feldman, K.A. (1986). The perceived instructional effectiveness of college teachers as related to their personality and attitudinal characteristics: A review and synthesis. *Research in Higher Education* 24: 139–213.

Feldman, K.A. (1987). Research productivity and scholarly accomplishment of college teachers as related to their instructional effectiveness: A review and exploration. *Research in Higher Education* 26: 227–298.

Feldman, K.A. (1988). Effective college teaching from the students' and faculty's view: Matched or mismatched priorities? *Research In Higher Education* 28: 291–344.

Feldman, K.A. (1989a). Instructional effectiveness of college teachers as judged by teachers themselves, current and former students, colleagues, administrators, and external (neutral) observers. *Research in Higher Education* 30: 137–194.

Feldman, K.A. (1989b). The association between student ratings of specific instructional dimensions and student achievement: Refining and extending the synthesis of data from multisection validity studies. *Research in Higher Education* 30: 583–645.

Feldman, K.A. (1990a). An afterword for "The association between student ratings of specific instructional dimensions and student achievement: Refining and extending the synthesis of data from multisection validity studies." *Research in Higher Education* 31: 315–318.

Feldman, K.A. (1990b). Instructional evaluation. *The Teaching Professor* 4: 5–7.

Feldman, K.A. (1992). College students' views of male and female college teachers: Part I—evidence from the social laboratory and experiments. *Research in Higher Education* 33: 317–375.

Feldman, K.A. (1993). College students' views of male and female college teachers: Part II—evidence from students' evaluations of their classroom teachers. *Research in Higher Education* 34: 151–211.

Feldman, K.A. (1994). *Identifying Exemplary Teaching: Evidence from Course and Teacher Evaluations*. Paper commissioned by the National Center on Postsecondary Teaching, Learning, and Assessment for presentation at the Second AAHE Conference on Faculty Roles and Rewards.

Feldman, K.A. (forthcoming). Identifying exemplary teaching: Using data from course and teacher evaluations. In M.D. Svinicki and R.J. Menges (eds.), *Honoring Exemplary Teaching* (New Directions for Teaching and Learning). San Francisco: Jossey-Bass.

122

Feldman, K.A., and Newcomb, T.M. (1969). *The Impact of College on Students*. San Francisco: Jossey-Bass.

Feldman, K.A., and Paulsen, M.B. (eds.) (1994). *Teaching and Learning in the College Classroom*. Needham Heights, MA: Ginn Press.

French-Lazovik, G. (1974). Predictability of students' evaluation of college teachers from component ratings. *Journal of Educational Psychology* 66: 373–385.

Frey, P.W. (1973). Student ratings of teaching: Validity of several rating factors. *Science* 182: 83–85.

Frey, P.W. (1976). Validity of student instructional ratings as a function of their timing. *Journal of Higher Education* 47: 327–336.

Frey, P.W., Leonard, D.W., and Beatty, W.W. (1975). Student ratings of instruction: Validation research. *American Educational Research Journal* 12: 435–444.

Garber, H., 1964. *Certain Factors Underlying the Relationship between Course Grades and Student Judgments of College Teachers*. Unpublished doctoral dissertation, University of Connecticut, Storrs.

Gigliotti, R.J., and Buchtel, F.S. (1990). Attributional bias and course evaluation. *Journal of Educational Psychology* 82: 341–351.

Good, K.C. (1971). *Similarity of Student and Instructor Attitudes and Student's Attitudes Toward Instructors*. Unpublished doctoral dissertation, Purdue University, West Lafayette.

Greenwood, G.E., Hazelton, A., Smith, A.B., and Ware, W.B. (1976). A study of the validity of four types of student ratings of college teaching assessed on a criterion of student achievement gains. *Research in Higher Education* 5: 171–178.

Grush, J.E., and Costin, F. (1975). The student as consumer of the teaching process. *American Educational Research Journal* 12: 55–66.

Harry, J., and Goldner, N.S. (1972). The null relationship between teaching and research. *Sociology of Education* 45: 47–60.

Harvey, J.N., and Barker, D.G. (1970). Student evaluation of teaching effectiveness. *Improving College and University Teaching* 18: 275–278.

Hativa, N., and Raviv, A. (1993). Using a single score for summative teacher evaluation by students. *Research in Higher Education* 34: 625–646.

Hoffman, R.G. (1978). Variables affecting university student ratings of instructor behavior. *American Educational Research Journal* 15: 287–299.

Hoyt, D.P. (1973). Measurement of instructional effectiveness. *Research in Higher Education* 1: 367–378.

Jiobu, R.M., and Pollis, C.A. (1971). Student evaluations of courses and instructors. *American Sociologist* 6: 317–321.

King, P.M., and Kitchener, K.S. (1994). *Developing Reflective Judgment: Understanding and Promoting Intellectual Growth and Critical Thinking in Adolescents and Adults*. San Francisco: Jossey-Bass.

Kulik, M.A., and McKeachie, W.J. (1975). The evaluation of teachers in higher education. In F.N. Kerlinger (ed.), *Review of Research in Education* (Vol. 3). Itasca, Il: F.E. Peacock.

Land, M.L. (1979). Low-inference variables of teacher clarity: Effects on student concept learning. *Journal of Educational Psychology* 71: 795–799.

Land, M.L. (1981). Actual and perceived teacher clarity: Relations to student achievement in science. *Journal of Research in Science Teaching* 18: 139–143.

Land, M.L., and Combs, A. (1981). *Teacher Clarity, Student Instructional Ratings, and Student Performance*. Paper read at the annual meeting of the American Educational Research Association.

Land, M.L., and Combs, N. (1982). Teacher behavior and student ratings. *Educational and Psychological Research* 2: 63–68.

Land, M.L., and Smith, L.R. (1979). The effect of low inference teacher clarity inhibitors and student achievement. *Journal of Teacher Education* 30: 55–57.

Land, M.L., and Smith, L.R. (1981). College student ratings and teacher behavior: An Experimental Study. *Journal of Social Studies Research* 5: 19–22.

Leftwich, W.H., and Remmers, H.H. (1992). A comparison of graphic and forced-choice ratings of teaching performance at the college and university level. *Purdue Universities Studies in Higher Education* 92: 3–31.

Leventhal, L. (1975). Teacher rating forms: Critique and reformulation of previous validation designs. *Canadian Psychological Review* 16: 269–276.

Levinson-Rose, J., and Menges, R.L. (1981). Improving college teaching: A critical review of research. *Review of Educational Research* 51: 403–434.

L'Hommedieu, R., Menges, R.J., and Brinko, K.T. (1988). *The Effects of Student Ratings Feedback to College Teachers: A Meta-analysis and Review of Research*. Unpublished manuscript, Northwestern University, Center for the Teaching Professions, Evanston.

L'Hommedieu, R., Menges, R.J., and Brinko, K.T. (1990). Methodological explanations for the modest effects of feedback. *Journal of Educational Psychology* 82: 232–241.

Maas, J.B., and Owen, T.R. (1973). *Cornell Inventory for Student Appraisal of Teaching and Courses: Manual of Instructions*. Ithaca, NY: Cornell University, Center for Improvement of Undergraduate Education.

Marsh, H.W. (1984). Students' evaluations of university teaching: Dimensionality, reliability, validity, potential biases, and utility. *Journal of Educational Psychology* 76: 707–754.

Marsh, H.W. (1987). Students' evaluations of university teaching: Research findings, methodological issues, and directions for future research. *International Journal of Educational Research* 11: 253–388.

Marsh, H.W. (1991a). Multidimensional students' evaluation of teaching effectiveness: A test of alternative higher-order structures. *Journal of Educational Psychology* 83: 285–296.

Marsh, H.W. (1991b). A multidimensional perspective on students' evaluations of teaching effectiveness: A reply to Abrami and d'Apollonia. *Journal of Educational Psychology* 83: 416–421.

Marsh, H.W. (in press). Weighting for the right criterion in the IDEA system: Global and specific ratings of teaching effectiveness and their relation to course objectives. *Journal of Educational Psychology*.

Marsh, H.W., and Dunkin, M.J. (1992). Students' evaluations of university teaching: A multidimensional approach. In J.C. Smart (ed.), *Higher Education: Handbook of Theory and Research* (Vol. 8). New York: Agathon Press.

Marsh, H.W., Fleiner, H., and Thomas, C.S. (1975). Validity and usefulness of student evaluations of instructional quality. *Journal of Educational Psychology* 67: 833–839.

Marsh, H.W., and Overall, J.U. (1980). Validity of students' evaluations of teaching effectiveness: Cognitive and affective criteria. *Journal of Educational Psychology* 72: 468–475.

McKeachie, W.J. (1979). Student ratings of faculty: A reprise. *Academe* 65: 384–397.

McKeachie, W.J. (1987). Instructional evaluation: Current issues and possible improvements. *Journal of Higher Education* 58: 344–350.

McKeachie, W.J., Lin, Y-G, and Mann, W. (1971). Student ratings of teacher effectiveness: Validity studies. *American Educational Research Association* 8: 435–445.

Miller, R.I. (1972). *Evaluating Faculty Performance.* San Francisco: Jossey-Bass.

Miller, R.I. (1974). *Developing Programs for Faculty Evaluation.* San Francisco: Jossey-Bass.

Mintzes, J.J., (1976–77). Field test and validation of a teaching evaluation instrument: The Student Opinion Survey of Teaching (A report submitted to the Senate Committee for Teaching and Learning, Faculty Senate, University of Windsor). Windsor, ON: University of Windsor.

Morgan, W.D., and Vasché, J.D. (1978). An Educational Production Function Approach to Teaching Effectiveness and Evaluation. *Journal of Economic Education* 9: 123–126.

Morsh, J.E., Burgess, G.G., and Smith, P.N. (1956). Student achievement as a measure of instructor effectiveness. *Journal of Educational Psychology* 47: 79–88.

Murray, H.G. (1980). *Evaluating University Teaching: A Review of Research.* Toronto: Ontario Confederation of University Faculty Associations.

Murray, H.G. (1983). Low-inference classroom teaching behaviors in relation to six measures of college teaching effectiveness. Proceedings of the Conference on the Evaluation and Improvement of University Teaching: The Canadian Experience (pp. 43–73). Montreal: McGill University, Centre for Teaching and Learning Service.

Murray, H.G. (1991). Effective teaching behaviors in the college classroom. In J.C. Smart (ed.), *Higher Education: Handbook of Theory and Research* (Vol. 7). New York: Agathon Press.

Orpen, C. (1980). Student evaluations of lecturers as an indicator of instructional quality: A validity study. *Journal of Educational Research* 74: 5–7.

Owen, P.H. (1967). *Some Dimensions of College Teaching: An Exploratory Study Using Critical Incidents and Factor Analyses of Student Ratings.* Unpublished doctoral dissertation, University of Houston, Houston.

Pascarella, E.T., and Terenzini, P.T. (1991). *How College Affects Students: Findings and Insights from Twenty Years of Research.* San Francisco: Jossey-Bass.

Perry, R.P. (1991). Perceived control in college students: Implications for instruction in higher education. In J.C. Smart (ed.), *Higher Education: Handbook of Theory and Research* (Vol. 7). New York: Agathon Press.

Plant, W.T., and Sawrey, J.M. (1970). Student ratings of psychology professors as teachers and the research involvement of the professors rated. *The Clinical Psychologist* 23: 15–16, 19.

Rankin, E.F., Jr., Greenmun, R., and Tracy, R.J. (1965). Factors related to student evaluations of a college reading course. *Journal of Reading* 9: 10–15.

Remmers, H.H. (1929). The college professor as the student sees him. *Purdue University Studies in Higher Education* 11: 1–63.

Remmers, H.H., Martin, F.D., and Elliott, D.N. (1949). Are students' ratings of instructors related to their grades? *Purdue University Studies in Higher Education* 66: 17–26.

Remmers, H.H., and Weisbrodt, J.A. (1964). *Manual of Instructions for Purdue Rating Scale of Instruction.* West Lafayette, IN: Purdue Research Foundation.

125

Rosenshine, B., Cohen, A., and Furst, N. (1973). Correlates of student preference ratings. *Journal of College Student Personnel* 14: 269–272.

Rubinstein, J., and Mitchell, H. (1970). Feeling free, student involvement, and appreciation. *Proceedings of the 78th Annual Convention of the American Psychological Association* 5: 623–624.

Sagen, H.B. (1974). Student, faculty, and department chairmen ratings of instructors: Who agrees with whom? *Research in Higher Education* 2: 265–272.

Sanders, J.A., and Wiseman, R.L. (1990). The effects of verbal and nonverbal teacher immediacy on perceived cognitive, affective, and behavioral learning in the multicultural classroom. *Communication Education* 39: 341–353.

Seldin, P. (1991). *The Teaching Portfolio*. Boston: Anker Publishing.

Shore, B.M., and associates (1986). *The Teaching Dossier: A Guide to Its Preparation and Use* (Rev. Ed.). Montreal: Canadian Association of University Teachers.

Smith, L.R., and Land, M.L. (1980). Student perception of teacher clarity in mathematics. *Journal for Research in Mathematics Education* 11: 137–146.

Sockloff, A.L. (1973). Instruments for student evaluation of faculty: Ideal and actual. In A.L. Sockloff (ed.), *Proceedings of the First Invitational Conference on Faculty Effectiveness as Evaluated by Students*. Philadelphia, PA: Temple University, Measurement and Research Center.

Solomon, D., Rosenberg, L., and Bezdek, W.E. (1964). Teacher behavior and student learning. *Journal of Educational Psychology* 55: 23–30.

Spencer, R.E. (1967). Analysis of the Instructor Rating Form—General Engineering Department. (Research Report No. 253). Urbana, Il: University of Illinois, Measurement and Research Division, Office of Instructional Resources.

Stumpf, S.A., and Freedman, R.D. (1979). Expected grade covariation with student ratings of instruction: Individual versus class effects. *Journal of Educational Psychology* 71: 293–302.

Theall, M., Franklin, J., and Ludlow, L. (1990a). Attributions and retributions: Student ratings and the perceived causes of performance. *Instructional Evaluation* 11: 12–17.

Theall, M., Franklin, J., and Ludlow, L. (1990b). *Attributions or Retributions: Student Ratings and the Perceived causes of Performance*. Paper presented at the annual meeting of the American Educational Research Association.

Turner, R.L. (1970). Good teaching and its contexts. *Phi Delta Kappan* 52: 155–158.

Turner, R.L., and Thompson, R.P. (1974). *Relationships between College Student Ratings of Instructors and Residual Learning*. Paper presented at the annual meeting of the American Educational Research Association.

Van Horn, C. *An Analysis of the 1968 Course and Instructor Evaluation Report*. (Institutional Research Bulletin No. 2–68). West Lafayette, IN: Purdue University, Measurement and Research Center.

Walker, B.D. (1968). *An Investigation of Selected Variables Relative to the Manner in which a Population of Junior College Students Evaluate their Teachers*. Unpublished doctoral dissertation, University of Houston,

Widlak, F.W., McDaniel, E.D., and Feldhusen, J.F. (1973). *Factor Analysis of an Instructor Rating Scale*. Paper presented at the annual meeting of the American Educational Research Association.

Williams, H.Y., Jr. (1965). *College Students' Perceptions of the Personal Traits and Instructional Procedures of Good and Poor Teachers*. Unpublished doctoral dissertation, University of Minnesota, Minneapolis.

APPENDIX

This appendix, with its listing of 28 instructional dimensions, first appeared in Feldman (1989b) in a slightly different version. For each of the instructional dimensions, examples of evaluation items that would be classified into it are given. For refinements and modifications to this list of dimensions and attendant coding scheme, see d'Apollonia, Abrami and Rosenfield (1993) and Abrami, d'Apollonia and Rosenfield (1996).

No. 1 *Teacher's Stimulation of Interest in the Course and Its Subject Matter:* "the instructor puts material across in an interesting way"; "the instructor gets students interested in the subject"; "it was easy to remain attentive"; "the teacher stimulated intellectual curiosity"; etc.

No. 2 *Teacher's Enthusiasm (for Subject or for Teaching):* "the instructor shows interest and enthusiasm in the subject"; "the instructor seems to enjoy teaching"; "the teacher communicates a genuine desire to teach students"; "the instructor never showed boredom for teaching this class"; "the instructor shows energy and excitement"; etc.

No. 3 *Teacher's Knowledge of Subject Matter:* "the instructor has a good command of the subject material"; "the teacher has a thorough knowledge, basic and current, of the subject"; "the instructor has good knowledge about or beyond the textbook"; "the instructor knows the answers to questions students ask"; "the teacher keeps lecture material updated"; etc.

No. 4 *Teacher's Intellectual Expansiveness (and Intelligence):* "the teacher is well informed in all related fields"; "the teacher has respect for other subject areas and indicates their relationship to his or her own subject of presentation"; "the teacher exhibited a high degree of cultural attainment"; etc.

No. 5 *Teacher's Preparation; Organization of the Course:* "the teacher was well prepared for each day's lecture"; "the presentation of the material is well organized"; the overall development of the course had good continuity"; "the instructor planned the activities of each class period in detail"; etc.

No. 6 *Clarity and Understandableness:* "the instructor made clear explanations"; the instructor interprets abstract ideas and theories clearly"; "the instructor makes good use of examples and illustrations to get across difficult points"; "the teacher effectively synthesizes and summarizes the material"; "the teacher answers students' questions in a way that helps students to understand"; etc.

No. 7 *Teacher's Elocutionary Skills:* "the instructor has a good vocal delivery"; "the teacher speaks distinctly, fluently and without hesitation"; "the teacher varied the speech and tone of his or her voice"; "the teacher has the ability to speak distinctly and be clearly heard"; "the instructor changed pitch, volume, or quality of speech"; etc.

No. 8 *Teacher's Sensitivity to, and Concern with, Class Level and Progress:* "the teacher was skilled in observing student reactions"; "the teacher was aware when students failed to keep up in class"; "the instructor teaches near the class level"; "the teacher takes an active personal interest in the progress of the class and shows a desire for students to learn"; etc.

127

No. 9 *Clarity of Course Objectives and Rdequirements*: "the purposes and policies of the course were made clear to the student"; "the instructor gave a clear idea of the student requirements"; "the teacher clearly defined student responsibilities in the course"; "the teacher tells students which topics are most important and what they can expect on tests"; "the instructor gave clear assignments"; etc.

No. 10 *Nature and Value of the Course Material (Including Its Usefulness and Relevance)*: "the teacher has the ability to apply material to real life"; "the instructor makes the course practical"; "there is worthwhile and informative material in lectures that doesn't duplicate the text"; "the course has excellent content"; "the class considers what we are learning worth learning"; etc.

No. 11 *Nature and Usefulness of Supplementary Materials and Teaching Aids*: "the homework assignments and supplementary readings were helpful in under-standing the course"; "the teacher made good use of teaching aids such as films and other audio-visual materials"; "the instructor provided a variety of activities in class and used a variety of media (slides, films, projections, drawings) and outside resource persons"; etc.

No. 12 *Perceived Outcome or Impact of Instruction*: "gaining of new knowledge was facilitated by the instructor"; "I developed significant skills in the field"; "I developed increased sensitivity and evaluative judgment"; "the instructor has given me tools for attacking problems"; "the course has increased my general knowledge"; "apart from your personal feelings about the teacher, has he/she been instrumental in increasing knowledge of the course's subject matter"; etc.

No. 13 *Teacher's Fairness; Impartiality of Evaluation of Students; Quality of Examina-tions*: "grading in the course was fair"; "the instructor has definite standards and is impartial in grading"; "the exams reflect material emphasized in the course"; "test questions were clear"; "coverage of subject matter on exams was comprehensive"; etc.

No. 14 *Personality Characteristics ("Personality") of the Teacher*: "the teacher has a good sense of humor"; "the teacher was sincere and honest"; "the teacher is highly personable at all times in dress, voice, social grace, and manners"; "the instructor was free of personal peculiarities"; "the instructor is not autocratic and does not try to force us to accept his ideas and interpretations"; "the teacher exhibits a casual, informal attitude"; "the instructor laughed at his own mistakes"; etc.

No. 15 *Nature Quality, and Frequency of Feedback from the Teacher to Students*: "the teacher gave satisfactory feedback on graded material"; "criticism of papers was helpful to students"; "the teacher told students when they had done a good job"; "the teacher is prompt in returning tests and assignments"; etc.

No. 16 *Teacher's Encouragement of Questions and Discussion, and Openness to Opinions of Others*: "students felt free to ask questions or express opinions"; the instructor stimulated class discussions"; "the teacher encouraged students to express differ-ences of opinions and to evaluate each other's ideas"; "the instructor invited criticisms of his or her own ideas"; "the teacher appeared receptive to new ideas and the viewpoints of others"; etc.

No. 17 *Intellectual Challenge and Encouragement of Independent Thought (by the Teacher and the Course)*: "this course challenged students intellectually"; "the teacher encouraged students to think out answers and follow up ideas"; "the teacher attempts to stimulate creativity"; "the instructor raised challenging questions and problems"; etc.

No. 18 *Teacher's Concern and Respect for Students; Friendliness of the Teacher*: "the instructor seems to have a genuine interest in and concern for students"; "the teacher took students seriously"; "the instructor established good rapport with students"; "the teacher was friendly toward all students"; etc.

No. 19 *Teacher's Availability and Helpfulness*: "the instructor was willing to help students having difficulty"; "the instructor is willing to give individual attention"; "the teacher was available for consultation"; "the teacher was accessible to students outside of class"; etc.

No. 20 *Teacher Motivates Students to Do Their Best; High Standard of Performance Required*: "Instructor motivates students to do their best work"; "the instructor sets high standards of achievement for students"; "the teacher raises the aspirational level of students"; etc.

No. 21 *Teacher's Encouragement of Self-Initiated Learning*: "Students are encouraged to work independently"; "students assume much responsibility for their own learning"; "the general approach used in the course gives emphasis to learning on the students' own"; "the teacher does not suppress individual initiative"; etc.

No. 22 *Teacher's Productivity in Research Related Activities*: "The teacher talks about his own research"; "instructor displays high research accomplishments"; "the instructor publishes material related to his subject field"; etc.

No. 23 *Difficulty of the Course (and Workload)—Description*: "the workload and pace of the course was difficult", "I spent a great many hours studying for this course"; "the amount of work required for this course was very heavy"; "this course required a lot of time"; "the instructor assigned very difficult reading"; etc.

No. 24 *Difficulty of the Course (and Workload)—Evaluation*: "the content of this course is too hard"; "the teacher's lectures and oral presentations are 'over my head'"; "the instructor often asked for more than students could get done"; "the instructor attempted to cover too much material and presented it too rapidly"; etc.

No. 25 *Classroom Management*: "the instructor controls class discussion to prevent rambling and confusion"; "the instructor maintained a classroom atmosphere conducive to learning"; "students are allowed to participate in deciding the course content"; "the teacher did not 'rule with an iron hand'"; etc.

No. 26 *Pleasantness of Classroom Atmosphere*: "the class does not make me nervous"; "I felt comfortable in this class"; "the instructor created an atmosphere in which students in the class seemed friendly"; "this was not one of those classes where students failed to laugh, joke, smile or show other signs of humor"; "the teacher is always criticizing and arguing with students"; etc.

No. 27 *Individualization of Teaching*: "instead of expecting every student to do the same thing, the instructor provides different activities for different students"; "my grade depends primarily upon my improvement over my past performance"; "in this class each student is accepted on his or her own merits"; "my grade is influenced by what is best for me as a person as well as by how much I have learned"; "the instructor evaluated each student as an individual"; etc.

No. 28 *Teacher Pursued and/or Met Course Objectives*: "the instructor accomplished what he or she set out to do"; "there was close agreement between the announced objectives of the course and what was actually taught"; "course objectives stated agreed with those actually pursued"; etc.

COMMENTARY AND UPDATE ON FELDMAN'S (1997) "IDENTIFYING EXEMPLARY TEACHERS AND TEACHING: EVIDENCE FROM STUDENT RATINGS"

Michael Theall* and Kenneth A. Feldman[†]

*Youngstown State University
mtheall@ysu.edu
[†]SUNY-Stony Brook

Abstract

In the original chapter (1997), Feldman explores how student ratings can be used to identify those teachers who are seen by students as exemplary, while noting certain precautions (which involve myths, half-truths and bias) in doing so. He also analyzes how exemplary teaching itself can be identified in terms of specific pedagogical dispositions, behaviors and practices of teachers. While the essential findings of this earlier analysis remain valid, there have been changes in the nature and focus of research on college teaching and its evaluation. As well, new challenges and developments are forcing higher education to rethink its paradigms and practices in such areas as teaching, the evaluation of faculty performance, and the kinds of support faculty need to meet the increasingly complex professional demands placed on the professoriate. The co-authors of the commentary and update (Theall and Feldman) review the principal findings of the original chapter, discuss the literature of the past decade, and offer suggestions for ways in which higher education and the professoriate can survive and flourish in the future

Key Words: College teaching; dimensions of teaching; exemplary teaching; student ratings of instruction; reliability and validity; myths vs. research evidence; faculty evaluation; the professoriate; higher education; paradigm shift; research and practice; faculty development; professional enrichment; faculty as meta-professionals; faculty careers

Reviewing the extant literature, Feldman (1997) explored how student ratings could be used to identify those persons who are seen by students as exemplary teachers, while noting certain precautions (involving current myths and half-truths as well as issues of bias) in doing so. He then analyzed how exemplary teaching itself can be identified in terms of specific pedagogical dispositions, behaviors and practices of teachers. He reviewed dimensions of teaching that are associated with student learning and with overall evaluations of teachers.

Since Feldman's chapter appeared, the number of publications about student ratings has not noticeably diminished nor has the amount of discussion abated. Although, in general, the major conclusions of his chapter still hold, two tracks of activity have become apparent— both of which we consider in various places in this commentary and update. One track is the continuation of scholarship by researchers and practitioners in the field with an increasing emphasis on bringing the research into practice. This activity has not gone unnoticed as evidenced by the fact that the 2005 American Educational Research Association's "Interpretive Scholarship, Relating Research to Practice Award" went to evaluation and ratings researchers doing just this kind of work. The second track has been less productive in terms of improving practice. It is represented by an array of opinion and reports of investigations attempting to prove that ratings are biased, are the cause of grade inflation, and are threats to promotion, tenure, academic freedom, and the general quality of higher education. One result of this activity has been the extension of misinformation and mythology surrounding ratings, which in effect has made improved practice more difficult (Aleamoni, 1987; Feldman, 1997).

GENERALIZATIONS AND CONCLUSIONS ABOUT RATINGS AS EVIDENCE OF EXEMPLARY TEACHERS AND TEACHING: SOME CAUTIONS

Feldman cautioned that his 1997 chapter was "...not intended as a comprehensive review of the research literature on evaluation of college students (ratings) of their teachers or on the correlates of effective teaching in college." (p. 385, parenthetical term added). This caution still applies for four reasons. First, it is clear that the number and variety of issues affecting teaching and learning is exceptionally large and complex, and thus beyond the scope of the present update. For example, recent work by Pascarella and Terenzini (2005) and Kuh et al. (2005) demonstrates that student performance is affected by a number of conditions beyond classroom teaching and other efforts of the faculty members. College instructors, existing in this same set of conditions, cannot help but be influenced as well, and thus their satisfaction as well as that of their students can affect their teaching and their students' perceptions of it (Cranton & Knoop, 1991). Ratings reflect students' opinions about teaching, and they do correlate with learning (Cohen, 1981), but to some degree they also indicate students' general satis-faction with their experiences. Environmental factors can affect those experiences and thus complicate an already complex measurement situation. Indeed, the complexity of the whole teaching-learning picture demands a broader view that both includes and goes beyond ratings as evidence of exemplary teaching.

A second reason for repeating the caveat is that while Feldman's chapter can remain essentially unchallenged in terms of its conclusions (because there is little in the way of substantial new evidence that contradicts his interpretations), at the same time there is an absence of new literature about exemplary teaching in contexts essentially nonexistent when the earlier analysis was completed. Of particular note, for example, is the growth of technologically enhanced instruction and on-line or other "distance" teaching and learning experiences. Thus, Feldman's (1989) work refining and extending the synthesis of data from multivalidation studies (reviewed in Feldman's 1997 chapter) remains a primary source of information about the dimensions of college teaching in traditional teaching and learning settings (also, see Abrami, d'Apollonia and Rosenfield, 1996). But, the 1997 chapter cannot be updated without also considering Feldman's (1998) chapter urging readers to consider the effects of context and "unresolved issues."

The growth of instruction in settings other than traditional classrooms raises questions about the extent to which established models and psychometric techniques can be transplanted into these new situations. Because there has not been a great deal of research on how to evaluate teaching in these contexts, these questions remain unresolved. Using the same traditional questionnaires and producing the same traditional reports raises serious validity issues. In addition, and given the number of references found in opinion pieces in the press and elsewhere, the emergence of private or for-profit on-line ratings has added to the faculty's legitimate concern about the misuse of ratings data. Clearly, the issues related to technological innovations are numerous, and while we note their impact here we cannot explore them in depth.

The third reason involves the nature and variety of publications specifically on student ratings. Earlier literature contained many in-depth analyses of ratings issues characterized by reports drawn from validation studies (e.g., Cashin, 1990, with IDEA; Centra, 1972, with SIR; Marsh, 1987, with SEEQ), syntheses or meta-analyses (e.g., Cohen, 1981; Feldman, 1989; Abrami, d'Apollonia and Rosenfield, 1996), the use of large databases to explore specific issues (e.g., Franklin and Theall, 1992, with TCEP), the involvement of scientists/researchers whose primary research emphases were teaching, learning, or ratings themselves (e.g., Doyle, 1975; Centra, 1979; Marsh, 1984) and, importantly, the extended discussion of reported results. An example of this last factor can be found in commentary and studies following the Naftulin, Ware and Donnelly (1973) "Dr. Fox" article. Commentaries were published in four issues of *Instructional Evaluation* between 1979 and 1982,[1] and Raymond Perry and associates conducted a series of studies on educational seduction and instructor expressiveness between 1979 and 1986, incorporating perceived control as a major variable in their later work.[2] Though there was public notice of the "Dr. Fox" study, the primary participants in the dialogue were the researchers themselves. This is less the case today, as almost any opinion from any quarter (it would seem) is deemed worthy of publication, and because communications technologies allow anyone to publish and widely circulate an opinion without the process required in traditional refereed environments.

Finally, affecting the scope of this update is the general descent of the status of the professoriate and higher education itself. Even respected academicians have produced work with clear sarcasm in their titles—for example, "Dry Rot in the Ivory Tower" (Campbell, 2000) and "Declining by Degrees" (Hersh and Merrow, 2005). A spate of books and opinions has inflamed the general public, editorial writers, and legislators who feel ever more comfortable demanding "accountability." The interesting irony is that if, to the joy of many critics, ratings were to be eliminated in favor of student learning as a measure of teaching excellence, then the same arguments used to question the reliability and validity of ratings would arise with respect to testing and grading. "Grade inflation," which according to these same critics (e.g., Johnson, 2003; Trout, 2000) is the by-product of ratings, would not disappear. Rather, grades might either become favored by faculty as evidence of teaching excellence ("Look how well I did. My students all got As!") or they would become the new criteria by which poor teaching would be characterized ("S/he must be a poor teacher! Look how many students got As). Thus, in this brave new world, teachers might

---

[1] *Instructional Evaluation* (now *Instructional Evaluation and Faculty Development*) is a semi-annual publication of the Special Interest Group in Faculty Teaching, Evaluation, and Development of the American Educational Research Association. Issues from 1996 are available on-line at: http://www.umanitoba.ca/uts/sigfted/backissues.php. Earlier issues can be purchased using information provided at: http://www.umanitoba.ca/uts/sigfted/iefdi/spring00/bkissues.htm.

[2] Studies with instructor expressiveness as a variable include Perry, Abrami and Leventhal (1979) through Perry, Magnusson, Parsonson and Dickens (1986). The conclusions of the research were that expressiveness alone does not enhance achievement but can influence ratings of specific presentation skills, and that in combination with appropriate content it can positively influence both ratings and achievement.

provide evidence of excellence by either "dumbing down" courses to maximize the numbers of As or, in the opposite perversion, failing as many students as possible.

THE PUBLIC DEBATE ON STUDENT RATINGS

Discussion of ratings issues has continued, and perhaps has even been unduly influenced by recent publications. For example, Johnson (2003) has supported a proposal at Duke University (see Gose, 1997) whereby class grade profiles would be used to rate classes so that the grades students received could then be given more or less weight in a calculation of the GPA. Such reaction and over-reaction seems based primarily on assumptions that grade inflation has been caused by the use of ratings and by a focus on learners as customers or consumers. The language of complaints almost always includes these issues in a simplistic way without crediting established findings (e.g., Cohen, 1981; Marsh, 1987) or taking account of the larger picture of improving evaluation and teaching in complimentary ways (e.g., Theall & Franklin, 1991).

Many recent publications are based on one-time and/or small-sample studies that vary substantially from methodologically accepted practice (e.g., Williams & Ceci, 1997), many include ratings issues in work from other disciplinary perspectives (e.g., Hamermesh & Parker, 2003), many are more opinion pieces than specific research on ratings (e.g., Trout, 2000), and few are by researchers whose primary emphasis has been faculty evaluation or student ratings (which would include all of the above-cited items). Many of these pieces have become well known by virtue of the interest of widely distributed publications (e.g., *Academe, The Chronicle of Higher Education*) in the controversy surrounding ratings.

One partial exception was the substantial work by Greenwald and Gillmore (1997a, 1997b) that culminated in a "Current Issues" section of *American Psychologist* (Vol. 52, No. 11) devoted to the topic of grade inflation and ratings. That was followed by an AERA symposium on the same topic. While there was considerable disagreement with Greenwald and Gillmore's contention that grading leniency was a "contaminant" of ratings to be statistically corrected, the point is that the work included a series of studies using a substantial database, and it was followed by an extended debate on the work and its conclusions by experienced ratings researchers. Nonetheless, the *Chronicle* published a lengthy article (Wilson, 1998) that contained errors serious enough to attract critical letters from many researchers who were quoted, including Gerald Gillmore himself.

This over-emphasis on criticisms of ratings has led to another problem: the propagation of the criticisms themselves as a separate and widely believed mythology about ratings. Arreola (2005a) maintains that these myths have become a kind of "...common knowledge, so pervasive that it far overshadows the 'truth' concerning student ratings and other faculty evaluation tools buried in the pages of psychometric journals" (p. 1). This pattern has even progressed to the point where writers critical of ratings (e.g., Johnson, 2003) refer to well-established and often-replicated ratings findings as "myths." Not surprisingly, there has been criticism of Johnson's book from within the community of ratings researchers and practitioners (e.g., Perry, 2004). One implication of Johnson's notoriety is that experienced evaluation and ratings researchers need to do a better job of putting their findings before two critical audiences: the faculty and administrators who use these data (Arreola, 2005a, 2005b).

A POSITIVE SHIFT IN EMPHASIS: RESEARCH INFORMING PRACTICE

Apart from the public debate on student ratings, there has been a shift in emphasis in recent years in the study and consideration of student ratings. Ratings researchers, writers, and practitioners have tended to move from necessary but sometimes narrow psychometric investigations concerned with validity and reliability of ratings, to the application of evaluation and ratings research to practice. Beginning as early as Theall and Franklin (1990a), through updates of previous work, this pattern has led to detailed descriptions of, and guidelines for, the development of "comprehensive evaluation systems" (Arreola, 2000). As recently as the 2005 meeting of the American Educational Research Association, the question, "Valid Faculty Evaluation Data: Are There Any?" was raised with an emphasis on improving evaluation practice rather than establishing or re-establishing the purely technical validity and reliability of ratings.

To a large extent this stream of thinking echoes Feldman's (1998) emphasis on the importance of a "continuing quest" (when analyzing the correlates and determinants of effective instruction) for "...establishing the conditions or contexts under which relationships become stronger or weaker...or change in some other way.... The quest calls attention to determining the importance of 'interaction effects' as well as 'main effects'" (p. 36). The context in which evaluation takes place has been shown to have a potentially serious effect on the way that ratings data can be both interpreted and used. For example, Franklin and Theall (1993) found gender differences in ratings in certain academic departments. Although women had lower average ratings, further exploration showed that in those departments women had been disproportionately assigned to teach large, introductory, required classes—those where teachers in general might be expected to have lower ratings. Replication of the study at another institution where course assignments were equally distributed found no gender differences. The information available to faculty and administrators rarely includes analysis that goes beyond mean scores or averages; thus, contextual subtleties are lost, misinterpretation is more likely, and integration of ratings research with practice is hindered.

Another contextual factor that can influence ratings is institutional type as exemplified, say, by the different emphases and operations of community colleges and research universities described by Birnbaum (1988). Such differences can affect the perceptions of faculty, students, and administrators at these institutions, thus influencing the expectations held for faculty work and the definitions of "exemplary teaching." Contextual differences can further occur across disciplines in average ratings of teachers and courses (Cashin, 1990); in instructional choices of faculty (Franklin & Theall, 1992); in their effects on students' assimilation into the disciplines (Smart, Feldman, and Ethington, 2000); and in the extent to which teachers communicate expectations about course work (Franklin & Theall, 1995).

IMPROVING THE PRACTICE OF RATING TEACHERS AND INSTRUCTION

In the past half-dozen years or so, there have been several new attempts to improve ratings and evaluation practice. Perhaps the most focused work is by Arreola (2000), who describes a detailed process for "Developing a Comprehensive Faculty Evaluation System." Arreola outlines an eight-step process that can be used to generate institutional dialogue on issues that need to be discussed before any evaluation or ratings process is begun. Theall and Franklin (1990b) proposed that ratings are only one part of "complex evaluation systems," and Arreola's (2000) process outline remains the only articulated approach that takes into account and deals with the contextual issues that greatly influence evaluation and ratings practice on a campus-by-campus basis.

Arreola has not been alone in pressing for improved practice. Indeed, no less than six volumes of the Jossey Bass "New Directions" series have been devoted to ratings issues since Feldman's (1997) chapter was published. The first contribution to this extended discussion was from Ryan (2000), who proposed a "Vision for the Future" based not only on sound measurement, but on "...philosophical issues that need to be addressed if faculty evaluation is to receive the respect and attention it deserves" (backpage, "From the Editor"). Theall, Abrami and Mets (2001) asked about ratings, "Are they valid? How can we best use them?" Included in their volume are chapters reminiscent of the depth and extent of earlier exemplary dialogue and debate in the field (noted earlier in the present commentary). Lewis (2001) edited a volume concentrating on "Techniques and Strategies for Interpreting Student Evaluations." In particular, this set of articles connects issues of accountability to the faculty evaluation process and considers ratings as existing within the context of department, college, and institutional imperatives (and as needing to be responsive to these pressures). This volume was immediately followed by one (Knapper & Cranton, 2001) presenting "Fresh Approaches to the Evaluation of Teaching." Colbeck (2002) took an appropriately broad view of "Evaluating Faculty Performance," noting that "Forces for change within and outside academe are modifying faculty work and the way that work is—or should be—evaluated" (p. 1). Finally, Johnson and Sorenson (2004) presented a specific discussion of a new aspect of the ratings and evaluation picture: the rapidly increasing use of on-line systems. Acknowledging that this rapid growth is occurring "...even amidst challenges and doubt" (p.1), they and other contributors present a balanced review of the advantages and disadvantages of on-line systems.[3]

BEYOND RATINGS AS EVIDENCE OF EXEMPLARY TEACHING: ENHANCING FACULTY CAREERS

It can be argued that college teaching and learning, evaluations of teachers, and higher education itself have changed to the point where it is no longer reasonable or prudent to consider student ratings of

---

[3] Although there is space only to list references here, in the past yen years or so various volumes of *Higher Education: Handbook of Theory and Research* have published articles dealing with evaluation of teaching, teaching effectiveness, and improvement in instructional practices: see, for example, Boice (1997), Feldman (1998), Murray (2001), Cashin (2003), and Centra (2004).

teaching effectiveness without also considering the context in which they occur. These ratings are or should be embedded in processes (faculty evaluation and development) that are connected to department and college issues (staffing, funding, competition for resources), institutional issues (assessment, accreditation, reputation) and other matters that extend beyond campus (public support, legislation, accountability). A systematic and ecological approach to evaluation and ratings is needed because effective practice is not possible without consideration of (and coordination with) these other issues.

Recent work (Arreola, 2005b, 2005c; Arreola, Theall, & Aleamoni, 2003; Theall, 2002)[4] has expanded on past approaches and incorporated a wider view that encompasses past literature on faculty evaluation and development, the professoriate, business, science, communications, and reaction to change, as well as new discussions of how contemporary changes and forces are affecting higher education and the professoriate (e.g., Hersh & Merrow, 2005; Newman, Couturier, & Scurry, 2004).

Defining the professoriate as requiring in-depth expertise in a disciplinary or "base profession" as well as professional skills in several other "meta-professional" areas, Arreola, Theall and Aleamoni (2003) have developed a two-dimensional matrix that arrays four faculty roles (Teaching, Scholarly and Creative Activities, Service, and Administration) against three base-profession skills (content expertise, practice/clinical skills, and research techniques), and twenty meta-professional skill sets (e.g., instructional design skills, group process and team-building skills, public speaking skills). The frequency of need for each skill-by-role cell in the matrix is indicated by color-coding. Five additional matrices are provided, in which the roles are broken down into component parts. For example, the "teaching" role has seven contextual components ranging from traditional classroom situations to on-line and distance learning. Scholarly and Creative Activities, Service, and Administration are also broken down into their contextual components, and a special matrix demonstrates how Boyer's (1990) "scholarship of teaching (and learning)" presents a special case of meta-professional requirements.

---

[4] The "Meta-Profession Project" is an ongoing effort to improve practice in faculty evaluation and development. It is based on the analysis of the roles faculty are required to fill and the skills necessary to successfully carry out role responsibilities. The basic roles and skill sets are displayed in a series of two-dimensional matrices available at the project website at http://www.cedanet.com/meta. The site also contains an overview of the concept and project, copies of various papers and publications, and related information.

The conceptualization of the meta-profession and the matrices provide a framework for exploring the nature and demands of faculty work on a campus-by-campus basis and thus for improving practice in faculty evaluation and development. Similarly, this exploration can lead to improved policy and provide numerous opportunities to investigate faculty work on a broad scale, particularly as it is affected by variables such as institutional type, individual and campus demographics, and changes in prevailing economic and other conditions.

A FINAL COMMENT

Clearly, various psychometric issues (including reliability and validity) are important to the study and improvement of student ratings (Feldman, 1998). Even so, and despite these technical requirements, faculty evaluation and the use of student ratings involve more than psychometric issues; important professional, political, social, personnel, and personal issues also come into play. Recent years have seen the potential threat of a seemingly endless and unproductive debate on reliability and validity issues—unproductive in the sense that what has been established in over fifty years of substantial research has been largely ignored for reasons that include administrative convenience, ignorance, personal biases, suspicion, fear, and the occasional hostility that surrounds any evaluative process.

Evaluation and student ratings are unlikely to improve until practice is based on a careful and accurate analysis of the work required of faculty, the skills required to do that work, and the levels of performance expected. Further, good practice requires the creation of complete systems that acknowledge the absolute need to blend professional and faculty development resources with those necessary for fair and equitable faculty evaluation. Student ratings form a part of this picture, but too often have been inappropriately employed with the result that there has been a disproportionate amount of attention, debate and dissension, accompanied by misinformation based on questionable research, a ratings mythology, and the propagation of a general sense that the use of ratings somehow demeans the teaching profession. To the extent that the negative feeling is based on a degree of truth that has its base in poor practice, then improving practice becomes a critical agenda.

REFERENCES

Abrami, P.C., d'Apollonia, S., and Rosenfield, S. (1996). The dimensionality of student ratings of instruction: What we know and what we do not. In J.C. Smart (ed.), *Higher Education: Handbook of Theory and Research*. New York: Agathon Press.

Aleamoni, L.M. (1987). Student rating myths versus research facts. *Journal of Personnel Evaluation in Education* 1: 111–119.

Arreola, R.A. (2000). *Developing a Comprehensive Faculty Evaluation System* (2nd edition). Bolton, MA: Anker Publishing Company.

Arreola, R.A. (2005a). Validity, like beauty is...Paper presented at the annual meeting of the American Educational Research Association. (Available at: http://www.cedanet.com/meta/ and http://www.umanitoba.ca/uts/sigfted/backissues.php)

Arreola, R.A. (2005b). Crossing over to the dark side: Translating research in faculty evaluation into academic policy and practice. Invited address presented at the annual meeting of the American Educational Research Association. (Available at: http://www.cedanet.com/meta/)

Arreola, R.A. (2005c). The monster at the foot of the bed. *To Improve the Academy* 24: 15–28.

Arreola, R.A., Theall, M., and Aleamoni, L.M. (2003). Beyond scholarship: Recognizing the multiple roles of the professoriate. Paper presented at the annual meeting of the American Educational Research Association. (Available at: http://www.cedanet.com/meta/)

Birnbaum, R. (1988). *How Colleges Work*. San Francisco: Jossey Bass.

Boice, B. (1997). What discourages research-practioners in faculty development. In J.C. Smart (ed.), *Higher Education: Handbook of Theory and Research* (Vol. 12). New York: Agathon Press.

Boyer, E.L. (1990). *Scholarship Reconsidered*. San Francisco: Jossey Bass.

Campbell, J.R. (2000). *Dry Rot in the Ivory Tower*. Lanhan, MD: University Press of America.

Cashin, W.E. (1990). Students do rate different academic fields differently. In M. Theall and J. Franklin (eds.), *Student Ratings of Instruction: Issues for Improving Practice* (New Directions for Teaching and Learning No. 43). San Francisco: Jossey Bass.

Cashin, W.E. (2003). Evaluating college and university teaching: Reflections of a practioner. In J.C. Smart (ed.), *Higher Education: Handbook of Theory and Research* (Vol. 18). Norwell, MA: Kluwer Academic Publishers.

Centra, J.A. (1972). The student instructional report: Its development and uses. (Student Instructional Report No. 1). Princeton, NJ: Educational Testing Service.

Centra, J.A. (1979). *Determining Faculty Effectiveness: Assessing Teaching, Research, and Service for Personnel Decisions and Improvement*. San Francisco: Jossey Bass.

Centra, J.A. (2004). Service through research: My life in higher education. In J.C. Smart (ed.), *Higher Education: Handbook of Theory and Research* (Vol. 19). Norwell, MA: Kluwer Academic Publishers.

Cohen, P.A. (1981). Student ratings of instruction and student achievement: A meta-analysis of multisection validity studies. *Review of Educational Research* 51: 281–309.

Colbeck, C.L. (ed.) (2002). *Evaluating Faculty Performance* (New Directions for Institutional Research No. 114). San Francisco: Jossey Bass.

Cranton, P.A., and Knoop, R. (1991) Incorporating job satisfaction into a model of instructional effectiveness. In M. Theall and J. Franklin (eds.), *Effective Practices for Improving Teaching* (New Directions for Teaching and Learning No. 48). San Francisco: Jossey Bass.

Doyle, K.O. (1975). *Student Evaluation of Instruction.* Lexington, MA: D. C. Heath.

Feldman, K.A. (1989). The association between student ratings of specific instructional dimensions and student achievement: Refining and extending the synthesis of data from multisection validity studies. *Research in Higher Education* 30: 583–645.

Feldman, K.A. (1997). Identifying exemplary teachers and teaching: Evidence from student ratings. In R.P. Perry and J.C. Smart (eds.), *Effective Teaching in Higher Education: Research and Practice.* New York: Agathon Press.

Feldman, K.A. (1998). Reflections on the effective study of college teaching and student ratings: One continuing quest and two unresolved issues. In J.C. Smart (ed.), *Higher Education: Handbook of Theory and Research* (Vol. 13). New York: Agathon Press.

Franklin, J., and Theall, M. (1992). *Disciplinary differences, instructional goals and activities, measures of student performance, and student ratings of instruction.* Paper presented at the annual meeting of the American Educational Research Association. (ERIC Document Reproduction Service No. ED 346 786)

Franklin, J., and Theall, M. (1993). Student ratings of instruction and gender differences revisited. Paper presented at the annual meeting of the American Educational Research Association.

Franklin, J., and Theall, M. (1995). The relationship of disciplinary differences and the value of class preparation time to student ratings of instruction. In N. Hativa and M. Marincovich (eds.), *Disciplinary Differences in Teaching and Learning: Implication for Practice* (New Directions for Teaching and Learning No. 64). San Francisco: Jossey-Bass.

Gose, B. (1997). Duke may shift grading system to reward students who take challenging classes. *The Chronicle of Higher Education* February 14: A43.

Greenwald, A.G., and Gillmore, G.M. (1997a). Grading leniency is a removable contaminant of student ratings. *American Psychologist* 52: 1209–1217.

Greenwald, A.G., and Gillmore, G.M. (1997b). No pain, no gain? The importance of measuring course workload in student ratings of instruction. *Journal of Educational Psychology* 89: 743–751.

Hamermesh, D., and Parker, A.M. (2003). Beauty in the classroom: Professors' pulchritude and putative pedagogical productivity. (NBER Working Paper No. W9853). Austin TX: University of Texas at Austin. Abstract available at: http://ssrn.com/abstract=425589

Hersh, R.H., and Merrow, J. (2005). *Declining by Degrees: Higher Education at Risk.* New York: Palgrave Macmillan.

Johnson, T., and Sorenson, L. (2004). *Online Student Ratings of Instruction* (New Directions for Teaching and Learning No. 96). San Francisco: Jossey Bass.

Johnson, V. (2003). *Grade Inflation: A Crisis in Higher Education.* New York: Springer Verlag.

Knapper, C., and Cranton, P.A. (eds.) (2001). *Fresh Approaches to the Evaluation of Teaching* (New Directions for Teaching and Learning No. 88). San Francisco: Jossey Bass.

Kuh, G.D., Kinzie, J., Schuh, J.H., Whitt, E.J., and Associates (2005). *Student Success in College: Creating Conditions That Matter.* San Francisco: Jossey-Bass.

Lewis, K.G. (ed) (2001). *Techniques and Strategies for Interpreting Student Evaluations* (New Directions for Teaching and Learning No. 87). San Francisco: Jossey Bass.

Marsh, H.W. (1984). Students' evaluations of university teaching: Dimensionality, reliability, validity, potential biases, and utility. *Journal of Educational Psychology* 76: 707–754.

Marsh, H.W. (1987). Students' evaluations of university teaching: Research findings, methodological issues, and directions for future research. *International Journal of Educational Research* 11: 253–388.

Murray, H.G. (2001). Low-interence teaching behaviors and college teaching effectiveness: Recent developments and controversies. In J.C. Smart (ed.), *Higher Education: Handbook of Theory and Research* (Vol. 16). New York: Agathon Press.

Naftulin, D.H., Ware, J.E., and Donnelly, F.A. (1973). The Dr. Fox lecture: A paradigm of educational seduction. *Journal of Medical Education* 48: 630–635.

Newman, F., Couturier, L., and Scurry, J. (2004). *The Future of Higher Education: Rhetoric, Reality, and the Risks of the Market.* San Francisco: Jossey Bass.

Pascarella, E.T., and Terenzini, P.T. (2005). *How College Affects Students, Volume 2: A Third Decade of Research.* San Francisco: Jossey Bass.

Perry, R.P. (2004). Review of a V. Johnson's *Grade Inflation: A Crisis in College Education. Academe* January-February: 10–13.

Perry, R.P., Abrami, P.C., and Leventhal, L. (1979). Educational seduction: The effect of instructor expressiveness and lecture contrent on student ratings and achievement. *Journal of Educational Psychology* 71: 107–116.

Perry, R.P., Magnusson, J.L., Parsonson, K.L., and Dickens, W.J. (1986). Perceived control in the college classroom: Limitations in instructor expressiveness due to non-contingent feedback and lecture content. *Journal of Educational Psychology* 78: 96–107.

Ryan, K.E. (ed.) (2000). *Evaluating Teaching in Higher Education: A Vision of the Future* (New Directions for Teaching and Learning No. 83). San Francisco: Jossey Bass.

Smart, J.C., Feldman, K.A., and Ethington, C.A. (2000). *Academic Disciplines: Holland's Theory and the Study of College Students and Faculty.* Nashville, TN: Vanderbilt University Press.

Theall, M. (2002). Leadership in faculty evaluation and development: Some thoughts on why and how the *meta*-profession can control its own destiny. Invited address at the annual meeting of the American Educational Research Association. (Available at: http://www.cedanet.com/meta/)

Theall, M., Abrami, P.C., and Mets, L.A. (eds.) (2001). *The Student Ratings Debate: Are They Valid? How Can We Best Use Them?* (New Directions for Institutional Research No. 109). San Francisco: Jossey Bass.

Theall, M., and Franklin, J.L. (eds.) (1990a). *Student Ratings of Instruction: Issues for Improving Practice* (New Directions for Teaching and Learning No. 43). San Francisco: Jossey Bass.

Theall, M., and Franklin, J.L. (1990b). Student ratings in the context of complex evaluation systems. In M. Theall and J. Franklin (eds.), *Student Ratings of Instruction: Issues for Improving Practice* (New Directions for Teaching and Learning No. 43). San Francisco: Jossey Bass.

Theall, M., and Franklin, J. (eds.) (1991). *Effective Practices for Improving Teaching* (New Directions for Teaching and Learning No. 48). San Francisco: Jossey Bass.

Trout, P. (2000). Flunking the test: The dismal record of student evaluations. *Academe* July-August: 58–61.

Williams, W.M., and Ceci, S.J. (1997). How'm I doing?: Problems with student ratings of instructors and courses. *Change* 29(5): 13–23.

Wilson, R. (1998). New research casts doubt on value of student evaluations of professors. *The Chronicle of Higher Education* January 16: A1, A16.

6. Low-inference Teaching Behaviors and College Teaching Effectiveness: Recent Developments and Controversies

Harry G. Murray

University of Western Ontario
murray@uwo.ca

Key Words: Teacher characteristics, low-inference teaching behaviors, student ratings of instruction, effective college teaching

INTRODUCTION

Research on teacher effectiveness in higher education attempts to specify characteristics of teachers that contribute to the cognitive or affective development of students (Murray, 1991). It is assumed that knowledge of teacher characteristics contributing to effective teaching will lead both to a better theoretical understanding of teaching and to the development of improved programs of faculty selection, faculty evaluation, and faculty development.

One of the first and most important problems that must be faced in teacher effectiveness research is that of criterion measurement. Measures of teaching effectiveness used in higher education studies to date have included: (1) student learning—for example, mean student performance on a common final examination in a multiple-section course; (2) student motivation for further learning—for example, frequency of students enrolling in advanced courses in the teacher's area of study; and (3) formal student ratings of instructional quality. Student instructional ratings, the most frequently used criterion measure in teacher effectiveness

This paper is based on an invited presentation to the Special Interest Group on Faculty Evaluation and Development, American Educational Research Association, at the 1997 AERA Annual Meeting in Chicago (Murray, 1997).

R.P. Perry and J.C. Smart (eds.), The Scholarship of Teaching and Learning in Higher Education: An Evidence-Based Perspective, 145–200.
© 2007 *Springer.*

research, provide both a direct measure of student satisfaction with instruction and an indirect or "proxy" measure of outcome variables such as student learning and student motivation. Evidence that student ratings are suitable or appropriate as a direct or indirect measure of teacher effectiveness includes the following: (1) high retest and inter-rater reliability; (2) moderate to high agreement with evaluations of the same instructors by other independent judges; (3) generally weak correlation with extraneous factors such as class size, strictness of grading, and course level; and (4) significant correlation with more objective indicators of teaching effectiveness, such as student learning and student motivation (Cohen, 1981; Feldman, 1989; Marsh and Dunkin, 1992).

Several different types of research design have been employed in teacher effectiveness research in higher education, including survey research, case studies, ethnography, classroom observation, and laboratory experimentation. The present review deals mainly with research using observational and experimental designs. In observational research, teachers are studied under natural conditions (usually in the classroom) with no manipulation or control of variables, and observed teacher characteristics are analyzed in relation to outcome measures such as student exam performance or student instructional ratings. Observational findings tend to be high in external validity but low in internal validity. In other words, research findings are generalizable to actual classrooms, but it is difficult to determine whether correlations found between teacher characteristics and outcome measures represent true cause-effect relationships. In experimental research, teachers are studied under laboratory or field conditions where one or more instructional variables are systematically manipulated by the investigator, with all other variables controlled or held constant. Under experimental conditions, it is possible to infer cause-effect relationships between teacher characteristics and measures of effectiveness (high internal validity), but the contrived artificiality of laboratory experiments may limit generalizability of results to real classrooms (low external validity). The ideal situation, of course, is for research findings to be replicated in both observational and experimental designs, so that the strengths of one type of design compensate for the weaknesses of the other, and the overall credibility of findings is maximized.

Two distinct types of instructional variables have been studied in teacher effectiveness research in higher education: high-inference and low-inference (Rosenshine and Furst, 1971). High-inference teacher characteristics are global, abstract traits such as "explains clearly" or "has good rapport," while low-inference characteristics are specific, concrete teaching behaviors, such as "signals the transition from one topic to the next" and "addresses individual students by name," that can be recorded with very little inference or judgement on the part of a classroom observer. Rosenshine and Furst's high-inference vs. low-inference dichotomy relates to Feldman's (1998) discussion of amount of inferring done by students in evaluating teachers as one of the dimensions contributing to the subjectivity-objectivity of student instructional ratings. Table 1 gives further examples of high-inference teacher traits and corresponding low-inference teacher behaviors. Although knowledge of both low-inference and high-inference characteristics is needed for a full understanding of teaching effectiveness, it can be argued that there are some definite advantages in focusing on specific, low-inference teaching behaviors. For one thing, such behaviors are relatively easy to manipulate or record for research purposes, and researchers are more likely to use consistent operational definitions of teaching when they are based on specific, concrete behaviors. Second, low-inference behaviors are valuable in teaching improvement programs because they provide specific, concrete examples of effective teaching that are easier to acquire or modify than high-inference characteristics such as "clarity" or "rapport." Finally, low-inference classroom teaching behaviors represent the "leading edge" of teaching, the point of direct contact between teacher and student, and thus (it would appear) are more likely to have a direct impact on student development than high-inference teacher characteristics such as subject knowledge, goals, planning. I don't mean to imply that we should ignore these high-inference characteristics in teaching, but it seems to me that good planning and good intentions on the part of the teacher will go for nought unless these plans and intentions are translated into specific, effective classroom behaviors.

Table 1: High-Inference vs. Low-Inference Teacher Characteristics

High-inference	Low-inference
Organization	Signals the transition from one topic to the next. Puts outline of lecture on blackboard or overhead. Explains how each topic fits into course as a whole. Give preliminary overview of lecture.
Enthusiasm	Moves about the room while teaching. Shows inflection and variation in tone of voice Gestures with hands and arms. Maintains eye contact with students.

This chapter provides a brief review of early research on low-inference teaching behaviors in relation to student instructional ratings, then a more detailed review of recent low-inference studies that have dealt with the following issues or questions: (1) Are low-inference teaching behaviors related to outcome measures other than student ratings, and if so, to what measures? (2) Is there a cause-effect relationship between low-inference teaching behaviors and measures of teaching effectiveness? (3) What are the cognitive or affective processes that underlie or mediate the relationship between low-inference teaching behaviors and student outcome measures? (4) Is the relationship between low-inference behaviors and student instructional ratings consistent across different situations or contexts? and (5) Can research on low-inference teaching behaviors be successfully applied to programs for improvement of teaching?

EARLY RESEARCH

Early research by myself and others showed that there is indeed a clear relationship between low-inference classroom teaching behaviors and student ratings of overall teaching effectiveness (e.g., Cranton and Hillgartner, 1981; Mintzes, 1979; Murray, 1983a, 1983b, 1985; Tom and Cushman, 1975). My own studies were designed to systematically observe and compare the teaching behaviors of instructors receiving low, medium, and high ratings from students, and thereby to determine specifically what it is that highly rated teachers actually *do* in the classroom, or less highly rated teachers fail to do. These studies involved sending trained observers into regular classes taught by participating faculty members. Typically each of 40 to 50 instructors was observed in three separate randomly selected one-hour class periods by each of 6 to 8 observers. The observers were undergraduate students who were paid, given preliminary training in recording teaching behaviors, and told to be as unobtrusive as possible in the classroom. The style of teaching was lecture or lecture-discussion, with a minimum class size of 30. Instructors gave informed consent for participation, but did not know the exact dates on which classroom observation would occur. Following their 3 hours of observation of a given instructor, observers completed an instrument known as the Teacher Behaviors Inventory (TBI), illustrated in part in Table 2,T2 which required ratings of the frequency of occurrence of each of 50 to 100 low-inference teaching behaviors on a 5-point scale ranging from 1 (almost never) to 5 (almost always). Ratings were averaged across observers to obtain mean

148

Table 2: Teacher Behaviors Inventory

Research Version
Instructions to observer In this inventory, you are asked to report your observations of the specific classroom teaching behaviors of a designated instructor. Please note that your reports should be "descriptive" rather than "evaluative," and should be based solely on your own classroom observations. Also, you should try to assess each teaching behavior independently of all other behaviors, rather than letting your overall impression of the instructor determine each individual rating.   Each section of the inventory begins with a definition of the category of teaching to be assessed in that section, followed by a list of specific teaching behaviors. Please use the 5-point rating scale shown below to estimate the *frequency of occurrence* with which the instructor shows each of the teaching behaviors in each category.

A	B	C	D	E
Almost Never	Rarely	Sometimes	Often	Almost Always

Clarity: teaching behaviors that serve to explain or clarify concepts and principles

1. gives several examples of each concept
2. uses concrete, everyday examples to explain concepts and principles
3. fails to define new or unfamiliar terms
4. uses graphs and diagrams to facilitate explanation
5. repeats difficult ideas several times
6. stresses most important points by pausing, speaking slowly, raising voice, etc.
7. suggests ways of memorizing complicated ideas
8. writes key terms on blackboard or overhead screen

frequency estimates for each teaching behavior and each instructor, then statistical analyses were run to identify specific teaching behaviors that correlated significantly with student ratings of overall teaching effectiveness, measured either by a single, global item or by the average of all items on a formal end-of-term teaching evaluation form. One advantage of the research design used in these studies is that classroom teaching behaviors are assessed in a relatively nonobtrusive or nonreactive way. Another advantage is that independent and dependent variables are measured in procedurally independent ways (i.e., low-inference teaching behaviors by classroom observers, overall teaching effectiveness by student raters), thus minimizing the possibility of spurious correlations between teaching behaviors and overall effectiveness ratings due to "halo effect" or "implicit personality theory."

Table 3: Factor Loadings, Interrater Reliabilities, and Correlations with Student Rating of Overall Teaching Effectiveness Rating for 27 Low-Inference Teaching Behaviors

			Correlation
	Factor	Interrater	with Student
Teaching Behavior	Loading	Reliability	Ratings
Clarity			
uses concrete examples	.57	.76	.47*
stresses most important points	.49	.78	.61*
repeats difficult ideas	.64	.66	.30*
Expressiveness			
shows facial expressions	.69	.84	.42*
gestures with hands and arms	.70	.89	.38*
speaks expressively or "dramatically"	.76	.78	.63*
Interaction			
addresses individual students by name	.51	.92	.36*
asks questions of class as a whole	.82	.86	.26*
praises students for good ideas	.54	.77	.36*
Organization			
puts outline of lecture on blackboard	.80	.81	.21
signals transition to next topic	.57	.66	.51*
summarizes periodically	.56	.75	.17
Task orientation			
states teaching objectives	.74	.77	.34*
sticks to point in answering questions	.59	.73	.22
provides sample exam questions	.72	.88	.17
Interest			
describes relevant personal experience	.74	.80	.23
points out practical applications	.58	.67	.39*
relates subject to student interests	.51	.80	.19
Rapport			
offers to help students with problems	.54	.83	.39*
announces availability for consultation	.66	.81	.43*
shows concern for student progress	.52	.69	.54*
Mannerisms			
avoids eye contact with students	.62	.92	−.38*
plays with chalk or pointer	.68	.78	−.17
says "um" or "ah"	.55	.89	−.19
Speech Quality			
voice fades in mid-sentence	.64	.64	−.48*
stutters, mumbles, or slurs words	.70	.70	−.44*
speaks softly	.62	.72	−.22*

(Pooled data for N = 424 teachers)

* Significant at .05 level

Table 3T3 shows the type of results found in these preliminary studies. Actually what is shown here are results for a subset of 27 different teaching behaviors combined across six different studies carried out over a period of several years, some unpublished and some published (e.g., Murray, 1983a, 1985), with a total combined sample size of 424 teachers. Three important findings may be noted in Table 3. First, outside observers showed reasonably high interrater reliability in their recording of low-inference classroom teaching behaviors. The average interrater reliability in Table 3 is .77, suggesting that different observers working independently arrived at similar estimates of the frequency of occurrence of a given teaching behavior for a given instructor. Second, observer ratings of classroom teaching behaviors showed a clear factor structure. Table 3 shows the individual teaching behaviors that loaded highest on each factor in a principal-components factor analysis of the combined data set for 424 teachers. For example, teaching behaviors such as "uses concrete examples" and "stresses most important points" tended to correlate or cluster together to define a factor interpreted as Clarity, whereas "speaks expressively" and "shows facial expressions" were part of a cluster identified as Expressiveness. Although exactly the same factors were not found in all studies, usually around 8 to 10 clearly defined factors were identified in a given study, with Clarity, Expressiveness, Interaction, Organization, and Disclosure found in all or nearly all studies. Third, there were many significant correlations between specific teaching behaviors and student ratings of overall teaching effectiveness. A total of 18 of the 27 teaching behaviors listed in Table 3 correlated significantly with overall effectiveness rating. These were distributed across several different factors, but correlations tended to be highest and most consistent across studies for teaching behaviors loading on the Clarity, Expressiveness, and Interaction factors. Using multiple regression analysis, it was possible to account for 50 to 70 percent of the variance in student ratings of teaching with a set of as few as 10 low-inference teaching behaviors loading on Clarity, Expressiveness, and Interaction factors as predictor variables.

In summary, early research on low-inference teaching behaviors showed that highly rated university teachers do in fact teach differently (i.e., exhibit different classroom teaching behaviors) than less highly rated teachers. Highly rated teachers are more likely to do certain specific things in the classroom and less likely to do other things. One implication of these results is that college and university teachers can improve their teaching substantially by acquiring low-

151

inference teaching behaviors known to contribute to overall effectiveness ratings. Another important, but frequently overlooked implication of these results is that they provide an alternative or supplementary source of evidence in support of the validity of student ratings of teaching. Most of the traditional evidence cited in support of student ratings validity comes studies in which instructors rated as effective by students are shown to be effective in other, more substantive ways, such as in terms of mean student performance on a common final exam in a multiple-section course (e.g., Cohen, 1981). From a teaching behaviors point of view, there are really two separate validity questions: (1) Do student ratings accurately reflect low-inference teaching behaviors of the instructor?, and (2) Are these teaching behaviors significantly related to student cognitive and affective outcomes? The fact that student ratings can be predicted with considerable accuracy from observation of classroom teaching behaviors suggests that student ratings are highly valid in the first sense, in that they are determined by how the teacher actually teaches rather than by extraneous factors such as "popularity" or "personal warmth." Evidence from multi-section predictive validity studies, as well as other data to be reviewed below, suggests that student ratings are also moderately valid in the second sense, in that teaching behaviors are significantly related to student achievement

ARE TEACHING BEHAVIORS RELATED TO OUTCOMES OTHER THAN STUDENT RATINGS?

An important question arising from preliminary research reviewed above is whether low-inference classroom teaching behaviors are related to measures of teaching effectiveness other than student instructional ratings. If low-inference behaviors are related only to student ratings and not to measures such as student learning of course content, it could be argued that low-inference behaviors contribute only to the "popularity" of teaching and not to the "substance" of teaching. Table 4T4 shows the results of a study by Murray (1983b) in which the classroom teaching behaviors of 36 instructors in a multiple-section Introductory Psychology course were studied in relation to 6 different measures of teaching effectiveness, including mean student ratings of overall teacher effectiveness and overall course quality, mean amount of studying per week reported by students, mean student performance on a common final exam, frequency of student registration in senior psychology courses, and mean student estimate of amount learned in the course. Please note that in this table, correlations are shown

Table 4: Correlations Between Teacher Behaviors and Criterion Measures (Murray 1983b)

Teacher Behavior Factor	Criterion Measure					
	Teacher Rating	Course Rating	Study Hours	Further Courses	Common Exam	Amount Learned Rating
Rapport	.62*	.43*	.14	.34*	.27	.17
Clarity	.78*	.55*	.20	.36*	.16	.29
Enthusiasm	.72*	.57*	.25	.45*	.36*	.28
Task orientation	.27	.41*	.39*	.33*	.38*	.39*
Organization	.34*	.38*	.14	.14	.25	.17
Speech quality	.64*	.36*	.05	.02	.29	.31
Use of class time	.22	.30	.12	.00	.41*	.25
Informality	.43*	.42*	.31	.35*	.08	.29
Nervousness	−.14	−.06	.13	.01	.24	.35*
Rate of speaking	.17	.20	.33*	.28	.31	.27
Use of media	.08	.17	.11	.20	−.23	.01
Criticism	−.34*	−.19	.01	−.21	−.25	−.20
Multiple R^2	.85*	.76*	.38*	.48*	.59*	.53*

Note: N = 36 instructors
*Significant at .05 level.

between outcome measures and teaching behavior factor scores rather than individual teaching behaviors, where factor scores were obtained by averaging frequency-of-occurrence ratings for all individual teaching behaviors that loaded .35 or higher on a given factor. For example, the factor score for "Rapport" was obtained by averaging across individual behaviors such as "addresses individual students by name," "talks with students before or after class," and "offers to help students with problems." As shown in the table, a total of 26 out of 78 correlations between teaching behavior factors and outcome measures were statistically significant, and multiple regression analyses showed that teacher behaviors collectively accounted for a substantial amount of variance in each outcome measure (ranging from 48% to 85%). In other words, it appears that low-inference teaching behaviors do indeed contribute to student outcomes other than instructional ratings. Specifically, the extent to which the student enjoys the course, studies a lot or a little, does well or poorly on the final examination, and enrolls in further courses in the same subject area appears to be determined, at least in part, by specific low-inference teaching behaviors of the instructor. On the other hand, relationships between teaching behaviors and outcome measures were not totally simple and straightforward, in that teaching behavior factors correlating significantly with one outcome measure often did not correlate similarly with other outcome measures. For example, Rapport correlated significantly with mean student rating of the teacher but not with mean performance on the common final examination, whereas Task Orientation correlated significantly with exam performance but not with teacher ratings. Enthusiasm, on the other hand, correlated significantly with both teacher rating and exam performance. This suggests that in order to be successful on a wide range of teaching outcome measures, an instructor must have a large and flexible repertoire of teaching behaviors!

Other research confirming that low-inference teaching behaviors correlate with outcomes other than student instructional ratings includes that of Hines, Cruikshank, and Kennedy (1985), Solomon, Rosenberg, and Bezdek (1964), and Tom and Cushman (1975). Hines, Cruikshank, and Kennedy investigated low-inference teaching behaviors in a sample of 32 student teachers enrolled in an experimental peer teaching program at Ohio State University. Each student was provided with a standard set of objectives and materials on the topic of matrix multiplication, and was allowed 2 days in which to prepare a 25-minute lesson to be presented to a group of 4 to 6 fellow students. Two observers viewed videotapes of the 32 mini-lessons and either counted or rated the frequency of occurrence of 29 low-inference teacher clarity behaviors. Additional data on teaching behaviors were obtained from student ratings and instructor self-ratings. Following instruction, students in each peer group rated their degree of satisfaction with the lesson and wrote a completion-type achievement test on matrix multiplication. Multiple regression analyses showed that observer estimates of low-inference clarity behaviors correlated strongly with both student instructional ratings and student performance on the achievement test, accounting for 36 percent of the variance in ratings and 52 percent of the variance in student achievement. The teacher clarity behaviors showing the strongest relationships to student ratings and student achievement included: "uses relevant examples," "asks questions of students," "reviews material," "repeats points when students do not understand," "teaches in a step-by-step manner," and "provides frequent examples." These behaviors are similar to items loading on the Clarity factor in the Murray (1983b) observational study reviewed above.

In summary, research evidence suggests that low-inference teaching behaviors do correlate with outcome measures other than student ratings, but correlations are not always consistent across different measures of teacher effectiveness.

IS THERE A TRUE CAUSE-EFFECT RELATIONSHIP BETWEEN TEACHING BEHAVIORS AND STUDENT OUTCOMES?

Given that low-inference teaching behaviors appear to be correlated with several different measures of teaching effectiveness, including student learning, it is fair to ask whether these correlations reflect a true cause-effect relationship between teaching behaviors and student outcomes. A significant correlation between teaching behaviors and student performance may or may not reflect an underlying "forward causation" model in which teaching behaviors represent the "cause" (or one of the causes) and student learning the "effect." Alternative causal models that could give rise to the same observed correlation include "backward causation," in which teaching behaviors are the result of prior student learning rather than the cause of present learning; and "third-variable causation," in which teaching behaviors covary with student learning because both are the result of some other variable. Establishing whether or not a forward cause-effect relationship exists between teaching behaviors and student outcomes is important not only for theoretical reasons but also for applied or practical reasons. From an applied point of view, it is counterproductive to encourage instructors to acquire or adopt particular teaching behaviors unless these behaviors have been shown to be causal antecedents of student learning. Adopting a teaching behavior that is a "correlate" but not a "cause" of student learning will fail to produce improved teaching effectiveness if the underlying causal pattern is either backward causation or third-variable causation.

Many procedures are available for clarifying the causal status of a correlation between teaching behaviors and student learning, but probably the best available option is to conduct a "true experiment," under either laboratory or field conditions, in which teaching behaviors are experimentally manipulated while all other variables that could potentially affect student learning are held constant or controlled. If teaching behaviors continue to be significantly related to student learning under controlled experimental conditions, then the relationship can be assumed to reflect forward causation rather than backward or third-variable causation.

Evidence that there is indeed a true cause-effect relationship between teaching behaviors and student learning comes from research involving experimental manipulation of low-inference teaching behaviors. Figure 1 shows the results of a study by Murray (1978) in which randomly assigned groups of subjects viewed four different

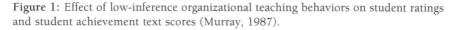

Figure 1: Effect of low-inference organizational teaching behaviors on student ratings and student achievement text scores (Murray, 1987).

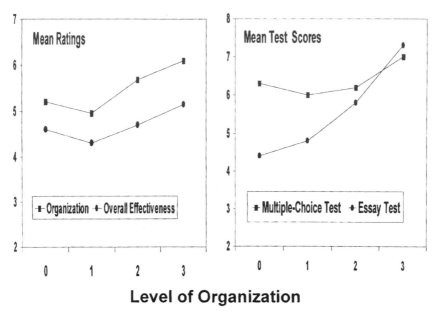

Level of Organization

versions of a 15-minute videotaped lecture on brain asymmetry under controlled laboratory conditions. The four versions of the lecture were identical in content, but varied in level of organization, or the extent to which they incorporated the following three low-inference "organizational" or "structuring" teaching behaviors: gives preliminary overview of the lecture, provides outline of lecture, and signals the transition between one topic and the next. In the control (Level 0) lecture, the instructor showed none of these behaviors, whereas in the three experimental conditions, the instructor either gave a preliminary overview of the lecture only (Level 1), gave a preliminary overview and put a topical outline on the blackboard (Level 2), or gave a preliminary overview, provided an outline, and explicitly signaled the transition from one topic to the next by pointing to the outline (Level 3). After viewing the lecture, subjects in all groups rated various aspects of quality of teaching on 7-point scales, answered a 10-item multiple-choice recall test assessing comprehension of lecture concepts, and wrote a short answer essay test assessing ability to apply, analyze and synthesize lecture concepts. As depicted in Figure 1, student ratings of both lecture organization and overall teacher effectiveness increased significantly with increased incorporation of low-inference organizational teaching behaviors, as did student performance on both multiple-choice and essay tests of amount learned. Given that extraneous variables were controlled in this study, the results suggest a true cause-effect relationship is operating between teaching behaviors and student outcomes. It is interesting to note that the positive impact of organizational teaching behaviors was more pronounced for the essay achievement test than for the multiple-choice test. This may suggest that organizational behaviors are particularly effective in helping students see the overall structure of topics and subtopics, and thus in transferring or applying knowledge to new situations.

Confirming evidence that low-inference teaching behaviors are causally related to student outcomes has been found in "true experiments" reported by Coats and Smidchens (1966), Land (1979), and Ware and Williams (1975), among others. Coats and Smidchens (1966) conducted a field experiment on the effects of teacher enthusiasm on student recall of lecture material. The subjects were 184 students enrolled in 8 introductory speech classes at the University of Michigan. Two instructors, graduate students in education, gave 10-minute guest lectures in 4 classes each. Lecture content was identical for all classes taught by a given instructor, but the lecture was presented in a "dynamic" fashion in two randomly selected classes, and in a "static" fashion in the two remaining classes. The dynamic condition included the usual behavioral ingredients of teacher enthusiasm: movement, gesturing, eye contact with students, vocal inflection, and minimal reliance on lecture notes. The static lecture was presented with good diction and volume, but was read verbatim from a manuscript, and included a minimum of eye contact, vocal inflection, and animation. Immediately following the lecture, students in all classes completed a 10-item multiple-choice test based on lecture material. It was found that students in the dynamic condition performed better on the recall test than students in the static condition. Mean recall was approximately 20 percent higher for dynamic lectures than for static lectures, and teacher enthusiasm accounted for 36 percent of the total variance in student recall scores.

Land (1979) evaluated the combined impact of 6 low-inference teacher clarity variables, including vagueness terms (i.e., inexact statements), transition signals (i.e., cues that mark the end of one topic and the beginning of another), and verbal mazes (i.e., false starts or halts in speech). Two versions of the same videotaped lesson, varying only in the presence or absence of the 6 clarity behaviors, were presented to students in an introductory education course. Students were told to take notes during the lesson, but were not allowed to use their notes during subsequent testing. The achievement test, consisting of 30 multiple-choice items written at the comprehension level of Bloom's taxonomy, was completed either immediately following the lesson or after a delay of one week. Statistical analysis showed that, for both immediate and delayed testing, comprehension scores were higher for the high-clarity lesson than for the low-clarity lesson. Land hypothesized that the use of explicit transition signals in classroom teaching assists students in organizing the subject matter, whereas the use of vagueness terms causes students to lose confidence in the instructor and thus in themselves.

In summary, evidence from both field and laboratory experiments suggests that the relationship between low-inference teaching behaviors and student learning generally conforms to a "forward causation" model in which teaching behaviors are the "cause" and student learning is the "effect." It should be noted, however, that some experiments (e.g., Anderson and Withrow, 1981) have failed to find any sort of significant cause-effect relationship between teaching behaviors and student learning.

WHAT ARE THE PROCESSES OR MECHANISMS UNDERLYING THE RELATIONSHIP BETWEEN TEACHING BEHAVIORS AND STUDENT LEARNING?

Given that teaching behaviors appear to be related to a wide range of student out-comes, including student learning, and given that this relationship appears to reflect a forward cause-effect pattern, what are the psychological processes or mechanisms that mediate this relationship? In other words, what are the cognitive or affective processes occurring in the student that give rise to the positive impact of teaching behavior X upon student learning? Among other things, it is possible that teaching behavior X causes students to perceive differences more accurately, to form more structured knowledge representations, to experience less anxiety, or to develop an improved self-concept. The question of underlying process is of course a theoretical question, but unfortunately research on low-inference teaching behaviors has tended to be rather atheoretical in nature. Most research to date has attempted to demonstrate empirical relationships between teaching behaviors and student outcomes rather than to identify processes or mechanisms underlying these relationships.

Although we still know very little about the psychological processes intervening between teaching behaviors and student learning, some promising leads in this area have been provided by Ray Perry's research on student attributions and perceived control in relation to classroom teaching behaviors, and by recent doctoral dissertations completed by Dieter Schonwetter at the University of Manitoba and Andrea Wood at the University of Western Ontario.

Research by Perry and colleagues, summarized in Perry (1991) has demonstrated that teacher expressiveness, defined by low-inference behaviors such as body movement, vocal variation, eye contact, and humor, has a stronger impact on student learning for students with internal success and failure attributions who perceive themselves to be in control of their environments, than for students with external attributions or lack of perceived control. This result suggests that lack of perceived control may interfere with processes normally activated by teacher expressiveness, such as increased attention to lecture material; or alternatively, that teacher expressiveness may facilitate student learning in part by creating a stronger sense of perceived control in students.

Schonwetter's (1996) doctoral research included a laboratory experiment assessing the interaction of two different categories of teaching behavior in determining student attention and learning: (1) teacher expressiveness, defined by eye contact, body movement, hand gestures, and use of humor; and (2) teacher organization, defined by providing an outline, using headings, and signalling topic transitions. A total of 380 students viewed one of four different versions of a videotaped economics lecture involving all possible combinations of low vs. high teacher expressiveness with low vs. high teacher organization (2×2 design). Student selective attention to lecture material was measured by self-report ratings and by a free recall test, whereas student learning was measured by post-lecture multiple-choice achievement tests assessing both recognition and application of concepts, and by self-ratings of amount learned. It was found that teacher organization had strong and significant effects on both student attention and student learning, whereas teacher expressiveness had weak and generally nonsignificant effects on both attention and learning. This result suggests (1) that low-inference teacher organization behaviors may be a more basic or prepotent factors in teaching effectiveness than low-inference teacher expressiveness behaviors, (2) that teacher organization may influence student learning by way of selective attention, and (3) that teacher expressiveness may affect student learning only if

159

the teacher is organized, rather than vice versa as suggested by Murray (1983a). Schonwetter points out, however, that the differentiation of low and high teacher expressiveness conditions in this study may not have been clear enough to result in statistically significant effects on student attention or learning.

Andrea Wood's (1998) doctoral thesis attempted to decide among three different models of the underlying process by which teacher enthusiasm affects student learning, namely selective attention, motivation to learn, and improved memory encoding. The selective attention model suggests that enthusiastic teaching behaviors such as body movement and vocal expressiveness improve learning by eliciting student attention to lecture material as opposed to distracting stimuli. The motivation model states that, perhaps through imitation or modeling on the part of student, enthusiastic teaching behaviors cause students to develop higher levels of motivation to learn the subject matter, both inside and outside the classroom. The memory encoding model assumes that expressive teaching behaviors improve learning by signalling important ideas in spoken text, and thus helping students understand the overall structure or "meaning" of the subject matter. To test among these three models, Wood conducted a laboratory experiment with videotaped lectures in a simulated classroom, where teacher enthusiasm was defined as the occurrence of the following low-inference teaching behaviors: vocal variation, movement and gesture, pausing to emphasize points, humor, facial expression, and eye contact. Three hundred introductory psychology students were randomly assigned to treatment groups receiving four different versions of a 16-minute lecture on memory theory, namely Low Enthu-siasm, High Enthusiasm/Strategic, High Enthusiasm/Random, and High Enthusiasm/Uniform. The Low Enthusiasm lecture included few if any enthusiastic teaching behaviors. The High Enthusiasm/Strategic lecture included a high frequency of enthusiastic teaching behaviors, and these low-inference behaviors were properly coordinated with the topic structure of the lesson. The High Enthusiasm/Random condition also included frequent use of enthusiastic behaviors, but these behaviors sometimes did and sometimes did not coincide with the topic structure of the lesson. The High Enthusiasm/Uniform condition featured frequent use of enthusiastic teaching behaviors, but their occurrence remained constant at all points throughout the lecture.

During the experiment, each of the three hypothesized mediating processes, namely selective attention, motivation, and memory encoding, was monitored by at least two different indicator variables.

Selective attention was measured by: (1) reaction time to a secondary tone detection task presented at random intervals during the video-taped lecture, and (2) observed frequency of on-task attending behavior during the lecture. It was expected that teacher enthusiasm would lead to *slower* secondary task reaction times, indicating greater attention to the lecture, and more frequent on-task behaviors. Student motivation was measured by: (1) a questionnaire assessing degree of interest in the lecture topic, and (2) observed frequency of written requests from students for mailed reading material relevant to the lecture. Memory encoding was measured by: (1) overall recall, defined as the total number of lecture propositions correctly recalled, (2) topic access, defined as the number of lecture topics for which at least one proposition was recalled, (3) conditional recall, the percentage of propositions recalled pertopic, given that at least one proposition was recalled, and (4) topic representation, defined as the degree of similarity (rank order correlation) between the subject's order of recalled topics and the actual order of presentation of topics in the lecture. The last three memory measures were intended to assess the extent to which participants had encoded the topical structure of the lecture as a whole, and as outlined further below, were expected to be facilitated by strategic, but not by random or uniform use of teacher enthusiasm. After viewing the videotaped lecture, subjects completed a multiple-choice test assessing learning of lecture content, and provided ratings of quality of teaching.

Table 5T5 summarizes the main results of the experiment, namely mean scores for the four treatment conditions on each of eight variables assessing potential mediators (2 attention, 2 motivation, 4 memory encoding) and each of two out-come measures (student learning, student ratings of lecture quality). It may be noted that subjects in the three High Enthusiasm conditions (Strategic, Random, and Uniform) tended to score higher than subjects in the Low Enthusiasm condition on all indicator variables assessing potential mediators, as well as on learning of lecture content and ratings of lecture quality. For example, subjects in the three High Enthusiasm conditions showed slower reaction times to the secondary task (indicating greater attention to the lecture), higher scores on the questionnaire assessing motivation for further learning, and better encoding of the topic structure of the lecture (as reflected in topic representation scores). These results suggest that any or all of the three hypothesized mediating processes (i.e., selective attention, motivation to learn, or memory encoding) could be responsible for the positive impact of teacher enthusiasm on

161

Table 5: Group Means Scores on Indicator Variables and Outcome Measures (Wood, 1998)

	Treatment Conditions				
	High Enthus Strategic	High Enthus Random	High Enthus Uniform	Low Enthus	Univariate F
Selective Attention					
Secondary Task Reaction Time	817.28	829.85	805.25	471.26	107.14*
On-Task Behavior	98.25	98.24	95.69	69.16	124.54*
Motivation					
Motivation Questionnaire	2.52	2.23	1.91	1.83	9.72*
Request for Further Reading	.24	.25	.17	.09	6.37
Memory Encoding					
Overall Recall	6.92	5.21	3.11	5.04	17.52*
Topic Access	3.64	2.87	1.99	2.87	13.10*
Conditional Recall	23.80	22.59	15.61	20.82	10.52*
Topic Representation	.72	.71	.58	.35	5.08*
Outcome Measures					
Multiple-Choice Test	8.76	6.79	6.48	6.05	21.05*
Ratings of Lecture Quality	5.21	4.64	4.78	2.51	55.90*

* Significant at .01 level

student learning. However, a more fine grained analysis of the data, as provided by planned comparison of treatment group mean scores, indicated that memory encoding does a better job of explaining group differences than selective attention or motivation. For example, only the memory encoding model is able to account for the fact that scores on the four measures of memory (overall recall, topic access, conditional recall, and topic representation), as well as scores on the multiple-choice test of student learning, tended to be significantly higher in the High Enthusiasm/Strategic condition than in the High Enthusiasm/Random and High Enthusiasm/Uniform conditions. The memory encoding hypothesis predicts that high levels of teacher enthusiasm should facilitate student achievement only when enthusiastic teaching behaviors are used strategically to signal important points in the lecture. Both the attention and motivation models predict, *incorrectly*, that student memory and learning scores should be facilitated equally by all three High Enthusiasm conditions. Converging evidence favoring the memory encoding model over the attention and motivation models of teacher enthusiasm was obtained from multiple regression analyses testing the role of selective attention, motivation, and memory encoding variables variable in mediating the relation between teacher enthusiasm (dummy coded) and student learning. It was found that the correlation between teacher enthusiasm and student learning was changed significantly only when memory encoding was entered or removed from the regression equation, indicating that although all three mediators may be involved to some degree, memory encoding plays a more decisive role in mediating the relationship between teacher enthusiasm and student learning than either selective attention or motivation. Although the memory encoding model generally provides a better account of the Wood findings than either the attention or the motivation model, it is not without problems. For example, it fails to account for the fact that conditional recall scores did not differ in Strategic vs. Random vs. Low Enthusiasm conditions, or for the fact that ratings of lecture quality were equally high in all three High Enthusiasm conditions.

The results of the Wood study provide preliminary evidence as to the specific underlying processes or mechanisms that mediate the relationship between teacher enthusiasm and student learning. Although all three hypothesized mediating processes (selective attention, motivation to learn, and memory encoding) may be involved to some degree in mediating the relationship between teacher enthusiasm and student learning, it appears that memory encoding plays a more decisive role than selective attention or motivation. Figure 2 shows one possible way in which memory encoding may interact with selective attention and motivation to mediate the effect of teacher enthusiasm on student learning. According to this model, teacher enthusiasm will facilitate student learning only if it activates memory encoding of text structure either directly or indirectly by way of selective attention. Reflecting its limited significance in the present study, motivation is treated as a secondary outcome or by-product of student learning in this model. One interesting implication of the Wood results is that teacher enthusiasm does not inevitably facilitate student learning in all cases. In order to contribute positively to student learning, enthusiastic teaching behaviors must be used strategically so as to emphasize the topic structure of the material to be learned.

In summary, recent research has provided preliminary evidence regarding the processes or mechanisms underlying the relationship

Figure 2: Interaction of selective attention, memory encoding, and motivation as mediators in the relationship between teacher enthusiasm and student learning.

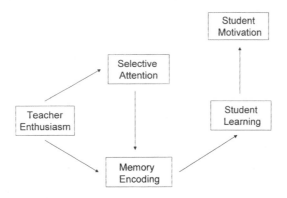

between low-inference teaching behaviors and student learning. However, only a few studies have been conducted to date, and these have tended to focus on only one type of teaching behavior, namely expressiveness or enthusiasm. One notable consistency between the Schonwetter (1996) and Wood (1998) studies is that in both cases, organizational teaching behaviors were found to be more basic or fundamental than expressive teaching behaviors, in the sense that teacher expressiveness was effective only to the extent that it was preceded by or operated through structuring of content. Further support for this hypothesis comes from meta-analyses reported by Feldman (1989, 1997) in which teacher organization, on average, correlated higher with student performance on common final exams in multiple-section courses than did teacher expressiveness.

IS THE RELATIONSHIP BETWEEN LOW-INFERENCE BEHAVIORS AND STUDENT INSTRUCTIONAL RATINGS CONSISTENT ACROSS DIFFERENT SITUATIONS OR CONTEXTS?

I now want to turn to some recent studies investigating the controversial question of whether or not the impact of low-inference teaching behaviors is consistent across different contexts or situations. Some writers do not consider this question to be controversial. They assert, sometimes with and sometimes without supporting empirical evidence, that teaching is contextual or context-dependent. Thus, teaching behaviors have no generality across situations, or what works in one situation will not necessarily work in another situation. For example, Brookfield (1990, page 12) reported that, "...every context in which I worked contained factors that prevented the neat application of principles and techniques of 'good' practice." Similarly, Shulman (1986) criticized teacher effectiveness research for failing to consider differences in subject matter, and for assuming "generic" teaching behaviors that are applicable in all contexts. Sheehan (1975) argued against the use of standardized teacher evaluation forms on the grounds that the characteristics assessed by such forms are not equally relevant in all contexts or for all types of students. Finally, Good and Brophy (1990, page 286) concluded from a review of teacher effectiveness research that, "Few if any instructional behaviors are appropriate in all teaching contexts,..."

Contrary to this popular line of thought, some researchers have reported that the impact of teacher characteristics is surprisingly consistent across different contexts or situations. Marques, Lane, and Dorfman (1979) asked students and faculty in four different academic divisions (humanities, engineering, natural sciences, social sciences) to rate the overall effectiveness of hypothetical instructors who varied systematically on specified dimensions. It was found that there was strong consensus between students and faculty and among respondents from different academic fields as to the relative importance of each instructional component or dimension in determining overall effectiveness, suggesting that perceived teaching effectiveness tends to be "transituationally invariant." Similarly, Pohlmann (1976) found that the correlation of overall teacher effectiveness ratings with specific instructional practices (e.g., encouraging student participation, specifying course objectives) did not differ significantly across five academic disciplines, indicating that what makes an effective teacher is basically the same regardless of what is taught. Finally, Roberts and Becker (1976) conducted an observational study of 123 instructors involved in one-to-one teaching of industrial and technical skills in high schools and community colleges, and found that the teaching behaviors differentiating between effective and ineffective instructors were remarkably similar to those reported for traditional large-class teaching.

Most of the previous research on the situational dependency of teaching has focused on high-inference rather than low-inference teacher characteristics, has relied on student raters to assess both teacher characteristics and overall teacher effectiveness (thus leading to possible spurious correlations due to judgement bias), and has dealt mainly with only one type of context variable, namely academic field. The studies reviewed below focus on specific low-inference teaching behaviors, use trained classroom observers to assess teaching behaviors, and report data on three different contextual variables, namely academic discipline, class size, and teacher gender. Also, these studies investigate the contextual dependency of low-inference teaching behaviors with respect to two different measures: (1) frequency of occurrence—e.g., does Behavior X occur more frequently in small classes than in large classes? and (2) correlation with outcome measures—e.g., does Behavior Y correlate higher with student ratings for Chemistry teachers than for Sociology teachers?

ACADEMIC DISCIPLINE

The first study, which compared teaching behaviors across three different academic discipline areas at the University of Western Ontario, was done in collaboration with Robert Renaud (Murray and Renaud, 1995). An aggregated sample of 401 teachers was obtained by combining data from seven previous studies involving classroom observation of faculty members teaching undergraduate lecture—or lecture discussion courses at the University of Western Ontario. In all of these studies, classroom observers summarized their 3 hours of classroom observation of a given teacher on the same 100-item version of the Teacher Behaviors Inventory. Overall teaching effectiveness was measured by end-of-term student ratings on a standardized teaching evaluation form administered in the same course and semester in which classroom observation took place. The three disciplinary groupings compared in this study were: Arts and Humanities (N = 117), Social Sciences (N = 149), and Science and Mathematics (N = 135). Mean observer ratings were calculated for each teacher on each of the 100 TBI items, then teaching behavior factor scores were obtained for each teacher by averaging TBI ratings across the teaching behaviors loading highest on each of 10 factors.

Table 6T6 shows the mean rated frequency of occurrence of teaching behaviors, or more accurately, teaching behavior factor scores, for Arts and Humanities vs. Natural Science vs. Social Science teachers. Statistical analysis of these data showed that 6 of 10 categories of teaching behavior differed significantly in frequency of occurrence across the three disciplinary groups, namely Interaction, Organization, Pacing, Disclosure, Rapport, and Mannerisms. For example, Arts and Humanities teachers were more likely than Social Science and Natural Science teachers to show behaviors in the Rapport and Interaction categories (e.g., encouraging student participation, addressing individual students by name), whereas teachers in Social Science and Natural Science were more likely than Arts and Humanities teachers to show behaviors loading on the Organization

166

Table 6: Mean Rated Frequency of Occurrence of Teaching Behaviors in Different Disciplinary Groups (Murray & Renaud, 1995)

Teaching Behavior Factor	Disciplinary Group		
	Arts and Humanities	Social Sciences	Natural Sciences and Mathematics
Clarity	3.44	3.57	3.52
Expressiveness	3.33	3.27	3.19
Interaction*	3.53	3.08	2.99
Organization*	2.86	3.21	3.20
Pacing*	3.71	3.90	3.74
Disclosure*	3.41	3.19	3.42
Interest	3.12	3.09	2.95
Rapport*	4.00	3.76	3.68
Mannerisms*	4.15	4.03	3.94
Speech Quality	4.10	4.01	3.99

* Differences among disciplinary groups are significant at .05 level.

and Pacing dimensions (e.g., putting outline on blackboard, sticking to the point in answering questions).

Table 7T7 compares Arts vs. Natural Science vs. Social Science teachers in terms of the magnitude and direction of correlations between teaching behavior factors and end-of-term student ratings of overall teaching effectiveness. As in previous research, all 10 teaching behavior dimensions showed generally positive correlations with student ratings of overall teaching effectiveness. Furthermore, and more relevant to the present issue, correlations between teaching behaviors and student ratings tended to be similar across academic fields. Statistical analysis of these data (using Fisher's r to z transformation and Fisher's test of the significance of differences between correlation coefficients, see McNemar, 1962, pages 139–140) indicated that of the 30 possible pairwise differences between academic disciplines in Table 7 (3 possible pairwise comparisons for each of 10 teaching behavior factors), only two were statistically significant. Specifically, Rapport correlated higher with overall teaching effectiveness ratings for both Social Science and Natural Science teachers than for Arts and Humanities teachers.

In summary, the results of this study suggest that teachers of different academic disciplines at the University of Western Ontario differed in the *frequency* with which they exhibited various low-inference teaching behaviors, but did not differ in the *correlation* of

Table 7: Correlation of Teaching Behaviors With Overall Teacher Effectiveness Ratings in Different Disciplinary Groups (Murray & Renaud, 1995)

Teaching Behavior Factor	Disciplinary Group		
	Arts and Humanities	Social Sciences	Natural Sciences and Mathematics
Clarity	.498	.562	.647
Expressiveness	.308	.402	.446
Interaction	.417	.441	.502
Organization	.359	.361	.439
Pacing	.511	.464	.609
Disclosure	.254	.405	.220
Interest	.352	.557	.435
Rapport*	.316	.591	.579
Mannerisms	.513	.455	.255
Speech Quality	.496	.625	.650

*One or more pairwise differences between disciplinary groups are significant at .05 level.

these teaching behaviors with student ratings of teaching effectiveness. For example, although teaching behaviors loading on the Organization and Pacing factors occurred more frequently in Science and Social Science teachers than in Arts teachers, the extent to which Organization and Pacing behaviors (and most other teaching behaviors) "paid off" or contributed to overall effectiveness ratings was essentially the same for Science and Social Science teachers as for Arts teachers. This result needs to be replicated in other teacher samples at other institutions. If so replicated, this result would suggest that the teaching behaviors that contribute to successful teaching are surprisingly similar in different academic disciplines, and would run directly counter to the widely shared belief that teaching effectiveness is highly context-dependent.

One practical implication of the above findings is that, contrary to the claim that we need to design separate and distinctively different faculty development and faculty evaluation programs for different academic fields (e.g., Sheehan, 1975), it may not be unreasonable, given that the correlation of teaching behaviors with overall effectiveness may be similar across academic disciplines, to offer the same types of teaching improvement programs for faculty in all disciplines, or to use a common form for student evaluation of teaching in all faculties or departments.

TEACHER GENDER

The same aggregated data set used above in comparing disciplinary groups provided data for a second study comparing samples of female (N = 60) and male (N = 364) teachers in terms of both frequency of occurrence of low-inference teaching behaviors and correlation of teaching behaviors with overall effectiveness ratings. It may be noted that females constituted about 14 percent of the aggregated sample, which is roughly equal to the percentage of female faculty at the University of Western Ontario at the time that this study was conducted. Results are summarized in Tables 8 and 9. Statistical analysis of the data in Table 8 indicated that 4 of 10 categories of teaching behavior showed significant differences in frequency of occurrence for female vs. male teachers, namely Interaction, Pacing, Disclosure, and Rapport. In general, it appears that female teachers were more likely to show behaviors such as encouraging student participation and showing concern for student progress, whereas male teachers were more likely to cover material at a rapid pace and provide information about tests and assignments. However, analysis of the data in Table 9 showed that the correlation of teaching behavior factors with teacher effectiveness rating differed significantly in female vs. male teachers for only one of 10 teaching behavior factors. As

Table 8: Mean Rated Frequency of Occurrence of Teaching Behaviors as a Function of Teacher Gender

	Teacher Gender	
Teaching Behavior Factor	Female	Male
Clarity	3.54	3.53
Expressiveness	3.27	3.23
Interaction*	3.33	3.12
Organization	3.09	3.15
Pacing*	3.83	3.93
Disclosure*	3.15	3.31
Interest	3.08	3.08
Rapport*	3.91	3.77
Mannerisms	4.13	4.04
Speech Quality	4.09	4.01
* Difference between gender groups is significant at .05 level.		

Table 9: Correlation of Teaching Behaviors With Overall Teacher Effectiveness Rating as a Function of Teacher Gender

Teaching Behavior Factor	Teacher Gender	
	Female	Male
Clarity	.530	.575
Expressiveness	.531	.377
Interaction	.521	.407
Organization	.445	.373
Pacing*	.267	.531
Disclosure	.397	.336
Interest	.601	.464
Rapport	.623	.504
Mannerisms	.314	.440
Speech Quality	.548	.590

* Difference between gender groups is significant at .05 level.

may be noted in the table, Pacing correlated significantly higher with overall effectiveness for males than for females. In summary, although male and female teachers differed in the frequency with which they exhibited certain teaching behaviors, they generally did not differ in the extent to which these behaviors correlated with or contributed to student ratings of overall teaching effectiveness. Consistent with what was found for academic disciplines, we again have evidence that teaching behaviors differed across situations or contexts (i.e., genders) in frequency of occurrence, but did not differ across contexts in correlation with student ratings of teaching. The low-inference classroom teaching behaviors that contributed to good teaching for male teachers are more or less the same as the teaching behaviors that contributed to teaching effectiveness for female teachers. Contrary to Basow and Distenfeld's (1985) laboratory-based finding that expressive teaching behaviors contributed more positively to student evaluation of teaching for male teachers than for female teachers, the present data indicate no significant gender difference in the correlation between teacher expressiveness and student ratings under field conditions (and in fact, the direction of the difference, although nonsignificant, is actually opposite to that reported by Basow and Distenfeld). As with the previously reported data for academic disciplines, the present results need to be replicated with other samples of teachers in other institutions.

CLASS SIZE

Research testing the consistency of teaching behaviors in small vs. large classes was reported in a Masters thesis by Andrea Wood (1994) at the University of Western Ontario. She studied a sample of 38 psychology professors, 19 of whom were teaching a large lecture-type class (mean size = 217, range = 25 to 400), and 19 of whom were teaching a small, seminar style class (mean size 21, range 7 to 40) during the same academic year. Similar to the academic discipline and gender data reported previously, this study found differences between small and large classes in the frequency of occurrence of low-inference teaching behaviors, but not in the correlation of teaching behaviors with student ratings of overall teaching effectiveness. Tables 10T10 and 11T11 summarize the frequency and correlation results respectively. It may be noted that the teacher behavior factor structure in this study was not exactly the same as in previous studies, in that only 8 rather than 10 factors were defined. Statistical analysis of the data in Table 10 indicated significant differences between small and large classes for 3 of the 8 teaching behavior factors. Specifically, Interaction and Rapport behaviors more frequent for teachers of small seminar classes than for teachers of large lecture classes, whereas Organization behaviors were more frequent in large classes than ine small classes. These results are not terribly surprising, and are more or less what Wood had predicted. However, what came as a big surprise was the fact that of the 8 teaching behavior factors listed in Table 11, none differed significantly across

Table 10: Mean Rated Frequency of Occurrence of Teaching Behaviors as a Function of Class Size (Wood, 1994)

Teaching Behavior Factor	Class Size	
	Small	Large
Clarity	3.59	3.82
Enthusiasm	3.59	3.47
Interaction*	3.62	3.30
Organization*	3.24	3.82
Pacing	3.83	3.79
Disclosure	3.37	3.46
Rapport*	4.00	3.43
Speech Quality	4.17	4.00

* Difference between small and large groups significant at .05 level.

Table 11: Correlation of Teaching Behaviors with Overall Effectiveness Ratings as a Function of Class Size (Wood, 1994)

Teaching Behavior Factor	Class Size	
	Small	Large
Clarity	.75	.83
Enthusiasm	.63	.41
Interaction	.23	.07
Organization	.57	.73
Pacing	.73	.73
Disclosure	.42	.55
Rapport	.07	.24
Speech Quality	.73	.59

* Difference between small and large groups significant at .05 level.

small seminar vs. large lecture classes in terms of correlation with overall effectiveness ratings. It was expected that interaction behaviors would not only occur more frequently in small than in large classes, but would contribute more to overall teaching effectiveness in small classes. Similarly, it was expected that organizational behaviors would both occur more often and correlate higher with overall effectiveness in lecture classes than in seminar classes. Contrary to expectation, neither interaction behaviors nor organization behaviors (nor any other type of teaching behavior) differed significantly between small and large classes in correlation with overall teacher ratings. So again we have suggestive evidence that although teaching behaviors may differ across situations or contexts in frequency of occurrence, they do not differ across situations in their correlation with student instructional ratings. Although small class teachers may be more likely to exhibit interactive teaching behaviors than large class teachers, the extent to which interactive behaviors "pay off" in higher teacher ratings may be just as high for large classes as it is for small classes. Similarly, although large class teachers tend to show organizational teaching behaviors more frequently, these behaviors may contribute to perceived teaching effectiveness just as much for small classes as for large classes. One possible criticism of the Wood study is that, contrary to instructor self-reports, the method or style of instruction used in small and large classes may in fact have been very similar or identical (for example, it is possible that teachers used 100 percent lecturing in both types of classes). Thus, what appeared to be a contextual difference may not have been a difference at all. This argument has intuitive appeal, but it will not account for the fact that there were significant differences in the *frequency* of teaching behaviors across small vs. large classes in the Wood study.

In summary, we have evidence from three separate studies that low-inference teaching behaviors showed surprising consistency across situations or contexts in their correlation with overall teaching effectiveness ratings. This finding runs counter to the popular view that what constitutes good teaching is embedded in context and varies systematically from one context or situation (e.g., Brookfield, 1990: Good and Brophy, 1990; Shulman, 1986). The "contextual dependency" view implies that the correlation between frequency of occurrence of specific teaching behaviors and measures of overall teaching effectiveness should differ significantly in different contexts. An alternative view, favored by the present author, is that there may be certain fundamental or generic teaching behaviors such as expressiveness, organization, clarity of explanation, and encouragement of student participation, that contribute more or less equally to teaching effectiveness in all or nearly all contexts ranging from teaching reading in Grade 1 to teaching biochemistry to graduate students. It makes sense to me that there may be certain key low-inference teaching behaviors that convey enthusiasm for the subject matter or contribute to clarity of explanation and are equally effective in all contexts. On the other hand, it is possible that there may be other low-inference teaching behaviors that do in fact differ significantly across contexts in their impact on teaching effectiveness. Obviously, this is a question that requires further investigation, and one can only hope that the eventual answer to this question be based on systematic empirical evidence rather than totally on anecdote or personal opinion.

CAN RESEARCH ON LOW-INFERENCE TEACHING BEHAVIORS BE APPLIED SUCCESSFULLY TO IMPROVEMENT OF TEACHING?

I want to turn now to some studies that have attempted to apply research on low-inference teaching behaviors to improvement of teaching. Given that there appear to be clear cause-effect relationships between specific classroom teaching behaviors and measures of teaching effectiveness, it would seem that university teachers could improve their effectiveness by acquiring or emulating some of the teaching behaviors found to be important in research. But we all know that there are at least two things in this world that are much easier said than done: (1) applying research findings to real world problems, and (2) acquiring new teaching behaviors. I will briefly review two studies that attempted to improve teaching by modifying low-inference teaching behaviors, one by way of feedback and one by way of training.

BEHAVIORAL FEEDBACK

One way of applying research on low-inference teaching behaviors is by developing better procedures for providing formative or diagnostic feedback to instructors on their classroom teaching. One obvious way of providing such feedback is by way of student ratings, but the typical student rating form in current use focuses primarily on global, high-inference teacher characteristics, and therefore is less than ideal for purposes of formative feedback. For example, a poor rating on a high-inference item such as "explains clearly" or "is well prepared" may signify that there is a problem with clarity or with preparation, but provides no hint as to specifically what the problem is, what is causing it, and what needs to done to bring about improvement. Over the years I have experimented with various "formative" or "diagnostic" student rating forms that focus on specific, low-inference teaching behaviors such as "maintains eye contact with students" and "signals the transition from one topic to the next," and thus are intended to give the instructor a much clearer signal as to what is wrong and what remedial action is needed.

Despite the intuitive appeal of this goal, early attempts to demonstrate beneficial effects of low-inference behavioral feedback from students (e.g., McLean, 1979; Froman and Owen, 1980; Creighton, 1990) met with very little success. One possible reason was the problem of finding a way to present behavioral feedback to faculty members in a succinct, understandable format. One thing we discovered in these early studies is that a computer printout showing means, standard deviations, and percentile scores for 100 teaching behaviors causes the eyes of most faculty members to glaze over instantly!

Murray and Smith (1989) constructed and evaluated a new, revised behavioral feedback form that was intended to solve these problems. Essentially this is a formative feedback version of the previously described Teacher Behaviors Inventory. The feedback version of the TBI consists of 50 or 60 items, each referring to a specific classroom teaching behavior that has been found in previous research to show adequate interrater reliability and to correlate significantly with student evaluation of overall teacher effectiveness. The difference is that the feedback version of the TBI is completed by students rather than outside observers and uses a very different type of rating scale. Instead of rating the frequency of occurrence of teaching behaviors, students rate each teaching behavior on a bipolar 5-point scale to indicate whether, for purposes of improving teaching, the behavior in question needs to be increased in frequency of occurrence (rating of +1 or +2), decreased in frequency of occurrence (rating of −1 or −2), or unchanged in frequency of occurrence (zero rating). The feedback version of the TBI is intended to provide behavioral feedback that is simple, direct, easy to interpret, and obvious in its implications for improvement. Instructors can obtain feedback on which teaching behaviors to change, and in what direction, simply by identifying TBI items where mean student ratings deviate noticeably from zero and have relatively small standard deviations.

To determine whether the revised TBI can in fact contribute to improvement of teaching, Murray and Smith (1989) conducted an experiment in which the instructors were 60 graduate students serving as teaching assistants in the Departments of Geography, Psychology, and English at the University of Western Ontario. Half of the instructors in each discipline were randomly assigned to receive midterm TBI feedback from students in their courses (experimental group), whereas half were assessed with the TBI at midterm but did not receive feedback of the results of this assessment (control group). Behavioral feedback consisted of the mean and standard deviation of student ratings for each item of the diagnostic TBI, plus brief instructions for interpreting the data provided. The experiment was conducted over an 8-month (September to April) academic term, with behavioral feedback provided at the approximate midpoint (late December). Thus the post-feedback interval was approximately 4 months, which is considerably longer than that used in most previous studies. Improvement of classroom teaching was measured by amount of pretest-to-posttest gain in student ratings of overall teaching effectiveness.

As may be noted in Figure 3, midterm behavioral feedback led to significant improvement of classroom teaching in all three academic departments, as indicated by significantly larger pretest (mid-term) to posttest (end-of-term) gains in student ratings of overall teaching effectiveness for experimental group instructors receiving behavioral feedback than for control instructors. Furthermore, the estimated effect size for behavioral feedback across all three departments was approximately .73 standard deviation units, which is considerably higher than the average effect size of .20 reported by Cohen (1980) for feedback from traditional high-inference student evaluation forms.

175

Figure 3: Effect of midterm behavioral feedback on end-of-term student ratings of teaching (Murray and Smith, 1989).

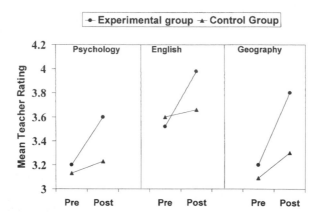

So, despite the pessimistic outcomes of earlier research, the Murray and Smith (1989) study suggests that, under the right conditions, feedback on low-inference teaching behaviors can contribute significantly to improvement of teaching. One of the "right conditions" for beneficial effects of behavioral feedback is that instructors are sufficiently motivated and open-minded about teaching to put effort into reading and thinking about the TBI feedback provided. This condition, in my experience, is more likely to be achieved with graduate student than with regular faculty instructors, and this may be one reason for the particularly clear results of the Murray and Smith study. Maybe, as the saying implies, it is easier to teach new tricks to young dogs than to old dogs?

BEHAVIORAL TRAINING

A second way of applying research on low-inference teaching behaviors to improvement of teaching is through the design of faculty development programs that provide intensive training on a limited subset of classroom behaviors known to contribute significantly to instructional outcome measures. As one example of this sort of effort, Murray and Lawrence (1980) assessed the impact of training in speech and drama skills on the classroom teaching of university professors. The rationale of such training is that the same expressive behaviors used by actors to convey meaning on the stage—for example, vocal variation, movement and gesture, facial expression, pausing and eye contact—can be used by teachers to communicate more effectively in the classroom. Given that teacher enthusiasm/expressiveness has consistently been found to correlate highly with student instructional ratings, it was expected that training of expressive teaching behaviors would produce significant improvement in rated teaching effectiveness. The impact of speech and drama training was assessed by a nonequivalent control group, pretest-posttest design in which the participating instructors were 24 fulltime faculty members in the Departments of Psychology, Sociology, and Physics at the University of Western Ontario. An experimental group of 12 teachers volunteered (and paid) for a series of 20 two-hour training sessions taught by a professional actor who also worked as a speech and drama instructor. Specific activities in weekly sessions included breathing and voice exercises, reading of monologues, acting out of short scenes from plays, and delivery of videotaped mini-lectures with corrective feedback from the instructor during playback. In all of these activities, participants were encouraged to make full use of expressive communication behaviors. A control group of 12 teachers, matched with the experimental group in terms of academic discipline and years of teaching, were assessed at pretest and posttest stages of the experiment, but received no behavioral training. Student ratings of both specific low-inference teaching behaviors and of overall teaching effectiveness were obtained just prior to (pretest) and immediately following (posttest) the 20-week training program for both experimental and control teachers. Similar overall effectiveness ratings were obtained for both groups in the four courses most recently taught by each teacher prior to the onset of the speech and drama program. As depicted in Figure 4, it was found that neither experimental nor control teachers showed improvement in teaching prior to the advent of the program, but experimental teachers then showed significant gains in student ratings from pretest to posttest, whereas control teachers showed no measurable change during the same time frame. The absence of improvement in experimental teachers prior to program onset suggests that pretest to posttest gains for the experimental group were due to behavioral training per se, rather than to greater motivation to improve in experimental teachers. To investigate further the impact of the program, the various low-inference teaching behaviors assessed at pretest and posttest stages were classified as either "target behaviors" that were expected to change as a result of the program (e.g., speaks expressively, lectures without notes, facial expressions) or "nontarget behaviors" that were not expected to change (e.g., provides sample exam questions, addresses students by name). As may be noted in Figure 5, the experimental group showed significantly larger pretest to posttest gains than the control group for target teaching behaviors

Figure 4: Impact of speech and drama training on teacher effectiveness ratings (Murray and Lawrence, 1980).

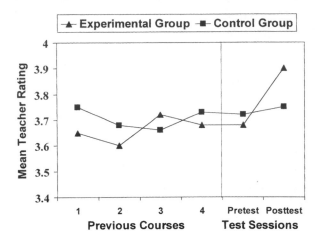

Figure 5: Impact of speech and Drama Training on Target vs. Nontarget Teaching Behaviors (Murray and Lawrence, 1980).

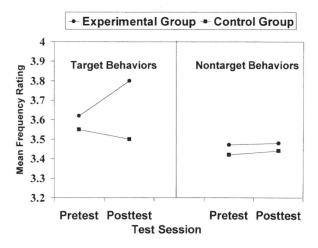

but not for nontarget behaviors. This result gives more credibility to the conclusion that the speech and drama program, rather than some extraneous variable, was responsible for the improvement in teaching exhibited by experimental teachers. Thus, as is the case with behavioral feedback, it appears that under the right conditions, a training or faculty development program focusing on a limited set of low-inference teaching behaviors can lead to significant improvement in quality of teaching.

In summary, it appears that research on low-inference teaching behaviors can provide a basis for effective programs for improvement of university teaching. Although teaching improvement is a complex, multifaceted, and long-term problem, with many possible models or approaches, there are some important advantages of incorporating low-inference teaching behaviors into teaching improvement programs. For one thing, because such behaviors tend to be very specific and concrete, they are relatively easy for faculty development consultants to define or describe. and relatively easy for faculty members to comprehend and modify. Second, because low-inference teaching behaviors can be viewed as the "leading edge" of teaching, the point of direct contact between teacher and student, it would seem that they are more likely to have an impact on student development than are more "abstract" or "cognitive" teacher characteristics such as goals, attitudes, knowledge, or planning. As a case in point, it does no good to be well-prepared for teaching or to be intensely enthusiastic about the subject matter in your own mind unless this preparation or enthusiasm is communicated by way of specific teaching behaviors that are observable to students in the classroom. Third, unlike some other models and approaches to teaching improvement, there is systematic research evidence that low-inference teaching behaviors are in fact causally related to student ratings as well as student learning, and can in fact contribute significantly to improvement of teaching.

CONCLUSIONS

Recent research on low-inference teaching behaviors and teaching effectiveness in higher education supports the following general conclusions:

1. There are specific, observable classroom teaching behaviors that account for a large proportion of the variance in student ratings of college and university teaching.
2. In addition to student ratings, low-inference teaching behaviors are related to a wide range of other measures of teaching effectiveness, including student learning and student motivation for further learning.
3. Low-inference teaching behaviors appear to be "causes" rather than simply "correlates" of various measures of teaching effectiveness, suggesting that incorporation of low-inference

behaviors into teaching improvement programs is likely to lead to actual improvement.

4. Very little is known about the cognitive or affective processes underlying the impact of low-inference teaching behaviors, but preliminary research suggests that teacher enthusiasm may affect student learning by way of memory encoding and cognitive structuring mechanisms. More research is desperately needed in this area.

5. Under the right conditions, feedback and training programs based on low inference teaching behaviors can lead to significant improvement in teaching.

6. Although low-inference teaching behaviors have been found to differ in frequency of occurrence across different contexts (academic disciplines, teacher genders, and class sizes), research conducted to date suggests that the contribution of specific teaching behaviors to overall teaching effectiveness tends to be consistent across different contexts or situations.

REFERENCES

Anderson, J.F., and Withrow, J.G. (1981). The impact of lecturer nonverbal expressiveness on improving mediated instruction. *Communication Education* 30: 342–353.

Basow, S.A., and Distenfeld, M.S. (1985). Teacher expressiveness: More important for male teachers than female teachers? *Journal of Educational Psychology* 77: 45–52.

Brookfield, S.D. (1990). *The Skillful Teacher*. San Francisco: Jossey-Bass.

Coats, W.D., and Smidchens, U. (1966). Audience recall as a function of speaker dynamism. *Journal of Educational Psychology* 57: 189–191.

Cohen, P.A. (1980). Effectiveness of student rating feedback for improving college instruction: A meta-analysis of findings. *Research in Higher Education* 13: 321–341.

Cohen, P.A. (1981). Student ratings of instruction and student achievement: A meta-analysis of multisection validity studies. *Review of Educational Research* 51: 281–309.

Cranton, P.A., and Hillgartner, W. (1981). The relationship between student ratings and instructor behavior: Implications for improving teaching. *Canadian Journal of Higher Education* 11: 73–81.

Creighton, A. (1990). *Impact of Behavioral versus Global Feedback on Improvement of University Teaching Performance*. Unpublished honors thesis, University of Western Ontario, London, Canada.

Feldman, K.A. (1989). The association between student ratings of specific instructional dimensions and student achievement: Refining and extending the synthesis of data from multisection validity studies. *Research in Higher Education* 30: 583–645.

Feldman, K.A. (1997). Identifying exemplary teachers and teaching: Evidence from student ratings. In R.P. Perry and J.C. Smart (eds.), *Effective Teaching in Higher Education: Research and Practice*. New York: Agathon Press.

Feldman K.A. (1998). Reflections on the study of effective teaching and student ratings: One continuing quest and two unresolved issues. In R.P. Perry and J.C. Smart (eds.), *Higher Education: Handbook of Theory and Research* (Vol. 13). New York: Agathon Press.

Froman, R.D., and Owen, S.V. (1980). *Influence of Different Types of Student Ratings Feedback upon Later Instructional Behavior*. Paper presented at annual meeting of American Educational Research Association, Boston.

Good, T.L., and Brophy, J. (1990). *Contemporary Educational Psychology* (5th Edition). White Plains, NY: Longmans.

Hines, C.V., Cruickshank, D.R., and Kennedy, J.J. (1985). Teacher clarity and its relationship to student achievement and satisfaction. *American Educational Research Journal* 22: 87–99.

Land, M.L. (1979). Low-inference variables of teacher clarity: Effects on student concept learning. *Journal of Educational Psychology* 71: 795–799.

Marques, T.E., Lane, D.M., and Dorfman, P.W. (1979). Toward the development of a system for instructional evaluation: Is there consensus regarding what constitutes effective teaching? *Journal of Educational Psychology* 71: 840–849.

Marsh, H.W., and Dunkin, M.J. (1992). Students' evaluations of university teaching: A multidimensional perspective. In J.C. Smart (ed.), *Higher Education: Handbook of Theory and Research* (Vol. 8). New York: Agathon Press.

McNemar, Q. (1962). *Psychological Statistics* (3rd edition). New York: Wiley.

Mintzes, J. J. (1979). Overt teaching behaviors and student ratings of instructors. *Journal of Experimental Education* 48: 145–153.

McLean, D.F. (1979). *The Effect of Mid-semester Feedback upon Weekly Evaluations of University Instructors.* Unpublished master's thesis, University of Western Ontario, London, Canada.

Murray, H.G. (1978). *Organizational Factors in Classroom Teaching.* Paper presented at annual meeting of Canadian Psychological Association, Ottawa.

Murray, H.G. (1983a). Low-inference classroom teaching behaviors and student ratings of college teaching effectiveness. *Journal of Educational Psychology* 75: 138–149.

Murray, H.G. (1983b). Low-inference classroom teaching behaviors in relation to six measures of college teaching effectiveness. In J.G. Donald (ed.), *Proceedings of the Conference on the Evaluation and Improvement of University Teaching: The Canadian Experience.* Montreal: Centre for Teaching and Learning Services, McGilll University.

Murray, H.G. (1985). Classroom teaching behaviors related to college teaching effectiveness. In J.G. Donald and A.M. Sullivan (eds.), *Using Research to Improve University Teaching.* San Francisco: Jossey-Bass.

Murray, H.G. (1991). Effective teaching behaviors in the college classroom. In J. C. Smart (ed.), *Higher Education: Handbook of Theory and Research.* (Vol. 7). New York: Agathon Press.

Murray, H.G. (1997). *Classroom Teaching Behaviors and Student Instructional Ratings: How Do Good Teachers Teach?* Presented at Annual Meeting of American Educational Research Association, Chicago.

Murray, H.G., and Lawrence, C. (1980). Speech and drama training for lecturers as a means of improving university teaching. *Research in Higher Education* 13: 73–90.

Murray, H.G., and Renaud, R.D. (1995). Disciplinary differences in classroom teaching behaviors. In N. Hativa, and M. Marincovich (eds.), *Disciplinary Differences in Teaching and Learning: Implications for Practice.* San Francisco: Jossey-Bass.

Murray, H.G., and Smith, T.A. (1989). *Effects of Midterm Behavioral Feedback on End-of-term Ratings of Instructor Effectiveness.* Paper presented at annual meeting of the American Education Research Association, San Francisco.

Perry, R.P. (1991). Perceived control in college students: Implications for instruction in higher education. In J.C. Smart (ed.), *Higher Education: Handbook of Theory and Research* (Vol. 7). New York: Agathon Press.

Pohlmann, J.T. (1976). A description of effective college teaching in five disciplines as measured by student ratings. *Research in Higher Education* 4: 335–346.

Roberts, C.L., and Becker, S.L. (1976). Communication and teaching effectiveness. *American Educational Research Journal* 13: 181–197.

Rosenshine, B., and Furst, N.F. (1971). Research on teacher performance criteria. In B.O. Smith (ed.), *Research in Teacher Education: A Symposium.* Englewood Cliffs, New Jersey: Prentice Hall.

Schonwetter, D.J. (1996). *Effective Instruction and Student Differences in the College Classroom.* Unpublished doctoral dissertation, University of Manitoba, Winnipeg, Canada.

Sheehan, D.S. (1975). On the invalidity of student ratings for administrative personnel decisions. *Journal of Higher Education* 46: 687–700.

Shulman. L.S. (1986). Those who understand: knowledge growth in teaching. *Educational Researcher* 15 (2): 4–14.

Solomon, D., Rosenberg, L., and Bezdek, W.E. (1964). Teacher behavior and student learning. *Journal of Educational Psychology* 55: 23–30.

Tom, F.K.T., and Cushman, H.R. (1975). The Cornell diagnostic observation and reporting system for student description of college teaching. *Search* 5 (8): 1–27.

Ware, J.E., Jr., and Williams, R.G. (1975). The Dr. Fox effect: A study of lecturer effectiveness and ratings of instruction. *Journal of Medical Education* 50: 149–156.

Wood, A.M. (1994). *Low-inference Classroom Teaching Behaviors in Lecture vs. Seminar Classes*. Unpublished masters thesis, University of Western Ontario, London, Canada.

Wood, A.M. (1998). Effects of teacher enthusiasm on student motivation, selective attention, and text memory. Unpublished doctoral dissertation, University of Western Ontario, London, Canada.

RESEARCH ON LOW-INFERENCE TEACHING BEHAVIORS: AN UPDATE

Harry G. Murray

University of Western Ontario
murray@uwo.ca

Abstract

This chapter provides an update to earlier reviews of research by the author (Murray, 1991, 2001) on the contribution of low-inference classroom teaching behaviors to university teaching effectiveness. Research reviewed here supports the following conclusions: (1) the covariance structure of low-inference student ratings resembles the covariance of actual teaching behaviours more closely than does the covariance structure of high-inference student ratings, indicating that low-inference ratings are higher in factorial validity; (2) low-inference teacher clarity behaviors contribute positively to both student achievement and student motivation, but contrary to expectation, these effects do not depend on student anxiety; and (3) high school student ratings of low-inference teaching behaviours show reasonable levels of rater accuracy and have potential as a source of formative feedback for high school teachers

Key Words: Teacher characteristics, low-inference teaching behaviors, student instructional ratings

The goal of research on teacher effectiveness in higher education is to identify characteristics of teachers that contribute significantly to student cognitive and attitudinal outcomes. It is assumed that knowledge of factors contributing to effective teaching will lead both to a better theoretical understanding of teaching and to the development of improved programs of faculty selection, evaluation, and development.

My own research on teacher effectiveness has focused mainly on specific, concrete "low-inference" classroom teaching behaviors, such as "signals the transition from one topic to the next", "provides a preliminary outline of the lecture", and "addresses individual students by name", that can be can be recorded objectively, with little or no judgement or inference, on the part of a classroom observer. High-inference teacher characteristics, on the other hand, are global, abstract traits such as "clarity" and "rapport", the assessment of which requires more inference or subjective judgement.

Although knowledge of both low-inference and high-inference characteristics is needed for a full understanding of teaching effectiveness, there are some definite advantages in focusing on low-inference teaching behaviors. Such behaviors are relatively easy to manipulate or record for research purposes, and feedback on low-inference behaviours is useful for faculty development purposes because it provides specific, concrete information on what needs to be done to improve teaching. Also, low-inference classroom teaching behaviors represent the "leading edge" of teaching, the point of direct contact between teacher and student, and thus would appear to have the most direct impact on student learning and development.

Previous research by myself and others, reviewed in earlier volumes of *Higher Education: Handbook of Theory and Research* (Murray, 1991, 2001), showed that there are clear relationships between low-inference classroom teaching behaviors and several outcome measures, including student ratings of instruction, student motivation, and student learning. This research included classroom observation studies, in which trained observers visited class sessions to record the frequency of occurrence of specific teaching behaviors, which were then related to student outcome measures; and experimental studies in which low-inference teaching behaviors were experimentally manipulated in a laboratory setting, with other variables controlled, to demonstrate cause-effect relations with outcome variables.

For purposes of classroom observation studies, I developed an instrument known as the Teacher Behaviors Inventory (TBI), which is used by classroom observers to estimate the frequency of occurrence of each of 50 low-inference teaching behaviors on a 5-point rating scale ranging from 1 (almost never) to 5 (almost always). There are actually two versions of the Teacher Behaviors Inventory: a Research Version, intended for research purposes as defined above, and a Feedback Version intended solely to provide diagnostic or formative feedback to instructors seeking to improve their teaching. The TBI Feedback Version consists of the same 50 low-inference behavioral items as the Research Version, but instead of rating frequency of occurrence per se, students or other observers use a bipolar 5-point rating scale to indicate whether, for purposes of teaching improvement, the instructor needs to increase (rating of +1 or +2), decrease (rating of −1 or −2), or make no change in (rating of 0) the frequency of occurrence of each low-inference teaching behavior. Both versions of the TBI are uncopyrighted, and may be viewed or copied online at the following website: www.ssc.uwo.ca/psychology/faculty/murray.

The remainder of this chapter provides an update of recent research on low-inference classroom teaching behaviours. Most of this research was conducted by graduate students I have worked with at the University of Western Ontario. Three different questions are addressed in this research: (1) the factorial validity of student ratings of low-inference teaching behaviours, (2) the interaction of low-inference teacher clarity behaviours with student anxiety, and (3) the validity and utility of high school student ratings of low-inference teaching behaviors.

FACTORIAL VALIDITY OF LOW-INFERENCE STUDENT RATINGS

This research was reported in a masters thesis by Robert Renaud (1996), and subsequently published by Renaud and Murray (2005). The goal of the research was to compare the factorial validity of student ratings of global, high-inference teacher characteristics vs. ratings of specific, low-inference teaching behaviors. Factorial validity is defined as the extent to which the correlation found among rated components of performance resembles the actual or true correlation of these components.

Although Cohen (1981) and Feldman (1989) have shown that student ratings of global, high-inference teacher characteristics such as clarity, rapport, and organization, are "valid" in the sense that they correlate significantly with student achievement on common final exams, it is possible that global components of teaching effectiveness are actually very low in factorial validity. Cronbach (1958) argues that people have a tendency to rate performance according to "what is thought to go with what", rather than "what actually goes with what", and this over-reliance on conceptual associations explains how traits can be rated as correlated when in reality they correlate little or not at all. For example, instructors who are well liked by students may be rated highly on both "Rapport" and "Organization", even though there is no actual or true tendency for teachers with good rapport to also be highly organized.

The recommended procedure for examining the impact of conceptual associations on performance ratings is to compare three correlation matrices: one based on ratings of component factors in performance, one based on conceptual associations among the same components, derived by having raters determine in their own minds how strongly each dimension is associated with each other dimension, and one based on direct observation of actual behaviors underlying each component of performance. Factorial validity is indicated if the rated component matrix shows a strong correlation with the actual behavior matrix, and a weaker correlation with the conceptual association matrix.

Although several previous studies (e.g., Cadwell & Jenkins, 1985; Whitely & Doyle, 1976) have reported that student ratings of teaching are strongly influenced by conceptual associations, an important limitation of these studies is that they failed to compare component ratings and similarity judgements to actual teaching behaviors. The degree to which ratings are influenced by conceptual associations is difficult to confirm in the absence of direct observation of teaching behaviors. Another limitation is that previous studies focused solely on student ratings of global, high-inference teacher characteristics, whereas higher levels of factorial validity might be found for student ratings of specific, low-inference teaching behaviours that require little subjective judgement on the part of the rater.

Data were obtained from 32 instructors videotaped during two 1-hour class periods, and from three separate groups of undergraduate students: the rating group, consisting of 622 students registered in the 32 classes taught by the participating instructors; the similarity judgement group, consisting of 43 students who provided pairwise similarity judgements of the same low- and high-inference teacher characteristics rated by the rating group; and the observer group, consisting of 256 students who recorded the frequency of occurrence of actual teaching behaviors from videotape of classes taught by the 32 instructors.

Four different teacher rating forms were used in this study. The first was an abbreviated version of the Teacher Behaviors Inventory, consisting of 16 low-inference classroom teaching behaviors representing 8 dimensions of teaching, with each behaviour rated on a 5-point frequency-of-occurrence scale (1 = "almost never", 5 = "almost always"). The second was the Teacher Rating Form (TRF), a newly developed 9-item form consisting of 8 high-inference items corresponding to the 8 dimensions represented on the TBI, plus a ninth item assessing overall teaching effectiveness. Each TRF item was rated on a 5-point scale ranging from 1 = "poor" to 5 = "excellent". The third rating form, used for the conceptual association task, included all possible pairs of items from the 16-item TBI, and all possible pairs of items from the 8-item TRF (excluding overall effectiveness). Subjects rated the degree of conceptual similarity of each pair of items on a scale ranging from −100 meaning "completely opposite" to 0 meaning "no similarity at all" to +100 meaning "completely similar". Finally, subjects in the observer group used a behavioural observation form to record each of the 16 TBI behaviors as either present or absent in each of 24 sequential 5-minute time segments, such that the recorded frequency of a behavior could range from 0 to 24 in 120 minutes of videotape.

Preliminary data analyses showed that the mean interrater reliability (intraclass correlation) of student ratings of the 16 low-inference TBI items was .82; whereas the mean interrater reliability of student ratings of the 8 high-inference TRF items was .80; and the mean interobserver reliability of counts of actual teaching behaviours was .88. Thus, reliability of measurement was generally high, particularly for direct observation or rating of specific classroom teaching behaviours.

Covariance matrices for low- and high-inference student ratings of teaching were obtained by intercorrelating all TBI or TRF items using instructor mean scores as the unit of analysis (N = 32). Corresponding matrices representing similarity judgements for TBI and TRF items were obtained by using the mean judgement of similarity for each pair of items for 43 judges. Thus, there were three 16×16 matrices representing the TBI items across each of the three tasks, and three 8×8 matrices representing the TRF items across the same three tasks.

To assess similarity of covariance structures across the three matrices for TBI and TRF items, each matrix was correlated with each other matrix by rearranging the values in the bottom half of each matrix into a column vector, and intercorrelating the three vectors. The top panel of Figure 1 shows correlations among the three matrices for low-inference TBI items. The pattern of covariation among teacher ratings corresponded closely to the pattern of similarity judgements, $r = .81$, $p < .01$, and also resembled the pattern of covariation among actual behaviors, $r = .54$, $p < .01$. Furthermore, to a slightly lesser degree, the pattern of covariation among actual behaviors was significantly related to the similarity judgements matrix, $r = .42$, $p < .05$. The bottom panel of Figure 1 shows correlations among the three matrices for high-inference TRF items. These data suggest a somewhat different

Figure 1: Correlations between teacher ratings, behaviour observations, and similarity judgements for low-inference (top panel) and high-inference (bottom panel) teacher characteristics.

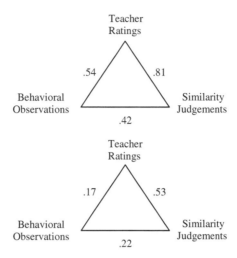

picture. Unlike the TBI matrices, the only significant relation among TRF matrices occurred between the ratings task and the similarity judgement task, $r = .53$, $p < .01$.

The results of this study are consistent with previous evidence (eg., Murray, 1983) that student ratings of low-inference teaching behaviors are slightly higher in interrater reliability than student ratings of high-inference teacher characteristics. Secondly, the present findings suggest that ratings of low-inference teaching behaviours are higher in factorial validity than high-inference ratings, in that the covariance pattern for low-inference ratings related not only to students' mental conceptions of which behaviors go together, but also to actual covariance of directly observed classroom teaching behaviours, whereas the covariance structure of high-inference ratings related only to student' conceptual associations.

Thus, when student ratings are used by promotion and tenure committees to judge teaching, or by faculty development specialists to improve teaching, particularly when components of teaching are used in a profile format to indicate areas of relative strength and weakness, low-inference student ratings may provide a more accurate and useful measure of relative performance on various components of teaching effectiveness than high-inference student ratings.

INTERACTION OF TEACHER CLARITY AND STUDENT ANXIETY

This research was part of a doctoral dissertation completed by Susan Rodger (2001) and since accepted for publication (Rodger, Murray & Cummings, 2007). A laboratory experiment was carried out to examine a possibility that teacher clarity and student test anxiety enter into an aptitude-treatment interaction (Cronbach & Snow, 1977), whereby the effect of teacher clarity is greater for high than for low anxiety students. The predicted aptitude-treatment interaction (ATI) was examined in relation to two different outcome measures, namely student achievement and student motivation for further learning.

Teacher clarity has consistently been found to positively influence student outcomes in previous research (Murray, 2001). In the present study, teacher clarity was a manipulated treatment variable, defined operationally by the following set of nine low-inference teaching behaviours: puts outline of lecture on projection screen, uses concrete examples, uses multiple examples of each concept, repeats difficult ideas, suggests practical applications, stresses important points, signals transitions between topics, summarizes periodically, and highlights similarities and differences between concepts.

Test anxiety has consistently been found to have a negative effect on student academic achievement and motivation (Hembree, 1988), possibly because it is associated with deficits in information processing. It was hypothesized that the positive effect of teacher clarity on student achievement and motivation would be larger for students high in test anxiety in the present study. One reason for expecting such an ATI is that the low-inference teaching behaviours underlying teacher clarity can be assumed to assist students in encoding and organizing new information, and highly anxious students with presumed deficits in information processing would be expected to benefit the most from high clarity teaching.

The research participants, 120 first-year psychology students, were randomly assigned to watch either a Low Clarity or High Clarity video-taped lecture on the topic of Memory and Amnesia and then read an assigned paper on the same topic. The two videotaped lectures were identical in content coverage and in length, the only difference being that the High Clarity lecture incorporated the 9 low-inference teaching behaviours listed above, whereas the Low Clarity lecture incorporated "filler material" such as historical facts and superfluous details. Test anxiety was measured by Spielberger's (1970) Test Anxiety Inventory

(TAI), and the 60 students at each level of teacher clarity were divided at the median TAI score to create Low Anxiety and High Anxiety conditions within a 2x2 factorial design. Student achievement was assessed by a multiple-choice and short-answer test based on the video-taped lecture and assigned reading, whereas student motivation was measured by Pintrich's et al.'s (1991) 17-item Motivated Strategies for Learning Questionnaire.

Students watched either the Low Clarity or High Clarity lecture in the first experimental session, then returned one week later after completing the assigned reading to take the achievement test covering both the lecture and reading. It was assumed that this design provided a laboratory simulation that replicated as closely as possible the conditions of real-world teaching and learning, including a lecture and assigned reading followed by a test.

The major results of the study are summarized in Figure 2. As may be noted in the top panel of the figure, both of the expected main effects were obtained for the student achievement measure, in

Figure 2: Effects of teacher clarity and student anxiety on student achievement (top panel) and student motivation (bottom panel).

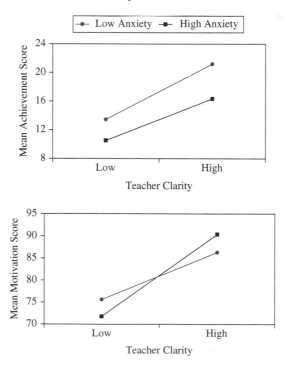

that students in the High Clarity condition scored significantly higher on the achievement test than students in the Low Clarity condition, and Low Anxiety students scored higher than High-Anxiety students. However, contrary to expectation, the interaction effect between Clarity and Anxiety was not significant, reflecting the fact that the facilitative effect of high teacher clarity was approximately equal for low and high anxious students.

The bottom panel of Figure 2 shows results for the second dependent variable, student motivation for further learning. It may be noted that motivation to learn was significantly higher for students receiving the High Clarity lecture than for students receiving the Low Clarity lecture, but there was no main effect for Test Anxiety and once again, no interaction effect between Clarity and Anxiety. Consistent with hypothesis, the effect of teacher clarity on student motivation was greater for high anxiety than for low anxiety students, but this difference was not large enough to produce a significant interaction in the ANOVA.

It should be noted that the above results for student achievement and student motivation were unchanged when the data were reanalysed (1) by hierarchical multiple regression with anxiety as a continuous variable, and (2) by multiple, planned comparisons of group means.

In summary, teacher clarity had significant positive effects on both student achievement and student motivation, whereas student test anxiety was negatively related to achievement but not to motivation. Furthermore, the predicted aptitude-treatment interaction effect, whereby the facilitative effect of teacher clarity was expected to be greater for high than for low anxious students, was not found in this study. The failure to find the interaction effect is surprising in that such an effect was reported by Dowaliby and Schumer (1973). The reason for this difference in results is not clear, but may be due to the fact that Dowaliby and Schumer focused on general or manifest anxiety, whereas the present study dealt with test anxiety.

The present results do provide important confirmation that teacher clarity, defined by low-inference classroom teaching behaviours, contributes positively to student learning for both low and high anxiety students. Whereas Hines, Cruikshank, and Kennedy (1985) and others have reported significant relationships between low-inference teacher clarity variables and student achievement, very few previous studies have examined the effects of teacher clarity on student learning under experimentally controlled conditions, as was done in the current study.

Thus, the present study shows that teacher clarity is a true causal antecedent, rather than merely a correlate, of student learning, and this increases our confidence that efforts by teachers to increase their use of low-inference "clarity" behaviours will actually pay off in terms of improvement in student achievement and motivation. The underlying process or mechanism whereby teacher clarity facilitates student learning is uncertain, but may relate to the role of underlying low-inference teaching behaviours in structuring information in short-term memory, thus leading to more meaningful encoding of information in long-term memory.

Another important contribution of this study is the demonstration that teacher clarity benefits student motivation as well as student learning. The theoretical explanation for this effect is also open to speculation, but it seems possible that teachers who use multiple examples, repeat difficult ideas, and provide a lecture outline create a sense of self-efficacy or personal control in students, thereby improving motivation to learn.

HIGH SCHOOL STUDENT RATINGS OF LOW-INFERENCE TEACHING BEHAVIORS

Two studies reported in a doctoral dissertation by Kristin Anglin-Bodrug (2005) were designed to investigate the validity and utility of high school student ratings of low-inference teaching behaviours. The goal of the first study was to compare low-inference ratings made by high school vs. university students in terms of Cronbach's (1955) four components of rating accuracy. As explained below, Cronbach's model assesses rating accuracy in terms of the extent to which student ratings of teaching are similar to those of expert raters.

The first component of accuracy in Cronbach's model, elevation (EL) is the degree to which a rater, on average, rates performance either too leniently or too severely relative to an expert rater. The second component, differential elevation (DE), is defined as the rater's ability, relative to that of an expert, to differentiate the performance levels of different individuals for summative evaluation, while controlling for overall rating elevation. Stereotype accuracy (SA), the third component, represents the rater's ability to distinguish between different performance items averaged across individuals, with overall elevation controlled. The fourth component of rating accuracy, differential accuracy (DA), measures the accuracy of identifying an individual's performance profile or pattern of strengths and weaknesses for purposes of formative evaluation.

There were three groups of raters in this study: experts, undergraduate students, and high school students, all of whom watched three videotaped simulations of high school teaching and then rated low-inference teaching behaviours. The sample of 16 expert raters included elementary school teachers, as well as graduate students and faculty members in educational psychology. The undergraduate students were 61 introductory psychology students, and the high school students were 164 volunteers, aged 14 to 19, representing all five grade levels in a local high school. Each of the three videotaped lessons was presented by a different experienced teacher, and each dealt with a separate topic relating to economic systems and the economy of China. The first videotape was used for practice and feedback purposes only, whereas the second and third videotapes were used to obtain rating accuracy estimates. Low-inference teaching behaviors in the three videos were evaluated using a subset of 15 items measuring three categories of teaching (clarity, enthusiasm, and voice quality) from the High School Teacher Behaviours Inventory (HSTBI). The HSTBI is a modified version of the Teacher Behaviours Inventory consisting of 58 items relevant to teaching at the high school level, each rated on a 5-point frequency-of-occurrence scale: *Almost Never* (1), *Rarely* (2), *Sometimes* (3), *Often* (4), and *Almost Always* (5).

High school and university students received rater training before rating the second and third videotapes. This consisted of definition of performance dimensions, examples of behaviours associated with various levels of performance, and practice in rating the first videotape followed by feedback relating their ratings to those of the expert raters. Rating accuracy scores for each of Cronbach's four components of accuracy on the second and third videotapes were calculated separately for each student and each teaching behaviour by comparing student ratings to mean expert ratings of the same behaviours.

Table 1 shows means and standard deviations of Cronbach rating accuracy scores averaged across all 15 HSTBI items for high school and undergraduate students. In general, rating accuracy was better (i.e., closer to zero) for undergraduate students than for high school students. Although high school students were slightly more accurate in terms of the elevation (EL) component of accuracy, undergraduate students were more accurate in terms of the other three Cronbach components, namely differential elevation (DE), stereotype accuracy (SA), and differential accuracy (DA). Across all four accuracy

Table 1: Means and Standard Deviations for Teacher Ratings by Student Group and Component of Accuracy

Accuracy Component	High school students			Undergraduate students		
	M	SD	n	M	SD	n
EL	.23	.17	155	.24	.17	60
DE	.39	.27	155	.23	.20	60
SA	.62	.16	155	.55	.12	60
DA	.59	.15	155	.54	.12	60

Note. Accuracy scores are based on a 5-point frequency rating scale; lower scores indicate greater accuracy. M = average accuracy score; EL = elevation; DE = differential elevation; SA = stereotype elevation; DA = differential accuracy.

components, the multivariate main effect for student group was significant in favour of university students. Further analyses of differences between university students and specific age groups at the high school level showed that ratings by 17, 18, and 19 year old high school students were significantly less accurate in terms of differential elevation (DE) than were ratings by undergraduate students, whereas 16 year old high school students gave significantly less accurate ratings in terms of stereotype accuracy (SA), and 15 year old high school students gave significantly less accurate ratings in terms of differential accuracy (DA). No other differences across age groups were significant.

The results of this study suggest that although there were significant differences between high school and university students for three of the four components of accuracy, these differences were not large or consistent or widespread. For example, ratings from 14 year old high school students did not differ significantly from undergraduate student ratings on any component of accuracy, and the oldest high school students were the least accurate in terms of distinguishing different performances across teachers (DE). In addition, high school students of varying ages did not differ significantly from each other. It appears that high school students are capable of rating teaching performance at close to the same level of accuracy as university students. Worrell and Kuterback (2001) reached a similar conclusion in a recent study where high school student ratings of low-inference teaching variables showed the same factor structure and same relationship to overall teaching effectiveness as has been reported at the university level.

Anglin-Bodrug (2005) conducted a second study to evaluate the effect of feedback from high school student ratings of low-inference teaching behaviours on the subsequent teaching performance of preservice teachers. High school students were asked to provide low-inference ratings of preservice teachers after two separate practice teaching placements, once at Time 1 and then again at Time 2. Preservice teachers were randomly assigned to either a feedback group or to a "waiting-list" control group. Those in the feedback group received the results of student ratings immediately after completing their Time 1 practice teaching placement, while the control group received feedback only after the study was completed (i.e., after Time 2). It was expected that the feedback group would show greater improvement in performance ratings from Time 1 to Time 2 than the control group.

The participants in this study were 93 preservice teachers who volunteered to participate, and were asked to select classes taught in their next two practice teaching placements wherein student ratings of teaching would be solicited. Student ratings of low-inference teaching behaviours were obtained via a subset of 28 items from the High School Teacher Behaviors Inventory, covering 7 dimensions of classroom teaching. The number of high school students providing HSTBI ratings was 901 at Time 1 and 946 at Time 2.

Preliminary analysis of data showed that, despite random assignment of subjects to conditions, self-ratings of teaching were significantly higher for the Control Group than for the Feedback Group prior to the onset of differential treatment. Figure 3 shows mean student ratings averaged across all 28 HSTBI items for Feedback and Control groups at Time 1 and Time 2, with self-ratings statistically controlled. It may be noted that mean student ratings were similar for Feedback and Control groups at Time 1, whereas at Time 2 there was an increase in student ratings for the Feedback Group, but no change in ratings for the Control Group. This pattern of results is consistent with expectation, but statistical analysis failed to show the expected Groups × Times interaction effect. This result is surprising for several reasons: (1) in terms of effect size, the present results look very much like those reported by Cohen (1980) for similar feedback studies at the university level; (2) teacher self-reports indicated that student feedback was helpful and beneficial; and (3) significant effects of high school student feedback on low-inference teaching behaviours were reported in a parallel study by Smits (2002). It is possible that the

Figure 3: Mean student HSTBI ratings for feedback and control groups at Time 1 and Time 2, with control for self-ratings.

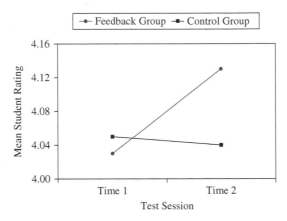

non-significant feedback effect in the present study was due to high within-group variability in student ratings and lack of statistical power.

In summary, the results of the two studies reported above suggest that high school student ratings of low-inference teaching behaviours could potentially be used for both summative and formative evaluation of teaching. The present research indicates that high school students of all age levels, like their university counterparts, can provide accurate low-inference teacher ratings, and these ratings could potentially be effective as a source of feedback to improve teacher performance.

CONCLUSIONS

The results of the three studies reviewed above confirm and extend previous evidence (Murray, 1991, 2001) demonstrating the value of focusing on specific, low-inference classroom teaching behaviours in research on teacher effectiveness, in evaluation of teaching, and in faculty development programs in higher education. The results of Study 1 suggest that student ratings of low-inference teaching behaviors are less influenced by implicit assumptions and conceptual associations than ratings of high-inference teacher characteristics, and thus are potentially useful for both summative and formative evaluation of teaching. Study 2 demonstrated a strong cause-effect relationship between teacher clarity and both student learning and student motivation. The fact that teacher clarity effects were similar for low and high anxiety students was contrary to prediction, but consistent with previous evidence (Murray, 2002) that effects of low-inference teaching behaviors are highly stable or robust across different contexts. The results of Study 3 suggest that high school students are capable of providing accurate ratings of low-inference teaching behaviours, and such ratings could potentially be used for both summative and formative purposes in high schools.

REFERENCES

Anglin-Bodrug, K.L. (2005). *Student Evaluation of High School Preservice Teachers: Rating Accuracy, Formative Feedback, and Concurrent Validity*. Unpublished doctoral dissertation, London, ON: University of Western Ontario.

Cadwell, J., and Jenkins, J. (1985). Effects of the semantic similarity of items on student ratings of instructors. *Journal of Educational Psychology* 77: 383–393.

Cohen, A.P. (1980). Effectiveness of student-rating feedback for improving collegein-struction: a meta-analysis of findings. *Research in Higher Education* 13: 321–341.

Cohen, P.A. (1981). Student ratings of instruction and student achievement: A meta-analysis of multisection validity studies. *Review of Educational Research* 51: 281–309.

Cronbach, L. (1955). Processes affecting scores on "understanding of others" and "assumed similarity." *Psychological Bulletin* 52: 177–193.

Cronbach, L.J. (1958). Proposals leading to analytic treatment of social perception scores. In R.Tagiuri and L. Petrulio (eds.), *Person Perception and Interpersonal Behavior* (pp. 351–379). Palo Alto, CA: Stanford University Press.

Cronbach, L., and Snow, R.E. (1977). *Aptitudes and Instructional Methods*. New York: Irvington.

Dowaliby, F.J., and Schumer, H. (1973). Teacher-centred versus student-centred mode of classroom instruction as related to manifest anxiety. *Journal of Educational Psychology* 64: 125–132.

Feldman, K.A. (1989). The association between student ratings of specific instructional dimensions and student achievement: Refining and extending the synthesis of data from multisection validity studies. *Research in Higher Education* 30: 583–645.

Hembree, R. (1988). Correlates, causes, effects and treatment of test anxiety. *Review of Educational Research* 58: 47–77.

Hines, C.V., Cruikshank, D.R., and Kennedy, J.J. (1985). Teacher clarity and its relationship to student achievement and satisfaction. *American Education Research Journal* 22: 87–99.

Murray, H.G. (1983). Low-inference classroom teaching behaviours and student ratings of college teaching effectiveness. *Journal of Educational Psychology* 75: 138–149.

Murray, H.G. (1991). Effective teaching behaviours in the college classroom. In J.C. Smart (ed.), *Higher Education: Handbook of Theory and Research* (Vol.7, pp. 135–172). New York: Agathon Press.

Murray, H.G. (2001). Low-inference teaching behaviours and college teaching effectiveness: Recent developments and controversies. In J.C. Smart and W.C. Tierney (eds.), *Higher Education: Handbook of Theory and Research* (Vol. 16, pp. 239–272). New York: Agathon Press.

Pintrich, P.R., Smith, D.R., Garcia, T., and McKeachie, W.J. (1991). A manual for the use of the Motivated Strategies for Learning Questionnaire (MSLQ). Ann Arbor, Michigan: University of Michigan.

Renaud, R.D. (1996). *Factorial Validity of Student Ratings of Instruction*. Unpublished M.A. thesis, London, ON: University of Western Ontario.

Renaud, R.D., and Murray, H.G. (2005). Factorial validity of student ratings of instruction. *Research in Higher Education* 46: 929–953.

Rodger, S.C. (2001). *Teacher Clarity and Student Anxiety: An Aptitude-Treatment Inter-action Experiment*. Unpublished doctoral dissertation, London, ON: University of Western Ontario.

Rodger, S., Murray, H.G., and Cummings, A.L. (2007). Effects of teacher clarity and student anxiety on student outcomes. *Teaching in Higher Education* 12: 91–104.

Spielberger, C.D., Gorsuch, R.L., and Lushene, R.E. (1970). *The State-trait Anxiety Test Manual*. Palo Alto, CA: Consulting Psychologists Press.

Smits, J.R. (2002). *Validity and Usefulness of a Low-Inference Student Evaluation of Teaching Questionnaire at the Secondary School Level*. Unpublished honours thesis, London, ON: University of Western Ontario.

Whitely, S., and Doyle, K.O. (1976). Implicit theories in student ratings. *American Educational Research Journal* 13: 241–253.

Worrell, F.C., and Kuterback, L.D. (2001). The use of student ratings of teacher behaviours with academically talented high school students. *Journal of Secondary Gifted Education* 14: 236–247.

7. TEACHERS' NONVERBAL BEHAVIOR AND ITS EFFECTS ON STUDENTS

Elisha Babad

Hebrew University of Jerusalem
elisha@VMS.HUJI.AC.IL

Abstract

This chapter presents the area of nonverbal (NV) behavior as it relates to teacher-student interaction, particularly in higher education. The first part covers research topics in NV psychology, the repertoire of NV behaviors, and topics of NV research pertinent to teaching. Microteaching is then discussed as a major application in teacher training involving NV behavior. The central part focuses on instructors' NV behavior and its effects on students. The "teacher enthusiasm" and "teacher immediacy" conceptualizations and research literatures are then discussed, wondering about their alienated isolation from each other, because both deal with the very same phenomenon of the contribution of instructors' NV enthusiasm to their teaching quality. Research on specifically-measured instructors' NV behaviors (opposed to global NV conduct as perceived by students) is then presented, demonstrating how thin slices (10 seconds) of teachers' NV behavior can predict student evaluations, and illuminating the NV profile of effective instructors

Key Words: Nonverbal (NV) behavior; NV psychology; teacher enthusiasm; teacher immediacy; Doctor Fox research; instructors' NV behavior; teachers' NV behavior; thin slices research; students' ratings of teaching (SRT); students' evaluations of teaching (SET); microteaching; teacher-student interaction; effective teaching; micro-analysis; NV profile of effective instructors

INTRODUCTION: IMPORTANCE OF NONVERBAL BEHAVIOR

We all live today in the era of the visual, of the nonverbal. People are continuously and excessively exposed to television, cinema and theater, and these media transmit a multitude of types and bits of information in nonverbal (NV) channels. From a young age children learn

R.P. Perry and J.C. Smart (eds.), The Scholarship of Teaching and Learning in Higher Education: An Evidence-Based Perspective, 201–261.
© 2007 *Springer.*

to understand the "NV language," to decipher implicit codes and to make meaning of social situations from numerous, often very subtle NV nuances (including lighting, camera angles, music, and certainly facial expressions and body language). People learn to understand situations without having to receive verbal explanations, such as knowing instantaneously whether they are provided with facts (news), told a story (movies or series) or being manipulated (advertising) the minute they turn on their TV. "NV behavior" includes all expressive aspects that are "non-verbal," that is, that they have no verbal content, words, or spoken and/or written language. NV research focuses on body language, facial expressions, gestures, postures, movements, vocal cues, attire, physical appearance, and behavioral patterns in interpersonal interaction.

The purpose of this chapter is to examine the area of NV behavior as it relates to higher education, and to focus particularly on the contributions of instructors' NV behavior to their teaching effectiveness. Commonsense would support the general notion that effective instructors are nonverbally expressive in addition to their verbal teaching qualities. But the extent, the unique impact, and the exclusivity of the NV aspects have been the grounds for much research and substantial controversy. In this chapter, I first provide some background information about NV research and its relevance to education. Subsequently I review the major conceptualizations, applications, and types of NV research in higher education, explicate methodological problems and overgeneralizations based on faulty research, and eventually lead to an up-to-date evaluation of the status and role of NV behavior in effective teaching.

In her review of NV behavior and self-presentation, Bella DePaulo (1992) described the special significance of NV behavior in several aspects: Its irrepressible nature, its links to emotion, its accessibility to observers, its speed, and the fact that it communicates unique meanings. To these factors, one can add the commonly-held belief that human deception can be detected through the examination of different NV channels – a belief that is borne out by a rich literature (e.g., Ekman, 1985; Ekman & Friesen, 1969b; Zuckerman, DePaulo, & Rosental, 1986). NV behavior simply exists and is enacted in almost every human situation, and therefore it is reasonable to assume that it is likely to influence the outcomes of human interactions of all kinds.

Therefore, NV behavior is part of the process of intended and/or unintended social influence, serving as a tool or a mediator toward the attainment of a wide spectrum of objectives. Some of these objectives are genuine, innocent and well-meaning, others might be devious, and some may be malicious. In education, students at all levels spend a huge number of cumulative hours with their teachers. The teachers have a clear agenda of influencing students and leading them to scholastic and cognitive attainments, but the students do not continuously share this agenda. Clearly, teachers' NV conduct must be meaningful in mediating the attainment of educational outcomes. Instructors' expressiveness can contribute to teaching effectiveness by maintaining student interest and preventing boredom; it may increase general or subject-specific student motivation as a function of instructor's enthusiasm; and it can often contribute directly to the quality of the verbal instruction through illustration and emphasis.

THE PSYCHOLOGY OF NV BEHAVIOR

RESEARCH TOPICS IN NV PSYCHOLOGY

Research on NV behavior grew out of the study of emotions and of the expression of emotions (dating back to Charles Darwin), and then expanded into social areas dealing with human communication, including the field of education. The central figure in NV psychology of emotions in the last half century has been Paul Ekman, who developed methods for identifying the basic human emotions in facial expressions, dealt with deception, detection and leakage, and has led research on NV behavior both conceptually and methodologically.

In their review of NV research in the fourth edition of the Handbook of Social Psychology, DePaulo and Friedman (1998) summarized the central research topics in contemporary NV psychology. The topics include person perception and personality judgments based on NV sensitivity; NV aspects in self-presentation (such as the expression of personal charisma and other attributes); the study of deception and detection of lying (either through leakage of false affect through people's differential ability to control the various NV channels, or through exaggeration); social influence and attempts to manipulate impressions (by politicians, for instance); NV aspects involved in interpersonal attraction; and the communication of interpersonal expectations (by judges, doctors, and of course teachers). Tests measuring sensitivity in NV decoding ability (by Rosenthal et al., 1979, and by Archer & Costanzo, 1988, see also Costanzo & Archer, 1993) led to a multitude of studies on NV behavior in different contexts, and to the development of applied practice to improve NV skills.

THE REPERTOIRE OF NV BEHAVIORS (EKMAN & FRIESEN, 1969A)

In a now-classic article, Ekman and Friesen (1969a) introduced and analyzed the five major types of NV behavior, laying the conceptual foundation for subsequent research on NV behavior. The five types are: Emblems; Illustrators; Affect displays; Regulators; and Adaptors, and they are delineated next, emphasizing their relevance to education when appropriate.

Emblems are "complete" NV acts that have a direct, clear and shared meaning, which usually has a verbal definition consisting of one or two words or a phrase. They are communicated intentionally and are meant to transmit a clear message or shared meaning. Examples of emblems include making a fist and various obscene or sexual gestures. The shared decoded meaning of emblems is either iconic or consensual (like pointing a figure at the temple to indicate confusion or the consensual emblems of sign language). Emblems are communicative and parsimonious, because they are complete, summative, consensual statements. Teachers often use emblems in providing explanations and in their interactions with students, although I did not come across any empirical study of teachers' emblems.

Illustrators are movements tied to speech, serving to illustrate what is being said verbally. They are learned with a communicative intent of emphasizing intended messages. Sometimes illustrators are emblems (though not always complete messages) and at other times they are facial affect displays (see next), and they are always intended to improve communication through illustration and amplification. Effective teachers use NV illustrators continuously, and this use is an important aspect of their effectiveness. In training for public speaking and in microteaching (see later discussion) people are taught and trained to use illustrators.

Affects displays are the movements of the facial muscles expressing the primary emotions. According to Ekman and Friesen, each of the primary emotions (happiness, surprise, fear, sadness, anger, disgust, and interest) has unique, distinctive movements of the facial muscles, and they are universal to the human race. Ekman developed coding systems (FAST and then FACS – Facial Action Coding System, see Ekman & Friesen, 1978) to code and quantify each emotion, and has led since then a wide field of the study of emotions and clinical applications. Later, Ekman also defined "display rules" – procedures for the management of affect displays in various social settings (when to over-intensify and when to de-intensify, when to emphasize and when

204

to conceal). Affect displays are extremely informative and influential, but they are not deliberate and do not have a communicative intent as emblems and illustrators. Affect displays can be consonant or dissonant with verbal messages, and much of the study of deception is based on affect displays and on gaps between channels. In education, teachers are supposed to be nonverbally expressive, and their genuine affect displays probably act as mediators in fostering student motivation and learning. Unfortunately, affect displays also play a crucial role in the transmission of teachers' negative expectancies, potentially hindering low-expectancy students.

Regulators are NV acts intended to regulate the back and forth interaction and control the behavior of the other(s). Examples of regulators include head nods, eye contact, slight movements forward or backward, eyebrow raising, hand movements, etc. Regulators do not have a universal content and they are not necessarily deliberate or intentional. Affective displays, illustrators or adaptors (next) can function as regulators. In education, regulators are critical in classroom management and in teacher-student interaction.

Adaptors are anti-communicative, transmitting that the person is busy with him/herself and his/her own needs, and is not attentive to the other. Examples of adaptors include self-referent behaviors such as grooming, nail-biting, head-scratching, fidgeting with self (self-touching) or with object (pencils, glasses, watch, etc.). Adaptors are directed "inside," toward the self and away from the other. In NV research, adaptors would usually found to be negative predictors, contributing to negative impressions and leading to negative reactions. People in interaction would usually prefer to ignore the adaptors of the other person, and preferably, not to be aware of them at all.

CATEGORIES OF NV RESEARCH PERTINENT TO TEACHING (SMITH, 1984)

In an article summarizing the state of the art of NV behavior in teaching, Howard Smith (1984, following Knapp, 1978) listed seven categories of NV research pertinent to teaching and learning. Although Smith did not refer particularly to higher education while most of the research discussed in the present chapter has been conducted after 1984 and was focused on higher education, the Smith categories are still helpful in the classification of NV research types at all levels of education.

Environmental factors involve the influence of the physical attributes and of school and classroom setting on students. The design and physical characteristics of the school, the arrangement of the classroom and the seating arrangement create the milieu and the atmosphere for learning. Today, such environmental factors would not be considered as representing "NV research" but would rather be classified as "environmental psychology."

Proxemics concerns the perception and use of personal space. The physical distance between teacher and students, the seating of students facing each other or seated in rows and columns, and the implicit norms concerning proxemics influence the learning climate and the nature of teacher-student interaction. In seating arrangement research, evidence shows that the most positive student attitudes and their best academic efforts are observed in the "activity zone" in the center of the classroom, close to the teacher (Moore & Glynn, 1984). Today, one of the most influential conceptions relating NV behavior and educational outcomes – "NV immediacy" – is defined by the "psychological closeness" between the teacher and the students.

Kinesics is probably the central category of NV behavior – including gestures, facial expressions, posture and body language, actually the entire range of expressive behavior. The study of instructor expressiveness and its relation to teaching effectiveness is the central theme of this chapter.

Touching behavior (also called haptics). In fact, educational research on touching behavior is quite rare. Although caring about children (and taking care of them) often includes touching, the issue of teachers touching students is a bit touchy and wrought with ethical limitations. Therefore, touching behavior would not be considered a major category of educational NV research today.

Physical characteristics of teachers and students, and *artifacts* are two Smith categories focusing on physical attractiveness and appearance, on clothes, jewelry, beauty aids and their influence on the perceivers. Frankly, it seems that not much educational research has focused on these features.

Paralanguage refers to the NV characteristics accompanying speech, such as voice pitch, volume, tempo, intensity, pauses, silences, etc. Today, research on instructors' enthusiasm and immediacy employs a global approach to the overall conduct of the instructor, including verbal behavior and the NV characteristics which accompany it. The total NV style of the teacher is considered to be a central mediator of teaching effectiveness, and teachers' paralanguage (which could represent illustrators, affect displays and regulators in Ekman and Friesen's terminology) is quite important.

PERSPECTIVES ON THE ROLE OF NV BEHAVIOR IN EDUCATION

THE SECONDARY ROLE OF NV BEHAVIOR IN EDUCATION

The origins of NV research are rooted in the study of emotions, and over the years it expanded to many fields focused on communication, including education. But given that the central objectives of schooling are cognitive development and scholastic achievement, it is then the *verbal* domain that is most significant in education, and NV research must take a secondary position. Beyond the curriculum, subject matter, didactic methods, cognitive strategies, and a host of other factors supposed to facilitate students' learning, instructors' NV behavior is important in the *delivery* of instruction and in the management of teacher-student interaction. As a mediator in the success of the verbal domain in achieving the central goals of education, NV behavior can be quite detrimental to teaching effectiveness. Bad instructors most often fail in their NV delivery, and excellence in teaching is probably due to a large extent to instructors' positive expressive style.

Thus, the main focus of NV research in education is on the instructors and their delivery of instruction, secondary to subject-matter concerns and didactic methods. Delivery of instruction has been the central focus of two separate conceptualizations and separate bodies of literature – "teacher enthusiasm" and "teacher immediacy." Both approaches are discussed in detail in this chapter, and it is argued that they investigate the very same phenomenon despite the distinct terminologies. Both phenomena focus on teacher expressiveness which is considered to contribute to creating the motivational and affective conditions that improve students' coping with learning materials and facilitate their learning and cognitive gains.

The goals of education might be construed in a wider perspective than cognitive learning, to include students' satisfaction, motivation and involvement as important objectives in their own right, not just as means for improving learning. In this broader perspective, the contribution of instructors' NV behavior becomes more central and more direct.

OVERALL "NV STYLE" VERSUS SPECIFIC "NV BEHAVIORS"

In educational research, the commonly-used definition of "NV behavior" is very global and generalized. At the other end of the specificity continuum, in Ekman's study of emotions, each emotion is defined by a particular profile of more than 40 facial muscles and characteristics. Similarly, in microanalysis, the method designed to trace specific NV behaviors contributing to global impressions (see later section on "Microanalysis"), dozens of specific NV behaviors are examined. And, in deception research, behavior is broken into different NV channels. In contrast, most of the NV research in higher education is focused on a single generalized concept (positive impression, enthusiastic, immediate, etc.) that sums up a host of specific variables. In fact, that generalized concept of overall style might include verbal behavior as well (e.g., use of humor), as long as the verbal content does not constitute of actual subject matter instructional material and is limited to the expressive domain. Thus, much of NV research in higher education is focused on generalized expressive style archetypes with no analysis of specific NV behaviors and their unique impact on students. I believe that a more exacting analysis of specific components of NV style has greater methodological and scientific value *and* greater potential applicability.

DISPARITY BETWEEN COLLEGE ENVIRONMENT AND ELEMENTARY/HIGH SCHOOL ENVIRONMENT

Because this chapter is almost exclusively focused on higher education, it is important to explicate the differences between the college and university environment on the one hand, and the elementary and high school classroom on the other hand, especially as far as research on NV behavior is concerned. The social nature and the organizational characteristics of the classroom and the role of the teacher/instructor differ considerably between the two settings. Therefore, the spectrum of (NV-related) issues relevant to higher education is more limited compared to school settings, and much of the NV research in elementary and high schools is mostly irrelevant to higher education.

Higher education is usually voluntary, the students are older and more mature, and they study the topics of their choice (indeed, some required, compulsory introductory courses in college are characterized as having "a high school atmosphere"). Instructors in higher education enjoy a higher status, they are almost totally exempt from administrative and classroom management duties, and they have to take a punitive stance very rarely. Their interaction with the students is less intense and looser than in the elementary and high school levels, and their role is almost exclusively focused on teaching their subject matter and field of expertise. In a way, the sense of coercion that often characterizes elementary schools and high schools is not felt in higher education, and it is less normative for college students to hate school. Finally, the average intellectual level of students in higher education is higher than in most public elementary and high schools, owing to the selective process, and most college and university classes are less heterogeneous than elementary and high school classes.

Therefore, NV research related to teachers' conduct in managing their classrooms and dealing with discipline problems is almost irrelevant to higher education. Moreover, the wide area of teachers' differential behavior (Babad, 1993) and the NV communication of teacher expectancies (Harris & Rosenthal, 1985, 2005) – a highly significant steppingstone in the development of NV research in elementary and high school education – is largely irrelevant to higher education. I might add that the standard questionnaires measuring college students' evaluations of their instructors – the dependent variables reflecting teaching effectiveness in research to be reviewed later in this chapter and a central focus of this entire book – are inappropriate for use with elementary and high school students in their conventional form.

MICROTEACHING – A MAJOR APPLICATION INVOLVING NV BEHAVIOR

Microteaching (MT) is the best known applied educational intervention involving NV behavior. The development of MT was not based on empirical research nor on a particular educational theory (although it might have been conceptually connected to the phenomenon of observational learning which evoked much attention in the early 1960s, see Bandura, 1977). MT followed the advances in video recording technology in the 1960s, when it became possible to videotape teaching sessions of sufficiently good technical quality without needing VCR experts and studios. Enthusiasm about it was probably fueled by the advances made in the 1960s in group-based methods of skill training within the (then growing) human relations movement. MT was developed by Dwight Allen and his colleagues at the Stanford University Teacher Education Program, and its popularity spread very quickly as a major intervention in teacher development and in teaching improvement programs worldwide (Allen & Ryan, 1969; Brown, 1975; Perrott, 1977). Today, it seems that the over-enthusiasm of the 1970s about MT has subsided somewhat (perhaps together with the decline of the group dynamics movement), and most practitioners now take a more realistic view of its potential for increasing teaching effectiveness. However, almost every teacher had participated at least once in a MT feedback session and examined her/his NV behavior in delivering instruction and interacting with students.

MT is essentially a data-based feedback intervention for teachers' self-inquiry ("reflection") and skills training. A teaching session is videotaped in a classroom or in a studio and the recording serves as raw "empirical" data. The recorded material constitutes the most complete coverage of all aspects of the teaching situation, and it provides the most reliable and unbiased evidence of teacher behavior (unlike supervisor's observation or self-report). In the MT training session, the videotaped material is viewed together by the videotaped teacher, the supervisor, and often by the teacher's peers as well, and the teacher receives personal feedback and supervision. The analysis of the videotaped data can take many forms, from open impressionistic discussion to more exacting analyses of pre-selected aspects. Statistical treatment of operationally defined and measured variables might be included as well.

MT was not intended initially to focus particularly on NV aspects, but was conceived as a general tool for the development of effective instruction. Undoubtedly, the analysis of the fully reconstructed verbal material and contentual flow of instruction is highly important, and much (if not most) work in MT sessions is focused on the (verbal) didactic aspects. Still, MT gained significance in the NV domain because of the unique power of the visual aspect. People are very excited to see themselves videotaped, and it seems that they are quite willing to receive feedback and constructive advice when the visual evidence of the finest nuances of their NV behavior can be seen in the recording. I would venture to say that most people show more readiness to be dissatisfied with themselves and to be less defensive when they are confronted with the videotaped evidence.

Therefore, the potential contribution of MT to the issue of NV behavior in instruction became significant several decades before researchers have begun to conduct systematic empirical research on teachers' NV behavior in the classroom. Long before the formulation of theoretical conceptions about teacher enthusiasm and teacher immediacy, it was clear that teachers' trainers and tutors had clear implicit (or explicit) theories about the role of teachers' NV behaviors in instruction and about the potential contribution of NV conduct to teaching effectiveness. The image of the successful teacher always included numerous NV aspects, and the evidence in the VCR recording made it possible to analyze each aspect and to provide teachers with corrective feedback (which could be examined in subsequent recordings).

Thus, MT highlights the role of NV behavior in teaching, and provides opportunities to include NV behavior in teacher training and in teaching improvement programs through "data-based" (however loosely defined) corrective feedback and supervision. Still, the basic problem was that the objective data exists in the videotaped pictures, but the interpretation of these data by supervisors and peers has been largely intuitive, not based on research and on valid findings showing systematic relationships between specific NV behaviors and defined educational outcomes.

TEACHER ENTHUSIASM IN HIGHER EDUCATION

Suppose we were interested in teaching excellence, and we would want to find out whether excellent (or good, or effective, or successful) teachers have in common behavioral characteristics that distinguish them from non-excellent or less successful teachers (see Theall and Feldman's chapter in this book). To find the answer, we would have to measure various behavioral characteristics of the teachers, to independently assess their success or effectiveness, and then to explore the relationships between the two measured clusters. Perhaps teaching excellence is expressed in unique, idiographic profiles, and no systematic differences would be found between the two groups of teachers, but it stands to reason that consistent differences would be found. Probably many, if not most of the behavioral correlates of teaching excellence would be verbal (e.g., giving clear explanation of terms and concepts, asking answerable questions, providing succinct overview and summary, etc.), but some correlates would be nonverbal (smiling, gesturing, showing enthusiasm, etc.), and still other predictors would be "organizational" (using a variety of media, access to students, structuring course assignments, etc.).

In a seminal study on teacher expressiveness and its relation to teaching effectiveness, Harry Murray (1983a) asked the question posed above, and examined it on a sample of 54 Canadian university professors. They were divided into three teaching effectiveness groups (high, medium, and low) according to averaged students' ratings of these instructors (SRT) in past courses. Each instructor was observed for 18–24 hours over a period of three months, and judges rated their behaviors on the 60-item Teacher Behavior Inventory. The Inventory included items in the following domains: Speech, NV behavior, explanation, organization, interest, task orientation, rapport, and participation. All items represented low inference measurement, describing specific, measurable behaviors, and they were summarized for each instructor for all observations of all judges.

Of the 60 behaviors, 26 showed significant differences among the low, medium and high SRT groups (see Murray's chapter in this book). The five teaching behaviors showing the largest differences were: (1) Speaks expressively or emphatically; (2) Shows strong interest in subject; (3) Moves about while lecturing; (4) Uses humor; and (5) Shows facial expressions. Murray saw these behaviors as communicating enthusiasm for the subject matter and thereby eliciting and maintaining student attention to lecture material. Factor analysis of the ratings yielded nine interpretable factors (Clarity; Enthusiasm; Interaction; Task orientation; Rapport; Organization; Use of media; Pacing; and Speech), and mean factor scores were computed. Three of the factors yielded substantial differences between the three groups of instructors – clarity, enthusiasm, and rapport.

On the basis of these results (Murray, 1983a), teacher enthusiasm was defined as consisting of the following expressive teaching behaviors (Wood, 1998):

1. Speaking in a dramatic or expressive way,
2. Variation in pitch and volume,
3. Vocal inflection,
4. Smiling or laughing while teaching,
5. Moving about while lecturing,
6. Gesturing with hands or arms,
7. Exhibiting facial gestures or expressions,
8. Eye contact,
9. Humor

Except for humor, which should be classified as a verbal behavior, all characteristics of teacher enthusiasm are NV. [The behavioral operational definition of instructor expressiveness used by Perry, Abrami, & Leventhal (1979, see later discussion of the Doctor Fox phenomenon) was virtually identical, defined as voice intonation (items 1–3 above, physical movement (items 4–7), eye contact, and content-relevant humor].

During the same year, Murray (1983b) published a second study which complemented the previous study by examining the relationship between instructor enthusiasm and students' actual learning outcomes.

In the 1983a study – as in most studies on NV behavior in education – educational outcomes were measured by students' self-reported evaluations of their instructors and of their own learning. Under ideal conditions, strong, valid, objective measures of learning and achievement are preferable to students' subjective self-reports, but such outcomes are hard to obtain in most studies.

Murray (1983b) focused his study on 36 instructors who taught sections of a multi-section introductory psychology course over a period of five years. The sample included 2,500 students who were randomly assigned to 10–15 sections per year. The same textbook, the same exam, and the same teacher and course evaluation forms were used in all sections, making it possible to include in the teaching effectiveness cluster SRT indices, students' achievement, and student motivation (self-reported amount of studying, and subsequent registration in senior psychology courses). The low-inference teaching behaviors of the 36 instructors were measured again by behavioral observations in the classrooms, using a 100-item version of the Teacher Behavior Inventory. Enthusiastic teaching behaviors based on the classroom observations correlated highly with SRT (for instructor rating, $r = .72$; for course rating, $r = .57$), with subsequent course registration ($r = .45$), *and* with final exam performance ($r = .36$). Thus, instructor enthusiasm was strongly related to students' evaluations of their instructors, and to a lesser extent but still demonstrating a very substantial effect, to actual student learning outcomes.

METHODOLOGICAL NOTE: MURRAY'S 1983 STUDIES AS MODEL RESEARCH

I chose to present Murray's two 1983 studies in great detail instead of covering many more studies about teacher enthusiasm in lesser detail. The reason is that I consider Murray's studies to be of special quality, with an excellent treatment of a host of issues, each of which constitutes a special problem in research on NV behavior in higher education.

1. Both studies were naturalistic field studies, with no unnatural manipulation or fabrication of NV behavior. As field studies, they were well-controlled and very strict methodologically. Many other studies were equally well-controlled and used strict methodology (see, for example, Perry et al., 1979; and Abrami, Leventhal, & Perry, 1982), but they used staged teaching simulations rather than naturally-occurring instructor behavior (see critique of the Doctor Fox studies in this chapter).

213

2. Murray used different measurement methods (SRTs by past students, behavioral observations, and exam performance of current students) coming from different sources. In too many studies, all data (on NV behavior and educational outcomes) consist of subjective self-reports of the same body of participating students.

3. Teachers' effectiveness/excellence was determined on the basis of averaged SRTs in all past courses (1983a).

4. NV behavior was measured by low inference, specific behaviors.

5. NV behavior was measured via behavioral observations made by trained observers. Instructor's score for each behavior was based on multiple observations, and therefore was of high validity.

6. The number of specific behaviors measured was very large (60 behaviors in 1983a, 100 behaviors in 1983b) and varied among different verbal and NV domains. Because the entire range of possible teacher behaviors was covered, the emergence of NV behaviors as most influential was doubly impressive and convincing. Many current studies focus exclusively on a narrow range of NV behaviors only.

7. In the 1983b study, the use of a multi-section course made it possible to obtain a credible evaluation of students' learning via exam performance. As will be seen later, the problems is assessing cognitive learning in NV research in higher education are almost insurmountable.

For all these reasons, I consider these studies to be "model research," and feel confident in their results.

Wood (1998) summarized a body of research on instructor enthusiasm, and the results seem to be consistent across research varieties and variations. Enthusiastic instructors seem to be more positively appreciated by their students, considered by students to have contributed to better learning outcomes, and to produce higher levels of student motivation and learning than non-enthusiastic instructors. The varieties of studies included field experiments, where instructor enthusiasm was manipulated in actual classrooms; laboratory studies conducted in artificial "classrooms;" studies focused on specific NV behaviors such as eye contact, voice intonation, and body movements and gestures; and studies measuring the effects of training programs to increase instructors' expressiveness and enthusiasm in their classrooms. Results are very consistent, and the same patterns of relations between instructor behavior and educational outcomes are repeatedly reported. Perry and his associates (Perry & Magnuson, 1987; Perry & Penner, 1990; Schonwetter, Perry, & Struthers, 1994) added a student dimension – perceived control – and demonstrated that achievement enhancing effects of instructor enthusiasm were found more strongly when students felt a sense of control over learning outcomes than when students felt helpless.

It seems reasonable to conclude that being nonverbally expressive is an important dimension of good teaching. Effective instructors show great interest and enthusiasm about their subject, they teach in a provocative and stimulating style, they use their faces, bodies, and voices to attract students' learning, and they take efforts to involve the students in the learning process. The common conceptual explanations of the effects of instructor enthusiasm on educational outcomes emphasize: (a) increased student motivation to learn better and to expand their learning, and (b) selective attention, enthusiastic instructor behavior serving an attention-getting role through the aroused interest and constant change in the classroom.

Wood (1998) conducted a laboratory experiment in a simulated, artificial classroom, comparing a low enthusiasm condition to three high enthusiasm conditions – strategic (coordinated with the topic structure and contingent with teaching goals), random, and uniform. Her results showed that instructor enthusiasm produced significant effects on student motivation, student attention, and student memory encoding. Strategic/contingent high enthusiasm produced the most positive outcomes. [See my later critique of experimental manipulations in NV research. Although I do not contest Wood's specific results, I have grave doubts about the appropriateness of fabricated experimental conditions in research involving NV behaviors].

THE DOCTOR FOX PHENOMENON

The "Doctor Fox" effect originates in the strong relation between instructor enthusiasm and teaching effectiveness. (Although the first Dr. Fox study preceded the above mentioned studies on instructor enthusiasm mentioned above, the belief about the expressiveness-effectiveness link has been common folklore). Specifically, this association raises the question whether the connection between expressiveness and other aspects contributing to instructional gains in good teaching is inherent, or conversely whether high expressivity might create an illusion of learning. In every university department one may find highly expressive instructors, admired and valued by their students

215

much more than by their colleagues. This question receives an extra impetus when teaching effectiveness – which can carry substantial weight in hiring and promotion procedures – is determined by student evaluations (SRT).

Naftulin, Ware, & Donnelly (1973) introduced "Dr. Myron L. Fox" to lecture to an audience of educators and mental health graduate students. He was actually a professional actor, and delivered his lecture in a charismatic, entertaining and highly expressive style, but the lecture was devoid of any meaningful content. Dr. Fox received surprisingly high evaluations from his audience. Naftulin et al. (1973) concluded that an instructor's charisma, wit, and expressive style can seduce students into the illusion of having learned.

The Doctor Fox study was widely cited, considered as a threat to the validity of SRT as a measure of teaching effectiveness. The controversy led many researchers – supporters and opponents – to conduct Doctor Fox studies over a span of two decades. In light of methodological and design criticisms of the 1973 study, Ware and Williams (1975) published a "corrected" Doctor Fox study, using a 2X3 factorial design, with two levels of teacher enthusiasm and three levels of lecture content amount. Students viewed one of the six 20-minute videotaped lectures, and subsequently filled out teacher evaluation forms (SRTs) and completed an achievement test on the content of the lecture. Ware and Williams found that students learned more and rated the instructor more favorably as a function of both instructor expressiveness and amount of content, with extremely high student ratings for the high-expressive instructor. They also reported an interaction effect, where for low expressiveness, high content produced higher student ratings than low content, but for high expressiveness, content did not affect the (high) student ratings. Ware and Williams suggested that SRT should not be used for faculty tenure and promotion decisions, because charismatic and enthusiastic instructors may receive high students' ratings regardless of how much their students learn.

Subsequently, Raymond Perry and his associates replicated the Doctor Fox study with several additional conditions at the University of Manitoba (Perry et al., 1979), and Marsh and Ware (1982) reanalyzed the data of the Ware and Williams study, concluding that the findings did not constitute a threat to the validity of SRT. Abrami et al., (1982) eventually published an article entitled "Educational seduction," in which they meta-analyzed a dozen Doctor Fox studies. They concluded that instructor expressiveness had a substantial impact on student ratings but a small impact on student achievement. In contrast, lecture content had a substantial impact on student achievement but a small impact on student ratings.

The Doctor Fox studies can be viewed from the perspective of NV research or from the perspective of SRT research. NV researchers would not have any problem accepting evidence indicating that instructor enthusiasm and charisma would lead students to report higher satisfaction with their teachers and even report better learning. NV researchers would also accept the proposition that subjective self reports about learning would be higher than empirical test findings on actual learning. Such findings are in line with the findings of the instructor enthusiasm studies reported earlier. It makes sense to view enthusiasm as a critical factor of effective teaching, contributing to student motivation and attention. In contrast, such findings would be more problematic in the SRT perspective because the stronger the effect of instructor enthusiasm independent of organizational and academic characteristics of instruction, the less one can trust SRT as a measure of teaching effectiveness. SRT advocates would probably reject the notion that student ratings may reflect only student satisfaction and enjoyment without necessarily assessing the quality and effectiveness of the actual scholastic teaching.

Today, following the various methodological and design criticisms and in light of the numerous studies that examined Doctor Fox effects under various reality conditions (see Perry et al., 1979 and Abrami et al., 1982), the original Doctor Fox argument is consensually rejected. Under reality conditions in regular university courses, it is not likely that a charismatic and entertaining instructor would receive high course evaluations if the presentation was devoid of any intellectual input and learning content. But some doubt may still linger that over-expressiveness might blind students somewhat for a certain period of time.

METHODOLOGICAL NOTE: EXPERIMENTAL MANIPULATION OF NV BEHAVIOR IS FAULTY

Much has been written and debated about the Doctor Fox effect, and there is no point in going into additional statistical discussions and arguments. However, these studies have not been examined from the perspective of NV research, and I believe that, from this unique perspective, the Doctor Fox design, as well as many other experimental studies manipulating instructors' NV expressive behavior is faulty and lacking in ecological validity.

In psychological research, experimentation is considered the best methodological solution for isolating variables and for examining a causal effect of one variable while controlling other variables. Experiments are usually conducted in artificial, simulated situations to ensure control that cannot be attained under field conditions. The relevant independent variables are operationally defined and manipulated in certain variations to experimental and control groups, and their "clean" impact on dependent variables is measured. But experimental results can be generalized beyond the specific simulated context only if the experimental situation can represent the "reality" of the investigated phenomenon in the field. Thus, the experiment must be unbiased and have high ecological validity. My argument is that, these demands can almost never be met in experiments on manipulated NV behavior (in Doctor Fox studies and in numerous other experiments) and therefore the experimental method is very problematic in educational NV research. [Perry et al. (1979) also reported that in the more ecological conditions, most closely approximating actual classrooms, the Doctor Fox effect was not replicated].

1. In the controlled experiments on teachers' NV behavior, students usually view a short video lesson on an unknown topic, and subsequently fill out teacher evaluations and sometimes also take a test on the lecture content. This presumably represents regular teaching throughout a university term (say, a 3-months semester). The student evaluations, as well as their achievements, are supposedly equivalent to those obtained in a regular university course. These assumptions can hardly be justified. The experimental situation is highly unusual and out of routine for the students in almost every aspect and it cannot be considered as representative of their normal student experience. Conventional SRTs are based on a long accumulation of continuous exposure to the instructors, including the variations in instructor behavior over time and exposure to rare, infrequent incidents that take place during the semester (see Babad, 2005a). Student achievement reflects a continuous, developing process that is also influenced by their motivation and diligence, and is not a one-shot simple occurrence. Thus, the experimental situation simply cannot be considered to represent the educational situation in which students achievements and evaluations of teaching are formed.

2. The NV behavior manipulated in the experimental videos is extremely exaggerated. Most students would never encounter

teachers who are so expressive and enthusiastic or so phleg-matic and dry as those depicted in such experiments. And if such rare teachers would have demonstrated such extreme behaviors continuously in the classroom for weeks (especially if they talk nonsense and teach nothing) – they would have been criticized rather than praised. The issue of internal validity is important, and the extreme low/high enthusiasm shows have no ecological validity. Students are certainly aware of the exaggeration (especially since this is conducted in an unnatural setting), and this must influence their reactions.

3. From the field studies (such as Murray's) and from the natural intuition of most educators, it is quite obvious that there is a natural covariation between expressive behavior and cognitive components in teaching, and effective instruction is based on a combination of both. This covariation is probably the underlying information processing scheme ("implicit corre-lation") employed by students when they are asked to evaluate their instructors. Their belief that instructor expressiveness and enthusiasm are part of effective teaching is, to a large extent, "truth" rather than bias. The artificial experimental attempt to separate the affective and cognitive components (an enthusi-astic instructor talking nonsense) violates the natural covari-ation and students' internal scheme. Because they are not aware of that, they would continue using their underlying scheme, attributing high learning gains to Doctor Fox. In reality, highly enthusiastic instructors who do not teach anything are quite rare, but when students discover such an instructor along the semester, they will probably allow an exception to their scheme and judge that instructor harshly.

4. The last point emphasizes the unique nature of NV behavior. As mentioned earlier, one of the central topics in NV research concerns detection of deception. A very extensive body of research confirms that the detection of lying and deception through NV behavior is far more effective than detection via verbal means. People have keen awareness to successfully trace deceptive affective messages through NV behavior (Ekman, 1985; Zuckerman, DePaulo, & Rosental, 1986), and students have an uncanny ability as "experts" to decipher hidden messages in teachers' NV behavior (Babad, 2005b). As Zuckerman et al. (1986) pointed out, exagger-ation is an important key to detection of deception. The

instructor expressive behavior manipulated in the experiments under discussion (highly enthusiastic versus blatantly non-enthusiastic teaching) is fabricated and unreal – especially when the same actor enacts both conditions. Obviously at least one of the behavioral patterns (or both, because of the necessary exaggeration) is unnatural to the actor. Therefore, the NV behavior in these experiments is deceptive, and likely to be detected as such by the students. I think that these NV situations cannot be considered as representing natural teaching, and the results of these experiments cannot be considered valid. In my own research, I have always taken extreme care to use in experimental conditions only recorded videotapes of naturally occurring NV behavior.

TEACHER IMMEDIACY IN HIGHER EDUCATION

Since the end of the 1970s, the majority of NV research in higher education was conducted in the field of "teacher immediacy." The bulk of instructor enthusiasm research originated in Psychology Departments in Canada, mostly at the University of Western Ontario and the University of Manitoba. Teacher immediacy research evolved in the Communication Department in West Virginia University by James McCroskey, Virginia Richmond and over a dozen doctoral students, headed by Janet Andersen, who actually "opened" this field in her dissertation. Most articles on teacher immediacy were published throughout the years in one journal – Communication Education.

As will be argued, the fields of teacher enthusiasm and teacher immediacy have strong conceptual and methodological affinity. Both present a holistic, global view of NV style, focusing on the integrated NV picture of instructor style in delivering instruction rather than on specific NV behaviors. Harris and Rosenthal (2005) saw an advantage in operationalizing NV behavior holistically because NV behaviors do not occur in isolation, and all behaviors are interpreted in a larger reality context. But they also saw a disadvantage in the holistic approach, because it is impossible to determine which discrete NV cues play a role in affecting student outcomes.

Teacher immediacy research began with Janet Andersen's (1978) doctoral dissertation under the supervision of James McCroskey. As McCroskey and Richmond (1992) described it, Andersen was searching for a conceptual structure to identify teachers' behaviors associated with effective instruction. She was influenced by Mehrabian (1969,

220

1971), who defined "immediacy" as the degree of physical or psychological closeness between people, expressed in positive affect and liking toward the other. Andersen took Mehrabian's idea and conceptualized "teacher immediacy" as instructors' NV behaviors that enhance closeness and interaction, positing that this is the major mechanism mediating teaching effectiveness. From my reading of the literature, it seems that Andersen did not continue working on teacher immediacy after the early 1980s, and McCroskey and Richmond continued developing and leading this field.

Andersen (1978, 1979) developed an observational methodology for measuring instructor immediacy (Behavioral Indicants of Immediacy), and found that observers' ratings of the specific NV behaviors correlated highly with ratings of students in the targeted courses. This opened the way to proceed to measure teacher immediacy exclusively by students' self-reported ratings of specific (low inference) instructor behaviors, dropping the expensive and cumbersome methodology of classroom observation. Andersen's initial findings showed that approximately 20% of the variance in student affect toward the subject matter, 46% of the variance in student affect toward the instructor, and 18% of the variance in motivation to take advanced courses in the area were predictable from instructors' scores on nonverbal immediacy (NVI). Students' test scores, which would have indicated cognitive learning, were not predictable from teachers' NVI scores.

In a doctoral dissertation conducted in the same department, Sorensen (1980) developed a measure of verbal immediacy, focused on instructors' self-disclosing statements and "we" statements. As had been expected, verbal and nonverbal immediacy were related to each other. However, most studies measured NVI exclusively, and Witt and Wheeless (2001), who compared predictions of educational outcomes from verbal and nonverbal immediacy, reported that verbal immediacy did not add much to the picture derived from measurement of NVI. In this chapter, the discussion centers on NVI.

The commonly-used NVI questionnaire (Richmond, Gorham, & McCroskey, 1987) consists of 14 items, six of them reversed in scoring:

1. Sits behind desk when teaching. (R)
2. Gestures when talking to the class.
3. Uses monotone/dull voice when talking to the class. (R)
4. Looks at the class when talking.
5. Smiles at the class as a whole, not just at individual students.
6. Has a very tense body position when talking to the class. (R)
7. Touches students in the class.

8. Moves around the classroom when teaching.
9. Sits on a desk or in a chair when teaching. (R)
10. Looks at board or notes when talking to the class. (R)
11. Stands behind podium or desk when talking to the class. (R)
12. Has a very relaxed body position when talking to the class.
13. Smiles at individual students in the class.
14. Uses a variety of vocal expressions when talking to the class.

Users of the 14-item NVI questionnaire found that some items were poor.

McCroskey, Sallinen, Fayer, Richmond, and Barraclough (1996) explained that college instructors virtually never touch their students (and therefore item # 7 was dropped), and that neither sitting nor standing while teaching is a reliable predictor of NVI (and therefore items # 1, 9, and 11 were dropped). Thus, NVI was measured in almost all studies by either the 10-item or the 14-item questionnaire.

METHODOLOGICAL/CONCEPTUAL NOTE: TWO CONCEPTIONS, TWO BODIES OF LITERATURE, BUT ONLY ONE PHENOMENON!

As I was covering the research literature on NV behavior in higher education, I was struck by the duality of the "enthusiasm" and "immediacy" literatures. The two bodies of research investigate the very same phenomenon and reach very similar conclusions, and yet they demonstrate total denial of each other, and one is not mentioned nor referred to in the other. For example, Wood's (1998) doctoral dissertation on teacher enthusiasm, with its extensive coverage of the relevant literature, had only *one* (marginal) reference to a teacher immediacy article among almost 100 items on her reference list! The situation is similar in all early and recent publications about immediacy. Could the amazing mutual denial between the two groups have been caused by faulty literature searches?

Murray's research originated from the SRT literature and was anchored in it. He searched for relevant instructor behaviors that would predict differences among low, medium, and highly-rated instructors, and discovered the cluster of NV behaviors he labeled "teacher enthusiasm." The West Virginia group started with a behavioral definition borrowed from Mehrabian, and then set out to construct outcome measures. In fact, immediacy researchers seldom made use of post-course SRT, preferring students' immediate self-report about their learning.

Presumably, the two literatures focus on distinct aspects in the delivery of instruction – "enthusiasm" would seem to emphasize instructors' expressive style in teaching their subject matter, whereas "immediacy" would seem to center on instructor-student interaction and closeness. However, scrutiny of the specific items which operationally define enthusiasm and immediacy demonstrates beyond doubt that the two instruments measure the very same phenomenon. Moreover, the above-listed items of the immediacy questionnaire could be condensed into the four behavioral components specified by Perry et al. (1979). To demonstrate the identity of the enthusiasm and immediacy questionnaires, the 10 items of the NVI questionnaire are listed next, showing for each item its equivalent in the list of behaviors defining teacher enthusiasm.

> *Item # 2*: Gestures when talking to the class. This item is equivalent to item # 6 (gesturing with hands and arms) and item # 7 (facial gestures or expressions) on the enthusiasm list.
>
> *Item # 3*: Monotone/dull voice (reversed item). Equivalent to item # 2 (pitch and volume variation) and item # 3 (vocal inflection) on the enthusiasm list.
>
> *Item # 4*: Looks at the class. Equivalent to item # 8 (eye contact).
>
> *Item # 5*: Smiles at the class as a whole. Equivalent to item # 4 (smiling or laughing).
>
> *Item # 6*: Tense body position. Reversed to item # 6 (gesturing with hands and arms) and other items on the enthusiasm list.
>
> *Item # 8*: Moves around. Equivalent to item # 5 (moving about).
>
> *Item # 10*: Looks at board or notes. Reversed to item # 8 (eye contact).
>
> *Item # 12*: Relaxed body position. No exact parallel exists for this item, but it is highly consonant with the entire enthusiasm list.
>
> *Item # 13*: Smiles at individual students. This is the only item which might tap an interactive characteristic of "closeness". It has no exact parallel in the enthusiasm list, although item # 8 (eye contact) and item # 4 (smiling) are quite equivalent. In any event, one item out of 10 or 14 items cannot have a substantial weight in the overall summary score.
>
> *Item # 14*: Vocal expressions. Equivalent to item # 1 (speaks in dramatic/expressive way), item # 2 (pitch and volume variations), and item # 3 (vocal inflection).

The additional four items dropped from the 14-item immediacy instrument do not change the picture. Touching (item # 7) is anyway very rare in college (McCroskey et al., 1996) and the sitting/standing items (# 1, 9, and 11) are in any event covered by equivalent items in the enthusiasm list.

Thus, my conclusion is that both instruments measure the very same phenomenon, and any conceptual distinctions between immediacy and enthusiasm are not reflected in the actual measurement instruments. Except for one immediacy item (# 13, smiling at individual students) any notion of interpersonal closeness in the immediacy items can hardly be noticed.

My sense is that the reference to "closeness" in the definition of teacher immediacy (which Andersen borrowed from Mehrabian) is misleading, because many readers might assume that the "closeness" is interpersonal in nature (that is, instructors being close to their students and caring about them personally). Perhaps the intended meaning was that instructors communicate to students their closeness to their subject matter (and their closeness might be contagious) – but still, the term "immediacy" was ill-chosen and is misleading, because immediacy and closeness are not measured at all

Although these two literatures ignore each other, the two bodies of research can be joined together. Almost all results in both literatures are consistent and very similar to each other, despite their unique methodological flaws.

MEASUREMENT OF NV IMMEDIACY AND EDUCATIONAL OUTCOMES

NV immediacy, as well as verbal immediacy, is measured exclusively via students' self-report about specific behaviors of their instructors. In an article summarizing the historical development of immediacy research, James McCroskey and Virginia Richmond (1992) justified that decision. They argued that the 10-item or 14-item NVI behavioral list consists of low inference behaviors that students know very well and can rate with high reliability, that students' self-reports were found highly correlated to behavioral observations, and that factor analysis yielded a simple one-factor solution with very high Alpha reliability.

McCroskey and Richmond left unsaid a more practical, highly important rationale justifying their scale: Measuring NVI through students' self-reports makes the administration very easy, enabling numerous researchers and graduate students to conduct immediacy research with relatively little investment of effort and resources. This fact may explain the great multitude of published investigations on teacher immediacy. Having experienced personally the great investment of effort and finance required for conducting NV research based on videotaped observations and subsequent judgment practices, I can only admire the simplicity of the self-report methodology. Because of my earlier-mentioned reservations about fabricated manipulations of NV behavior in controlled experiments, the self-report measure remains the central effective tool in immediacy research. However, the measurement is wrought with methodological flaws.

The NVI score is a statistical composite of all (10 or 14) items. Harris and Rosenthal (2005) argued that the immediacy scale items are certainly broad in scope, and we do not yet have exact empirical evidence of the relative contribution of these individual behaviors to producing immediacy. Harris and Rosenthal concluded (following McCroskey et al., 1996) that vocal variety, eye contact, smiling, and relaxed body position were probably the stronger contributors to immediacy.

A very interesting innovation in the self-report measurement of NVI is the fact that students are asked to rate "the instructor in the last class you had before this one" rather than the present instructor. McCroskey and Richmond (1992) argued that poor instructors and those who do not value social science research are often unwilling to cooperate with research that may involve evaluation of their teaching behaviors. The "previous class" method (if it is ethically permissible because instructors are not asked for their consent) ensures great variability in the samples of instructors and courses. However, McCroskey and Richmond were well aware of the fact that this strategy complicates the subsequent measurement of cognitive learning.

Because of the retrospective nature of the students' ratings of the NVI items, it must be understood that students actually rate "instructor's style" rather than "instructor's behavior." Their retrospective judgments reflect their recollections of the instructor's most typical conduct, but they do not rate specific behavioral instances. Therefore, we are not dealing here with a pure "low inference measurement."

METHODOLOGICAL NOTE: N = STUDENTS VERSUS N = TEACHERS

Cronbach (1976) and Cooper and Good (1983) emphasized the difference between educational research based on N = Students and educational research based on N = Teachers/Classrooms. They warned against aggregating all students into one sample if classroom phenomena are investigated. When the investigated phenomenon involves the entire classroom or the instructor, and we investigate, for example, 20 classrooms with 25 students in each class, we cannot analyze our data for $N = 500$ students but must rather analyze $N = 20$ instructors, using averaged scores for each class. This requirement complicates educational research and makes it very expensive, and Cronbach, as well as Cooper and Good lamented that it might destroy educational research. Clearly teacher immediacy is a classroom phenomenon, in which a single instructor affects the entire class, and therefore $N = $ Instructors is the appropriate way for analyzing the data. Indeed, Murray's (1983a, 1983b) seminal studies were conducted using $N = $ Instructors (samples of 54 and 36 instructors). Christophel (1990a, 1990b) did likewise in her early investigation of teacher immediacy (with $N = 60$ classrooms).

The use of the self-report methodology in the measurement of immediacy turned the research into $N = $ Students type. Because each student reports about a different instructor and a different course, the design actually becomes one of $N = $ Students $= $ Instructors, and the evidence on each instructor is derived from $N = 1$ Student. I suppose that Cronbach would *not* have accepted this approach, and would have demanded more robust data about each instructor. Because the results of enthusiasm and immediacy research are so consistent (see next), this issue has not been dealt with as yet (except for a comment in passing in McCroskey and Richmond's, 1992, account).

To assess the impact of teacher immediacy, educational outcomes must be measured – constituting the dependent variables (in experimental research) or criteria (in correlational research) representing teaching effectiveness. In enthusiasm research, the investigators used students' post-course evaluations (SRT), which are the conventional and most widely used instruments worldwide. Their advocates maintain that SRT instruments measure teaching effectiveness with high validity (see Marsh's chapter in this book). Even their critics concede that SRT instruments measure students' satisfaction and affective reactions to their teachers (see also Special Section of Journal of Educational Psychology, Perry, 1990).

Immediacy researchers chose to ignore SRT and course grades. (Indeed, when the research is not conducted in the $N = $ Instructors approach, mean course SRT and grades are not available at all). McCroskey and Richmond (1992) described their deliberations and how they settled on students' self-report about their learning. The choice is practical, because all data on both instructor immediacy and educational outcomes are collected in one short session, necessitating no search for data from other sources.

To measure cognitive learning, students are asked two questions: (1) How much did you learn in this class? (2) How much do you think you could have learned in this class had you had the ideal instructor? By subtracting the first score from the second, a variable labeled "learning loss" was created, and was expected to correlate negatively with teacher immediacy scores. Both the raw learning (first item) and the learning loss scores are used to measure students' reports of their learning. Psychometric analyses which would have examined the validity of this measure of cognitive learning have not been provided, and meta-analyses (to be reported later) could not ascertain its validity.

METHODOLOGICAL NOTE: THE POSSIBILITY OF HALO EFFECT

The methodology of accepting students' self-reports about their learning gains is very problematic. Students report about the instructor who taught them at their previous class. They characterize the instructor's behaviors on a 10–14 item scale, and then immediately proceed to evaluate how much they have learned from that instructor, and how committed they feel to study more in the same area and/or from the same instructor. Almost all data of the field studies in immediacy research have been collected in this manner.

Harris and Rosenthal (2005) were worried that a halo effect might influence the students' ratings. Halo effect is the phenomenon where one's overall reaction to a target person (e.g., liking) influences all other, presumably independent ratings to be consonant with the overall impression. Because *all* measures (of instructor's NVI and students' affective learning, behavioral intentions, and cognitive learning) are filled out by the responding student in a single short session, and furthermore, given that each instructor is represented in this research by $N = 1$ Student, the possibility of inflated correlations due to halo effect is quite real.

Feeley (2002), who has been investigating halo effects in different areas, conducted one study on halo effect in immediacy research. He asked 128 students to evaluate the same instructor on the three conventional measures: NV immediacy, teaching effectiveness, and attitudes toward course content. To these measures he added two variables irrelevant to teaching effectiveness (physical attractiveness and vocal clarity) that should have been equally rated by all students (and to yield zero correlations with the other measures), because only one instructor was evaluated. Feeley found significant correlations among all five measures, indicating the presence of a halo effect. When the irrelevant variables appeared at the end of the questionnaire, their correlations with the other three variables grew higher. Thus, the typical relationships found in the conventional self-report measurement of all variables in immediacy research probably over-estimates the intensity of the relationships between instructor immediacy and educational outcomes.

META-ANALYSES OF NV IMMEDIACY RESEARCH

Two recent meta-analyses summarized the research on instructor immediacy and its relations to educational outcomes, one by Witt, Wheeless, and Allen (2004), the other by Harris and Rosenthal (2005). Witt and his associates are researchers in the field of teacher immediacy, and Witt's (2003) doctoral dissertation consisted of an experimental study comparing educational outcomes for 2X2 combinations of verbal and NV immediacy (see also Witt & Wheeless, 2001). The meta-analysis reported by Witt et al. (2004) was based on 81 studies of verbal and NV immediacy.

Harris and Rosenthal (2005) are "veteran" meta-analysts, having published several meta-analyses on various topics over the last 20 years. Rosenthal is one of the world leading experts on meta-analysis. Their meta-analysis on NVI was based on 37 studies. The difference between the number of studies included in the two meta-analyses stems from different search methods and differing criteria for inclusion in the analysis (e.g., including or not including studies of verbal immediacy, including or rejecting M.A. theses or unpublished reports, etc.).

The measures employed in two meta-analyses were as follows:

1. *Teacher immediacy*. Harris and Rosenthal included only studies involving NVI, Witt et al. included both verbal and NV immediacy.
2. *Affective learning*. Students' evaluative reaction either toward the course or the instructor. This is an affective measure of satisfaction.
3. *Cognitive learning*. Students' self-report about their learning, usually including both "raw learning" and (the reversed) "learning loss" scores.
4. *Cognitive performance*. Objective measures of achievement in the form of grades or exam performance. Only few of the meta-analyzed studies included such measures, and these studies were mostly experimental manipulations of NVI.

228

5. *Behavioral intentions* to take another course with the same instructor or on the same subject. Only Harris and Rosenthal included this index in the analysis.

The results of both meta-analyses (Table 1)T1 were quite similar, although Witt et al. (2004) reported higher effect sizes than Harris and Rosenthal (2005) for affective learning and self-reported cognitive learning. In both reports, the meta-analytic results for the few experimental studies showed much smaller effects sizes compared to the field studies.

Witt et al. (2004) concluded that teacher immediacy has a substantial relationship with certain attitudes and perceptions of students in relation to their learning and their instructors, but only a modest relationship with cognitive learning performance. Harris & Rosenthal (2005) concluded that the results of the meta-analysis reveal that NV immediacy is strongly related to many positive student outcomes: Liking for the course and the instructor, willingness to take more classes with the instructor and more classes in that subject, and students' perceptions that they have learned a lot in the class. What is not yet clear in their minds is the degree to which these positive outcomes are translated into gains in actual student achievement.

McCroskey and Richmond would have probably reacted to these meta-analyses by arguing that, due to inevitable methodological shortcomings, the meta-analytic effect size reported here for objective achievement ($r = .14$ to $r = .17$) underestimated the real life magnitude of the impact of teacher immediacy on actual achievement. In my opinion, the gap between the associations of NVI with students' affective outcomes and with objective student achievements is quite reasonable and makes sense. Instructors' enthusiasm, immediacy and expressiveness indeed contribute to student satisfaction. It stands to reason that a student who is very satisfied with his instructor's

Table 1: Effect Sizes in Meta-analyses of Teachers' Nonverbal Immediacy Research

Correlations of NVI with:	Harris & Rosenthal (2005)	Witt, Wheeless, and Allen (2004)
1. Affective Learning	$r = .43$	$r = .49$
2. Behavioral Intentions	$r = .32$	$r = .51$
3. Cognitive Learning (Self Report)	$r = .36$	$r = .17$
4. Cognitive Performance (Objective Grades)	$r = .14$	

expressive style and delivery of instruction, a student who enjoyed the course (see Pekrun's chapter in this book), would react more positively, report higher motivation, and may also have an inflated sense of learning gains. Objective cognitive learning probably requires many additional causal factors that are not included in the immediacy conception – including students' differential intellectual abilities and their interest in the subject, the intellectual and teaching ability of the instructor, clarity of presentation and course organization, the structure of the syllabus and the assignments. Excellent teaching (see Theall and Feldman's chapter in this book) would combine both affective (NV) and intellectual qualities of the instructor, and would influence both affective and cognitive student outcomes.

THE BIG PICTURE OF INSTRUCTORS' GLOBAL NV STYLE AND STUDENT OUTCOMES: CONCEPTUAL SYNOPSIS

SUMMARY OF THE MAJOR FINDINGS ON GLOBAL NV STYLE AND STUDENT OUTCOMES

Thus far, the presentation in this chapter was focused on instructors' global NV style, that is, summary measures of their overall NV expressiveness. The accumulated results from the numerous studies on immediacy and enthusiasm are very consistent, despite the numerous methodological problems and flaws. We know that the expressive style of instructors in higher education is consistently related to (and probably causes) positive outcomes among the students: Positive affect toward the instructor and toward the subject, an increase in motivation and commitment, improvement in attention, and positive self-reports about cognitive learning. As to the influence of teacher expressive style on objective achievement outcomes and students' academic/intellectual learning, effect sizes are much smaller, the findings are not as robust, and there is no clear indication that instructor expressiveness leads to improved academic gains.

The extensive, cumulative research literature on SRT has demonstrated beyond any shadow of doubt the covariation between academic and affective components of effective instruction (see chapters by Abrami, Rosenfield, & Dedic and by Marsh in this book). Therefore, the positive expressive characteristics in enthusiasm and immediacy research probably constitute a necessary, but not sufficient condition for effective instruction. Students' implicit theory about effective teaching includes a belief about such covariation of academic and affective components of instructor style, and subsequently expressive instructors would usually tend to be (and believed to be) effective instructors. The great instructors who are sought out by students and who are remembered forever by their former students are probably excellent in both expressive and intellectual components. Very poor instructors that students try to avoid are probably lacking in both affective and academic components. Low quality of a given instructor in either the academic or the affective component would probably lead students to a negative view of that instructor's teaching effectiveness.

CENTRAL PROBLEMS WITH RESEARCH ON GLOBAL NV STYLE

As has been demonstrated thus far in this chapter, the study of global NV style is wrought with conceptual, methodological and measurement problems. First and above all, we face the absurd situation of discovering two bodies of literature that are focused on the very same phenomenon and yet are totally alienated from each other. I have never experienced such estrangement between related conceptualizations, especially when the main instruments for defining and measuring the central phenomenon are almost identical. The irony of this situation is the fact that the findings in the enthusiasm and immediacy literatures are highly consistent with each other!

The larger body of literature – on teacher immediacy – is characterized by several faults:

1. The main concept – "immediacy" – is borrowed from Mehrabian and is not consonant with operational definition of the concept as apparent in the measurement tool. Therefore, the term "teacher immediacy" is misleading.
2. The field research is almost exclusively based on students' subjective and retrospective self-reports. Data on both instructor NVI and student outcomes are collected in one short questionnaire, with no safeguards against halo effects.
3. Every instructor is represented by $N = 1$ Student only.
4. Cognitive learning gains are evaluated via students' uncorroborated self-reports, with no established validity for the measurement of this most problematic cluster.
5. The few experimental studies of instructor immediacy are based on deceptive and exaggerated (staged) NV behaviors that have no ecological validity and are inappropriate for NV research.

231

Last, but not least, the undifferentiated focus on "global NV style" and its global correlates in students' impressions severely limits the efficacy and utility of this research. To advance our knowledge on instructor's classroom NV behavior and its (correlates or) effects on students, we need to isolate and carefully investigate specific NV behaviors, different types of courses and students, various types of instructional situations, and separate aspects of student outcomes.

A PROFESSIONAL DILEMMA: METHODOLOGICAL QUALITY VERSUS CONSISTENCY OF RESULTS

The situation described in the last two sections evokes a professional dilemma. On the one hand, most of the immediacy studies have serious methodological flaws that should inevitably lead to discounting them. In our professional training, we tell our students that faulty research must be discarded regardless of its results. On the other hand, the results of almost all published studies and of the meta-analyses are very systematic, showing highly consistent associations between instructors' global expressive style and students' outcomes. Even the distinction between affective and academic measures of student learning gains is systematic in this body of literature. Should we accept methodologically faulty research if the accumulated findings are consistent and systematic? The only "solution" to this dilemma is to give highest credence to studies that seem to be of higher methodological quality and to be more carefully designed.

A FINAL REFLECTION ON DOCTOR FOX EFFECTS

The Doctor Fox phenomenon has maintained its salience over several decades because it symbolizes the ambivalence of many experts in the field of teaching and learning in higher education about the power of instructors' NV behavior. On the one hand it is consensually held that effective teaching requires enthusiasm and expressiveness on the part of the instructor. On the other hand, excellence in teaching must be based on certain academic and intellectual aspects (clarity of presentation, intellectual challenge, and so on). The Doctor Fox study fueled the nightmarish notion that the showy, theatrical aspects *alone* might lure students into the illusion of having learned, thus destroying the foundations of students' evaluations of instruction.

As a scientist, I concur with the various critics that the claimed Doctor Fox effect has no validity, and cannot be considered as a threat to the validity of SRT in real university settings. As a former dean and a member of various academic committees, I cannot deny that suspicion about potential inflation of student evaluations as a function of instructors' charisma and over-expressiveness always lingers on... We do not want to have a Doctor Fox (or even a "partial" Doctor Fox) on the staff of our departments, and we would like to believe that unlike their reported susceptibility in a one-shot Doctor Fox simulation, students' diagnostic abilities would lead them to react appropriately to charismatic instructors who fail to deliver the academic goods week after week. If Hans Christian Anderson's famous king would have appeared in his "new clothes" again and again week after week, it stands to reason that everybody would eventually discover the nature of the new attire.

CROSS CULTURAL DIFFERENCES IN NV CONDUCT

McKroskey and Richmond (1992) summarized the questions that remain to be resolved by research in the field of teacher immediacy. The first question concerned cross cultural differences in NV conduct, wondering whether findings on teacher immediacy obtained in the USA can be generalized to other cultures. Questions were raised about the stability of the relationship between teacher immediacy and educational outcomes, about cross cultural differences in absolute levels of teacher immediacy (as a function of cultural norms and expectations about expressivity), and about inter-cultural teacher-student interaction in American education (See McCkroskey et al., 1996, who compared teacher immediacy in Australia, Finland, Puerto Rico and the USA; Neulip, 1997, and Pribyl, Sakamoto, and Keaten, 2004, who compared Japan to the USA; Myers, Zhong, and Guan, 1998, who compared the USA and China; Roach and Byrne, 2001, who compared Germany and the USA; and Johnson and Miller, 2002, who compared Kenya and the USA). Without going into the details of those studies, tentative conclusions claimed consistency across cultures in the pattern of relationship between teacher immediacy and educational outcomes; showed cultural differences in absolute levels of immediacy; and indicated that unique combinations due to different cultural expectations might be expected. Several researchers investigated inter-racial teacher-student interaction in American education (see Feldman, 1985; Feldman & Saletzky, 1986; Neulip, 1995, and Rucker and Gendrin, 2003).

CAN TEACHER ENTHUSIASM/IMMEDIACY BE TRAINED?

In the earlier discussion of microteaching, the importance of applied training in NV behavior to improve teaching effectiveness was emphasized. In the final analysis, the significance of research on NV behavior in education lies in the possibility of using the research outcomes for corrective purposes. Because this chapter is written from a research perspective and it is based on empirical research publications, the problem must be faced that the number of published research studies reporting outcomes of applied interventions of NV training is very small. Only few researchers choose to conduct and publish research on applied interventions, and probably there is a lot more applied work being conducted in the field.

The problem gets worse because of the explicit focus of this chapter on higher education. In most countries, formal teacher training is required for early childhood education, for elementary, middle and high school education, but not for higher education. Many educators (and certainly university students) lament the fact that most instructors in higher education have not undergone formal teacher training. They are hired on the basis of their scientific and research potential much more than on the basis of their teaching ability. It is true that many universities and colleges invest effort and resources in the improvement of teaching, but participation in training programs is usually voluntary, and the volunteer participants are most often self-selected – they are the most interested and motivated instructors who do not need the training too urgently. The weak instructors who need training interventions more urgently, often tend to be those who resist change efforts and would not voluntarily participate in such programs. The situation is less problematic in the K-12 level, because the investment in initial teacher training is enormous, and it is normative for teachers to continue their in-service training throughout their careers. In my country, Israel, continued in-service training is mandatory and rewarded, and therefore K-12 teachers seek opportunities for continued training. Because there is a demand, many professional (formal and informal) organizations offer training services of various kinds. Thus, it should not be surprising that of the few references to training in NV behavior which I have found, only a fraction dealt with higher education.

In both teacher immediacy and teacher enthusiasm literatures, one high quality study on applied NV training was published by the researchers leading those fields – Murray and Lawrence (1980) in teacher enthusiasm, and Richmond, McCorskey, Plax, and Kearney

(1986) in teacher immediacy. Richmond et al. (1986) conducted their study in high school (grades 7–12). Teachers were trained in NV communication generally and NV immediacy behaviors specifically. They were matched with teachers in their schools who taught the same subjects but had no NV training. Measures of NV immediacy and affective learning were administered to the students of both groups of teachers. The trained teachers were perceived as more immediate than the untrained teachers, and their students reported more positive affect for both the teacher and the subject matter than did the students of the untrained teachers. Richmond et al. (1986) concluded that research results on teacher immediacy in the classroom could be translated and applied to real improvements in teachers' NV behavior and to lead to real increases in student learning.

Murray and Lawrence (1980) conducted their NV training research on a sample of university lecturers. Twelve instructors participated in 20 2-hour speech and drama training workshops, and learned how to apply acting techniques (body movement, expressive speech, etc.) to classroom teaching. They were compared to twelve matched controls with comparable pre-treatment ratings of teaching effectiveness. Teaching effectiveness was assessed by a student rating form completed before the beginning and after the end of the 20-week program. Independence of pretest and posttest was guaranteed by using different random samples of student raters at pretest and posttest. The experimental instructors significantly improved their effectiveness ratings whereas control teachers did not. In addition to the change in the mean overall effectiveness rating, the improvements of the experimental instructors included the following ratings: (1) shows concern for student progress; (2) is friendly and approachable; (3) shows facial expressions; (4) asks questions; (5) suggests supplementary reading; and (6) lectures without notes. Wood (1998) concluded that the Murray and Lawrence (1980) study was a significant contribution to the teacher effectiveness research because it demonstrated that enthusiasm training in the form of speech and drama workshops generalized to the classroom and produced improvement in teacher effectiveness ratings and specific teaching behaviors. In reading this report, I was disappointed that Murray and Lawrence had not used a later posttest in addition to the immediate posttest, to examine whether the new style of teacher behavior still held after the excitement of the workshops wore off.

Wyckoff (1973) also developed a teacher enthusiasm training program, and examined its effects with 12 teachers who were randomly selected from among 90 student teachers attending a MT lab. They received training in (1) gesturing, (2) pausing while lecturing, and (3) moving around the classroom. Then they taught two distinct lecture topics to groups of four students, one presented with enthusiasm as trained, the other with minimal stimulus variation, sitting at a desk and reading from notes. The student groups consisted of elementary and secondary school children. The results showed that the secondary school students retained more information in the enthusiastic condition, whereas elementary school students did more poorly in that condition. Wyckoff (1973) thought that the enthusiasm and animation of the teachers might have distracted the younger children. McKinney et al. (1983), who compared the effects high, medium and low enthusiasm conditions on 4th grade students, found increased classroom management problems in the high enthusiasm condition.

The McKinney et al. (1983) study was not an applied training study, but an experimental study. It highlighted the issue of *exaggerated* enthusiasm and its potential of hindering students. The danger of over-enthusiasm or excessively high immediacy is quite apparent, especially when the advantages of this expressive style are zealously preached. In another experimental (non-training) study, Comstock, Rowell, and Bowers (1995) compared low, moderately high, and excessively high NV immediacy, and found a curvilinear inverted U relationship, where moderately high immediacy resulted in higher cognitive, affective, and behavioral learning.

Klinzing and Jackson (1987) wrote about issues in training teachers in NV sensitivity and NV behavior, and assessed various methods and techniques as means of improving teachers' NV abilities. Klinzing (1983) developed a training program for secondary school teachers on the basis of the NV descriptors of enthusiastic learning, including vocal delivery, eye contact, facial expression, gestures, and body movement. He conducted four field studies using several combinations of the training elements. Klinzing reported that the studies provided consistent evidence of the trainability of teachers' NV sensitivity.

Within the teacher immediacy framework, Hunnicutt's (1999) doctoral dissertation at Georgia Southern University carefully examined the effects of training in the use of selected NV behaviors in reducing student disruptions in the classroom. The experimental group of pre-service elementary and middle school teachers-in-training received training in the use of NV behaviors in expectancy, immediacy, withitness, dress, haptics, kinesics, prosody, and proximity. The equivalent control group did not receive such training. Classroom observations focused on seven distinct categories of student disruptions. Hunnicutt did not find significant differences between the behaviors of the students in the classrooms of the experimental and control teachers, However, the pattern and consistency of the differences along the different categories of disruptive behaviors were clear, showing some effectiveness of the NV training program in reducing classroom disruptions. I believe that the findings could have been more instructive had they been discussed in terms of effect sizes (as is customary today) and not in terms of statistical significance.

CONCEPTUAL VARIETIES OF TRAINING IN NV BEHAVIOR

Conceptually, implementation of a training intervention for changing teachers' NV behavior can be viewed in three perspectives:

1. *Holistic approach.* The holistic approach puts the entire NV style of the teacher in focus, and they are taught about expressive style as an integrated whole. Such intervention would probably include an extensive theoretical component, where instructors would learn about the overall phenomenon and the research findings supporting it. Perhaps they would view videotapes of enthusiastic or immediate instructors in their classrooms and would compare them to non-enthusiastic or non-immediate instructors, and the practical training would deal with the overall impression each trainee creates while teaching. This perspective is quite consonant with the holistic nature of the definitions and the findings in both teacher enthusiasm and teacher immediacy fields. In the training studies described above, both the Richmond et al. (1986) and Murray and Lawrence (1980) studies represented this perspective, and both reported positive outcomes demonstrating the effectiveness of the training. (The studies by McKinney et al. (1983) and Streeter (1986) could also be considered as representing this perspective).

2. *Specific behavioral approach.* In this perspective, the training is concentrated on pre-selected specific behaviors considered critical for improving teaching effectiveness, and the training is focused on these behaviors only. Klinzing (1983) examined specific training combinations of several pre-defined behaviors, and Wyckoff (1973) chose three defined behaviors. Hunnicutt's (1999) research could be classified as falling between the holistic and the specific behavioral approach, as she had pre-selected eight different behaviors.

Some years ago, in the 1970s, a colleague in Philadelphia (Norman Newberg, personal communication) did an impressive piece of training work with one single, isolated NV behavior. In that period, verbal and NV research in the elementary school focused on teachers' expectancy-related differential behavior, following "Pygmalion in the classroom" (Rosenthal & Jacobson, 1968). Eye contact was one of the distinct differential NV behaviors considered to mediate teacher expectancy effects (Brophy, 1983; Harris & Rosenthal, 1985; see also Babad, 1993), with evidence that teachers held shorter duration eye contact with low-expectancy students, especially following wrong answers or failure to respond. When teachers do not expect those students to do better, they shift their eyes more quickly to other students. Newberg decided to train teachers to intentionally prolong eye contact with low-achievers. The participating teachers reported that the changed pattern of eye contact affected classroom atmosphere and motivated weak students to more active participation.

In a somewhat paradoxical way, the specific behavioral approach to NV training can be conceptually justified by the holistic nature of teacher enthusiasm and teacher immediacy. Because of the covariation between the different behaviors comprising enthusiasm or immediacy, it might sometimes be sufficient to change one specific behavior or one aspect, and other behaviors and aspects would follow suit and change in covariation with that specific change. I think that this happened in the classrooms of the teachers in Newberg's intervention. This idea is certainly not new; it is one of the cornerstones of behavior therapy and biofeedback, where a change in one specific behavior can trigger a chain of subsequent changes in related behaviors.

3. *Diagnostic approach.* In this commonly-used approach, training is flexible, with no pre-selection of change objectives. Diagnostic change means that each participant must be observed via MT or another form of observation, and individual strengths and weaknesses must be diagnosed and measured. Expert supervisors then analyze the instructor's data, make judgments about aspects that are more readily changeable, and design training particularly tailored to that instructor, to strengthen certain changeable behaviors and/or weaken other behaviors through behavioral training. Other members of the trained group of instructors can learn vicariously from that individualized training undergone by their peer. This approach is widely-used as individually-tailored consultation and can potentially be very successful, but it does not lend itself readily to systematic evaluation research.

PREDICTING STUDENT EVALUATIONS FROM THIN SLICES OF TEACHERS' NV BEHAVIOR

GLOBAL NV STYLE VERSUS SPECIFIC NV BEHAVIORS

The research described thus far, especially teacher immediacy research, deals with "NV style" rather than "NV behavior." It presents the averaged sum total of the instructor's most typical and most frequent behaviors, as these are recalled retrospectively by the students. One cannot determine the differential weighting of specific behaviors and the degree to which each behavior or various combinations of behaviors contribute to predict the student outcomes (are facial gestures more important than hand and body motion? how do smiling, voice pitch, and relaxed body compare to each other? etc.). In the NV research perspective, attention is focused on specific NV behaviors as they are enacted, and attempts are made to isolate specific behaviors and defined situations and to reduce the impact of the overall context and the verbal, contextual characteristics.

CONTEXT MINIMAL NV RESEARCH

The studies discussed thus far in this chapter dealt with NV behavior while maintaining the full (or almost full) context of the classroom. The immediacy questionnaire presumably consists of low-inference NV behaviors, but students report their retrospective memories about teacher's typical style of enacting each behavior, and do not rate at all any specific behavioral instance. In NV research, most investigations of NV behavior are carried out in minimal (or limited) contexts, where judges' exposure to the person whose behavior is to be judged is controlled. Context minimal NV research would usually include some or all of the following characteristics: (1) It would focus on isolated behaviors rather than on a continuous flow; (2) It might separate NV channels (face, body, voice, etc.); (3) It would eliminate verbal content; (4) It would focus on the judged target (e.g., the instructor) and not show the other parties in a given social interaction; (5) It might use brief exposure to behavioral instances; and (6) NV behavior would be rated by outside judges rather than by the actual participants in the interaction. NV researchers argue that only through isolation of variables and maximal control of "noise" variation it is possible to examine the impact of specific NV behaviors.

The issue of classroom context has long been debated among educational researchers, and the interest in NV research in education sharpened the debate (see Galloway, 1984; Woolfolk & Galloway, 1985). Some educational researchers (Doyle, 1977, 1981, 1983; Fenstermacher, 1979) were apprehensive about research methods that ignore the natural setting and flow of the intact classroom, believing that all relevant characteristics of the classroom must be included in "proper" educational research. In their view, the true meanings of an educational situation are embedded *only* in its fullest context, and therefore a minimized context cannot be considered to represent the actual classroom situation. If one accepts this approach, educational research on NV behavior would be seriously limited. The mere term "NV" means that verbal content must be ignored and the focus should be on NV aspects only! Beyond that, the purpose of thin slices research is to isolate single behaviors and to examine them under the most controlled conditions.

It must be made clear that a minimized context can be of high ecological validity. "Ecological validity" means that the investigated unit represents reality and is not faked or artificial, whereas "minimal context" refers to the length of the investigated unit. The manipulation of enthusiasm and immediacy in experiments such as the Doctor Fox studies was criticized earlier in this chapter, because the behavior enacted in these situations was faked and exaggerated, and did not represent naturally (or ecologically) occurring behavior. But exposure of ten seconds to the face of a teacher (without hearing anything) can be of high ecological validity if this expression was recorded in a real classroom interaction. The empirical test of such recorded behavior would be if it would predict, on its own, certain student outcomes.

THIN SLICES RESEARCH

A recent development in NV research is the investigation of thin slices of NV behavior (Ambady & Rosenthal, 1992; Ambady, Bernieri, & Richeson, 2000). Thin slices research continues the trend of measuring NV sensitivity through judgments of very brief instances of NV behavior that started in the PONS Test (Profile of Nonverbal Sensitivity, Rosenthal et al., 1979). In the PONS, decoding ability is tested by deciding which of two alternative descriptions for each brief item accurately describes the meaning of the enacted NV behavior (e.g., goes to church or goes to supermarket; scolds or praises her child). But whereas the PONS also separated channels such as face, body and voice, in thin slices research the full NV context is shown, only that exposure time is extremely short. Raters are exposed to very brief instances of NV behavior – a few seconds of trial judges delivering instructions to jurors; of job applicants in the first few seconds of job interviews; of doctors communicating to patients; of TV interviewers; of experimenters reading instructions; and recently, also of teachers and instructors – and subsequently rate their impressions of these target persons. These ratings are then correlated with a variety of criteria characterizing these target people, with a diagnostic and/or predictive objective (e.g., judges' verdicts, applicant success in job interviews, interviewers' bias or equity, SRT). It turns out that perceivers absorb considerable amounts of information even from extremely brief exposure to target persons, and they are therefore capable of making accurate judgments that are not inferior to judgments made on the basis of much longer exposure.

Thin slices research often evokes a "Wow!" reaction in its audience. To quote a few dramatic examples, Babad, Bernieri, and Rosenthal (1991) and Babad and Taylor (1992) demonstrated that, after viewing unknown, foreign teachers for 10 seconds without under-standing their speech content, 4th-grade students could accurately guess whether the teachers were interacting with unseen high- or low-achievers. Blanck, Rosenthal, and Cordell (1985) showed that ratings of brief excerpts of judges' NV behavior while delivering instruc-tions to jurors in actual criminal trials were correlated with judges' expectations for the trial outcomes and with the criminal history of the defendants. Using these videotapes of trial judges from actual trials in mock jury research, Hart (1995) found that even when admonished to disregard the judge's behavior, participants returned verdicts concordant with the judges' bent. Babad (1999) demonstrated that thin-slices (averaging 7 seconds) of content-free NV behavior of television interviewers provided ample information to accurately detect interviewers' favoritism and preferential treatment. Gada-Jain (1999) examined NV behavior in job interviews, focusing on initial greeting and settling into chairs, and reported that thin slices depicting the initial handshake and introduction predicted the outcome of the subsequent structured employment interview. Finally, Babad (2005b) demon-strated that after viewing 10-second clips depicting unknown teachers lecturing to their entire classrooms, 11th graders could accurately guess those teachers' differential treatment of unseen low- and high-expectancy students in other classroom situations.

METHODOLOGICAL NOTE: EXPENSES AND NEEDED RESOURCES IN THIN SLICES RESEARCH

Thin slices research is quite complicated and expensive to run, especially compared to the administration of a short questionnaire to students in measurement of NV immediacy. In this slices research, appropriate samples of instructor behavior must be videotaped in the classroom, following strict procedures. The necessary lab work must then be done to select clips and record them on master cassettes. Next, these clips are administered to groups of judges/raters who are unfamiliar with the videotaped instructors. "In return" for this investment, thin slices research can demonstrate in a dramatic and clear manner the tremendous informational value of specific, isolated NV behaviors, even with the briefest and most minimal exposure.

In thin slices research in higher education, we investigate whether ratings of very brief clips depicting instructors' classroom NV behavior can systematically predict students' post-course evaluations (SRT). This question is similar to the general question of teacher enthusiasm and teacher immediacy research, namely, whether instructor expressive style contributes to teaching effectiveness. But the thin slices research differs from the other types of research in that it is completely context minimal: The judges/raters are not familiar at all with the videotaped instructors; exposure time is very short and measured in seconds; there is no flow or continuity to the videotaped material; and there is no comprehension of any verbal content. Finally, unlike NVI research, the measurement of NV conduct and the measurement of teaching effectiveness are totally independent of each other in thin slices research.

If very brief instances of instructors' content-free NV behavior would be found to predict students' post-course evaluations of these instructors, a conceptual issue would have to be resolved. Would such a finding be considered a threat to the validity of SRT (as had been claimed following the Doctor Fox studies), or would it actually strengthen the validity of SRT? The challenge would then be to define the conditions and specific findings that could lead to support one interpretation or the other.

THE AMBADY AND ROSENTHAL (1993) STUDY – "HALF A MINUTE"

Ambady and Rosenthal (1993) used very short NV clips (lasting 30 seconds) in which 13 junior instructors (graduate students) at Harvard University were videotaped while lecturing in sections of undergraduate courses. The clips (video only, no sound) were judged on a series of dimensions by students who were not familiar with the instructors. Ambady and Rosenthal examined the correlations between these judgments (each separately and as a composite) and the mean end-of-semester (SRT) "overall course" and "overall instructor" evaluations given by the students in these courses. They found very high correlations between the judgments of NV behavior and SRT. The correlations were not reduced when the clips were shortened from 30 seconds to 6 seconds for another sample of judges.

The importance of Ambady and Rosenthal's (1993) study was in the initial demonstration of the intense predictive power of thin slices of NV behavior in the context of higher education. As thin slices research advanced during that decade, Ambady et al. (2000) argued that thin slice ratings are context dependent, and therefore more differential predictions must be made from particular stimulus situations to particular criteria. In a replication and extension of the 1993 study, Babad, Avni-Babad, and Rosenthal (2004) examined the prediction of SRT aspects from brief instances of professors' NV behavior in defined instructional situations.

THE BABAD, AVNI-BABAD, AND ROSENTHAL (2004) STUDY – INSTRUCTIONAL SITUATIONS

The Babad et al. (2004) study was designed to replicate the Ambady and Rosenthal (1993) study and extend it in several directions. The sample consisted of 47 experienced professors who taught in 67 courses of various types and sizes (20 professors were videotaped in two courses – a small and a large one).

The 1993 study was confined to lecturing behavior, when instructors addressed their entire classes. In the 2004 study, each professor was videotaped in four distinct situations, and the relationship between instructor's NV behavior and SRT was examined separately for each situation. The four situations were:

1. The first minute of the first class session (initial exposure of the students to the professor – "first impression").
2. Lecturing to the entire class.
3. Interacting with students in an instructional dialogue. The interaction clips did not show any student at all, focusing only on the interacting instructor.
4. Talking about the course to the camera in the professor's office.

The distinction between "talking about" and "talking to" yielded interesting results in studies of psychotherapists (Rosenthal et al., 1984) and teachers (Babad et al., 1989).

In the Ambady and Rosenthal (1993) study, the judges viewed the clips of the instructors in a silent video, to prevent any influence of the verbal content on their judgments. Babad's method has been to use judges in a foreign country who did not understand the Hebrew-speaking teachers (Babad & Taylor, 1992) and TV interviewers (Babad, 1999, 2005c). They can hear the speech and are therefore exposed to the NV characteristics of the voice. In the 2004 study, Babad et al. also used American judges who did not comprehend the Hebrew speech content of the videotaped instructors. Each group of foreign judges viewed the 67 instructors in one of the four instructional situations, and rated each instructor on three scales: Friendly, Competent, and Interesting. A fourth score, an overall composite averaging the three ratings, was added following reliability checks and principal components analyses.

All students in the 67 courses filled out the SRT questionnaire close to the end of the term (long after the videotaping in the classroom had been completed). Ambady and Rosenthal (1993) used a global SRT index, averaging the "overall course" and "overall instructor" student evaluations as the measure of teaching effectiveness. The overall ratings are considered in the SRT literature as being potentially prone to bias (Cohen, 1990; Theall & Franklin, 1990), and it is recommended to use more distinct components and aspects (Marsh, 1984, 1987, see also chapter in this book). In the Babad et al. (2004) study, the specific SRT ratings were clustered into four composite scores following principal components analyses:

Academic: Learning value, intellectual quality and challenge, breadth of coverage, contribution of readings, and presenting different points of view.

Instructional: Instructor's humor, enthusiasm, clarity, and expressive style.

Students: Questioning students and encouraging their participation, interest in students and accessibility to them.

Difficulty: Course workload and difficulty, and fairness of assignments, exams, and grading (difficult courses considered as less fair).

Predicting SRT from professors' NV behavior. Because of the complexity of the findings, it is important that the overall conclusions from the Babad et al. (2004) college study (and the complementary findings from the Babad et al., 2003 high school study) be stated first to provide "the big picture." The shift from the analysis of a global NV style that is over-generalized beyond all situational nuances to a careful and exacting analysis focused on specific aspects in defined instructional situations demonstrated that the associations between aspects of instructors' NV behavior and students' educational outcomes are very complex, with no one monolithic global prediction! Instructors' NV behaviors in one instructional situation can predict certain SRT aspects (but not all aspects); NV behaviors of the same instructors in another instructional situation may not predict SRT (but might be related to other course characteristics); and NV behaviors in yet another teaching situation may be found to be a *negative* predictor of SRT aspects, mediated by course characteristics that had not been considered at all in previous research. Moreover, the specific NV behaviors of the same instructors vary from one instructional situation to the other and are largely unrelated to each other! Beyond all that, and still without tiring the readers with detailed findings, I argue that in the big picture, the findings support the validity of SRT measurement, and the relevant NV aspects are predictors (of moderate effect size) of the relevant student outcomes.

Table 2T2 presents the correlations between the averaged judges' ratings of professors' NV behavior in the four instructional situations and the averaged ratings of the professors by their actual students in those courses at the end of the term (SRT). Because all data points for all variables in these analyses consisted of group means for each professor, all correlations are reduced compared to results in a N = Students design.

As can be seen, the correlations for the clips videotaped at the first class session (top of Table 2) showed almost no association between judges' ratings of NV behavior in the first minute of the course and students' SRT. Students' post-course SRTs are probably based on numerous impressions, and first impressions might be modified by further exposure to the teacher. The correlations for ratings of the professors' NV behavior while talking about their courses in their offices (bottom of Table 2) also showed no association with SRT. Thus, an important conclusion is that not *every* sample of instructors' NV behavior can predict SRT.

The stronger associations between ratings of instructors' NV classroom behavior and end-of-course SRTs were found for the two instructional situations that represented the central activities of

Table 2: Correlations between Professors' NV Behavior in Four Instructional Situations and Components of Students' Post-course Evaluations (Adapted from Babad et al., 2004)

NV Behav. In Instructional *Situation*	SRT Components and Overall Evaluations					
	Academic Factors	Insructional Style	Interact Students	Difficulty Level	Overall Course	Overall Instruct
First Class Session	−0.14	−0.09	0.17	0.22*	−0.18	−0.05
Lecturing	0.08	0.29**	0.08	0.10	0.20*	0.20*
Interacting W. Students	−0.25*	−0.20*	−0.12	0.33**	−0.30**	−0.22*
Talking About Course	0.08	0.10	0.15	0.16	0.08	0.09

$^*p < .10$ $^{**}p < .05$

university teaching – lecturing and interacting with students. However, patterns of correlations for lecturing and for interacting with students were not consistent with each other! This incompatibility was counter-intuitive and required further thinking and analysis.

For lecturing, the correlations for the thin slices of instructors' NV behavior supported what we know from enthusiasm and immediacy research. Being rated more positively on the 9-second clip depicting NV behavior while lecturing was positively related to the overall course and overall instructor global ratings, more strongly related to the instructional component of SRT which includes instructor's expressive style, and unrelated to the other three SRT components. The fact that three of the four specific SRT components were not related to the NV lecturing behaviors adds to the credibility of the relationship found for the instructional component.

The negative correlations between instructors' NV behavior while interacting with students and SRT components were unexpected and surprising. The more positively professors were rated by the foreign judges for their NV behavior while interacting with students, the more they received *negative* course evaluations from their students for the academic and instructional SRT components and for the two SRT overall ratings. In light of the findings for lecturing behavior, in light of the Ambady and Rosenthal (1993) findings, and in light of most teacher enthusiasm and teacher immediacy research reviewed earlier, a positive relationship should have been expected! Why should these NV-SRT correlations be negative?

Babad et al. (2004) thought that the key to understanding this pattern lies in the positive correlation of the NV interaction ratings with the difficulty component in SRT. This correlation (r = .33) was the highest in Table 2. Professors' NV behavior while interacting with students was rated by the judges of the brief clips more positively in the difficult courses and less positively in the easy courses (with "easy" and "difficult" determined by the actual students' responses about "course workload and difficulty and fairness of assignments" in the SRT questionnaire). Babad et al. speculated that perhaps the professors were aware that some of their courses were considered difficult by the students, and in these courses they tried harder to be more communicative and to provide the best explanations. This compensation was probably manifested most clearly in their interaction with students, answering questions and explaining difficult issues. Therefore, NV Interaction behavior was judged more positively in the more difficult courses. This explanation could account for the negative correlation of the NV interaction clips with the overall course evaluations and the other SRT components in Table 2: The difficulty component was found in that study (in analyses not reported here) to be negatively related to all other SRT components (correlations ranging from $r = -.40$ to $r = -.54$ with all other SRT components and overall composites), difficult courses (where professors' NV Interaction behavior was judged more positively) receiving lower SRTs. Thus, self awareness of the difficulty of their courses probably moved instructors to try harder to demonstrate a more positive behavior in their interaction with students, but students anyway evaluated the difficult courses more negatively.[1]

---

[1] I am aware that the findings touch the controversial and much-debated issue of the nature of the relationship between course difficulty and student evaluations. In the present study course difficulty (consisting of ratings of workload and fairness) was negatively related to the other components of SRT, and more difficult courses received lower evaluations. Marsh (1984, 1987, see also chapter in this book) claimed that course difficulty is positively related to other aspects of SRT, and Marsh and Roche (2000) claimed to have debunked the popular myth that student evaluations are substantially biased by course workload. The myth that difficult courses might "cost" instructors in low ratings is indeed popular (see Greenwald & Gillmore, 1997a, 1997b). In my opinion, the issue is complicated, and no overall global conclusion would be valid. Different types of "difficulty" (e.g., grading leniency, workload of readings and assignments, number and format of exams, difficulty of exams, course tempo, level of difficulty of the subject, difficulties in understanding the instructor, etc.) probably interact with course characteristics (e.g., required versus elective courses, focused seminars versus broad lecture courses, beginners versus advanced courses, etc.) and with students' expectations to determine differential patterns of relationships. With regard to this issue, difficult courses were clearly evaluated more negatively by the students in the 67 courses in the Babad et al. (2004) study. With regard to NV research, the notable finding was that instructors' NV behavior while interacting with students was rated more positively in the more difficult courses!

METHODOLOGICAL NOTE: EXAMINATION OF COURSE DIFFICULTY
AS A MODERATING VARIABLE IN NV-SRT RELATIONS
FOR INTERACTING WITH STUDENTS

In essence, the above argument puts course difficulty as a moderating variable in the NV-SRT relations for teachers' NV behaviors while interacting with students. Babad et al. (2004) computed a series of partial correlations for the NV-SRT relations for NV behaviors while interacting with students, controlling for course difficulty. And indeed all correlations dropped considerably: None of the NV–SRT partial correlations was significant or even close to significant, the median correlation was $r = -.07$ and the highest was $r = -.14$. Thus, course difficulty probably was the key moderating variable in the negative correlations between professors' NV Interaction behaviors and SRT: Professors invested more effort in conducting positive interactions with students in difficult courses (as perceived by the judges of their NV behavior), but, being harder courses, the students in these courses gave them anyway more negative evaluations.

Course-size effects. Babad et al. (2004) examined whether ratings of instructors' NV behavior varied as a function of course size. Only a very weak, nonsignificant trend was detected for smaller courses to receive slightly higher ratings of instructors' NV behavior. However, an interesting fact was discovered when comparing the NV ratings for the 20 professors who were videotaped in both a small and a large course. Of the four instructional situations, differences in judges' ratings of the NV behaviors of these 20 professors were found only for talking about the course. Professors' NV behavior when talking about their smaller classes was rated more positively than their behavior when talking about their larger classes. Professors seem to like and enjoy their smaller courses more than their larger courses, and their feelings were picked up by the judges from 10 seconds of their NV behavior when they talked about these courses. At the same time, no differences were found for the ratings of their actual NV behavior in the classrooms! This finding adds to the credibility of the examination of thin slices of NV behavior in different instructional situations.

HIGH SCHOOL (2003) VERSUS UNIVERSITY STUDIES
(2004) – DISPARATE PATTERNS

Concurrently with their investigation (2004) of instructors' NV behavior in higher education, Babad et al. (2003) conducted a parallel study in a high school context. A high school study is pertinent to this chapter's focus on higher education for one of two alternative reasons: (a) Either it confirms the validity and generality of the patterns discovered in the university context; (b) Or it uncovers different patterns of findings which would limit the generalization across educational contexts. Ambady and Rosenthal (1993) also conducted parallel investigations in college and in high school, and their results (for teaching effectiveness ratings provided by the school principals due to the lack of appropriate SRT instruments for high school populations) confirmed the generality of the reported pattern. The results of the Babad et al. (2003) high school study differed radically from the 2004 college study, illuminating fundamental conceptual issues concerning the role of teachers' NV behavior in the teaching/learning process.

Groups of foreign judges rated the NV behavior of 28 experienced high school teachers in seven separate instructional situations: (1) Administrative behavior; (2) Disciplinary action; (3) Using the board; (4) Frontal teaching (lecturing) to the entire class; (5) Interaction with students ("at large," that is, students identified as neither high-achieving or low-achieving); (6) Interactions with high-achieving students; (7) Interactions with low-achieving students. Students' evaluations of their teachers were collected in a SRT questionnaire (especially designed to fit the high school classroom) and in a second questionnaire measuring students' perceptions of each teacher's differential behavior toward high- and low-achieving students.

As in the 2004 university study, Babad et al. (2003) found again in high school that the prediction of SRT aspects from ratings of teachers' NV behavior varied greatly among the instructional situations, with no overall generalized pattern. For administrative behavior and using the board, no predictive NV-SRT correlations were found at all. The instructional situation for which the most positive predictions of SRT were found was disciplinary behavior, with correlations up to $r = .40$. The more teachers were rated positively by the foreign judges for their brief NV behavior while disciplining students, the more they received positive evaluations from their students at the end of the year. Frontal lecturing to the entire class, which was found to be the positive predictor of SRT in the university study (2004), was found in high school to be a *negative* predictor, and all 40 relevant correlations for this instructional situation were negative! The teachers who were rated higher by the foreign judges for their NV behavior while lecturing were more disliked by their students, and they received more negative evaluations from them.

A NV behavior index of teachers' differential behavior was computed by subtracting the ratings (of one group of foreign judges) of each teacher's NV behavior in interaction with a low-achiever from the ratings (of another group of foreign judges) of the teacher's NV behavior while interacting with a high-achiever. The greater this difference, the more differential a teacher was considered. This empirical differentiality, based on NV behaviors in 10-second clips, was related to extreme dislike toward the teacher by the classroom students, with negative correlations ranging from $r = -.47$ to $r = -.63$ with SRT components.

Thus, the high school students liked teachers whose NV behavior while dealing with discipline problems was more positive, and disliked unfair, inequitable teachers who treated high-achievers differently than low-achievers. They also disliked the more positively rated lecturers and considered them unfair.

As in the other study, Babad et al. (2003) conducted partial correlation analyses to examine potential moderator variables that might explain the surprising finding that highly rated lecturing was associated with more negative student evaluations. It turned out that higher ratings of NV behavior in frontal lecturing to the entire class were related to greater teacher differentiality (which was disliked by students). The negative NV-SRT correlations for lecturing indeed dropped after the effect of teacher differentiality was partialled out. In a subsequent study, Babad (2005b) showed the frontal lecturing thin slice clips to high school students in another town in Israel, and asked the students to make guesses about each (unknown) teacher's differential behavior when s/he would interact with low- and with high-achievers in other instances. And indeed, correlations around $r = .40$ indicated that high school students were able to guess teacher differentiality from their NV behavior while addressing their entire classrooms. Adult judges could *not* guess teacher differentiality. Babad concluded that students were "experts" in picking up and interpreting very fine and subtle nuances in teachers' NV behavior.

In conclusion, the findings on specific NV behaviors in defined instructional situations stand in contrast with the sweeping generalizations about the overall impact of global NV style on students' outcomes emerging from the teacher immediacy and enthusiasm literatures. NV behaviors can indeed predict aspects of teaching effectiveness, but such associations are context specific (differing between college and high school) and situation specific (as a function of the nature of specific instructional situations). The stronger NV-SRT predictions were found for the instructional situations reflecting students' central needs and concerns – learning from instructors' lecturing activity in college, and disciplinary action and teachers' fairness and equal treatment of all students in high school.

MICROANALYSIS : THE NV PROFILE OF THE "GOOD LECTURER"

The final section in this chapter brings the different literatures on teachers' NV behavior to some closure and integration through the discussion of microanalysis – the method for analyzing NV profiles and illuminating the molecular behaviors contributing to overall impression. When thin slices research yields dramatic predictions of various outcomes after an extremely brief exposure to the target person, the question that pops up in everybody's mind is: "What did they (teachers, judges, TV interviewers, doctors, job applicants) specifically *do* in those few seconds that could predict future outcomes?" The microanalytic technique is quite simple: A few judges scrutinize each brief clip of NV behavior by viewing it again and again. They are given a long list of molecular variables which isolate all possible elements of each gesture, expression, movement and body position. A list of microanalytic variables would include separate lists of variables for the face, the head, the hands, the body, and the voice (e.g., nods head, leans forward, blinks, fidgets with object, etc.). Ekman's Facial Action Coding System (FACS, Ekman & Friesen, 1978) uses essentially the same methodology for identifying all human emotions from the analysis of facial molecular elements.

For molar judgments (like those presented in the previous section), judges viewed each clip only once and then filled out their global impression (e.g., competent, interesting, etc.). For molecular analysis the clips are viewed again and again, until the judges feel that they had examined each specific aspect and rated it satisfactorily. The microanalytic ratings for each clip are then correlated with the molar judgments for those clips, to examine the extent to which each element had contributed to the overall impression. Microanalysis can illuminate the molecular NV profile of good teachers, TV interviewers, trial judges, etc. In studies where multiple brief clips of a given target person are available (see Babad, 1999, on TV interviewers), micro-analysis can be used to characterize the unique individual NV style of each target person. But usually the microanalysis is conducted on the entire target group (e.g., all teachers) where each person is represented by one brief clip only, and then microanalysis is used to discover a generalized profile. [In a way, it might be said that Murray (1983a) used a microanalytic approach in his study of teacher enthusiasm, only that he used molar observer judgments of classroom-observed NV behaviors rather than molecular elements].

Babad (2005a) pointed out that microanalysis can often be quite disappointing. Many variables can be quite elusive and difficult to rate and sometimes the analysis does not yield meaningful results. Sometimes only universal components emerge out of the microanalysis, such as smiling contributing to a positive impression or shouting contributing to a negative impression, and at other times sporadic findings cannot be integrated into a meaningful pattern.

Ambady and Rosenthal (1993) conducted microanalyses on the NV behaviors of 13 junior lecturers, using a dozen molecular behaviors (on arms, gaze, frown, nod, fidgeting, laughing, smiling, leaning, etc.) plus four "position" variables (of hands, legs, torso, and sitting versus standing). The microanalytic ratings were then correlated with the judges' molar ratings of the videotaped instructors, and also with the educational outcomes. The results were quite disappointing, and did not reveal a systematic and consistent profile of good lecturers. In a way, they might have uncovered in that analysis the NV characteristics of *bad* lecturers, as the highest (negative) correlations were found for frowning and for Ekman and Friesen's (1969) adaptors – fidgeting with hands, legs, and objects.

Babad et al. (2004) conducted a microanalysis on the 67 clips depicting professors' NV behavior in lecturing to their classes. As mentioned above, the molar judgments for this instructional situation positively predicted the relevant aspects of SRT, and the objective of the microanalysis was to search for the NV profile of the good lecturer. Table 3T3 presents the correlations between 42 microanalytic molecular behaviors and the global (molar) impressions of the foreign judges based on the intact 9-second clips. Of the 42 correlations in the Table, 25 were statistically significant, and some reflected very strong relationships.

Because of the significance of the profile of the good lecturer derived from molecular elements of their NV lecturing behavior, I next list all the specific behaviors found significantly related to the global impression, re-ordered in meaningful conceptual clusters. The professors who received more positive molar ratings by the foreign judges on the basis of 9 seconds of their lecturing, demonstrated more overall NV emphasis ($r = .52$); voice intent toward students to

Table 3: The NV Profile of a Good Lecturer: Correlations between Microanalytic Molecular Behaviors and Molar Judgments for NV Lecturing Clips in 67 University Courses (Adapted from Babad et al., 2004)

Microanalytic NV Behavior	Correlation with Molar Judgment	Microanalytic NV Behavior	Correlation with Molar Judgment
Face Variables		*Body Variables*	
Smile	.44**	Sitting vs. standing	.42**
Frown	−.42**	Moving in space	.28*
Gaze down	−.36*	Body expressiveness	.33*
Eye contact	.34*	Lean forward	−.38*
Blinking	−.14	Lean backward	.09
Wide vs. narrow eyes	−.12	Lean sideways	−.35*
Tense vs. relaxed face	.31*	Orientation to audien.	.34*
Sarcasm	.30*	Fidgeting with body	−.25*
Gen. face expression	.20	Fidgeting with object	−.05
Head Variables		*Changes*	
Movement, expression	.10	Body & posture shift	.38**
Nod head	.03	Change NV express.	−.13
Shake head	−.18	Change in intensity	.42**
Thrust head	−.02	*Global Variables*	
Touch head	−.18	Regulators	−.11
Hands Variables		Illustrators	.16
Hold hands	−.23	Tense vs. relaxed	.31*
Movement, expression	.50**	Overall emphasis	.52**
Beating movement	.39**	*Voice Variable*	
Round movement	.30*	Intensity (volume)	.43**
Hands in pockets	.32*	Soft vs. hard	−.34*
Hands folded together	−.23	Voice change	.42**
		Voice emphasis	.41**
		Slow/fast tempo	.45**
		Intent toward student	.40**

*$p < .05$ **$p < .001$
Note: Voice variables were judged while hearing professors' voice. All other microanalytic judgments were made without hearing professors' voice.

make them understand (.40); and body orientation toward students (.34). They were more expressive, showing more movement and expressions of their hands (.50); hand beating movements and round movements (.39 and .30, respectively); body expressiveness (.33) and body movement in the classroom space (.28), while standing rather than sitting (.42). The more positively-rated professors demonstrated more changes in intensity (.42); body and posture shifts (.38); voice change (.42); and voice emphasis (.41). But interestingly, the professors judged as better lecturers were also more relaxed (relaxed face .31, and overall relaxation .31), and they refrained from negative behaviors (negative correlations): frowning (−.42); gazing down (−.36); and fidgeting with body (−.25). Among the different clusters in Table 3, the use of voice was particularly important in predicting the judges' molar ratings, and all correlations for the voice variables were quite substantial: Volume and intensity (.43); soft voice (−.34); voice change (.42); voice emphasis (.41); fast tempo (.45); and voice seemingly intended to make students understand (.40).

Together with the analysis of the significant molecular predictors of effective lecturing, it is important to inspect the molecular behaviors that were *un*related to the molar judgments. In Table 3, the nonsignificant correlates were noted for several miscellaneous behaviors (e.g., blinking, wide-narrow eyes, leaning backwards, etc.), but more notably for the cluster of head variables (head movement, nodding, shaking, thrusting, etc.). This is interesting, because in a parallel microanalysis of the NV profile of effective TV interviewers (Babad, 1999; see next discussion), head variables – especially head thrust and nodding – were found to be significant predictors of molar impressions. Perhaps TV interviewers, who are seated and cannot move about, need to use their heads for "expressive purposes" more than college instructors, who are free to move about in the classroom space.

This profile of effective lecturing – derived from exacting analysis of extremely brief samples of instructors' NV behavior under context-minimal conditions and with no comprehension of verbal content - was quite clear, consistent, and rich in detail. Highly-rated lecturers are very expressive in their faces, hands, voices, and body orientation toward their audience. They make continuous shifts in the various channels of their NV behavior, thereby preventing boredom and increasing student interest. And yet, despite their high level of activity, they are quite relaxed and avoid showing negative behaviors.

These findings are consonant with the various lines of research discussed in this chapter. They lend validity to teacher enthusiasm and teacher immediacy field research and experimental studies, despite the numerous flaws and methodological faults in many studies. Still, new elements emerged in the microanalysis that could not have emerged in all previous analyses. Most important is the fact that effective lecturers are quite relaxed despite their high level of face, body, and voice activity. Unlike many other life situations, their over-expressiveness is not a sign of tension or anxiety, and they even seem to enjoy the commotion. The other element concerns the finding that effective lecturers refrain from manifesting negative behaviors such as frowning, gazing down, and Ekmen-type adaptors. The absence of influence of such negative predictors enhances the effectiveness of their positive expressive characteristics.

MICROANALYTIC COMPARISON OF EFFECTIVE LECTURERS EFFECTIVE TV INTERVIEWERS

The utility of microanalysis can be enhanced if it can demonstrate distinct and unique profiles of effective NV behavior in different social roles and different contexts. Beyond the universal meaning of some NV behaviors – such as smiling being positive or Ekman-type adaptors being negative – "success" in a particular social role would require a different profile of NV behaviors than in another role, dependent upon contextual aspects and normative demands. Babad (1999) investigated the NV behavior of TV interviewers with the objective of tracing preferential behavior, and that study included a microanalysis of seven prominent Israeli TV interviewers. The same set of microanalytic variables was used in the Babad et al. (2004) study, and therefore it was possible to compare the NV profile of positively-rated professors and TV interviewers.

Comparison of the 1999 and 2004 microanalyses showed that a substantial number of variables predicted the molar judgments in the same direction in both analyses (such as positive correlations for smiling, relaxed face and round hand movements, and negative correlations for frowning, gazing down, blinking, and fidgeting with self and objects). However, a substantial number of microanalytic variables that were found to be negative predictors for TV interviewers, emerged as positive predictors for effective teachers. Such a reversed pattern was found for sarcasm, head shaking, hand movements and gestures, beating hand movements, body mobility, body and posture shifts, changes in intensity, and several voice variables.

Thus, changes in NV behavior and shifts in intensity, as well as "strong" expressive behaviors, are negative indicators in the tense and confrontational setting of the TV interview. These same behavioral aspects become positive indicators in the more relaxed, less confrontational atmosphere of the university lecture, and intensive and strong NV behaviors contribute to lecture effectiveness rather than hindering it. The same behavior might be perceived and interpreted as "aggressive" in one context and as "enthusiastic" in another setting. Therefore, the conclusion presented earlier for thin slices research, that a NV behavior attains its particular meaning only in the context and the situation within which it is enacted, is further confirmed by evidence from the microanalytic research.

CONCLUSION

The profile of successful lecturers, derived from very fine and exacting molecular aspects of extremely brief behavioral instances, does not tell a new story about effective teaching. It consistently confirms the picture emerging from a multitude of studies in several separate literatures, and supports the intuitive common sense of educators and teacher training specialists that instructors' expressive behavior and enthusiastic (NV) conduct contribute to students' interest, satisfaction, and motivation to pursue their studies. However, the specific NV research and the microanalytic research add more specific and particular details, uncovers some counter-intuitive findings and illuminates non-findings. Most importantly, it shows how the various details are integrated into a whole picture. Thus, we can feel confident that teachers' expressive style in higher education, as delineated and investigated in various methodologies and measurement designs, is strongly related to, and probably accounts for major elements of "effective teaching."

REFERENCES

Abrami, P., Leventhal, L., and Perry, R. (1982). Educational seduction. *Review of Educational Research* 52: 445–464.

Allen, D., and Ryan, K. (1969). *Microteaching*. Reading, MA: Addison-Welsey.

Ambady, N., Bernieri F., and Richeson, J. (2000). Toward a histology of social behavior: judgmental accuracy from this slices of the behavioral stream. In M. Zanna (ed.), *Advances in Experimental Social Psychology* (Vol. 32, pp. 201–271). Boston: Academic Press.

Ambady, N., and Rosenthal, R. (1992). Thin slices of behavior as predictors of inter-personal consequences: A meta-analysis. *Psychological Bulletin* 111: 256–274.

Ambady, N., and Rosenthal, R. (1993). Half a minute: predicting teacher evaluations from thin slices of behavior and physical attractiveness. *Journal of Personality and Social Psychology* 64: 431–441.

Andersen, J. (1978). *The Relationship between Teacher Immediacy and Teaching Effectiveness*. Unpublished doctoral dissertation, West Virginia University, Morgantown, W. Va.

Andersen, J. (1979). Teacher immediacy as a predictor of teaching effectiveness. In D. Nimmo (ed.), *Communication yearbook 3* (pp. 543–559). New Brunswick, NJ: Transaction Books.

Archer, D., and Costanzo., M. (1988). *The Interpersonal Perception Task*. Berkeley, CA: University of California Extension Media Center.

Babad, E. (1993). Teachers' differential behavior. *Educational Psychology Review* 5: 347–376.

Babad, E. (1999). Preferential treatment in television interviewing: Evidence from nonverbal behavior. *Political Communication* 16: 337–358.

Babad, E. (2005a). Nonverbal behavior in education. In J. Harrigan, R. Rosenthal and K. Scherer (eds.), *The New Handbook of Methods in Nonverbal Behavior Research* (pp. 283–311). Oxford: Oxford University Press.

Babad, E. (2005b). Guessing teachers' differential treatment of high- and low achievers from thin slices of their public lecturing behavior. *Journal of Nonverbal Behavior* 29: 125–134.

Babad, E. (2005c). The psychological price of media bias. *Journal of Experimental Psychology: Applied* 11: 245–255.

Babad, E., Avni-Babad, D., and Rosenthal, R. (2003). Teachers' brief nonverbal behaviors in defined instructional situations can predict students' evaluations. *Journal of Educational Psychology* 95: 553–562.

Babad, E., Avni-Babad, D., and Rosenthal, R. (2004) Prediction of student's evaluations from professors' nonverbal behavior in defined instructional situations. *Social Psychology of Education* 7: 3–33.

Babad, E., Bernieri, F., and Rosenthal, R. (1989). When less information is more informative: Diagnosing teacher expectancies from brief samples of behavior. *British Journal of Educational Psychology* 59: 281–195.

Babad, E., Bernieri, F., and Rosenthal, R. (1991). Students as judges of teachers' verbal and nonverbal behavior. *American Educational Research Journal* 28: 211–234.

Babad, E., and Taylor, P. (1992). Transparency of teacher expectations across language, cultural boundaries. *Journal of Educational Research* 86: 120–125.

Bandura, A. (1977). *Social Learning Theory*. Englewood Cliffs, NJ: Prentice-Hall.

Blanck P., Rosenthal, R., and Cordell, L. (1985). The appearance of justice: Judges' verbal and nonverbal behavior in criminal jury trials. *Stanford Law Review* 38: 89–164.

Brophy, J. (1983). Research on the self-fulfilling prophecy and teacher expectations. *Journal of Educational Psychology* 75: 631–661.

Brown, G. (1975). *Microteaching: A Program of Teaching Skills*. London: Methuen & Co.

Christophel, D. (1990a). *The Relationships among Teacher Immediacy Behaviors, Student Motivation, and Learning*. Unpublished doctoral dissertation, West Virginia University, Morgantown, W. Va.

Christophel, D. (1990b). The relationships among teacher immediacy behaviors, student motivation, and learning. *Communication Education* 37: 323–340.

Cohen, P. (1990). Bringing research into practice. In M. Theall and J. Franklin (eds.), *Student Ratings of Instruction: Issues for Improving Practice* (pp. 123–132). San Francisco: Jossey-Bass.

Comstock, J., Rowell, E., and Bowers, J. (1995). Food for thought: Teacher nonverbal immediacy, student learning, and curvilinearity. *Communication Education* 44: 251–266.

Cooper, H., and Good, T. (1983). *Pygmalion Grows Up: Studies in the Expectation Communication Process*. New York: Longman.

Costanzo, M., and Archer, D. (1993). *The Interpersonal Perception Task-15 (IPT-15)* [Videotape] Berkeley: University of California Extension Media Center.

Cronbach, L. (1976). *Research on Classroom and Schools: Formulation of Questions, Design and Analysis*. Stanford evaluation consortium, Eric document no. ED 135 801, Stanford University, CA.

DePaulo, B. (1992). Nonverbal behavior and self-presentation. *Psychological Bulletin* 111: 203–243.

DePaulo, B., and Friedman, H. (1988). Nonverbal communication. In D. Gilbert, S. Fiske and G. Lindzey (eds.), *The Handbook of Social Psychology* (4th edition, pp. 3–40). Boston: McGraw-Hill.

Doyle, W. (1977). Paradigms for teacher education research. In L. Shulman (ed.), *Review of Research in Education* (Vol. 5, pp. 163–198). Itasca, IL: Peacock.

Doyle, W. (1981). Research on classroom contexts. *Journal of Teacher Education* 32: 3–6

Doyle, W. (1983). Academic work. *Review of Educational Research* 53: 159–200.

Ekman, P. (1985). *Telling Lies*. New York: Norton.

Ekman, P., and Friesen, W. (1969a). The repertoire of nonverbal behavior: Categories, origins, usages and coding. *Semiotica* 1: 49–98.

Ekman, P., and Friesen, W. (1969b). Nonverbal leakage and clues to deception. *Psychiatry* 32: 88–106.

Ekman, P., and Friesen, W. (1978). *Facial Action Coding System: A Technique for the Measurement of Facial Movement*. Palo Alto, CA: Consulting Psychologistm Press.

Feeley, T. (2002), Evidence of halo effects in students evaluations of communication instruction. *Communication Education* 51: 225–236.

Feldman, R. (1985). Nonverbal behavior, race, and the classroom teacher. *Theory into Practice* 24: 45–49.

Feldman, R., and Saletzky, R. (1986). Nonverbal communication in interracial teacher-student interaction. In R. Feldman (ed.), *The Social Psychology of Education: Current Research and Theory* (pp. 115–131). NY: Cambridge University Press.

Fenstermacher, G. (1979). A philosophical consideration if recent research on teaching effectiveness. *Review of Research in Education* 6: 157–185.

Gada-Jain, N. (1999). *Intentional Synchrony Effects on Job Interview Evaluation*, Unpublished Master Thesis, University of Toledo.

Galloway, C. (1984). Nonverbal behavior and teacher-student relationships: An intercultural perspective. In A. Wolfgang (ed.), *Nonverbal Behavior: Perspectives, Applications, and Intercultural Insights* (pp. 411–430). Toronto: Hogrefe.

Greenwald, A., and Gillmore, S. (1977a). No pain, no gain? The importance of measuring course workload in student ratings of instruction. *Journal of Educational Psychology* 89: 743–751.

Greenwald, A., and Gillmore, S. (1977b). Grading leniency is a removable containment of student ratings. *American Psychologist* 52: 1209–1217.

Harris, M., and Rosenthal, R. (1985). Mediation of interpersonal expectancy effects: 31 meta-analyses. *Psychological Bulletin* 97: 363–386.

Harris, M., and Rosenthal, R. (2005). No more teachers' dirty looks: Effects of teacher nonverbal behavior on student outcomes. In R. Riggio and R.S. Feldman (eds.), *Applications of Nonverbal Communication* (pp.157–192).

Hart, A. (1995). Naturally occurring expectation effects. *Journal of Personality and Social Psychology* 68: 109–115

Hunnicutt, V. (1999). Training in the use of selected nonverbal behaviors to reduce student disruptions in the classroom. *Dissertation Abstracts International, Section A: Humanities & Social Sciences*. US, 1999 April 59 (10-A): p. 3726.

Johnson, S., and Miller, A., (2002). A cross-cultural study of immediacy, credibility & learning in the U.S. and Kenya. *Communication Education* 51: 280–292.

Klinzing, H. (1983). Effects of a training program on expressive non-verbal behavior. Paper presented at the Annual Meeting of the American Educational Research Association (Montreal, Canada, April 1983).

Klinzing, H., and Jackson, I. (1987). Training teachers in nonverbal sensitivity and nonverbal behavior. *International Journal of Educational Research* 11:589–600.

Knapp, M. (1978). *Nonverbal Communication in Human Interaction* (2nd edition). New York: Holt, Rinehart & Winston.

Marsh, H. (1984). Student evaluation of university teaching: Dimensionality, reliability, validity, potential biases, and utility. *Journal of Educational Psychology* 76: 707–754.

Marsh, H. (1987). *Students' Evaluation of University Teaching: Research Findings, Methodological Issues and Directions for Future Research*. Elmford, NY: Pergamon.

Marsh, H., and Roche, L. (2000). Effects of grading leniency and low workload on students' evaluation of teaching: Popular myth, bias, validity, or innocent bystanders? *Journal of Educational Psychology* 92: 202–228.

Marsh, H., and Ware, J. (1982). Effects of expressiveness, content, coverage and incentive on multidimensional student rating scales: New interpretations of the Dr. Fox effect. *Journal of Educational Psychology* 74: 126–134.

McCroskey, P., and Richmond, J. (1992). Increasing teacher influence through immediacy. In V. Richmond and J. McCroskey (eds.), *Power in the Classroom: Communication, Control and Concern* (pp.101–119). Hillsdale, NJ: Erlbaum.

McCroskey, J., Sallinen, A., Fayer, J., Richmond, V., and Barraclough, R. (1996). Nonverbal immediacy & cognitive learning: A cross-cultural investigation. *Communication Education* 45: 200–211.

McKinney, C., Larkins, A., Kazelkis, R., Ford, M., Allen, J., and Burts, D. (1983). Some effects of teacher enthusiasm on student achievement in fourth grade social studies: *Journal of Educational Research* 76: 249–253.

Mehrabian, A. (1969). Some referents and measures of nonverbal behavior. *Behavioral Research Methods and Instrumentation* 1: 213–217.

Mehrabian, A. (1971). *Silent Messages*. Belmont, CA: Wadsworth.

Moore, D., and Glynn, T. (1984). Variation in question rate as a function of position in the classroom. *Educational Psychology* 4: 233–248.

Murray, H. (1983a). Low-inference classroom teaching behaviors and students' ratings of college teaching effectiveness. *Journal of Educational Psychology* 75: 138–149.

Murray, H (1983b). Low- inference classroom teaching behaviors in relation to six measures of college teaching effectiveness. In J.G. Donald (ed.), *Proceedings of the Conference on the Evaluation and Improvement of University Teaching: The Canadian Experience*. Montreal: Center for Teaching and Learning Services, McGill University.

Murray, H., and Lawrence, C. (1980). Speech and drama training for lectures as a means of improving university teaching. *Research in Higher Education* 13: 73–90.

Myers, S., Zhong, M., and Guan, S. (1998). Instructor immediacy in the Chinese college classroom. *Communication Studies* 49: 240–254.

Naftulin, D., Ware, J., and Donnelly, F. (1973). The doctor fox lecture: A paradigm of educational seduction. *Journal of Medical Education* 48: 630–635.

Neulip, J.W. (1995). A comparison of teacher immediacy in African-American & Euro-American classrooms. *Communication Education* 44: 267–267.

Neulip, J.W. (1997). A cross-cultural comparison of teacher immediacy in American and Japanese college classrooms. *Communication Research* 24: 431–452.

Perrott, E. (1977). *Microteaching in Higher Education: Research, Development and Practice*. Surrey, GB: Society for Research into Higher Education.

Perry, R. (1990). Introduction to the special section. *Journal of Educational Psychology* 82: 183–188.

Perry, R., Abrami, P., and Leventhal, L., (1979). Educational seduction: The effect of instructor expressiveness & lecture content on student rating and achievements. *Journal of Educational Psychology* 71: 107–116.

Perry, R., and Magnuson, J. (1987). Effective instruction and students' perception of control in the college classroom: Multiple-lecture effects. *Journal of Educational Psychology* 79: 453–460.

Perry, R., and Penner, K. (1990). Enhancing academic achievement in college students through attributional retraining and instruction. *Journal of Educational Psychology* 82: 262–271.

Pribyl, C., Sakamoto, M., and Keaten, J. (2004). The relationship between nonverbal immediacy, student motivation, and perceived cognitive learning among Japanese college students. *Japanese Psychological Research* 46: 73–85.

Richmond, V., Gorham, J., and McCroskey, J. (1987). The relationship between selected immediacy behaviors and cognitive learning. In M. McLaughlin (ed.), *Communication yearbook 10* (pp. 547–590). Newbury Park, CA: Sage.

Richmond, V., McCorskey, J., Plax, T., and Kearney, P. (1986). Teacher nonverbal immediacy training and student affect. *World Communication* 15: 181–194.

Roach, K., and Byrne P. (2001). A cross-cultural comparison of instructor communication in American & German classrooms. *Communication Education* 50: 1–14.

260

Rosenthal, R., Blanck, P., and Vannicelli, M. (1984). Speaking to and about patients: Predicting tone of voice. *Journal of Consulting and Clinical Psychology* 52: 679–686.

Rosenthal, R., Hall, J., Archer, D., DiMatto, M., and Rogers, P. (1979). *The Pons Test Manual: Profile of Nonverbal Sensitivity*. New York: Irvington Publishers.

Rosenthal, R., and Jacobson, L. (1968). *Pygmalion in the Classroom*. New York: Holt, Rinehart & Winston.

Rucker, M., and Gendrin, D. (2003). The impact of ethnic identification on student learning in the HBCU classroom. *Journal of Instructional Psychology* 30: 207–215.

Schonwetter, D., Perry, R., and Struthers, C. (1994). Student perceptions of control and success in college classroom: Affects and achievement in different instructional conditions. *Journal of Experimental Education* 61: 227–246.

Smith, H. (1984). Nonverbal behavior aspects of teaching. In A. Wolfgang (ed.), *Nonverbal Behavior: Perspectives, Applications, Intercultural Insights* (pp. 171–202). Toronto: Hogrefe.

Sorensen, G. (1980). *The Relationship between Teachers' Self-disclosive Statement and Student Learning*. Unpublished doctoral dissertation, West Virginia University, Morgantown, W. Va.

Streeter, B. (1986). The effect of training experienced teachers in enthusiasm on students' attitudes toward reading: *Reading Psychology* 7: 249–259.

Theall, M., and Franklin, J. (eds.). (1990). *Student Rating of Instruction: Issues for Improving Practice*. (New Directions for Teaching and Learning, No.43). San Francisco: Jossey-Bass.

Ware, J., and Williams, R. (1975). The Dr. Fox effect: A study of lecturer effectiveness and ratings of instruction. *Journal of Medical Education* 40: 149–156.

Witt, P. (2003). An experimental study of teachers' verbal and nonverbal immediacy, student motivation, and cognitive learning in video instruction. *Dissertation abstracts International, Section A: Humanities & Social Sciences*. Vol 63 (9-A): p. 3060.

Witt, P., and Wheeless, L.(2001). An experimental study of teachers' verbal and nonverbal immediacy and students' affective and cognitive learning. *Communication Education* 50: 327–342.

Witt, P., Wheeless, L., and Allen, M. (2004). A meta-analytical review of the relationship between teacher immediacy and student learning. *Communication Monographs* 71: 184–207.

Wood, A. (1998). The effects of teacher enthusiasm on student motivation, selective attention, and text memory. Doctoral dissertation, University of Western Ontario. *Dissertation abstracts International, Section A: Humanities & Social Sciences*. US, 1999 March 59 (9-A): p. 3355.

Woolfolk, A., and Galloway, C. (1985). Nonverbal communication and the study of teaching. *Theory Into Practice* 24: 77–84.

Wyckoff, W. (1973). The effect of stimulus variation on learning from lecture. *Journal of Experimental Education* 41: 85–90.

Zuckerman, M., DePaulo, B., and Rosenthal, R. (1986). Humans as deceivers and lie detectors. In P. Blanck, R. Buck and R. Rosenthal (eds.), *Nonverbal Communication in the Clinical Context* (pp. 13–35). University Park, PA: Pennsylvania State University Press.

8. Faculty Cultures and College Teaching

Paul D. Umbach

University of Iowa
paul-umbach@uiowa.edu

Abstract

College faculty members work and live in a web of varying cultures, all of which influence their work with undergraduates in and out of the classroom. In this chapter, I explore the influence that various faculty cultures (professional, institutional, and disciplinary) have on how faculty teach and interact with students. I begin by defining culture and its manifestations followed by a discussion of research on faculty subcultures. I then propose a model for studying faculty cultures as they relate to teaching and use my work and the work of others as examples of the effects of cultural contexts on teaching. Finally, I conclude by describing the implications that this research and the conceptual model have for practice and future research

Key Words: College faculty, culture, subcultures, teaching, student-faculty interactions, effective educational practices, instruction, pedagogy

From an organizational perspective, it is difficult to study how faculty teach and to understand why they teach the way they do. College faculty are embedded in an organizational matrix made up of disciplinary contexts and institutional alliances (Austin, 1990, p. 66; Clark, 1983, 1987a, 1987b; Kuh & Whitt, 1988; Ladd & Lipset, 1975; Ruscio, 1987). Distinct and fragmented disciplinary and institutional differences have created a diverse profession with varied teaching goals, values, and pedagogical techniques. This fragmentation has caused one scholar to suggest that "the academic man [and woman] is a myth (Light, 1974, p. 14)." Given these complicated, overlapping, and loosely-arranged structures, how does one make sense, in meaningful and useful ways, of the ways faculty deliver undergraduate instruction?

In their attempt to explain their functioning, scholars have characterized colleges and universities as loosely coupled systems

R.P. Perry and J.C. Smart (eds.), *The Scholarship of Teaching and Learning in Higher Education: An Evidence-Based Perspective*, 263–317.
© 2007 *Springer*.

(Weick, 1976), and as having problematic goals, unclear technologies, and fluid participation (Cohen & March, 1974). They also have described institutions of higher education as anarchical and irrational with high levels of ambiguity and uncertainty (Birnbaum, 1988; Cohen & March, 1974). Given these descriptions of how colleges are organized and the fragmented nature of the professoriate, it would seem that a cultural framework, which relies heavily on symbols to make sense of complex organizations and to provide direction in ambiguous environments, would be particularly useful in understanding faculty work. In fact, as early as the 1960s (Clark, 1962), researchers have used a cultural lens to explore and explain differences in faculty work, attitudes and beliefs. Since that time, dozens of studies have applied culture to the study of college faculty (e.g., Becher, 1981, 1987; Becher & Trowler, 2001; Clark, 1987a; Feldman & Paulsen, 1999; Freedman, 1979; Gaff & Wilson, 1971; Kuh & Whitt, 1988; Masland, 1982; Paulsen & Feldman, 1995a; Tierney & Bensimon, 1996; Tierney & Rhoades, 1993; Toma, 1997; Toma, Dubrow, & Hartley, 2005).

Interestingly, few, if any, researchers have conducted empirical research using culture to study faculty teaching. Burton Clark (1987a) perhaps offers the most extensive and compelling cultural analysis of college faculty, yet his work is nearly 20 years old and does not examine college teaching, either pedagogy or interactions with undergraduates, in any detail. Those who have applied the concept of culture to college teaching have made important contributions, but their work either lacks extensive empirical evidence (e.g., Austin, 1990; Austin, 1996; Feldman & Paulsen, 1999; Neumann, Parry, & Becher, 2002; Paulsen & Feldman, 1995a), focuses solely on disciplinary cultures (e.g., Becher & Trowler, 2001; Neumann et al., 2002), or emphasizes only institutional cultures (e.g., Ruscio, 1987). A few studies (e.g., Smart & Ethington, 1995) identify both institutional and disciplinary differences in faculty goals for undergraduate education, but they do so without an integrative conceptual framework. An integrated framework supported by empirical analysis of faculty cultures and college teaching seems important for two reasons. First, a framework will provide a comprehensive lens through which researchers can explore, understand, and study college teaching. Rather than attempt to explain each of the parts, a cultural framework may help make sense of the whole. Second, college campuses and disciplinary leaders seeking to create environments that emphasize effective teaching will benefit from an understanding of the complex nature of faculty cultures and subcultures. Without this knowledge, they are driving without a roadmap.

In this chapter, I apply a cultural lens to explore the influence that various faculty cultures (professional, institutional, and disciplinary) have on how faculty teach and interact with students. I begin my defining culture and its manifestations followed by a discussion of research on faculty subcultures. I then propose a model for studying faculty cultures as they relate to teaching. Using my work and the work of others as examples, I will examine the artifacts, behaviors, values, and underlying assumptions associated with teaching within each of the cultural contexts. Finally, I delineate the implications that this research and the conceptual model have for practice and future research.

DEFINITION OF CULTURE

Using culture as a framework to study organizations came in vogue in the late 1970s and the 1980s as researchers began to emphasize the importance of symbols within organizations and to move away from rational aspects of organizational functioning. A brief review of the literature suggests a large variety of definitions of culture. Some have suggested that this diversity can be attributed to culture's intellectual foundation in three disciplines: cultural anthropology, sociology, and psychology (Cameron & Ettington, 1988; Kuh & Whitt, 1988; Toma et al., 2005). Definitions of culture are as varied as their disciplinary underpinnings. Below are just a few examples of definitions of culture.

"A pattern of shared basic assumptions that the group learned as it solved its problems of external adaptation and internal integration, that has worked well enough to be considered valid and, therefore, to be taught to new members as the correct way to perceive, think, and feel in relation to those problems" (Schein, 1992, p. 12).

"Deeply embedded patterns of organizational behavior and the shared values, assumptions, beliefs, or ideologies that members have about their organization or its work" (Peterson & Spencer, 1990, p. 6).

"Historically transmitted pattern of meanings embodied in symbols, a system of inherited conceptions expressed in symbolic forms by means of which [people] communicate, perpetuate, and develop their knowledge about and attitudes toward life" (Geertz, 1973, p. 891).

"Both a product and a process, the shaper of human interaction and the outcome of it, continually recreated by people's ongoing interactions" (Jelinek, Smircich, & Hirsch, 1983, p. 331).

"The pattern of development reflected in a society's system of knowledge, ideology, values, laws, and day-to-day ritual" (Morgan, 1997, p. 120).

Given the array of definitions of culture, one is faced with the challenge of adopting a definition that has its shortcomings. Nevertheless, for this analysis of faculty cultures, I adopt the Kuh and Whitt (1988, pp. 12–13) definition that suggests culture in higher education "is the collective, mutually shaping patterns of norms, values, practices, beliefs, and assumptions that guide the behavior of individuals and groups...and provides a frame of reference within which to interpret the meaning of events and actions." It is important to note that this definition not only encompasses the idea of shared norms and values, but it suggests that culture is socially constructed. In other words, individuals form their realities in a process that of enactment or the interpretation of the manifestations of culture (Weick, 1979).

These definitions lead me to argue that faculty cultures play an important role in guiding faculty teaching behaviors. Faculty cultures serve as a guide for faculty in the ways in which they interpret and making meaning of their roles as teachers. What is taught and how it is taught is framed by the professional, institutional, and disciplinary of college faculty. Simply put, I argue that the professional, institutional, and disciplinary cultures of college faculty shape the way faculty members teach and interact with undergraduate students. In turn, these teaching behaviors and interactions influence student learning. In its simplest form, my proposed model for faculty cultures and college teaching can be depicted in the following way: Faculty subcultures (professional, institutional, and disciplinary)→faculty teaching→student learning. Before I explore these varying faculty cultures and their relation to college teaching in greater detail, it is important to understand how culture might manifest itself in colleges and universities.

MANIFESTATIONS OF CULTURE

I integrate the work of Schein (1992), Peterson and Spencer (1990), and Hofstede, Neuijen, Ohayv, Daval and Sanders (1990) to frame my discussion of four manifestations of culture: artifacts, behavioral patterns and processes, espoused values, and basic underlying assumptions. Figure 1F1 summarizes the four levels of culture. Artifacts are the tangible elements of an organization, everything that one can see, hear, or feel. These include architecture, language, ceremonies, myths,

Figure 1: Manifestations of culture.

	Definition	Examples related to college teaching
Artifacts	architecture, geo-spatial environment, rituals, traditions, myths, symbols, structures	teaching awards, centers for teaching and learning, representation of groups on campus
Behavioral Patterns	manifested behaviors that are sustained and repeated over time	classroom emphases, student evaluations, reward systems (tenure and promotion)
Espoused values and beliefs	Stated goals, strategies, missions, philosophies	teaching is important, faculty should be available to students
Underlying assumptions or embedded values and beliefs	taken-for-granted beliefs; provide a real sense of meaning of their organizational enactment	autonomy, academic freedom

Notes: Adapted from Schein (1993) and Peterson and Spencer (1990)

rituals, organizational structures, sagas, and traditions (Clark, 1972; Hofstede et al., 1990; Kuh & Whitt, 1988; Ott, 1989; Peterson & Spencer, 1990; Riley, 1983; Schein, 1992; Trice & Beyer, 1993). Artifacts serve as symbols that are particularly important in loosely coupled systems where are often uncoordinated (Weick, 1976). Symbols can help individuals make sense of organizational goals and focus attention on organizational values (Geertz, 1973; K. E. Weick, 1982). Examples of artifacts as they relate to college teaching might be an annual teaching award or a presentation by the college center for teaching and learning at new faculty orientation. Others might be structures that support the recruitment and retention of faculty of color.

Behavioral patterns and processes are enduring behavioral activities with standardized form and content, either formally defined or informally developed by organizational members (Peterson & Spencer, 1990). These behaviors are part of an organization's operations and often create the structure for social interaction. Behavioral patterns might be interpreted as specific teaching behaviors such as rapport, task orientation, organization, and enthusiasm (See Marsh in this book for a full review of teaching behaviors). Other possible examples of these as they relate to teaching and learning are what faculty members choose to emphasize in the classroom, enduring pedagogical strategies, and student evaluations. Others might consider the specific processes associated with the tenure process, such as peer evaluation of teaching, as behavior patterns.

Espoused values and beliefs are the stated values that organizational members openly communicate (Peterson & Spencer, 1990; Schein, 1992). These values and beliefs help create the institutional identity but are often present only in the ideal. Common examples of these are stated goals and missions. For example, a college may indicate in their mission that they are a learning college that focuses its efforts on holistic student growth and development. Another institution might indicate that they believe diversity is important on their campus and they work to create a supportive environment that utilizes diversity to enhance learning.

The final manifestation of culture is underlying assumptions or embedded values (Schein, 1992) and beliefs (Peterson & Spencer, 1990). Underlying assumptions are the taken-for-granted beliefs that help people make meaning of an organization. People are not conscious of these beliefs and values, yet they guide their daily actions. Some faculty may consider autonomy and academic freedom to be an example of these embedded values. Faculty at one institution, perhaps a liberal arts college, may also believe that teaching and service to undergraduates is central to their work and their behaviors follow this belief.

It is important to note that these manifestations may not be discrete in nature. For example, the tenure process may be considered a behavioral pattern in that junior faculty submit dossiers for review, senior faculty evaluate teaching, faculty members (often in the form of committees) meet and vote on candidates, and administrators weigh in on a candidate's worthiness. The process also serves as a symbol and helps junior faculty interpret what is important to an organization (Tierney & Bensimon, 1996). Tenure processes may also reveal much about the espoused and embedded values of a college. A college may indicate that teaching is of central importance in the promotion and tenure process (espoused values); yet, the same college's tenure and promotion committee may spend most of their time deliberating the scholarly significance of a junior faculty member's work and conduct only a cursory review of their teaching (embedded values). Regardless of overlap, exploring the manifestations of culture is often the only way to study and understand cultures.

To understand faculty cultures and how they shape teaching, we must explore these various manifestations of culture. The artifacts, behavioral patterns and processes, espoused values, and basic underlying assumptions of the profession, institutions, and academic disciplines help faculty members make meaning of their roles as teachers and provide a guide for how to teach. These manifestations also are a way that researchers can view, explore, and understand teaching cultures.

FACULTY SUBCULTURES

Within a single college or university, numerous subcultures may be operating (Tierney, 1988). Bolton and Kammeyer (1972, pp. 381–382) define a subculture as "A normative value system held by some group or persons who are in persisting interaction, who transmit the norms and values to newcomers by some communicated process, and who exercise some sort of control to ensure conformity to the norms." Members of subgroups interact with one another because of formal and informal purposes, shared values, similar work roles, physical proximity, and history (Van Maanan & Barley, 1985). Through these interactions, a collective understanding is developed and a subculture formed. It is important to note that a subculture may share some values and attitudes and not be entirely in opposition with the host organizational culture (Broom & Selznick, 1973; Kuh & Whitt, 1988).

Some have described the academic profession as a complex matrix of sub-professions (Bess, 1982), a web of many professions (Ruscio, 1987), or a fragmented series of unrelated parts (Light, 1974). I adhere to the argument made by many higher education scholars in that the professoriate is made up of three overlapping subcultures: professional, institutional, and disciplinary (Austin, 1990; Clark, 1987a; Kuh & Whitt, 1988). I explore each of these subcultures in the following sections, particularly in ways that relate to undergraduate instruction, and propose a theoretical framework for studying college teaching that integrates the theory described above with the concept of faculty subcultures.

THE ACADEMIC PROFESSION AS A SUBCULTURE

Although the professoriate is segmented and made up of disciplinary and institutional subcultures, researchers have found that it

269

is bound together in a culture based on a few basic concepts and symbols (Bowen & Schuster, 1986; Clark, 1987a; Kuh & Whitt, 1988; Ruscio, 1987). The extent to which the professional culture emphasizes good teaching affects how faculty teach. Clark (1987a) suggests that the academic profession holds three universal values or norms: the pursuit and dissemination of knowledge, academic honesty, and academic freedom. Nearly all academics seek to advance knowledge, answer questions, solve problems, and transmit understanding through teaching (Bowen & Schuster, 1986). Many contend that teaching, compared with research, holds greater or equal import among faculty members. Recent research suggests that faculty continue to "express normative unity about the value of teaching and the satisfaction they derive from it" (Leslie, 2002, p. 70). The extent to which the culture of the profession places a priority on teaching can have profound effects on instruction. A culture that rewards teaching is likely to have good teachers.

INSTITUTIONAL SUBCULTURES

Where a faculty member is employed "defines the institutional career, strongly affecting the duties, opportunities, rewards, relationship with the discipline, and prestige of the faculty member experiences" (Austin, 1990, p. 66). Mission, academic program, governance structures, academic standards, reward structures, size, location, physical environment, saga, and distinctive themes, all contribute to an institution's faculty culture and how faculty teach and interact with students (Austin, 1990; Clark, 1962, 1970; Kuh & Whitt, 1988; Ruscio, 1987).

Colleges and universities affect faculty cultures through recruitment, interpersonal socialization, and work socialization (Clark, 1962). Institutions recruit faculty that they believe hold the same values, beliefs, and attitudes. In other words, they try to find the right fit for the position and the institution. In turn, the recruit is socialized through interpersonal interactions with faculty and administration. The newcomer is oriented to the priorities and goals of the institution, which already presumably match the character and personality of the newcomer. The demands and rewards of the work further induce the faculty members to adopt institutional values and beliefs.

Researchers have used institutional classification systems (e.g., Carnegie Classification) to uncover differences between faculty teaching roles (Austin, 1990; Clark, 1962, 1987a, 1987b; Fairweather, 1996; Kuh & Whitt, 1988). While the different types of faculty varies between colleges and universities, institutions of similar type tend to have similar faculty cultures. For example, faculty members at liberal arts colleges are likely to be focus on teaching (Clark, 1962). They have heavy teaching loads, interact frequently with undergraduates, tend to be less specialized, and have little interest in the application of knowledge (Austin, 1990; Clark, 1987a; Kuh & Whitt, 1988). These colleges tend to emphasize teaching excellence and the development of undergraduates as whole persons. Compared with faculty at other institution types, faculty at liberal arts colleges are more likely to emphasize the acquisition and integration of knowledge (Smart & Ethington, 1995). Recent research on undergraduate students also suggests a distinctive culture at liberal arts colleges where faculty teaching and interactions with students emphasizes good practices in undergraduate education (Kuh, 2001, 2003; Pascarella & Terenzini, 2005; Pascarella, Wolniak, Seifert, Cruce, & Blaich, 2005).

In contrast, faculty members at major research universities tend to be emphasize research and consulting and place a lower priority on teaching (Clark, 1962). They identify more strongly with their disciplines, place a priority on research, spend more time teaching and advising graduate students, and have lighter teaching loads (Astin & Chang, 1995; Austin, 1990, 1996; Bowen & Schuster, 1986; Clark, 1962, 1987a; Kuh & Whitt, 1988). In many cases, they are cosmopolitans and their disciplinary affiliation is stronger than their institutional ties.

Faculty at state colleges and universities have high teaching loads and little time for research or time to cultivate affiliations beyond the local community (Clark, 1962, 1987a; Fairweather, 1996). In recent years, a paradox has developed at many of these institutions. Many have increased their expectations for faculty research productivity, while maintaining high course loads (Perry, Clifton, Menec, Struthers, & Menges, 2000; Perry et al., 1997).

Community colleges faculty place nearly all of their emphasis on teaching. They have high teaching load and varied service expectations, it is little surprise that community college faculty develop strong commitments to their institution and pragmatically avoid time-consuming affiliations beyond their local community(Clark, 1962).

Others have described structural characteristics of colleges and universities that extend beyond institutional type and signal distinctive faculty cultures. For example, small institutions appear to have unique cultures that often translate into an instructional culture that benefits students (Clark, 1970; Kuh, 2001, 2003; Kuh & Whitt, 1988).

DISCIPLINARY SUBCULTURES

As Becher (1981, p. 109) suggests, "academic disciplines are also a cultural phenomena: they are embodied in collections of like-minded people, each with their own codes of conduct, sets of values and distinctive intellectual tastes." In fact, identification with the culture of the academic discipline is often stronger than with the institution of employment (Blau, 1973; Clark, 1983; Ruscio, 1987). Newcomers learn the content of the discipline, its language, ways members interact with one another, and pedagogical techniques. (Becher, 1987; Becher & Trowler, 2001). Members of disciplines regularly interact with both local and national colleagues. This interaction encourages cooperation among members and affirms a discipline's goals, values, and beliefs with regard to teaching and research (Becher, 1981, 1987; Becher & Trowler, 2001; Clark, 1987a).

A relatively large body of research suggests that what is taught and how it is taught is largely shaped by these disciplinary cultures. Currently, it seems that two models of classifying academic disciplines predominate the study of college faculty: those developed by Biglan (1973a, 1973b) then later extended by Becher (1987; Becher & Trowler (2001), and the application of Holland's (1966, 1973, 1985, 1997) work on careers to academic environments. I summarize these classification schemas in Figure 2 and briefly describe them below. I also provide some examples of the research done on teaching using each of the schemas. Using these classification systems helps researchers make sense of the values, beliefs, and attitudes of disciplinary cultures. For detailed description of each of these typologies, consult Braxton and Hargens (1996), Becher and Trowler (2001), and Smart, Feldman, and Ethington (2000).

Biglan and Becher disciplinary groupings. More than 30 years ago, Lodahl and Gordon (1972) applied Kuhn's (1962) paradigm development to academic fields, which was soon to become an important concept for the study of disciplinary differences. They argued that fields with established paradigms have a high degree of consensus about theory, methods, and problems. Their analyses supported this assertion, and they identified physics and chemistry as having high levels of paradigm development and political science and sociology as having low paradigm development.

Building on this work and the earlier work of Storer (1967, 1972), Biglan (1973a, 1973b) developed an empirically derived three dimensional classification schema (See Figure 2 for a description of the

Figure 2: Descriptions of Biglan[1], Becher[2], and Holland[3] disciplinary groupings.

Disciplinary category	Description	Example disciplines
Biglan[1]		
Hard	Disciplines have a high degree of paradigm development, thus members share consensus about theory, methods, techniques, and problems.	Engineering, math, physics
Soft	Disciplines have a low degree of paradigm development, thus members hold varying beliefs about theory, methods, techniques, and problems.	History, anthropology, economics
Pure	Disciplines traditionally have little concern for practical application.	Chemistry, political science, foreign languages
Applied	Disciplines traditionally emphasize the practical application of knowledge.	Computer science, , accounting, agronomy
Life	Disciplines involved with organic or living forms of study.	Biology, psychology, sociology
Non-life	Disciplines involved in the study of inorganic or non-living things.	Astronomy, math, English, finance
Becher[2]		
Hard-pure	Disciplines focus discovery through simplification and quantification. Knowledge is cumulative in nature, is neatly divided, and grows from a main body of research. The culture is competitive, highly collaborative, with a high publication rate.	Biology, chemistry
Soft-pure	Disciplinary focuses on discovery through interpretation and tend to use qualitative techniques. Researchers focus on particulars in an attempt to understand, not simplify. The culture focuses on the individual, is characterized as loosely structured, and	English, philosophy, psychology
Hard-applied	Disciplines are pragmatic in their pursuit with the mastery of the physical environment. Their work results in products and techniques. The culture is characterized as entrepreneurial and focuses on patents rather than publications.	Mechanical engineering, computer science
Soft-applied	Disciplines focus on function and the utilitarian application of knowledge resulting in protocols and procedures. Culture is characterized by status uncertainty, pursuit of power, and a reduction in publication as a result of consultancies.	Education, finance, accounting
Holland[3]		
Realistic	Environments focus on concrete, practical activities that often use machines and tools and little emphasis is placed on human relations skills. Outputs are often practical, concrete, and tangible.	Electrical engineering, mechanical engineering, military science
Investigative	Environments emphasize activities that focus on the creation and use of knowledge and emphasize analytical, scientific, and mathematical competencies. The goal is the acquisition of knowledge through investigation and problem solving.	Biology, mathematics, sociology, economics, civil engineering
Artistic	Environments are concerned with creative activities and emphasize ambiguous, unstructured endeavors. These environments encourage imagination and the acquisition of innovative and creative competencies.	Arts, English, architecture, speech, music, theater
Conventional	Environments focus on meeting requirements or needs through the use of numbers or machines. They emphasize a conventional outlook and are concerned with orderliness and routines.	Accounting, data processing
Enterprising	Environments are oriented toward personal or organizational goal attainment through leadership or manipulation. They emphasize leadership development and reward popularity, self-confidence, and aggressiveness.	Business, journalism, communications, computer science
Social	Environments focus on the healing or teaching of others. They emphasize the acquisition of interpersonal competencies and focus little attention on technical competencies. Members are regarded for sociability, understanding, empathy, and generosity.	Political science, nursing, special education, philosophy, history

[1] Adapted from Biglan (1973a, 1973b) and Braxton and Hargens (1996)

[2] Adapted from Becher (1987) and Becher and Trowler (2001)

[3] Adapted from Smart, Feldman and Ethington (2000) and Holland (1997)

schema). The first dimension, labeled the hard versus soft dimension, reflects the existence of a paradigm in a discipline. Hard disciplines, such as physical sciences and mathematics, sit on one end of the paradigmatic continuum and have a high degree of consensus. On the other side of the continuum are soft disciplines, such as the humanities and education, which have a low degree of consensus. The second dimension, applied versus pure, reflects the degree to which fields emphasize the practical application of knowledge. On one end of the dimension are applied fields (e.g., education, accounting, and engineering) that typically focus on practical applications of their work. Pure disciplines (e.g., mathematics, physical sciences, and history) are on the other end of the continuum and hold little concern for the practical application of knowledge. The final dimension, life versus non-life, focuses on the degree to which disciplines focus on living systems. Life disciplines, such as biological sciences and sociology, are typically involved with organic or living forms of study. In contrast, non-life disciplines, such as astronomy, mathematics, and computer science, focus on inorganic and non-living systems.

Some have suggested that the Biglan schema is atheoretical and empirically driven, and that the body of knowledge derived from the schema has yielded stronger theoretical work than the schema itself (Bayer, 1987). Becher (1987; Becher & Trowler, 2001) is one who built upon this work and created a four-group classification system (Hard-pure, soft-pure, hard-applied, and soft-applied) using culture to ground his work. Members of hard-pure disciplines emphasize simplification and quantification in their pursuit of knowledge, and they contend that knowledge is cumulative in nature and neatly divided. In contrast, soft-pure disciplines emphasize discovery through interpretation and tend to use qualitative techniques. Researchers focus on particulars in an attempt to understand, not simplify. Soft-pure cultures are described as person-centered and loosely structured. Generally, faculty in soft-pure disciplines have a low publication rate. The culture of hard-applied disciplines is competitive, highly collaborative, and members have a high publication rate. Members are pragmatic in their pursuit with the mastery of the physical environment. Becher characterizes the culture of hard-applied disciplines as entrepreneurial and suggests that it focuses on patents rather than publications. Finally, faculty members in soft-applied disciplines focus on function and the utilitarian application of knowledge, and their efforts resulting in protocols and procedures. Culture in soft-applied disciplines is characterized by status uncertainty, pursuit of power, and a reduction in publication because of consultancies.

Regardless of the criticisms related to the atheoretical nature of the Biglan (and Becher) schema, it has been cited widely in higher education literature and has proven to be a useful tool for viewing disciplinary values, norms, and beliefs as they relate to teaching. We can draw several conclusions about the cultural values based on the research using Biglan. For example, faculty in soft fields place greater emphasis on student character development than faculty in hard fields

(Smart & Elton, 1982). Others have suggested that both hard and soft disciplines emphasize the learning of facts and concepts, but soft disciplines also place a high priority on the development of cognitive skills such as critical thinking (Lattuca & Stark, 1995). In terms of course planning, faculty in soft disciplines tend to focus more on student needs, growth, and development than faculty in hard disciplines (Stark, Lowther, Bentley, & Martens, 1990).

Smart and Ethington (1995) used all three Biglan dimensions to examine differences in the importance placed on various undergraduate goals. They found that faculty in soft disciplines placed greater emphasis on knowledge acquisition and knowledge integration than do faculty in hard disciplines. Compared with their colleagues in soft disciplines, faculty in hard disciplines attach greater importance on the application knowledge. Faculty in applied disciplines place greater emphasis on knowledge application and knowledge integration than do faculty in pure disciplines, while the latter places greater importance on knowledge acquisition. Interestingly, faculty are not significantly different on the life-non-life dimension in the importance they attach to undergraduate goals.

In terms of pedagogy and assessment of learning, faculty vary along the hard-soft continuum. Faculty in soft fields attach greater emphasis to active learning methods than faculty in hard disciplines (Braxton, Olsen, & Simmons, 1998; Lattuca & Stark, 1995); yet faculty in hard fields value undergraduate research more than their peers in soft fields (Lattuca & Stark, 1995). Faculty in soft disciplines are also more likely than their colleagues in hard disciplines to interact with student, communicate high expectations, and respect diverse talents and ways of knowing (Braxton et al., 1998). An analysis of examination questions reveals that faculty in soft disciplines are more likely than faculty in hard disciplines to ask questions that require students to us higher-order cognitive skills (e.g., synthesis, application) (Braxton, 1993; Braxton & Nordvall, 1988).

Holland's theory of academic environments. The atheoretical nature of Biglan has caused many in recent years to be drawn to the application of Holland's (1966, 1973, 1985, 1997) theory of careers to the study of academic disciplinary environments. Holland's theory as applied to college environments relies on three central premises. First, the choice of a career or field of training is an expression of one's personality and most people can be classified into six personality types (Realistic, Investigative, Artistic, Social, Enterprising, Conventional; see Figure 2 for a description of the different Holland environments) based on

275

their distinctive patterns of attitudes, interests, and abilities. Second, these personality types have six corresponding academic environments, each dominated by their analogous personality type. Third, the extent to which members' attitudes, interests, and abilities are congruent with their academic environments is related to higher levels of stability, satisfaction, and achievement. Extensive empirical evidence generally supports the validity of each of the three premises of Holland's theory, though the amount and strength of the evidence varies across the three assumptions (see Assouline & Meir, 1987; Holland, 1997; Smart, Feldman, & Ethington, 2000; Spokane, Meir, & Catalano, 2000; Tsabari, Tziner, & Meir, 2005).

A central component of Holland's (1997) theory is the socialization hypothesis. This socialization process occurs through efforts of environmental members to stimulate others' participation in the preferred activities of the environment, to encourage them to see themselves in ways consistent with the preferred values of the environment, and to reward them for the display of the preferred values of the environment. Faculty members are thus rewarded for behaviors, values, attitudes, and beliefs that match those of the academic environment.

Holland's theory has proved useful in understanding differences in college student development and attitudes, as well as differences in teaching preferences among college faculty. For example, Peters (1974) found that faculty in Investigative and Realistic academic environments were more likely to use structured and formal instructional approaches such as lecture-discussion format, while their colleagues in Artistic and Social environments tended to utilize more student-centered approaches such as small-group activities. Similarly, Morstain and Smart (1976) found that faculty varied greatly in their educational orientations when viewed through the lens of Holland's academic environments. For example, faculty in Realistic and Investigative academic environments emphasized structured learning environments (e.g., lecture-discussion), placed a high priority on evaluation in the form of grades and examinations, and preferred more formal, distant relationships with students. In contrast, Social and Artistic faculty emphasized an unstructured and independent teaching and learning process, believed that students work best on their own, and preferred to share course responsibilities with students in a collegial environment (e.g., small-group discussions). Finally, Smart, (1982) found that faculty in Realistic, Enterprising, and Conventional academic environments were more likely to emphasize vocational preparation than their colleagues in Social, Artistic, and Investigative environments; whereas, faculty in Social and Artistic academic environments placed greater emphasis on character development than do their counterparts in Investigative and Realistic environments.

FACULTY ATTRIBUTES/GROUP SUBCULTURES

Although I am reluctant to label them as subcultures, some have argued that specific groups of faculty (e.g., part-time faculty, faculty of color, women faculty, experience) may develop their own subcultures (Kuh & Whitt, 1988). If we rely on Van Maanan and Barley's (1985) components necessary to be considered a subculture (e.g., members of subgroups interact with one another because formal and informal purposes, shared values, similar work roles, physical proximity, and history), then one might assume that these groups are in fact subcultures. Regardless of whether one considers these groups as subcultures or simply faculty attributes that affect teaching, it is clear that they deserve consideration in the study of college teaching. I will describe two faculty subcultures or attributes here.

Research suggests that the racial/ethnic diversity of the faculty members of a college creates a unique culture for learning (Hurtado, 2001; Hurtado, Milem, Clayton-Pedersen, & Allen, 1999; Milem, 2001; Smith, 1989). Diversification of faculty increases the variation of perspectives and approaches creating a richer learning environment for students (Smith 1989). Hurtado (2001) suggests that institutions with higher proportion of faculty of color are more likely to incorporate a wider range of pedagogical techniques. While the body of evidence is growing, some have suggested that contribution faculty of color make to the undergraduate experience remains in the realm of conjecture rather than empirically demonstrated facts (Cole & Barber, 2003).

Faculty members in part-time and full-time non-tenure-track appointments, a group that has grown substantially in recent years, may also create a distinct subculture. Between 1975 and 1995, the number of part-time faculty increased by 103%, and the number of full-time tenure-ineligible faculty by 93%. Meanwhile, the number of probationary, tenure-track faculty decreased by 12%. The most recent estimates suggest that more than half of all instructional staff are contingent faculty in that they work in part-time or in full-time, but tenure-ineligible, positions (American Association of University

Professors, 2001; Baldwin & Chronister, 2002; Gappa, 2001; U. S. Department of Education, 2000).

Researchers argue that the shrinking number of tenure-track positions will erode academic freedom and irreparably damage the academic profession (Clark, 1987a; Finkin, 2000; Tierney, 1998). Although some have made assertions that the reliance on contingent appointments negatively impacts undergraduate education (Benjamin, 1998a, 1998b, 2002), few, if any, have asked whether the increasing dependence on contingent faculty affects undergraduate education. Several scholars have suggested that contingent faculty are as effective, and in some cases more effective, in delivering instruction when compared with their tenured or tenure-track counterparts (Baldwin & Chronister, 2001; Chronister & Baldwin, 1999; Gappa & Leslie, 1993; Roueche, Rouche, & Milliron, 1995). Few, if any, of these claims, either positive or negative, are supported with empirical evidence; leaving the issue of the effect of employing contingent faculty on undergraduate education unresolved (Baldwin & Chronister, 2002; Benjamin, 2002).

Other characteristics or subcultures have proven salient in the prediction of teaching behaviors. Researchers (Fairweather, 1996; Finkelstein, Seal, & Schuster, 1998; Milem, 2001; Statham, Richardson, & Cook, 1991; Umbach & Wawrzynski, 2005) have found gender to be a strong predictor of faculty teaching behaviors. Women tend to employ a broader range of pedagogical techniques and tend to engage students in activities that are found to be related with positive student outcomes. Others have found that younger people are more innovative and more likely to take risks in the classroom (Mulkay, 1972).

Proposed Conceptual Model

It is clear that college faculty work in a complex web of interconnected cultures that effects their teaching and interactions with undergraduates. The evidence presented also suggests that these cultures are particularly important to faculty as they develop their teaching values, attitudes, and behaviors. Building on this work, I propose a conceptual model that integrates the research on faculty cultures and offers a framework for the study of faculty cultures and college teaching (See Figure 3).F3 This model suggests that behaviors, attitudes, and values related to college teaching are influenced by the three overlapping subcultures in which faculty members find themselves. These subcultures are often interrelated and in many cases affect each other. For example, structural elements of colleges and universities,

Figure 3: Culture and college teaching: A conceptual model.

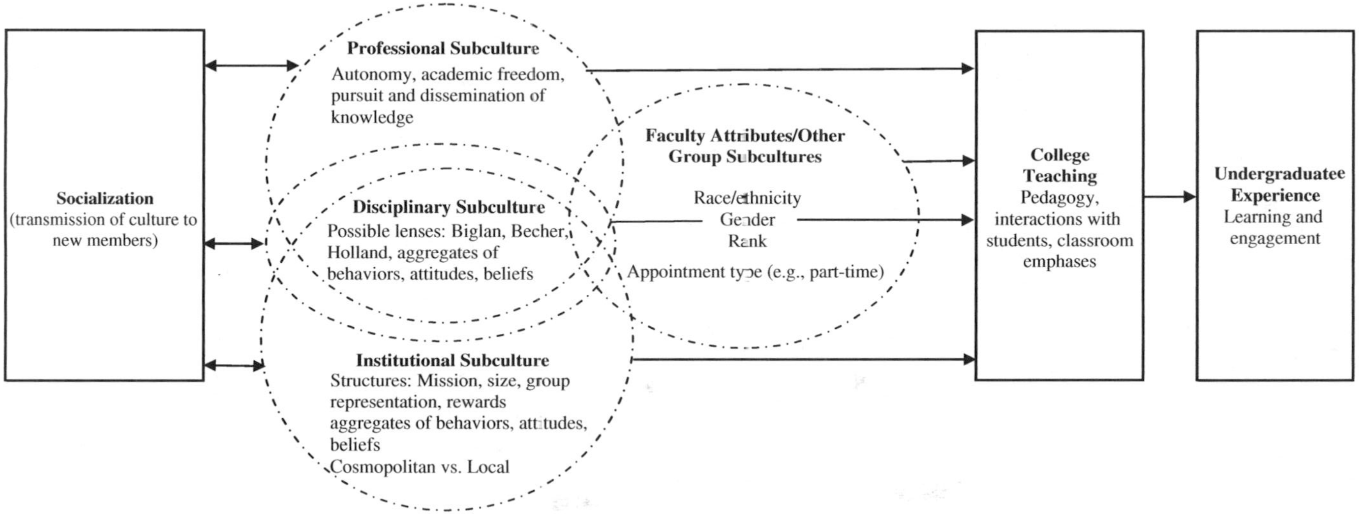

such as size and mission, affect disciplinary cultures. Larger institutions are more likely to have faculty with stronger disciplinary alliances than smaller institutions (Clark, 1983, 1987a), resulting in greater instructional variation. Faculty at liberal arts colleges are more likely than their counterparts at research universities to emphasize high quality teaching, have larger teaching loads, and emphasize education of the whole person, regardless of disciplinary affiliation. Size and other institutional characteristics may also increase the proliferation of other subcultures, such as part-time faculty groups and junior faculty groups (Kuh & Whitt, 1988); therefore, I have overlapped faculty attributes/other subcultures with institutional, professional, and disciplinary subcultures. In sum, these three subcultures affect pedagogical techniques, classroom emphases, attitudes about undergraduate education, and types of interactions with students.

Two other components of the model are worthy of note. First, the model highlights the critical role that socialization into all three subcultures has in shaping how college faculty teach and interact with undergraduates. Second, while the focus of the model is college faculty, subcultures have a profound effect not only on teaching but also on the undergraduate experience. Little research examines the effect that the organizational behaviors of colleges and universities have on the student experience (Berger & Milem, 2000), and this framework may begin to provide a lens for understanding these complex relationships.

I also offer a few words of caution about the study of cultures, and assert some of my assumptions. The varied theoretical underpinnings of culture present challenges in the study of organizations that require researchers to make some assumptions. One must decide whether culture is an independent variable, as is often the case in sociological research, or whether it is more like a dependent variable, as it tends to be in the anthropological tradition (Cameron & Ettington, 1988; Smircich, 1983). As the theoretical models suggests, I assume the sociological tradition and argue that organizations or groups *have* cultures, rather than the anthropological tradition that suggests that organizations *are* cultures (Cameron & Ettington, 1988), and these cultures are independent variables that affect college teaching and the undergraduate experience. This approach has its shortcomings in that it assumes a simplicity and linearity of attitudes and behaviors that may not exist in complex organizations. Nevertheless, the application of the proposed model and the assumptions that go with its application are useful in helping us make sense of a complex array of subcultures and their members' attitudes, values, behaviors, and beliefs.

The differences in the fundamental concept of culture also highlight the continuing controversy about how to investigate culture. Some suggest that quantitative techniques that rely on survey data are inappropriate for the study of cultures because they measure climates rather than enduring cultures (Cameron & Ettington, 1988). Opponents of quantitative techniques argue that culture can be understood only through qualitative research with thick descriptions (Peterson & Spencer, 1990). However, numerous studies (e.g., Cameron & Ettington, 1988; Hofstede et al., 1990; Kuh, 1990; Mirvis, 1985; Selvin & Hagstrom, 1996) have utilized quantitative techniques or described ways quantitative data can be used to explore culture and its manifestations, revealing a great deal about organizations and their functioning.

APPLICATION OF THE PROPOSED CULTURAL FRAMEWORK

Much of my work on college faculty (Kuh, Nelson Laird, & Umbach, 2004; Smart & Umbach, in press; Umbach, 2006, 2007) and college students (Kuh & Umbach, 2004, 2005; Milem, Umbach, & Liang, 2004; Umbach & Kuh, 2006; Umbach & Milem, 2004) contributes to the proposed framework and uncovers some important cultural evidence of disciplines and institutions related to college teaching, as well as their affects on the undergraduate experience. I present and summarize some of these findings in the next three sections.

This line of research relies heavily on the large body of literature that suggests engagement in educationally purposeful activities contributes to high levels of learning and personal development (Kuh, 2001, 2003; Pascarella & Terenzini, 1991, 2005). Astin's (1993) model of inputs-environments-outcomes assesses the impacts that various institutional practices and environmental experiences (e.g., faculty-student contact, pedagogical techniques) has on student outcomes (e.g., student engagement and student learning). Astin argues that student involvement (e.g., involvement with student peer groups and involvement with faculty) enhances almost all aspects of learning and academic performance. Moreover, the amount of time and physical and psychological energy that students invest influences their development (Astin, 1993).

Chickering and Gamson (1987) outline seven effective educational practices that influence the quality of students' learning and their educational experiences. Four of the principles advanced by

281

Chickering and Gamson focus specifically faculty behaviors and attitudes (encouraging cooperation among students, encouraging active learning, communicating high expectations, encouraging contact between students and faculty, and including diverse perspectives in the classroom) and are directly relevant to the research described below. I also extend this work by including other relevant faculty behaviors and attitudes said to enhance student learning (Kuh, 2001, 2003), such as an emphasis on higher-order cognitive activities and the importance that faculty place on enriching educational activities.

EVIDENCE OF INSTITUTIONAL CULTURE AND COLLEGE TEACHING

Evidence of the influence of institutional culture on college teaching comes from a series of studies on college faculty (see Kuh et al., 2004; Smart & Umbach, in press; Umbach, 2006, 2007; Umbach & Wawrzynski, 2005). The sample of faculty used in these studies comes from a survey administered at 137 colleges and universities in spring 2003. Full-time and part-time faculty members who taught at least one undergraduate course in the 2002–2003 academic year are included in the data set. The instrument was designed to measure faculty expectations for student engagement in educational practices that are known to be linked with high levels of learning and development (Astin, 1993; Kuh, 2001; Pascarella and Terenzini, 1991, 2005). Additionally, the instrument examined how faculty members structure their classroom and out-of-class work. Approximately 43%, or 14,336 faculty members, completed the survey.

For some of the analyses, I also include data on college students from National Survey of Student Engagement (NSSE). The NSSE survey is designed to assess the extent to which students are engaged in empirically derived good educational practices and what they gain from their college experience (Kuh, 2001). Only NSSE students from the same 137 schools that surveyed their faculty were included in the analyses (see above). The sample for this study consisted of 20,226 senior students and 22,033 first-year students who completed the NSSE in spring 2003.

Institutional culture of engagement. The first set of analyses integrates work from two studies (see Kuh et al., 2004 and Umbach & Wawrzynski, 2005) that explore the culture created by faculty that leads to higher levels of engagement, growth, and learning. We constructed a series of hierarchical linear models (HLM) to explore the effect of institutional aggregates of faculty behaviors and attitudes

282

(faculty interactions with students, active and collaborative instructional techniques, emphasis on higher order thinking, instructional emphasis on diversity, academic challenge, importance of enriching activities) on student engagement (student-faculty interations, active and collaborative learning, higher order activities, academic effort, and diversity experiences) and student self-reported growth and development (gains in personal and social development, gains in general education knowledge, gains in practical competencies). In other words, we tested the effects of aggregated faculty behaviors at an institution on student experiences at that institution, controlling for a number of individual-level student characteristics (student age, race, gender, transfer status, residence, athlete, Greek affiliation, major, full-time, and parents' education) and institution-level attributes (urbanicity, size, sector, selectivity, and Carnegie Classification). Appendix A presents the constructs and reliabilities used in these analyses.

These analyses and the others (unless noted) presented in this chapter use hierarchical linear modeling (HLM). Using HLM overcomes the problems associated with complex multilevel data by simultaneously estimating equations for both individual and institutional effects (see Ethington, 1997; Heck & Thomas, 2000; Kreft & de Leeuw, 1998; Luke, 2004; see Raudenbush & Bryk, 2002). HLM also is a useful tool in assessing contextual or cultural effects. By partitioning the variance between individuals and institutions and allows for modeling of institutional averages, HLM allows for the modeling of organizational that extend beyond mere individual-level effects.

Table 1 summarizes our model results. A + sign denotes a statistically significant positive relationship, and a − sign indicates a statistically significant negative relationship. With few exceptions, aggregate faculty behaviors and attitudes have a positive effect on both first-year and senior student engagement in effective educational practices. Not surprisingly, average faculty member reports of behaviors were significantly positively related to student reports of similar activities. In other words, on campuses where faculty create expectations for their students, structure their classrooms using effective practices and engage students out of the classroom, students engage in effective educational practices. For example, students report interacting more frequently with faculty on campuses where faculty average reports of interactions with students are high. What is compelling is the positive relationship that faculty aggregates have on engagement of unrelated student behaviors, suggesting a culture of good practices in undergraduate education. For example, students report greater

Table 1: The Effects of Institutional Aggregates of Faculty Behaviors and Attitudes on Student Engagement

Campus aggregates of faculty behaviors and attitudes	Student reports of engagement									
	Student-faculty interactions		Active and collaborative learning		Higher-Order Activities		Academic Effort		Diversity Experiences	
	FY	SR	FY	SR	FY	SR	FY	SR	FY	SR
Faculty interactions with students	+	+	+	+	+	+	+	+		
Active and Collaborative Techniques	+	+	+	+	+	+	+	+	+	+
Emphasis on higher order thinking	+		+	+	+	+	+	+	+	+
Emphasis on diversity	+	+	+	+	+	+	+	+	+	+
Academic Challenge	+		+	+	+	+	+	+	+	+
Importance of Enriching Activities	+	+	+	+	+	+	+	+	+	+
Cultural emphasis on practices	+	+	+	+	+	+	+	+	+	+

Notes: + denotes a statistically significant (p < .05) positive relationship; − denotes a statistically significant (p < .05) negative relationship
FY-First-year students; SR-Seniors
Adapted from Kuh et al. (2004) and Umbach & Wawrzynski (2005)
Level-one controls included student age, race, gender, transfer status, residence (on or off campus), athlete, greek, major, full-time, and parents' education. Level-two controls included urbanicity, size, sector, selectivity, and Carnegie Classification.

effort on academics on campuses where faculty utilize diversity in the classroom, interact frequently with students, employ active and collaborative instructional techniques, and place high levels of importance on enriching activities.

To test further the cultural context created by faculty on college campuses, I created a composite variable combining the six faculty aggregates used separately in our other models. Combining group-level attributes in level-two models is a common technique used by multi-level modelers to explore cultural effects. The last row in Table 1 presents the effects that the cultural context created by faculty. Without exception, on campuses where faculty create a culture that values good practices, students are more engaged. Worthy of note is the fact that the observed effects of cultural emphasis variable are present after controlling for a number of structural characteristics, such as size, urbanicity, Carnegie Classification, sector and selectivity.

The next model summary, shown in Table 2,T2 extends the concept of cultural effects of faculty by exploring the impact of aggregated faculty behaviors on student reports of gains in learning and development. For both seniors and first-year students, self-reported gains were positively related to faculty aggregates of interactions with students, active and collaborative instructional techniques, diversity emphasis, and importance placed on enriching educational activities reported. Students on campuses where faculty emphasize higher-order cognitive activities reported greater gains in general education knowledge. On campuses where faculty require high levels of effort, students report greater gains in general education. Likewise, the culture created by faculty related to best practices significantly affects student perceptions of gains. Students on campuses where faculty emphasize best practices report greater gains in personal/social development, general education knowledge, and practical competencies.

Institutional differences in faculty behaviors and attitudes. Table 3T3 summarizes the results of our level two models (institution level) predicting faculty behaviors and attitudes (taken from Umbach, 2006, 2007; Umbach & Wawrzynski, 2005). Again, we ran a series of HLMs but used the faculty attitudes, beliefs, and behaviors measures from the previous analyses as dependent measures. At level-two, we included institutional artifacts such as urbanicity, size, sector, selectivity, Carnegie Classification, percent faculty of color, and percent contingent faculty (part-time and full-time, untenurable). The level-one models included controls for race/ethnicity, gender, age, years teaching, rank, appointment type, and academic discipline.

Table 2: The Effects of Institutional Aggregates of Faculty Behaviors and Attitudes on Student Self-reported Gains in Student Learning and Development

Campus aggregates of faculty behaviors and attitudes	Student self-reported gains					
	Personal/social gains		Gains in general education		Gains in practical competencies	
	FY	SR	FY	SR	FY	SR
Faculty interactions with students	+	+	+	+	+	+
Active and Collaborative Techniques	+	+	+	+	+	+
Emphasis on higher order thinking		+	+	+		
Emphasis on diversity	+	+	+	+	+	+
Academic Challenge	+	+	+	+	+	+
Importance of Enriching Activities	+	+	+	+	+	+
Cultural emphasis on practices	+	+	+	+	+	+

Notes: + denotes a statistically significant (p < .05) positive relationship; – denotes a statistically significant (p < .05) negative relationship

FY–First-year students; SR–Seniors

Adapted from Kuh et al. (2004) and Umbach & Wawrzynski (2005)

Level-one controls included student age, race, gender, transfer status, residence (on or off campus), athlete, greek, major, full-time, and parents' education. Level-two controls included urbanicity, size, sector, selectivity, and Carnegie Classification.

Table 3: Institutional Differences in Faculty Behaviors and Attitudes

Independent Variables	Dependent Variables					
	Faculty interactions with students	Active and collaborative	Higher-order cognitive emphasis	Academic challenge	Importance of enriching activities	Emphasis on diversity
Doctoral Research – Extensive	−		−	−	−	−
Doctoral Research – Intensive	−	−		−	−	−
Masters I and II	−	−	−	−	−	−
Baccalaureate – General			−	−	−	−
Other Carnegie	−			−	−	−
Liberal arts college (reference group)						
Private	+				+	+
Suburban						
Rural			−	−		
Urban (reference group)						
Selectivity	+	−	−			−
Size						
% Faculty of color			+			+
% Contingent faculty	−					

Notes: + denotes a statistically significant (p < .05) positive relationship; − denotes a statistically significant (p < .05) negative relationship
Adapted from Umbach (2006, 2007) and Umbach & Wawrzynski (2005)
Level-one controls include race/ethnicity, gender, age, years teaching, rank, appointment type, and academic discipline.

In general, faculty at Liberal Arts Colleges (LAC) employ good practices more frequently than their peers at other institutional types. Compared to their peers at all other institution types, LAC faculty provide higher levels of challenge, place greater importance on enriching, and more frequently emphasized diversity in the classroom. With the exception of Baccalaureate-General College faculty, LAC faculty interact with students more frequently than faculty at other institution types. They also employ active and collaborative instructional techniques more often than faculty at and Master's Colleges and Universities. Other than Doctoral Research-Intensive University faculty, LAC professors place greater emphasis on higher-order cognitive skills than professors at other institution types. My work (Kuh & Umbach, 2004, 2005; Umbach & Kuh, 2006) and the work of others (Kuh, 2001, 2003; Pascarella & Terenzini, 2005; Pascarella et al., 2006) suggests similar institution-type differences between college students and further highlight the unique culture at LACs.

It also seems that private colleges tend to have a culture where faculty engage students in good educational practices. Compared with the public-college peers, faculty at private colleges interact with students more frequently, place a greater importance on enriching educational activities, and more frequently use diversity in classroom instruction.

Selectivity has a mixed relationship with faculty behaviors and attitudes. Faculty at selective institutions interact with students more frequently than faculty at less selective colleges. However, these same faculty employ active and collaborative techniques in their instruction less frequently, emphasize higher order cognitive skills less often, and utilize diversity in their classroom less frequently. Although these findings may be surprising to some, recent work I conducted with a number of colleagues suggests that students at less selective institutions are engaging in good practices at the same rate, and at times at a greater rate, as students from selective institutions (Pascarella et al., 2006).

Institutional size, as measured by undergraduate headcount, does not seem to distinguish between instructional behaviors and attitudes. Perhaps after we control for mission (as proxied by Carnegie Classification), sector, and urbanicity, size does not matter for faculty. This runs counter to research that suggests that college students on small campuses are more engaged (Kuh, 2001, 2003; Pascarella & Terenzini, 2005) It also is important to note that urbanicity did not seem to affect most of the models. Only in the case of higher-order cognitive emphasis and academic challenge, where urban faculty scored higher than rural faculty, did differences exist.

Very recently, I have begun to explore other structural factors that may affect collegiate instruction (presented in the last two rows of Table 3). For example, I found that the representation of faculty of color on a campus has a positive effect on the emphasis that faculty place on higher-order cognitive abilities and the frequency with which faculty use diversity in their classroom instruction. These effects hold true regardless of individual faculty attributes, such as race/ethnicity and a series of institutional controls. I argue that the representation of faculty of color on a college campus acts a symbol of an institution's commitment to diversity, creating a culture where diversity is highly valued. This symbol allows faculty to make sense (Weick, 1979) of institutional values and priorities as they relate to diversity. In turn, faculty act in a way that is compatible with institutional goals and priorities related to diversity. Another structural characteristic, the percentage of non-tenure-track faculty (both full-time and part-time) on a college campus, has a negative relationship with the frequency that faculty interact with students. In addition to being symbols, these structural characteristics also might be evidence of what some (Austin, 1990; Kuh & Whitt, 1988; Ruscio, 1987) have suggested as faculty group subcultures based on race/ethnicity or contract type.

RECENT EVIDENCE OF DISCIPLINARY CULTURES AND COLLEGE TEACHING

Some of my recent work also highlights important cultural differences between academic disciplines in instructional techniques and relationships with students. In all the examples provided here, I use Holland's theory of careers and code faculty into academic environments using the *Educational Opportunities Finder* (Rosen, Holmberg, & Holland, 1997). Table 4T4 summarizes the level-one (individual level) results from three recent studies of college faculty (Umbach, 2006, 2007; Umbach & Wawrzynski, 2005) controlling for a series of institution-level characteristics (urbanicity, size, sector, selectivity, and Carnegie Classification).

The last seven rows indicate differences between Holland academic environments with Social as the omitted group. In general, faculty in Social disciplines more frequently use effective educational practices than their peers. Compared with other academic environments, they interact with students more frequently. Given the personalities of

Table 4: Individual Differences in Faculty Behaviors and Attitudes

Independent Variables	Dependent Variables					
	Faculty interactions with students	Active and collaborative	Higher-order cognitive emphasis	Academic challenge	Importance of enriching activities	Emphasis on diversity
African American	+	+	+	+	+	+
Latino/a		+	+	+	+	+
Asian Pacific American	+	+	+	+	+	−
Native American	+	+			+	+
Other race	+	+	+	+	+	+
White (reference group)						
Female	+	+	+	+	+	+
Age	+	+	+	+	+	+
Years teaching	−	−	−	−	−	
Associate professor	+	+				
Assistant professor		+			+	
Other rank		+	−			
Professor (reference group)						
Part-time	−	−			−	
Full-time, untenurable	−			−		
Tenured\tenure-track (reference group)						
Holland academic environments						

Table 4: *(Continued)*

	Dependent Variables					
Independent Variables	Faculty interactions with students	Active and collaborative	Higher-order cognitive emphasis	Academic challenge	Importance of enriching activities	Emphasis on diversity
Realistic discipline	–	+	+			–
Investigative discipline	–	–	–	–	–	–
Artistic discipline	–	–		+		–
Conventional discipline	–	–	–		–	–
Enterprising discipline	–			+	–	–
Other discipline	–	+		–		–
Social discipline (reference group)						

Notes: + denotes a statistically significant (p < .05) positive relationship; − denotes a statistically significant (p < .05) negative relationship
Adapted from Umbach (2006, 2007) and Umbach & Wawrzynski (2005)
Level-two controls include urbanicity, size, sector, selectivity, and Carnegie Classification.

individuals in Social academic environments, this finding is expected. Similarly, Social faculty use diversity-related activities more frequently than any other faculty. Conventional, Realistic, and Investigative faculty are less likely than other faculty to use diversity in classroom instruction. Research on college students differences between Holland academic major environments and diversity experiences parallels (Milem & Umbach, 2003; Milem et al., 2004; Umbach & Milem, 2004) these findings.

Similar to previous research (Morstain & Smart, 1976; Peters, 1974), Realistic, Investigative, and Conventional faculty are among the least likely to employ active and collaborative learning. The models suggest statistically significant and substantive differences between disciplines in the use of higher-order activities. Investigative and conventional faculty are the least likely to emphasize higher-order cognitive activities in their classes, while Realistic are the most likely to emphasize these activities. Artistic and Enterprising require the greatest amount of effort from their students, and Investigative and Conventional faculty require the least amount of effort. Social faculty members hold greater importance on enriching activities than Investigative, Conventional, and Enterprising disciplines.

John Smart and I (Smart & Umbach, in press) recently conducted a study using the same data set used in the studies described above. We selected a set of items that assessed the extent to which faculty members structured their undergraduate courses to foster student learning and development in twelve different areas. Faculty members were asked to indicate the extent to which they structured their selected course section so that students learn and develop in each of the twelve areas using a four-point response scale (4 = very much, 3 = quite a bit, 2 = some, 1 = very little). These areas include the following: Acquiring a broad general education; Acquiring job or work-related; Writing clearly and effectively; Speaking clearly and effectively; Thinking critically and analytically; Analyzing quantitative problems; Using computing and information; Working effectively with others; Learning effectively on their own; Understanding themselves; Understanding people of other; and solving complex real-world problems. Because there were an insufficient number of faculty members in Realistic and Conventional academic environments, our final sample included only faculty in Investigative, Artistic, Social, and Enterprising academic environments.

We then used discriminant analysis procedures to assess the magnitude and nature of differences among faculty in the four academic environments of Holland's theory. Three statistically significant discriminant functions emerged. Figure 4 displays a summary of the results of our analysis. The first discriminant function reflects the extent to which faculty members structure their course to emphasize analyzing data versus understanding people in their courses. The positive side of the first function is defined by analyzing quantitative problems and using computing and information technology, while the negative side is defined by understanding themselves and understanding people of other racial and ethnic backgrounds. This dimension suggests that Artistic and Social (positive end of the discriminant function) faculty place greater emphasis on understanding people when compared with their colleagues in Investigative and Enterprising (negative end of the discriminant function) environments, who place greater emphasis on analyzing data. These findings mirror research that found college students in Social and Artistic majors are more likely than their peers in other majors to emphasize racial and ethnic diversity issues in their classroom discussions and assigned readings (Milem & Umbach, 2003; Milem et al., 2004; Umbach & Milem, 2004).

The second discriminant function distinguishes between faculty members whose courses emphasize independent thinking versus solving interpersonal problems. The positive end of this dimension represents an emphasis on teaching students to learn effectively on their own and to think critically and analytically, while negative end represents an emphasis on solving complex real-world problems and understanding people of other racial and ethnic backgrounds. Faculty in Social environments place a higher priority on solving interpersonal problems compared with their colleagues in Artistic environments (and to a lesser extent those in Investigative and Enterprising environments) who place greater emphasis on the development of independent thinking.

Figure 4: Differences in faculty classroom emphases by Holland academic environments.

Notes: Based on results reported in Smart and Umbach (in press).

293

The third function is one dimensional and reflects the extent to which faculty members structure their courses to emphasize the acquisition of work-related knowledge and skills. This dimension is comes primarily from two questions that measure the extent to which faculty emphasize acquiring job or work-related knowledge and skills and using computing and information technology. This function discriminates between faculty in Enterprising environments, who place the greatest emphasis on work-related knowledge and skills, and their colleagues in the three other academic environments.

FACULTY ATTRIBUTES/OTHER GROUP SUBCULTURES

Table 4 summarizes the level-one (individual level) results from three recent studies of college faculty (Umbach, 2006, 2007; Umbach & Wawrzynski, 2005) controlling for a series of institution-level characteristics (urbanicity, size, sector, selectivity, and Carnegie Classification). Several patterns emerge from the summary of results. First, it is clear that faculty of color use good practices more frequently than do their White colleagues. Compared with Whites, all minority groups employ active and collaborative instructional techniques more frequently, require more effort from their students, and attach greater importance to enriching activities. African American and Native American faculty interact with students more frequently than do Whites. With the exception of Native Americans, faculty of color are more likely than Whites are to emphasize higher-order cognitive activities. Finally, faculty of color, with the exception of Asian Pacific Americans, are more likely than White faculty to emphasize diversity in their classroom instruction. Women also scored higher on all dependent measures than did men.

Appointment type, rank, and experience also have a significant relationship with some of the components faculty teaching. In general, the other variables in the model, experience is negatively related with the use of good practices. Associate professors more frequently interact with student than do full professors. Compared with full professors, all ranks employ active and collaborative learning techniques more frequently. Assistant professors place greater importance on enriching activities than do full professors. In many cases, contingent faculty members utilize good practices less frequently than do their more permanent colleagues. Compared with tenured and tenure-track faculty, part-time faculty interact less frequently with students (even after controlling for number of courses taught), employ active and collaborative instructional techniques less frequently, and attach less importance to enriching activities. Full-time, non-tenure-track faculty members interact with students less frequently and require less effort from their students than do tenured and tenure-track faculty.

DISCUSSION

Researchers often talk of two dominant and often divergent cultures in institutions of higher education: a culture of research and a culture of teaching (Paulsen & Feldman, 1995a). Very often prestige is tied more closely with research and has caused institutions that do not normally emphasize a research ideal to increase efforts in this area (Bowen & Schuster, 1986). The result is a hierarchy of prestige with research universities having the highest status, followed in order by doctoral universities, comprehensive state colleges and universities, liberal arts colleges, and community colleges (Clark, 1987a). The result is the greatest paradox of academic work in that "most professors teach most of the time, and large proportions of them teach all of the time, but teaching is not the activity my rewarded by the academic profession nor most valued by the system at large" (Clark, 1987a, pp. 98–99).

The findings from this line of inquiry suggest that faculty cultures extend well beyond the institution and exist in a complex, interconnected web of professional, disciplinary, and institutional cultures, all of which have a profound effect on college teaching and the undergraduate experience. As the model and the findings presented here suggest, it is quite evident that institutions, disciplines, and perhaps even other faculty groups create distinct cultures related to teaching and the undergraduate experience. Beyond that, these findings offer three important insights. First, while some institution types tend to place a high priority on teaching (e.g., LACs), it seems that cultures that emphasize and support teaching can occur within any institution type. Although faculty behaviors and attitudes clearly vary by type, size, sector, and other institutional characteristics, the evidence presented here suggests that cultures of good practices transcend institutional type and structures. Even after controlling for a variety of structural characteristics and institution type, some colleges and universities were more likely than others to create a culture of good practices that engage students in and out of the classroom.

Second, the findings suggest that disciplinary cultures play a central role in shaping how faculty teach, what faculty emphasize in their classroom instruction, and how faculty interact with students. Faculty in the disparate academic environments in Holland's theory design and structure their courses in order to foster and promote differential patterns of student learning and development are consistent across. It seems that "the disciplinary tendency is as much in the nature of things as the institutional linkage" (Clark, 1987, p. 26). This finding suggests that Holland's theory is equally applicable in guiding research on the socialization mechanisms of academic environments in diverse institutional settings.

Finally, these findings suggest that faculty characteristics, such as race, gender and appointment type, affect teaching. Some may argue that these groups are in fact subcultures in that they share similar values, attitudes, and beliefs and may interact on a college campus with some frequency. Further support for this subculture argument can be found in the fact that the proportion of faculty of color and contingent faculty on a campus affects instruction. At the very least, when high numbers of these groups serves as a symbol about the priorities of an institution.

College campuses and disciplinary associations that seek to improve faculty instruction by creating teaching cultures might gain some insight using the framework presented in this chapter. Clearly, the model does not paint a simple picture to direct efforts, nor does it suggest a simple set of procedures to change the direction of a campus. Cultural change is not that easy. My intent in presenting evidence of this complexity was not to complicate the discussion of factors that affect teaching, but to provide a framework that allows faculty members, faculty developers, and campus leaders to consider how they might view their campuses to determine the best way to create a culture of teaching. This complexity presents unique challenges for leaders hoping to change the culture of a campus, but understanding these complexities will aid in change efforts. Likewise, anyone leading change efforts must be aware that cultures, by definition, are slow to change (Peterson & Spencer, 1990).

Nevertheless, the proposed framework and supporting evidence do have implications for policy and practice. As has been suggested by others, many of these suggestions focus on organizational structures and policies, all outward manifestations of culture (Austin, 1990; Feldman & Paulsen, 1999; Paulsen & Feldman, 1995a). However, these structural components play an important and often symbolic role in shaping the values of cultural members. I integrate and expand upon previous research on teaching cultures (see Austin, 1990, 1996;

Feldman & Paulsen, 1999; Massy, Wilger, & Colbeck, 1994; Paulsen & Feldman, 1995a) and make nine recommendations that seem particularly salient.

Assess the culture of your campus. Before any efforts are made, it is important to understand the campus culture and subcultures. A cultural audit using interview and survey data will provide insight into the espoused and embedded values of the subcultures on campus. Carefully worded survey instruments combined with in-depth interviews also will allow leaders and faculty groups to assess the mixture of subcultures (e.g., disciplinary, contingent) on a campus. If they do not fully understand the campus cultures, administrators and faculty leaders are in danger of implementing policies or structural changes that run counter to those cultures. The resulting policies are not likely to yield positive outcomes, or worse, yield outcomes that run counter to the policies' intentions.

This implies that policies, procedures, and structures are likely to be most effective if they take into account the varied disciplinary and other group subcultures on campus, as well as the professional culture of college campuses. Practices that run counter to the beliefs, attitudes, and values of disciplinary subcultures are likely to fail before they even begin. Although it may be obvious, it is worth stating that practices that run counter to the values (e.g., autonomy) of the professional culture of faculty are likely to be unsuccessful.

Be intentional in the socialization of newcomers. Socialization of new faculty is often random, disjointed, and disorganized (Austin, 2002; Tierney & Bensimon, 1996). Beginning with anticipatory socialization, institutions and their departments should be intentional in the way they socialize faculty in their teaching role. Hiring processes should communicate to applicants and interviewees the importance of teaching. Along with traditional research materials, campuses might require applicants to include sample syllabi, student evaluations, and teaching statements in their dossiers. As part of the campus interviews, search committees might require a teaching demonstration or pedagogical colloquium that requires a faculty member to describe systematically their approach to teaching (Paulsen & Feldman, 1995a; Rice & Austin, 1990). These practices are symbols that newcomers will use to determine what is important to a college.

Departments might also assign new faculty members a teaching mentor. The teaching mentors may simply serve as sounding boards for new faculty members or they might attend classes and provide suggestions for improvement. Departments should be careful to utilize

297

the teaching mentor as a tool for support and not evaluation, and they should communicate this to the new faculty member. Perhaps using an untenured, but more senior, colleague, or using a faculty member from outside the newcomer's department will help in that regard.

It is important to remember that socialization occurs well before the acculturation of interviewees and new faculty members. Graduate programs and their faculty play a central role in transmitting cultural values related to teaching. Training of future professors occurs almost entirely at large research universities where research is emphasized. They see that faculty are rewarded for research behaviors and often learn that shirking teaching responsibilities does little to affect success (Austin, 1990, 2002) Thus, new faculty arrive on campus placing a high priority on research efforts and a low priority on good teaching. Some have begun to call for national reform of graduate student socialization in hopes of attaching greater emphasis to teaching (Austin, 1990, 2002).

Recruit and retain faculty who place a high priority on teaching and work to diversify the racial/ethnic composition of the faculty. Perhaps more important is that colleges and universities hire faculty members who value teaching. One straightforward way to create a culture of teaching is to screen and hire faculty members who place a high priority on teaching. A campus that turns over even a small percentage of its faculty each year will experience a dramatic shift in its culture in five to ten years, if it begins to hire and retain faculty who teach well.

Colleges and universities also should consider their efforts in the recruitment and retention of faculty of color. Faculty of color not only provide a diversity of perspectives that enhances learning, they appear to be more likely than their White peers to engage students in effective educational practices. Placing a high priority on the recruitment and retention of faculty of color serves as a symbol of the importance of diversity on campus, and it creates a culture that embraces diversity in the learning process and emphasizes higher order cognitive skills in classroom instruction.

Reward good teaching in the tenure and promotion process. In addition to hiring good teachers, colleges and universities seeking to foster a teaching culture conduct rigorous peer and student evaluations of teaching. Equally important is connecting these evaluations to the tenure and promotion process. Research suggests that campuses with teaching cultures recognize and connect evaluations of teaching to promotion and tenure process (Paulsen & Feldman, 1995a). In order to affect culture, these efforts need to be more than a mere nod at teaching effectiveness, but senior faculty need to use and weigh heavily student teaching evaluations in tenure and promotion decisions.

Of course, the challenge is to define what good teaching is. Faculty and administrative leaders should be cognizant of important and valuable disciplinary differences when establishing policies about what constitutes good teaching. In most cases, for policies to gain any real traction, colleges and universities would be wise to allow departments to establish their own procedures and standards and provide the support needed to accomplish their goals.

Some have called for the broadening of the concept of scholarship (Boyer, 1990; Paulsen & Feldman, 1995a, 1995b). Boyer (1990) suggests that scholarship should not be defined solely by the pursuit of knowledge, that that it should include discovery, integration, application, and teaching. A multidimensional definition that includes engaging and fostering student learning requires a major cultural shift in thinking and the way in which faculty are evaluated. This may be attractive to many because "it allows faculty to build on their own scholarly strengths and be rewarded for them" (Rice & Austin, 1990, p. 33). It is a matter of speculation whether we have witnessed such a shift in the 15 years since Boyer (1990), but the concept of a broader definition may be an important step in creating a professional culture of teaching.

Establish tangible symbols that signal to members that effective teaching is valued. It is not uncommon for college campuses to have annual awards for exceptional teachers. Other campuses offer fellowships or grants to support innovative and effective new teaching efforts or specialized training. Such awards, if given high visibility by senior administration, serve as important symbols of the value of teaching. Campuses should seek creative ways to make such awards distinctive and prestigious. Disciplinary associations often award faculty for research and service efforts, but the extent to which disciplinary associations can effectively award teaching may be worth investigation. Such awards would provide a powerful symbol about the value that the discipline places on teaching.

Disciplinary journals dedicated to teaching (e.g., *Teaching Sociology*) not only provide an important outlet for the scholarship of teaching and learning, they also symbolize the importance the discipline places on teaching endeavors. One concern is that these journals become marginalized among the array of publishing outlets. The placement of well-respected teachers and researchers on the editorial boards disciplinary journals dedicated to teaching will enhance their credibility and felt importance.

Provide opportunities for faculty to interact and collaborate within and across disciplines. Institutional cultures that support teaching encourage and provide opportunities for interaction among faculty regarding teaching (Austin & Baldwin, 1991; Massy et al., 1994; Paulsen & Feldman, 1995a). Teaching-related interactions have been proven to improve teaching, increase intellectual stimulation, and reduce the isolation typically associated with teaching (Austin & Baldwin, 1991). Institutions and departments might create and support formal sessions or groups that meet to discuss teaching. Institutions might consider offering rewards or incentives for participating in these discussions. National and regional conferences might also have roundtables or special interest groups that foster discussions about teaching.

These discussions are likely to be enhanced if groups include faculty from diverse backgrounds and disciplines. Clearly much is to be learned from disciplines other than one's own. For example, Social disciplines may be able to share with Investigative disciplines the ways they use diversity in the classroom. This may not result in a direct application, but it will allow for faculty to reflect on ways they might be able to integrate diverse perspective into their teaching.

Create and/or elevate the status of centers for teaching and learning and faculty development programs. Faculty cultures that value teaching tend to have extensive faculty development programs typically coordinated by teaching centers (Feldman & Paulsen, 1999; Paulsen & Feldman, 1995a; Rice & Austin, 1990). In most cases, these centers are funded by the college or university and are housed within academic affairs. The can offer consultations, workshops, seminars, training programs, conferences, teaching assistant orientations.

These centers serve two very important purposes. First, they provide important support mechanisms. If campuses seek to challenge their faculty to be better teachers, they must provide them with the appropriate supports. Second, they serve as a symbol of the importance the campus places on teaching. If placed centrally in academic affairs divisions and supported by senior administrators, centers for teaching serve as meaningful symbol of the importance of teaching.

Establish institutional priorities by communicating a commitment to teaching. Language is an important manifestation of culture and plays an important role in creating a culture that supports teaching. Senior administrators need to communicate the campus' commitment to teaching in speeches, interviews, and informal discussions. Behavioral patterns need to follow the rhetoric so that faculty know that the commitment is not merely words.

Mission statements and strategic plans should reflect the priority placed on teaching, if campuses which to create a teaching culture. Often, these written documents do not create direct tangible results, but they provide faculty with a roadmap that helps them make meaning of values and priorities of the institution.

Do not forget contingent faculty members. Given that contingent faculty members now make up more than half of the professoriate, colleges and universities would be advised to consider how to socialize these temporary employees in a way that signals a culture that emphasizes good teaching. While the findings presented in this chapter suggest some deficiencies among contingent faculty, it is important not to lay blame entirely on faculty in these appointments. Faculty in contingent appointments earn low wages, receive little support for professional development, and work in environments that often marginalize them (Baldwin & Chronister, 2001; Gappa & Leslie, 1993). They also are not afforded the same socialization activities, such as orientation and mentoring, as tenured and tenure-track peers and may not fully understand institutional values and priorities. Given these work conditions, it should surprise few that contingent faculty display a lack of commitment and perform less effectively than their tenured and tenure-track peers.

For part-time faculty, Gappa and Leslie (1993) offer a number of suggestions for creating a culture that is more inclusive. Among them, they recommend that colleges offer benefits, conduct regular performance reviews, provide instructional support and professional development, develop a salary scale, create standards for progression through the salary scale, and provide equitable compensation to part-time faculty. Baldwin and Chronister (2001) provide similar suggestions to institutions when working with full-time tenure-ineligible faculty, but offer some additional recommendations. They suggest institutions create a defined probationary period and explicit evaluation criteria for contingent faculty. They also recommend that contingent faculty be allowed to participate in campus governance and curriculum development.

In addition to providing a framework to view policy and practice, the proposed model may provide a lens through which future researchers may explore teaching and learning. As with most research endeavors, the model and its supporting analyses leave many questions unanswered and provide avenues for future research. As I noted earlier in the chapter, many argue that culture cannot be studied effectively using quantitative methods. While I do not fully subscribe to this opinion, I do believe that the proposed model should be tested and revised through in-depth ethnographic research. Studies that seek to gain some depth of understanding will provide additional insights into faculty cultures and college teaching that cannot be determined through quantitative work. For example, from my quantitative analyses, I can only surmise the meaning that faculty make of symbols and other artifacts. I also cannot fully uncover the embedded values and beliefs of a culture.

Future research might also explore departmental cultures. Academic departments are organizational units that serve as an intersection of campus and disciplinary cultures. Academic departments should probably be included in the model, but the bulk of the theoretical research (see Austin, 1990; Becher, 1981, 1987; Becher & Trowler, 2001; Biglan, 1973a, 1973b; Clark, 1962, 1987a, 1987b; Smart et al., 2000) I relied upon for this chapter did not include departments in their discussions of faculty cultures. I was unable to uncover more than a modest body of empirical studies that explore departmental cultures. Nor was I able to rely on my own research to make an argument for the inclusion of departmental cultures. A cross-institution, department-level study would provide a great deal of valuable information about the effects of departmental cultures on teaching.

Recent work by Austin (2002) provides valuable information about the socialization of graduate students and their acquisition of professional, disciplinary, and institutional values. Extending this work to explore the changes that occur during graduate school, prior to getting the first faculty job, and while on the tenure track would provide compelling evidence about the socialization of new faculty and the role this socialization has in creating a teaching culture. A longitudinal panel survey or a long-term qualitative analysis would answer many questions about socialization of newcomers to the faculty ranks and the changes that occur during the process.

Others might apply a cultural framework to the study of how specific faculty groups come to understand professional, institutional, and disciplinary values as they relate to teaching. A study of contingent faculty seems important given their prevalence in higher education and some of their teaching deficiencies described in this chapter. Others might also explore in greater depth the role that culture plays in the way that faculty of color approach undergraduate instruction.

Several questions arise from the current analyses of disciplinary cultures. I offer two suggestions. First, does the proportional representation of faculty within disciplines affect the culture of a campus? In the late 1960s and early 1970s, Astin and Richards (along with their colleagues) used the Holland typology to conduct a series of studies that explored this question, and found that the distribution of faculty and students in the six Holland personality types affects perceptions of college environments (Astin, 1963, 1968; Astin & Holland, 1962; Richards, Rand, & Rand, 1966; Richards, Seligman, & Jones, 1970). An update of this body of literature would be valuable to campus leaders seeking insight into their campus cultures. Second, in what ways do the two disciplinary classification models presented here – Holland and Biglan – intersect to provide additional information about faculty teaching? Given the variety within each of the categories of the two schemas, a great deal may be learned by integrating the two to create a matrix that would provide a more detailed analysis of disciplinary attitudes.

Others might also conduct empirical research on Clark's (1962) four faculty types (Teacher, Demonstrator, Scholar-researcher, and Consultant). Given that campuses have varying combinations of these faculty types, it would be particularly useful to determine the representation of faculty on a campus and to explore how this mix relates to teaching and learning on that campus.

Finally, in a small way, this chapter begins to explore the effects of organizational structures on the undergraduate experience. We have long understood that college faculty are one of the strongest influences on college students (Astin, 1993; Pascarella & Terenzini, 1991, 2005). The research summarized in this chapter and the work of Berger and Milem (2000) suggest that institutional cultures, and more specifically faculty cultures, play an important role in the way students engage in educationally purposeful activities in and out of the classroom. Additional studies that examine the intersection of faculty cultures and student cultures would contribute significantly to this line of inquiry.

CONCLUSION

More than anything, this chapter proposes a framework that provides a starting point for understanding faculty cultures and college teaching. College faculty work and live in a web of varying cultures, all of which influence their work with undergraduates in and out of the classroom. Understanding this web and all of its complexities will greatly extend our knowledge of what motivates faculty to become good teachers.

REFERENCES

American Association of University Professors. (2001). *Policy Documents and Reports*. Washington, DC: American Association of University Professors.

Assouline, M., and Meir, E.I. (1987). Meta-analysis of the relationship between congruence and well-being measures. *Journal of Vocational Behavior* 31(3): 319–332.

Astin, A. (1993). *What Matters in College: Four Critical Years Revisited*. San Francisco: Jossey-Bass.

Astin, A.W. (1963). Further validation of the environmental assessment technique. *Journal of Educational Psychology* 54: 217–226.

Astin, A.W. (1968). *The College Environment*. Washington, DC: American Council on Education.

Astin, A.W., and Chang, M.J. (1995). Colleges that emphasize research and teaching: Can you have your cake and eat it too. *Change* 27(5): 45–49.

Astin, A.W., and Holland, J.L. (1962). The environmental assessment technique: A way to measure college environments. *Journal of Educational Psychology* 52: 308–316.

Austin, A.E. (1990). Faculty cultures, faculty values. In W.G. Tierney (ed.), *Understanding Academic Climate and Culture and Climate* (Vol. 68, pp. 61–74). San Francisco, CA.

Austin, A.E. (1996). Institutional and departmental cultures: The relationship between teaching and research. In J. M. Braxton (ed.), *Faculty Teaching and Research: Is there a Conflict* (Vol. 90, pp. 61–74). San Francisco, CA.

Austin, A.E. (2002). Preparing the next generation of faculty: Graduate school as socialization to the academic career. *Journal of Higher Education* 73(1): 94–122.

Austin, A.E., and Baldwin, R.G. (1991). *Faculty Collaboration: Enhancing the Quality of Scholarship and Teaching* (Vol. 7). Washington, DC: George Washington University.

Baldwin, R., and Chronister, J. (2001). *Teaching without Tenure: Practices and Policies for a New Era*. Baltimore, MD: Johns Hopkins University Press.

Baldwin, R., and Chronister, J. (2002). What happened to the tenure track. In R. Chait (ed.), *The Questions of Tenure* (pp. 125–159). Cambridge, MA: Harvard University Press.

Bayer, A.E. (1987). The 'biglan' model' and the smart messenger: A case study of eponym diffusion. *Research in Higher Education* 26: 212–223.

Becher, T. (1981). Towards a definition of disciplinary cultures. *Studies in Higher Education* 6(2): 109–122.

Becher, T. (1987). The disciplinary shaping of the profession. In B.R. Clark (ed.), *The Academic Profession: National, Disciplinary, and Institutional Settings* (pp. 271–304). Berkeley, CA: University of California Press.

Becher, T., and Trowler, P. (2001). *Academic Tribes and Territories: Intellectual Enquiry and the Cultures of Discipline* (2nd edition). Buckingham: Open University Press.

Benjamin, E. (1998a). Declining faculty availability to students is the problem – but tenure is not the explanation. *American Behavioral Scientist* 41(5): 716–735.

Benjamin, E. (1998b). Variations in the characteristics of part-time faculty by general fields of instruction and research. In D. W. Leslie (ed.), *The Growing Use of Part-time Faculty: Understanding the Causes and Effects* (pp. 45–59). San Francisco: Jossey-Bass.

Benjamin, E. (2002). How over-reliance on contingent appointments diminishes faculty involvement in student learning. *Peer Review* 5(1): 4–10.

Berger, J.B., and Milem, J.F. (2000). Organizational behavior in higher education and student outcomes. In J.C. Smart (ed.), *Higher Education: Handbook of Theory and Research* (Vol. 15, pp. 268–338). New York: Agathon Press.

Bess, J.L. (1982). *University Organization: A Matrix Analysis of Academic Professions.* New York, NY: Human Services Press.

Biglan, A. (1973a). The characteristics of subject matter in different academic areas. *Journal of Applied Psychology* 57(3): 195–203.

Biglan, A. (1973b). Relationships between subject matter characteristics and the structure and output of university departments. *Journal of Applied Psychology* 51: 204–213.

Birnbaum, R. (1988). *How Colleges Work: The Cybernetics of Academic Organization and Leadership.* San Francisco, CA: Jossey-Bass.

Blau, P.M. (1973). *The Organization of Academic Work.* New York: John Wiley & Sons.

Bolton, C.D., and Kammeyer, K.C.W. (1972). Campus cultures, role orientations, and social types. In K.A. Feldman (ed.), *College and Student: Selected Readings in the Social Psychology of Higher Education.* New York, NY: Pergamon Press.

Bowen, H.R., and Schuster, J.H. (1986). *American Professors: A National Resource Imperiled.* New York: Oxford University Press.

Boyer, E.L. (1990). *Scholarship Reconsidered: Priorities of the Professoriate.* Princeton, NJ: The Carnegie Foundation for the Advancement of Teaching.

Braxton, J.M. (1993). Selectivity and rigor in research universities. *Journal of Higher Education* 64: 657–675.

Braxton, J.M., and Hargens, L.L. (1996). Variation among academic disciplines: Analytical frameworks and research. In J.C. Smart (ed.), *Higher Education: Handbook of Theory and Research* (Vol. 11, pp. 1–46). New York: Agathon Press.

Braxton, J.M., and Nordvall, R.C. (1988). Quality of graduate department origin of faculty and relationship to undergraduate course examination questions. *Research in Higher Education* 28: 145–159.

Braxton, J.M., Olsen, D., and Simmons, A. (1998). Affinity disciplines and the use of principles of good practice for undergraduate education. *Research in Higher Education* 39(3): 299–318.

Broom, L., and Selznick, P. (1973). *Sociology: A Text with Adapted Readings.* New York, NY: Harper and Row.

Cameron, K.S., and Ettington, D.R. (1988). The conceptual foundations of organizational culture. In J.C. Smart (ed.), *Higher Education: Handbook of Theory and Research* (Vol. 4, pp. 356–396). New York: Agathon Press.

Chickering, A.W., and Gamson, Z.F. (1987). Seven principles for good practice in undergraduate education. *AAHE Bulletin* 39(7): 3–7.

Chronister, J., and Baldwin, R. (1999). Marginal or mainstream? Full-time faculty off the tenure track. *Liberal Education* 85(4): 16–23.

Clark, B.R. (1962). Faculty culture. In T.F. Lunsford (ed.), *The Study of Campus Cultures* (pp. 39–54). Boulder, CO: Western Interstate Commission for Higher Education.

Clark, B.R. (1970). *The Distinctive College: Antioch, Reed and Swarthmore.* Chicago, IL: Aldine Publishing Company.

Clark, B.R. (1972). The organizational saga in higher education. *Administrative Science Quarterly* 17(2): 178–184.

Clark, B.R. (1983). *The Higher Education System: Academic Organization in Cross-national Perspective*. Berkeley, CA: University of California Press.

Clark, B.R. (1987a). *The Academic Life: Small Worlds, Different Worlds*. Princeton, NJ: The Carnegie Foundation for the Advancement of Teaching.

Clark, B.R. (ed.) (1987b). *The Academic Profession: National, Disciplinary, and Institutional Settings*. Berkeley, CA: University of California.

Cohen, M.D., and March, J.G. (1974). *Leadership and Ambiguity: The American College President*. New York, NY: McGraw-Hill.

Cole, S., and Barber, E. (2003). *Increasing Faculty Diversity: The Occupational Choices of High-Achieving Minority Students*. Cambridge, MA: Harvard University Press.

Ethington, C.A. (1997). A hierarchical linear modeling approach to studying college effects. In J. Smart (ed.), *Higher Education Handbook of Theory and Research* (Vol. 12, pp. 165–194). Edison, NJ: Agathon.

Fairweather, J.S. (1996). *Faculty Work and Public Trust: Restoring the Value of Teaching and Public Service in American Academic Life*. Boston, MA: Allyn and Bacon.

Feldman, K.A., and Paulsen, M.B. (1999). Faculty motivation: The role of a supportive teaching culture. In M. Theall (ed.), *Motivations from Within: Approaches for Encouraging Faculty and Students to Excel* (Vol. 78). San Francisco: Jossey-Bass.

Finkelstein, M.J., Seal, R.K., and Schuster, J.H. (1998). *The New Academic Generation: A profession on Transformation*. Baltimore, MD: The Johns Hopkins University Press.

Finkin, M.W. (2000). The campaign against tenure. *Academe* 86(3): 20–21.

Freedman, M. (1979). *Academic Culture and Faculty Development*. Berkeley, CA: University of California Press.

Gaff, J.G., and Wilson, R.C. (1971). Faculty cultures and interdisciplinary studies. *Journal of Higher Education* 42(3): 186–201.

Gappa, J.M. (2001). Academic careers for the 21st centure: More options for new faculty. In J.C. Smart (ed.), *Higher Education: Handbook of Theory and Research* (Vol. 17, pp. 425–475). Dordrecht, Netherlands: Kluwer Academic Publishers.

Gappa, J.M., and Leslie, D.W. (1993). *The Invisible Faculty: Improving the Status of Part-timers in Higher Education*. San Francisco, CA: Jossey-Bass.

Geertz, C. (1973). *The Interpretation of Cultures*. New York, NY: Basic Books.

Heck, R.H., and Thomas, S.L. (2000). *An Introduction to Multilevel Modeling Techniques*. Mahwah, NJ: Lawrence Erlbaum Associates.

Hofstede, G., Neuijen, B., Ohayv, D.D., and Sanders, G. (1990). Measuring organizational cultures: A qualitative and quantitative study across twenty cases. *Administrative Science Quarterly* 35(2): 286–316.

Holland, J.L. (1966). *The Psychology of Vocational Choice*. Waltham, MA: Blaisdell.

Holland, J.L. (1973). *Making Vocational Choices: A Theory of Vocational Personalities and Work Environments*. Engelwood Cliffs, NJ: Prentice-Hall.

Holland, J.L. (1985). *Making Vocational Choices*. Englewood Cliffs, NJ: Prentice-Hall.

Holland, J.L. (1997). *Making Vocational Choices: A Theory of Vocational Personalities and Work Environments*. Odessa, FL: Psychological Assessment Resources.

Hurtado, S. (2001). Linking diversity and educational purpose: How diversity affects the classroom environment and student development. In G. Orfield and M. Kurlaender (eds.), *Diversity Challenged: Evidence on the Impact of Affirmative Action*. Cambridge, MA: Harvard University Press.

Hurtado, S., Milem, J., Clayton-Pedersen, A., and Allen, W. (1999). *Enacting Diverse Learning Environments: Improving the Climate for Racial/Ethnic Diversity in Higher Education*. Washington, DC: The George Washington University.

Jelinek, M., Smircich, L., and Hirsch, P. (1983). Introduction: A code of many colors. *Administrative Science Quarterly* 28(3): 331–338.

Kreft, I.G.G., and de Leeuw, J. (1998). *Introducing Multilevel Modeling*. London; Thousand Oaks, CA: Sage.

Kuh, G.D. (1990). Assessing student culture. In W.G. Tierney (ed.), *Understanding Academic Climate and Culture and Climate* (Vol. 68, pp. 47–60). San Francisco, CA.

Kuh, G.D. (2001). Assessing what really matters to student learning: Inside the national survey of student engagement. *Change* 33(3): 10–17, 66.

Kuh, G.D. (2003). What we're learning about student engagement from nsse. *Change* 35(2): 24–32.

Kuh, G.D., Nelson Laird, T.F., and Umbach, P.D. (2004). Aligning faculty activities and student behavior: Realizing the promise of greater expectations. *Liberal Education* 4(24–31).

Kuh, G.D., and Umbach, P.D. (2004). College and character: Insights from the national survey of student engagement. In J. Dalton and T. Russell (eds.), *Assessing Character Outcomes in College. New Directions in Institutional Research* (vol. 122, pp. 37–54). San Francisco, CA: Jossey-Bass.

Kuh, G.D., and Umbach, P.D. (2005). Experiencing diversity: What can we learn from liberal arts colleges? *Liberal Education* 91(1): 14–20.

Kuh, G.D., and Whitt, E.J. (1988). *The Invisible Tapestry: Culture in American Colleges and Universities*. Washington, DC: The George Washington University.

Kuhn, T.S. (1962). *The Structure of Scientific Revolutions*. Chicago, IL: University of Chicago Press.

Ladd, E.C., and Lipset, S.M. (1975). *The Divided Academy*. New York, NY: Norton.

Lattuca, L.R., and Stark, J.S. (1995). Modifying the major: Discretionary thoughts from ten disciplines. *Review of Higher Education* 18(2): 315–344.

Leslie, D.W. (2002). Resolving the dispute: Teaching is academe's core value. *Journal of Higher Education* 73(1): 49–73.

Light, D. (1974). The structure of academic professions. *Sociology of Education* 47(1): 2–28.

Lodahl, J.B., and Gordon, G.G. (1972). The structure of scientific fields and the functioning of university graduate departments. *American Sociological Review* 37(1): 57–72.

Luke, D.A. (2004). *Multilevel Modeling*. Thousand Oaks, CA: Sage Publications.

Masland, A.T. (1982). Organizational culture and the study of higher education. *Review of Higher Education* 8(2): 157–168.

Massy, W.F., Wilger, A.K., and Colbeck, C. (1994). Overcoming 'hallowed' collegiality. *Change* 26(4): 11–20.

Milem, J.F. (2001). Diversity is not enough: How campus climate and faculty teaching methods affect student outcomes. In G. Orfield (ed.), *Diversity Challenged: Legal Crisis and New Evidence* (pp. 233–249). Cambridge, MA: Harvard Education Publishing Group.

Milem, J.F., and Umbach, P.D. (2003). Examining the perpetuation hypothesis: The influence of pre-college factors on students' predispositions regarding diversity activities in college. *Journal of College Student Development* 45(5): 611–624.

Milem, J.F., Umbach, P.D., and Liang, C. (2004). Exploring the perpetuation hypothesis: The role of colleges and universities in desegregating society. *Journal of College Student Development* 45(6): 688–700.

Mirvis, P.H. (1985). Managing research while researching managers. In P.R. Frost, L.F. Moore, M.R. Louis, C.C. Lundberg and J. Martin (eds.), *Organizational Culture* (pp. 201–221). Beverly Hills, CA: Sage.

Morgan, G. (1997). *Images of Organization* (2nd edition). Thousand Oaks, CA: Sage.

Morstain, B.R., and Smart, J.C. (1976). Educational orientations of faculty: Assessing a personality model of the academic professions. *Psychological Reports* 39(1199–1211).

Mulkay, M. (1972). *The Social Process of Innovation: A Study in the Sociology of Science.* London: Macmillan Press.

Neumann, R., Parry, S., and Becher, T. (2002). Teaching and learning in their disciplinary contexts: A conceptual analysis. *Studies in Higher Education* 27(4): 405–417.

Ott, J.S. (1989). *The Organizational Culture Perspoective.* Chicago, IL: Dorsey.

Pascarella, E.T., Cruce, T.M., Umbach, P.D., Wolniak, G.C., Kuh, G.D., Hayek, J.C., et al. (2006). College selectivity and good practices in undergraduate education: How strong is the link? *Journal of Higher Education* 77(2): 251–285.

Pascarella, E.T., and Terenzini, P.T. (1991). *How College Affects Students: Findings and Insights from Twenty years of Research.* San Francisco: Jossey-Bass.

Pascarella, E.T., and Terenzini, P.T. (2005). *How College Affects Students: A Third Decade of Research.* San Francisco: Jossey-Bass.

Pascarella, E.T., Wolniak, G., Seifert, T., Cruce, T., and Blaich, C. (2005). *Liberal Arts Colleges and Liberal Arts Education: New Evidence on Impacts.* San Francisco, CA: Jossey-Bass.

Paulsen, M.B., and Feldman, K.A. (1995a). *Taking Teaching Seriously: Meeting the Challenge of Instructional Improvement.* Washington, DC: The George Washington University.

Paulsen, M.B., and Feldman, K.A. (1995b). Toward a reconceptualization of scholarship: A human action system with functional imperatives. *Journal of Higher Education* 66(6): 615–614.

Perry, R.P., Clifton, R.A., Menec, V.H., Struthers, C.W., and Menges, R.J. (2000). Faculty in transition: A longitudinal analysis of perceived control and type of institution in the research productivity of newly hired faculty. *Research in Higher Education* 41(2): 165–194.

Perry, R.P., Menec, V.H., Struthers, C.W., Hechter, F.J., Schonwetter, D.J., and Menges, R.J. (1997). Faculty in transition: A longitudinal analysis of the role of perceived control and type of institution in adjustment ot postsecondary institutions. *Research in Higher Education* 38(5): 519–556.

Peters, D.S. (1974). The link is equitability. *Research in Higher Education* 2: 57–64.

Peterson, M.W., and Spencer, M.G. (1990). Assessing climates and cultures. In W.G. Tierney (ed.), *Understanding Academic Climate and Culture and Climate* (Vol. 68, pp. 3–18). San Francisco, CA.

Raudenbush, S.W., and Bryk, A.S. (2002). *Hierarchical Linear Models: Applications and Data Analysis Methods.* Thousand Oaks, CA: Sage Publications.

Rice, R.E., and Austin, A.E. (1990). How administrators can improve teaching. In P. Seldin (ed.), *Organizational Impacts on Faculty Morale and Motivation to Teach.* San Francisco, CA: Jossey-Bass.

Richards, J.M., Rand, L.P., and Rand, L.M. (1966). Description of junior colleges. *Journal of Educational Psychology* 57: 207–214.

Richards, J.M., Seligman, R., and Jones, P.K. (1970). Faculty and curriculum as measures of college environment. *Journal of Educational Psychology* 61: 324–332.

Riley, P. (1983). A structurationist account of political culture. *Administrative Science Quarterly* 28(3): 414–437.

Rosen, D., Holmberg, K., and Holland, J.L. (1997). *The Educational Opportunities Finder*. Odessa, FL: Psychological Assessment Resources.

Roueche, J.E., Rouche, S.D., and Milliron, M.D. (1995). *Strangers in their Own Land: Part-time Faculty in American Community Colleges*. Washington, DC: Community College Press.

Ruscio, K.P. (1987). Many sectors, many professions. In B.R. Clark (ed.), *The Academic Profession: National, Disciplinary, and Institutional Settings*. Berkeley, CA: University of Califronia.

Schein, E.H. (1992). *Organizational Culture and Leadership* (2nd edition). San Francisco, CA: Jossey-Bass.

Selvin, H.C., and Hagstrom, W.O. (1996). The emperical classification of formal groups. In T.M. Newcomb and E.K. Wilson (eds.), *College Peer Groups: Problems and Prospects for Research*. Chicago, IL: Aldine.

Smart, J.C. (1982). Faculty teaching goals: A test of Holland's theory. *Journal of Educational Psychology* 74(4): 180–188.

Smart, J.C., and Elton, C.F. (1982). A validation of the biglan model. *Research in Higher Education* 17(2): 213–229.

Smart, J.C., and Ethington, C.A. (1995). Disciplinary and institutional differences in undergraduate education goals. In *New Directions for Teaching and Learning* (Vol. 64, pp. 49–57). San Francisco, CA: Jossey-Bass.

Smart, J.C., Feldman, K.A., and Ethington, C.A. (2000). *Academic Disciplines: Holland's Theory and the Study of College Students and Faculty* (1st edition). Nashville: Vanderbilt University Press.

Smart, J.C., and Umbach, P.D. (in press). Faculty and academic environments: Using Holland's theory to explore differences in how faculty structure undergraduate courses. *Journal of College Student Development*.

Smircich, L. (1983). Concepts of culture and organizational analysis. *Administrative Science Quarterly* 28(3): 339–358.

Smith, D.G. (1989). *The Challenge of Diversity: Involvement or Alienation in the Academy*. Washington, DC: The George Washington University.

Spokane, A.R., Meir, E.I., and Catalano, M. (2000). Person-environment congruence and Holland's theory: A review and reconsideration. *Journal of Vocational Behavior* 57(2): 137–187.

Stark, J.S., Lowther, M.A., Bentley, R.J., and Martens, G.G. (1990). Disciplinary differences in course planning. *Review of Higher Education* 13(2): 141–165.

Statham, A., Richardson, L., and Cook, J. (1991). *Gender and University Teaching: A Negotiated Difference*. Albany, NY: SUNY Press.

Storer, N.W. (1967). The hard sciences and the soft: Some sociological observations. *Bulletin of the Medical Library Association* 55(1): 75–84.

Storer, N.W. (1972). Relations among scientific disciplines. In S.Z. Nagi and R.G. Corwin (eds.), *The Social Contexts of Research*. New York, NY: Wiley.

Tierney, W.G. (1988). Organizational culture in higher education: Defining the essentials. *Journal of Higher Education* 59(1): 2–21.

Tierney, W.G. (1998). Tenure is dead. Long live tenure. In W.G. Tierney (ed.), *The Responsive University: Restructuring High Performance*. Baltimore, MD: The Johns Hopkins University Press.

Tierney, W.G., and Bensimon, E.M. (1996). *Promotion and Tenure: Community and Socialization in Academe*. Albany, NY.

Tierney, W.G., and Rhoades, R.A. (1993). *Enhancing Promotion, Tenure, and Beyond: Faculty Socialization as a Cultural Process*. Washington, DC: Association for the Study of Higher Education.

Toma, J.D. (1997). Alternative inquiry paradigms, faculty cultures, and the definition of academic lives. *Journal of Higher Education* 68(6): 679–705.

Toma, J.D., Dubrow, G., and Hartley, M. (2005). *The Uses of Institutional Culture: Strengthening Identification and Building Brand Equity in Higher Education*. San Francisco, CA: Jossey-Bass.

Trice, H.M., and Beyer, J. (1993). *Cultures of Work Organizations*. Englewood Cliffs, NJ: Prentice Hall.

Tsabari, T., Tziner, A., and Meir, E.I. (2005). Updated meta-analysis of the relationship between congruence and satisfaction. *Journal of Career Assessment* 13(2): 216–232.

U. S. Department of Education. (2000). *IPEDS Fall Staff Survey of Postsecondary Institutions*. Washington, DC: U.S. Department of Education.

Umbach, P.D. (2006). The contribution of faculty of color to undergraduate education. *Research in Higher Education* 47(3): 317–345.

Umbach, P.D. (2007). How effective are they? Exploring the impact of contingent faculty on undergraduate education. *Review of Higher Education* 30(2): 91–123.

Umbach, P.D., and Kuh, G.D. (2006). Student experiences with diversity at liberal arts colleges: Another claim for distinctiveness. *Journal of Higher Education* 77(1): 169–192.

Umbach, P.D., and Milem, J.F. (2004). Applying Holland's typology to the study of differences in student views about diversity. *Research in Higher Education* 45(6): 625–649.

Umbach, P.D., and Wawrzynski, M.R. (2005). Faculty do matter: The role of college faculty in student learning and engagement. *Research in Higher Education* 46(2): 153–184.

Van Maanan, J., and Barley, S.R. (1985). Cultural organization: Fragments of a theory. In P.R. Frost, L.F. Moore, M.R. Louis, C.C. Lundberg and J. Martin (eds.), *Organizational Culture*. Beverly Hills, CA: Sage.

Weick, K.E. (1976). Educational organizations as loosely coupled systems. *Administrative Science Quarterly* 21: 1–19.

Weick, K.E. (1979). *The Social Psychology of Organizing*. New York, NY: McGraw-Hill.

Weick, K.E. (1982). Administering education in loosely coupled schools. *Phi Delta Kappan* 63(10): 673–676.

APPENDIX A: CONSTRUCTS USE IN MODELS

Constructs and Variables	Question Response Sets
FACULTY CONSTRUCTS	
Interactions with students ($\alpha = .72$)	
Discuss grades or assignments with you	None, 1–24%, 25–49%, 50–74%, 75% or higher
Talk about career plans with you	None, 1–24%, 25–49%, 50–74%, 75% or higher
Discuss ideas from readings or classes with you outside of class	None, 1–24%, 25–49%, 50–74%, 75% or higher
Use e-mail to communicate with you	None, 1–24%, 25–49%, 50–74%, 75% or higher
Working with students on activities other than course work (committees, organizations, student life activities, orientation, intramurals, etc)	Hours/week: 0,1–4,5–8,13–16,17–20,21–30, more than 30
Other interactions with students outside of the classroom	Hours/week: 0,1–4,5–8,13–16,17–20,21–30, more than 30
Advising undergraduate students	Hours/week: 0,1–4,5–8,13–16,17–20,21–30, more than 30
Working with undergraduates on research	Hours/week: 0,1–4,5–8,13–16,17–20,21–30, more than 30
Supervising internships or other field experiences	Hours/week: 0,1–4,5–8,13–16,17–20,21–30, more than 30
Active and Collaborative Learning ($\alpha = .78$)	
Working effectively with others	Very much, quite a bit, some, very little
Work with other students on projects during class	Very important, important, somewhat important, not important
Work with classmates outside of class to prepare class assignments	Very important, important, somewhat important, not important
Tutor or teach other students (paid or voluntary)	Very important, important, somewhat important, not important
Discuss ideas or readings from class with others outside of class (other students, faculty members, coworkers, etc.)	Very important, important, somewhat important, not important
Ask questions in class or contribute to class discussions	None, 1–24%, 25–49%, 50–74%, 75% or higher

(cont.)

311

(Continued)

Constructs and Variables	Question Response Sets
Teacher-student shared responsibility (seminar, discussion, etc.)	%of class time: 0, 1–9,10–19,20–29,30–39,40–49,75 or more
Student presentations	% of class time: 0, 1–9,10–19,20–29,30–39,40–49,75 or more
Small group activities	% of class time: 0, 1–9,10–19,20–29,30–39,40–49,75 or more
In-class writing	% of class time: 0, 1–9,10–19,20–29,30–39,40–49,75 or more

Academic Challenge ($\alpha = .72$)

Writing clearly and effectively	Very much, quite a bit, some, very little
Work on a paper or project that requires integrating ideas or information from various sources	Very important, important, somewhat important, not important
Prepare two or more drafts of a paper or assignment before turning it in	Very important, important, somewhat important, not important
Work harder than they usually do to meet your standards	None, 1–24%, 25–49%, 50–74%, 75% or higher
Mark the box that represents the extent to which your evaluations of student performance (e.g., examinations, portfolio) challenge students in your selected course section to do their best work?	1 (very little), 2,3,4,5,6,7 (very much)
Number of written papers of more than 10 pages	0,1–4,5–8,9–12,13–16,17–20,21–30, More than 31
Number of assigned textbooks, books, and/or book length packs of course readings	0,1–4,5–8,9–12,13–16,17–20,21–30, More than 31
Number of homework assignments that take your students more than one hour to complete	0,1–4,5–8,9–12,13–16,17–20,21–30, More than 31
Number of written papers between 5 and 10 pages	0,1–4,5–8,9–12,13–16,17–20,21–30, More than 30
In a typical 7-day week, about how many hours do you think your students actually spend preparing for your class (studying, reading, writing, rehearsing, and other activities related to your course)	0, 1–2,3–4,5–6,7–8,9–10,11–12, More than 12

In a typical 7-day week, about how many hours do you expect your students to spend preparing for your class (studying, reading, writing, rehearsing, and other activities related to your course)	0, 1–2,3–4,5–6,7–8,9–10,11–12, More than 12

Faculty emphasis on diversity
(a = .83)

Have serious conversations in your course with students who are very different from them in terms of their religious beliefs, political opinions, or personal values	Never, sometimes, often, very often
Have class discussions or writing assignments that include diverse perspectives (different races, religions, genders, political beliefs, etc.)	Never, sometimes, often, very often
Have serious conversations in your course with students who are very different from them	Never, sometimes, often, very often
Understanding people of other racial and ethnic backgrounds	Very much, quite a bit, some, very little

Higher-Order Cognitive Activities
($\alpha = .78$)

Thinking critically and analytically	Very much, quite a bit, some, very little
Synthesizing and organizing ideas, information, or experiences into new, more complex interpretations and relationships	Very much, quite a bit, some, very little
Solving complex real-world problems	Very much, quite a bit, some, very little
Making judgments about the value of information, arguments or methods such as examining how others	
gathered and interpreted data and assessing the soundness of their conclusions	Very much, quite a bit, some, very little
Applying theories or concepts to practical problems or in new situations	Very much, quite a bit, some, very little

Importance of Enriching Activities[a]($\alpha = .77$)

Analyzing the basic elements of an idea, experience or theory, such as	Very much, quite a bit, some, very little

(cont.)

313

(Continued)

Constructs and Variables	Question Response Sets
examining a particular case or situation in depth, and considering its components	
Put together ideas or concepts from different courses when completing assignments or during class discussions	Very important, important, somewhat important, not important
Community service or volunteer work	Very important, important, somewhat important, not important
Participation in a learning community or some other formal program where groups of students take two or more classes together	Very important, important, somewhat important, not important
Study abroad	Very important, important, somewhat important, not important
Independent study	Very important, important, somewhat important, not important
Self-designed major	Very important, important, somewhat important, not important
Culminating senior experience	Very important, important, somewhat important, not important
Practicum, internship, field experience, co-op experience	Very important, important, somewhat important, not important
Work on a research project with you outside of course program requirements	Very important, important, somewhat important, not important
Foreign language coursework	Very important, important, somewhat important, not important

STUDENT CONSTRUCTS

Student Engagement

Level of Academic Challenge (First-year student $\alpha = .74$, Senior $\alpha = .75$)

Hours per week preparing for class (studying, reading, writing, rehearsing, and other activities related to your academic program)	0, 1–5, 6–10, 11–15, 16–20, 21–25, 26–30, More than 30
Worked harder than you thought you could to meet an instructor's standards or expectations	Very often, often, sometimes, never
Number of assigned textbooks, books, or book-length packs of course readings during the current school year	None, 1–4, 5–10, 11–20, more than 20

314

Number of written papers or reports of 20 pages or more during the current school year	None, 1–4, 5–10, 11–20, more than 20
Number of written papers or reports between 5 and 19 pages during the current school year	None, 1–4, 5–10, 11–20, more than 20
Number of written papers or reports of fewer than 5 pages during the current school year	None, 1–4, 5–10, 11–20, more than 20
Coursework emphasizes: Analyzing the basic elements of an idea, experience, or theory	Very much, quite a bit, some, very little
Coursework emphasizes: Synthesizing and organizing ideas, information, or experiences into new, more complex interpretations and relationships	Very much, quite a bit, some, very little
Coursework emphasizes: Making judgments about the value of information, arguments, or methods	Very much, quite a bit, some, very little
Coursework emphasizes: Applying theories or concepts to practical problems or in new situations	Very much, quite a bit, some, very little
Campus environments emphasize: Spending significant amounts of time studying and on academic work	Very much, quite a bit, some, very little

Active and Collaborative Learning (First-year student $\alpha = .61$, Senior $\alpha = .62$)

Asked questions in class or contributed to class discussions	Very often, often, sometimes, never
Made a class presentation	Very often, often, sometimes, never
Worked with other students on projects during class	Very often, often, sometimes, never
Worked with classmates outside of class to prepare class assignments	Very often, often, sometimes, never
Tutored or taught other students (paid or voluntary)	Very often, often, sometimes, never
Participated in a community-based project as part of a regular course	Very often, often, sometimes, never

Student Faculty Interaction (First-year student $\alpha = .73$, Senior $\alpha = 75$)

Discussed grades or assignments with an instructor	Very much, quite a bit, some, very little

(cont.)

315

(Continued)

Constructs and Variables	Question Response Sets
Discussed ideas from your readings or classes with others outside of class (students, family members, coworkers, etc.)	Very often, often, sometimes, never
Discussed ideas from your readings or classes with faculty members outside of class	Very much, quite a bit, some, very little
Received prompt feedback from faculty on your academic performance (written or oral)	Very much, quite a bit, some, very little
Talked about career plans with a faculty member or advisor	Very much, quite a bit, some, very little
Gains in Learning and Intellectual Development	
Gains in Personal and Social Development (First-year student $\alpha = .80$, **Senior** $\alpha = .81$)	
Contributed to: Developing a personal code of values and ethics	Very much, quite a bit, some, very little
Contributed to: Understanding people of other racial and ethnic backgrounds	Very much, quite a bit, some, very little
Contributed to: Understanding yourself	Very much, quite a bit, some, very little
Contributed to: Improving the welfare of your community	Very much, quite a bit, some, very little
Contributed to: Learning effectively on your own	Very much, quite a bit, some, very little
Contributed to: Working effectively with others	Very much, quite a bit, some, very little
Gains in General Education (First-year student $\alpha = .79$, **Senior** $\alpha = .80$)	
Contributed to: Writing clearly and effectively	Very much, quite a bit, some, very little
Contributed to: Speaking clearly and effectively	Very much, quite a bit, some, very little
Contributed to: Thinking critically and analytically	Very much, quite a bit, some, very little
Contributed to: Acquiring broad general education	Very much, quite a bit, some, very little
Contributed to: Analyzing quantitative problems	Very much, quite a bit, some, very little

Contributed to: Solving complex real-world problems	Very much, quite a bit, some, very little
Experiences with diversity (First-year student a = .70, Senior a = .72)	
Have serious conversations in your course with students who are very different from them in terms of their religious beliefs, political opinions, or personal values	Very often, often, sometimes, never
Have class discussions or writing assignments that include diverse perspectives (different races, religions, genders, political beliefs, etc.)	Very often, often, sometimes, never
Have serious conversations in your course with students of a different race or ethnicity than their own	Very often, often, sometimes, never

9. Students' Evaluations of University Teaching: Dimensionality, Reliability, Validity, Potential Biases and Usefulness

Herbert W. Marsh*

Oxford University
herb.marsh@edstud.ox.ac.uk

Abstract

Students' evaluations of teaching effectiveness (SETs) have been the topic of considerable interest and a great deal of research in North America and, increasingly, universities all over the world. Research reviewed here indicated that SETs are:

- multidimensional;
- reliable and stable;
- primarily a function of the instructor who teaches a course rather than the course that is taught;
- relatively valid against a variety of indicators of effective teaching;
- relatively unaffected by a variety of variables hypothesized as potential biases; and
- Seen to be useful by faculty as feedback about their teaching, by students for use in course selection, and by administrators for use in personnel decisions

Key Words: Teaching effectiveness; reliability; construct validity; multidimensionality; bias; feedback interventions; longterm stability; profile analysis

Students' evaluations of teaching effectiveness (SETs) are commonly collected in U.S. and Canadian universities (Centra, 2003), are increasingly being used in universities throughout the world (e.g., Marsh &

*This chapter is a substantially revised version of the much longer chapter by Marsh and Dunkin (1997; also see Marsh 1984, 1987). I would like to thank particularly co-authors of earlier studies summarized in this review and colleagues who have offered suggestions on this and on my previous reviews of SET research. Requests for further information about this investigation should be sent to Professor Herbert W. Marsh, Department of Educational Studies, University of Oxford, 15 Norham Gardens, Oxford OX2 6PY UK; E-mail: *herb.marsh@edstud.ox.ac.uk*.

R.P. Perry and J.C. Smart (eds.), The Scholarship of Teaching and Learning in Higher Education: An Evidence-Based Perspective, 319–383.
© 2007 *Springer.*

Roche, 1997; Watkins, 1994), are widely endorsed by teachers, students, and administrators, and have stimulated much research spanning nearly a century. Numerous studies have related SETs to a variety of outcome measures broadly accepted by classroom teachers (e.g., learning inferred from classroom and standardized tests, student motivation, plans to pursue and apply the subject, positive affect, experimental manipulations of specific components of teaching, ratings by former students, classroom observations by trained external observers, and even teacher self-evaluations of their own teaching effectiveness). Considered here are the purposes for collecting SETs, SET dimensions, issues of reliability, validity and generalizability, potential biases in SETs, and the use of SETs for improving teaching effectiveness. As literally thousands of papers have been written, a comprehensive review is beyond the scope of this chapter. The reader is referred to reviews by: Aleamoni (1981); Braskamp, Brandenburg, and Ory (1985); Braskamp and Ory (1994); Cashin (1988); Centra (1979, 1989, 1993); Cohen, (1980, 1981); Costin, Greenough and Menges (1971); de Wolf (1974); Doyle (1975; 1983); Feldman (1976a, 1976b, 1977, 1978, 1979, 1983, 1984, 1986, 1987, 1988, 1989a, 1989b, 1992, 1993); Kulik and McKeachie (1975); Marsh (1982b, 1984, 1985, 1987); Marsh and Dunkin (1992, 1997); Marsh and Dunkin (1997, 2000); McKeachie (1963, 1973, 1979); Murray (1980); Overall and Marsh (1982); Remmers (1963); and Rindermann (1996).

PURPOSES FOR COLLECTING SETs

SETs are collected variously to provide:

- diagnostic feedback to faculty for improving teaching;
- a measure of teaching effectiveness for personnel decisions;
- information for students for the selection of courses and instructors;
- one component in national and international quality assurance exercises, designed to monitor the quality of teaching and learning; and
- an outcome or a process description for research on teaching (e.g., studies designed to improve teaching effectiveness and student outcomes, effects associated with different styles of teaching, perspectives of former students).

The first purpose is nearly universal, but the next three are not. Systematic student input is required before faculty are even considered for promotion at many universities, but not at all at some others. At a few universities, students buy summaries of SETs in bookstores for purposes of course selection, but they are provided no access to the ratings in many other universities. The publication of SETs is controversial (Babad, Darley, & Kaplowitz, 1999; Perry, Abrami, Leventhal, & Check, 1979) and, not surprisingly, is viewed more positively by students than by teachers (Howell & Symbaluk, 2001). The existence of a program of students' evaluations of teaching is typically considered as one requirement of a good university in quality assurance exercises. Surprisingly, SET research has not been systematically incorporated into broader studies of teaching and learning (see Marsh & Dunkin, 1997).

DIMENSIONS OF SETs

Researchers and practitioners (e.g., Abrami & d'Apollonia, 1991; Cashin & Downey, 1992; Feldman, 1997; Marsh & Roche, 1993) agree that teaching is a complex activity with multiple interrelated components (e.g., clarity, interaction, organization, enthusiasm, feedback). Hence, it should not be surprising that SETs—like the teaching they are intended to represent—are also multidimensional. Particularly formative/diagnostic feedback intended to be useful for improving teaching should reflect this multidimensionality (e.g., a teacher can be organized but lack enthusiasm).

SET instruments differ in the quality of items, the way the teaching effectiveness construct is operationalized, and the particular dimensions that are included. The validity and usefulness of SET information depends upon the content and coverage of the items and the SET factors that they reflect. Poorly worded or inappropriate items will not provide useful information, while scores averaged across an ill-defined assortment of items offer no basis for knowing what is being measured. In practice, most instruments are based on a mixture of logical and pragmatic considerations, occasionally including some psychometric evidence such as reliability or factor analysis (Marsh & Dunkin, 1997). Valid measurement, however, requires a continual interplay between theory, research and practice. Careful attention should therefore be given to the components of teaching effectiveness that are to be measured. Whereas the usefulness of a SET program depends on more than having a well-designed instrument, this is an important starting point. Several theoretically defensible instruments with a well-defined factor structure have been reviewed (see Centra, 1993; Marsh 1987;

Marsh & Dunkin, 1997), but few have been evaluated extensively in terms of potential biases, validity, and usefulness of feedback.

IDENTIFYING THE DIMENSIONS TO BE MEASURED

Marsh and Dunkin (1997) noted three overlapping approaches to the identification, construction and evaluation of multiple dimensions in SET instruments: (1) empirical approaches such as factor analysis and multitrait-multimethod (MTMM) analysis; (2) logical analyses of the content of effective teaching and the purposes the ratings are intended to serve, supplemented by reviews of previous research and feedback from students and instructors (see Feldman, 1976b; also see Table 1); and (3) a theory of teaching and learning. In practice, most instruments are based on either of the first two approaches— particularly the second. The SET literature contains examples of instruments that have a well-defined factor structure, such as the four instruments presented by Marsh (1987; also see Centra, 1993; Jackson, Teal, Raines, Nansel, Force, Burdsal, 1999; Marsh & Dunkin, 1997; Richardson, 2005). Factor analyses have identified the factors that each of these instruments is intended to measure, demonstrating that SETs do measure distinct components of teaching effectiveness. The systematic approach used in the development of these instruments, and the similarity of the factors that they measure, supports their construct validity.

An important, unresolved controversy is whether the SET instruments measure effective teaching or merely behaviors or teaching styles that are typically correlated with effective teaching. In particular, is a teacher necessarily a poor teacher if he/she does not use higher order questions, does not give assignments back quickly, does not give summaries of the material to be covered, etc. (For further discussion, see McKeachie 1997; Scriven, 1981). Unless SETs are taken to be the criterion of good teaching, then it may be inappropriate to claim that a poor rating on one or more of the SET factors necessarily reflects poor teaching. Indeed, an often-cited complaint of SETs is that their use militates against some forms of effective teaching (see discussion on biases). Nevertheless, there is little or no systematic evidence to indicate that any of the typical SET factors is negatively related to measures of effective teachings (see discussion on validity). Furthermore, taken to its extreme, this argument could be used to argue against the validity of the type of behaviors that Scriven advocates should be measured by SETs or any other measure of effective teaching. Because teaching

Table 1: Categories of Effective Teaching Adapted From Feldman (1976b) and the Students' Evaluations of Educational Quality (SEEQ) and Endeavor factors Most Closely Related to Each Category

Feldman's Categories	SEEQ Factors
1) Stimulation of interest (I)	Instructor Enthusiasm
2) Enthusiasm (I)	Instructor Enthusiasm
3) Subject knowledge (I)	Breadth of Coverage
4) Intellectual expansiveness (I)	Breadth of Coverage
5) Preparation and organisation (I)	Organisation/Clarity
6) Clarity and understandableness (I)	Organisation/Clarity
7) Elocutionary skills (I)	None
8) Sensitivity to class progress (I/II)	None
9) Clarity of objectives (III)	Organisation/Clarity
10) Value of course materials (III)	Assignments/Readings
11) Supplementary materials (III)	Assignments/Readings
12) Perceived outcome/impact (III)	Learning/Value
13) Fairness, impartiality (III)	Examinations/Grading
14) Classroom management (III)	None
15) Feedback to students (III)	Examinations/Grading
16) Class discussion (II)	Group Interaction
17) Intellectual challenge (II)	Learning/Value
18) Respect for students (II)	Individual Rapport
19) Availability/helpfulness (II)	Individual Rapport
20) Difficulty/workload (III)	Workload/Difficulty

Note. The actual categories used by Feldman in different studies (e.g., Feldman, 1976, 1983, 1984) varied somewhat. Feldman (1976b) also proposed three higher-order clusters of categories, which are identified by I (presentation), II (facilitation), and III (regulation) in parentheses following each category.

effectiveness is a hypothetical construct, there is no measure (SETs or any other indicators) that IS effective teaching—only measures that are consistently correlated with a variety of indicators of teaching effectiveness.

THE STUDENTS' EVALUATION OF EDUCATIONAL QUALITY (SEEQ) INSTRUMENT

Strong support for the multidimensionality of SETs comes from research based on the SEEQ instrument (Marsh, 1982b; 1987; Marsh & Dunkin, 1997; Richardson, 2005). SEEQ measures nine factors (See Table 1). In the development of SEEQ, a large item pool was obtained from a literature review, from forms in current usage, and interviews with faculty and students about what they saw as effective teaching. Students and teachers were asked to rate the importance of items; teachers were asked to judge the potential usefulness of the items as a basis for feedback, and open-ended student comments were examined to determine if important aspects had been excluded. These criteria, along with psychometric properties, were used to select items and revise subsequent versions, thus supporting the content validity of SEEQ responses. Marsh and Dunkin (1992, 1997; Marsh & Roche, 1994) also demonstrated that the content of SEEQ factors is consistent with general principles of teaching and learning, with particular emphasis on theory and research in adult education that is most relevant to higher education settings. As noted by Richardson (2005), the SEEQ instrument continues to be the most widely used instrument in published research. In summary, there is a strong empirical, conceptual, and theoretical basis for the SEEQ factors.

Factor analytic support for the SEEQ scales is particularly strong. The factor structure of SEEQ has been replicated in many published studies, but the most compelling support is provided by Marsh and Hocevar (1991a). Starting with an archive of 50,000 sets of class-average ratings (reflecting responses to 1 million SEEQ surveys), they defined 21 groups of classes that differed in terms of course level (undergraduate/graduate), instructor rank (teaching assistant/regular faculty), and academic discipline. The 9 a priori SEEQ factors were identified in each of 21 separate factor analyses. The average correlation between factor scores based on each separate analysis and factor scores based on the total sample was over .99. Whereas most SEEQ research has focused on student responses to the instrument, the same nine factors were identified in several large-scale studies of teacher self-evaluations of their own teaching using the SEEQ instrument (Marsh, Overall, & Kesler, 1979b; Marsh, 1983; also see Marsh, 1987, p. 295).

Studies using the "applicability paradigm" (see reviews by Marsh, 1986; Marsh & Roche, 1992; 1994; Watkins, 1994) in different Australian and New Zealand universities, in a cross-section of Australian Technical and Further Education institutions, and universities from a variety of different countries (e.g., Spain, Papua New Guinea, India, Nepal, Nigeria, the Philippines, and Hong Kong) provide support for the applicability of the distinct SEEQ factors outside the North American context in which they were developed. Watkins (1994) critically evaluated this research in relation to criteria derived from cross-cultural psychology. He adopted an "etic" approach to cross-cultural comparisons that seeks to evaluate what are hypothesized to be universal constructs based on the SEEQ factors. Based on his evaluation of the applicability paradigm, Watkins (1994, p. 262) concluded, "the results are certainly generally encouraging regarding the range of university settings for which the questionnaires and the underlying model of teaching effectiveness investigated here may be appropriate."

OLDER, EXPLORATORY AND NEWER, CONFIRMATORY APPROACHES TO FACTOR ANALYSIS

Confirmatory factor analysis (CFA) has largely superseded traditional applications of exploratory factor analysis (EFA), and this has created an interesting disjuncture between SET research based on older instruments, derived from EFA and newer studies based on CFA (see related discussion by Abrami, d'Apollonia, & Rosenfield, 1993; 1997; Jackson et al., 1999; Marsh, 1987; 1991a; 1991b; Marsh & Dunkin, 1997; Toland & De Ayala, 2005). This is an important issue, because different practices in the application of EFA and CFA may give the appearance of inconsistent results if not scrutinized carefully (e.g., Toland & De Ayala, 2005). Given the extensive EFA evidence for SEEQ having a clearly defined, replicable structure, why would CFA provide apparently conflicting results?

The resolution of this dilemma is that the CFAs are typically based on a highly restrictive "independent clusters" model in which each item is allowed to load on one and only one factor, whereas exploratory factor analysis allows each item to cross-load on other factors. The exclusion of significant non-zero cross-loadings in CFA not only results in a poor fit to the data, but also distorts the observed pattern of relations among the factors. Although there are advantages in having "pure" items that load on a single factor, this is clearly not a requirement of a well-defined, useful factor structure, nor even a requirement of traditional definitions of "simple structure". The extensive EFA results summarized here clearly demonstrate that the SEEQ factor structure is well-defined, replicable over a diversity of settings, and stable over time, whereas the independent cluster model (e.g., Toland & De Ayala, 2005) does not provide an appropriate representation of the factor structure. In addressing this issue, Marsh (1991a, 1991b) also noted that an independent cluster model did not provide an adequate fit to the data, as many items had minor cross-loading on other factors. He randomly divided a large sample of classes into groups, used empirical techniques to determine additional parameters, and then showed that this post hoc solution cross-validated well with the second sample. Thus, the existence of an a priori model based on CFA is the key to resolving the apparent anomaly identified by Toland and De Ayala.

An alternative solution to this problem is illustrated by Jackson et al. (1999), who compared CFA and EFA solutions based on analyses of a new set of 7,000 university classes from the Student's Perceptions of Teaching Effectiveness. This is an older instrument that has a well-established multidimensional structure with factors similar to those of SEEQ. Jackson et al. tested the replicability of an EFA solution based on previous results with a CFA based on new data, but allowed minor loadings for items with moderate cross-loadings in the original EFA. This a priori factor structure did not have an independent cluster solution, but the CFA model resulted in a good fit to the data and cross-validated well with EFAs based on both the new and the old data sets.

In summary, CFA offers important advantages over older, EFA approaches, but researchers must use care to evaluate appropriate models that accurately reflect factor structures and relations among variables. Whereas factor analytic research with appropriately designed instruments clearly supports a multidimensional perspective (e.g., the nine-factor solution for SEEQ), a more critical question is whether there is support for the discriminant validity and usefulness of the multiple factors in other research, such as studies evaluating relations with validity criteria, potential biases, and the usefulness of SETs for the purposes of improving teaching effectiveness.

LOGICAL APPROACHES TO THE IDENTIFICATION OF DIMENSIONS OF TEACHING

Feldman (1976b; also see Table 1) logically derived a comprehensive set of components of effective teaching by categorising the characteristics of the superior university teacher from the student's point of view. He reviewed research that either asked students to specify these characteristics or inferred them on the basis of correlations with global SETs. In a content analysis of factors identified in well-defined multidimensional SET instruments, Marsh (1987) demonstrated that Feldman's categories tended to be more narrowly defined constructs than the empirical factors identified in many instruments—including SEEQ. Whereas SEEQ provided a more comprehensive coverage of Feldman's categories than other SET instruments considered, most SEEQ factors represented more than one of Feldman's categories (e.g., Feldman's categories "stimulation of interest" and "enthusiasm" were both included in the SEEQ "instructor enthusiasm" factor). Surprisingly, there seems to have been no attempt to design and rigorously test an instrument based on Feldman's theoretical model of the components of effective teaching (but see Abrami et al., 1997).

GLOBAL SET RATINGS

Global or "overall" ratings cannot adequately represent the multidimensionality of teaching. They may also be more susceptible to context, mood and other potential biases than specific items that are more closely tied to actual teaching behaviors, leading Frey (1978) to argue that they should be excluded. In the ongoing debate on the value of global ratings, Abrami & d'Apollonia (1991; Abrami, d'Apollonia, & Rosenfield, 1997) seemed to initially prefer the sole use of global ratings for personnel decisions, whereas Marsh (1991b; Marsh & Bailey, 1993) preferred a profile of scores—including the different SEEQ factors, global ratings, expected grades, and prior subject interest ratings. In support of global ratings, Abrami et al argue the correlation between SETs and student learning in multisection validity studies is higher for global ratings than the *average* correlation based on specific rating factors. However, it is important to emphasize that student learning is systematically more highly correlated with specific components of SETs more logically related to SETs than to global SETs (see subsequent discussion of multi-section validity studies of student learning). Abrami et al. also argue that there exist a plethora of SET instruments that reflect a lack of clear consensus about the specific dimensions of SETs that are assessed in actual practice. However, it is also important to point out that Feldman (1976b) provided a comprehensive map of the specific SET dimensions that have been identified in empirical research that provides a basis for assessing those that are included on any particular instrument (see Table 1).

Although this debate continues, there is apparent agreement that an appropriately weighted average of specific SET factors may provide a workable compromise between these two positions. Along with other research exploring higher-order (more general) factors associated with SET dimensions (Abrami et al., 1997), this compromise acknowledges the underlying multidimensionality of SETs (Marsh & Roche, 1994). However, it also raises the thorny question of how to weight the different SET components. Marsh and Roche (1994) suggested that for purposes of feedback to instructors (and perhaps for purposes of teacher input into personnel decisions), it might be useful to weight SET factors according to their importance in a specific teaching context as perceived by the teacher. Unresolved issues concerning the validity and utility of importance-weighted averages (e.g., Marsh, 1995), however, dictate caution in pursuing this suggestion.

Recent reviews of SET research (e.g., Apodaca & Grad, 2005; Hobson & Talbot, 2001) also noted that whereas there is general agreement on the appropriateness of a multidimensional perspective of SETs for purposes of formative feedback and instructional improvement, the debate about the most appropriate form of SET for summative purposes is unresolved: overall ratings, a multidimensional profile of specific SET factors, or global scores based on weighted or unweighted specific factors. Indeed, Marsh (1987; Marsh & Dunkin, 1997) recommended that teachers preparing a teaching portfolio for purposes of personnel decisions should be given the opportunity to use a multidimensional profile of SET scores to defend their approach to effective teaching—thereby implicitly endorsing use of a weighted-average approach.

In an attempt to discover how students weight different SET components in forming an overall evaluation, Ryan and Harrison (1995; Harrison, More & Ryan, 1996) conducted a policy-capturing experiment (also see Marsh & Groves, 1987) in which descriptions of hypothetical teachers were experimentally manipulated in relation to SEEQ factors. Results indicated that students demonstrated insight in forming overall SET ratings, using an appropriate weighting scheme that was consistent across students, thus supporting the use of a weighted-average approach based on weights derived from students.

Harrison, Douglas, and Burdsal (2004) specifically compared the usefulness of different strategies for obtaining global ratings (overall ratings, weighted averages with weights determined by students and teachers, unweighted averages, or higher-order factors based on higher-order factor analysis). Whereas they expressed a preference for a higher-order SET factor, they noted that results from all these approaches were highly correlated—suggesting that there was little empirical basis for choosing one over the others. However, conceptually and strategically there are apparently important differences that may affect the acceptability of SETs to academics, administrators, and students.

UNIT OF ANALYSIS PROBLEM

Misunderstanding about the appropriate unit of analysis continues to be a source of confusion and a critical methodological issue in SET research. Because of the nature of SETs, it is feasible to consider variation at the level of the individual student, the class or teacher, the department or faculty, or even an entire university. Fortunately, however, there is a clear consensus in SET research that the class-average or individual teacher is the appropriate unit of analysis, rather than the individual student (e.g., Cranton & Smith, 1990; Gilmore, Kane, & Naccarato, 1978; Howard & Maxwell, 1980; Marsh, 1987). As emphasized by Kane, Gillmore and Crooks (1976, p. 172), "it is the dependability of the class means, rather than the individual student ratings, that is of interest, and the class is the appropriate unit of analysis." Thus, support for the construct validity of student evaluation responses must be demonstrated at the class-average level (e.g., relations with class-average achievement, teacher self-evaluations), support for the factor structure of SETs should be based on a large, diverse set of class-average ratings, the reliability of responses is most appropriately determined from studies of interrater agreement among different students within the same course (also see Gilmore et al., 1978 for further discussion), and studies of potential bias (expected grades, class size, prior subject interest, workload/difficulty) should be based on class-average ratings.

Historically, due largely to limitations in statistical analysis available to them, SET researchers have had to choose a single unit of analysis. In such cases, the class-average is almost always the appropriate unit of analysis. However, as suggested by Marsh and Dunkin (1997; Marsh, 1987), advances in the application of multilevel modeling open up new opportunities for researchers to simultaneously consider more than one unit of analysis (e.g., individual student and class) within the same analysis.

Although commercial packages have greatly facilitated the application of multilevel modeling, there are only a few examples of multilevel modeling in SET research (e.g., Marsh and Hattie, 2002; Marsh, Rowe, and Martin, 2002; Ting, 2000; Toland & De Ayala, 2005; Wendorf & Alexander, 2004). It is important to emphasize that the typical analysis of class-average SETs is not invalidated by the existence of a multilevel structure to the data, in which there is significant variation at both the individual student and class levels, but this multilevel structure does invalidate most analyses conducted at the individual student level. More importantly, a systematic evaluation of the multilevel structure of the data allows researchers to pursue new questions not adequately addressed by conventional analyses. Thus, for example, whereas researchers have routinely evaluated variance components associated with individual students and classes, a more complete analysis of the multilevel structure might address, for example, how SETs vary from department to department and the characteristics of departments associated with this variation, or even differences between entire universities (Marsh, Rowe, and Martin, 2002). In the near future it is likely that multilevel modeling will become widely used in SET research.

IMPLICIT THEORIES AND THE SYSTEMATIC DISTORTION HYPOTHESIS

Theoretical work on the implicit theories that people use to make ratings and the systematic distortion hypothesis based largely on personality research (e.g., Cronbach, 1958) has been applied to SET research to provide an alternative explanation for the robustness of factor structures based on a well-designed, multidimensional SET instrument. Marsh (1984; also see Marsh, 1987) noted, for example, that if a student's implicit theory of behavioral covariation suggests that the occurrences of behaviors X and Y are correlated and if the student rates the teacher high on X, then the teacher may also be assumed to be high on Y, even though the student has not observed Y. The systematic distortion hypothesis predicts that traits can be rated as correlated (based on implicit theories), whereas actual behaviors reflecting these traits are not correlated.

In a study particularly relevant to implicit theories, Cadwell and Jenkins (1985) specifically noted the factor analytic research based on SEEQ was "particularly impressive" (p. 383), but suggested that the strong support for the factor structure was due to semantic similarities in the items. To test this speculation, they asked student to make ratings of teaching effectiveness based on scripted scenarios (sets of 8 one-sentence descriptions depicting the presence or absence of each behavior) derived from various combinations of SEEQ items. However, in their critique of the Cadwell and Jenkins (1985) study, Marsh & Groves (1987) noted many methodological problems and conceptual ambiguities; thus, interpretations should be made cautiously. In particular, students were given inadequate or conflicting information that required them to rely on implicit theories and re-interpretations of the meaning of the behaviors to make sense of the task. For example, students were told whether or not an instructor "often summarized material in a manner that aided comprehension" (p. 386) and "presented a brief overview of the lecture content" (p. 386), as a basis for responding to the SEEQ item "the objectives of the course were clearly stated and pursued", but were given no information about the actual pursuit of course objectives. Even more problematic, students were asked to make ratings on the basis of apparently contradictory behavioral descriptions. For example, they were told that the same instructor "summarized material in a manner that aided comprehension" (p. 386) but did *not* "present a brief overview of the lecture content" (p. 386). Hence, students in this study were forced to make inferences about SEEQ items based on the information available or to devise plausible explanations for apparently contradictory information, to make sense of the task. Marsh and Grove argued that these and other conceptual and methodological problems precluded any justifiable conclusions about the effect of semantic similarities and implicit theories. Nevertheless, Cadwell and Jenkins did find that most of the systematic variation in responses to each SEEQ item was associated with differences in the experimentally manipulated teaching behaviors designed to parallel that item, thus supporting the construct validity of SEEQ responses.

More recently, Renaud and Murray (2005) conducted one of the most detailed tests of the systematic distortion hypothesis in relation to implicit theories. Noting the failure of most previous research, such as the Caldwell and Jenkins (1985) study, to include behaviors based on actual classrooms, they considered: (a) student ratings of teaching effectiveness (SETs) under typical conditions for a sample of 32 teachers; (b) frequency counts of observable teaching behaviors based on videotapes of these same teachers; and (c) ratings of the conceptual similarity of all possible pairs of items used in these tasks. In support of the validity of students' implicit theories, covariation between SET items was substantially related to covariation among teaching behaviors. However, covariation between SETs and similarity ratings was somewhat higher, suggesting the possibility of a semantic distortion in addition to covariation among ratings consistent with actual behaviors. However, whereas the application of implicit theories to SET research has been heuristic, apparently inherent complexities and difficult methodological problems like those discussed by Marsh & Groves (1987) and by Renaud and Murray (2005) mean that unambiguous interpretations are unlikely to result from these studies.

Summary of the Dimensionality of SETs

Many SET instruments are not developed using a theory of teaching and learning, a systematic logical approach that ensures content validity, or empirical techniques such as factor analysis. Appropriately constructed SET instruments and particularly research based on SEEQ provide clear support for the multidimensionality of the SET construct. Whereas some instruments based on far fewer items provide evidence of fewer factors, it is clear that students are able to differentiate between distinct components of effective teaching. Indeed, the classification scheme developed by Feldman (1987; see Table 1) provides an appropriate framework for evaluating the comprehensiveness of any particular instrument. The debate about which specific components of teaching effectiveness can and should be measured has not been resolved, although there seems to be consistency in those identified in response to the most carefully designed instruments such as SEEQ, which are apparently applicable to a wide diversity of educational settings. Furthermore, it is important to note that many poorly constructed student evaluation surveys fail to provide a comprehensive multidimensional evaluation, thus undermining their usefulness, particularly for diagnostic feedback. "Home-made" SET surveys constructed by lecturers themselves, or by committees, are particularly susceptible to such deficiencies, and compounded by the likelihood that aspects of teaching excluded from the survey are those which tend to be the most neglected in practice. Such "one shot" instruments are rarely evaluated in relation to rigorous psychometric considerations and revised accordingly. SET instruments should be designed to measure separate components of teaching effectiveness, and support for both the content and the construct validity of the multiple dimensions should be evaluated.

RELIABILITY, STABILITY, GENERALIZABILITY, AND APPLICABILITY

Reliability

Traditionally, reliability is defined on the basis of the extent of agreement among multiple items designed to measure the same underlying construct, using indexes such as coefficient alpha. This approach, although potentially useful, does not provide an adequate basis for assessing the reliability of SET responses. The main source of variability is lack of agreement among different students' ratings of the same teacher rather than lack of agreement among different items. Hence, the reliability of SETs is most appropriately determined from studies of interrater agreement that assess lack of agreement among different students within the same course (see Gilmore et al., 1978 for further discussion). The correlation between responses by any two students in the same class (i.e., the single rater reliability; Marsh, 1987) is typically in the .20s but the reliability of the *class-average* response depends upon the number of students rating the class: .95 for 50 students, .90 for 25 students, .74 for 10 students, and .60 for five students. Given a sufficient number of students, the reliability of class-average SETs compares favourably with that of the best objective tests.

Although there are more sophisticated approaches to error that can incorporate both lack of agreement among items and students as well as other sources of error, such generalizability research typically shows that lack of agreement among students is by far the largest source of error (see Gilmore et al., 1978 for further discussion). In these analyses, differences between responses by individual students are typically considered to reflect random measurement error. More recent developments of multilevel modeling allow researchers to simultaneously incorporate both the class and the individual student into the same analysis. This would allow researchers to determine, for example, individual student characteristics that may explain variation among students nested within classes, how these individual characteristics might affect class-average ratings, and how these might interact with class-level characteristics to influence class-average ratings.

STABILITY

Sadly, there is a broad range of cross-sectional and longitudinal research demonstrating that teaching effectiveness—no matter how measured—tends to decline with age and years of teaching experience (see reviews by Marsh, 1987; Marsh & Dunkin, 1997). At best, there is limited evidence of an increase in teaching effectiveness over the first few years of teaching, followed by a gradual decline in teaching effectiveness. Hence, it is not surprising that cross-sectional studies typically report that SETs are also negatively related to age and years of teaching experience (Feldman, 1983; Renaud & Murray, 1996), although there is some suggestion that SETs may increase slightly during the first few years of teaching (Marsh & Dunkin, 1997). Also, this effect may vary somewhat with the particular SET dimension. Furthermore, these results are typically based on average responses aggregated across many teachers so that, perhaps, there are large individual differences for particular teachers—some improving and others declining—that are lost when averaged across teachers. Cross-sectional studies provide a poor basis for inferring how ratings of the same person will change over time.

In a true longitudinal study, Marsh and Hocevar (1991b) examined changes in ratings of a diverse sample of 195 teachers who had been evaluated continuously over a 13-year period. Based on an average of more than 30 sets of ratings for each teacher, they found that the mean ratings for their cohort of 195 teachers showed almost no systematic changes in any of the SEEQ factors for the total group or for subsamples with little, intermediate, or substantial amounts of teaching experience at the start of the 13-year longitudinal study. Furthermore, whereas there were some individual differences in this trend, there was only a small number of teachers who showed systematic increases or decreases over time. Although it is discouraging that the feedback from the ratings alone did not lead to systematic improvement, it is encouraging that this group of teachers who had received so much SET feedback did not show the systematic declines in teaching effectiveness that appear to be the norm (also see Kember, Leung, & Kwan, 2002). The Marsh and Hocevar study is particularly important in showing the stability of the SEEQ factor structure over time and the stability of SETs over an extended period of time.

GENERALIZABILITY

Student versus alumni ratings. Some critics suggest that students cannot recognize effective teaching until being called upon to apply their mastery in further coursework or after graduation. However, cross-sectional studies show good agreement between responses by current students and alumni (see Marsh, 1987; Centra, 1979, 1989). In a true longitudinal study (Overall & Marsh, 1980), ratings in 100 classes correlated .83 with ratings by the *same* students when they again evaluated the same classes retrospectively several years later, at least one year after graduation. These studies demonstrate that SETs for alumni and current students are very similar.

Teacher versus course effects. Researchers have also explored the correlation of SETs in different courses taught by the same instructor or in the same course taught by different teachers. Results (Marsh, 1987; Marsh & Dunkin, 1997; also see Rindermann & Schofield, 2001) demonstrate that SETs are primarily due to the instructor who teaches a class and not the particular class being taught. Thus, for example, Marsh (1987, p. 278) reported that for the overall instructor rating, the correlation between ratings of different instructors teaching the same course (i.e., a course effect) was −.05, while correlations for the same instructor in different courses (.61) and in two different offerings of the same course (.72) were much larger. These results support the validity of SETs as a measure of teacher effectiveness, but not as a measure of course effectiveness independent of the teacher.

This research on teacher and course effects also has important implications for the compilation of normative archives used to assess teaching effectiveness, based on ratings of the same teacher over time in different courses. Gilmore, Kane, and Naccarato (1978), applying generalizability theory to SETs, suggested that ratings for a given instructor should be averaged across different courses to enhance generalizability. If it is likely that an instructor will teach many different classes during his or her subsequent career, then tenure decisions should be based upon as many different courses as possible—Gilmore, Kane, and Naccarato, suggest at least five. These recommendations require that a longitudinal archive of SETs is maintained for personnel decisions. These data would provide the basis for more generalizable summaries, the assessment of changes over time, and the determination of which particular courses are best taught by a specific instructor. Indeed, the evaluation of systematic change in SETs of the same teacher over time would also provide an alternative basis of comparison that was not based on how ratings of a given teacher compared with those by other teachers. It is most unfortunate that some universities systematically collect SETs, but fail to keep a longitudinal archive of the results.

GENERALIZABILITY OF PROFILES

Marsh and Bailey (1993) used multivariate profile analysis to demonstrate that each teacher has a characteristic profile on the 9 SEEQ scores (e.g., high on organisation and low on enthusiasm). For each teacher who had been evaluated continuously over 13 years, Marsh and Bailey determined a characteristic profile of SEEQ factors based on all the SETs of each teacher. Each teacher's characteristic profile was distinct from the profiles of other teachers, generalised across course offerings over the 13-year period, and even generalised across undergraduate and graduate level courses. Indeed, the generalizability of the profile of SEEQ scores was as strong as or stronger than the generalizability of the individual SEEQ factors and global ratings over time. Similarly,

335

Hativa (1996) also demonstrated that SETs were highly stable in terms both of the level and profile based on multiple ratings of the same teachers teaching the same course on multiple occasions. These results provide further support for the multidimensionality of SETs and their generalizability.

This support for the existence of teacher-specific profiles also has important implications for the use of SETs as feedback and for the relation of SETs to other criteria such as student learning. For example, presentation of an appropriate profile of SET factors (Marsh, 1987) provides clear evidence about relative strengths and weaknesses in teaching effectiveness. Given this stability of profiles, Marsh and Bailey lament that so little research has evaluated how specific profiles of SETs are related to student learning, other validity criteria, potentially biasing factors, and other correlates of SETs. For example, meta-analyses show that SETs are related to student learning and feedback interventions, and that the effect sizes vary systematically and logically with the specific SET component. However, there has been almost no research to establish how characteristic profiles are related to these criteria. Thus, for example, a profile in which both enthusiasm and organization are high might be particularly conducive to learning—beyond what can be explained in terms of either of these SET factors considered in isolation.

STUDENT WRITTEN COMMENTS—GENERALITY ACROSS DIFFERENT RESPONSE FORMS

Braskamp and his colleagues (Braskamp et al., 1985; Braskamp, Ory, & Pieper, 1981; Ory, Braskamp & Pieper, 1980) examined the usefulness of students' written comments and their relation to SET rating items. Student comments were scored for overall favorability with reasonable reliability and these overall scores correlated with responses to the overall rating item ($r = .93$), close to the limits of the reliability of the two indicators (Ory, Braskamp & Pieper, 1980). Braskamp, Ory, & Pieper (1981) sorted student comments into one of 22 content categories and evaluated comments in terms of favorability. Comment favorability was again highly correlated with the overall instructor rating (.75).

In a related study, Ory and Braskamp (1981) simulated results about a hypothetical instructor, consisting of written comments in their original unedited form and rating items—both global and specific. The rating items were judged as easier to interpret and more comprehensive for both personnel decisions and self-improvement, but other aspects of the written comments were judged to be more useful for purposes of self-improvement. Speculating on these results, the authors suggested that "the nonstandardized, unique, personal written comments by students are perceived as too subjective for important personnel decisions. However, this highly idiosyncratic information about a particular course is viewed as useful diagnostic information for making course changes" (pp. 280–281). However, Murray (1987) reported that for purposes of feedback, teachers more strongly endorsed ratings of specific components of teaching effectiveness (78%) than written comments (65%), although global ratings were seen as even less useful (54%).

Lin, McKeachie, and Tucker (1984) reported that the impact of statistical summaries based on specific components of SETs was enhanced by written comments for purposes of promotional decisions—although the effects of research productivity were much larger. However, because they did not consider comments alone, or comments that were inconsistent with the statistical summaries in their experimental simulation study, there was no basis for comparing the relative impact of the two sources of information. Perhaps, because student comments are not easily summarized (due to the effort required as well as their idiosyncratic nature, which is dependent upon the specific class context), it may be more appropriate simply to return written comments to teachers along with appropriate summaries of the SET ratings. A useful direction for further research would be to evaluate more systematically whether this lengthy and time consuming exercise provides useful and reliable information that is not obtainable from the more cost effective use of appropriate multidimensional rating items. Unfortunately, there has apparently been no research to compare results of multidimensional content categories based on written comments with a well-defined multidimensional profile of SET ratings to evaluate the convergent and discriminant validity of both sources of information.

VALIDITY

THE CONSTRUCT VALIDATION APPROACH TO VALIDITY

SETs, as one measure of teaching effectiveness, are difficult to validate, since no single criterion of effective teaching is sufficient. Historically, researchers have emphasised a narrow, criterion-related approach to validity in which student learning is the only criterion of effective teaching. This limited framework, however, inhibits a better understanding of what is being measured by SETs, of what can be inferred from SETs, and how findings from diverse studies can be understood within a common framework. Instead, Marsh (1987) advocated a construct validation approach in which SETs are posited to be positively related to a wide variety of other indicators of effective teaching and specific rating factors are posited to be most highly correlated with variables to which they are most logically and theoretically related. Although student learning—perhaps inferred in a variety of different ways—is clearly an important criterion of effective teaching, it should not be the only criterion to be considered. Hence, within this broader framework, evidence for the long-term stability of SETs, the generalizability of ratings of the same instructor in different courses, and the agreement in ratings of current students and alumni can be interpreted as support for the validity of SETs.

The most widely accepted criterion of effective teaching, appropriately, is student learning. However, other criteria include changes in student behaviors, instructor self-evaluations, ratings by colleagues and administrators, the frequency of occurrence of specific behaviors observed by trained observers, and experimental manipulations. A construct validity approach to the study of SETs now appears to be widely accepted (e.g., Cashin, 1988; Howard, Conway, & Maxwell, 1985). A difficulty in this approach is obtaining criterion measures that are reliably measured and that validly reflect effective teaching. If alternative indicators of teaching effectiveness are not reliable and valid, then they should not be used as indicators of effective teaching for research, policy formation, feedback to faculty, or personnel decisions.

STUDENT LEARNING—THE MULTISECTION VALIDITY STUDY

The most widely accepted criterion of student learning is performance on standardized examinations. However, examination performance typically cannot be compared across different courses except in specialized settings. In order to address this issue, SET researchers have proposed the multisection validity paradigm in which it may be valid to compare teachers in terms of operationally defined learning, and to relate learning to SETs.

In the ideal multisection validity study (Cohen, 1981; Feldman, 1989b; Marsh, 1987; Sullivan & Skanes, 1974) there are many sections of a large multisection course; students are randomly assigned to sections so as to minimize initial differences between sections; pretest measures that correlate substantially with final course performance serve as covariates; each section is taught completely by a separate instructor; each section has the same course outline, textbooks, course objectives, and final examination; the final examination is constructed to reflect the common objectives and, if there is a subjective component, it is graded by an external person; students in each section evaluate teaching effectiveness on a standardized evaluation instrument, preferably before they know their final course grade and without knowing how performances in their section compare with those of students in other sections; and section-average SETs are related to section-average examination performance, after controlling for pretest measures.

Despite methodological problems (Abrami, d'Apollonia, & Cohen, 1990; Marsh & Dunkin, 1992, 1997; Marsh & Roche, 1994), meta-analyses of multisection validity research have supported the validity of the SETs by demonstrating that the sections that evaluate the teaching as most effective are also the sections that perform best on standardized final examinations (Cohen, 1981, 1987; Feldman, 1989b). Cohen (1987), in his summary of 41 "well-designed" studies, reported that the mean correlations between achievement and different SET components were Structure (.55), Interaction (.52), Skill (.50), Overall Course (.49), Overall Instructor (.45), Learning (.39), Rapport (.32), Evaluation (.30), Feedback (.28), Interest/Motivation (.15), and Difficulty ($-.04$), in which all but the last two were statistically significant. Feldman (1989b) extended this research by demonstrating that many of Cohen's broad categories were made up of more specific components of SETs that are differentially related to student achievement. Thus, for example, Cohen's broad "skill" category was represented by 3 dimensions in Feldman's analysis, which correlated with achievement .34 (instructor subject knowledge), .56 (clarity and understandableness), and .30 (sensitivity to class level and progress). Cohen (1987; also see Feldman, 1989b; 1990) also reported that correlations were higher when specific SET components were measured with multi-item scales instead of single items. This research demonstrates that teachers who receive better SETs are also the teachers from whom students learn the most. Perhaps more than any other area of SET research, results based on the multisection validity paradigm support the validity of SETs.

EVALUATIONS OF TEACHING EFFECTIVENESS BY DIFFERENT
EVALUATORS

Teaching effectiveness can be evaluated by current students, former
students, the instructor him/herself, colleagues, administrators, or
trained external observers.

Self-evaluations. Instructors can be asked to evaluate themselves in a
wide variety of educational settings, even using the same instrument
used by their students, so as to provide tests of convergent and
divergent validity. Despite the apparent appeal of instructor self-
evaluations as a criterion of effective teaching, it has had limited
application. Feldman's (1989b) meta-analysis of correlations between
SETS and self-evaluations, based on only 19 studies, reported a mean
r of .29 for overall ratings and mean *r*s of .15 to .42 for specific
SET components. Marsh (1982c, 1987; Marsh, Overall, & Kesler,
1979b) conducted two studies in which large numbers of instructors
evaluated their own teaching on the same multifaceted evaluation
instrument that was completed by students. In both studies: separate
factor analyses of SETs and self-evaluations identified the same SEEQ
factors; student-teacher agreement on every dimension was significant
(median *r*s of .49 and .45) and typically larger than agreement on
overall teaching effectiveness (*r*s of .32); mean differences between
student and faculty responses were small and unsystematic. Particularly important for the multidimensional perspective of SETs, MTMM
analyses provided support for both convergent and discriminant
validity of the ratings. Hence, not only was there general student-
teacher agreement on teaching effectiveness overall, the student-teacher
agreement was specific to each of the different SET factors (e.g., organization, enthusiasm, rapport).

Peer evaluations. Colleague, peer, and administrator ratings that are
not based upon classroom visitation are sometimes substantially correlated with SETS, but it is likely that colleague ratings are based on
information from students (Marsh, 1987; Marsh & Dunkin, 1992,
1997; Marsh & Roche, 1994). In contrast, colleague and administrator
ratings based on classroom visitation do not appear to be very reliable
(i.e., ratings by different peers do not even agree with each other) or to
correlate substantially with SETs or with any other indicator of effective
teaching (see Marsh, 1987; Centra, 1979). While these findings neither
support nor refute the validity of SETs, they suggest that the colleague
and administrator ratings based on classroom visitation are not valid
indicators of teacher effectiveness (also see Murray, 1980).

External observer ratings. Murray (1980) concluded that SETs "can be accurately predicted from external observer reports of specific classroom teaching behaviors" (1980, p. 31). For example, Cranton and Hillgartner (1981) examined relationships between SETs and specific teaching behaviors observed on videotaped lectures in a naturalistic setting; SETs of organisation were higher "when instructors spent time structuring classes and explaining relationships;" SETs of effectiveness of student-teacher interaction and discussion were higher "when professors praised student behavior, asked questions and clarified or elaborated student responses" (p. 73).

In one of the most ambitious observation studies, Murray (1983) trained observers to estimate the frequency of occurrence of specific teaching behaviors of 54 university instructors who had previously obtained high, medium or low SETs in other classes. A total of 18 to 24 sets of observer reports were collected for each instructor. The median of single-rater reliabilities (i.e., the correlation between two sets of observational reports) was .32, but the median reliability for the average response across the 18–24 reports for each instructor was .77. Factor analysis of the observations revealed nine factors, and their content resembled factors in SETs described earlier (e.g., clarity, enthusiasm, interaction, rapport, organisation). The observations significantly differentiated among the three criterion groups of instructors. Unfortunately, Murray only considered SETs on an overall instructor rating item, and these were based upon ratings from a previous course rather than the one that was observed. Hence, MTMM-type analyses could not be used to determine if specific observational factors were most highly correlated with matching student rating factors. The findings do show, however, that instructors who are rated differently by students do exhibit systematically different observable teaching behaviors, and provide clear support for SETs in relation to these specific behaviors.

Multiple evaluators with different perspectives. Howard, Conway, and Maxwell (1985; also see Feldman, 1989a and discussion of his review by Marsh and Dunkin, 1992, 1997) compared multiple indicators of teaching effectiveness for 43 target teachers who were each evaluated in one course by: current students in the course (mean $N = 34$ per class); former students who had previously taken the same or similar course taught by the target teacher (minimum $N = 5$); one colleague who was knowledgeable of the course content and who attended two class sessions taught by the target teacher; and 8 advanced graduate students specifically trained in judging teaching effectiveness, who attended two class sessions taught by the target teacher. Howard et al. concluded that "former-students and student ratings evidence substantially greater validity coefficients of teaching effectiveness than do self-report, colleague and trained observer ratings" (p. 195). Whereas self-evaluations were modestly correlated with current SETs (.34) and former SETs (.31), colleague and observer ratings were not significantly correlated with each other, current SETs, or self-evaluations.

EXPERIMENTALLY MANIPULATED TEACHER BEHAVIORS

A limited amount of research has related SETs to experimentally manipulated teaching situations. Studies of teacher clarity and teacher expressiveness (see reviews by Marsh, 1987; Marsh & Dunkin, 1992, 1997; Marsh & Roche, 1994) demonstrate the important potential of this approach. Both these teaching behaviors are amenable to experimental and correlational designs, can be reliably judged by students and by external observers, are judged to be important components of teaching effectiveness by students and by teachers, and are related to student achievement in naturalistic and experimental studies. In experimental settings, scripted lessons which differ in these teaching behaviors are videotaped, and randomly assigned groups of subjects view different lectures, evaluate teaching effectiveness, and complete achievement tests. Manipulations of these specific behaviors are significantly related to SETs and substantially more strongly related to matching SET dimensions than to nonmatching SET dimensions. These results support the inclusion of clarity and expressiveness on SET instruments, demonstrate that SETs are sensitive to natural and experimentally manipulated differences in these teaching behaviors, and support the construct validity of the multidimensional SETs with respect to these teaching behaviors. More generally, the direct manipulation of teaching behaviors and the experimental control afforded by laboratory studies are an important complement to quasi-experimental and correlational field studies.

SUMMARY AND IMPLICATIONS OF VALIDITY RESEARCH

Effective teaching is a hypothetical construct for which there is no adequate single indicator. Hence, the validity of SETs or of any other indicator of effective teaching must be demonstrated through a construct validation approach. SETs are significantly and consistently related to the ratings of former students, student achievement in multisection validity studies, faculty self-evaluations of their own teaching effectiveness, and, perhaps, the observations of trained observers on specific processes such as teacher clarity. This provides support for the construct validity of the ratings. In contrast, colleague and administrator ratings based on classroom visitation are not systematically related to SETs or other indicators of effective teaching, which calls into question their validity as measures of effective teaching.

Nearly all researchers argue that it is necessary to have multiple indicators of effective teaching whenever the evaluation of teaching effectiveness is to be used for personnel decisions. It is, however, critical that the validity of *all* indicators of teaching effectiveness, not just SETs, be systematically examined before they are actually used. The heavy reliance on SETs as the primary measure of teaching effectiveness stems in part from the lack of support for the validity of any other indicators of effective teaching. This lack of viable alternatives—rather than a bias in favor of SETs—seems to explain why SETs are used so much more widely than other indicators of effective teaching.

Whereas SET validity research has been dominated by a preoccupation with student achievement and the multisection validity paradigm, there is too little research relating SETs to other criteria. Thus, for example, Marsh (1987; Marsh & Dunkin, 1992, 1997; Marsh & Roche, 1994) discussed the validity of SETs in relation to student motivation, self-concept, affective criteria, subsequent coursework selection, student study strategies and the quality of student learning. Whereas he argued that it is imperative to expand the range of validity criteria in SET research substantially, this plea has apparently not been pursued in subsequent published research. There is also surprisingly little research validating SETs in relation to experimentally manipulated teaching situations, even though there are some good demonstrations of this approach based on teacher clarity and teacher expressiveness (see Marsh, 1987).

Practitioners and researchers alike give lip-service to the adage that teaching effectiveness should be evaluated with multiple indicators of teaching—not just SETs. To this prescription I would like to add the caveat that all indicators of teaching effectiveness for formative or summative assessment should be validated from a construct validity approach prior to being integrated into practice. However, there are few other indicators of teaching effectiveness whose use is systematically supported by research findings. As noted by Cashin (1988), "student ratings tend to be statistically reliable, valid, and relatively free from bias, probably more so than any other data used for faculty evaluation" (p. 5).

RESEARCH PRODUCTIVITY: A TEACHING-RESEARCH NEXUS

Teaching and research are typically seen as the most important products of university academics. Marsh (1987; Marsh and Hattie, 2002) contrasted opposing theoretical perspectives positing that indicators of the two activities should be positively correlated, negatively correlated, or uncorrelated.

There is a clear rationale for a positive nexus of reciprocal relations between teaching and research. Teachers who are active researchers are more likely to be: on the cutting edge of their discipline; aware of international perspectives in their field; and convey a sense of excitement about their research and how it fits into a larger picture. The process of teaching forces academics to clarify the big picture into which their research specialization fits, clarifying their research and reinforcing research pursuits through sharing it with students. Indeed, without this positive relation between teaching and research, one basis for funding modern research universities to pursue research as well as providing teaching is undermined.

The case can also be made as to why teaching and research are incompatible. Blackburn (1974) noted, for example, that unsatisfactory classroom performance might result from academics neglecting their teaching responsibilities in order to pursue research. The time and energy required to pursue one is limited by the time demands of the other, whereas the motivation and reward structures that support the two activities might be antagonistic as well.

Hattie and Marsh (1996) conducted a comprehensive meta-analysis of the relation between teaching and research among University academics. Based on 58 articles contributing 498 correlations, the overall correlation was 0.06 (see also Feldman, 1987; Centra, 1983). They searched for mediators and moderators to this overall correlation, with little success. The overall conclusion of a zero relation was found across: disciplines, various measures of research output (e.g., quality, productivity, citations), various measures of teaching quality (student evaluation, peer ratings), and different categories of university (liberal, research). Based on this review they concluded that the common belief that research and teaching are inextricably entwined is an enduring myth. At best, research and teaching are loosely coupled.

Marsh and Hattie (2002) pursued suggestions from the literature to better understand this belief in a positive nexus between teaching and research, and to discover situations or characteristics that reinforce a positive teaching-research relation. Data were based on a representative sample of academics from one research university who had extensive data on teaching effectiveness (SETs), externally monitored research productivity over three years, and completed a detailed survey on teaching and research constructs (self-ratings of ability, satisfaction, personal goals, motivation, time spent, supporting activities, and beliefs in a nexus). They began by testing Marsh's (1984; 1987) theoretical model in which the near-zero relation between teaching and research outcomes is a function of the counterbalancing positive relation between teaching and research abilities and the negative relation between time required to be effective at teaching and research and, perhaps, the motivation to be a good researcher and a good teacher. They found limited support for theoretical predictions. Whereas there was a substantial negative relation between time spent on teaching and research and no significant relation between teaching and research outcomes, there were no statistically significant relations between teaching and research ability or between teaching and research motivation.

Consistently with predictions, teaching ability had a moderate effect on teaching effectiveness and research ability had a substantial effect on research publications. The corresponding motivation and time variables had no significant effect on the teaching and research outcome variables (beyond what can be explained in terms of ability). In support of the posited antagonism between teaching and research, research ability had positive effects on research motivation and time, but negative effects on teaching motivation and time. Teaching ability had no significant effect on teaching motivation or teaching time, but it had a negative effect on research motivation. However, there was no support for the fundamental assumption that the ability to be a good teacher and the ability to be a good researcher are positively related. Indeed, because self-ratings are likely to be positively biased by potential biases (e.g., halo effects), it was quite surprising that these self-rating variables were not positively correlated.

Marsh and Hattie (2002) explored further research and teaching variables that might mediate the relations between ability and outcomes, including the belief that there is a nexus—that teaching contributes to research, or vice versa. Academics who believed that research contributes to teaching had more research publications and

345

higher self-ratings of research. However, beliefs in this nexus had no relation to the corresponding measures of teaching. In contrast, the belief that teaching contributes to research was not significantly related to self-ratings or outcomes for either teaching or research. Using multi-level modeling techniques they found that the near-zero correlation between teaching and research was consistent across the 20 academic departments included in their research, suggesting that differences in departmental ethos (or any other departmental characteristic) apparently had little impact on the teaching-research relation. They also explored a wide variety of potential moderators of the teaching-research relation to predict those who were high in both, but these results were also non-significant and supported the generality of the near-zero correlation between teaching and research.

In summary, this research supports the notion of teaching and research as reasonably independent constructs. While these findings seem neither to support nor refute the validity of SETs, they do demonstrate that measures of research productivity cannot be used to infer teaching effectiveness or vice versa. However, this research program has also stimulated a fierce debate about its implications. Particularly in the UK, the findings have been interpreted to mean that research and teaching functions of universities should be separated, fuelling further outrage within an academic community whose beliefs of integration prevail. It is noted, however, that a zero correlation need not lead to this separation—it means that there are just as many good teachers and researchers, not so good teachers and researchers, good researchers and not so good teachers, and good teachers and not so good researchers—independence of association does not mean that the two are necessarily "separate" for all. For those who believe so fervently that there is a positive teaching-research nexus, the failure to demonstrate it is seen to reflect inappropriate research. My belief is that a positive teaching-research nexus should be a goal of universities (to increase the number of academics who are both good teachers *and* good researchers), but empirical research provides little evidence that universities have been successful in doing so.

POTENTIAL BIASES IN STUDENTS' EVALUATIONS

The voluminous literature on potential biases in SETs is frequently atheoretical, methodologically flawed, and not based on well-articulated operational definitions of bias, thus continuing to fuel (and to be fuelled by) myths about bias (Feldman, 1997; Marsh,

1987; Marsh & Dunkin, 1997). Marsh listed important methodological problems in this research including: (a) implying causation from correlation; (b) use of an inappropriate unit of analysis (the class-average is usually appropriate, whereas the individual student is rarely appropriate); (c) neglect of the multivariate nature of SETs and potential biases; (d) inappropriate operational definitions of bias and potential biasing factors; and (e) inappropriate experimental manipulations.

Proper evaluation of validity, utility, and potential bias issues in SETs (see Feldman, 1998; Marsh & Dunkin, 1992; Marsh & Roche, 1997) demands the rejection of such flawed research, including narrow criterion-related approaches to bias. Instead, as for validity research, I use a broad construct validity approach to the interpretation of bias, which recognizes that (a) effective teaching and SETs designed to measure it are multidimensional; (b) no single criterion of effective teaching is sufficient; and (c) theory, measurement, and interpretations of relations with multiple validity criteria and potential biases should be evaluated critically across different contexts and research paradigms. Recognition of the *multidimensionality* of teaching and of SETs is fundamental to the evaluation of competing interpretations of SET relations with other variables. Although a construct validity approach is now widely accepted in evaluating various aspects of validity, its potential usefulness for the examination of bias issues has generally been ignored.

Marsh and Dunkin (1997; also see Centra, 1979; Marsh, 1987; also see Table 2 for a summary of typical relations between SETs and potential biases, based on earlier reviews by Marsh, 1987, and by Marsh and Dunkin, 1997) reviewed several large studies of the multivariate relationship between a comprehensive set of background characteristics and SETs. In two such studies (see Marsh, 1987), 16 background characteristics explained about 13% of the variance in the set of SEEQ dimensions, but varied substantially depending on the SEEQ factor. Four background variables could account for most of the explained variance: SETs were correlated with higher prior subject interest, higher expected grades, higher levels of workload/difficulty, and a higher percentage of students taking the course for general interest only. Path analyses demonstrated that prior subject interest had the strongest impact on SETs, and that this variable also accounted for about one-third of the expected-grade effect. Expected grades had a negative effect on workload/difficulty in that students in classes expecting to receive lower grades perceived the course to be more difficult. Even these relatively modest relations, however, need not be interpreted as reflecting bias.

Table 2: Overview of relationships found between student ratings and background characteristics

Background characteristics	Summary of findings
Prior subject interest	Classes with higher interest rate classes more favorably, though it is not always clear if interest existed before start of course or was generated by course/instructor
Expected grade/actual grades	Class-average grades are correlated with class-average SETs, but the interpretation depends on whether higher grades represent grading leniency, superior learning, or pre-existing differences
Reason for taking a course	Elective courses and those with higher percentage taking course for general interest tend to be rated higher
Workload/difficulty	Harder, more difficult courses requiring more effort and time are rated somewhat more favorably
Class size	Mixed findings but most studies show smaller classes rated somewhat more favorably, though some find curvilinear relationships where large classes are also rated favorably
Level of course/year in school	Graduate level courses rated somewhat more favorably; weak, inconsistent findings suggesting upper division courses rated higher than lower division courses
Instructor rank	Mixed findings, but little or no effect
Sex of instructor and/or student	Mixed findings, but little or no effect
Academic discipline	Weak tendency for higher ratings in humanities and lower ratings in sciences, but too few studies to be clear
Purpose of ratings	Somewhat higher ratings if known to be used for tenure/promotion decisions
Administrative conditions	Somewhat higher if ratings not anonymous and instructor present when being completed

Table 2: *(Continued)*

Background characteristics	Summary of findings
Student personality	Mixed findings, but apparently little effect, particularly since different "personality types" may appear in somewhat similar numbers in different classes

Note. For most of these characteristics, particularly the ones that have been more widely studied, some studies have found results opposite to those reported here, while others have found no relationship at all. The size of the relationships often varies considerably, and in some cases even the direction of the relationship, depending upon the particular component of student ratings that is being considered. Few studies have found any of these characteristics to be correlated more than .30 with class-average student ratings, and most reported relationships that were much smaller.

POTENTIAL BIASES AS A SOURCE OF VALIDITY

Support for a bias hypothesis, as with the study of validity, must be based on a construct validation approach. Indeed, it is ironic that consumers of SET research who have been so appropriately critical of studies claiming to support the validity of SETs have not applied the same level of critical rigor to the interpretation of potential biases in SETs. If a potential biasing factor actually does have a valid influence on teaching effectiveness and this influence is evident in different indicators of teaching effectiveness (e.g., SETs, teacher self-evaluations, student motivation, subsequent course choice, test scores), then it may be possible that the influence reflects support for the validity of SETs (i.e., a valid source of influence in teaching effectiveness is reflected in SETs) rather than a bias. If a potential bias has a substantial effect on specific SET components to which it is most logically related (e.g., class size and individual rapport) but has little or no relation to other SET components (e.g., organization) and this pattern of relations is consistent across multiple methods of measuring teaching effectiveness (e.g., SETs and teacher self-evaluations), again this influence may reflect the validity of SETs rather than a bias. Whereas this still leaves the tricky question of how to control for such differences most appropriately when interpreting SETs, this is a separate question to the most appropriate interpretation of relations between SETs and potential bias factors. Thus, for example, apparently no one would argue that student learning as articulated in multisection validity studies is a bias to student ratings rather than a source of validity or that student learning should be partialled from SETs to provide a more valid summary of the SETs.

Following Marsh (1987), Centra's (2003) operationalization of bias is consistent with the perspective taken here: "*Bias exists when a student, teacher, or course characteristic affects the evaluations made, either positively or negatively, but is unrelated to any criteria of good teaching, such as increased student learning*". Although a thorough discussion of potential biases is beyond the scope of this review (see Marsh, 1984; 1987; Marsh & Dunkin, 1997; Marsh & Roche, 1997; 2000; Marsh, 2001), we briefly present the argument for why many of the most widely posited potential biases to SETs actually support their validity.

Class size. Class size has a small negative relationship with SETs, which is sometimes uncritically interpreted as a bias. However, class size is moderately correlated with factors to which it is most logically related (group interaction and individual rapport, rs as large as -0.30). In contrast, it is almost uncorrelated with other SET factors and global ratings and somewhat positively correlated with organization (i.e., teachers are somewhat more organized in large lecture classes than small seminar classes). Importantly, there is a similar pattern of domain specific relations between class size and teacher self-evaluations of their own teaching (Marsh, Overall, & Kesler, 1979a). Also, the class-size effect is nonlinear, such that SETs increase with increasing enrolment beyond an inflection point, such that ratings are as high in very large classes as in small classes. Marsh and Dunkin (1997; also see Marsh, 1987) suggested this reflects more appropriate large-class teaching strategies when class size is very large. Also, students are more likely to enroll in courses taught by the best teachers, suggesting that the direction of causation might be from teaching effectiveness to SETs. Particularly the specificity of the class size effect to SET factors most logically related to this variable, and the similar results for teacher self-evaluations, argues that class size does not bias SETs. Rather, class size has moderate effects on the aspects of effective teaching to which it is most logically related (group interaction and individual rapport) and these effects are accurately reflected in the SETs. Clearly, the nature of class size effect demonstrates that relations must be carefully scrutinized from a construct validity approach before bias interpretations are offered on the basis of correlations.

Prior subject interest. Marsh and Dunkin, 1997; also see Feldman, 1977; Howard & Maxwell, 1980; Howard & Schmeck, 1979) reported that prior subject interest was the most strongly related to SETs of any of the 15 other background variables they considered. In different studies, prior subject interest was consistently more highly correlated with learning/value (rs about 0.4) than with any other SEEQ dimensions (rs between 0.3 and −0.12). Instructor self-evaluations of their own teaching were also positively correlated with both their own and their students' perceptions of students' prior subject interest, particularly learning/value. The specificity of the prior subject interest effect to dimensions most logically related to this variable, and the similarity of findings based on SETs and teacher self-evaluations argues that this effect is not a "bias" to SETs. Rather, prior subject interest is a variable that influences some aspects of effective teaching, particularly learning/value, and these effects are accurately reflected in both the SETs and in instructor self-evaluations.

Workload/difficulty. Workload/difficulty is frequently cited by faculty as a potential bias to SETs in the belief that offering less demanding courses will lead to better SETs. However, of critical importance to its interpretation, the direction of the workload/difficulty effect is opposite to that predicted by a bias hypothesis; workload/difficulty is positively—not negatively—correlated with SETS, the direction of the effect generalizing over several different large scale studies based on millions of students, thousands of teachers, and hundreds of universities (see Marsh & Dunkin, 1997; Marsh & Roche, 2000; Marsh, 2001). Overall & Marsh (1979) also reported that instructor self-evaluations of their own teaching effectiveness tended to be positively related to workload/difficulty.

Subsequent research suggests that the workload/difficulty effect is more complicated. For example, Marsh and Roche (2000); Marsh (2001) demonstrated a small non-linear component to the workload effect. For most of the range of the workload/difficulty factor the relation was positive (better SETs associated with higher levels of workload/difficulty). However, they also identified a non-linear component with an inflection point near the top of the workload continuum where SETs levelled off and then decreased slightly. In his recent analysis of 55,549 classes from a diverse sample of universities, Centra (2003) reported a similar nonlinear relation between workload/difficulty and overall teacher evaluations. However, Marsh (2001) found no non-linearity in the positive relation between workload and learning/value. Since the direction of the workload/difficulty effect was opposite to that predicted as a potential bias, and since this finding is consistent for both SETs and instructor self-evaluations, workload/difficulty does not appear to constitute a bias to SETs.

In a reanalysis of Greenwald and Gillmore's (1997a, 1997b) data, Marsh (2001) found two nearly uncorrelated components of Workload (also see Gillmore & Greenwald, 1994; Frankin & Theall, 1996); good workload was positively related to SETs and learning, but bad workload (time spent that was not valuable) had negative relations. Because the majority of the workload was seen as valuable, the total workload factor was positively related to SETs. Whereas Marsh was able to replicate the non-linear relation between good workload (a positive relation with an inflection point near the top of the workload continuum), the negative relation between SETs and bad workload was linear. Although the results suggest that it is possible to have too much of a good thing, it is important to note that few classes had good workload levels beyond the inflection point. Implications are that most teachers in order to be good teachers – as well as improving their SETs, should increase good workload, but decrease bad workload.

GRADING LENIENCY/EXPECTED GRADE EFFECT

The effect of class-average expected grades and grading leniency on SETs is the most controversial and, perhaps, most misunderstood potential bias in this area of research. Class-average grades are not substantially correlated with SETs. Marsh and Dunkin (1997; Marsh & Roche, 2000) reported that class-average grades correlated .20 with overall teacher ratings in SEEQ research, and this finding is consistent with the extensive review of this relation reported by Feldman (1976a; 1997). Marsh and Dunkin suggested that the best single estimate of the relation between overall teacher rating and expected grades was probably the .2 value reported by Centra and Creech (1976) based on 9,194 class-average responses from a diversity of different universities, courses, settings, and situations. However, Centra (2003), in subsequent research based on a much larger, diverse sample of 55,549 classes, found a slightly lower correlation of only .11. Although the relation is small, it is important to pursue at least three very different interpretations of this relation (Marsh & Dunkin, 1997; Marsh, 2001):

- The *grading leniency hypothesis* proposes that instructors who give higher-than-deserved grades will be rewarded with higher-than-deserved SETs, and this constitutes a serious bias to SETs. According to this hypothesis it is not grades per se that influence SETs, but the leniency with which grades are assigned.

- The *validity hypothesis* proposes that better expected grades reflect better student learning, and that a positive correlation between student learning and SETs supports the validity of SETs.
- The *prior student characteristics hypothesis* proposes that pre-existing student variables such as prior subject interest may affect student learning, student grades, and teaching effectiveness, so that the expected-grade effect is spurious.

While these and related explanations of the expected-grade effect have quite different implications, actual or expected grades must surely reflect some combination of student learning, the instructor's grading standards, and student characteristics.

In evaluating these alternative interpretations, it is important to emphasize that the critical variable is grading leniency rather than expected grades per se. To the extent that higher expected grades reflect better student learning (instead of lenient grading), the positive relation between class-average expected grades and SETs represents a valid influence, as posited in the validity hypothesis. However, except in special circumstances like the multisection validity study, it is difficult to unconfound the effects of expected grades and grading leniency.

Domain specificity. Marsh and Dunkin (1997; Marsh, 2001; Marsh & Roche, 2000) reported that expected grades correlated between 0 and .30 with different SEEQ factors. The highest correlation is for the learning factor, and this is consistent with the validity hypothesis (that higher grades reflect greater levels of mastery as a result of more effective teaching). Because this relation is reduced substantially by controlling prior subject interest, there is also support for a prior characteristics hypothesis. A similar pattern of results was found with teacher self-evaluations of their own teaching. Expected grades are also moderately correlated with group interaction. This apparently indicates that students tend to receive higher grades in advanced level seminar courses where student-teacher interaction may be better. In support of this interpretation, controlling for class size and class-average year in school substantially reduced this effect, consistent with the prior characteristics hypothesis.

Multisection validity studies. In these studies (reviewed earlier), sections of student in a multi-section course that performed best on a standardized final examination also gave the most favorable SETs.

353

Because pre-existing differences and grading leniency are largely controlled in these studies, the results provide strong support for the validity hypothesis. Because the size of correlations between actual achievement and SETs in multisection validity studies tends to be as large as or larger than the typical expected-grade correlation, it seems that much of this relation reflects the valid effects of student learning on SETs. This research provides the strongest basis for the interpretation of the expected-grade effect of any research considered here.

Perceived learning. Ideally, it would be useful to control class-average expected grades for the amount students actually learned as an operational definition of grading leniency. However, this is not typically possible in a cross-section of different classes. This is why the results based on multisection validity studies are so important, demonstrating that learning is positively related to SETs when grading leniency (and many other characteristics) are held constant.

In an alternative approach, several research groups (Cashin, 1988; Centra, 1993; Greenwald & Gillmore, 1997a; Howard & Maxwell, 1982) have devised measures of perceived learning as an alternative measure of student learning. These consisted of student self-ratings of progress on specific learning outcomes related to the quality and quantity of learning (e.g., factual knowledge, appreciation, problem solving, real-world application, creativity), rather than teaching effectiveness per se. Consistent with a validity hypothesis—and in direct contradiction to a grading leniency hypothesis—Marsh and Roche (2000) demonstrated that the relation between class-average expected grades and SETs was eliminated once the effect of student perceptions of learning was controlled. Centra (2003) reached a similar conclusion based on his large, diverse sample of 55,549 classes, leading him to conclude that once student ratings of learning outcomes (perceived learning) were controlled, there was no effect of expected grades. Although Marsh and Roche offer cautions about the interpretation of perceived learning as a surrogate of actual student learning, these studies represent one of the few attempts to unconfound expected grades from student learning as must be done if the effects of grading leniency are to be evaluated.

Direct measures of grading leniency. In one of the few studies to measure teacher perceptions of their grading leniency directly, Marsh and Overall (1979) reported that correlations between teacher self-perceptions of their own "grading leniency" (on an "easy/lenient grader" to "hard/strict grader" scale) were significantly correlated with student ratings of grading lenience. Importantly, both student and teacher ratings of grading leniency were not substantially related to either student and teacher-self evaluations of effective teaching (rs between $-.16$ and $.19$), except for ratings of workload/difficulty (rs of $.26$ and $.28$) and teacher self-evaluations of examinations/grading ($r = .32$). In a separate study, Marsh (1976) found that teachers who reported that they were "easy" graders received somewhat (significantly) *lower* overall course and learning/value ratings. Hence, results based on this direct measure of grading leniency argue against the grading leniency hypothesis.

Path analytic approaches. Path analytic studies (see Marsh, 1983, 1987) demonstrate that about one-third of the expected-grade effect is explained in terms of prior subject interest. This supports, in part, the prior characteristics hypothesis.

Experimental field studies. Marsh and Dunkin (1992; Marsh & Roche, 1997; 2000; Marsh, 2001; also see Abrami, Dickens, Perry, & Leventhal, 1980; Centra, 2003; Howard & Maxwell, 1982) reviewed experimental field studies purporting to demonstrate a grading leniency effect on SETs. However, they concluded that this research was flawed in terms of design, grading leniency manipulations, interpretation of the results, and ambiguity produced by deception research. More methodologically adequate studies along the lines of this historical set of studies have not been conducted, because current ethical standards have precluded the type of deception manipulations used in these studies. In contrast, Abrami et al. (1980) conducted what appears to be the most methodologically sound study of experimentally manipulated grading standards in two "Dr. Fox" type experiments (see subsequent discussion) in which students received a grade based on their actual performance but scaled according to different grading standards (i.e., an "average" grade earning a B, C+, or C). Students then viewed a similar lecture, evaluated teacher effectiveness, and were tested again. The grading leniency manipulation had no effect on achievement and weak inconsistent effects on SETs. Whereas the findings do not support a grading-leniency effect, the external validity of the grading manipulation in this laboratory study may also be questioned.

Other approaches. Marsh (1982a) compared differences in expected grades with differences in SETs for pairs of offerings of the same course taught by the same instructor on two different occasions. He reasoned that differences in expected grades in this situation probably represent differences in student performance, since grading standards are likely to remain constant, and differences in prior subject interest were small (for two offerings of the same course) and relatively uncorrelated with differences in SETs. He found even in this context that students in the more favorably evaluated course tended to have higher expected grades, which argued against the grading leniency hypothesis.

Peterson and Cooper (1980) compared SETs of the same instructors by students who received grades and those who did not. The study was conducted at two colleges where students were free to cross-enrol, but where students from one college were assigned grades but those from the other were not. Whereas class-average grades of those students who received grades were correlated with their class-average evaluations, their class-average evaluations were in substantial agreement with those of students who did not receive grades. Hence, receiving or not receiving grades did not affect SETs. Because grading leniency was unlikely to affect students who did not receive grades, these results suggest that the expected grade effect was not due to grading leniency.

Grade inflation. Even if grading leniency and workload are not significantly related to SETs, a belief that they are may prompt academics to assign grades more leniently and reduce levels of workload, on the assumption that they will be rewarded with higher SETs. In one of the most systematic evaluations of this possibility, Marsh and Roche (2000) evaluated changes in SETs, expected grades, and workload over a 12-year period at one university. Workload did not decrease, but increased slightly over this period; grades neither systematically increased nor decreased over this time period. Although there was a very small increase in SETs over time (0.25% of variance explained), these were not related to changes either in expected grades or workload. However, based on a similar analysis over 40 semesters at a single university, Eiszler (2002) found small increases in both expected grades and SETs, leading him to suggest grade inflation may be related to changes in SETs. Curiously, controlling for cumulative GPA did not substantially reduce the relation between expected grades and SETs, as would be expected if both GPA and expected grades were influenced by grade inflation. Although there were important differences between the two studies (Marsh and Roche based results on class-average means whereas Eiszler, apparently inappropriately, based analyses on semester-average scores aggregated across class-average means), both studies suffered in that they were based on responses from a single university. It would be useful to pursue grading leniency bias in related analyses based upon a large diverse sample of universities such as that used by Centra (1993, 2003) for different purposes.

Summary of grading leniency/expected grades effects. In summary, evidence from a variety of different studies clearly supports the validity and student characteristics hypotheses. Whereas a grading-leniency effect may produce *some* bias in SETs, support for this suggestion is weak, and the size of such an effect is likely to be insubstantial.

THE "DR. FOX" EFFECT

The "Dr. Fox" effect is defined as the overriding influence of instructor expressiveness on SETs, and has been interpreted to mean that an enthusiastic lecturer can "seduce" students into giving favorable evaluations, even though the lecture may be devoid of meaningful content (see Marsh & Dunkin, 1997; Marsh, 1987). In the standard Dr. Fox paradigm, a series of six videotaped lectures—representing three levels of course content (the number of substantive teaching points covered) and two levels of lecture expressiveness (the expressiveness with which a professional actor delivered the lecture)—were all presented by the same actor. Students viewed one of the six lectures, evaluated teaching effectiveness on a multidimensional SET instrument, and completed an achievement test based upon all the teaching points in the high content lecture. In their meta-analysis of this research, Abrami, Leventhal, and Perry (1982) concluded that expressiveness manipulations had substantial impacts on overall SETs and small effects on achievement, whereas content manipulations had substantial effects on achievement and small effects on ratings.

In their reanalysis of the original Dr. Fox studies, Marsh and Ware (1982) identified five SET factors that were differentially affected by the experimental manipulations. Particularly in the condition most like the university classroom, where students were given incentives to do well on the achievement test, the Dr. Fox effect was *not* supported in that: (a) the instructor expressiveness manipulation only affected ratings of instructor enthusiasm, the factor most logically related to that manipulation, and (b) content coverage significantly affected ratings of instructor knowledge and organization/clarity, the factors most logically related to that manipulation. When students were given no added incentives to perform well, instructor expressiveness had more impact on all five student rating factors (though the effect on instructor enthusiasm was still largest), but the expressiveness manipulation also had more impact on student achievement scores than did the content manipulation (i.e., presentation style had more to do with how well students performed on the examination than did the number

357

of questions that had been covered in the lecture). Hence, as observed in the examination of potential biases to SETs, this reanalysis indicates the importance of considering the multidimensionality of SETs. An effect, which has been interpreted as a "bias" to SETs, seems more appropriately interpreted as support for their validity with respect to one component of effective teaching.

UTILITY OF STUDENT RATINGS

Using a series of related logical arguments, many researchers and practitioners have made the case for why the introduction of a broad institutionally-based, carefully planned program of SETs is likely to lead to the improvement of teaching (see Marsh & Dunkin, 1997; Murray, 1987): (a) SETs provide useful feedback for diagnosing strengths and weaknesses in teaching effectiveness; (b) feedback can provide the impetus for professional development aimed at improving teaching; (c) the use of SETs in personnel decisions provides a tangible incentive to working to improve teaching; and (d) the use of SETs in tenure decisions means that good teachers are more likely to be retained. In support of his argument, Murray (1987; also see Marsh & Dunkin, 1997) summarized results of published surveys from seven universities that asked teachers whether SETs are useful for improving teaching. Across the seven studies, about 80% of the respondents indicated that SETs led to improved teaching. None of these observations, however, empirically demonstrate improvement of teaching effectiveness resulting from SETs.

In most studies of the effects of feedback from SETs, teachers are randomly assigned to experimental (feedback) and one or more control groups; SETs are collected during the course (i.e., midterm ratings); midterm ratings of the teachers in the feedback group are returned to instructors as quickly as possible; and the various groups are compared at the end of the term on a second administration of SETs and sometimes on other variables as well. There are, of course, many variations to this traditional feedback design.

SEEQ Feedback Research

Multisection feedback design. In two early feedback studies with the SEEQ instrument, a multisection feedback design was used in which experimental and control teachers taught different sections of the same multisection course. In the first study, results from an abbreviated form of the survey were simply returned to faculty; the impact of the feedback was positive, but very modest (Marsh, Fleiner, & Thomas, 1975). In the second study (Overall & Marsh, 1979) researchers actually met with instructors in the feedback group to discuss the evaluations and possible strategies for improvement. In this study, students in the feedback group subsequently performed better on a standardized final examination, rated teaching effectiveness more favorably at the end of the course, and experienced more favorable affective outcomes (i.e., feelings of course mastery, and plans to pursue and apply the subject).

Particularly the Overall and Marsh study was significant, as it was apparently the first to include student learning and other outcomes not easily implemented in studies with diverse courses. However, Hampton and Reiser (2004) replicated the Overall-Marsh multisection design, demonstrating the effectiveness of feedback and consultation compared to a randomly assigned no-feedback control group in terms of instructional practice of the teachers and SETs. Whereas student learning and student motivation were positively correlated with use of instructional activities—a focus of the intervention differences between experimental and control groups did not reach statistical significance. Even though the multisection feedback design is rarely used, this set of studies highlights important advantages that can be implemented in future research.

Feedback consultation intervention. A critical concern in feedback research is that nearly all of the studies are based on midterm feedback from midterm ratings. This limitation probably weakens effects, in that many instructional characteristics cannot be easily altered within the same semester. Furthermore, Marsh and Overall (1980) demonstrated in their multisection validity study that midterm ratings were less valid than end-of-term ratings.

Marsh and Roche (1993) addressed this issue—as well as others noted in their review of previous research—in an evaluation of a feedback/consultation intervention adapted from Wilson (1986). More specifically, a large, diverse group of teachers completed self-evaluations and were evaluated by students at the middle of Semester 1, and again at the end of Semesters 1 and 2. Three randomly assigned groups received the intervention at midterm of Semester 1, at the end of Semester 1, or received no intervention (control).

A key component of the intervention was a booklet of teaching strategies for each SEEQ factor. Teachers selected the SEEQ factor to be targeted in their individually structured intervention and then selected

359

the most appropriate strategies from the book of strategies for that SEEQ factor. Ratings for all groups improved over time, but ratings for the intervention groups improved significantly more than those for the control group. The intervention was particularly effective for the initially least effective teachers and the end-of-term feedback was more effective than the midterm feedback.

For the intervention groups (compared to control groups), targeted dimensions improved substantially more than nontargeted dimensions. The study further demonstrated that SET feedback and consultation are an effective means to improve teaching effectiveness and provided a useful procedure for providing feedback/consultation.

Critical features of the Marsh and Roche (1993) intervention were the availability of concrete strategies to facilitate efforts to improve teaching effectiveness in relatively less effective areas that the teacher perceived to be important, the facilitator role adopted by the consultant in this intervention, the personal commitment obtained from the teacher—facilitated by the face-to-face interaction between teacher and consultant, and the multidimensional perspective embodied in feedback booklets and the SEEQ instruments. Fundamental assumptions underlying the logic of the intervention are that teaching effectiveness and SETs are multidimensional, that teachers vary in their effectiveness in different SET areas as well as in perceptions of the relative importance of the different areas, and that feedback specific to particular SET dimensions is more useful than feedback based on overall or total ratings, or that provided by SET instruments which do not embody this multidimensional perspective. Indeed, this intervention can only be conducted with a well-designed, multidimensional instrument like SEEQ and feedback booklets specifically targeted to the SEEQ factors.

META-ANALYSES OF FEEDBACK RESEARCH

In his classic meta-analysis, Cohen (1980) found that instructors who received midterm feedback were subsequently rated about one-third of a standard deviation higher than controls on the total rating (an overall rating item or the average of multiple items), and even larger differences were observed for ratings of instructor skill, attitude toward subject, and feedback to students. Studies that augmented feedback with consultation produced substantially larger differences, but other methodological variations had little effect (also see L'Hommedieu,

Menges, & Brinko, 1990). The most robust finding from the feedback research reviewed here is that consultation augments the effects of written summaries of SETs, but insufficient attention has been given to determine the type of consultative feedback that is most effective.

L'Hommediu, Menges, and Brinko (1990) critically evaluated feedback studies. They concluded that the overall effect size attributable to feedback was probably attenuated due to a number of character-istics of the traditional feedback paradigm, and developed method-ological recommendations for future research. Among their many recommendations, they emphasized the need to: use a larger number of instructors; more critically evaluate findings within a construct validity framework, as emphasized by Marsh (1987); more critically evaluate the assumed generalizability of midterm feedback to end-of-term feedback; base results on well-standardized instruments such as SEEQ; and use more appropriate no-treatment controls. In their meta-analysis, they considered three forms of feedback that differed system-atically in their effect sizes: written feedback consisting of printed summaries of SETs (Mean effect = .18); personal feedback consisting of summary material delivered in person, sometimes accompanied by interpretations, discussion, and advice (mean effect = .25); and consul-tative feedback that combines SET feedback and professional devel-opment (mean effect = .87). Consistently with Cohen (1980) they concluded that "the literature reveals a persistently positive, albeit small, effect from written feedback alone and a considerably increased effect when written feedback is augmented with personal consultation" (1990, p. 240), but that improved research incorporating their sugges-tions would probably lead to larger, more robust effects.

More recently, Penny and Coe (2004) conducted a meta-analysis of 11 studies that specifically contrasted consultative feedback based on a dialogue with a consultant, with randomly assigned control groups. They found an overall effect size of .69, consistent with earlier results. Although they did not find significant study-to-study variation, they pursued a systematic evaluation of moderator effects. The largest effects were associated with the use of a well-standardized rating instrument, and consultations that incorporated a consultative or educational approach (rather than a purely diagnostic approach that focused on interpretation of the ratings). Whereas they offered heuristic recommendations about providing consultation, their sample size was so small that highlighted differences rarely achieved statistical significance. As advocated by Penny and Coe, there is need for further research to explore more fully their recommendations.

OTHER USES OF SETs

Personnel decisions. In research reviewed by Marsh and Dunkin (1997) there is clear evidence that the importance and usefulness of SETs as a measure of teaching effectiveness have increased dramatically during the last 60 years. Despite the strong reservations of some, faculty are apparently in favor of the use of SETs in personnel decisions—at least in comparison with other indicators of teaching effectiveness. In order to evaluate experimentally the importance of teaching effectiveness in personnel decisions, Leventhal, Perry, Abrami, Turcotte and Kane (1981), and Salthouse, McKeachie, and Lin (1978) composed fictitious summaries of faculty performance that systematically varied reports of teaching and research effectiveness, and also varied the type of information given about teaching (chairperson's report, or chairperson's report supplemented by summaries of SETs). Both studies found reports of research effectiveness to be more important in evaluating total faculty performance at research universities, although Leventhal et al. found teaching and research to be of similar importance across a broader range of institutions. While teaching effectiveness as assessed by the chairperson's reports did make a significant difference in ratings of overall faculty performance, neither study found that supplementing the chairperson's report with SETs made any significant difference. However, neither study considered SETs alone, or even suggested that the two sources of evidence about teaching effectiveness were independent. Information from the ratings and the chairperson's report was always consistent, so that one was redundant, and it would be reasonable for subjects in these studies to assume that the chairperson's report was at least partially based upon SETs. These studies demonstrate the importance of reports of teaching effectiveness, but apparently do not test the impact of SETs.

In other research related to the use of SETs for personnel decisions, Franklin and Theall (1989) argue that SETs can be misused or misinterpreted when making personnel decisions. This introduces another source of invalidity in the interpretation of SETs—even if the SETs are reliable and valid in relation to the traditional psychometric criteria considered in this chapter. Here, as in other areas of research on how SETs are most appropriately used to enhance their utility, there is a dearth of relevant research.

Usefulness in Student Course Selection. Little empirical research has been conducted on the use of ratings by prospective students in the selection of courses. UCLA students reported that the Professor/Course

Evaluation Survey was the second most frequently read of the many student publications, following the daily, campus newspaper (Marsh, 1987). Similarly, about half the Indiana University students in Jacob's (1987) study generally consulted published ratings prior to taking a course. Leventhal, Abrami, Perry and Breen (1975) found that students say that information about teaching effectiveness influences their course selection. Students who select a class on the basis of information about teaching effectiveness are more satisfied with the quality of teaching than are students who indicate other reasons (Centra & Creech, 1976; Leventhal, Abrami, & Perry, 1976; also see Babad et al. 1999; Perry et al., 1979). In an experimental field study, Coleman and McKeachie (1981) presented summaries of ratings of four comparable political science courses to randomly selected groups of students during preregistration meetings. One of the courses had received substantially higher ratings, and it was chosen more frequently by students in the experimental group than by those in the control group. Hence, apparently SETs are useful for students in the selection of instructors and courses.

USE OF NORMATIVE COMPARISONS

In many programs, the SET raw scores are compared with those obtained by large representative groups of classes in order to enhance the usefulness of the feedback. Although arguments for and against the use of normative comparisons and related issues have tended to be overly simplistic, this is a complicated issue fraught with theoretical, philosophical, and methodological quagmires for the unsuspecting. Here I distinguish between three related issues: use of norms to enhance the usefulness of SETs, the construction of norms to control potential biases to SETs, and the setting of standards.

Enhancing the usefulness of SETs. Traditionally, one of the key differences between broad, institutionally developed programs of SETs and ad hoc instruments has been the provision of normative comparisons. Marsh (1987; Marsh & Dunkin, 1997), like many others, argued that the usefulness of the raw scores is enhanced by appropriate normative comparisons, because raw score ratings on SET factors, global rating items, and specific rating items are likely to be idiosyncratic to the particular wording of the item. Furthermore, scores on different items and SET factors are not directly comparable in the original raw score metric. The metric underlying raw scores is not well defined and varies from item to item (and from factor to factor).

363

Hence, the normative comparisons provide information on how ratings on different SET factors for a given teacher compare with those based on a suitably constructed normative group of teachers and classes, and how scores from different SET items and factors for the same teacher compare to each other.

McKeachie (1996) provoked an interesting debate about the desirability of normative comparisons. Although he did not necessarily question the potential usefulness of appropriate normative comparisons, he argued that the unintended negative consequences might outweigh potential benefits. Thus, because nearly all class-average student ratings fall above the mid-point of the rating scale (e.g., above 3.0 on a typical 1–5 scale in which 5 is the highest rating), teachers can feel good about themselves even if they fall below the normative average response. According to McKeachie, if teachers are demoralized by low ratings, then the consequences may be more negative than if this supplemental information were not made available.

My perspective, although sympathetic with the potential dangers of social comparison on self-perceptions and implications for future performance (Marsh & Hau, 2003) is quite different. Indeed, I argue that it may be unethical—certainly patronizing—to deny teachers potentially useful information based on the assumption that we know what is best for them. Gillmore (1998), also arguing for the usefulness of normative comparisons, suggested that a strategic compromise might be to provide extensive norms via the web that are readily accessible, but not to provide these normative comparisons as part of the standard feedback presented to academics. My recommendation is that raw scores and scores normed in relation to at least one appropriately constructed normative comparison group should be included as part of the feedback given to teachers (Marsh, 1987).

Control for potential biases. Even if the usefulness of normative comparisons is accepted, there are critical issues involved in the construction of appropriate norms. For example, some researchers advocate that SETs should be adjusted for potential biases to the SETs (e.g., class size, expected grades, prior subject interest, workload/difficulty) based on multiple regression. I also dispute the appropriateness of this approach on methodological and philosophical grounds. As I have argued here, bias can only be inferred in relation to a well-defined operational definition of bias. At least based on the definition of bias used here (also see Centra, 2003), there is little support for any of these characteristics as biases to SETs. The adjustment rationale may, perhaps, be more appropriate in a relation to a definition of bias based on a fairness notion. Hence, to the extent that some characteristic is not under the control of the teacher, it might be "fair" to adjust for this characteristic. Logically, such adjustments should be based on characteristics that are readily discernible prior to the start of actual instruction, to avoid potential confounding of factors that influence the SETs, rather than being influenced by teaching effectiveness. This would preclude, for example, adjustments to class-average actual or expected grades, which are clearly under the control of the teacher and influenced by teaching effectiveness. Whereas it may, for example, be reasonable to adjust for prior subject interest, it could be argued that some of the class-average prior subject interest ratings collected at the end of the course might reflect effective teaching in addition to the effect of prior subject interest in ratings of this construct collected prior to the start of the class. Even a characteristic such as class size is not completely unproblematic if students choose teachers on the basis of teaching effectiveness, such that teaching effectiveness causes class size.

An alternative, somewhat more acceptable compromise is to construct separate normative comparison groups of similar courses. Thus, for example, Marsh (1987) described how SEEQ ratings are normed in relation to courses from three groups (Teaching Assistants, undergraduate courses taught by regular teachers, and graduate level courses) and there is provision—subject to adequate sample sizes—to form norm groups specific to a particular discipline (Marsh & Roche, 1994). This solution, although overcoming some of the problems associated with statistical adjustment, would still be problematic if norm groups were formed on the basis of class characteristics that reflect teaching effectiveness instead of (or in addition to) a source of bias or unfairness. Thus, for example, I would argue against the construction of norm groups based on class-average expected grades.

Other standards of comparison. Particularly when normative comparisons are presented, there is an emphasis on how the ratings of a teacher compare with those obtained by other teachers. This social comparison emphasis, as noted by McKeachie (1996), might have unintended negative consequences. In contrast, rating profiles (see earlier discussion of profile analyses) focus more specifically on the relative strengths and weaknesses in relation to the different SEEQ factors. Whereas the "level" of the profile for any given factor reflects a normative comparison with an appropriate norm group, the differences between the different factors (the "shape" component in profile analyses) are a more salient feature of this graphical presentation.

365

So long as SET programs retain appropriate archives over an extended period of time, it is also possible to use the graphical profile to compare one set of ratings with those based on previous ratings by the same teacher. Thus, for example, the profile graphs presented by Marsh and Bailey (1993) were based on many sets of ratings by the same teacher. They noted, however, it would be easy to extend these graphs to show the current set of ratings simultaneously, to allow the teacher to easily evaluate progress in relation to his or her own previous performance—further de-emphasizing the normative comparisons with other teachers.

Focusing on the use of different SET factors as a basis of improvement, Marsh and Roche (1994) asked teachers to focus improvement efforts on a specific SET factor—one on which their ratings were low relative to other SEEQ factors in a multidimensional profile based on their previous ratings, and one that they rated as important in self-evaluations of their own teaching.

In summary, alternative frames of reference against which to judge SETs include the performance of other teachers, previous ratings by the same teacher, or the ratings on one SET factor in relation to those of other SET factors. Particularly when the focus of the SET program is on the improvement of teaching effectiveness, it is appropriate for teachers to set their own standards for what they hope to accomplish in relation to ratings of other teachers, their own previous ratings, or even the relative performance on different SET factors.

Goals and standards of comparison. In considering the use of norms, it is important to distinguish between normative comparisons and standards of what is acceptable, appropriate, or good benchmarks of effective teaching. For present purposes we focus on the use of SETs but it is important to emphasize that there are many criteria of effective teaching—some of which are idiosyncratic to a particular course. A critical aspect of feedback relates to the goals or intended standards of performance. Effective goals involve challenge and commitment (Hattie, 2003; Hattie, Biggs & Purdie, 1996). They inform individuals "as to what type or level of performance is to be attained so that they can direct and evaluate their actions and efforts accordingly. Feedback allows them to set reasonable goals and to track their performance in relation to their goals so that adjustments in effort, direction, and even strategy can be made as needed" (Locke & Latham, 1990, p. 23). As a consequence of feedback, it is critical for teachers to set appropriately challenging goals. When goals have appropriate challenge and teachers are committed to these goals, then a clearer understanding of the appropriate success criteria is likely to be understood and shared. This focus on having teachers select the most appropriate areas to improve teaching, using prior SETs as a basis of comparison for evaluating improvement, fostering a sense of commitment in achieving improved teaching effectiveness in relation to specific targeted factors, and providing concrete strategies on how to achieve this goal is at least implicit in SET feedback studies (e.g., Marsh & Roche, 1994). However, there is clearly a need to integrate more fully lessons on effective forms of goal setting and feedback (e.g., Hattie, 2003; Hattie et al., 1996; Locke & Latham, 1990) into SET research.

Summary. In summary, normative comparisons provide a valuable additional source of information in the interpretation of SETs. Rather than denying teachers this valuable source of information, it is more appropriate to develop normative comparisons that are more useful to teachers. Here, for example, I emphasize the usefulness of multi-dimensional profiles that focus on a comparison of relative strengths and weakness for the different components of teaching effectiveness, and on longitudinal comparisons that focus on changes over time in the ratings of the same teacher. Nevertheless, the theoretical, methodological, and philosophical issues inherent in the construction of appropriate normative comparisons are important areas in need of further research. Clearly the appropriate construction of normative comparison groups is an important issue that has received surprisingly little research. Hence, instead of getting rid of norms, we need to enhance their usefulness.

SUMMARY OF STUDIES OF THE UTILITY OF STUDENT RATINGS

With the possible exception of feedback studies on improving teaching based on midterm ratings, studies of the usefulness of SETs are infrequent and often anecdotal. This is unfortunate, because this is an area of research that can have an important and constructive impact on policy and practice. Critical, unresolved issues in need of further research were identified.

- For administrative decisions, SETs can be summarized by responses to a single global rating item, by a single score representing an optimally-weighted average of specific components, or a profile of multiple components, but there is limited research on which is most effective.

- Debates about whether SETs have too much or too little impact on administrative decisions are seldom based upon any systematic evidence about the amount of impact they actually do have.
- Researchers often indicate that SETs are used as one basis for personnel decisions, but there is a dearth of research on the policy practices that are actually employed in the use of SETs.
- Rather than to deny the usefulness of normative comparisons, more research is needed on the most appropriate strategies to construct normative comparisons that enhance the usefulness of SETs. Whereas normative comparisons are an important basis of comparison, too little work has been done on alternative standards of effective teaching.
- A plethora of policy questions exists (e.g., how to select courses to be evaluated, the manner in which rating instruments are administered, who is to be given access to the results, how ratings from different courses are considered, whether special circumstances exist where ratings for a particular course can be excluded, either a priori or post-hoc, whether faculty have the right to offer their own interpretation of ratings, etc.), which are largely unexplored despite the wide use of SETs.
- Anecdotal reports often suggest that faculty find SETs useful, but there has been little systematic attempt to determine what form of feedback to faculty is most useful (although feedback studies do support the use of services by an external consultant), and how faculty actually use the results which they do receive.
- Some researchers have cited anecdotal evidence for negative effects of SETs (e.g., lowering grading standards or making courses easier) but these are also rarely documented in systematic research. Critics suggest that SETs lead to more conservative teaching styles, but Murray (1987) counters that highly rated teachers often use nontraditional approaches and that teaching is less traditional today than it was before SETs were used widely.
- McKeachie (personal communication, 19 March, 1991) noted that SETs are typically used constructively, encouraging instructors to think of alternative approaches and to try them out. He also suggested, however, that if SETs are used destructively so that teachers feel that they are in competition with each other—"that they must always be wary of the sword of student ratings hanging over their head"—poor ratings may increase

anxiety and negative feelings about students so that teaching and learning may suffer. Again, research is needed to examine whether teachers react constructively or destructively to SETs and whether there are individual differences that influence these reactions.

• Although SETs are sometimes used by students in their selection of courses, there is little guidance about the type of information which students want and whether this is the same as is needed for other uses of SETs. Typically, publication of SET results is a highly controversial issue.

These, and a wide range of related questions about how SETs are actually used and how their usefulness can be enhanced, provide a rich field for further research.

USE OF SETS TO BENCHMARK UNIVERSITIES: QUALITY ASSURANCE

In Australia, UK, Hong Kong, and many other countries, there are major governmental initiatives to enhance the accountability of universities by collecting comparable data for purposes of benchmarking and comparing different universities, different disciplines, and different disciplines within universities. Thus, for example, highly standardized and audited measures of research productivity are sometimes used to rank universities and disciplines within universities that determine, in part, the research funding that different universities receive. Hence, the Australian government commissioned the development and evaluation of the Postgraduate Research Experience Questionnaire (PREQ) to provide a multidimensional measure of the experience of postgraduate research students. An initial trial of the PREQ led to very positive recommendations about its psychometric properties (factor structure and reliability) and its potential usefulness as part of a large-scale national benchmarking exercise for Australian universities (Marsh et al., 2002). However, the unit of analysis was a critical issue in this research, as the intended focus was on the overall postgraduate experience at the broad level of the university, and disciplines within a university, rather than the effectiveness of individual supervisors. Indeed, students were specifically asked not to name their supervisor, and some of the factors focused on departmental or university level issues.

Marsh, Rowe, and Martin (2002) evaluated PREQ, a multidimensional measure of PhD and research Masters students' evaluation of the quality of research supervision, that was administered to graduates ($n = 1832$) from 32 Australian and New Zealand Universities. At the level of the individual student, responses had reasonable psychometric properties (factor structure and internal consistency estimates of reliability). Consistent with the potential use of these instruments to benchmark the quality of supervision across all Australian universities, Marsh et al. evaluated the extent to which responses reliably differentiated between universities, academic disciplines, and disciplines within universities. Based on fitting two-level (individual student, university) and three-level (individual student, discipline, university) multilevel models, the responses failed to differentiate among universities, or among disciplines within universities. Although there were small differences between ratings in a few disciplines, even these small differences were consistent across different universities. The results demonstrate that PREQ responses that are adequately reliable at one level (individual student) may have little or no reliability at another level (university). Marsh et al. concluded that PREQ responses should not be used to benchmark Australian universities or disciplines within universities. Furthermore, Marsh, et al. argued that PREQ responses, as presently formulated, were unlikely to be useful for most other conceivable purposes.

The most salient finding of this study was that PREQ ratings did not vary systematically between universities, or between disciplines within universities. This has critically important methodological and substantive implications for the potential usefulness of the PREQ ratings. Because there was no significant variation at the university level, it follows that the PREQ ratings were completely unreliable for distinguishing between universities. This clearly demonstrates why it is important to evaluate the reliability of responses to a survey instrument in relation to a particular application and the level of analysis that is appropriate to this application. Although PREQ ratings were reliable at the level of individual students, these results are not particularly relevant for the likely application of the PREQ ratings to discriminate between universities. Whereas SET research suggests that PREQ ratings might be reliable at the level of the individual supervisor, the number of graduating PhD students associated with a given supervisor in any one year might be too small to achieve acceptable levels of reliability, and there are important issues of anonymity and confidentiality. There are apparently no comparable studies of the ability of SET ratings to differentiate between universities or even departments within universities, but I suspect that the results would be similar.

Substantively, the Marsh, Rowe, and Martin (2002) study questions is the potential usefulness of PREQ ratings in benchmarking different universities, although the Australian government is continuing to use them for this purpose. More generally, it calls into question research or practice that seeks to use SETs as a basis for comparing universities as part of a quality assurance exercise. Clearly this is an area in need of further research. Although the existence of an effective SET program coupled with a program to improve teaching effectiveness is clearly a relevant criteria upon which to evaluate a university in relation to quality assurance, it is not appropriate – or at least premature – to use SETs from different universities to evaluate differences in teaching effectiveness at those universities.

HOW SETs SHOULD NOT BE USED

There is broad acceptance that SETs should not be the only measure of teaching effectiveness used, particularly for personnel decisions. Indeed, there are a number of areas in which results based on SETs should be supplemented with other sources of information. Thus, for example, whereas students provide relevant information about the currency of materials and the breadth of content coverage, this is clearly an area in which peer evaluations of the course syllabus and reading list should provide major input.

There are other areas where SETs, perhaps, should not be used at all. Particularly for universities with a clear research mission, a major component of the personnel decisions should be based on appropriate indicators of research. The results of the present investigation indicate that SETs—particularly at the level of the individual teacher—are nearly unrelated to research productivity. Highly productive researchers are equally likely to be good teachers as poor teachers. Hence, SETs should not be used to infer research productivity. However, because most universities have at least an implicit mission to enhance the nexus between teaching and research, this is an appropriate area in which to seek student input, and warrants further research.

At least for the type of items used on instruments like SEEQ and dimensions like those summarized by Feldman (1987; also see Table 1), SETs reflect primarily the teacher who does the teaching rather than the particular course that is taught. Even when students are specifically asked to evaluate the course rather than the teacher (i.e., overall course ratings as opposed to overall instructor ratings) the ratings are primarily a function of the teacher and do not vary systematically with the course. These results greatly enhance the usefulness of SETs for purposes of the evaluation of teachers, but seriously undermine their usefulness for purposes of the evaluation of courses independent of the teacher. It may be possible to construct different items reflecting different dimensions that are useful for evaluations of courses rather than the teacher, and there may be idiosyncratic circumstances in which differences between courses are much more important than particular teachers, but the SET research does not appear to provide support for these suppositions. On this basis, I recommend that SETs not be used to evaluate courses independently of the teachers who teach the course.

Increasingly, SETs are being incorporated into quality assurance exercises like that based on the PREQ research. Clearly, it is appropriate to evaluate the quality of the SET program instituted by a university and provision for systematic programs to improve teaching effectiveness. A useful contribution would be to develop appropriate checklists for indicators of an effective SET program for use in quality assurance exercises. However, the PREQ research suggests that it would be inappropriate to use SETs to evaluate the quality of teaching across different universities or even departments within universities. Nevertheless, recommendations based on ratings of research supervision by PhD students are not a fully satisfactory basis of inference about SETs based on classroom teaching. Particularly given the exciting advances in the application of multilevel modeling, there are likely to be new developments in this area. However, pending results of new research, I recommend that the actual numerical ratings based on SETs should not be used to compare universities in quality assurance exercises.

OVERVIEW, SUMMARY AND IMPLICATIONS

Research described in this chapter demonstrates that SETs are multi-dimensional, reliable and stable, primarily a function of the instructor who teaches a course rather than the course that is taught, relatively valid against a variety of indicators of effective teaching, relatively unaffected by a variety of potential biases, and seen to be useful by faculty, students, and administrators. I recommend that researchers adopt a construct validation approach in which it is recognised that: effective teaching and SETs designed to reflect teaching effectiveness are multidimensional; no single criterion of effective teaching is sufficient; and tentative interpretations of relations with validity criteria and with potential biases should be evaluated critically in different contexts and in relation to multiple criteria of effective teaching. In contrast to SETs, however, there are few other indicators of teaching effectiveness whose use is systematically supported by research findings. As noted by Cashin (1988), "student ratings tend to be statistically reliable, valid, and relatively free from bias, probably more so than any other data used for faculty evaluation" (p. 5). Of particular importance, the review demonstrates that the combined use of a good evaluation instrument like SEEQ and an effective consultation procedure like that adapted from Wilson (1986) can lead to improved university teaching.

Despite the many positive features identified in this review, there are a host of critical, unanswered questions in need of further research. Particularly discouraging is the observation that—with a few major exceptions—SET research during the last decade seems not to have adequately addressed these issues that were clearly identified a decade ago. Indeed, relative to the heydays of SET research in the 1980s, the amount and quality of SET research seems to have declined. This is remarkable, given the ongoing controversies that SETs continue to incite, the frequency of their use in universities in North America and, increasingly, throughout the world, and important advances in statistical and methodological tools for evaluating SETs.

Particularly critical issues have to do with the appropriate form to present SETs to enhance their usefulness for formative and summative feedback, and how most appropriately to integrate SETs into programs to enhance teaching effectiveness. Perhaps the most damning observation is that most of the emphasis on the use of SETs is for personnel decisions rather than on improving teaching effectiveness. Even here, however, good research on how SETs are most appropriately used to inform personnel decisions is needed. Although much work is needed on how best to improve teaching effectiveness, it is clear that relatively inexpensive, unobtrusive interventions based on SETs can make a substantial difference in teaching effectiveness. This is not surprising, given that university teachers typically are given little or no specialized training on how to be good teachers and apparently do not know how to fully utilize SET feedback without outside assistance. Why do universities continue to collect and disseminate potentially demoralising feedback to academics without more fully implementing programs to improve teaching effectiveness? Why is there not more SET research on how to enhance the usefulness of SETs as part of a program to improve university teaching? Why have there been so few intervention studies in the last decade that address the problems identified in reviews of this research conducted a decade ago?

Indeed, it is remarkable that after nearly a century of extensive research, there is apparently no general theory of college teaching that has arisen from SET research. Clearly, the science to support a theory of college teaching does exist in the communal agreement on the key dimensions of effective teaching, appropriate outcome variables, well-established research paradigms, design features, statistical analyses, meta-analyses, and the accumulated findings from a diverse range of laboratory, quasi-experimental, field, longitudinal, and correlational studies. Given the ongoing interest in the science, analysis, interpretation and uses of SETs the time for this type of unified theory building is long overdue.

REFERENCES

Abrami, P.C., and d'Apollonia, S. (1991). Multidimensional students' evaluations of teaching effectiveness: Generalizability of $N = 1$ research, Comment on Marsh (1991). *Journal of Educational Psychology* 30: 221–227.

Abrami, P.C., d'Apollonia, S., and Cohen, P.A. (1990). Validity of student ratings of instruction: What we know and what we do not. *Journal of Educational Psychology* 82: 219–231.

Abrami, P.C., d'Apollonia, S., and Rosenfield, S. (1997). The dimensionality of student ratings of instruction: What we know and what we do not. In J.C. Smart (ed.), *Higher Education: Handbook of Theory and Research* (Vol. 11, pp. 213–264). New York: Agathon.

Abrami, P.C., d'Apollonia, S., and Rosenfield, S. (March, 1993). *The Dimensionality of Student Ratings of Instruction*. Paper presented at the Annual Meeting of the American Educational Research Association, Atlanta, GA.

Abrami, P.C., Leventhal, L., and Perry, R.P. (1982). Educational seduction. *Review of Educational Research* 52: 446–464.

Abrami, P.C., Dickens, W.J., Perry, R.P., and Leventhal, L. (1980). Do teacher standards for assigning grades affect student evaluations of instruction? *Journal of Educational Psychology* 72: 107–118.

Aleamoni, L.M. (1981). Student ratings of instruction. In J. Millman (ed.), *Handbook of Teacher Evaluation* (pp. 110–145). Beverly Hills, CA. Sage.

Apodaca, P., and Grad, H. (2005). The dimensionality of student ratings of teaching: integration of uni- and multidimensional models. *Studies in Higher Education* 30: 723–748.

Babad, E., Darley, J., and Kaplowitz, H. (1999). Developmental aspects in students' course selection. *Journal of Educational Psychology* 91: 157–168.

Blackburn, R.T. (1974). The meaning of work in academia. In J.I. Doi (ed.), Assessing faculty effort. New Directions for Institutional Research (Vol. 2, pp. 75–99). San Francisco: Jossey-Bass.

Braskamp, L.A., Brandenburg, D.C., and Ory, J.C. (1985). *Evaluating Teaching Effectiveness: A Practical Guide*. Beverly Hills, CA: Sage.

Braskamp, L.A., Ory, J.C., and Pieper, D.M. (1981). Student written comments: Dimensions of instructional quality. *Journal of Educational Psychology* 73: 65–70.

Braskamp, L.A., and Ory, J.C. (1994). *Assessing Faculty Work: Enhancing Individual and Institutional Performance*. San Francisco, Jossey-Bass.

Cadwell, J., and Jenkins, J. (1985). Effects of the semantic similarity of items on student ratings of instructors. *Journal of Educational Psychology* 77: 383–393.

Cashin, W.E. (1988). *Student Ratings of Teaching. A Summary of Research*. (IDEA paper No. 20). Kansas State University, Division of Continuing Education. (ERIC Document Reproduction Service No. ED 302 567).

Cashin, W.E., and Downey, R.G. (1992). Using global student rating items for summative evaluation. *Journal of Educational Psychology* 84: 563–572.

Centra, J.A. (1979). *Determining Faculty Effectiveness*. San Francisco, CA: Jossey-Bass.

Centra, J.A. (1983). Research productivity and teaching effectiveness. *Research in Higher Education* 18: 379–389.

Centra, J.A. (1989). Faculty evaluation and faculty development in higher education. In J.C. Smart (ed.), *Higher Education: Handbook of Theory and Research. Supplementary* (Vol. 5,pp. 155–179). New York: Agathon Press.

Centra, J.A. (1993). *Reflective Faculty Evaluation.* San Francisco, CA: Jossey-Bass.

Centra, J.A. (2003). Will teachers receive higher student evaluations by giving higher grades and less course work? *Research in Higher Education* 44(5): 495–518.

Centra, J.A., and Creech, F.R. (1976). *The Relationship between Student, Teacher, and Course Characteristics and Student Ratings of Teacher Effectiveness* (Project Report 76–1). Princeton, NJ: Educational Testing Service.

Cohen, P.A. (1980). Effectiveness of student-rating feedback for improving college instruction: A meta-analysis. *Research in Higher Education* 13: 321–341.

Cohen, P.A. (1981). Student ratings of instruction and student achievement: A meta-analysis of multisection validity studies. *Review of Educational Research* 51: 281–309.

Cohen, P.A. (April, 1987). *A Critical Analysis and Reanalysis of the Multisection Validity Meta-analysis.* Paper presented at the 1987 Annual Meeting of the American Educational Research Association, Washington, DC (ERIC Document Reproduction Service No. ED 283 876).

Coleman, J., and McKeachie, W.J. (1981). Effects of instructor/course evaluations on student course selection. *Journal of Educational Psychology* 73: 224–226.

Costin, F., Greenough, W.T., and Menges, R.J. (1971). Student ratings of college teaching: Reliability, validity and usefulness. *Review of Educational Research* 41: 511–536.

Cranton, P.A., and Hillgartner, W. (1981). The relationships between student ratings and instructor behavior: Implications for improving teaching. *Canadian Journal of Higher Education* 11: 73–81.

Cranton, P., and Smith, R.A. (1990). Reconsidering the unit of analysis: A model of student ratings of instruction. *Journal of Educational Psychology* 82: 207–212.

Cronbach, L.J. (1958). Proposals leading to analytic treatment of social perception scores. In R. Tagiuri and L. Petrullo (eds.), *Person Perception and Interpersonal Behavior* (pp. 351–379). Stanford University Press.

de Wolf, W.A. (1974). *Student Ratings of Instruction in Post Secondary Institutions: A Comprehensive Annotated Bibliography of Research Reported Since 1968* (Vol. 1). University of Washington Educational Assessment Center. Educational Assessment Center.

Doyle, K.O. (1975). *Student Evaluation of Instruction.* Lexington, MA: D. C. Heath.

Doyle, K.O. (1983). *Evaluating Teaching.* Lexington, MA: Lexington Books.

Eiszler, C.F. (2002). College students' evaluations of teaching and grade inflation. *Research in Higher Education* 43(4): 483–501.

Feldman, K.A. (1976a). Grades and college students' evaluations of their courses and teachers. *Research in Higher Education* 4: 69–111.

Feldman, K.A. (1976b). The superior college teacher from the student's view. *Research in Higher Education* 5: 243–288.

Feldman, K.A. (1977). Consistency and variability among college students in rating their teachers and courses. *Research in Higher Education* 6: 223–274.

Feldman, K.A. (1978). Course characteristics and college students' ratings of their teachers and courses: What we know and what we don't. *Research in Higher Education* 9: 199–242.

Feldman, K.A. (1979). The significance of circumstances for college students' ratings of their teachers and courses. *Research in Higher Education* 10: 149–172.

Feldman, K.A. (1983). The seniority and instructional experience of college teachers as related to the evaluations they receive from their students. *Research in Higher Education* 18: 3–124.

Feldman, K.A. (1984). Class size and students' evaluations of college teacher and courses: A closer look. *Research in Higher Education* 21: 45–116.

Feldman, K.A. (1986). The perceived instructional effectiveness of college teachers as related to their personality and attitudinal characteristics: A review and synthesis. *Research in Higher Education* 24: 139–213.

Feldman, K.A. (1987). Research productivity and scholarly accomplishment: A review and exploration. *Research in Higher Education* 26: 227–298.

Feldman, K.A. (1988). Effective college teaching from the students' and faculty's view: Matched or mismatched priorities. *Research in Higher Education* 28: 291–344.

Feldman, K.A. (1989a). Instructional effectiveness of college teachers as judged by teachers themselves, current and former students, colleagues, administrators, and external (neutral) observers. *Research in Higher Education* 30: 137–194.

Feldman, K.A. (1989b). Association between student ratings of specific instructional dimensions and student achievement: Refining and extending the synthesis of data from multisection validity studies. *Research in Higher Education* 30: 583–645.

Feldman, K.A. (1990). An afterword for "the association between student ratings of specific instructional dimensions and student achievement: Refining and extending the synthesis of data from multisection validity studies". *Research in Higher Education* 31: 315–318.

Feldman, K.A. (1992). College students' views of male and female college teachers. Part I-Evidence from the social laboratory and experiments. *Research in Higher Education* 33: 317–375.

Feldman, K.A. (1993). College Students' Views of Male and Female College Teachers. Part II-Evidence from Students' Evaluations of Their Classroom Teachers. *Research in Higher Education* 34: 151–211.

Feldman, K.A. (1997). Identifying exemplary teachers and teaching: Evidence from student ratings. In R.P. Perry and J.C. Smart, (eds.), *Effective Teaching in Higher Education: Research and Practice* (pp. 368–395). New York: Agathon.

Feldman, K.A. (1998). Reflections on the effective study of college teaching and student ratings: one continuing quest and two unresolved issues. In J.C. Smart (ed.), *Higher Education: Handbook of Theory and Research* (pp. 35–74). New York: Agathon Press.

Franklin, J.L., and Theall, M. (1989). *Who Reads Ratings. Knowledge, Attitudes, and Practices of Users of Student Ratings of Instruction.* Paper presented at the 70th annual meeting of the American Educational Research Association. San Francisco: March 31.

Franklin, J., and Theall, M. (1996). *Disciplinary Differences in Sources of Systematic Variation in Student Ratings of Instructor Effectiveness and Students' Perceptions of the Value of Class Preparation Time: A Comparison of Two Universities' Ratings Data.* Paper presented at the annual meeting of the American Educational Research Association, New York.

Gilmore, G.M. (1988). *Grades, Ratings and Adjustments.* Instructional Evaluation and Faculty Development (available on internet: http://www.umanitoba.ca/uts/sigfted/backissues.php, 25 August, 2006).

377

Gillmore, G.M., and Greenwald, A.G. (1994). *The Effects of Course Demands and Grading Leniency on Student Ratings of Instruction*. Office of Educational Assessment (94–4), University of Washington, Seattle.

Gilmore, G.M., Kane, M.T., and Naccarato, R.W. (1978). The generalizability of student ratings of instruction: Estimates of teacher and course components. *Journal of Educational Measurement* 15: 1–13.

Greenwald, A.G., and Gillmore, G.M. (1997a). Grading leniency is a removable contaminant of student ratings. *American Psychologist* 52: 1209–1217.

Greenwald, A.G., and Gillmore, G.M. (1997b). No Pain, No Gain? The importance of measuring course workload in student ratings of instruction. *Journal of Educational Psychology* 89: 743–751.

Hampton, S.E., and Reiser, R.A. (2004). Effects of a theory-based feedback and consultation process on instruction and learning in college classrooms. *Research in Higher Education* 45(5): 497–527.

Harrison, P.D., Douglas, D.K., and Burdsal, C.A. (2004). The relative merits of different types of overall evaluations of teaching effectiveness. *Research in Higher Education* 45(3): 311–323.

Harrison, P.D., More, P.S., and Ryan, J.M. (1996) College student's self-insight and common implicit theories in ratings of teaching effectiveness. *Journal of Educational Psychology* 88: 775–782.

Hattie, J.A. (2003). Why is it so difficult to enhance self-concept in the classroom: The power of feedback in the self-concept–achievement relationship. Paper presented at the International SELF conference, Sydney, Australia.

Hattie, J.A., Biggs, J., and Purdie, N. (1996). Effects of learning skills intervention on student learning: A meta-analysis. *Review of Research in Education* 66: 99–136.

Hattie, J., and Marsh, H.W. (1996). The relationship between research and teaching—a meta-analysis. *Review of Educational Research* 66: 507–542.

Hativa, N. (1996). University instructors' ratings profiles: Stability over time, and disciplinary differences *Research In Higher Education* 37: 341–365.

Hobson, S.M., and Talbot, D.M. (2001). Understanding student evaluations: What all faculty should know. *College Teaching* 49(1): 26–31.

Howard, G.S., Conway, C.G., and Maxwell, S.E. (1985). Construct validity of measures of college teaching effectiveness. *Journal of Educational Psychology* 77: 187–196.

Howard, G.S., and Maxwell, S.E. (1980). The correlation between student satisfaction and grades: A case of mistaken causation? *Journal of Educational Psychology* 72: 810–820.

Howard, G.S., and Maxwell, S.E. (1982). Do grades contaminate student evaluations of instruction? *Research in Higher Education* 16: 175–188.

Howard, G.S., and Schmeck, R.R. (1979). Relationship of changes in student motivation to student evaluations of instruction. *Research in Higher Education* 10: 305–315.

Howell, A.J., and Symbaluk, D.G. (2001). Published student ratings of instruction: Revealing and reconciling the views of students and faculty. *Journal of Educational Psychology* 93: 790–796.

Jackson, D.L., Teal, C.R., Raines, S.J., Nansel, T.R., Force, R.C., and Burdsal, C.A. (1999). The dimensions of students' perceptions of teaching effectiveness. *Educational and Psychological Measurement* 59: 580–596.

Jacobs, L.C. (1987). *University Faculty and Students' Opinions of Student Ratings*. Bloomington, IN: Bureau of Evaluative Studies and Testing. (ERIC Document Reproduction Service No. ED 291 291).

Kane, M.T., Gillmore, G.M., and Crooks. T.J. (1976). Student evaluations of teaching: The generalizability of class means. *Journal of Educational Measurement* 13: 171–184.

Kember, D., Leung, D.Y.P., and Kwan, K.P. (2002). Does the use of student feedback questionnaires improve the overall quality of teaching? *Assessment & Evaluation in Higher Education* 27: 411–425.

Kulik, J.A., and McKeachie, W.J. (1975). The evaluation of teachers in higher education. *Review of Research in Higher Education* 3: 210–240.

L'Hommedieu, R., Menges, R.J., and Brinko, K.T. (1990). Methodological explanations for the modest effects of feedback. *Journal of Educational Psychology* 82: 232–241.

Leventhal, L., Abrami, P.C., and Perry, R.P. (1976). Teacher rating forms: Do students interested in quality instruction rate teachers differently? *Journal of Educational Psychology* 68: 441–445.

Leventhal, L., Abrami, P.C., Perry, R.P., and Breen L.J. (1975). Section selection in multi-section courses: Implications for the validation and use of student rating forms. *Educational and Psychological Measurement* 35: 885–895.

Leventhal, L., Perry, R.P., Abrami, P.C., Turcotte, S.J.C., and Kane, B. (1981, April). *Experimental Investigation of Tenure/Promotion in American and Canadian Universities*. Paper presented at the Annual Meeting of the American Educational Research Association, Los Angeles.

Lin, Y., McKeachie, W.J., and Tucker, D.G. (1984). The use of student ratings in promotion decisions. *Journal of Higher Education* 55: 583–589.

Locke, E.A., and Latham, G.P. (1990). *A Theory of Goal Setting and Task Performance*. Englewood Cliffs, NJ: Prentice Hall.

Marsh, H.W. (1976). *The Relationship between Background Variables and Students' Evaluations of Instructional Quality*. OIS 76–9. Los Angeles, CA: Office of Institutional Studies, University of Southern California.

Marsh, H.W. (1982a). Factors affecting students' evaluations of the same course taught by the same instructor on different occasions. *American Educational Research Journal* 19: 485–497.

Marsh, H.W. (1982b). SEEQ: A reliable, valid, and useful instrument for collecting students' evaluations of university teaching. *British Journal of Educational Psychology* 52: 77–95.

Marsh, H.W. (1982c). Validity of students' evaluations of college teaching: A multitrait-multimethod analysis. *Journal of Educational Psychology* 74: 264–279.

Marsh, H.W. (1983). Multidimensional ratings of teaching effectiveness by students from different academic settings and their relation to student/course/instructor characteristics. *Journal of Educational Psychology* 75: 150–166.

Marsh, H.W. (1984). Students' evaluations of university teaching: Dimensionality, reliability, validity, potential biases, and utility. *Journal of Educational Psychology* 76: 707–754.

Marsh, H.W. (1985). Students as evaluators of teaching. In T. Husen and T.N. Postlethwaite (eds.), *International Encyclopedia of Education: Research and Studies*. Oxford: Pergamon Press.

Marsh, H.W. (1986). Applicability paradigm: Students' evaluations of teaching effectiveness in different countries. *Journal of Educational Psychology* 78: 465–473.

379

Marsh, H.W. (1987). Students' evaluations of university teaching: Research findings, methodological issues, and directions for future research. *International Journal of Educational Research* 11: 253–388. (Whole Issue No. 3)

Marsh, H.W. (1991a). A multidimensional perspective on students' evaluations of teaching effectiveness: A reply to Abrami and d'Apollonia (1991). *Journal of Educational Psychology* 83: 416–421.

Marsh, H.W. (1991b). Multidimensional students' evaluations of teaching effectiveness: A test of alternative higher-order structures. *Journal of Educational Psychology* 83: 285–296.

Marsh, H.W. (1995). Still weighting for the right criteria to validate student evaluations of teaching in the idea system. *Journal of Educational Psychology* 87: 666–679.

Marsh, H.W. (2001). Distinguishing between good (useful) and bad workload on students' evaluations of teaching. *American Educational Research Journal* 38(1):183–212.

Marsh, H.W., and Bailey, M. (1993). Multidimensionality of students' evaluations of teaching effectiveness: A profile analysis. *Journal of Higher Education* 64: 1–18.

Marsh, H.W., and Dunkin, M. (1992). Students' evaluations of university teaching: A multidimensional perspective. *Higher Education: Handbook on Theory and Research*(Vol. 8, pp. 143–234). New York: Agathon.

Marsh, H.W., and Dunkin, M.J. (1997). Students' evaluations of university teaching: A multidimensional perspective. In R.P. Perry and J.C. Smart (ed.), *Effective Teaching in Higher Education: Research and Practice* (pp. 241–320). New York: Agathon.

Marsh, H.W., Fleiner, H., and Thomas, C.S. (1975). Validity and usefulness of student evaluations of instructional quality. *Journal of Educational Psychology* 67: 833–839.

Marsh, H.W., and Groves, M.A. (1987). Students' evaluations of teaching effectiveness and implicit theories: A critique of Cadwell and Jenkins. *Journal of Educational Psychology* 79: 483–489.

Marsh, H.W., and Hattie, J. (2002). The relationship between research productivity and teaching effectiveness: Complimentary, antagonistic or independent constructs. *Journal of Higher Education* 73: 603–642.

Marsh, H.W., and Hau, K.T. (2003). Big fish little pond effect on academic self-concept: A cross-cultural (26 country) test of the negative effects of academically selective schools. *American Psychologist* 58: 364–376.

Marsh, H.W., and Hocevar, D. (1991a). The multidimensionality of students' evaluations of teaching effectiveness: The generality of factor structures across academic discipline, instructor level, and course level. *Teaching and Teacher Education* 7: 9–18.

Marsh, H.W., and Hocevar, D. (1991b). Students' evaluations of teaching effectiveness: The stability of mean ratings of the same teachers over a 13-year period. *Teaching and Teacher Education* 7: 303–314.

Marsh, H.W., and Overall, J.U. (1979). Long-term stability of students' evaluations. *Research in Higher Education* 10: 139–147.

Marsh, H.W., Overall, J.U., and Kesler, S.P. (1979a). Class size, students' evaluations, and instructional effectiveness. *American Educational Research Journal* 16: 57–70.

Marsh, H.W., Overall, J.U., and Kesler, S.P. (1979b). Validity of student evaluations of instructional effectiveness: A comparison of faculty self-evaluations and evaluations by their students. *Journal of Educational Psychology* 71: 149–160.

Marsh, H.W., and Overall, J.U. (1980). Validity of students' evaluations of teaching effectiveness: Cognitive and affective criteria. *Journal of Educational Psychology* 72: 468–475.

Marsh, H.W., and Roche, L.A. (1992). The use of student evaluations of university teaching in different settings: The applicability paradigm. *Australian Journal of Education* 36: 278–300.

Marsh, H.W., and Roche, L.A. (1993). The use of students' evaluations and an individually structured intervention to enhance university teaching effectiveness. *American Educational Research Journal* 30: 217–251.

Marsh, H.W., and Roche, L.A. (1994). *The Use of Students' Evaluations of University Teaching to Improve Teaching Effectiveness*. Canberra, ACT: Australian Department of Employment, Education, and Training.

Marsh, H.W., and Roche, L.A. (1997). Making students' evaluations of teaching effectiveness effective. *American Psychologist* 52: 1187–1197.

Marsh, H.W., and Roche, L.A. (2000). Effects of grading leniency and low workloads on students' evaluations of teaching: Popular myth, bias, validity or innocent bystanders? *Journal of Educational Psychology* 92: 202–228.

Marsh, H.W., Rowe, K., and Martin, A. (2002). PhD students' evaluations of research supervision: Issues, complexities and challenges in a nationwide Australian experiment in benchmarking universities. *Journal of Higher Education* 73(3): 313–348.

Marsh, H.W., and Ware, J.E. (1982). Effects of expressiveness, content coverage, and incentive on multidimensional student rating scales: New interpretations of the Dr. Fox Effect. *Journal of Educational Psychology* 74: 126–134.

McKeachie, W. (1963). Analysis and investigation of teaching methods. In N.L. Gage (ed.), *Handbook of Research on Teaching* (pp. 448–505). Chicago: Rand McNally.

McKeachie, W.J. (1973). Correlates of students' ratings. In A.L. Sockloff (ed.), *Proceedings: The First Invitational Conference on Faculty Effectiveness Evaluated by Students* (pp. 213–218). Temple University.

McKeachie, W.J. (1979). Student ratings of faculty: A reprise. *Academe* 65: 384–397.

McKeachie, W.J. (1996). Do we need norms of student ratings to evaluate faculty? *Instructional Evaluation and Faculty Development* 14: 14–17.

McKeachie, W.J. (1997). Student Ratings: The Validity of Use. *American Psychologist* 52: 1218–25.

Murray, H.G. (1980). *Evaluating University Teaching: A Review of Research*. Toronto, Canada, Ontario Confederation of University Faculty Associations.

Murray, H.G. (1983). Low inference classroom teaching behaviors and student ratings of college teaching effectiveness. *Journal of Educational Psychology* 71: 856–865.

Murray, H.G. (April, 1987). *Impact of Student Instructions Ratings on Quality of Teaching in Higher Education*. Paper presented at the 1987 Annual Meeting of the American Educational Research Association, Washington, DC. (ERIC Document Reproduction Service No. ED 284 495).

Ory, J.C., and Braskamp, L.A. (1981). Faculty perceptions of the quality and usefulness of three types of evaluative information. *Research in Higher Education* 15: 271–282.

Ory, J.C., Braskamp, L.S., and Pieper, D.M. (1980). Congruency of student evaluative information collected by three methods. *Journal of Educational Psychology* 72:321–325.

Overall, J.U., and Marsh, H.W. (1979). Midterm feedback from students: Its relationship to instructional improvement and students' cognitive and affective outcomes. *Journal of Educational Psychology* 71: 856–865.

Overall, J.U., and Marsh, H.W. (1980). Students' evaluations of instruction: A longitudinal study of their stability. *Journal of Educational Psychology* 72: 321–325.

Overall, J.U., and Marsh, H.W. (1982). Students' evaluations of teaching: An update. American Association for Higher Education Bulletin 35(4): 9–13 (ERIC Document Reproduction Services No. ED225473).

Penny, A.R., and Coe, R. (2004). Effectiveness of consultation on student ratings feedback: A meta-analysis. *Review of Educational Research* 74(2): 215–253.

Perry, R.P., Abrami, P., Leventhal, L., and Check, J. (1979). Instructor reputation: An expectancy relationship involving student ratings and achievement. *Journal of Educational Psychology* 71: 776–787.

Peterson, C., and Cooper, S. (1980). Teacher evaluation by graded and ungraded students. *Journal of Educational Psychology* 72: 682–685.

Remmers, H.H. (1963). Rating methods in research on teaching. In N.L. Gage (ed.), *Handbook of Research on Teaching* (pp. 329–378). Chicago: Rand McNally.

Renaud, R.D., and Murray, H.G. (2005). Factorial validity of student ratings of instruction. *Research in Higher Education* 46: 929–953.

Renaud, R.D., and Murray H.G. (1996). Aging, Personality, and Teaching Effectiveness in Academic Psychologists. *Research in Higher Education* 37: 323–340.

Richardson, J.T.E. (2005). Instruments for obtaining student feedback: a review of the literature. *Assessment and Evaluation in Higher Education* 30(4): 387–415.

Rindermann, H. (1996). On the quality of students' evaluations of university teaching: An answer to evaluation critique. *Zeitschrift Für Pädagogische Psychologie* 10(3–4): 129–145.

Rindermann, H., and Schofield, N. (2001). Generalizability of multidimensional student ratings of university instruction across courses and teachers. *Research in Higher Education* 42(4): 377–399.

Ryan, J.M., and Harrison, P.D. (1995). The relationship between individual characteristics and overall assessment of teaching effectiveness across different instructional contexts. *Research in Higher Education* 36: 577–594.

Salthouse, T.A., McKeachie, W.J., and Lin, Y.G. (1978). An experimental investigation of factors affecting university promotion decisions. *Journal of Higher Education* 49: 177–183.

Scriven, M. (1981). Summative Teacher Evaluation, in J. Millman (ed.), *Handbook of Teacher Evaluation* (pp. 244–71). Beverley Hills, CA: SAGE.

Sullivan, A.M., and Skanes, G.R. (1974). Validity of student evaluation of teaching and the characteristics of successful instructors. *Journal of Educational Psychology* 66(4): 584–590.

Ting, K. (2000). Cross-level effects of class characteristics on students' perceptions of teaching quality. *Journal of Educational Psychology* 92: 818–825.

Toland, M.D., and De Ayala, R.J. (2005). A Multilevel Factor Analysis of Students' Evaluations of Teaching. *Educational and Psychological Measurement* 65: 272–296.

Watkins, D. (1994). Student evaluations of teaching effectiveness: A Cross-cultural perspective. *Research in Higher Education* 35: 251–266.

Wendorf, C.A., and Alexander, S. (2005). The influence of individual- and class-level fairness-related perceptions on student satisfaction. *Contemporary Educational Psychology* 30: 190–206.

Wilson, R.C. (1986). Improving faculty teaching: Effective use of student evaluations and consultants. *Journal of Higher Education* 57: 196–211.

10. THE DIMENSIONALITY OF STUDENT RATINGS OF INSTRUCTION: WHAT WE KNOW AND WHAT WE DO NOT*

Philip C. Abrami[†], Sylvia d'Apollonia[‡] and Steven Rosenfield[§]

[†]*Concordia University*
abrami@education.concordia.ca
[§]*Vanier College*

Key Words: Student ratings, effective teaching, post-secondary education, meta-analysis

Sometime during the second half of almost all college and university courses offered in North America, a brief ritual occurs. Students take out their sharpened pencils (number two lead, if you please) and quickly answer a series of multiple choice questions covering a range of issues about the course and their instructor. Student rating forms often contain specific items, which are purported to reflect a number of distinct dimensions of instructional effectiveness, as well as a few global items, which reflect students' overall impressions of the instructor and the course. Examples of specific items include: "Does the instructor have a good command of the subject matter?" "Does the instructor use class time well?" "Is the instructor friendly?" "Does

*An earlier version of this paper was presented at the annual meeting of the American Educational Research Association, Atlanta, Georgia, April, 1993 as part of a symposium entitled: "Student ratings of instruction: Meta-analysis of their dimensionality."

This research was supported by grants from the Social Sciences and Humanities Research Council (Government of Canada) and Fonds pour la formation de chercheurs et l'aide à la recherche (Government of Quebec).

The authors gratefully acknowledge the constructive feedback received from Harris Cooper, Kenneth Feldman, Wilbert McKeachie, Herbert Marsh, Raymond Perry, and an anonymous reviewer who read earlier versions of this manuscript.

Address reprint requests to: Dr. Philip C. Abrami, Centre for the Study of Classroom Processes, Concordia University, 1455 DeMaisonneuve Blvd. W., Montreal, Quebec CANADA H3G 1M8.

R.P. Perry and J.C. Smart (eds.), The Scholarship of Teaching and Learning in Higher Education: An Evidence-Based Perspective, 385–456.
© 2007 *Springer.*

the instructor assign difficult reading?" "Does the instructor facilitate class discussion?" "Does the instructor keep students informed of their progress?" Examples of global items include: "How would you rate the instructor in overall ability?" "How would you rate the quality of this course?" "How much have you learned in this course compared to others?" Many student rating forms also provide students with the opportunity to provide narrative feedback about the course, the instructor, and their learning. While the rating ritual ends quickly, the implications of the results can be far reaching, for student ratings are used for a variety of important purposes.

In many circumstances ratings are the most influential or only source of information on teaching available for decisions about promotion, tenure, or merit. Typically, personnel committees use ratings to judge teaching effectiveness by comparing individual faculty results with departmental norms. Ratings are also widely used for instructional improvement to provide feedback to instructors on the quality of their courses. Faculty use ratings feedback to identify both areas of strength that should be maintained and areas of weakness that require modification. Ratings are occasionally used by students as a guide to course selection. For example, some students may use ratings information to select the highest rated instructors, while others may use ratings information to select the easiest courses. Thus, student ratings serve widespread and important practical purposes.

Student ratings also serve important theoretical purposes by providing researchers with information on the teaching-learning process. For example, such information may be useful in assessing the effectiveness of innovative pedagogical techniques such as cooperative learning, in understanding the relationship between instructional preparation and delivery as they affect multiple outcomes of instruction, and in judging the impact of instructional strategies for different students, courses, and settings.

The practical and theoretical utility of student ratings depends on the extent to which ratings meet psychometric standards of excellence. Concerns about the reliability, validity, and generalizability of student ratings include: Are rating results consistent over time? Are students uniform in their assessments of instructors? Are ratings free from the influence of biasing characteristics? What is the dimensionality of student ratings? Are these dimensions consistent across students, courses, settings, and rating forms? Which dimensions reflect the impact of instruction on student learning and other outcomes?

This paper is concerned with the dimensionality of instruction as reflected in student ratings. Research on the dimensions of effective teaching is not new. There are numerous studies which have explored this issue and notable disagreements (e.g., Abrami, d'Apollonia and Cohen, 1990; Marsh, 1987) regarding, in particular, whether and how data from multidimensional student rating forms should be used in summative decisions about teaching (e.g., promotion, merit, tenure, etc.). This paper critically examines many of these issues and reaches important conclusions about the dimensionality of teaching as reflected in student ratings, makes practical suggestions, as well as suggests directions for future research.

In the first section, three alternative definitions of effective teaching are presented and critically analyzed: the product definition, the process definition, and the process-product definition. We contend that the relationships between teaching processes and teaching products is of major interest to researchers and practitioners.

The second section provides a general discussion of methods for empirically determining effective teaching with special emphasis on the use of student ratings for each of the three definitions of effective teaching. We comment on the difficulties of directly assessing the products of instruction and suggest the use of a table of specifications as one way to develop a rating form to indirectly measure what and how students have learned. We suggest that student ratings as process measures must contain items which assess the relevant aspects of teaching accurately in each instructional context. We note that the dimensionality of student ratings varies with course characteristics and we suggest that some items which evaluate specific aspects of teaching vary in relevance across contexts. We show that multidimensional student rating forms do not contain items which evaluate the same, specific teaching qualities; the rating forms lack both comprehensiveness and uniformity. We conclude that since the qualities of teaching evaluated by different student rating forms appear to differ both in their nature and structure, it is of value to explore the forms further and determine if there are dimensions of teaching common to a collection of student rating forms.

The third section concentrates on the strengths and weaknesses of three validation designs—the laboratory design, the multisection validation design and the multitrait-multimethod design—for empirically determining the relationship between the processes and products of teaching. The laboratory design uses the experimental manipulation of instructional conditions to study the causal effects of instruction on students. It is often considered low in external validity. The multisection validation design uses multiple sections of the same course taught by different instructors employing common measures of student ratings and student learning. The correlations between course section means for student ratings and means for student achievement explore the relationship between instructional processes and an important instructional product. We consider the multisection design particularly strong because it reduces the probability of rival explanations to instructor impacts and is high in generalizability to classrooms. In the multitrait-multimethod design, student ratings and several criterion measures (e.g., instructor self-ratings) are collected across a wide range of courses, without controlling for biasing or extraneous influences. We consider this design weaker both in internal validity, since controls are lacking, and in external validity, since important product measures of instruction (e.g., student learning) are not included. We conclude that studies employing the multisection design are worthy of special attention.

The fourth section examines the quantitative reviews of the 43 multisection validity studies. We describe what we have learned from these studies and what remains to be learned of the relationship between what instructors do when they teach and how this affects student learning. We note that reviews to date suggest that the specific dimensions of teaching appear to differentially and, in some cases, poorly predict instructor impacts on learning compared to global ratings. We suggest that there are several limitations of prior reviews. First, the reviews include only a fraction of the findings from the original studies. Second, there is the lack of a comprehensive, empirically validated system for organizing the findings from different rating forms into a common framework. Third, study features which may explain the variability in study findings remain unexplored. Consequently, a more comprehensive research integration is called for using an empirically determined scheme for coding the findings from different rating forms.

The fifth section summarizes our attempt to identify the common dimensions of effective teaching as reflected in student ratings. First, we summarize our reanalysis of Marsh in which we failed to find many specific teaching dimensions but found a general teaching factor instead. Since our ultimate goal is to explore the relationship between process and product, we concentrate on the rating forms used in the 43 multisection validity studies. We quantitatively integrate the results from 17 inter-item correlation matrices by: a) coding the items using a common scoring scheme, b) eliminating items which were heterogeneous within categories, and c) factor analyzing the aggregate correlation matrix.

Our factor analysis indicates that there is a common structure to instruction. Four factors emerged of which the largest ones were highly correlated. We conclude that existing analyses provide support for a large underlying general trait although it may not be the only trait. We also believe that effective teaching is multidimensional but that there are differences across rating forms concerning the specific dimensions which underlie effective instruction. These differences suggest that student ratings of specific teaching dimensions should not be used indiscriminately for summative decisions about teaching effectiveness. Now that we have identified the common structure of student ratings, the next phase of research will be to use the techniques of quantitative research integration to explore the relationship between this structure and teacher-produced student achievement as well as the substantive and methodological variables which explain inconsistencies in the relationships.

DEFINITIONS OF EFFECTIVE TEACHING

Effective teaching can be defined from several perspectives. In the first perspective, effective teaching is defined in terms of affecting student products. In the second perspective, effective teaching is defined in terms of the processes which instructors enact. These views are elaborated and contrasted below. The relationship between process and product views is also presented. The relationship between the process and product views of effective teaching seeks to find the links between what teachers do and whether and how students change as a result.

The Product Definition of Effective Teaching

Broadly speaking, effective teaching from the product view can be defined as the positive changes produced in students in relevant academic domains including the cognitive, affective, and occasionally the psychomotor ones (to use the general taxonomic classifications developed by Bloom et al., 1956). Included in the cognitive domain are both specific cognitive skills (e.g., subject matter expertise), general cognitive skills (e.g., analytical thinking), and meta-cognitive skills (e.g., error correction). Included in the affective domain are attitudes and interests toward the subject matter in particular and learning in general as well as interpersonal skills and abilities relevant to learning and working in a social context. Finally, included in the psychomotor domain are physical skills and abilities ranging from those acquired in a physical education to precise motor skills acquired in a fine arts education.

This definition concentrates on the products that effective teaching promotes in students. The definition has several corollaries. First, there is not a single product of effective teaching; there are many. Second, there is no *a priori* theoretical requirement that the products are inter-related either within or across domains. For example, it is not necessarily the case that increased student knowledge of basic facts will result in increased analytical and synthesis skills or vice versa. Third, the value attached to individual products is often situation-specific, requiring adjustments to meet the local needs described by students, departments, and colleges. Fourth, greater teaching effectiveness is not necessarily associated with the number of products affected. Fifth, the definition makes no prediction about the (casual) sequences or paths among products. For example, it does not explicate whether student casual beliefs about learning affect academic self-concept or vice versa.

The product definition of effective teaching recognizes that there is widespread disagreement in the academic community about both the objectives and goals of instruction and the ways to achieve them. For example in the social sciences, clinical practitioners may dispute experimental researchers about the importance of developing the affective skills of students. While almost all faculty will agree with the preeminence of developing the cognitive abilities of students, there is less general agreement over the form that development takes. For example, in the natural sciences physicists may dispute whether to teach about the many concepts of the discipline or how to teach students to discover a few fundamentals.

THE PROCESS DEFINITION OF EFFECTIVE TEACHING

The process definition of effective teaching emphasizes the acts of teaching rather than the consequences of those actions. The process definition is meant to include instructor activities which occur both before (preparatory) and during (delivery) teaching. Preparation may include such wide-ranging activities as: developing content expertise; preparing course outlines, activities, and objectives; selecting a teaching method; assigning course workload; and setting evaluation practices and procedures. The delivery procedures may include classroom activities and abilities such as organization, dynamism, enthusiasm, and rapport, and outside classroom activities such as availability to, and friendliness toward, students.

The process definition has several corollaries. First, there is not a single process of effective teaching; there are many. The definition recognizes that effective teaching is multidimensional consisting of numerous and apparently distinct acts. Second, the definition is tentative regarding the specific acts which constitute the process. One purpose of our research is to determine empirically whether there is uniformity and consistency to these acts. Third, it is also possible that these distinct acts represent different operationalizations of an underlying construct or constructs. For example, "instructor clarity" may consist of clarity of speech, audibility, pace, comprehensibility, etc. Furthermore, these constructs may be both additive and hierarchical. This is also an empirical question. Fifth, the term "effective teaching" means that there is an evaluative component to the process. This evaluative component regards both the instructor's choice of acts and the quality and quantity with which they are enacted. In other words, ineffective instructors may emphasize the wrong acts when they teach or enact them poorly.

It is also unclear whether generally static personal characteristics or traits (e.g., gender, race, age, personality, etc.) form part of the process definition. They are qualities which are beyond the control of the instructor but which may nevertheless indirectly influence both the acts of teaching and the products of teaching. These are sometimes referred to as biasing characteristics in recognition both of their potential for influence and the undesirability of that influence.

THE PROCESS-PRODUCT DEFINITION OF EFFECTIVE TEACHING

What activities differentiate good instructors from poor ones in promoting students' critical thinking, task engagement, and persistence? Is instructor enthusiasm an important teaching process because enthusiasm motivates students to learn? Important questions such as these speak to the inexorable link between teaching processes and products.

It is our contention that the relationships between teaching processes and teaching products is of major interest. The link between process and product raises new questions about the meaning of the term "effective teaching." Now, rather than effective teaching being defined only in terms of either process or product, we may combine the two. Doing so helps identify links between what teachers do and whether and how students change as a result.

Broadly speaking, effective teaching from the process-product view can be defined as the instructor activities which occur both before (preparatory) and during (delivery) teaching which produce positive changes in students in relevant academic domains including the cognitive, affective, and occasionally the psychomotor ones.

We hypothesize that the varied products of effective teaching are affected by different teaching processes. But we cannot describe with any great confidence the specific nature of these causal relationships.

We further hypothesize that the causal relationship between any one teaching process and any one teaching product will vary as a function of external influences including student, course, and setting influences. As stated previously, there appears to be important disagreements among faculty on what to teach and how to teach it.

To summarize, we have briefly explored three alternative definitions of effective teaching: the product definition, the process definition, and the process-product definition. We believe the relationship between teaching processes and teaching products is of major interest.

EMPIRICALLY DETERMINING EFFECTIVE TEACHING

In this section we consider ways to determine effective teaching empirically for the three definitions of teaching presented. We concentrate, in particular, on the use of student ratings for these purposes.

EMPIRICALLY DETERMINING THE PRODUCTS OF EFFECTIVE TEACHING

According to the product definition, effective teaching produces changes in such student outcomes as content knowledge, analytic ability, academic self-concept, motivation to learn, aesthetic appreciation, and so on. Unfortunately, the authors are unaware of individual studies that attempt to systematically and inclusively describe college teaching from a product-based perspective. There are studies that explore outcomes singly, particularly those that examine the effects of teaching on (undifferentiated) student learning of course content. Therefore, it may be profitable to apply the techniques of quantitative research integration to the literature on instructional products to better and more completely understand the effects of teaching.

In recent years, Seldin (1991), Shore et al. (1986), and others have argued for the use of the teaching portfolio, a comprehensive collection of descriptive and evaluative information on individual faculty teaching, which might include a statement of teaching responsibilities, course syllabi, instructor self evaluations, a description of improvement efforts, peer assessments, participation in teaching conferences, videotapes of instruction, student exams and essays, alumni ratings, and so on. The portfolio is to be used both for teaching improvement purposes and for summative decisions.

Judging teaching effectiveness by examining the evidence of student accomplishments—tests, papers, and projects—generally requires that two criteria are met: a) the data presented are representative of the faculty member's effect on students and b) the results of faculty can be objectively compared. Meeting the first criterion requires examining the results either of all students or a random sample of students. Submitting the best student products as evidence of teaching effectiveness, a common practice, does little to allow accurate judgments of how well instructors promote student learning.

Meeting the second criterion requires measures of student productivity that can be compared across courses. Unfortunately, this has rarely been accomplished. For example, it is extremely difficult to compare the achievement of students enrolled in an introductory Physics course with the achievement of students enrolled in an advanced, upper-level Physics course in order to judge which instructor best promotes student learning. Are differences in achievement between the two courses due to the quality of the students enrolled? The difficulty of the tests used? The nature of the material learned? The quality of the instruction given? Similarly, it is tenuous to assume that changes from pretest examination scores at the beginning of term to posttest examination scores at the end reflect only the impacts of instruction. In contrast, it is less difficult to compare student achievement on a final, common examination when the students are enrolled in different sections of the same course, especially when it is reasonable to assume that students selected course sections more or less at random. Under circumstances resembling the latter, using product measures to compare and judge instruction seems quite defensible and its use should be more widespread. In general, however, product measures of effective teaching are seldom practical to use and rarely provide accurate data for judging quality teaching.

Student ratings as direct product measures. Student ratings measure directly one product of instruction; namely, student satisfaction with teaching. For many, measuring student satisfaction with teaching is a sufficient reason to use student ratings. Proponents of the use of ratings as satisfaction measures argue that if students are the consumers of the teaching process, then student satisfaction with teaching should be a component of instructional evaluation.

Otherwise, student ratings do not measure *directly* how much or how well a class of students has learned or any other aspect of achievement in the cognitive domain including how well the content is retained. Student ratings also do not often measure directly: most affective products of instruction such as student expectations, beliefs, and concepts about themselves as learners; student attitudes, values, and interests toward the subject matter including enrolling in other courses in the area or adopting the area as a field of major study; student interpersonal and social skills generally and such skills within the context of executing a complex academic task; etc.

Student ratings as **indirect** *product measures.* Student ratings are often used as convenient alternative measures of most instructional products. Ratings are used to *infer* that highly rated instructors positively affect instructional products. Student ratings provide a basic yardstick for these judgments when product measures are unavailable, when the product measures are of questionable quality, or when conditions (such as differences in the level or type of course) do not allow for fair comparisons of products across instructors.

To what extent do student ratings reflect the impact of instructors on students learning of course content, their motivation to learn, development of interpersonal skills, and so on? There is a reasonable body of well-designed research, reviewed more extensively elsewhere in this paper, which suggests that, on average, there is a modest, positive relationship between global ratings of instruction and instructor-produced student learning of lower-level academic skills (e.g., knowledge of basic facts, simple comprehension, etc.). Much less is known about the validity of ratings as predictors of other outcomes of instruction.

Improving student ratings as **indirect** *product measures.* Consider the following item from a student rating form: "Rate the extent to which your instructor motivated you to learn." Does this item ask students to describe an instructional process or an instructional product? The item does not ask students to judge instructor preparation or delivery but the consequences of teaching. It is, therefore, not a measure of a teaching process. But is it is an accurate, *indirect* assessment of an instructional product? It is accurate only to the extent that student self-report of motivation reflects student persistence at learning, the intensity of student effort, student choice of tasks to learn, etc. Rating forms occasionally include items that ask students to assess the success of instructors at encouraging them to learn but seldom include items that assess the specific behaviors associated with that motivation.

Table 1: Table of Specifications for Student Ratings of Course Content in Psychological Statistics

Instructions: Please use this rating form to assess how well your instructor taught you the content of this course. Begin by assigning your instructor an overall rating for the amount you learned in the course. Use the box with the darkest shading for this purpose. The major content areas of the course are listed in the *rows* of the table. For each content area or row assign your instructor an *overall* rating using the scale shown below. For example, if your instructor taught you descriptive statistics extremely well assign an overall rating of 5 for descriptive statistics. The major cognitive objectives of the course are listed as *columns* in the table. For each cognitive objective or column assign your instructor an *overall* rating. For example, if your instructor taught you to apply the content extremely well assign an overall rating of 5 for application. Finally, use each box to give your instructor a rating for both what you learned and how you learned it. For example, assign your instructor a "4" if (s)he did a very good job teaching you to evaluate uses of the t-test.							

Use the following rating scale in making your judgments:
1—Poor
2—Fair
3—Good
4—Very good
5—Excellent
NA—*Not applicable*

Course Content	How the Content Was Learned						
	Knowledge	Compre-hension	Appli-cation	Analysis	Synthesis	Evaluation	OVERALL RATING
Descriptive statistics							
The t-test							
Oneway Anova							
Factorial Anova							
Nonparametrics							
OVERALL RATING							

Similarly, rating forms do not often contain items that ask students to assess an instructor's impact on specific cognitive and meta-cognitive achievements. Instead, rating forms more frequently ask students to rate: "How much have you learned in this course compared with others?" A questionnaire can be designed so that ratings items may be made more precise by asking students to judge how well they learned from the instructor in each content area of the course as well as the depth to which they learned. (See Table 1, page 222.)

The table of specifications or teaching blueprint presented in Table 1 illustrates a student rating form for an undergraduate course in psychological statistics. The rows represent the content to be learned.

The columns represent how the content is to be learned. The cells or boxes represent the combination of what is to be learned and how it is to be learned. Students may use this type of evaluation form to judge an instructor's effectiveness: overall in promoting student learning, in particular content areas of the course, and in promoting different types and levels of learning. The evaluation form also allows for very specific feedback on particular aspects of teaching. For example, was the instructor effective at promoting higher level skills in more complex areas of the course?

Not all the content areas of the course are equally important, nor is every type of learning of equal value and emphasis. For example, the instructor may need to spend considerable time on some topics (e.g., descriptive statistics) and not others (e.g., factorial ANOVA). Similarly, some topics may require substantial efforts devoted to basic knowledge and comprehension while other topics may require greater efforts devoted to analysis, synthesis, and evaluation.

Prior to the evaluation, the instructor and/or students may wish to estimate the amount of time devoted to each content area and type of learning. First, estimate the percent of course time devoted to each content area. The sum of the row percentages should be 100%. Next estimate the percent of course time devoted to each cognitive objective. The sum of the column percentages should be 100%. Next, fill in each cell or box percentage. Note that the precision of the table of specifications rating form in assessing student learning remains to be determined empirically.

Finally, not all rating items seem as logically defensible as indirect measures of instructional products as the self report items described above. For example why should instructor friendliness and openness toward students necessarily reflect student understanding of thermodynamics? Indeed, we recall rather heated discussions by some faculty that they do not. Therefore, such items are better understood to reflect student ratings of the processes of effective teaching. An interest in whether such items and similar items can be used to assess instructor impacts on student learning and other outcomes is, consequently, an interest in the relationship between process and product.

Empirically Determining the Processes of Effective Teaching

Many studies have attempted to determine empirically the dimensions, clusters, factors or major characteristics that college instructors employ. Are these characteristics too many or too varied to describe succinctly?

Do faculty and students agree on the characteristics they describe? Can these characteristics be grouped together?

A major portion of the research has relied on empirical methods for identifying teaching dimensions, chiefly through the use of factor analysis. Marsh (1987) summarized research on one instrument, Students' Evaluations of Educational Quality (SEEQ), which identified nine factors of instruction. Marsh (1987) argued for consideration of these nine factors when summative evaluations of teaching are made (e.g., for promotion and tenure decisions).

Feldman (1976) reviewed studies in which students were asked to describe the characteristics of best teachers, or of ideal teachers, or of good teaching. He identified 19 dimensions which he used to classify the descriptions. Later, Feldman (1988) reviewed studies comparing faculty and student specifications of the instructional characteristics they considered particularly important to good teaching and effective instruction. In the latter review, Feldman (1988) identified 22 instructional dimensions. The average correlation between students and faculty in their judgement of these components was +0.71. Feldman (1988) concluded that there was general agreement between faculty and students in their views of good teaching as reflected in the importance the two groups placed on the components of teaching.

Feldman (1976) and Kulik and McKeachie (1975) reviewed factor analytic research of student ratings of instruction. Feldman (1976) employed 19 categories to categorize the items from 60 studies. He then fit the dimensions into three major clusters. Kulik and McKeachie (1975) reviewed 11 studies and identified four commonly found factors.

In sum, there appeared to be encouraging evidence regarding the processes of effective teaching. Descriptions of teaching by students appeared to fit into a reasonably finite set of categories. Faculty and students showed reasonable agreement as to the characteristics they considered important. When students rated faculty on these characteristics, groups of items formed into factors that reviewers were able to organize further. In light of such findings, it seemed reasonable to ask students to rate faculty to measure teaching processes. After all, students had the greatest exposure to faculty teaching and should be in a good position to judge.

Such thinking, however, depended first on showing that students were accurate, consistent, and unbiased judges. Second, it depended on showing that the teaching qualities students were asked to judge were always relevant and appropriate and took into account innovative teaching methods[1] It also depended on showing that different rating forms contained items which tapped the same teaching qualities. Finally, it depended on showing that the results of specific ratings could be effectively used.

The accuracy of student ratings. The validity of student ratings as process measures of effective teaching depends on showing that the ratings of students are accurate and reliable descriptions of preparation and delivery activities. The reliability of student ratings is not a contested issue: the stability of ratings over time and the consistency of ratings over students (especially in classes of ten or more) compares favorably with the best objective tests (Feldman, 1977; Marsh, 1987; Marsh and Dunkin, 1992).

The accuracy of student ratings of teaching process is a concern about criterion-related validity. Are students able to accurately judge whether (quantity) and how well (quality) instructors teach according to the dimensions specified on the rating form? In general,

---

[1] Feldman (1976, 1988, 1989a, 1989b, 1990) among others has explored the relationship between global ratings of teaching effectiveness and dimensional ratings as a way of showing the validity of dimensional ratings as indices of teaching processes. The value of such an approach depends on making a case for the link between specific teaching processes and student perceptions of the general quality of teaching received. Feldman (1988) puts the case this way:

> If it is assumed that each student's overall evaluation of an instructor is an additive combination of the student's evaluation of specific aspects of the teacher and his or her instruction, weighted by the student's estimation of the relative importance of these aspects to good teaching, then it would be expected that students' overall assessment of instructors would be more highly associated with instructor characteristics that students generally consider to be important to good teaching than with those they consider to be less important. (p. 314)

The assumption of a link between global ratings and specific ratings is, in our view, highly plausible but an assumption that can be challenged on both conceptual and empirical grounds. Is it not also plausible that students' impressions have either: a) a general component and specific components or b) only specific components? If either of these alternative views is plausible, it would be erroneous to invalidate ratings of teaching dimensions that do not correlate with global assessments. For example, the social psychology literature suggests several models of impression formation including the three dimensions of evaluative judgment (good-bad, weak-strong, and fast-slow) offered by Osgood, Suci, and Tannenbaum (1957) as well as the weighted averaging model of overall impressions (Anderson, 1968).

However, what is fundamentally important is not the structure of student impressions but the structure of what teachers actually do when they teach. Consequently, the plausibility of the assumption that students form general impressions may be reasonable for the *judgment* of teaching process that students utilize but the assumption becomes much less reasonable and much less plausible when one is utilizing student ratings to develop a theoretical *description* of the teaching process. Is teaching a series of discrete actions? Do these actions meld into a single collection of actions or several collections of actions? It remains uncertain which of these ways is best to describe teaching.

criterion-related validation studies require alternative measures of the teaching process in addition to student ratings. For example, to assess the criterion-related validity of ratings as process measures requires examining studies comparing faculty (peer) and chair ratings with student ratings, trained observers ratings with student ratings, instructor self-ratings with student ratings, etc. The data suggest that students are reasonably accurate judges of most teaching processes (Marsh, 1987; Marsh and Dunkin, 1992).

The criterion validation of student ratings as measures of teaching processes is not to be confused with the validation of student ratings as measures of teaching products. As Doyle noted:

> In instructional evaluation validity studies, ratings of instructor characteristics are compared with student learning. But student learning is not an alternative measure of, say, an instructor's effectiveness in engaging student attention. Alternative measures of engaging student attention might include observer's counts of students dozing or staring out the window, or student reports of boredom, or even galvanic skin response. (1981, p. 24)

The content validity of student ratings. The validity of student ratings as process measures of effective teaching also depends on showing that the items on the rating form have content validity and are a representative sample of items from the larger population of items. The requirement of content validity suggests that if a single form is used it is equally applicable in a variety of instructional contexts and not just the lecture format for which most rating forms were designed. These instructional contexts include different pedagogical methods (e.g., small and large class lecturing, tutoring and advising, studio classes, discussion and small group methods including cooperative learning, individualized and mastery learning, etc.), academic disciplines, student and setting characteristics, etc.

Abrami, d'Apollonia and Cohen (1990) argued that a student rating form should contain items equally relevant to each of the instructional situations for which it was designed. Consequently, items such as "Students were encouraged to participate in class discussion" and "Instructor was friendly towards individual students" would not be equally relevant in small and large classes, regardless of whether those items retained the same interrelationship with other items across instructional contexts. For example, imagine several items (e.g., friendliness, openness, encouraging, and warmth) which assess instructor rapport. It is quite easy to see how scores on these items would be inter-related regardless of instructional context. If you are not very friendly, you are probably not seen as especially open, encouraging, or warm. This may explain why Marsh and Hocevar (1984, 1990) report some evidence of the factorial validity of the SEEQ.

But it is equally easy to envision how instructor rapport with students might be more critical in a small class than a large one. And it is also possible that because different teaching behaviors are important in different contexts, instructor mean ratings might vary across contexts. That is, instructors may concentrate on the qualities important in that context and receive higher ratings on context-relevant teaching skills. Fernald (1990) found that items on a multidimensional rating form varied greatly with regard to student perceptions of item relevance to the course. Furthermore, the degree of item relevance was correlated with student ratings of instruction: the higher the item relevance score, the higher the student rating score.

In our hypothetical example, rapport mean ratings would vary significantly in small classes versus large classes even though the under-lying relationship among rapport items remained the same. Unfortunately, mean scores, not interitem correlations, are used by promotion committees to make summative decisions about effective teaching. In this case, irrelevant items bias the case against the instructor of large classes.

Comprehensiveness and uniformity of student rating forms. Another type of evidence concerning the validity of rating forms comes from comparisons of items on different rating forms. Abrami, d'Apollonia and Cohen (1990) reasoned that if effective teaching was substantially invariant, then one would expect the same teaching qualities to emerge on each multidimensional rating form; there would not be substantial variability across forms in the factors of effective teaching which are assessed. Moreover, the relative type and proportion of items repre-senting these factors would also not vary across forms.

To assess the comprehensiveness and uniformity of existing multi-dimensional rating forms, we used an early version of our coding scheme to sort the rating items found in 43 studies assessing the validity of student ratings to predict teacher-produced student learning. There were 154 study findings in the 43 studies (e.g., studies that report the findings for more than one course). There were 742 validity coefficients or correlations between scores on the rating forms and student learning. For example, a multidimensional rating form would yield several rating-achievement correlations. We first determined the number of times a category was found in the study findings. The comprehensiveness index represents the portion of times a teaching category is represented in the 154 findings. We then computed a uniformity index, which is a measure of the unidimensionality of reported validity coefficients across forms, for each instructional dimension. The uniformity index is the average proportion of items within a specific dimension, computed across 154 study findings. Thus, a high uniformity index indicates that the reported validity coefficients tend to represent a single dimension. The results of the uniformity and comprehensiveness analyses are presented in Table 2. The results suggest that both the items that appear on multidimensional student rating forms and the factors that these items represent vary across study findings.

Table 2: Uniformity and Comprehensiveness Analysis of Student Rating Forms (N = 154 study findings)

Dimension	N	CI[1]	UI[2]
Stimulation of interest	88	0.57	0.25
Enthusiasm	30	0.19	0.23
Knowledge of the subject	43	0.28	0.36
Intellectual expansiveness	35	0.23	0.11
Preparation and organization	89	0.58	0.33
Clarity and understandableness	112	0.73	0.30
Elocutionary skills	54	0.35	0.13
Class level and progress	76	0.49	0.20
Clarity of course objectives	68	0.44	0.25
Relevance and value of materials	46	0.30	0.38
Supplementary materials	26	0.17	0.36
Workload	84	0.55	0.45
Perceived outcome	75	0.49	0.47
Fairness of evaluation	69	0.45	0.39
Classroom management	79	0.51	0.25
Personality characteristics	54	0.35	0.25
Feedback	66	0.43	0.24
Encouragement of discussion	90	0.58	0.35
Intellectual challenge	35	0.23	0.24
Concern and respect for students	75	0.49	0.22
Availability and helpfulness	68	0.44	0.29
Overall course	92	0.60	0.51
Overall instructor	109	0.71	0.61
Miscellaneous	47	0.31	0.23

[1]CI =Comprehensiveness Index [2]UI =Uniformity Index
Adapted from Abrami, d'Apollonia and Cohen (1990).

The uniformity indices for teaching dimensions were as low as 0.11 (instructor expansiveness ratings); these dimensional indices contrast with global indices that were 0.51 (overall course rating) and 0.61 (overall instructor rating). Especially at the level of asking specific questions about instruction (i.e., low-inference questions) multidimensional student rating forms are composed of a diverse collection of items. Furthermore, even as the items are organized into factors, a considerable lack of uniformity remains.

Student ratings and innovative teaching methods. As never before, college instructors are using innovative teaching methods in place of, or in addition to, the traditional lecture method. One method that shows special promise for enhancing student achievement as well as developing communication and interpersonal skills, is cooperative learning (Abrami et al., 1995; Cooper et al., 1990: Johnson, Johnson, and Smith, 1991). Cooperative learning relies on students learning actively and purposefully together in small groups. Two key elements of cooperative learning are positive interdependence and individual accountability. Positive interdependence exists when students perceive that their success at learning has a positive influence on their teammates' successes and vice versa. Individual accountability exists when students perceive that they are responsible for their own learning and for the learning of their teammates. The instructor's role in cooperative learning is different than in whole class instruction. Because students spend a considerable amount of time attending to their classmates, much less class time is devoted to lecturing. Instead, the instructor usually gives only a brief overview of important ideas and then allows student teams to explore these ideas further.

The distinctiveness of cooperative learning compared with lecturing suggests that the specific instructional processes involved will be different. For example, in whole class instruction almost all of class time is devoted to the instructor talking and students listening. Clarity of explanation should be more important in classes designed for lecturing than in classes where the instructor presents for only a portion of the time.

In a cooperative classroom, the instructor's primary role is to insure that teams are viable and that teammates are effectively instructing one another. In particular, the instructor insures that group tasks are appropriate for learning and that students are operating together as a team with each member of the team holding a personal stake in the outcome. Furthermore, the instructor insures that each team has the necessary skills and abilities to learn. When necessary, the instructor may intervene to motivate students and to facilitate their learning. Thus, differences in instructional methods suggest that a student rating form consisting of one set of specific teaching dimensions will not have uniform content validity.

Factorial invariance? An underlying assumption of the multidimensional approach to the evaluation of instruction is that the characteristics of effective teaching are substantially invariant across situations (Marsh and Hocevar, 1984). In general, the qualities important to effective teaching are not expected to vary from course to course, from department to department, or from university to university. Marsh and Hocevar (1984, 1990) provide some evidence of the factorial invariance of one student rating form across different groups of students, academic disciplines, instructor levels, and course levels. That is, the factor structure of the rating form (i.e., the number and nature of the teaching dimensions found) and thus the relationships among perceived characteristics of teaching, was stable across contexts. However, differences in pedagogical methods were not explored for possible influences on factor structure.

A study by Smith and Cranton (1992) reached different conclusions about the influence of course characteristics. They found that student perceptions of the amount of improvement needed in the four dimensions of a student rating form differed significantly across levels of instruction and class size. They concluded that the relationships between course characteristics and student ratings are not general but specific to the instructional setting. They suggested several practical implications of their results. First, for instructional improvement, a faculty member should not assume that all items on a student rating form are of equal importance in planning changes. Second, faculty who want to determine criteria for the interpretation of their ratings by comparing themselves to others would likely be making a mistake. Third, personnel decisions using data from student ratings should not be based on a comparisons among faculty or across courses without considering the instructional setting.

Utility of student rating forms. Finally, one cannot expect untrained administrators or non-experts in evaluation to properly weigh the information provided by factor scores in arriving at a single decision about the quality of an instructor's teaching (Franklin and Theall, 1989). One cannot expect administrators to have the expertise of faculty developers, nor are there precise and defensible procedures for synthesizing the information from factor scores. Experience suggests that administrators weigh factor scores equally or look for particularly strong or weak areas of teaching. What if these low scores occurred because the dimensions were low in relevancy? Cashin and Downey (1992) studied the usefulness of global items in predicting weighted composite ratings with a sample of 17,183 classes from 105 institutions. Their results were that global items accounted for a substantial amount of the variance (more than 50%). They concluded: "The results of this study have supported that single, global items—as suggested by Abrami (1985)—can account for a great deal of the variance resulting from a weighted composite of many multidimensional student rating items" (Cashin and Downey, 1992, p. 569). They recommended that short student rating forms should be used for summative evaluations and longer forms should be reserved for teaching improvement.

Ratings and the processes of instruction: Where do we go from here? The interests of many researchers and practitioners alike appears to have focused on finding a rating form capable of identifying the major qualities or traits essential to the process of effective teaching. Analytical strategies such as factor analysis concentrate on identifying what is common to teaching and generally disregard what is unique.

The alternative view we argue for here suggests that the search for a collection of the invariant dimensions of effective instruction may underemphasize the importance of the local context. We are reminded, in particular, of the endless discussions among faculty over the merits of including particular items on student rating forms. Comments such as "What does____have to do with good teaching?" are reflections of the possible problems associated with employing a single definition of instruction when many are needed. Consequently, research and practice may need to be more sensitive to situational influences and make greater allowances for multiple approaches to the definition and evaluation of effectiveness.

Nevertheless, there are both theoretical and practical reasons to continue to examine, describe, and classify instructional processes. We decided, therefore, to explore further the research on the dimensionality of the processes of effective teaching by quantitatively integrating the results of many studies using a collection of different student rating forms. We believe that a systematic effort to integrate this corpus of research may better answer questions about teaching. Is there a core set of teaching qualities that emerge from every one of the studies? Do these qualities form into the same factors? How much does context matter? By integrating the existing research, we hoped to be better able to separate common dimensions of teaching from unique qualities that may only be appropriate for particular instructional context. We describe our findings in a later section. Before doing so, we consider research linking the processes and the products of effective teaching.

EMPIRICALLY DETERMINING THE LINKS BETWEEN THE PROCESSES AND PRODUCTS OF EFFECTIVE TEACHING

According to the process-product view of effective instruction, a valid student rating must assess accurately, if not directly, instructor impacts on both processes and products. That is, we wish to know not only the extent student ratings reflect what instructors do when they teach but also the extent to which students learn course content, are motivated, and develop critical skills as a result. Consequently, the principal consideration for a research design is that it allows one to assess the degree to which student ratings reflect what teachers do (process) and the impact teachers have on students (product). In particular, the design must control for plausible rival explanations to the causal effects of instructors.

Generally, these plausible rival explanations center around the effects of "biasing" characteristics, mainly student characteristics (e.g., ability), but also course and setting effects (e.g., size), and extraneous instructor characteristics (e.g., grading standards). Thus, our first consideration is that the design controls for plausible threats to internal validity (Campbell and Stanley, 1963).

Our second consideration is that the design allows us to generalize the results across students, instructors, courses and other setting characteristics, various rating instruments and importantly, different products of effective instruction. For example, we wish to conclude that ratings predict teacher impacts in a variety of courses and for a variety of instructor effectiveness measures. Thus, our second consideration is that the design controls for plausible threats to external validity (Campbell and Stanley, 1963). The strongest design will control for plausible threats to both internal and external validity.

In this section three research designs—the laboratory design, the multisection validation design and the multitrait-mutimethod design (MTMM)—are critically reviewed. In the typical laboratory design, students are randomly assigned to instructional treatment conditions that attempt to simulate certain classroom features. After a brief exposure to the treatment (often as short as 20 minutes), students are asked to complete ratings and other measures. In the multisection validation design, researchers correlate mean student ratings and mean student achievement on a common examination from multiple sections of a college course. A large positive correlation is taken as evidence of rating validity, establishing a link between what instructors do when they teach and their impact on students. In the MTMM design, student ratings factors and several criterion measures (e.g., instructor self-ratings) are collected across a wide range of courses, and the convergent and discriminant validity of ratings are assessed.

LABORATORY DESIGNS

To explore simply and conclusively the causal relationships between particular instructional processes and particular products requires experiments that manipulate what teachers do and that measure how students change as a result (see Murray, 1991, for a review). Laboratory designs are the strongest designs for controlling threats to internal validity because they manipulate instructional conditions and control for the effects of students through random assignment. However, they are the weakest designs for controlling for threats to external validity.

The laboratory studies on instructor expressiveness and lecture content (educational seduction or the Dr. Fox effect; Abrami, Leventhal, and Perry, 1982) examined the effects of two instructional delivery processes—expressiveness and content—on two instructional products—student satisfaction and low-level student learning. But Abrami, Leventhal, and Perry (1982) argued that these laboratory studies suffered shortcomings in both the comprehensiveness of the process variables studied and the representativeness of the values of the process variables manipulated. The laboratory studies lacked comprehensiveness because they failed to represent the many instructor characteristics that may affect ratings and learning. The laboratory manipulations of instructor characteristics lacked representativeness because they failed to represent actual differences among instructors in the field. The lack of both comprehensiveness and representativeness means that laboratory studies cannot be used to estimate the *extent* to which ratings predict student learning. For example, the laboratory findings that instructor expressiveness affects ratings substantially ($r = .70$) and achievement slightly ($r = .12$) suggests only that the correlation between ratings and achievement falls somewhere in the range of $+.84$ to $-.56$. Instead, laboratory studies are best used to explain *why* ratings and achievement are related by identifying the instructional processes which *causally* affect instructional products.

MULTISECTION VALIDATION DESIGN

To date, more than 40 studies have appeared using the multisection validation design. The design has several features that make it high in internal validity. Using class section means rather than students (or students pooled across classes) as the units of analysis emphasizes instructor effects on ratings and achievement. Furthermore, in many of these studies, section differences in student characteristics were controlled experimentally, via random assignment, or statistically, using ability pretests. Similarly, section differences in setting effects were often minimized with the use of a common syllabus, common textbook, similar section sizes, and so on. Finally, the effect of instructor grading standards was reduced by the use of a common examination for all sections. Thus, the design minimizes the extent to which the correlation between student ratings and achievement can be explained by factors other than instructor influences. However, unlike laboratory studies, instructional variables are not manipulated but only measured by the student rating instrument.

One of the strongest features of the design is that the validity criterion, mean section examination performance, is relatively high in external validity. Examination scores are both a direct and important measure of one of the products of effective instruction, designed to assess what students have learned of the course material (and to assign grades). Consequently, we believe that multisection validation designs are especially useful in determining the extent to which ratings of particular instructional processes are valid indices of important instructional products, particularly student learning of course content.

Substantive criticisms of multisection validation designs. Feldman (1989a, 1990) expressed a different view of the value of multisection validity studies:

> Although the data for the present analysis comes from what are called "multisection validity studies," the analysis herein was not an attempt to validate specific ratings of instructors. While it makes sense to seek information about the validity of overall or global ratings of instructors by correlating these ratings with student achievement, it makes less sense to do so for specific ratings because student achievement is not necessarily a direct or meaningful validity criterion for each of the instructional dimensions...

The present analysis accepted the specific rating items, scales, and factors of the studies under review as valid indicators of instructional characteristics. It sought to find out which of them are most highly associated with student achievement under the presumption that the higher the correlation the more facilitative is the instructional characteristic of student achievement. (1989, pp. 624–625)

We do not share completely Feldman's interpretation of the value of multisection validity studies. We agree that understanding the relationship between global ratings and student achievement is extremely important and can be used in judging the validity of global ratings. However, we believe that understanding the relationship between specific ratings and student achievement is also important and can be used to judge the validity of specific ratings since it sheds light on the link between what instructors do when they teach and their impact on students. According to the process-product view, ratings dimensions *are* validated to the extent they reflect instructor-produced student learning.

Methodological criticisms of the multisection design. Abrami (Abrami, Cohen, and d'Apollonia, 1988; Abrami, d'Apollonia and Cohen, 1990) and Marsh (1987; Marsh and Dunkin, 1992) disagree over the strengths of the multisection design. Marsh gives several reasons why the design of multisection validity studies is "inherently weak" and notes that "there are many methodological complications in its actual application" (1987, p. 289). First, the sample size of course sections in any study is almost always quite small, adversely affecting sampling error. Second, variance in achievement scores is mostly attributable to student variables (e.g., ability) and researchers are generally unable to find appreciable effects due to teachers, especially in multisection designs where many of the setting effects are held constant. In addition, the reliability of section average differences is unstudied but may be small and unreliable, attenuating the size of the ratings-achievement correlation. Third, the comparison of findings across different multisection validity studies is problematic since most use different operationalizations both of student ratings and achievement. Fourth, other criteria of teaching effectiveness besides objectively scored tests, and more generally student learning, need to be considered. Fifth, pretest scores on student ability should be used to statistically equate course sections even when students are randomly assigned to the sections, since randomization is not a guarantee of section equivalence. Furthermore, the multisection design does not constitute an experimental design in which students are randomly assigned to treatment groups that are varied systematically in terms of experimentally manipulated variables, and so the advantages of random assignment are not so clear. Finally, the grading satisfaction hypothesis may explain the ratings-achievement correlation. According to the grading satisfaction hypothesis students reward teachers who assign high grades by rating instructors highly regardless of how much students actually learned.

Response to criticisms of the multisection design. We agree with Marsh on several points. First, integrating the findings from the collection of multisection courses helps overcome sample size problems in analyzing single studies. The research we report here and elsewhere is an attempt at such integration. Second, the statistical control of student characteristics in combination with randomization can be superior to randomization alone. However, failing this and faced with a choice of design strategies, we prefer the use of experimental control of nuisance variables over statistical control for two reasons: a) the as-yet unstudied effect of poor randomization on the validity coefficient must certainly be less than when students self-select course sections; and b) statistical control requires that these nuisance variables are known and uncorrelated with instructor effects, while random assignment does not.

Third, we agree that the products of effective instruction are multi-dimensional. But a call for the inclusion of measures other than student learning is not, by itself, an identification of a methodological weakness in multisection designs. It does identify a limitation of existent studies and suggests a direction for future research. Furthermore, the learning measures studied in multisection investigations do represent multiple operationalizations of student learning since test item content varies from study-to-study. Finally, instructor self-ratings, colleague or peer ratings, and the ratings of trained observers could be incorporated into studies employing the multisection design.

We disagree with Marsh on several points. First, the restriction of range problem in the achievement criterion does not hold unless it can be shown that the sample of instructors studied is unrepresentative and the criterion measure lacks sensitivity to instructor effects. Otherwise the experimental control of extraneous influences which affect the criterion is desirable, not undesirable. In both laboratory and field investigations, Abrami (Abrami, Perry, and Leventhal, 1982; Abrami and Mizener, 1985) found that student ratings were more sensitive than student achievement to differences in instruction. Instructors may have genuinely small effects on what students learn. In addition, the use of locally developed or teacher-made tests in some of the validation studies is a double-edged sword. On the one hand, teacher-made tests are likely to be less psychometrically sound but, on the other hand, are often more sensitive to instructor effects than standardized tests.

Second, mono-operationalizations of measures (i.e., using the same instruments throughout) reduce, but do not eliminate, the interpretive problems involved in making inferences across multi-section validity studies. Important uncontrolled differences in student, instructor, course, and setting characteristics may also be responsible for study-to-study differences therefore lowering the internal validity of cross-study comparisons. However, cross-study comparisons can be useful for judging the external validity of findings where it seems reasonable to explore whether different student ratings instruments are correlated with different student learning measures.

Third, the unsystematic nature of the treatment (i.e., differences in instruction) in multisection designs does not detract from the value of random assignment of students. Random assignment helps insure that the relationship between ratings and achievement was produced by differences in instruction rather than differences in students. This insurance of internal validity can be the starting point for further explorations of the treatment. For example, Sullivan and Skanes (1974) used the multisection design to explore the influence of instructor experience on the ratings-achievement relationship.

Finally, the grading satisfaction hypothesis may be one mechanism by which students rate faculty, but it is not an alternative explanation of the validity of ratings when section differences in students are controlled and instructor grading practices, including timing, are uniform across classes. The alleged effect of grading satisfaction will operate consistently, if at all, in each section of a multisection course unless instructors *first* produce differences in student learning. Under these conditions, grading satisfaction cannot explain mean section differences in either student ratings or student achievement. However, the problem is especially pronounced when one is studying multiple classes outside the multisection paradigm where there is more variability in instructor grading practices.[2]

---

[2] Marsh and Dunkin (1992) suggest several fallacies with our reasoning: First, the implicit assumption that all section differences are instructor-produced is completely unrealistic. Even random differences in section mean examination performances will produce inflated validity

MULTITRAIT-MULTIMETHOD DESIGNS

Marsh (1987) and others (Howard, Conway, and Maxwell, 1985) have argued in favor of a MTMM approach to the validation of ratings. To be superior to the multisection design, the MTMM design requires greater control of threats to internal validity, external validity, or both. Specifically, the design must reasonably show that threats to internal validity are controlled in order to attribute class mean differences in ratings and the criterion measures to instructors, and not to extraneous characteristics such as students, the course, and setting variables.

coefficients due to grading satisfaction effects. Second, there is no way to unconfound the influence of grades and satisfaction with grades. Third, the problem is pronounced outside the multisection paradigm and, therefore, the paradigm is unrepresentative. Finally, the reliability of section-average differences in achievement is a critical problem when the section-average scores are similar to one another and within-section differences.

Our response follows: First, if there were unwanted systematic differences in section means they would be much smaller than validation designs without controls for student differences. (The point of our argument has always been that the multisection design is relatively one of the strongest designs, not that it is a perfect design.) It is also unclear what effect random differences in examination performance will have on the ratings-achievement relationship. In general, unsystematic differences tend to attenuate the size of a correlation, whereas Marsh and Dunkin (1992) claim the opposite will occur due to grading satisfaction. It is also the case that inferential statistics were conceived on the notion of random fluctuation both between and within groups. This random fluctuation or sampling error does not need to be zero for valid statistical tests to be performed, although reductions in error variability increase the power or sensitivity of the tests. Random or unsystematic fluctuation, a tolerable problem, is not to be confused with systematic bias or contaminants which are alternative explanations of teacher effects, a more serious problem.

Second, we agree that the grading satisfaction effect cannot be disentangled from the effect of grading per se in existing multisection studies although it could be incorporated into the design of future multisection studies. Our claim is that the temporal sequence of influence (i.e., instructor produced learning affects grades which affects satisfaction which may affect ratings) coupled with the use of uniform grading standards removes grading satisfaction as a source of bias. Marsh's claim is the influence of learning and grade satisfaction on ratings are dissimilar. For example, small differences in learning produce large differences in grading satisfaction which, in turn, have a meaningful impact on student ratings. Thus, if this were the case it would be seen in individual validation studies incorporating a grading standards variable or by comparing multisection validation studies where grading standards were not uniform with validation studies where grading standards were uniform.

Finally, we believe that Marsh's concern for the reliability of section mean differences in achievement should be extended both to all student ratings and criterion measures and to all designs, not only multisection validation designs, using the correct unit of analysis for exploring instructor influences which is the class mean or section average. For example, in 1990 we wrote: "if we adjusted a validity coefficient of .43 (which is the average value reported by P.A. Cohen, 1981, for overall instructor ratings) for the reliability of ratings (estimated to be .70), the corrected coefficient would be .51. If we then adjusted the validity coefficient further for an equal degree of error in the criterion measure, the corrected coefficient would be .61" (Abrami et al., 1990, p. 227).

This can be partly achieved if the criterion measures of effective instruction—possibly instructor self-ratings, alumni or former student ratings, peer ratings, and ratings of trained observers—are less sensitive to extraneous influences than course examinations. If so, one may compute the validity correlation between student ratings and scores on the criterion measure(s) for a host of courses, not just multisection ones, and may thereby greatly enhance external validity. But without evidence to the contrary, designs which do not control statistically or experimentally for extraneous influences on the criterion do not represent good alternatives to the multisection validation design in concluding that differences in the criterion measure were caused by instructors. Furthermore, these designs do not control for extraneous influences on student ratings. Thus, even if it could be shown that the criterion was unaffected, the validity coefficient might be affected.

To show advantages in external validity, one must also show that the alternatives to student learning such as instructor self-ratings, former student ratings, and peer ratings represent adequate product measures of instruction. Yet whether these measures (and student ratings) represent adequate criteria of effective instruction has been seriously questioned (Gaski, 1987). Maxwell and Howard (1987) acknowledge these criticisms as well-taken (see also Feldman, 1989b). In our view, such measures help establish the validity of ratings as measures of teaching processes but not as measures of the products of instruction.

Thus, we conclude the MTMM validation designs provide weaker evidence for the validity of student ratings as measures of instructional effectiveness than multisection validation designs. The MTMM designs are generally weaker in internal validity and employ criterion measures which are either less defensible as or less important measures of good teaching than student learning.

THE CHOICE OF DESIGNS

In choosing among research designs, one must consider whether threats to internal and external validity are addressed. The multisection validation design has advantages over MTMM designs in determining whether ratings reflect instructional processes and products. The multi-section design is generally higher in internal validity and typically incorporates an important product measure of effective instruction, student learning, contributing to its external validity. The multisection design is also superior to laboratory studies when the validity question addresses the practical concern of the degree to which ratings predict teacher-produced outcomes in typical classroom settings. For these reasons, multisection validation studies are singularly important to concerns about validity and deserve special attention.

MULTISECTION VALIDITY STUDIES: WHAT HAVE THEY TOLD US SO FAR?

What can one conclude about the validity of ratings from multisection validation studies? Do global ratings predict student learning? Are there particular instructional processes, as reflected in student ratings, which are related to student learning or other outcomes? Are the findings from the collection of studies uniform? If not, are there substantive or methodological features that explain variability in study findings? Do reviewers agree on what the findings mean? Is there more to learn: Are there inadequacies in either the literature or reviews of the literature?

THE RELATIONSHIP BETWEEN RATINGS AND STUDENT LEARNING

Abrami, Cohen, and d'Apollonia (1988) compared six published, quantitative reviews of the findings from multisection designs (Abrami, 1984; Cohen, 1981, 1982, 1983; Dowell and Neal, 1982; McCallum, 1984) to identify their agreements and disagreements. Unfortunately, the reviews differed in several important ways including: a) the specification of the criteria used to include studies; b) comprehensiveness or the extent to which each review included studies meeting inclusion criteria (where the proportion of studies included per review ranged from .13 to .88); c) the presence and completeness of study feature coding used to explain study-to-study variability; d) the extraction and calculation of individual study outcomes (where there was only 47% agreement among the reviews); and e) procedures for data analysis, especially variability in study outcomes. These difference help explain why the conclusions reached by the reviewers were markedly different:

> The present meta-analysis provides strong support for the validity of student ratings as measures of teaching effectiveness. Teachers whose students do well on achievement measures receive higher instructional ratings than teachers whose students do poorly. This study demonstrates that the relationship between ratings and achievement is slightly stronger and more consistent than was previously thought. (Cohen, 1981, pp. 300–301)

> The literature can be seen as yielding unimpressive estimates of the validity of student ratings. The literature does not support claims that the validity of ratings is a consistent quantity across situations. Rather the evidence suggests that the validity of student ratings is modest at best and quite variable. (Dowell and Neal, 1982, p. 59)

There have been further attempts to summarize the findings from the multisection validity studies and analyze variability in study findings (Abrami and d'Apollonia, 1987, 1988; Abrami, d'Apollonia and Cohen, 1990; Cohen, 1986, 1987; d'Apollonia and Abrami, 1987, 1988; Feldman, 1989a, 1990). The average validity coefficients found by the reviewers using two different coding schemes for categorizing the results from different rating forms are presented in Tables 3 and 4.

Collectively, the results of the reviews suggest that some specific rating dimensions, as well as student global ratings, are moderately correlated with student learning in multisection college courses. On average, there exists a reasonable, but far from perfect, relationship between some student ratings and learning. To a moderate extent, student ratings are able to identify those instructors whose students learn best. Furthermore, regardless of the coding scheme used, the average of global ratings of instructional effectiveness explains a greater percentage of variance in student learning than the average of specific ratings. It also appears that not all specific ratings are related to achievement; for example, ratings of course difficulty generally do not predict student achievement at all. Consequently, we recommend

Table 3: Mean Validity Coefficients in the Multisection Validity Studies: Cohen Dimensions (Cohen, 1987)

Type	Dimension	N[1]	VC[2]	Mean	SE[3]	Range
Global	Overall Instructor	59	0.44	0.45	0.012	[0.44, 0.48]
	Overall Course	21	0.48			
	Skill	44	0.41			
	Rapport	35	0.30			
	Structure	29	0.55			
	Difficulty	25	0.00			
Specific	Interaction	20	0.45	0.34	0.053	[0.00, 0.55]
	Feedback	7	0.29			
	Evaluation	25	0.23			
	Learning Progress	17	0.46			
	Interest/Motivation	12	0.26			

Table 4: Mean Validity Coefficients in the Multisection Validity Studies: Feldman Dimensions (d'Apollonia, and Abrami, 1988)

Type	Dimension	N[1]	VC[2]	Mean	SE[3]	Range
Global	Overall instructor	44	0.30	0.32	0.019	[0.30, 0.36]
	Overall course	18	0.36			
	Stimulates interest	34	0.37			
	Enthusiasm	11	0.25			
	Knowledge	12	0.21			
	Expansiveness	4	0.03			
	Preparation	33	0.43			
	Clarity/understandable	46	0.42			
	Elocutionary skills	8	0.26			
	Concern for progress	19	0.30			
	Clarity of objectives	25	0.33			
	Course materials	19	0.29			
	Supplemental materials	12	0.17			
Specific	Perceived outcome	32	0.39	0.20	0.015	[0.03, 0.45]
	Instructor's fairness	29	0.31			
	Personality	4	0.45			
	Feedback	15	0.11			
	Openness	27	0.29			
	Intellectual challenge	11	0.34			
	Concern for students	26	0.24			
	Availability	22	0.30			
	Course difficulty/workload	29	0.03			
	Classroom management	13	0.13			
	General	16	0.31			

using the results of specific rating dimensions to judge which teachers best promote student learning with caution especially when making promotion and tenure decisions. The same caution is not necessary when using global ratings of instruction.

Finally, the nature and number of the specific rating dimensions used in the two schemes appears different. In the Cohen (1987) coding scheme, the findings are arranged according to two global dimensions and nine specific dimensions. This coding scheme is not without limitations. For example, it relies on the factor analytic findings from a single instrument (Isaacson et al., 1964) which may not allow the results from all instruments to be properly represented. This may have resulted in validity coefficients being either forced into categories, creating heterogeneous categories, or dropped from the meta-analysis.

d'Apollonia and Abrami (1988) used Feldman's scheme to report the average validity coefficients for 22 specific rating dimensions, more than twice the number reported by Cohen. This coding scheme has been used and refined repeatedly by Feldman (1976, 1983, 1984, 1989a) using a conceptual approach to comprehensively represent the items from many forms without preference toward any one instrument or its factor structure. Nevertheless, questions remain about which way to organize items and whether any coding scheme can be empirically validated.

d'Apollonia and Abrami (1988) and Abrami et al. (1990) also observed that the multisection studies contained a large number of validity coefficients that were not all represented when other reviewers reported mean coefficients. In 43 multisection validation studies we found a total of 742 ratings-achievement correlations reported. Yet only a small fraction of these correlations were included in other reviews.

LOOKING FURTHER AT THE MULTISECTION VALIDITY STUDIES

Research integrations are seldom necessary when the findings in an area are uniform. Reviews become necessary especially when the results of research on a topic appear heterogeneous. The research findings from the multisection validity studies seem to vary widely. The range of reported validity coefficients is −0.75 to +0.92. There is one study finding of a strong negative relationship between ratings and achievement—the highest rated instructors had the lowest performing students. There is also one study finding showing the opposite, a near perfect positive relationship between ratings and achievement. In a quantitative review, the reviewer searches for ways to explain the variability in study findings. The range of findings in the multisection validity studies is a reason to explore the findings further to explain these inconsistencies.

Cohen (1981) was the first quantitative reviewer to attempt a systematic exploration of the variability in study findings. He explored the relationship between 20 study and methodological features of the primary research and the validity coefficients extracted from this research. Three of the features together accounted for approximately thirty percent of the variance in the validity coefficients for Overall Instructor ratings: control for bias in evaluating achievement (i.e., Was the test graded by the instructor?); time at which ratings were administered (i.e., Were the ratings collected before final grades?); and instructor experience (i.e., Were the instructors graduate students?).

416

Abrami et al. (1990) examined these findings further. First, they showed that individual study features did not explain a significant amount of variability in the validity coefficients because of low statistical power. The analyses often lacked the sensitivity necessary to identify characteristics that explain a medium size effect on the relationship between ratings and achievement. More of the study features might prove to be useful predictors in future if either additional primary studies are conducted or more powerful statistical procedures of research integration were employed. Until then, one can neither accept nor reject claims that these other explanatory factors are trivial.

Second, the 20 study features employed by Cohen (1981) to explain variability in validity outcomes did not generalize across global and specific aspects of teaching. Since rating factors are regarded by some as distinct and uncorrelated (e.g., Marsh, 1987) there is little reason to suspect that these factors will be uniformly affected by biasing characteristics. Characteristics that predicted the relationship between student perceptions of teaching and instructor impacts on learning varied with the aspect of teaching being investigated. Unfortunately, the precise nature of this pattern of effects could not be elaborated. (For one, the sample sizes were too small to confidently make fine distinctions.) However, the findings were sufficiently clear to urge users of multidimensional rating forms away from the common practice of universally controlling for "biasing" characteristics (e.g., course level) and further complicate the use of specific ratings in summative decisions about teaching.

Third, Abrami et al. (1990) employed nomological coding to identify the investigated, accounted for, and mentioned characteristics in the forty-three validity studies. They uncovered 75 study features that could be used to explain variability in the findings of the multi-section validity studies. Since this was a substantial increase in the explanatory features used previously (almost four times the number of factors explored by Cohen, 1981), Abrami et al. (1990) concluded that prior reviews did not comprehensively identify potential predictive characteristics.

WHERE DO WE GO FROM HERE?

Reviews of the multisection validity studies on the relationship between ratings and achievement suggest there is much yet to be learned of the relationship between what instructors do when they teach and how this affects student learning and other products of instruction. Abrami

417

et al. (1990) recommended that another quantitative review should be undertaken with alternative systems for coding the rating dimensions, the use of the 75 study features they identified, and more powerful analysis strategies (e.g., tests of homogeneity, Hedges and Olkin, 1985) using the 742 validity coefficients extracted from the literature. As a major step in this process, we first embarked on research to identify the common dimensions of teaching as represented in the rating forms used in the multisection validity studies. Before presenting the results of the integration of many forms, we discuss some of the complications with the factor analysis of a single form.

FACTOR ANALYSIS AND THE DIMENSIONS OF EFFECTIVE INSTRUCTION

Recent research by Marsh (1991) attempted to address questions about the dimensionality of student ratings through the application of confirmatory factor analysis (CFA). Using data from a single rating form—the SEEQ—Marsh (1991) evaluated four higher-order factor models. The results provided support for the nine first-order factors the SEEQ is designed to measure and, of the higher-order models, particularly for the four factor approach. Marsh concluded:

Considerable information is lost when the student ratings are summarized with a single score or even a small number of scores. The challenge for future research—particularly in terms of personnel decisions—is how to most appropriately use the information that is available in student ratings rather than throw it away. (Marsh, 1991, p. 13).

The validity of this conclusion rests in large part on the adequacy of the SEEQ to represent the qualities of effective teaching. As is evident from Abrami, d'Apollonia and Cohen (1990), different student rating forms assess different dimensions of effective instruction. This point is also demonstrated by Marsh (1991, see Table 1, p. 15) where the dimensional categories of the Endeavor rating form (Frey, 1978) were compared with the SEEQ and shown to be different. It is also not surprising that Marsh's (1991) confirmatory analyses generally conform to prior analyses with the same instrument—they amount to grand tests of instrument reliability. What is surprising is that the nine factor a priori model... "is not fully adequate" (Marsh, 1991, p. 9).

In addition, note that Marsh (1991) was able to describe not one but four higher order models from prior research and reviews. But even these models do not adequately describe the diversity and complexity of findings regarding the dimensionality of instruction. In his reviews of student rating forms, Feldman (1976, 1988) noted that rating form items are often intercorrelated despite their apparent conceptual independence. For example, the instructor's stimulation of interest, clarity and comprehensibility, course preparation, and organization and enthusiasm are frequently highly correlated. Kulik and McKeachie's (1975) review of student ratings suggested a general Skill factor on which many items (including global items) load highly. Global items are included in the specific factors from the SEEQ: *Overall course rating* is included in the *Learning/Value* factor and *Overall instructor rating* is included in the *Instructor Enthusiasm* factor. These interrelationships among items and between global items and specific factors create interpretive difficulties when one argues for the dimensionality of instruction. Should one interpret this covariance to mean that specific dimensional ratings predict global ratings or that students' responses to specific items are influenced by their overall assessments? Indeed, Feldman's reviews have often been predicated on the assumption that specific dimensional ratings should predict student global ratings.

LIMITATIONS OF FACTOR ANALYSIS

Implicit in Marsh's conclusion is that CFA can "disconfirm" the theory that a few general or global dimensions capture the structure of student ratings. An alternative conclusion is that it is not the theory which needs revision but the instruments and methods used in testing it.

The use of factor analysis alone to determine the structure of a phenomenon is inconclusive since different analysis methods are based on different assumptions. Each analysis is, therefore, designed to "discover" the structure favored by the assumptions. For example, principal components extraction, the most frequently used extraction method, was pioneered by Spearman to extract mutually independent components such that the first or principal component resolves the maximum amount of variance with subsequent factors explaining progressively less variance. Thus, factor analysis without rotation is designed to resolve one general or global component explaining most of the variance and a few less important, subsidiary components. Thurstone objected to this hierarchical interpretation of the components and developed rotation to redistribute the variance explained by the general factor over the subsidiary factors. This increased the variance the subsidiary factors explained.

419

The two solutions resolve exactly the same amount of total variance, therefore, which one "best" describes reality cannot be determined empirically. Moreover, both solutions are affected by the choice of items in the instrument(s) in question. The selection of unique items that are highly positively correlated favors a principal components solution while the selection of clusters of similar items favors a rotated solution elucidating a number of equally important factors. Clearly, the use of any one student rating form in a CFA is not an adequate test for the presence of a particular higher order factor structure. An adequate test requires the use of a diversity of student ratings.

SECONDARY ANALYSES OF SEEQ DATA

There are a number of decisions made during a factor analysis that affect the final results and their interpretation. Some of these are: a) the items included in the correlation matrix, b) the number of factors extracted, c) whether the axes are rotated, d) if rotated, whether rotated orthogonally or obliquely, and e) if oblique rotation is selected, the degree of obliqueness. In order to investigate the possibility that Marsh's conclusions reflected his methodological choices rather than the multidimensionality of instruction (as determined by the SEEQ), Abrami and d'Apollonia (1991) conducted a secondary analysis of the SEEQ data from Marsh and Hocevar (1984) and replicated in Marsh (1991). Marsh and Hocevar (1984) obtained a nine factor solution using oblique rotation with delta set at approximately −2.0.

Abrami and d'Apollonia (1991) reconstructed the reproduced correlation matrix by premultiplying the factor pattern correlation matrix by the oblique factor matrix and postmultiplying it by the transpose of the oblique factor pattern matrix (Tabachnick and Fidell, 1983). Abrami and d'Apollonia (1991) estimated the observed correlation matrix by replacing the diagonal elements of the reproduce correlation matrix with 1's. Since the communalities were very high, they were able to replicate the results within rounding error. They then factor analyzed the correlation matrix of the 35 items using SPSS (SPSS Inc., 1990).

The results of the Abrami and d'Apollonia re-analysis (see Table 5) were: a) Thirty-one of the items load highly on the principal component (> .63) with Overall Instructor and Overall Course being the most highly loading items (both .94), indicating that the first component was a general or global factor. This global factor explained almost 60% of the total variance in ratings. The four remaining items, concerning course difficulty and workload, loaded heavily on a second component

Table 5: Nonrotated Factor Pattern Matrix with Six Components Extracted via Principal Components Analysis[1]

SEEQ Item	Factor loadings on first six components					
	I	II	III	IV	V	VI
Course challenging	.893	.392	.017	−.109	.037	−.056
Learned something valuable	.873	.262	.021	−.148	.133	−.080
Increased subject interest	.868	.122	−.013	−.226	.153	−.031
Understood subject matter	.760	−.182	−.094	−.167	.201	−.142
Overall course rating	.940	.176	−.032	−.085	.017	−.120
Enthusiastic about teaching	.886	.017	.039	−.082	−.308	−.073
Dynamic and energetic	.875	.104	.045	−.133	−.324	−.156
Enhanced presentation with humor	.787	.009	.039	−.158	−.315	−.152
Teaching style held interest	.884	.075	.012	−.147	−.249	−.208
Overall instructor rating	.941	.058	−.037	−.024	−.181	−.105
Explanations clear	.868	−.057	−.180	−.076	−.072	−.121
Materials prepared and clear	.857	.065	−.300	.052	−.064	−.060
Objectives stated and pursued	.855	.130	−.255	.125	.056	−.094
Lectures facilitated note taking	.649	.153	−.485	.118	−.158	.043
Encouraged class discussions	.741	−.390	.389	−.233	.104	−.068
Students shared ideas/knowledge	.688	−.479	.394	−.226	.136	−.046
Encouraged questions and answers	.852	−.303	.237	−.108	.047	−.070
Encouraged expression of ideas	.780	−.414	.349	−.131	.084	−.016
Friendly towards students	.769	−.370	.256	.258	−.097	.117
Welcomed seeking help or advice	.756	−.310	.246	.393	−.122	.184
Interested in individual students	.817	−.277	.261	.303	−.089	.117
Accessible to individual students	.678	−.180	.138	.471	−.108	.298
Contrasted implications	.803	.010	−.205	−.156	−.016	.418
Gave background of ideas/concepts	.819	−.024	−.237	−.201	.033	.398
Gave different points of view	.818	−.107	−.207	−.158	.060	.375
Discussed current developments	.743	.035	−.142	−.270	.030	.340
Examination feedback valuable	.776	−.061	−.163	.336	.064	−.182
Examination methods fair	.808	−.149	−.163	.328	.069	−.146
Exams emphasized course content	.794	−.064	−.242	.289	.071	−.187
Readings/texts valuable	.639	.168	−.045	.131	.563	−.018
Added to course understanding	.754	.175	−.007	.122	.476	−.098
Course difficulty	.333	.840	.181	.075	−.068	.046
Course workload	.336	.793	.351	.037	.034	.065
Course pacing	.238	.794	.182	.092	−.100	.037
Hours/week outside class	.305	.726	.384	.068	.065	.115
Factor eigenvalues	20.67	3.95	1.75	1.42	1.18	1.05
% variance explained	59.1	11.3	5.0	4.0	3.4	1.9

Source: Abrami and d'Apollonia (1991), p. 414.

which explained an additional 11% of the variance. Interestingly, Cohen (1981) found that course difficulty items were poor in construct validity, predicting student learning near zero. The remaining four components explained only 5%, 4%, 3%, and 2%, respectively, and did not contain any items that did not load heavily on one of the first two factors.

In response, Marsh (1991) claimed that the most serious problem with the critiques of Abrami and d'Apollonia (1991) and Abrami (1988, 1989a, 1989b) was the failure to operationalize criteria for unidimensionality or multidimensionality. Further, Marsh claimed that. . ." the most defensible approach to evaluating unidimensionality is to test the existence of one latent trait underlying the data" (Marsh, 1991, p. 417). Consequently, one purpose of our analysis of the collection of rating forms was to explore the underlying nature of student perceptions of instruction across many rating forms as the first step towards testing the existence of one global trait.

In the past, Abrami (1985, 1988, 1989a, 1989b) and Abrami, d'Apollonia and Cohen (1990, 1991) have been critical of the methodological and substantive difficulties with factor-analytic research on student ratings. These problems have not led us to deny that teaching is multidimensional—it clearly is—but to suggest that research to date does not justify the use of factor scores from a single instrument in making summative decisions about teaching effectiveness. By determining whether there exists a "common" core among the collection of rating forms used in multisection validation studies we believe we will take a step toward overcoming some of the limitations described above.

THE DIMENSIONALITY OF INSTRUCTION: IS THERE A "COMMON" CORE?

In this section we explore the unidimensionality-multidimensionality issue further by applying the techniques of quantitative synthesis to a collection of student rating forms. In this way, we will be able to explore the dimensionality of ratings with a higher degree of generalizability than ever attempted before.

A problem that reviewers of the multisection validity literature face is that there appears no consensus, across student rating forms, of what constitutes the structure or dimensionality of instructional effectiveness as perceived by students. The effectiveness of postsecondary instruction is, like the elephant in *The Blind Men and the Elephant* (John Godfrey Saxe), a beast with many different characteristics. Each reviewer has attempted to examine this issue, and like the blind men of the poem, is convinced that he/she has discovered the true and accurate representation. What the following analysis attempts is to fit together the pieces to form a picture. But the analogy of the blind men and the elephant is not entirely correct. Each researcher does not hold only a unique piece of the puzzle but rather may hold some pieces in common with one or more other researchers, as well as some unique pieces.

The question of the dimensionality or structure of instructional effectiveness across student rating forms can be approached in two ways: conceptually or empirically. In a conceptual or logical approach, theoretical models are used to develop a hierarchical structure or taxonomy. Borich (1977) suggests three stages in the development of a valid system of evaluating teacher effectiveness. The first stage is to search the literature for significant relationships and rationally select promising behaviors and skills. The second stage is to build a nomological network indicating antecedent, intervening and terminal behaviors, to test the validity of the above relationships, and to sequentially order the behaviors and skills. The third stage is to construct a taxonomy or hierarchy of behaviors emphasizing the important distinctions and minimizing the superfluous ones. Thus, the three stages are: selecting variables on the basis of the literature, chunking variables on the basis of relationships, and proposing higher-order structures on the basis of theory. The proposed hierarchical relationships among variables can then be empirically tested on a second sample via confirmatory factor analysis (CFA) or linear structured relationships (LISREL) (Hill, 1984).

There have been some studies attempting to elucidate empirically the structure of the student rating forms used in the multisection validity literature (Widlak et al., 1973; Kulik and McKeachie, 1975; Marsh, 1987, 1991). However, in general, one student rating form is factor analyzed and no attempt is made to compare it's factor structure to those of other rating forms purporting to measure the same dimensions of effective instruction. One exception is Marsh (1987) who commented on the similarity of specific factors in a number of student rating forms. However, this was done on the basis of a logical analysis and not empirically. Marsh (1991) analyzed logically the correspondence among the SEEQ, the Endeavor and Feldman's categories. He concluded that: Feldman's categories were much more specific than factors from either the SEEQ or the Endeavor; the SEEQ represented more of Feldman's categories than the Endeavor represented; and many SEEQ factors contained more than one Feldman category.

In the last few years, we have been using multivariate approaches to meta-analysis to explore the "common" factor structure across multiple student rating forms (Rosenfield, d'Apollonia, and Abrami, 1993; d'Apollonia, Abrami, and Rosenfield, 1993). Thus, we have combined both conceptual and empirical approaches. Figure 1 illustrates our goals. Take the large rectangle that surrounds the illustration. This represents all the qualities of teaching that could be represented in student rating forms. Any one rating form is represented by a smaller rectangle. Hence, two rating forms are illustrated in the figure. Each rating form rectangle is a subset of the whole. Furthermore, the rating form rectangles do not perfectly overlap, suggesting they represent somewhat different aspects of instruction. The circle within each rating form rectangle represents the rating form variability explained by a particular factor analysis of student responses to the rating form. Finally, there is an area of overlap between the circles representing the two rating forms. This is what is common to the factor analyses of the two rating forms. The non-intersecting part of the two circles represents what is unique to each of the factor analyses.

Figure 1: Hypothetical illustration of the underlying traits "common" to two rating forms.

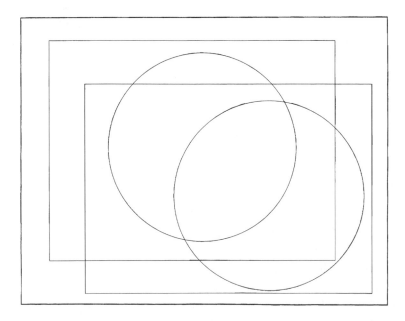

Now, imagine a more complex figure with 17 rating form rectangles and their 17 circles within. Bits of intersecting circles represent what is common to two or more rating forms. But the union of all the circles represents the qualities of teaching represented by factors underlying all of the forms together.[3]

"COMMON" DIMENSIONS OF TEACHING

We decided to employ the Feldman coding scheme to further explore the dimensionality of student ratings of instruction and the validity of those dimensions to predict the products of instruction, particularly, student achievement. We found several difficulties with the scheme: a) lack of operational definitions for the categories (use of exemplars only); b) high intercoder agreement by us (Cohen's kappa = .93) but lower agreement (.60) with items categorized by Feldman; and c) internal inconsistencies including ambiguity, multidimensionality, and overlap among the categories. Using Feldman's coding scheme as the basis of our work, we decided to revise the scheme using the following principles:

1. The coding scheme should not be ambiguous. The categories used to code items should be clear, comprehensive and succinct. The categories should be of more or less equal breadth.
2. The bipolar values of a category should be contained within it; for example, clear and unclear presentations, authoritarian and participatory class management, etc.
3. Both the product and the process orientations to a teaching behavior should be in the same category; for example, the instructor presenting the subject as interesting and the students being interested in the subject.
4. Since global evaluations (course instructor, perceived learning) are included, the remaining categories should only include specific statements.

We defined our coding scheme based upon the 1,184 items collected from the student rating forms used in the *multisection validity studies*. Two coders subsequently coded the above items and obtained a 91.5%

---

[3] For methodological reasons associated with the aggregated correlation matrix, we were only able to examine that part of the union of the 17 circles that lay entirely encompassed within the largest circle.

intercoder agreement. The items from the *factor analytic studies* are a subset of the above items. The definition of each category is presented in Appendix A, beginning on page 253. The appendix also includes all items whose correlation were used to form the aggregate correlation matrix.

Collection of Factor Studies

We first collected studies that reported either complete factor matrices or correlation matrices for the student rating forms used in the multi-section validity studies. We collected seventeen studies representing most of the rating forms in the validity set (excluding the in-house forms). One student rating form, the form used by Wherry (1951), supplied almost 50% of the items in the data set. It thus furnished a large portion of the interitem correlation coefficients. As expected, the global items are underrepresented in the factor set relative to the validity set.

Extraction and Coding of Outcomes

The outcome variables of interest for the integration of factor studies are the interitem correlation coefficients for each student rating form. These were estimated from the reproduced correlation matrices computed from the factor loading matrix of the items in the student rating forms (if rotated orthogonally), or from the pattern matrix and factor correlation matrix (if rotated obliquely). The 458 items from the factor studies were initially placed into 40 categories. These categories are listed and briefly defined in Appendix A.

Pruning and Synthesis of Aggregate Correlation Matrix

In order to aggregate the interitem correlation coefficients, one must first establish that the values being aggregated are homogeneous. If the set is not homogeneous, the (weighted) mean correlation does not properly represent the set of studies. There are a number of possible causes for heterogeneity: a) the items are ambiguous and/or multidimensional; b) the categories are ambiguous and/or multidimensional; and c) the relationship between items varies with setting, subject, etc.

    The first two reasons speak to technical problems with the coding schema and certain student rating forms. Unfortunately, these problems confound questions concerning the dimensionality of

426

effective instruction. Therefore, if one wishes to address the latter question, one must first reduce these technical problems. We therefore, eliminated (pruned) items and categories that were heterogeneous in the following manner.

We pruned items and categories from our data set in two stages. In the first stage we eliminated items that contributed to "poor" correlations between items belonging to the same category. We subdivided the complete set of interitem correlations (21,383 correlations) into 40 sets of interitem correlations between items belonging to the same category. We assumed that if the categories were unidimensional and generalizable, sets of interitem correlation coefficients should be uniform across student rating forms and the mean interitem correlation coefficient for the set should approach 1.0. In other words, the mean interitem correlation coefficient for the subset is analogous to a reliability coefficient. For each set, we identified items that contributed to correlations that were below 0.5, or that lowered the mean interitem correlation coefficient for a category consistently below .65. We scrutinized these items for ambiguous wording, reversed polarity, negative wording, compound statements, etc. We subsequently dropped these items. For each set, we continued pruning until the set was homogeneous (*i.e.* the coefficient of variability was .20 or less). We eliminated three categories, *appropriate use of materials, low-level cognitive outcomes*, and *overall learning* because of insufficient data.

In the second stage we eliminated items that contributed to heterogeneous correlations between items in different categories. This is a more difficult task in that since the correlations for items belonging to different categories are not known we can no longer assume that the correlations should approach 1. However, we can still expect that there should be a tight cluster of values about the weighted mean.

We subsequently subdivided the remaining 8,131 correlations into 666 sets representing the intercorrelations between items belonging to different categories. Taking one set at a time, we identified the items that contributed to correlations at the extremes of the distribution. We eliminated those items that consistently contributed to the heterogeneity of the set. Finally, after all pruning had been done, we reviewed all decisions to see if later decisions to drop items would allow us to reinsert some dropped items. Note that two items contributed to a correlation that was an "outlier." In some cases the "poor" item could be easily identified because of poor wording, double negatives, compound items, etc. However in other cases, the choice of item to be eliminated was somewhat arbitrary. That is, there is not one unique set of items which if eliminated produce homogeneous sets. Rather, there are a number of possible sets. Moreover, interitem correlations exist only between items in the same student rating form. Therefore the distribution of items per category/per rating form influences which items can be considered for elimination. That is, there have to be at least two items within a category from the same rating form for either item to be considered for pruning at the first stage. Therefore, some of the items that were retained at both pruning stages were retained not because they are "superior" items, but rather because they were never considered for elimination.

In addition, we eliminated two more categories, *time management* and *workload*, because we were not able to reduce the heterogeneity without deleting all the items in some sets. Less than 2% of the 595 sets that remained are heterogeneous. We decided not to drop any other categories or items since they did not consistently produce heterogeneity across all sets.

Thus, we constructed a 35 by 35 correlation matrix. This matrix represented the aggregation of 6,788 interitem correlations computed for 225 items from 17 rating forms. These items, sorted by category, are presented in Appendix A.

Of the 40 Feldman instructional categories, only five were missing from this correlation matrix because of either excessive heterogeneity or insufficient data. These five categories were: *appropriate use of methods/materials, low-level cognitive outcomes, overall learning, time management* and *workload*.

Factor Analysis

Factors were extracted from the aggregate correlation matrix produced above using SPSS (SPSS Inc., 1990). Factors with eigenvalues greater than 1.0 were extracted. The solution was then rotated obliquely using OBLIMIN with a delta of .2. Four factors were extracted via principal components extraction. The percent variance extracted by each factor, in decreasing magnitude, were 62.8%, 4.2%, 3.7, and 2.9%. Of the 35 categories, all except *course objectives, knowledge of domain*, and *supervision and disciplinary activities* had loadings of at least .62 on the first component. Thus there clearly is a large general factor which explains about 63% of the variance in student ratings.

In order to improve interpretability, the solution was rotated obliquely; thus, the variance was redistributed over the four factors.

The four factors, in order of importance as judged by the sum of squared loadings, are described below.

Thirteen categories load on Factor 1 (loadings > .55): *choice of supplementary materials, relevance of instruction, overall course, monitoring learning, general knowledge and cultural attainment, research productivity and reputation, motivating students to greater effort, enthusiasm for teaching, high-level cognitive outcomes, clarity of instruction, stimulation of interest, preparation,* and *management style.* We note that most of these categories pertain to the instructor viewed in an instructional role. The sum of the squared loadings is 8.0 and, therefore, this factor appears to be the most important factor in instructional effectiveness.

Sixteen categories load on factor 2 (loadings > .38): *personal appearance, health, and attire, general attitudes, dramatic delivery, concern for students, vocal delivery, answering questions, knowledge of teaching, tolerance of diversity, availability, overall instructor, interaction and discussion, respect for others, enthusiasm for students, friendly classroom climate, enthusiasm for subject,* and *personality characteristics.* We note that most of these categories pertain to the instructor viewed as a person. The sum of the squared loadings is 5.6 and, therefore, the second factor is almost as important as the first factor.

Two categories load on Factor 3 (loadings > .75): *evaluation* and *feedback.* We note that these two categories pertain to the instructor viewed as a regulator. The sum of the squared loadings is 2.5 and, therefore, this factor is considerably less important than the previous two.

Four categories load on Factor 4. These are *supervision and disciplinary actions, knowledge of domain, choice of required materials,* and *objectives.* The sum of the squared loadings is 1.8 and, therefore, this factor is the least important factor. We note that it is difficult to interpret this factor, but it is considerably less important than the previous three and may not be stable. It is also the only factor that is not correlated with the other factors.

Since we aggregated items within categories and factor analyzed relatively homogeneous categories, one would expect to extract "higher-order" factors representing the "common" aspects of instruction across situations. We extracted 62.8% of the variance across the interitem correlations in the first principal component. All items load heavily on this component, suggesting it is an overall instructional skill factor. Such a general skill factor has been proposed by Kulik and McKeachie (1975). Rotation results in the redistribution of variance such that three correlated factors emerged, along with one subsidiary uncorrelated factor. These three correlated factors are similar to the three factors proposed by Widlak, McDaniel, and Feldhusen (1973) describing three roles: instructor, actor, and director. They subsequently factor analyzed responses to the 18 item Course-Instructor-Evaluation form from Purdue and obtained three highly correlated factors.

Feldman (1976) also investigated the pattern of relationships among factors from 60 factor studies. He reported that "despite the profusion of connections..., a fairly consistent and meaningful pattern does emerge: indeed, this pattern supports the view of Widlak et al. (1973) that instructors primarily enact three different roles." Feldman called these roles presentation, facilitation, and regulation.

To address concerns related to both the number of items pruned and the possibility of alternative pruned sets, we ran similar factor analyses of the complete data set, and alternative pruned sets. In all cases the same general factor emerged. Differences occurred primarily in those categories having moderate loadings (e.g., those mentioned above as loading on two factors).

Our factor analysis across the multiple rating forms indicates that there is a "common" structure to instructional effectiveness. Four factors were obtained, three of which were highly correlated. Global items were loaded highly on the first two factors.

The finding that the factors were correlated may obscure setting differences. For example, some students (e.g., engineering students in calculus classes) may respond favorably to the clarity of instruction and give especially high mean ratings for clarity, while other students (e.g., psychology students in clinical classes) may respond favorably to an interactive classroom climate and give especially high mean ratings for interaction and discussion. Despite situational differences in mean ratings, a "common" correlated factor structure would emerge.

Whatever the reason for the high correlations between the factors, the finding that there is such a large global component and that it is highly correlated with the other components argues against the utility of using specific factors or teaching categories to make summative assessments of instruction. We believe that the logical and empirical analyses already presented by us and others provide support for a large, underlying general trait "effective teaching" although it may not be the only trait. In addition, we believe that effective teaching is multi-dimensional but that there is inconsistency concerning the teaching dimensions, particularly across rating forms (i.e., operationalizations of different latent traits). This inconsistency suggests that any one of the existing multidimensional rating forms may not represent teaching for all instructors, courses, and settings. Therefore, we recommend that specific ratings should be used cautiously for summative decisions about teaching. If one uses an existing rating form, computing a composite score based on the categories and items that formed the general factor of our analysis would appear to be superior to using separate dimensional scores. If one prepares a customized form, only those items and categories that loaded highly on the first principal component of our analysis should be included and their scores averaged. Finally, it remains our opinion that the best alternative to averaging across specific items is to base summative decisions of teaching effectiveness on global ratings.

CONCLUSIONS

Numerous studies have explored the dimensions of effective college instruction. Yet there remain notable disagreements regarding whether and how data from multidimensional student rating forms should be used in summative decisions about teaching. This paper critically examined a host of issues associated with the dimensions of instructional effectiveness as reflected in student ratings of teaching. We discussed effective teaching from both product and process views. From the product view, effective teaching can be defined as the positive cognitive, affective, and/or psychomotor changes produced in students. From the process view, effective teaching can be defined as the teaching activities that occur both before (preparatory) and during (delivery) teaching. We subsequently discussed the need for research exploring the impact of process variables on product variables. The second section provided a general discussion of methods for empirically determining effective teaching. The third section concentrated on the strengths and weaknesses of three validation designs—the laboratory design, the multisection design and the multitrait-multimethod design. The fourth section summarized the quantitative literature reviews of the 43 multisection validity studies. Finally, the fifth section considered factor analysis and the dimensions of effective teaching. We summarized our attempts to quantitatively integrate the results from seventeen correlation matrices by coding the items using a common scoring scheme, eliminating items that were heterogeneous within categories, and factor analyzing the aggregated correlation matrix.

We conclude that existing analyses provide support for a large underlying general trait although it may not be the only trait. We also believe that effective teaching is multidimensional but that there are differences across rating forms concerning the specific dimensions that underlie effective instruction. These differences suggest that student ratings of specific teaching dimensions should not be used indiscriminately for summative decisions about teaching effectiveness.

In this paper we have presented many lines of evidence that suggest that although instructional effectiveness is multidimensional, global items should be used for the purposes of summative decisions. First, when examining many rating forms one is immediately struck by the fact that, despite their differences, what they share is a similar set of global items. Second, global items, more so than many specific instructional dimensions, have relatively high validity coefficients. Third, different instructional settings are likely to have larger effects on specific dimensions than on global items. Fourth, even in well designed multidimensional forms, such as the SEEQ, global items load most strongly on the first few factors. Finally, our factor analysis across seventeen rating forms confirms the four points listed above.

APPENDIX A: STUDENT RATING ITEMS AND THEIR CATEGORIES

In the list below, categories are arranged alphabetically. The five categories not used in the final analysis are presented solely for completeness and are marked with an asterisk (*). These categories are listed with definitions while all other categories contain definitions as well as all items retained for final analysis. Note that items are presented as in original sources. If an item appeared in multiple sources it presented multiply. A quadruple of numbers appears immediately after the name of the category (used in the final analysis) to represent: a) the initial number of items code; b) the number of items retained through all stages; c) the number of items dropped at the stage when interitem correlations **within** each category were examined; and d) the number of items dropped at the stage when interitem correlations **between** categories were examined).

Answering Questions (9/6/2/1): The students are evaluating the extent to which the instructor encouraged students to ask questions and responded to students' questions appropriately.

> Rate the instructor on the basis that he answers student's questions in a clear and concise manner.
> Rate the extent to which the instructor responded effectively to student questions.
> Encouraged questions and answers.
> The instructor encouraged and readily responded to student questions.
> Became angry when questions were asked.
> No questions allowed between explanations.

*Appropriate Use of Methods/Materials (2/2/0/0): The students are evaluating the extent to which the instructor uses appropriate instructional methods and materials in class, including appropriate use of textbook and tests for learning.

Availability (7/4/0/3): The students are evaluating the extent to which the instructor was available outside of the classroom for assistance or extra-curricular activities.

> Rate the instructor on the basis of the ease at which an office appointment can be made.
> Welcomed seeking help and advice.
> Accessible to individual students.
> Welcomed conferences.

Choice of Required Materials (8/4/1/3): The students are evaluating the qualities of the required course materials including textbooks, assignments, etc.

> The textbook was very good.
> Readings and text valuable.
> Assignments added to course understanding.
> Did not go to trouble of making up assignments.

Choice of Supplementary Materials (4/2/0/2): The students are evaluating the qualities of the supplementary materials (e.g., film, audio-visuals, etc.). That is, they are evaluating whether they were interesting, valuable, or personally relevant. Unless explicitly labeled "supplementary" such materials are considered to be required.

> The outside assignments for this course are just about the right length/somewhat too long/somewhat too short/much too long/much too short.
> Had varied illustrations about topic covered.

Clarity of Instruction (25/15/3/7): The students are evaluating the extent to which the instructor delivers clear, concise, understandable and accurate instruction (e.g., lectures, laboratories, etc.).

> Presentation of subject matter.
> Rate the instructor on the basis of the organized class presentation.
> Rate the instructor on the basis that she makes clear or simple the difficult ideas or concepts in this course.
> The instructor did not synthesize ideas.
> Rate the extent to which the instructor was successful in explaining the course material.
> Presentations clarified material.
> Presented clearly and summarized.
> Instructor's explanations clear.
> Presentation well prepared and integrated.
> He explained clearly and his explanations were to the point.
> Instructions not complete.
> Covered subject well.
> Made subject clear.
> Presentations of materials especially good.
> Students in constant state of uncertainty.

Concern for Students (8/6/0/2): The students are evaluating the extent to which the instructor was concerned and helpful about student difficulties

> The instructor seemed genuinely concerned with student's progress and was actively helpful.
> The instructor seemed to be concerned with whether the students learned the material.
> Listened and willing to help.
> Concerned about student difficulties.
> The instructor maintained a generally helpful attitude toward students and their problems.
> Too busy for talks with students.

Dramatic Delivery (5/3/2/0): The students are evaluating the extent to which the instructor delivered instruction in an expressive, dynamic, dramatic or exaggerated manner.

> Dynamic and energetic.
> Talked with back to class.
> Hard to believe.

Enthusiasm for Students (11/9/2/0): The students are evaluating the extent to which the instructor communicates his/her enthusiasm, interest or liking for students as people.

> Sympathetic attitude toward students.
> Rate the instructor on the basis of the instructor's apparent interest in working with students.
> The instructor seemed to be interested in students as persons.
> Interested in individual students.
> Was the instructor considerate of and interested in his students?
> Always suspicious of students.
> Afraid of students.
> Lacked interest in students.
> Kept up with student affairs.

Enthusiasm for Subject (3/3/0/0): The students are evaluating the extent to which the instructor communicates his/her enthusiasm, interest or liking for the subject.

> Interest in subject.
> The instructor was enthusiastic when presenting course material.
> Interested in all aspects of subject.

Enthusiasm for Teaching (4/3/0/1): The students are evaluating the extent to which the instructor communicates his/her enthusiasm, interest or liking for teaching.

> The instructor seemed to consider teaching as a chore or routine activity.
> Enthusiastic about teaching.
> Enjoyed teaching class.

Evaluation (27/8/11/8): The students are evaluating the extent to which the instructor's tests were appropriate in terms of content, frequency, time allocation, weight, difficulty, validity and learning opportunity. They are also evaluating the instructor's fairness and consistency in grading.

> The types of test questions used were good.
> Fair and impartial grading.
> Grading reflected performance.
> Grading indicated accomplishments.
> Evaluation methods fair and appropriate.
> Exams emphasized course content.
> Tests indicated careful preparation.
> Would not explain grading system.

Feedback (16/5/8/3): The students are evaluating the instructor's use of review and feedback (frequency, positive/negative) and its effect on students.

> Instructor did not review promptly and in such a way that students could understand their weaknesses.
> The instructor made helpful comments on papers or exams.
> Rate the instructor on the basis of the information or feedback provided concerning the nature and quality of my work (considering all the factors involved in teaching this course).
> Examination feedback valuable.
> Reviewed test questions that majority of students missed.

Friendly Classroom Climate (8/6/2/0): The students are evaluating the extent to which the instructor modeled, encouraged and achieved a friendly and safe classroom.

> He was friendly.
> Friendly towards students.
> Discouraged students.
> Made students feel very insecure.
> Very much at ease with the class.
> Students often returned to chat with teacher.

General Attitudes (4/3/1/0): The students are evaluating the instructor's general attitudes. (An attempt is first made to fit items into the other, more specific instructional dimensions. Only if they do not fit elsewhere are they classified here.)

> Liberal and progressive attitude.
> Had unethical attitudes.
> Did not approve of extracurricular activities.

General Knowledge and Cultural Attainment (2/2/0/0): The students are evaluating the instructor's general knowledge and cultural attainment beyond the course.

> Admired for great intelligence.
> Large background of experience made subject more interesting.

High-level Cognitive Outcomes (32/11/21/0): The students are evaluating the extent to which the instructor is promoting high-level cognitive outcomes such as writing skills, reasoning, meta-cognition, problem solving, etc.

> The instructor encouraged students to think for themselves.
> The instructor encouraged the development of new viewpoints and appreciations.
> Understand advanced material.
> Ability to analyze issues.
> I can think more coherently.
> Developing a sense of personal responsibility (self-reliance, self-discipline).
> Discovering the implications of the course material for understanding myself (interests, talents, values, etc.).
> Developing specific skills, competencies and points of view that I can use later in life.
> Intellectual curiosity in subject stimulated.
> Gained general understanding of topic.
> Encouraged students to think out answers.

Interaction and Discussion (15/6/1/8): The students are evaluating the extent to which the instructor modeled, encouraged and achieved interactive classes in which both students and instructor contributed to the class.

> Encouraged class discussions.
> Encouraged expression of ideas.
> Students would not cooperate in class.
> Group discussions encouraged.
> Nothing accomplished in classroom discussions.
> Very skillful in directing discussion.

Knowledge of Domain (4/1/2/1): The students are assessing the instructor's knowledge of the specific course subject matter and its applications.

> Did not need notes.

Knowledge of Teaching and of Students (1/1/0/0): The students are evaluating the instructor's knowledge of pedagogy (e.g., knowledge of students, student learning, and/or of instructional methods).

> No ability to handle students.

Low-level Cognitive Outcomes: The students are evaluating the extent to which the instructor is promoting low-level cognitive outcomes (e.g., recall, recognition, knowledge, etc.).

Management Style (23/10/12/1): The students are evaluating the instructor's management style (e.g., authoritarian/participatory, formal/informal) and method of handling issues of classroom control (e.g., noise, order, seating, calling on students).

> The demands of the students were not considered by the instructor.
> He decided in detail what should be done and how it should be done.
> He was permissive and flexible.

Knack in dealing with all types of problems.
Never deliberately forced own decisions on class.
Classes always orderly.
Conducted class smoothly.
Never considered what class wanted.
Maintained a well organized classroom.
Weak in leadership questions.

Monitoring Learning (7/5/1/1): The students are evaluating the extent to which the instructor monitored students' reactions and taught at the appropriate individual and class level.

The instructor was skilful in observing student reactions.
Skilled at bringing out special abilities of students.
Worked with students individually.
Aware of individual differences in pupils.
Sensed when students needed help.

Motivating Students to Greater Effort (18/9/3/6): The students are evaluating the extent to which the instructor motivated students to more effort, intellectual curiosity, love of learning, high academic aspirations, etc.

Stimulating intellectual curiosity.
Rate the instructor on the basis that the teaching methods inspire, stimulate or excite me intellectually.
Rate the instructor on the basis that she motivates me to think rather than just memorize material.
I developed motivation to do my best work.
Plan to take more courses.
Inspired many students to do better work.
Motivated students to work.
Instilled spirit of research.
Inspired class to learn.

Objectives (11/4/3/4): The students are evaluating the extent to which the instructor communicated performance criteria and deadlines for assignments and tests.

The direction of the course was adequately outlined.
Detailed course schedule.
The instructor was clear on what was expected regarding course requirements, assignments, exams, etc.
Students always knew what was coming up next day.

Overall Course (8/5/2/1): The students are evaluating the overall worth and quality of the course.

You generally enjoyed going to class.
Overall course rating.
How would you rate the overall value of this course?
Have you enjoyed taking this course?
Students discouraged with course.

Overall Instructor (13/12/1/0): The students are evaluating the overall effectiveness of the instructor.

> Rate the overall teacher's effectiveness.
> General teaching ability.
> Attitudes about teaching.
> Would you recommend this course from this instructor?
> Overall instructor rating.
> Would you recommend this course from this instructor?
> How would you rate your instructor with respect to general (all-around) teaching ability?
> Overall evaluation of instructor.
> Would like instructor as personal friend.
> Learned a lot from teacher.
> Students avoided this teacher's class.
> Not qualified as a teacher.

*****Overall Learning:** The students are evaluating the overall quality and relevance of the perceived learning that took place including the achievement of short and long term objectives.

Personal Appearance, Health, and Attire (11/5/6/0): The students are evaluating the instructor's personal appearance, health and attire.

> Personal appearance.
> Teacher very careless about dress.
> Very pleasing appearance.
> Wore wrinkled clothes.
> Poor posture.

Personality Characteristics and Peculiarities (24/20/4/0): The students are evaluating the instructor's general personality characteristics and peculiarities not directly related to teaching (e.g., maturity, irritability, confidence, paranoia, cynicism, etc.).

> Sense of proportion and humor.
> Personal peculiarities.
> Rate the instructor on the basis of poise and classroom mannerisms.
> The instructor exhibited professional dignity and bearing in the classroom.
> Enhanced presentations with humor.
> Crabby.
> Good natured.
> Consistent.
> A typical old maid (or bachelor) personality.
> Immature emotionally.
> Very prejudiced.
> Considerate.
> No sense of humor.
> Tactless.
> Wonderful sense of humor.
> Cynical attitude repels students.

Did not inspire confidence.
Magnetic personality.
Tried to show off.
Well-rounded personality.

Preparation and Organization (13/8/2/3): The students are evaluating the extent to which the instructor prepared himself/herself for instruction. (This category only related to preparation, not presentation. Any items that are ambiguous in terms of whether they relate to preparation or presentation are classified as presentation are classified as presentation are classified as presentation since students judge on the basis of presentation.)

Course material was poorly organized.
Generally the course was well organized.
Rate the extent to which the instructor's lectures were well prepared.
The instructor was consistently prepared for class.
Rate the extent to which the instructor's lectures and other material were well prepared.
Absolutely no previous preparation for class.
Became confused in class.
Best organized of any class I have had.

Relevance of Instruction (11/7/3/1): The students are evaluating the extent to which the instructor emphasizes the relevance of the provided information, including recent research.

The instructor's use of examples or personal experiences helped to get points across in class.
Good use of examples.
Contrasted implications.
Gave background of ideas and concepts.
Gave different points of view.
Discussed current developments.
Related subject to everyday life.

Research Productivity and Reputation (3/2/1/0): The students are evaluating the instructor's research productivity and reputation.

Cooperative with other teachers.
Looked to for advice.

Respect for Others (28/15/13/0): The students are evaluating the extent to which the instructor modeled, encouraged and showed trust, respect, and consideration for others (e.g., listened without interruption, did not not belittle or criticize others' criticism, treated others as equals, was punctual, etc.).

The instructor's attendance and punctuality have been consistently good.
He listened attentively to what class members had to say.
Irritated easily.
Very impatient with less able students.
Carried friendliness outside of classroom.

Built up confidence in students.
Gained class confidence very quickly.
Made students feel at ease.
Sarcastic if disagreed with.
Students did things to make teacher mad.
Always very polite to students.
Humiliated students.
Publicly ridiculed some students.
Ridiculed students.
Very sincere when talking to students.

Stimulation of Interest in the Course (21/13/4/4): The students are evaluating the extent to which the instructor stimulated their interest in the course by using a variety of activities, manifested by the extent to which good attendance, increased interest, outside reading, and liking/enjoyment for the subject matter were exhibited.

Rate the instructor on the basis that she presents the material or content of this course in an interesting manner.
Rate the extent to which the instructor stimulated your interest in the course.
Increased subject interest.
Teaching style held your interest.
Rate the extent to which the instructor stimulated your interest in the course.
Do you now enjoy reading more than you used to?
Gained interest in American government.
Do more reading on topic.
Everyone attended regularly.
Knew how to hold attention in presenting materials.
Made lectures stimulating.
No attempt to make course interesting.
Students counted the minutes until class was dismissed.

Supervision and Disciplinary Actions (3/1/2/0): The students are evaluating the extent to which the instructor supervised tests and handled disciplinary actions when disruptions occurred.

Never had to discipline the students.

*****Time Management**: The students are evaluating the extent to which the instructor handled class time.

Tolerance of Diversity (12/6/3/3): The students are evaluating the extent to which the instructor modeled, encouraged and achieved tolerance for a diversity of opinions, ideas and viewpoints and an absence of prejudice in the classroom.

The instructor was open to other viewpoints.
Rate the instructor on the basis that he considers opposing viewpoints or ideas.
The instructor appeared receptive to new ideas and others' viewpoints.
Intolerant.
Presented both sides of every question.
Blinded to all viewpoints but own.

440

Vocal Delivery (7/5/2/0): The extent to which the instructor demonstrated skill in vocal delivery.

> Rate the instructor on the basis that she speaks clearly and is easily heard.
> The instructor is clear and audible.
> Speech very fluent.
> Lectured inaudibly.
> Occasional bad grammar detracted from speech.

*Workload: The students are evaluating the performance standards and the workload (amount, difficulty) of the course and assignments.

REFERENCES

Abrami, P.C. (1984, February). Using meta-analytic techniques to review the instructional evaluation literature. *Postsecondary Education Newsletter* 6: 8.

Abrami, P.C. (1985). Dimensions of effective college instruction. *Review of Higher Education* 8: 211–228.

Abrami, P.C. (1988). SEEQ and ye shall find: A review of Marsh's "Students' evaluation of university teaching." *Instructional Evaluation* 9(2): 19–27.

Abrami, P.C. (1989a). SEEQing the truth about student ratings of instruction. *Educational Researcher* 43(1): 43–45.

Abrami, P.C. (1989b). How should we use student ratings to evaluate teaching? *Research in Higher Education* 30: 221–227.

Abrami, P.C., Chambers, B., Poulsen, C., DeSimone, C., d'Apollonia, S., and Howden, J. (1995). *Classroom Connections: Understanding and Using Cooperative Learning.* Toronto, Ontario: Harcourt Brace.

Abrami, P.C., Cohen, P.A., and d'Apollonia, S. (1988). Implementation problems in meta-analysis. *Review of Educational Research* 58: 151–179.

Abrami, P.C., and d'Apollonia, S. (1987, April). *A Conceptual Critique of Meta-analysis: The Literature on Student Ratings of Instruction.* Paper presented at the annual meeting of the American Educational Research Association, Washington, DC.

Abrami, P.C., and d'Apollonia, S. (1988, April). *The Literature on Student Ratings of Instruction: A Conceptual Solution to Some Implementation Problems of Meta-analysis.* Paper presented at the annual meeting of the American Educational Research Association, New Orleans, LA.

Abrami, P.C., and d'Apollonia, S. (1990). The dimensionality of ratings and their use in personnel decisions. In M. Theall and J. Franklin (eds.) *Student Ratings of Instruction: Issues for Improving Practice. New Directions for Teaching and Learning.* Number 43, pp. 97–111. San Francisco: Jossey-Bass.

Abrami, P.C., and d'Apollonia, S. (1991). Multidimensional students' evaluations of teaching effectiveness-Generalizability of "N = 1" research: Comment on Marsh (1991). *Journal of Educational Psychology* 83: 411–415.

Abrami, P.C., d'Apollonia, S., and Cohen, P.A. (1990). The validity of student ratings of instruction: What we know and what we do not. *Journal of Educational Psychology* 82: 219–231.

Abrami, P.C., Leventhal, L., and Perry, R.P. (1982). Educational seduction. *Review of Educational Research* 52: 446–464.

Abrami, P.C., and Mizener, D.A. (1985). Student/instructor attitude similarity, student ratings, and course performance. *Journal of Educational Psychology* 77: 693–702.

Anderson, N.H. (1968). Likableness ratings of 555 personality-trait words. *Journal of Personality and Social Psychology* 9: 272–279.

Borich, G.D. (1977). *The Appraisal of Teaching: Concepts and Process.* Reading, MA: Addison-Wesley

Bushman, B.J., Cooper, H.M., and Lemke, K.M. (1991). Meta-analysis of factor analyses: An illustration using the Buss-Durke Hostility Inventory. *Personality and Social Psychology Bulletin* 17: 344–349.

Bloom, B.S., Engelhart, M.D., Frost, E.J., Hill, W.H., and Krathwohl, D.R. (1956). *Taxonomy of Educational Objectives. Handbook I: Cognitive Domain.* New York: David McKay.

Campbell, D.T., and Stanley, J.C. (1966). *Experimental and Quasi-experimental Designs for Research*. Boston: Houghton-Mifflin.

Cashin, W.E., and Downey, R.G. (1992). Using global student rating items for summative evaluations. *Journal of Educational Psychology* 84: 563–572.

Cohen, P.A. (1981). Student ratings of instruction and student achievement: A meta-analysis of multisection validity studies. *Review of Educational Research* 51: 281–309.

Cohen, P.A. (1982). Validity of student ratings in psychology courses: A meta-analysis of multisection validity studies. *Teaching of Psychology* 9: 78–82.

Cohen, P.A. (1983). Comment on a selective review of the validity of student ratings of teaching. *Journal of Higher Education* 54: 448–458.

Cohen, P.A. (1986, April). *An Updated and Expanded Meta-analysis of Multisection Student Rating Validity Studies*. Paper presented at the annual meeting of the American Educational Research Association, San Francisco. CA.

Cohen, P.A. (1987, April). *A Critical Analysis and Reanalysis of the Multisection Validity Meta-analysis*. Paper presented at the annual meeting of the American Educational Research Association, Washington, DC.

Cooper, J., Prescott, S., Cook, L., Smith, L., Mueck, R., and Cuseo, J. (1990). *Cooperative learning and College Instruction: Effective Use of Student Learning Teams*. Long Beach, CA: California State University Foundation on behalf of California State University Institute for Teaching and Learning, Office of the Chancellor.

d'Apollonia, S. and Abrami, P.C. (1987, April). *An Empirical Critique of Meta-analysis: The Literature on Student Ratings of Instruction*. Paper presented at the annual meeting of the American Educational Research Association, Washington, DC.

d'Apollonia, S. and Abrami, P.C. (1988, April). *The Literature on Student Ratings of Instruction: Yet Another Meta-analysis*. Paper presented at the annual meeting of the American Educational Research Association, New Orleans, LA.

d'Apollonia, S., Abrami, P., and Rosenfield, S. (1993, April). *The Dimensionality of Student Ratings of Instruction: A Meta-analysis of the Factor Studies*. Paper presented at the annual meeting of the American Educational Research Association, Atlanta, GA.

d'Apollonia, S., Abrami, P., and Rosenfield, S. (in preparation). A multivariate meta-analysis of the multisection validity studies.

Doyle, K.O., Jr. (1981). Validity and perplexity: An incomplete list of disturbing issues. *Instructional Evaluation*, 6(1): 23–25.

Doyle, K.O., and Crichton, L.I. (1978). Student, peer, and self-evaluations of college instructors. *Journal of Educational Psychology* 5: 815–826.

Feldman, K.A. (1976). The superior college teacher from the student's view. *Research in Higher Education* 5: 243–288.

Feldman, K.A. (1977). Consistency and variability among college students in rating their teachers and courses: A review and analysis. *Research in Higher Education* 6: 223–274.

Feldman, K.A. (1983). Seniority and experience of college teachers as related to evaluations they receive from students. *Research in Higher Education* 18: 3–214.

Feldman, K.A. (1984). Class size and college students' evaluations of teachers and courses: A closer look. *Research in Higher Education* 21: 45–116.

Feldman, K.A. (1988). Effective college teaching from the students' and faculty's view: Matched or mismatched priorities? *Research in Higher Education* 28: 291–344.

Feldman, K.A. (1989a). The association between student ratings of specific instructional dimensions and student achievement: Refining and extending the synthesis of data from multisection validity studies. *Research in Higher Education* 30: 583–645.

Feldman, K.A. (1989b). Instructional effectiveness of college teachers as judged by teachers themselves, current and former students, colleagues, administrators, and external (neutral) observers. *Research in Higher Education* 30: 137–194.

Feldman, K.A. (1990). An afterword for "The association between student ratings of specific instructional dimensions and student achievement: Refining and extending the syn<??>hesis of data from multisection validity studies." *Research in Higher Education* 31: 315–318.

Fernald, P.S. (1990). Students' ratings of instruction: Standardized and customized. *Teaching of Psychology* 17: 105–109.

Franklin, J., and Theall, M. (1989, April). *Rating the Readers: Knowledge, Attitude, and Practice of Users of Student Ratings of Instruction.* Paper presented at the Annual Meeting of the American Educational Research Association, San Francisco.

Frey, P.W. (1978). A two dimensional analysis of student ratings of instruction. *Research in Higher Education* 9: 69–91.

Gaski, J.F. (1987). On "Construct validity of measures of college teaching effectiveness." *Journal of Educational Psychology* 79: 326–330.

Gorsuch, R.I. (1983). *Factor Analysis.* Hillsdale, NJ: Lawrence Erlbaum.

Hedges, L.V., and Olkin, I. (1985). *Statistical Methods for Meta-analysis.* Orlando, FL: Academic Press.

Hill, P.W. (1984). Testing hierarchy in educational taxonomies: A theoretical and empirical investigation. *Evaluation Education* 8: 181–278.

Howard, G.S., Conway, C.G., and Maxwell, S.E. (1985). Construct validity of measures of college teaching effectiveness. *Journal of Educational Psychology* 77: 187–196.

Isaacson, R.L., McKeachie, W.J., Milholland, J.E., Lin, Y.G., Hofeller, M., Baerwaldt, J.W., and Zinn, K.L. (1964). Dimensions of student evaluations of teaching. *Journal of Educational Psychology* 55: 344–351.

Johnson, D.W., Johnson, R.T., and Smith, K.A. (1991). *Active Learning: Cooperation in the College Classroom.* Edina, MN: Interaction Book Co.

Kaiser, H.F., Hunka, S., and Bianchini, J.C. (1969). *Relating Factors Between Studies Based Upon Different Individuals.* In H.J. Eysenck (ed.), Personality Structure and Measurement. San Diego, CA: Knapp.

Kulik, J.A., and McKeachie, W.J. (1975). The evaluation of teachers in higher education. *Review of Research in Education* 3: 210–240.

Linn, R.L., Centra, J.A., and Tucker, L. (1975). Between, within, and total group factor analysis of student ratings of instruction. *Multivariate Behavioral Research* 10: 277–288.

Marsh, H.W. (1987). Students' evaluations of university teaching: Research findings, methodological issues, and directions for future research. *International Journal of Educational Research* 11: 253–388.

Marsh, H.W. (1991). Multidimensional students' evaluations of teaching effectiveness: A test of alternative higher-order structures. *Journal of Educational Psychology* 83: 285–296.

Marsh, H.W. (1991). A multidimensional perspective on students' evaluations of teaching effectiveness: Reply to Abrami and d'Apollonia. *Journal of Educational Psychology* 83: 416–421.

Marsh, H.W., and Dunkin, M.J. (1992). Students' evaluations of university teaching: A multidimensional perspective. In J. Smart (ed.), *Higher Education: Handbook of Theory and Research*, Vol. VIII. New York: Agathon Press.

Marsh, H.W., and Hocevar, D. (1984). The factorial invariance of student evaluations of college teaching. *American Educational Research Journal* 21: 341–366.

Marsh, H.W., and Hocevar, D. (1991). The multidimensionality of students' evaluations of teaching effectiveness: The generality of factor structures across academic discipline, instructor level, and course level. *Teaching and Teacher Education* 7: 9–18.

Maxwell, S.E., and Howard, G.S. (1987). On the underdetermination of theory by evidence. *Journal of Educational Psychology* 79: 331–332.

McCallum, L.W. (1984). A meta-analysis of course evaluation data and its use in the tenure decision. *Research in Higher Education* 21: 150–158.

Murray, H.G. (1991). Effective Teaching Behaviors in the College Classroom. In J. Smart (ed.), *Higher Education, Handbook of Theory and Research* (Vol. 6) New York: Agathon.

Murray, H.G., Rushton, J.P., and Paunonen, S.V. (1990). Teacher personality traits and student instructional ratings in six types of university courses. *Journal of Educational Psychology* 82: 250–261.

Osgood, C.E., Suci, G.J., and Tannenbaum, P.H. (1957). *The Measurement of Meaning*. Urbana, IL: University of Illinois Press.

Rosenfield, S., d'Apollonia, S., and Abrami, P.C. (1993, April). *The Dimensionality of Student Ratings of Instruction: Aggregating Factor Studies*. Paper presented at the annual meeting of the American Educational Research Association, Atlanta, GA.

Seldin, P. (1991). *The Teaching Portfolio*. Bolton, MA: Anker Publishing Co.

Shore, B.M., Foster, S.F., Knapper, C.K., Nadeau, C.G., Neill, N., and Sim, V.W. (1986). *The Teaching Dossier: A Guide to Its Preparation and Use*. Ottawa: Canadian Association of University Teachers.

Smith, R.A., and Cranton, P.A. (1992). Students' perceptions of teaching skills and overall effectiveness across instructional settings. *Research in Higher Education* 33: 747.

Sullivan, A.M., and Skanes, G.R. (1974). Validity of student evaluations of teaching and the characteristics of successful instructors. *Journal of Educational Psychology* 66: 584–590.

Tabachnick, B.G., and Fidell, L.S. (1983). *Using Multivariate Statistics*. New York: Harper and Row.

Thomson, B. (1989). Meta-analysis of factor structure studies: A case study example with Bem's Androgyny measure. *Journal of Experimental Education* 57: 182, 197.

Wherry, R.L. (1951). *The Control of Bias in Ratings: Factor Analysis of Rating Item Content*. Columbus: The Ohio State University Research Foundation, United States Army, AGO, Personnel Research Branch, PRB Report No. 919.

Widlak, F.W., McDaniel, E.D., and Feldhusen, J.F. (1973). *Factor Analyses of an Instructor Rating Scale*. Paper presented at the annual meeting of the American Educational Research Association, New Orleans. (ERIC Document Reproduction Service ED 079324).

The Dimensionality of Student Ratings of Instruction: An Update on What We Know, Do not Know, and Need to Do

Philip C. Abrami*, Steven Rosenfield† and Helena Dedic†
*Concordia University
abrami@education.concordia.ca
†Vanier College

Abstract

Analysis ten years ago of seventeen multidimensional student rating forms revealed that all included global items measuring one underlying general trait: effective teaching. Differences existed across rating forms concerning which other underlying dimensions were included, which led to the conclusion that only student ratings of global items, not those concerning specific teaching dimensions, should be used for summative decisions about teaching effectiveness. In response to society's current transition into the Information and Communication Age, a transformation of learning environments has begun, without parallel changes in rating forms. Thus, summative use of dimensions other than the general trait of effective teaching, now even less relevant to, perhaps even biased against, teachers transforming their learning environments, may be slowing educational reform.

Key Words: student ratings, effective teaching, post-secondary education, science education, metanalysis

In our earlier article for *Higher Education: A Handbook of Teaching and Learning*, Abrami, d'Apollonia, and Rosenfield (1996) explored the dimensionality of instruction as reflected in student ratings. While ten years does not seem like a terribly long time in the social sciences, we worked on this update wondering whether our conclusions stood the test of time.

Abrami et al. (1996) was divided into five sections. In the first section, we explored three alternative definitions of effective teaching.

* Address inquires to: Philip C. Abrami, Centre for the Study of Learning and Performance, Concordia University, 1455 DeMaisonneuve Blvd. W., Montreal, Quebec Canada H3G 1M8. E-mail: abrami@education.concordia.ca. Website: http://doe.concordia.ca/cslp/. Support for the preparation of this article was provided by grants to the authors from Fonds québécois de la recherche sur la société et la culture, Government of Quebec. The authors are solely responsible for the content of the article.

In section two, we discussed methods of empirically determining effective teaching. In section three, we concentrated on the strength and weaknesses of student ratings validation designs. In section four, we examined the quantitative reviews of the validation studies. And in section five, we summarized our analyses of the common dimensions of effective teaching as reflected in student ratings by integrating the results of seventeen correlation matrices.

We concluded "existing analyses provide support for a large underlying general trait although it may not be the only trait. We also believe that effective teaching is multidimensional but that there are differences across rating forms concerning the specific dimensions that underlie effective teaching. These differences suggest that student ratings of specific teaching dimensions should not be used indiscriminately for summative decisions about teaching effectiveness.

In this paper we have presented many lines of evidence that suggest that although instructional effectiveness is multidimensional, global items should be used for the purposes of summative decisions. First, when examining many rating forms one is immediately struck by the fact that, despite these differences, what they share is a similar set of global items. Second, global items, more so than many specific instructional dimensions, have relatively high validity coefficients. Third, different instructional settings, involving disciplinary differences, year, career path, etc. are likely to have larger effects on specific dimensions than on global items. Fourth, even in well designed multidimensional forms, such as the SEEQ, global items load most strongly on the first few factors. Finally, our factor analysis across seventeen rating forms confirms the four points listed above" (Abrami et al., 1996, p. 357).

In preparing the current update, we focus on two aspects of student ratings that build upon our earlier findings. The first concerns a contrast between student-centred and teacher-centred learning environments and how student ratings of specific teaching qualities should vary across these environments. The second concerns the use of ratings for summative decisions about teaching effectiveness.

STUDENT-CENTRED AND TEACHER-CENTRED LEARNING ENVIRONMENTS

In this section we will discuss the results of a study (Rosenfield et al., 2005) of learning environments in post-secondary science classrooms. This study was undertaken in large part because reports indicate a looming shortage of graduates in science and engineering from our universities in North America (OECD, 2005; Baillargeon et al., 2001; Crimmins, 1984). There have also been strident warnings about the danger this shortfall poses for North American economies in the twenty-first century, particularly given the increasing competition from the rising Asian giants, India and China. No less than the President of United States, George Bush, in his 2006 State of the Union address, took note of the problem proclaiming an "American Competitiveness Initiative"..."to give our nation's children a firm grounding in math and science" and promising to hire 70,000 new high-school mathematics and science teachers. It is to be noted that our Asian competitors have the edge not only in the number of graduates, but in the quality of those graduates. This situation must be fairly evident when even a newspaper comic strip, Doonesbury, runs a strip in which a character is described as outsourcing his own job to an Indian software engineer, but has to have the engineer mess up every few weeks so that the American employer won't guess what has happened (Trudeau, 2005).

One essential element underlying this shortage of graduates has been our failure to successfully adapt our teaching methods to the changes in students and the demands placed on them during and after their studies (Tobias, 1990; Seymour, 1992, 1995; Seymour & Hewitt, 1997). This failure to adapt how we teach is not because educational researchers have not been able to determine what kinds of changes in pedagogy would be useful (American Psychological Association, 1997). On the contrary, there is evidence that in student-centred learning environments, learners are actively-engaged and acquire improved conceptual understanding in contrast to their peers in teacher-centred learning environments (Hake, 1998a, 1998b). In a policy forum on education called "Scientific Teaching", Handelsman et al. (2004) state that "since publication of the AAAS (editor's note: American Association for the Advancement of Science) 1989 report "Science for all Americans", commissions, panels and working groups have agreed that reform in science education should be founded on "scientific teaching", in which teaching is approached with the same rigour as science at its best. Scientific teaching involves active learning strategies to engage students in the process of science and teaching methods that have been systematically tested and shown to reach diverse students." Handelsman et al. (2004) cite about a half-dozen specific examples of successful experiments at modifying

teacher-centred learning environments that focus on the transmission of knowledge to something stimulating active engagement,
and evidence of resultant improvements in problem-solving ability,
conceptual understanding, and success in subsequent courses
compared with peers experiencing traditional teacher-centred learning
environments.

Despite this evidence the problem of improving science is still
not solved. That is, even though some post-secondary institutions
have implemented changes in the learning environment with success,
such change has not become the norm in post-secondary pedagogy
(Handelsman et. al., 2004). A recent study following a large cohort of
students (N = 1452) through their first two years of post-secondary
science studies (Rosenfield et al., 2005) assessed both faculty and
students' perceptions concerning the learning environments they face
in mathematics and science classrooms came to a similar conclusion.
This assessment focussed primarily on the process definition of
teaching. Analysis of teacher data from this study (Dedic, Dickie,
Rosenfield, & Rosenfield, 2005b) showed that 36% (sample N = 84)
of instructors engaged in teaching acts associated with student-centred
learning environments (called in that study "fostering environments").
A sample item indicates the type of teaching acts engaged in by this
group of instructors, "I encourage students to discuss ideas amongst
themselves as a way to improve their understanding." while the
remaining instructors did not consider such teaching acts as useful.
The focus of the former group of instructors on the learning process.
For example, they are significantly more likely than their peers to
assess students' prior knowledge before teaching a new topic. Interestingly, the 36% of instructors who rated the environments that they
created as high in "fostering" and low in "transmission" were significantly more likely to have knowledge of education research than
their colleagues. These results support the claims of Handelsman et al.
(2004) that required changes in learning environments by and large
are not happening, and instructors are not cognizant of educational
research results.

In the study by Rosenfield et al. (2005) there were two versions of
a forty item assessment of learning environments instrument: one for
students and one for instructors. Factor analysis of both instructor and
student data revealed the same two major factors: both groups viewed
the learning environments as being teacher-centred ("transmission")
and/or student-centred ("fostering"). To illustrate these views, a sample

item on the teacher-centred scale reads "Students should spend most of their time in class taking notes" (instructor version) or "I spent most of my time in class copying the teacher's notes" (student version), and a sample item on the student-centred scale is "I encourage students to develop their own methods for solving typical problems" (instructor version) or "The teacher encouraged me to think for myself" (student version). A cluster analysis of student data reveals three groups of students: 1) those who perceive the environment largely as student-centred; 2) those who perceive the environment as both student-centred and teacher-centred; 3) those who perceive the environment as largely teacher-centred. Students in cluster 1) who perceived the environment as largely student-centred had significantly (p < .001) higher academic performance (measured by average grade in mathematics and science courses), higher affect and self-efficacy than their peers in cluster 3), and they were also more likely to persevere (Dedic, Rosenfield, Dickie, & Rosenfield, 2005a).

One further finding from the Rosenfield et al. (2005) study is that the cluster 1) students, who rated the learning environment as largely student-centred, as opposed to their peers, rated their instructors as more effective in helping them learn (p < .001). We reason from this that if summative assessment decisions were made on the basis of responses to the global item "The teacher was effective in making me learn.", and teachers were made aware of the link between this global item and student-centred teaching acts, then there would be an incentive amongst instructors to move toward student-centred learning environments. This belief is fostered by the apparent ability of teachers, just like their students, to distinguish between teaching acts that are student-centred versus those that are teacher-centred.

One caveat, this research took place in four post-secondary institutions with no summative instructor evaluation policy. That is, student rating forms are not used for hiring, firing or tenure type decisions. Instead, the objective of departmental evaluation is solely to provide feedback to instructors to help guide professional development.

However, student rating forms can be an obstacle to professional development. Kolitch and Dean (1999) examined the Student Evaluation of Instruction (SEI) form used at the State University of New York, from the point of view of both the transmission or teacher-centred model of teaching and the "engaged-critical" model of teaching (their term for what was called above "fostering" or student-centred), and found implicit assumptions built into the SEI that favoured the teacher-centred model over the student-centred one. Student rating forms, which were developed to rate instruction that was presumed to use the prevailing paradigm of post-secondary instruction which is teacher-centred, that is, transmission of knowledge, have not changed over the last two decades. If non-global items from such rating forms are used for summative decisions, instructors may feel obliged to pander to the built in bias these forms exhibit towards teacher-centred learning environments, and so the rating forms themselves would become a major obstacle to adoption of more student-centred active learning strategies that educational research has shown to promote conceptual change.

Abrami, Theall and Mets (2001) raised similar concerns about the philosophies and approaches to postsecondary instruction under-going major change from traditional didactic forms of instruction to more learner-centred approaches. When using cooperative learning techniques. We may wish to include items that assess whether the instructor facilitated positive interdependence (e.g., Were students responsible for the learning of their peers?) and individual account-ability (e.g., Were teammates responsible for their individual learning?) We may also wish to ask about how well instructors facilitated problem-based inquiry and whether and how students were scaffolded to engage in self-regulated learning. In addition, the use of technology for learning, both as a way to supplement traditional instruction and as a means to deliver instruction at a distance, may require a rethinking about the qualities of effective teaching and its evaluation, especially with regard to specific teaching dimensions.

Like the perennial question about "the chicken and the egg", which comes first: changes in student rating forms or changes in post-secondary learning environments? Even as some departments or faculties move towards adding emphasis to the teaching component of tenure decisions, evaluation of teaching continues to be made on the basis of forms designed with the intention of determining if the instructor is a good transmitter of knowledge. Currently it would be foolhardy for young instructors hoping for tenure to create active-engagement learning environments that depend more on students working collaboratively, with or without technology enhancements, despite the overwhelming evidence that such active learning strategies improve learning, knowledge retention, and persistence in science studies.

These concerns reinforce our prior recommendations (Abrami et al., 1996) concerning the use of global ratings, instead of dimen-sional ratings, for summative purposes. In brief, we recommend that only global ratings be used for summative decisions, and that there is evidence that this can help persuade teachers to move towards more student-centred learning environments. Also, in the last ten years, with the rise of student-centered approaches, it has become clear that we need new evaluation approaches, not biased towards teacher-centred approaches, for formative assessment as well to help teachers see how to change.

USING STUDENT RATINGS FOR SUMMATIVE DECISIONS

Expert consensus regarding the use of student ratings for promotion and tenure purposes is that global ratings can reliably distinguish among outstanding, average and poor instructors. That is, broad categorizations of teaching quality are possible but fine distinctions go beyond what the instruments are capable of. Nevertheless, there is much anecdotal evidence that administrative uses of student ratings are improper, making small differences among instructors into fateful hiring and promotion recommendations. It is a problem of misplaced precision.

We are decidedly against removing human judgment from the process of judging teaching effectiveness. At the same time, we want to take the accumulated scientific evidence and see that it forms part of the decision process. Chief amongst our recommendations is to use statistical hypothesis testing to insure that judgments about excellence do not capitalize on chance fluctuation. In addition, we recommend that measurement error be more carefully reflected in how student ratings data are used.

More precisely, Abrami (2001) presented a method for insuring the appropriate precision in using student ratings for summative decisions:

1. Report the average of several global items or a weighted average of specific items, if global items are not included in the student rating form.
2. Combine the results of each faculty member's courses together. Decide in advance whether the mean will reflect the average rating for courses (i.e., unweighted mean) or the average rating for students (i.e., weighted mean).
3. Decide in advance on the policy for excluding student rating scores by choosing one of the following alternatives: a) include student ratings for all courses; b) include student ratings for

all courses after they have been taught at least once; c) include student ratings for all courses but those agreed upon in advance (e.g., exclude small seminars); or d) include student ratings for the same number of courses for all faculty (e.g., include best ten rated courses).

4. Choose between norm-referenced and criterion-referenced evaluation. If norm-referenced, select the appropriate comparison group and relative level of acceptable performance in advance. If criterion referenced, select the absolute level of acceptable performance in advance.

5. Follow the steps in statistical hypothesis testing: a) state the null hypothesis; b) state the alternative hypothesis; c) select a probability value for significance testing; d) select the appropriate statistical test; e) compute the calculated value; f) determine the critical value; g) compare the calculated and critical values in order to choose between the null and alternative hypotheses.

6. Provide descriptive and inferential statistics and illustrate them in a visual display which shows both the point estimation and interval estimation used for statistical inference.

7. Incorporate student rating validity estimates into statistical tests and confidence intervals. Norm-based statistical procedures with a correction for measurement error:

$$t_{vc} = \frac{\overline{Y}_i - \overline{Y}_g}{\sqrt{\frac{s_i^2}{n_i} + \frac{s_g^2}{n_g} \frac{1}{1-vc}}} \text{ for } df = n_i \mid n_g - 2.$$

where $\overline{Y}$ is the mean TRF score, s^2 is the unbiased variance, n is sample size, vc is the validity coefficient, and df is the degrees of freedom.

In addition, one can calculate a confidence interval for the calculated value of t_{vc}:

$$CI = (\overline{Y}_i - \overline{Y}_g) \pm t_\alpha s_{Dvc}$$

where t_α is critical value of t at a particular alpha level and

$$s_{Dvc} = \sqrt{\frac{s_i^2}{n_i} + \frac{s_g^2}{n_g} \frac{1}{1-vc}}$$

8. Since we are interested in instructor effectiveness and not student characteristics, consider using class means and not individual students as the units of analysis.
9. Decide whether and to what extent to weigh sources of evidence other than student ratings.

If promotion and tenure committees are provided with evidence that takes into account the general impact of extraneous influences more correct decisions about teaching quality will be reached. Providing clear data and interpretative guidelines does not mean that human judgment will be ignored. Promotion and tenure committees may elect to confirm the results of statistical testing or disconfirm them, especially if a reasoned argument is provided. The wise use of statistical tools and procedures can go a long way towards overcoming the covert and overt forms of bias that characterize uneducated subjective judgment.

CONCLUSION

Ten years ago, we argued that the multidimensional nature of teaching was not uniquely captured by a single rating form and, furthermore, that dimensional ratings were highly intercorrelated. All together, we argued for the use of multidimensional ratings especially for summative decisions and for the use of global ratings.

Ten years later we have added further to that argument in two respects. First, an emphasis on student-centred learning has made traditional forms of student ratings of questionable relevance as a universal approach to judging teaching effectiveness. Second, we need to pay greater attention to how ratings are used to make summative decisions about teaching effectiveness. Global ratings are the best for doing so, especially if we provide guided and scaffolded support to their use and interpretation.

The one constancy in the twenty-first century, the Age of Information and Communication, is change, and at that, there is an increasing rate of change in how we work and what we work at. With changes in technology and work have come, perhaps unbidden, changes in societal mores and beliefs. Whatever one's moral or political philosophy, whether one is happy or unhappy with the changes that are taking place, denying either the existence of change or the large role it plays in shaping the lives and characters of our youth is pointless. Nations that fail to recognize the impact of change, and do not successfully adapt, are in danger of becoming "have nots".

REFERENCES

Abrami, P.C. (2001). Improving judgments about teaching effectiveness using teacher rating forms. In M. Theall, P.C. Abrami and L.A. Mets (eds.), *New Directions for Institutional Research: No.109. The Student Ratings Debate: Are They Valid? How Can We Best Use Them?* (pp. 59–87). San Francisco: Jossey-Bass.

Abrami, P.C., d'Apollonia, S., and Rosenfield, S. (1996). The dimensionality of student ratings of instruction: What we know and what we do not. In J. Smart (ed.), *Higher Education: Handbook of Theory and Research* (Vol.11, pp. 213–264). New York, NY: Agathon Press.

Abrami, P.C., Theall, M., and Mets, L.A. (2001). Introduction to the student ratings debate. In M. Theall, P. Abrami and L.A. Mets (eds.), *The Student Ratings Debate: Are They Valid? How Can We Best Use Them?* (Vol. 109, pp. 1–6). San Francisco: Jossey-Bass.

American Psychological Association. (1997). *Learner-centered Psychological Principles: A Framework for School-Redesign and Reform.* Washington, DC: http://www.apa.org/ed/lcp.html accessed July 30, 2005.

Baillargeon, G., Demers, M., Ducharme, P., Foucault, D., Lavigne, J., Lespérance, A., Lavallée, S., Ristic, B., Sylvain, G., and Vigneault, A. (2001). *Education Indicators, 2001 edition.* Québec City: Ministère de l'Éducation, Gouvernement du Québec.

Crimmins, J.C. (1984). *A Report on the Crisis in Mathematics and Science Education: What Can Be Done Now?* New York, NY: American Association for the Advancement of Science.

Dedic, H., Rosenfield, S., Dickie, L., and Rosenfield, E. (2005a). *Post-Secondary Science Students: Academic Performance, Persistence and Perceptions of the Learning Environment*, paper presented to American Educational Research Association 2006 annual meeting.

Dedic, H., Dickie, L., Rosenfield, E., and Rosenfield, S. (2005b). *Post-Secondary Science Instructors: Motivation and Perception of the Learning Environment*, paper presented to American Educational Research Association for 2006 annual meeting.

Hake, R.R. (1998a). Interactive-engagement vs traditional methods: A six-thousand-student survey of mechanics test data for introductory physics courses. *American Journal of Physics* 66(1): 64–74.

Hake, R.R. (1998b). Interactive-engagement methods in introductory mechanics courses. unpublished manuscript; on line as ref 25 at <http://www.physics.indiana.edu/~hake>, accessed Sept 21 2003.

Handelsman, J., Ebert-May, D., Beichner, R., Bruns, P., Chang, A, DeHaan, R., Gentile, J., Lauffer, S., Stewart, J., Tilghman, S., and Wood, W. (2004). Scientific Teaching, a policy forum in *Science* 304: 521–522.

Kolitch, E., and Dean, A.V. (1999). Student ratings of instruction in the USA: Hidden assumptions and missing conceptions about "good" teaching. *Studies in Higher Education.* Routledge, Vol. 24, #1, pp. 27–42.

OECD. (2005). Education at a Glance 2005. 520 pp., ISBN 9264011919 http://www.oecd.org/document/34/0,2340,en_2649_34515_35289570_1_1_1_1,00.html accessed January 31, 2006.

Rosenfield, S., Dedic, H., Dickie, L., Rosenfield, E., Aulls, M.W., Koestner, R., Krishtalka, A., Milkman, K., and Abrami, P. (2005). *Étude des facteurs aptes à influencer la réussite et la rétention dans les programmes de la science aux cégeps*

455

anglophones, Final Report submitted to Fonds de recherche sur la société et la culture, October 2005, at <http://sun4.vaniercollege.qc.ca/fqrsc/reports/fr_22.pdf>, accessed October 31, 2005.

Seymour, E. (1992). "The Problem Iceberg" in science, mathematics, and engineering education: Student explanations for high attrition rates. *Journal of College Science Teaching* 21: 230–238.

Seymour, E. (1995). Revisiting the 'Problem Iceberg': Science, Mathematics, and Engineering Students Still Chilled Out, *Journal of College Science Teaching* 24(6): 392.

Seymour, E. and Hewitt, N. (1997). *Talking about Leaving: Why Undergraduates Leave the Sciences*. Boulder, CO: Westview.

Tobias, S. (1990). *They're not Dumb, They're Different: Stalking the Second Tier. An Occasional Paper on Neglected Problems in Science Education*. Tucson, AR: Research Corporation.

Trudeau, G.B. (2005) Doonesbury, Flashback, *The Montreal Gazette*, October 29.

11. GOOD TEACHING MAKES
A DIFFERENCE—AND WE KNOW WHAT IT IS*

W. J. McKeachie
billmck@umich.edu

Key Words: College teaching; dimensions of teaching; student ratings of instruction; reliability and validity; faculty evaluation; faculty development

Harry Murray began his chapter with the question, "Do teachers differ significantly in their impact on student cognitive and affective development?" The preceding chapters clearly demonstrate that they do and that we can measure the differences and the impact that teaching makes.

The basic aim of this chapter is to review and highlight aspects of the previous chapters in ways that will be helpful to faculty developers or faculty members involved in programs for improving teaching and evaluation of teaching. However these chapters stimulated my thinking, as they no doubt have stimulated yours, and I include here some additional thoughts about the topics they covered. I should also state at the outset that what seemed a daunting task when I began reading these chapters in order to prepare my review turned out instead to be one of real delight. Each is excellent! My hope is that this chapter in no way diminishes the superb job they have done. I have organized the review around four questions:

1. Does teaching make a difference?
2. How do teachers differ from one another?
3. Can teachers learn how to be more effective?
4. Why do effective teaching methods result in better learning?

*I am grateful for the comments of Herb Marsh and Ray Perry on an earlier version of this chapter.

R.P. Perry and J.C. Smart (eds.), The Scholarship of Teaching and Learning in Higher Education: An Evidence-Based Perspective, 457–474.
© 2007 *Springer.*

DOES TEACHING MAKE A DIFFERENCE?

One of the barriers to the improvement of teaching is the still not uncommon belief that all that is required for good college teaching is knowledge of the subject matter. This attitude was exemplified by one of the speakers at the 1993 Council meeting of the American Psychological Association. The Board of Educational Affairs had proposed that the Association's criteria for accreditation of doctoral programs should consider whether or not the program provided training for teaching. One Council member stated with great fervor, "Those who attempt to give training in methods of college and university teaching are usually themselves poor teachers and certainly have nothing to offer to any professor who has a good command of the subject matter."

The average person would have no doubt that good teaching methods make a difference, but ever since the review by Dubin and Taveggia (1968) suggesting that most comparisons of teaching methods found no statistically significant differences, some academicians have argued that even though some teachers may make a difference for some students, on the average differences in teaching don't make much difference in student learning.

We thought we had pretty well silenced that argument by our review of the research literature (McKeachie and Birney, 1955) showing that even though many studies of teaching lacked sufficient statistical power to show differences at the 5% level of confidence, the direction of the results was quite consistent; e.g. classes taught by discussion were superior to lecture classes in 13 out of 14 comparisons that used measures of thinking, retention after the final examination, motivation, or attitude change. Similarly early studies of student ratings of teachers by Remmers and his students showed that teachers differ in effectiveness (Remmers, 1927, 1958). As we have also seen in the previous chapters, clearly teachers and teaching methods do make a difference!

Research on teaching flourished in the decades following World War II, but in the past couple of decades the focus of attention has shifted from teaching to the *learner*. While the earlier discounting of the importance of the teacher was largely a function of naiveté, current emphasis on the learner with less focus on teaching results from sophisticated research and theory. With the hegemony of cognitive psychology, we became more aware that learning was not simply a matter of stimulus-response-feedback, but rather that learners construct knowledge, actively seeking to understand—interpreting and encoding information in relation to their prior knowledge. Thus in any classroom, no two learners represent new knowledge in the same way. Some faculty members may take this to mean that the responsibility for learning is now solely that of students. Such an abdication of responsibility is, however, uncommon. Clearly teaching and learning are intimately intertwined (See Shuell, 1993). The great bulk of research on student studying, reading, writing, and experiencing has occurred in the last 20 years. This has given us much valuable knowledge about how students learn. Nonetheless, as Murray suggests, "what," "how," and "how much" a student studies is to some extent a function of the teaching. To the degree that teachers make challenging assignments, encourage competency, give thought-provoking tests, and use other means to promote active learning, students will make their learning meaningful so that it will stick with them for later use. If in recent years we have overemphasized learning at the expense of teaching, the chapters in this section help to restore the balance.

Each of the preceding chapters presents evidence that teaching makes a difference. Murray shows that low inference behaviors can reliably differentiate effective from less effective teachers; this is true both for cognitive and motivational outcomes. Feldman and Marsh and Dunkin give a wealth of evidence that effective teachers are different from less-effective teachers on dimensions that appear even in cross-cultural studies. This section of my chapter can be brief because the evidence in the previous chapters is compelling. Thus we can turn to the broader question of what makes the difference between effectiveness and ineffectiveness. To answer that question we need first to understand how teachers differ.

HOW DO TEACHERS DIFFER FROM ONE ANOTHER?

Marsh and Dunkin's analysis of primary and higher order factors found in student ratings to teaching clearly indicates the multi-dimensionality and complexity of teaching. Marsh's nine primary factors—Instructor enthusiasm, Breadth of coverage, Organization/clarity, Assignments/reading, Learning/value, Examinations/grading, Group interaction, Individual rapport, and Workload/difficulty—indicate that student ratings of teaching involve a mix of personality characteristics and characteristics related to the content and assessment of achievement, broadly paralleling the two factors—"Empathy" and "Professional Maturity"—found in the first factor analysis of student ratings (Smalzreid and Remmers, 1943). "Empathy" included "sympathetic attitude toward students" and "liberal and progressive attitude" while "Professional Maturity" included "presentation of subject-matter."

I like factor analysis, and I enjoyed thinking about the differences between Marsh's nine dimensions, Feldman's twenty-eight, and Abrami, d'Apollonia, and Rosenfeld's four. In many ways their disagreement parallels that between Spearman and Thurstone in the early factor analytic studies of intelligence. However, it seems to me that the key issue is how one wants to use these findings. For certain research and personnel purposes, only a general factor, such as Abrami, d'Apollonia and Rosenfield's general factor or Marsh's higher order factors may be sufficient; for analyzing a particular course, in helping a particular group of teachers to improve, or for research on the effect of interventions in teaching, a finer cut, such as Feldman's, may be more useful.

As Abrami, d'Apollonia and Rosenfield suggest, we need a theoretical description of the teaching process. Factor analysis is only one means to stimulate theoretical thinking; we need to approach theory not only through factor analysis but also from other approaches as well. Much of the work on student ratings deals not so much with process as with characteristics of teachers; we need also to think not only of teaching processes but also of cognitive processes of student learners. Following are examples of two approaches—one related to teacher characteristics; the other to cognitions of learners.

With respect to teacher characteristics one way of relating student rating dimensions to a larger body of research and theory would be to see how they fit with the "Big Five" dimensions of personality, (Norman, 1963; Tupes and Christal, 1961) which are now generally accepted as the basic taxonomic basis for research in personality structure.

While researchers differ somewhat in the names they attach to the Big Five, the following are reasonably acceptable labels:

  I. Extraversion-introversion
  II. Agreeableness
  III. Conscientiousness
  IV. Emotional stability-neuroticism
  V. Culture (Openness to experience).

Marsh's "Instructor enthusiasm" falls into Factor I—*extraversion.* "Organization" is found in Factor III—*conscientiousness,* and "Fairness in examinations and grading" also falls in Factor III. "Individual rapport" clearly belongs in *agreeableness.* "Breadth of coverage" might well fall in Factor V. Surprisingly *Emotional stability vs. neuroticism* doesn't appear in Marsh's list even though it seems likely that this dimension is also important in teaching effectiveness. Feldman's dimension 14, "Teacher personality," with items such as "good sense of humor," "sincere and honest," "highly personable," "casual, informal, attitude," and "free of personal peculiarities" seems to capture some of the emotional stability dimension.

Why should we care about relating our student ratings of teachers to the basic dimensions of personality? The practical implications are not immediately apparent. Yet, recognizing this relationship does help in giving us confidence that the dimensions found by Marsh and others are not arbitrary; they do make sense in terms of the basic theory of personality structure. While the Big 5 dimensions have been most often applied in personnel selection, personnel psychologists see them as also being valuable in performance appraisal and training (Barrick and Mount, 1991). Thus those who work in appraisal and training of college teachers may find useful relationships to the broader work in other areas. Equally important is that the Big 5 gives us access to the several thousand words describing the Big 5 personality characteristics, roles, and motives. This can give us a richer understanding of what is represented by the dimensions and how the items making up the dimensions of student rating scales are likely to be related to other human characteristics.

Another theoretical approach is to look at cognitive and instructional theory to see what tools they provide for thinking about the dimensions uncovered by factor analysis. For example, we might look at the dimensions revealed in Marsh's analysis to see how they relate to the major categories of theoretical variables that predict student learning—cognition and motivation. (Marsh and Dunkin's chapter relates their nine dimensions to principles of learning in adult education and have covered some of the points that I shall develop from a related but slightly different perspective.) While there are overlaps between motivational and cognitive aspects of the Marsh dimensions, most can be fairly easily classified as affecting either student motivation or cognition. I like the way Murray linked "enthusiasm" to attention, "clarity" to encoding and "interaction" to active learning. Moreover, I think we can go beyond this. Thus, "instructor enthusiasm" seems to me to affect student motivation as well as attention, while "organization/clarity" affects the meaningfulness and organization of student learning.

461

"Group interaction" has both motivational and cognitive effects. "Interaction" provides opportunities to reveal and clear up confusion, to practice problem solving, to permit elaboration or deep processing of the subject matter, and also to stimulate motivation by social facilitation and the opportunity to relate material to student interests. "Rapport" is also related to motivation for learning.

"Workload/difficulty" can pose cognitive problems, but also may be a factor either in stimulating curiosity and challenge or alternatively leading to discouragement and loss of motivation. Brady (1994) showed that in general students prefer professors who are demanding, a result reinforced by Feldman's finding that intellectual challenge is more positively related to mean student ratings of teaching effectiveness than to mean student achievement.

As an aside, I would note that Abrami, d'Apollonia, and Rosenfield's comment that "ratings of course difficulty do not predict student learning at all" is what one would expect on the basis of cognitive and motivational theory. The relationship between difficulty and learning should be curvilinear; i.e. the best learning should occur when a course is perceived as difficult enough to be achievable— challenging one to do well—but not when it is so easy that it is not challenging, or so difficult that mastery is hopeless. As a further aside, I would note that one of the difficulties with factor analysis, as well as with product-moment correlations, is that they assume linearity and are likely to miss curvilinear relationships.

In any case Marsh gives us a framework for looking at teacher differences. Both personality and cognitive theories as well as research evidence indicate that these dimensions are important in determining teacher effectiveness.

CAN TEACHERS LEARN HOW TO BE MORE EFFECTIVE?

Once again we can give a resoundingly positive answer. Each chapter presents encouraging evidence, ranging from the specific training of behavior by Murray through the feedback of student rating studies reviewed by Perry and Marsh to the more extensive programs of faculty development reviewed by Weimer and Lenze.

Although feedback of student ratings alone has positive but mixed effects, feedback with consultation or with written descriptions of strategies, such as the booklets developed by Wilson (1986) and Marsh and Roche (1993), enhances the likelihood of improvement.

462

The improvement in teaching demonstrated is encouraging, but I fully agree with Murray and Weimer and Lenze that we need more research on teacher thinking to get a better idea of how feedback and various forms of training are incorporated into planning and moment-to-moment decision making in the classroom. Is our training primarily effective through its effect upon teacher thinking? Upon development of skills? Or does it obtain its results through its effect on motivational variables such as goals and self-efficacy? Probably all occur, with different effects in different contexts.

In any case we have made significant gains since the early studies validating the importance of instructor enthusiasm and clarity. (Remmers, Martin, and Elliott, 1949; Morsh, Burgess, and Smith, 1956)

Murray shows the specific behaviors that mark the enthusiastic teacher—vocal variation, movement and gesture, facial expression, and humor. While I had always thought that changing a teacher's enthusiasm was well nigh impossible, I now believe that Murray has given us some handles that will help. Movement, gesture, and vocal variation are trainable characteristics. We are probably not going to transform a quiet, monotone into a manic who rushes up and down the aisles shouting, but we can move them toward the middle of the expressiveness scale and Murray's research demonstrates that such training produces significant changes in student ratings of effectiveness.

Teaching "clarity" is, I think, an easier task when we are given Murray's list of associated behaviors. Using concrete examples, providing an outline, signaling transitions—these are clearly teachable skills.

And I learned very early in training graduate teaching assistants that encouraging them to learn student names and to use the students' names when questioning or responding—such simple things made a significant difference in student-teacher "rapport."

Marsh and Dunkin's and Feldman's superb reviews of research on student ratings of teaching, together with Murray's research, should convince any rational person of the value of collecting student ratings, but college faculty members are not noted for their rationality in faculty debates about higher education policy. As one of my distinguished colleagues said when Herb Marsh mildly suggested that there was relevant research on the issue being discussed, "We don't care about the research findings. We have our own experience."

Such an attitude may help us understand why there is general acceptance of peer ratings of research as highly valid despite data indicating relatively low agreement among ratings of research articles while discounting the voluminous validity data presented by Marsh with respect to student ratings of teaching.

I suspect that the validity data for student ratings of instruction are about as extensive as for any psychological tests except intelligence tests. Nonetheless we still have points of vulnerability. Most validity studies relating mean student ratings to mean achievement of students are carried out in large multi-section courses at the introductory level. As Feldman notes, the typical criterion is a final examination consisting mostly of multiple-choice or true-false questions testing simple knowledge of isolated facts and involving little higher order thinking. This probably explains why Feldman found that ratings of "intellectual challenge" and "encouragement of students' independent thought" were highly correlated with students' overall evaluation of instruction but not highly correlated with mean student achievement. To me this indicates that students are more sophisticated in their view of the goals of education than we may have thought. They value an emphasis on thinking even if the criterion examinations on which they are graded do not require it.

Faculty resistance to student ratings: An aside. While the research on the impact of feedback from student ratings indicates that there is some improvement in teaching, the amount of improvement is small unless the feedback involves consultation. A major reason for this rather disappointing result is that many faculty members resist using them. Even though student ratings of teaching have been in widespread use at the University of Michigan for 45 years there is still much resistance and hostility toward their use. Yet our experience at the Center for Research on Learning and Teaching is that there is great faculty enthusiasm for *midterm* feedback from students. How can we account for this phenomenon?

Marsh and Dunkin analyze the problem of faculty resistance in some depth, and I shall simply endorse and elaborate on their discussion. As I see it, a major difference between end-of-term student ratings and collection of student reactions at mid-term is in the projected use of the student opinions. In the case of midterm feedback, the instructor has personal control of the use of the results. One can determine which aspects to attend to and which are less important. The use of the ratings is within the faculty member's own control— and autonomy is one of the motives that is particularly high for faculty members as compared with individuals in other occupations. Perry shows the importance of perceived personal control in student motivation, and faculty members are, if anything, even more motivated for personal control than the average person.

End-of-the-term ratings that may be used for determination of salary increases or promotion are quite another matter. Here the faculty member has no control over the interpretation or use of the ratings. As I wrote two decades ago, most humans do not enjoy being evaluated unless we are confident that the results will be highly positive (McKeachie, 1973). Ratings used for personnel decisions represent the power and control of the institution over the individual—a condition that is not conducive to positive feelings.

Why then do we accept peer evaluation of our research— a dimension of academic performance carrying even more weight in promotion decisions? The answer, I believe, is that these evaluations are almost always positive. As a department chair and member of our college executive committee, I have been involved in reviewing hundreds—probably well over a thousand—such letters. My experience (lacking knowledge of relevant research) is that negative letters are about as common as palm trees above the Arctic circle. It is true that one reads between the lines—even the absence of superlatives is sometimes taken to be negative—but I can never remember a letter stating bluntly that a candidate's research is poor.

Now as it happens, student ratings are also mostly positive. At the University of Michigan 90% of our faculty are rated as excellent by over half of their students. Why then are student ratings feared?

I believe that there are two reasons.

The first is that the ratings are on numerical scales that are normed. In the late 1940s, when the University of Michigan faculty first debated the used of student ratings, one faculty member argued that good teaching could not be measured. I argued that anything that existed, existed in a quantifiable fashion. Thus it was appropriate to use quantifiable ratings. I now feel that that was a mistake. Not that qualities of teaching are not quantifiable. Numbers are often useful. The fault is not in the numbers, but rather in their use. Once numbers are assigned, faculty promotion committees begin to make comparisons between teachers and assume that if one number is larger than another, there is a real difference between the teachers to whom the numbers have been assigned.

Moreover faculty members are supplied with norms indicating the average ratings on each item. Thus a faculty member whose students all "agree" that he or she is an excellent teacher will find that he or she is "below average" as a teacher because other faculty members have some students who "strongly agree" on that item. Finding that one is "below average" is unlikely to increase one's enthusiasm for teaching, and it certainly does not lead to greater enthusiasm for student ratings.

Nira Hativa, in a recent article in *Instructional Evaluation and Faculty Development* (Hativa, 1993), argues persuasively against comparative ratings. She suggests that we simply consider absolute levels of student satisfaction or, as I would prefer, judgments of learning. Abrami, d'Apollonia, and Rosenfield's chapter provides additional support for the notion that faculty members should not use student ratings to compare themselves with other teachers.

We do not assign numbers in our letters evaluating the research of a faculty member being considered for promotion to tenure. It is very unlikely that a solid, but not outstanding researcher, will be categorized as "below average." I believe that we should simply report the number of students at each point on the rating scale for each item rather than reporting means and norms. However using the distribution of student responses, or even mean ratings, to track one's improvement over time is a worthwhile use of numbers. Marsh and Bailey (1993) show how profile comparisons over time can be of value.

If one is concerned about using ratings to improve the quality of teaching, the finding that most faculty are rated positively should not be taken as a damning indictment of student ratings. Rather, even elementary motivation theory would say that this is exactly the sort of result that is likely to increase faculty member's motivation for teaching.

The second reason for the distrust of student ratings is that evaluation of teaching in many universities is seldom used as a positive factor in determining the promotion of faculty members. Rather, as Salthouse, Lin and I (1978) showed in our studies of the use of student ratings in promotion and salary decisions, poor ratings of teaching had a negative effect, but good ratings had little impact. Thus a teacher being evaluated runs the risk of negative results with little chance of positive rewards.

For decades those who study student ratings of faculty have suggested that we should make a cleaner separation between the formative and summative uses of student ratings of teaching. Rather than requiring that ratings be given routinely at the end of the semester, let us get feedback from students early in the term—perhaps at the end of the first month or at midterm. The feedback could well be on the sort of items studied by Murray or Marsh, could be on specific aspects of the course, or could be open-ended. For example, I sometimes ask my students or my teaching assistants' students two questions:

What have you liked about the course so far?
What suggestions do you have for improvement?

These questions are not likely to produce comments that will be devastating to the beginning teacher and usually provide useful ideas for improvement.

Similarly Bob Boice (1992) has developed a painless set of items for collecting student feedback. His "Informal Student Evaluation" form asks students to rate aspects of teaching that the instructor does well and the directions in which it might be changed (with no good or bad endpoints). Whatever the method of collecting feedback, improvement is more likely to occur if the feedback is discussed with a consultant.

End of the term student opinion need not be collected in every course to be valid data for personnel purposes. Faculty members should be asked to include data from several classes in their portfolio, but they should be free to opt out when they are trying new methods or developing a risky innovation, just as they are free to avoid publishing research that didn't pan out.

Helping faculty members and administrators become more sophisticated users of student ratings of teaching. Those of us involved in faculty development and evaluation of teaching have, I believe, done a creditable job in developing and validating forms for collecting student opinion. Students have generally done a fairly good job in filling out the forms. The problems encountered in evaluation of faculty seem to me to lie primarily on the doorsteps of faculty members, administrators, and faculty developers. As a faculty member, a sometime administrator and faculty developer, I admit culpability in all three roles.

The basic problem is that neither administrators, nor faculty members who serve on committees responsible for faculty evaluation, are well-trained for the task. Those of us responsible for evaluative decisions accept with little question letters about research that have limited reliability and unknown validity. In evaluating teaching we often fail to gather relevant data such as examinations, papers, reports, or other student products indicative of achievement, and only with the current popularity of the portfolio have many departments examined syllabi, reading lists, course requirements, and other evidence of course planning and content. We focus on classroom performance and neglect important out-of-class contributions to education. We look at mean ratings of teaching and because the results are reported statistically, the numbers are given magical significance. As Abrami, d'Apollonia and Rosenfield demonstrate, we include information from student rating items that are inappropriate for courses that do not fit the conventional classroom lecture format. We fail to take account of contextual variables.

Feldman's review of the myths and half-truths believed by many faculty members illustrates the seriousness of the problem of resistance by faculty members and misuse by faculty committees and administrators.

Nonetheless professionals in faculty development must share the blame. We have done all too little to supply information in ways that will reduce misuse; we have failed to provide training for personnel committees and administrators, not only in interpreting student ratings, but also in evaluating course materials and other kinds of evidence. We have not succeeded in helping faculty members understand the basic research and theories having to do with the goals of education and the nature of effective teaching and learning. We have done little to help students be better observers and judges of their own learning.

The ethics of evaluation of teaching. There is also an ethical problem in requiring student time for the collection of student opinions of teaching. I believe that if you are taking students' (or anyone's) time, you have an ethical obligation to insure that it is educational, interesting, fun, or in some way rewarding to them. For midterm evaluations, one can argue that the students will benefit from whatever improvements follow from their feedback. But I would argue that there is a more important value that we have failed to emphasize in our use of student ratings of teaching. This is the educational value to the student of filling out student rating forms.

Systems of student evaluation of teaching should encourage students to think about their own educational experiences—to develop clearer conceptions of the kinds of teaching and educational experiences that contribute most to their learning. The student opinion form could, and should, be educational in the highest sense—helping students gain a better understanding of the goals of education, stimulating them to think more metacognitively about their own learning, motivating them to continue learning, and encouraging them to accept responsibility for their learning.

I believe that we could do a much better job of introducing these educational objectives for filling out the rating forms. We can certainly create forms that encourage student metacognition. The form I developed and published in my book, *Teaching Tips*, (7th edition, 1978; McKeachie and Svinicki, 2006) asks students to think about the impact of the course upon their own gains on several dimensions of education. Items are also included dealing with the student's own responsibility for learning. I am pleased that Abrami, d'Apollonia and Rosenfeld also endorse this approach.

Discussion with students aimed at sensitizing them to evaluating their own learning and the conditions that contribute to learning is important in developing their ability to learn more effectively. Such a discussion before ratings are collected and discussion of the results after the ratings have been summarized should not only result in more useful feedback for teachers but also help students become better learners.

At this point we have linked dimensions of teaching and teaching behaviors to teaching effectiveness empirically, but we have only touched upon the theory underlying our conception of effective teaching. Let us now return to the theory of instruction.

WHY DO EFFECTIVE TEACHING METHODS RESULT IN BETTER LEARNING?

Even in the 1940's and 1950's we theorized about teaching effectiveness. In my doctoral dissertation (McKeachie, 1949) I talked about student "gut learning"—essentially the kind of learning that might now be labeled as "deep processing." We used terms like "groupiness" or "group cohesion" to describe the sense of trust, cooperation and motivation characterizing effective discussion groups. Today we emphasize the value of collaborative or cooperative learning, sometimes based upon cognitive theory of elaboration or levels of processing and upon motivation and social psychological theories of social facilitation, or sometimes simply on the practical argument that skills in cooperation are important in employment after college. Even though it might seem from comparing the research and theory of research in college teaching in the 1950's with that of the 1990's that the themes are much the same, there has been progress. As I see it, three areas of theoretical development have particular significance for our thinking about teaching.

One of these is the importance of *context*. Feldman points out that many aspects of teaching that one would expect to be highly related to teaching effectiveness have rather modest correlations with outcomes. *Feedback*, for example, does not correlate particularly well with student achievement. But we now know that feedback can have unintended effects depending upon the context and the student's attributions. Criticism, for example, may be taken by a student as evidence that he or she lacks the ability to succeed, or it may be interpreted as evidence that the teacher thinks that one has the ability to improve. Thus the kind of feedback and the previous relationship between the teacher and the student may determine whether the feedback produces a reduction in motivation or increased motivation.

Similarly *organization* has a rather tricky relationship to student prior knowledge, the difficulty of the material, and the heterogeneity of the students in a class. Clearly students will remember better if they have some organized framework within which to encode facts and concepts. But they will remember the material best if they have developed the organization for themselves. Teachers with heterogeneous classes, therefore, are faced with the dilemma that if they provide a high level of organization, they diminish the learning of students with the ability to organize for themselves; if the teachers fail to provide an organization, students with less prior knowledge will be left in confusion. Hartley's comparisons of providing complete lecture notes, skeletal notes, or no notes suggest that skeletal notes are an effective compromise in the typical lecture class (Hartley and Davies, 1978), but clearly the value of organization is affected by the context.

A second area where we have made progress is in a much more detailed understanding of what is going on in the students' heads—the **cognitive processes** affected by teaching. As discussed earlier, teacher *enthusiasm* enhances student attention; teacher *clarity* aids encoding; *interaction* of students and teachers promotes the surfacing of misunderstanding, and permits clarification and elaboration.

Students create learning out of the interaction of what is already in their heads with the learning experiences we provide in and out of the classroom. Because only the students know what is in their minds, peer observations can never take the place of the students' own ratings of their educational experiences. This does not mean that student introspections are flawless, but they do provide information that is important for understanding teaching and learning.

Important as are the gains in our understanding of cognition, equally important progress has been made, as Perry suggests (Perry, 1991) in the area of **motivation**. Both expectancy-value theory and attribution theory have given a better understanding of the way in which teaching affects motivation for learning.

Teacher *enthusiasm* has important motivational as well as cognitive effects. The teacher's enthusiasm about the interest and value of the subject acts as a model that influences the value students place upon learning the material; moreover, as Feldman notes, teacher enthusiasm includes spontaneity and variability, which not only affects attention but is also relevant to curiosity and interest.

Similarly *interaction* of students and teachers increases opportunity for students to feel a greater sense of personal control—an important motivational variable both in increasing the student's self-efficacy and expectancy of success and also in affecting attributions of success to one's own ability and effort rather than to external causes.

Motivation theory also helps us understand the problems of faculty motivation for teaching, such as the heavy extrinsic pressures exerted by evaluation for tenure, with a likely result of a loss of intrinsic satisfaction. (Deci, 1971)

CONCLUSION

So, we have seen that good teaching makes a difference. What can we do with the information?

There are a number of implications for teachers and academic administrators in the preceding chapters and I have mentioned several in this chapter. Like Mary Ellen Weimer I would call them tentative rather than hard and fast rules. Nonetheless I would take a somewhat more strongly positive stance than Weimer in encouraging teachers, administrators, and faculty developers to think about the implications suggested by the researchers and to try out their own versions, using the suggestions heuristically rather than as recipes for improvement. In any case here are some that are particularly worthy of the attention of administrators and faculty developers:

1. Workshops and other forms of training (as reviewed by Weimer and Lenze) can help faculty members communicate greater enthusiasm, teach them methods of establishing rapport, help develop greater skills in organization and clarity, assist in developing other skills, and enhance motivation.
2. Consultation (See Weimer and Lenze) can greatly improve the value of feedback from student ratings, videotapes, or other information gathering methods.
3. No one is too old to learn. With the end of mandatory retirement in the United States, it will become even more important that older faculty members maintain their vitality by developing new skills and understanding of teaching.
4. As Weimer and Lenze indicate, training in basic skills as well as continuing social support can increase the likelihood that

471

the early teaching experiences of teaching assistants and new faculty members will be intrinsically satisfying. Just as intrinsic interest in learning and deeper processing of content reciprocally reinforce one another; so too intrinsic satisfactions in teaching and development as a teacher go hand in hand.

5. Weimer and Lenze, reviewing each of the categories of interventions designed to help teachers improve, repeatedly stress the necessity of better evaluative data particularly in actual teaching situations. I join in that plea. We can seldom do an ideal evaluation, but we should do much more than we have thus far in linking our efforts to changes in teacher motivation, thinking, and behavior that seem likely to result in better student learning. I would not ask that we always go to our ultimate criterion—student learning—because as I have pointed out elsewhere, (McKeachie, 1990) student learning is affected by so many variables that the effects of any one intervention are not likely to make a big difference, particularly in the relatively insensitive and marginally valid typical final examination.

Although there is still much to be done, we have come a long way since Remmers' 1927 monograph. I have no doubt that college and university teaching has improved and that we have gained enough knowledge to facilitate continued improvement.

Reprinted by permission of Agathon Press, New York.

REFERENCES

Barrick, M.R., and Mount, M.K. (1991). The Big Five personality dimensions and job performance: A meta-analysis. *Personnel Psychology* 44: 1–26.

Boice, R. (1992). Countering common misbeliefs about student evaluations of teaching. *Chalkboard*. Fall 1992, University of Missouri-Columbia, Program for Excellence in Teaching.

Brady, P.J. (1994). How likeability and effectiveness ratings of college professors by their students are affected by course demands and professors' attitudes. *Psychological Reports* 74: 907–913.

Deci, E.L. (1971). *Intrinsic Motivation* New York: Plenum.

Dubin, R., and Taveggia, T.C. (1968). *The Teaching-Learning Paradox*. Eugene, Oregon: University of Oregon.

Hartley, J., and Davies, I.K. (1978). Note-taking: A critical review. *Programmed Learning and Educational Technology* 15(3): 207–224.

Hativa, N. (1993) Student ratings: A non-comparative interpretation. *Instructional Evaluation and Faculty Development* 13(2): 1–4.

Marsh, H.W., and Bailey, M. (1993). Multidimensionality of students' evaluations of teaching effectiveness: A profile analysis. *Journal of Higher Education* 64: 1–18.

Marsh, H.W., and Roche, L. (1993). The use of students' evaluations and an individually structured intervention to enhance teaching effectiveness. *American Educational Research Journal* 30: 217–251.

McKeachie, W.J. (1949) Individual conformity to attitudes of classroom groups. Doctoral dissertation published in *Journal of Abnormal and Social Psychology*, 1954: 49, 282–289.

McKeachie, W.J. (1973). Resistances to evaluation of teaching. *Occasional Paper No. 2.* Evanston, IL: The Center for Teaching Professions, Northwestern University.

McKeachie, W.J. (1990). Learning, thinking, and Thorndike. *Educational Psychologist* 25(2): 127–141.

McKeachie, W.J. (1978). *Teaching Tips*. Lexington, MA: D.C.Health.

McKeachie, W.J., and Birney, R. (1955). The teaching of psychology: A survey of research since 1942. *Psychological Bulletin* 51: 51–68.

McKeachie, W.J., and Svinicki, M. (2006). *McKeachie's Teaching Tips: Strategies, Research, and Theory for College and University Teachers* (12th edition). Boston, MA: Houghton-Mifflin.

Morsh, J.E., Burgess, G.G., and Smith, P.N. (1956). Student achievement as a measure of instructor effectiveness. *Journal of Educational Psychology* 47: 79–88.

Norman, W.T. (1963) Toward an adequate taxonomy of personality attributes: Replicated factor structure in peer nomination personality ratings. *Journal of Abnormal and Social Psychology* 66: 574–583.

Perry, R.P. (1991). Perceived control in college students: Implications for instruction in higher education. In J.C. Smart (ed.), *Higher Education: Handbook of Theory and Research*, Vol. VII. New York: Agathon Press (*included in this volume*).

Remmers, H.H. (1927). The college professor as the student sees him. *Purdue University Studies in Higher Education* No.11.

Remmers, H.H. (1958). On students' perceptions of teacher effectiveness. In W.J. McKeachie (ed.), *The Appraisal of Teaching in Large Universities*. Ann Arbor: University of Michigan.

Remmers, H.H., Martin, F.D., and Elliott, D.N. (1949). Are students' ratings of instructors related to their grades? *Purdue Studies of Higher Education* 66: 17–26.

Salthouse, T.A., McKeachie, W.J., and Lin, Y-G, (1978). An experimental investigation of factors affecting university promotion decisions: A brief report. *Journal of Higher Education* 49: 177–183.

Shuell, T.J. (1993). Toward an integrated theory of teaching and learning. *Educational Psychologist* 28(4): 291–311

Smalzreid, N.T., and Remmers, H.H. (1943). A factor analysis of the Purdue rating scale for instructors. *Journal of Educational Psychology* 34: 363–367.

Tupes, E.C., and Christal, R.E. (1961). Recurrent personality factors based on trait ratings. (USAF ASD Tech. Rep. No. 61–97). Lackland Air Force Base, TX: U.S. Air Force.

Wilson, R.C. (1986). Improving faculty teaching: Effective use of student evaluations and consultants. *Journal of Higher Education* 57: 196–211.

SECTION III: RESEARCH ON LEARNING IN HIGHER EDUCATION

12. PERCEIVED (ACADEMIC) CONTROL AND SCHOLASTIC ATTAINMENT IN HIGHER EDUCATION

Raymond P. Perry[†], Nathan C. Hall[‡] and Joelle C. Ruthig[§]

[†]*University of Manitoba Canada*
rperry@cc.umanitoba.ca
[‡]*University of California at Irvine*
[§]*University of North Dakota*

Key Words: Perceived control, paradox of failure, attribution theory, causal attributions, academic motivation and achievement, academic engagement, achievement striving

The geopolitical climate of late 18th century France described by Charles Dickens as "the best of times, the worst of times" is no less true today of postsecondary institutions in North America. "The best of times" are seen in the dramatic expansion of the postsecondary education system in the last 50 years — more openings are available and a greater diversity of groups have access to those openings. In Canada, for example, the number of undergraduate students increased from approximately 115,000 in 1960 to almost 850,000 in 2000, while Canada's population grew by less than 2-fold (Canadian Association of University Teachers,

*The research described here was supported by grants from the Social Sciences and Humanities Research Council of Canada (91–1296; 95–0152; 99–0435; 2003–0059), the Alexander von Humboldt Foundation (Germany), and the Max Planck Society (Germany) to the senior author, and doctoral fellowships from the Social Sciences and Humanities Research Council of Canada to the two junior authors. The efforts of Steve Hladkyj, Verena Menec, and Ward Struthers in the coordination and development of the Motivation and Academic Achievement (MAACH) Research Laboratory described here are greatly appreciated, as are the contributions of many others who participated. Raymond Currie, Dean of Arts (1991 to 1999) provided critical institutional support to the overall development of this research and Judy G. Chipperfield contributed insightful ideas concerning various research projects. Please address correspondence to Raymond P. Perry, Department of Psychology, University of Manitoba, Winnipeg, Manitoba, CANADA, R3T 2N2. Email: rperry@cc.umanitoba.ca. The MAACH research group web site can be found at the following address: http://www.umanitoba.ca/faculties/arts/psychology/maach

R.P. Perry and J.C. Smart (eds.), The Scholarship of Teaching and Learning in Higher Education: An Evidence-Based Perspective, 477–551.
© 2007 *Springer.*

2003; Clifton, 2000; Sokoloff, 2004). During this same period, female undergraduate participation rates have risen from less than 25% in 1960, to 50% in 1980, and over 57% in 2000 (Clifton, 2000; Sokoloff, 2004). Compared to the 4-fold increase for male undergraduates, the number of female undergraduates increased by more than 14 times. Participation rates in the U.S. postsecondary education system are comparable (National Center for Educational Statistics, 2004).

With an expanding postsecondary system comes substantial economic benefits for students as well as for the broader society. According to Paulsen (1998), earnings for male college students were superior to high-school-educated males, when all fields and levels of experience are combined, by 40% in 1963, 48% in 1971, and 58% in 1989 (Murphy and Welch, 1992). Studies of identical twins indicate that earnings increase roughly 12% to 16% with each additional year of college education (Ashenfelter and Krueger, 1994; Miller, Mulvey, and Martin, 1995). Moreover, the type of college plays an instrumental role in the occupational status attained by students in professional and nonprofessional jobs (Smart, 1986) and in their eventual income levels (Smart, 1988). Within the broader societal context, Leslie and Slaughter (1992) showed that each $1 million invested by a four-year college in its budget results in $1.8 million in additional business spending and 53 new jobs, with similar figures reported by Creech, Carpenter, and Davis (1994).

Meanwhile, "the worst of times" are reflected in the accelerating failure rates and the decreasing quality of graduates. An unacceptable number of undergraduates leave college prematurely and many new graduates are deficient in basic numeracy and literacy skills that were commonplace decades ago. Surveys of participation rates in U.S. postsecondary institutions show that approximately 50% of graduating high school students enroll in college, but of these, 27% leave at the end of their first year, and fewer than 55% of those remaining graduate after five years (Desruisseaux, 1998; Geraghty, 1996). Of every 100 high school students in Grade 11, no more than 14 will graduate from college after five years. Figures for Canadian postsecondary institutions are equally disconcerting, as for example, at our own university, only 55% of first-year students will graduate within six years after entering their respective undergraduate programs.

More opportunity to pursue postsecondary studies, it would seem, is inextricably linked to a higher incidence of failure — an unanticipated nexus of access and failure that embraces both optimistic and pessimistic perspectives. Greater institutional choice also means that college students have more responsibility for their academic

478

development. Never before have personal autonomy, independence, and self-reliance played such a large role in college students' educational experiences. In this context, we view quality of educational experience broadly in terms of teaching and learning processes that promote academic motivation and achievement-striving, as expressed in cognitive, affective, and performance outcomes in students.

The present chapter examines student differences in perceived control within higher education settings and how these differences impact students' achievement, persistence, and overall scholastic development. As part of this analysis, we consider other academic differences among college students, such as course-related emotions and perceptions of success, that interact with perceived control to enhance or impede academic motivation and achievement striving. Finally, the chapter explores the interaction between academic control in students and classroom instructional practices as a form of aptitude-treatment interaction described by Cronbach and Snow (1977). In this context, we introduce an instructional practice that is an educational treatment intervention expressly designed to assist failure-prone college students by enhancing their academic control, referred to as Attributional Retraining.

PERCEIVED ACADEMIC CONTROL: A RESEARCH PERSPECTIVE

Our main thesis in this chapter is that students who describe themselves as psychologically "in control" work harder, feel better about their studies, obtain better grades, and have more productive academic careers than their "out of control" counterparts. Simply put, two students who are equally capable intellectually may perform very differently in their courses, because of the level of control they believe they have over their academic performance. For our purposes, *perceived academic control* refers to students' beliefs about whether they possess certain attributes, such as intellectual ability, physical stamina, effort expenditure, task strategies, social skills, and educational experience, and whether such attributes make a difference to their scholastic performance (cause-effect contingencies). In this context, student differences in perceived academic control can be viewed as a continuum anchored by two distinct student groupings: *low-control students* who are failure-prone and helpless-oriented, and *high-control students* who are academi cally successful and mastery-oriented. Within this framework, low-control students are expected to have very different academic trajectories than their high-control counterparts in terms of cognitive, affective, motivational, and achievement outcomes. Both types of students are assumed to be represented in a typical college classroom, along with other students (moderate-control) who occupy the middle of the control continuum.

Two fundamental questions must be addressed when considering the role of perceived academic control in the scholastic development of college students. First, what is the effect of academic control on achievement motivation and scholastic performance when students enter college initially, and relatedly, throughout their undergraduate training? Embedded within this first research question are two related issues concerning the relative effects of perceived control compared to traditional predictors such as intelligence, prior knowledge, and socio-economic status, and the sustainability of perceived control effects on academic development over time. These two issues are of interest not just to students, but to instructors and postsecondary institutions as well. Instructors want to know, for example, whether differences between college students in academic control influence scholastic performance separately from aptitude and other student differences pertinent to learning and performance; and if so, by how much and for how long.

The second question concerns whether classroom instructional methods can offset the deleterious consequences uniquely associated with low academic control. Low control in college students is particularly worrisome when normally effective teaching methods are ineffective with low-control students. If differences in academic control are critical, then instructors may want to tailor their teaching methods to students differing in control. The discussion method of instruction, for example, may be suitable for high-control students because of its open-ended structure, but not so for low-control students for the same reason; or, the lecture method may appeal to low-control students because of its highly structured and predictable nature, but not to high-control students because of the lack of autonomy. Control-enhancing educational interventions would have special appeal to classroom instructors if they can be readily incorporated into their teaching methods to assist low-control students in getting better grades and staying in college. In the context of this second question, we introduce *Attributional Retraining (AR)* as a control-enhancing treatment designed to assist failure-prone, low-control students which can be readily incorporated into instructors' classroom teaching methods (see Attributional Retraining: A Control-Enhancing Instructional Treatment section below).

Over the past two decades, we conducted a number of experimental studies to explore these two basic research questions in both laboratory and field settings (Perry, 1991, 2003). A common core 2×2 factorial design was used to test the effects of academic control (low, high) and instructional treatments (control-enhancing treatment, no treatment) on performance and achievement-related measures involving cognition, emotion, and motivation. The first question concerning individual differences in academic control is a main effect question which statistically addresses whether high-control students perform better than low-control students in their first year of college and throughout their undergraduate studies. The second instructional treatment question is examined in two ways: first, with a control-enhancing treatment main effect which examines whether both low- and high-control students perform better after receiving the treatment, compared to those not receiving the treatment; and second, with an academic control × treatment interaction which is a type of aptitude-treatment interaction (Cronbach and Snow, 1977). This interaction question considers whether the AR educational treatment intervention (treatment vs. no treatment) improved the performance of some students (low control), but not others. The bulk of the chapter is devoted to a detailed exploration of these research questions.

PERCEIVED CONTROL AND ACADEMIC ACHIEVEMENT SETTINGS

Although college students are selected for their intellectual and academic capabilities, surprising numbers fail, even as the criteria for admission to postsecondary institutions become increasingly stringent. As shown by Anastasi (1988) and Britton and Tesser (1991), pre-college aptitude determines only 16% to 20% of variance in college grades, a finding replicated with increasing frequency. Presumably, admissions criteria should increase students' success rates, yet college students are taking longer to graduate or are simply withdrawing from postsecondary education entirely. Perry, Hladkyj, Pekrun, and Pelletier (2001) describe this deficiency in traditional selection criteria as a *paradox of failure* to describe outwardly bright, motivated college students who subsequently fail despite having met stipulated admissions criteria. They argue that an accurate account of this paradox must include psychosocial variables, notably perceived control, in addition to typical academic and demographic selection criteria involving intellectual aptitude, disciplinary knowledge, academic skills, socioeconomic status, gender, and English-language fluency. Considerable latitude exists in the research literature in the specification of psychosocial variables, however, they are generally considered to include a host of noncognitive variables related to personality, attitudes, creativity, curiosity, motivation, emotion, and so on, but exclude sociodemographic and cognitive variables.

A wealth of empirical evidence supports the importance of psychosocial variables for scholastic attainment in college in addition to more traditional, aptitude and cognitively-based criteria such as SATs and GREs (cf., Pascarella and Terenzini, 1991). For example, in a two-semester longitudinal study, Perry *et al.* (2001) assessed first-year college students' beliefs about their control over academic outcomes and about their preoccupation with success and failure, using covariate analysis to adjust for intellectual aptitude. Students who believed they had control over academic outcomes and who were preoccupied with failure had better grades than all other students at the end of the course, and had better GPAs in all courses taken over a three-year period (Perry, Hladkyj, Pekrun, Clifton, and Chipperfield, in press). Harackiewicz, Barron, Tauer, and Elliott's (2002) seven-year longitudinal follow-up study demonstrated the importance of achievement goals for academic success in college. As expected, ability and high school performance predicted academic success on entry to college and thereafter, but in addition, achievement goals also played a major role in students' scholastic development. Studies by Eaton and Bean (1995) and House (1995) also underscore the importance of psychosocial variables in the academic development of college students. In Robbins *et al.*'s (2004) meta-analytic review of the role of psychosocial factors in college success, perceived control (self-efficacy) and achievement motivation were the strongest predictors of college GPA and persistence (retention) of all psychosocial factors considered, and were superior to socioeconomic status, standardized achievement, and high school GPA.

Perceived (Academic) Control

What is variously labeled autonomy, independence, or self-reliance in common parlance, is viewed here as perceived control, a psychological construct that has received widespread interest in the social sciences over the last five decades. As a construct, it has evolved from Rotter's (1966) conception of it as an individual difference variable (locus of control) and Glass and Singer's (1971) depiction of it as an environmental (contextual) stressor, to a critical component in many present day social cognition theories, including competence motivation (White, 1959), personal causation (DeCharms, 1968), learned helplessness (Seligman, 1975), mastery (Dweck, 1975), reactance (Wortman and

Brehm, 1975), self-efficacy (Bandura, 1977), self-determination theory (Deci and Ryan, 1985), primary/secondary control (Rothbaum, Weisz, and Snyder, 1982), action control (Kuhl, 1985), causal attributions (Weiner, 1985), and mindfulness (Langer, 1989). It is also featured prominently in research on academic achievement (Dweck, 1975; Stipek and Weisz, 1981), health (Chipperfield and Greenslade, 1999; Thompson, Sobolew-Shubin, Galbraith, Schwankovsky, and Cruzen, 1993), stress (Folkman, 1984), depression (Garber and Seligman, 1980), aging (Rodin, 1986), and human mortality (Chipperfield, 1993).

Perceived control is a person's subjective estimate of his or her capacity to manipulate, influence, or predict some aspect of the environment. In the research literature, the prevailing view is that higher perceptions of control are more advantageous than lower perceptions of control. As Skinner's (1996) seminal review so aptly illustrates, the construct continues to evolve to an ever-expanding list of terminology and complexities. In general, perceived control refers to beliefs about the predictability of life's daily events and about the capacity to influence such events, with "perceived" reflecting subjective rather than objective capacity. This phenomenological distinction between "perceived" and "actual" capacity results in the correlation between subjective and objective control ranging from positive to negative (cf., Thompson et al., 1993). Some people assume they have more or less capacity to influence and to predict events than they have in reality, whether as a stable and enduring part of their personality, or as a temporary and transient experience.

These stable and transient forms of perceived control can be thought of as being trait- and state-like manifestations of perceived control, somewhat comparable to trait/state distinctions in personality theory (cf., Eysenck, 1997; Wiggins, 1996). *Stable perceived control* is more enduring and is an integral part of an individual's personality makeup, the result of biology and past learning experiences. In contrast, *transient perceived control* is much less enduring and a product of temporary and ongoing intrusions of daily life. Within college classrooms, the learning contingencies can cause the level of transient control in students to fluctuate widely (see Academic Control and Low-Control Learning Environments section below). As such, an individual's level of stable perceived control can vary as a function of changing levels of transient perceived control created by situational factors. Research perspectives on perceived control typically differ with regard to trait generality, as for example, Bandura (1997) who considers self-efficacy to be a domain-specific entity, whereas Rotter (1975) considers locus of control to be a general attribute. These differences between individuals in perceived control, stable or transient, generate cognitive, emotional, and behavioral consequences, leading people with greater perceived control to think, feel, and respond differently than those with less perceived control.

In achievement settings, we view *perceived academic control* as a relatively stable psychological disposition affecting students' motivation and achievement-striving as revealed in class tests, term assignments, course grades, GPA, etc. It is deemed to be "relatively" stable because assessments of trait perceived control may include the effects of transient elements as well, assuming that periodic environmental intrusions can affect a person's general sense of control to some degree (e.g., Rotter, 1975; Skinner, Connell, and Zimmer-Gembeck, 1998). Initially, we assessed academic control using a single-item, domain-specific measure (Perry and Dickens, 1984), but subsequently expanded this to a multi-item scale (Perry, Hladkyj, and Pekrun, 1998; Perry *et al.*, 2001) incorporating primary academic control, secondary academic control (Rothbaum *et al.*, 1982), and desire for control (Burger, 1989). This reconfiguration follows from the social cognition literature in which perceived control has been defined with a variety of single- and multiple-item measures (Skinner, 1996).

Within this framework, perceived academic control is deemed to be a personal attribute students bring to the classroom that interacts with various aspects of the classroom environment, the most salient being the teaching methods employed by instructors. In addition to academic control beliefs, other dispositional (stable) student characteristics that contribute to students' scholastic development would include constructs such as optimism, self-worth, perceptions of success, and so on. How these stable, personality-like variables relate to academic control goes beyond the scope of this chapter, however, in our own studies academic control has been found to relate positively to: optimism ($rs = .26–.34$), self-esteem ($rs = .40–.44$), cognitive elaboration ($rs = .22–.26$), desire for control ($rs = .34–.51$), procrastination ($.18$), and Big 5 Personality constructs involving Extraversion ($.17$), Agreeableness ($.18$), Openness to Experience ($.23$), and Conscientiousness ($.16$).

DESIRE FOR CONTROL

In considering pre-existing dispositional differences in control among students, it is important to recognize that students' "perceptions of control" differ from their "desire for control" (Burger, 1995; Schulz and Heckhausen, 1996). Despite individual differences in levels of perceived academic control, both low- and high-control students share a common *desire* to influence their scholastic endeavors, although the level of desire may vary across academic tasks. Some students may believe they can control certain academic outcomes, yet view that control as unimportant (i.e., high control/low desire), as in the case of students taking a "practice test," completing an assignment not worth any formal marks, or taking an elective course. These students believe they will perform well on the practice test, but this control is of little value (low desire) to them because the outcome (test score) is unimportant. Similarly, students taking piano lessons or engaged in an athletic sport, but who have little interest in the activity, may perform poorly, even though they have ample talent to excel in the task. In such cases, students having little interest in or desire for their academic endeavors (low desire) does not necessarily imply a lack of control in those circumstances.

The reverse is also the case, however, where students want to influence academic outcomes (high desire), but perceive themselves as having little control over those outcomes, no matter how badly they may want more control (i.e., low control/high desire). Many students, for example, want to perform well in their courses, but are nevertheless uncertain about how to achieve optimal outcomes. Moreover, because academic performance is such an important aspect of their lives, students are likely to desire a considerable amount of control over their achievement outcomes. This desire for control fuels the development of perceptions of control by regulating the type of goals and situations that individuals pursue and their capacity to deal with those situations (Burger, 1995; Burger and Cooper, 1979).

Covington (1992) has argued persuasively that students' self-worth is intricately interwoven with their desire to do well in academic settings. He points out that students tend to equate their own sense of worth with their competitively determined academic accomplishments (e.g., grades assigned by their instructors). As such, the top priority among these students is to strive for academic success and avoid failure, the latter viewed as a sign of incompetence. Thus, a key assumption in academic control research is that students generally want to control their educational experiences. Instances in which this is not the case are of special interest.

ACADEMIC FAILURE

Academic failure, its consequences, and its remediation are critical not just to perceived control researchers, but also to the students themselves, their instructors, and the institutions they attend. For college students, the psychological consequences of failure can threaten their self-worth, erode their perseverance, and undermine their career goals. Moreover, the financial burden of failing a course or changing programs can lengthen graduation completion time substantially, adding thousands of dollars in direct educational costs, as well as indirect costs in lost wages. In contrast, highly motivated students with good academic skills and who receive effective instruction complete their education in much less time, incur far fewer personal and institutional expenses, and have better career options available to them when they graduate. For postsecondary institutions, student failure can amount to tens of thousands of dollars per year in administrative costs for course and program changes, for counseling services, for remedial skills courses, and so on. When academic failure leads to withdrawal from the university, lost tuition revenues for as few as 100 students can add up to $500,000 a year, based on a conservative estimate of tuition costs of $5,000 per year.

Weiner's theory of achievement motivation and emotions (1985, 1995; see below) provides insight into academic failure in college classrooms. Academic failure initiates a causal search in students to identify the reasons (i.e., causes, explanations) for poor performance. The resulting causal attributions can have significant consequences for students' more immediate scholastic performance and for their overall academic career development. A student who attributes a series of failures on course tests to a lack of effort has a better prognosis academically than a student who attributes such failures to a lack of ability. The "low ability" student will experience a loss of perceived control, negative emotions, lack of motivation, and an increased probability of failing subsequent tests and withdrawing from college. Unfortunately, failure is all too common in college, particularly in the first year when students are making the transition from the comfortable realities of high school to the unknown realities of college. How students' perceptions of academic control are affected by both success and failure experiences is discussed in greater detail below in the context of Weiner's theory of achievement motivation (see An Attributional Framework for Perceived Control in College Classrooms).

The remediation of failure is pertinent to all students who struggle at some point in their academic careers, but more so for those who fail repeatedly. Furthermore, postsecondary institutions are also becoming more concerned about failure remediation because of its relevance to student access and attrition. Many colleges and universities have implemented remedial programs to assist failure-prone students and access programs designed for students whose qualifications and experiences may impede entry into higher education. Obviously then, policies and procedures intended to reduce student failure are of significant financial value to and practical importance for postsecondary institutions. In a later section, we examine in detail how Attributional Retraining can offer a viable failure-remediation solution for college students and post-secondary institutions alike.

ACADEMIC CONTROL AND LOW-CONTROL LEARNING ENVIRONMENTS

For over three decades, perceived control researchers have demonstrated how unpredictable or noncontingent events can produce loss of perceived control and helplessness in animals and humans (see Skinner, 1996 for a review). When outcomes and events in the environment are unpredictable and/or cannot be influenced by a person, perceived control is reduced, giving rise to helplessness and hopelessness (Garber and Seligman, 1980; Glass and Singer, 1971; Weiner, 1980). The emphasis on "perceived" in perceived control means that the objective realities of predictability and contingency are inferred by the person in a given situation. Thus, a situation that is objectively predictable or controllable may be perceived as a low-control situation by one person and as high-control by another. Or, a situation that is objectively unpredictable and/or uncontrollable may nevertheless be perceived as a high-control situation. In most instances, the correspondence between the objective and subjective reality of a given situation is reasonably isomorphic, although perceived differences between objective and subjective reality can exist for a given individual or between individuals in the same situation. Situations which limit perceived predictability and/or the perceived capacity to influence events create optimal conditions for observing the impact of academic control on scholastic attainment.

Though academic experiences in college may be "objectively" controllable, students' subjective (phenomenological) or perceived controllability is the operative reality here (Weiner, 1985, 1995), sometimes causing objectively controllable learning experiences to be perceived as uncontrollable, or objectively uncontrollable learning situations as controllable. For some students, any number of academic demands and tasks can be sufficiently novel and unfamiliar as to create unpredictable and noncontingent conditions, that in combination, generate a highly aversive, control-threatening classroom learning environment. But for other students, these same classroom conditions are commonplace, having been part of previous academic experiences, and are seen as reasonably predictable and contingent. Each occurrence can represent some combination of unfamiliarity, challenge, unpredictability, or failure, any one of which portending a loss of perceived control (Skinner, 1996; Weary, Gleicher, and Marsh, 1993).

Thompson *et al.* (1993) describe life situations which inundate individuals with objectively unpredictable events and outcomes as *low-control environments* because they create a psychological state of being "out of control." Perry (1991, 2003) argues that such low-control environments can develop at different levels of the educational system when a disproportionate number of unpredictable and/or uncontrollable achievement events occur in classrooms and other academic contexts. The first year of college can be a prototypic control-threatening learning environment to the extent that students' academic and social experiences undermine their perceived control as a result of heightened academic competition, increased pressure to excel coupled with more frequent failure, unfamiliar academic tasks, critical career choices, new social networks, etc. To the extent that these experiences occur within classrooms, they can be described as low-control learning environments. Because of this, in college classrooms, in contrast to high school classrooms, failure experiences can be more common. At the same time, however, the potential for control, and related successes, is also greater, which in itself may pose a threat to control for some students.

These experiences are assumed to occur with greater regularity during transition periods throughout students' educational development, such as the first year of college, and create more low-control perceptions relative to other years in college (Perry, 2003). Within the K-16 education system, such classroom conditions are more likely during transition years, as might occur in kindergarten, grade 1, grade 7, grade 10, or first-year university. These low-control transition periods, in turn, can have a direct, though temporary, influence on students' perceived academic control. For students continuing their education beyond K-16, additional low-control transition periods would include the first year of graduate or professional school and beginning a new job or career (cf., Bess, 1973; Menges *et al.*, 1999; Perry *et al.*, 1997, 2000; Smart, 1990).

In contrast to these episodic, educationally-contextualized experiences, perceived control has stable and enduring qualities that the student brings to an achievement setting, low-control or otherwise. In transition periods characterized by a high frequency of unpredictable achievement episodes, stable differences between students in personal control and transient control will jointly determine achievement motivation and performance, with students high in academic control outperforming their low-control counterparts. How state- and trait-like factors contribute to overall perceived control is not precisely clear in the literature (cf., Skinner, 1996), however, both are obviously important. Aside from affecting students' transient academic control, repeated experiences with low-control classroom settings likely are incorporated into their more enduring sense of control. In our research discussed below, we focused on the first year of college as a "low-perceived-control" experience in which student differences in perceived academic control are expected to be more pronounced.

AN ATTRIBUTIONAL FRAMEWORK FOR PERCEIVED CONTROL IN COLLEGE CLASSROOMS

Our perspective on perceived academic control in college students begins with the conventional position that perceived control is determined by two broad categories of variables, namely the characteristics of the individual and the properties of the environment. In achievement settings, perceived control is deemed to be a personal quality that students bring to the classroom, like intellectual aptitude, gender, socioeconomic status, discipline knowledge, intrinsic motivation, etc., which is influenced by, yet separate from, the properties of the classroom itself (Glass and Singer, 1971; Perry, 1991, 2003). Perceived academic control is considered to be one such characteristic that students bring to the classroom and a major individual difference directly affecting motivation and performance. Classroom properties also can contribute to a student's sense of academic control and would include not just the physical aspects of the setting, but also such factors as instructional quality, instructor's grading standards, classroom discipline, course level, curriculum structure, class composition and size, and so on.

Within this dichotomy of student characteristics and classroom properties, we adopt an attributional perspective on perceived academic control which focuses on the causal attributions students use to explain their academic successes and failures (cf., Weiner, 1985, 1995). Assuming that college students are actively engaged in trying to make sense of their classroom experiences in order to succeed, they will search for explanations (causal attributions) of their successes and failures within themselves and within the educational context. The personal characteristics of students offer a rich source of possible causes for their successes and failures, the most salient being intelligence, prior knowledge, motivation, and personal goals (Van Overwalle, 1989, 1997). For college students, their quest for causal explanations is manifest in a preoccupation with their personal attributes, reflected in such questions as, "Am I smart enough?" "Can I hang in there long enough?" and so on. Such questions highlight students' concerns about how their attributes affect their performance in comparison to other students, or to some absolute standard. The classroom properties category also presents numerous possibilities for explaining academic success and failure, the most prominent being instructional quality, content difficulty, and grading criteria, but also class size, temperature, lighting, etc. (Van Overwalle, 1989).

According to control theory, perceptions of control depend on perceived contingency between action and outcome (Rothbaum *et al.*, 1982; Rotter, 1966). Thus, within an academic context, perceived control refers to students' perceived influence over and responsibility for their academic performance (Perry, 1991) which involves a perceived contingency between the student's actions (e.g., studying) and subsequent academic outcomes (i.e., success or failure). Perceived contingency between actions and outcomes is inferred by students from their attributions for those outcomes. Consequently, to influence an outcome students must perceive the outcome as being dependent on their own actions or personal qualities. In this sense, perceived control is a product of a student's belief in the contingency between his or her actions and an outcome, with the contingency relation being determined by the causal attributions selected. The stronger the perceived contingency, the greater the sense of control. If success on a class test is attributed to internal, controllable causes (e.g., one's own effort), for example, a student is likely to view performance on a task as dependent on his actions, resulting in an increase in perceived control, motivation, and performance (Weiner, 1986). Thus, in terms of motivation, students' subjective indicators of control are often more important than objective indicators of their actual control (Shapiro, Schwartz, and Astin, 1996).

The phenomenological basis of perceived academic control can be understood from the perspective of Weiner's attribution theory of motivation and performance (1985, 1995) which has had a major impact on several areas of psychology, including clinical, educational, social, developmental, and learning (cf., Fiske and Taylor, 1991).

490

Weiner argues that students' explanations for their successes and failures are pivotal to achievement-striving and academic performance. Weiner proposes that people routinely seek to understand why they succeed and fail in life's challenges. They are constantly trying to explain the world around them with such questions as: "Why did that happen?" "Why did she say that?" "Why didn't he do that?" People's answers to these "why" questions are the basis for their subsequent thoughts, feelings, and actions in future situations. The process of identifying explanations or reasons for these "why" questions is referred to as *causal search*. Within this perspective, we would expect that students who explain their successes and failures using controllable causes should have more perceived control than those who attribute such outcomes to uncontrollable causes.

According to Weiner, all attributions resulting from causal search have three properties or dimensions: *locus of causality*, which refers to whether the causes of success or failure reside within (e.g., aptitude) or outside (e.g., chance) the individual; *stability*, which describes whether the causes are stable (e.g., industriousness) or transient (e.g., fatigue); and *controllability*, which indicates whether the causes can or cannot be influenced by the individual or someone else (e.g., laziness versus economic recession). In its simplest representation, the three dimensions of the taxonomy can be dichotomized and depicted as a locus (internal, external) by stability (unstable, stable) by controllability (uncontrollable, controllable) $2 \times 2 \times 2$ factorial matrix, although in reality each dimension represents a continuum and not a dichotomy. Given that every causal attribution possesses these three properties, any attribution can be placed within one of the eight cells of this simple framework.

These dimensional properties of causal attributions determine subsequent cognitions, affect, and motivation, all of which, in turn, contribute to action. For instance, the stability dimension influences future expectations: a stable attribution (aptitude) about an outcome implies that it is more likely to reoccur than would an unstable attribution (chance). Each of the three dimensions also determines specific emotions which, in combination with expectations generated by the stability dimension, lead to motivated behavior. Feelings of guilt occur when a controllable attribution (low effort) is used to explain failure, or feelings of hopelessness can result if a stable attribution (low ability) is used to explain failure. Thus, the unique locus, stability, and controllability properties of an attribution can substantially alter a person's motivation and behavior regarding future actions. A more complete account of this model is provided elsewhere (Weiner, 1985, 1986, 1995).

Consider Weiner's theory applied to an achievement setting in which a student fails an important test and, in seeking an explanation, attributes the poor performance to lack of ability. Because ability is typically viewed as an internal, stable, and uncontrollable cause, the student would regard himself/herself as personally responsible for the negative outcome and would experience shame, sadness, lowered self-esteem, and in extreme cases, depression. These negative emotions would make the course much less attractive to the student and lead to avoidance. Coupled with high expectations of continued failure, assuming lack of ability is perceived as stable, these negative emotions would undermine the student's motivation to succeed, thereby jeopardizing future perfor-mance and continuation in the course. In contrast, internal, unstable, and controllable attributions, such as effort, would have very different academic consequences. Similar to a lack of ability attribution, a lack of effort attribution for failure would generate negative affect (guilt vs. shame) because the student feels responsible for the poor performance, but it would be far less harmful. Shame is less likely to occur, self-esteem is less threatened, and other negative emotions are infrequent. More importantly, expectations about future success versus failure would be more positive because lack of effort is regarded as an unstable and controllable cause that can be modified. This suggests an optimistic scenario in which failure resulting from lack of effort can be changed to success by trying harder (more effort) next time. Thus, the student may not feel good about the course, but will strive to do better anyway.

This stability/controllability difference between ability and effort, and any other causal attributions, lies at the heart of achievement motivation and performance. Although both are internal attribu-tions for failure, helplessness is more likely to result from a lack of ability attribution (stable/uncontrollable factor), whereas mastery is more probable from a lack of effort attribution (unstable/controllable factor). External attributions, such as fate or task difficulty, would create less negative affect, less harm to a student's self-esteem, and less helplessness. Simply put, the more in control we feel, the more motivated we are; conversely, the less control, the less motivated. Thus, our explanations, or causal attributions, for why we succeed and fail directly affect our motivation because they imply that our academic performance is either controllable or uncontrollable. So, when "lack of ability" (low intelligence) or "poor instruction" are deemed to be the cause of failure, attributions which are not controllable by us and are stable, we experience a loss of control which, in turn, leads to low motivation and weak performance.

In contrast, "lack of effort," "bad strategy," or "poor note-taking," are all controllable and changeable causes of failure. They can be altered by trying harder, using a better strategy, or taking clearer notes, thereby enhancing perceived control and strengthening motivation and performance. Controllable attributions give students a greater sense of personal control over academic performance, and in turn, more motivation to achieve; uncontrollable attributions engender less personal control and less motivation to succeed. Thus, differences in perceived control result from the three dimensional properties of attributions acting together such that an internal, stable, and uncontrollable attribution (ability) for failure would lead to a loss of perceived control, whereas an internal, unstable, and controllable attribution (effort) for the same failure would enhance perceived control.

In sum, perceived academic control is a function of causal attributions which provide students with the specific reasons for various achievement outcomes. Weiner's theory explicitly describes the cognitive, affective, and motivational consequences of controllable and uncontrollable attributions which underpin students' belief patterns of perceived control. Weiner's attribution theory is particularly well-suited for deriving manipulations, measures, and predictions related to academic performance and has several major advantages for studying linkages between academic markers and teaching and learning processes: a primary emphasis on achievement; a broad range of cognitive, affective, and motivational outcomes; and, a clearly delineated framework for testing their sequential developments. This explicit sequencing of variables lends itself to unraveling the complexities underpinning perceived academic control and the scholastic attainment of college students.

The remainder of the chapter is devoted to two main themes: first, that perceived academic control is a critical individual difference in students (academic marker) affecting their scholastic attainment; and secondly, that Attributional Retraining (AR), designed as a cognitive intervention to enhance students' academic control, can be viewed as an instructional treatment that positively influences achievement motivation and performance.

ACADEMIC CONTROL IN ACHIEVEMENT SETTINGS

Thus far, the chapter has dealt with the conceptual foundation of perceived control within higher education settings. We shift now to focus on student differences in academic control and how they affect the motivation, performance, and overall scholastic development of college students. In the process, we examine other academic differences among students, such as course-related emotions and perceptions of success, that interact with perceived control to enhance or impede academic motivation and achievement striving. Finally, we consider students' academic control in relation to classroom instructional practices as a form of an aptitude-treatment interaction (Cronbach and Snow, 1977).

ACADEMIC CONTROL IN ELEMENTARY AND HIGH SCHOOL STUDENTS

Beginning in the early school years through to high school, perceived academic control has been found to positively affect several aspects of students' educational development (Musher-Eizenman, Nesselroade, and Schmitz, 2002; Stipek and Weisz, 1981; Yamauchi, Kumagai, and Kawasaki, 1999). For example, in a series of studies conducted by Skinner and her colleagues (e.g., Skinner, Wellborn, and Connell, 1990; Skinner *et al.*, 1998), school-age children's achievement and perceived control were found to be reciprocal in nature: greater percep-tions of control enhanced subsequent academic achievement, and achievement, in turn, enhanced perceptions of control over future academic outcomes. Moreover, children who had teachers described as warm and contingent were more likely to develop optimal profiles of control that emphasized internal causes, resulting in greater classroom engagement and achievement. Conversely, unsupportive teaching was associated with less perceived control, which predicted academic apathy and lower achievement. These findings indicate that teachers can actively shape children's control beliefs and academic motivation by providing a warm and contingent learning environment (Clifton and Roberts, 1992; Skinner *et al.*, 1990).

Other research involving school-age children reveals that greater academic control enables children to understand course content better and use more effective learning strategies (Yajima, Sato, and Arai, 1996). These benefits of academic control are not limited to the general school population, but extend to learning-disabled children as well. Specifically, perceived control can enhance achievement motivation among children with learning disabilities or those who are at risk academically (Dev, 1998). Dicintio and Gee (1999), for example, found that among unmotivated students who were deemed to be at risk academically, perceived control was associated with greater task

494

involvement and feelings of competency, and conversely, with less boredom, confusion, and interest in doing other things. Thus, even among school-age children who experience academic failure due to learning or motivational difficulties, perceived control can improve their educational development.

Of note, perceived control may be more critical than other factors previously thought to influence children's scholastic development. In a longitudinal study, Ross and Broh (2000) examined both perceived control and self-esteem among 10th grade children in an attempt to determine which individual difference factor was a stronger predictor of academic achievement in grade 12. While prior academic achievement and parental support assessed in grade 8 enhanced both self-esteem and perceived control in grade 10, only perceived control influenced subsequent academic achievement in grade 12. Similar results were found by Leondari and Gialamas (2000), where high perceived control was associated with better performance and no direct link was found between self-esteem and achievement. Together, these findings show that perceived control can be more critical than self-esteem to students' academic achievement. More generally, the research findings in K-12 students point to the significance of perceived control for their overall academic development and serve to highlight its potential importance for college students. Notably, levels of perceived control do appear to increase somewhat from one grade to the next, but then stabilize during high school. And because intellectually capable high school students are most likely to advance to college (Rotter, 1975; Stipek and Weisz, 1981), perceived academic control is likely to play a larger role in their scholastic development in college than in high school (Cassidy and Eachus, 2000; Perry, 2003).

ACADEMIC CONTROL IN COLLEGE STUDENTS

Although perceptions of control over academic outcomes are important for school-age children, they may be even more critical for students making the transition from high school into college. At this critical point in their lives, college students are free to pursue various career options; parental authority and influence are reduced, as are relationship or familial restraints — all of which enhance students' focus on autonomy and independence, more so than in primary, middle, or secondary school. At the same time, college students must assume responsibility for their education and contend with a greater emphasis on academic competition and success. It is also during this

495

transition phase that a stronger tie develops between self-concept and achievement, so that one's identity is linked to one's academic performance (Perry, 1991).

Because perceived control over academic-related outcomes is especially crucial to college students' scholastic success, this transitional period from high school into college can be particularly problematic to the extent that it constitutes a low-control learning environment (Perry, 2003). Low-control situations are not uncommon within the education system, particularly when certain grades or transition years are infused with a disproportionate number of unpredictable achievement events or episodes. The first year of college is notable in this regard because it can undermine students' efforts to gain a sense of control and autonomy by repeatedly exposing them to novel and unexpected experiences such as increased emphasis on performance, heightened competition, pressure to excel, more frequent failure, unfamiliar academic tasks, new social networks, and critical career choices (Perry, 1991, 2003).

Thus, while perceived academic control is key to success in college, maintaining that sense of control presents an enormous challenge to first-year college students in particular. Students who have a higher sense of academic control are more likely to conquer many of the challenges presented to them in their first year of college because they believe the onus is on them to invest more effort, to adjust their study strategies, and to seek assistance from their instructors as needed. In contrast, students with a lower sense of academic control often feel utterly helpless when faced with the daunting challenges of their first year at college. We have chosen to focus on this struggle to maintain a sense of control in low-control situations faced by college students, and in research conducted in both laboratory and field settings, we have consistently found that academic control benefits first-year college students in terms of their academic-related emotions, cognitions, motivation, and achievement. The following sections review this research, and consequently, address one of the fundamental questions posed at the beginning of this chapter concerning the positive impact of academic control on student scholastic development.

EMOTIONAL CONSEQUENCES

Academic control has been found to positively influence college students' emotional experiences in their courses. Schönwetter, Perry, and Struthers (1993), for example, showed that academic control affected students' achievement-related emotions in their introductory psychology course wherein students with greater levels of control felt more pride and less shame concerning their course performance compared to students with less control. Aside from shame, other negative course-related emotions are also minimized by academic control, as seen in Perry et al.'s (2001) study in which high-control students reported less course-related anxiety and boredom than their low-control counterparts. Research by Wise and colleagues (Wise, 1994; Wise, Roos, Leland, Oats, and McCrann, 1996; Wise, Roos, Plake, and Nebelsick-Gullett, 1994) revealed that students' desire for control within testing situations, coupled with a greater sense of control over the situation, was associated with less test anxiety. Similarly, students who have a greater sense of control over questions that would be potentially included on their introductory psychology tests experience less stress than students who feel they have no control over the test questions (DasGupta, 1992). Thus, perceptions of control over course exams and other academic outcomes can enhance both the positive emotions *and* reduce the negative emotions that students experience toward their college courses.

COGNITIVE AND MOTIVATIONAL CONSEQUENCES

In addition to influencing their academic-related emotions, perceived control also enhances students' cognitive and motivational experiences within the college setting. Academic control can bolster achievement motivation so that high-control college students put more effort into academic tasks, are more motivated to learn, believe they are more successful in their courses (Perry et al., 2001), and are more likely to persist in their college courses than students with less control (Ruthig, Hladkyj, Hall, Pekrun, and Perry, 2002). Furio (1987) also found that higher perceptions of control were associated with increased learning and motivation to work and study. Finally, research by Cassidy and Eachus (2000) showed that students with higher academic control engaged in more effective study strategies involving time management and organization, which in turn, predicted better academic achievement.

In the realm of metacognitive strategies, academic control is positively associated with cognitive elaboration and self-monitoring. High-control students tend to engage in more cognitive elaboration strategies such as finding common themes throughout their courses and relating new course material to prior knowledge, as well as active

497

learning and more self-monitoring (i.e., capacity to determine how well they understand course material) than their low-control counterparts (Cassidy and Eachus, 2000; Perry *et al.*, 2001). Taken together, these research findings indicate that perceptions of academic control contribute significantly to students' emotional, cognitive, and motivational experiences during their college education.

ACHIEVEMENT CONSEQUENCES

Aside from these affective and cognitive benefits, academic control positively influences students' academic performance in terms of class tests, assignments, and final grades in college courses. For example, in a one-year longitudinal field study involving academic control, we found a dramatic difference between high- and low-control students in their final introductory psychology course grades. Students with a greater sense of academic control at the start of the year obtained a final grade of B+ in the course at the end of the year, in comparison to their low-control counterparts who obtained a C+ (Perry *et al.*, 2001). This variation in students' perceptions of control resulted in a performance difference of roughly two letter grades. Our academic control research has included both single-course achievement measures (i.e., final course grades) and performance indicators from all courses in which students enroll over an entire academic year, namely cumulative grade point average (Hall, Perry, Ruthig, Hladkyj, and Chipperfield, 2005; Ruthig, Hladkyj, Perry, Clifton, and Pekrun, 2001). In these longitudinal studies involving large, diverse samples, high-control students had greater overall GPAs than low-control students, providing evidence that academic control benefits student achievement, both at the course-specific level ($r = .18$) and across numerous courses and different classroom situations ($rs = .18$–$.25$).

In addition to academic performance, we have examined the relation between academic control and college persistence as reflected in students' intentions to remain in or withdraw from these courses. Ruthig *et al.* (2002), for example, showed that academic control significantly predicted persistence in an introductory psychology course, where the more academic control students felt they had at the beginning of the term, the less likely they were to subsequently drop their introductory psychology course. In keeping with this focus on cumulative measures of academic achievement, our recent research efforts have examined the effects of perceived academic control on attrition from students' cumulative voluntary withdrawal from all courses taken during the academic year. To this end, Hall, Perry, Ruthig, Hladkyj,

498

et al. (2005) found that students with higher levels of perceived academic control were also less likely to withdraw from other courses during their first year of college than were low-control students. Thus, academic control not only contributes to better achievement in first-year courses, it also increases students' persistence in those courses (e.g., Ruthig *et al.*, 2005; Perry *et al.*, in press).

In studying the effects of academic control on first-year achievement and persistence we have controlled for aptitude differences in students. A confound can arise when the relationship between academic success and control is reciprocal: academic success promotes academic control which, in turn, fosters academic success. For instance, high-aptitude students are more successful and their successes contribute to higher levels of perceived control (e.g., Barling and Snipelisky, 1983; Edmonds, 2003; El-Hindi and Childers, 1996; Yan and Gaier, 1991). Accordingly, a measure of high school performance is routinely included as a covariate in our analyses to account for potential differences in aptitude upon entering college. Thus, we can be confident that differences in academic performance after the first year of college are less likely due to preexisting differences in high school aptitude.

Because our research is based on Canadian university students who are not required to write SATs, we have relied on other measures of high school aptitude. High school achievement has been assessed using self-reported high school grade, a subjective average of students' grades in their final year of high school, which correlates strongly with students' final course grades in college, $rs = .39–.54$ (e.g., Hall, Perry, Chipperfield, Clifton, and Haynes, in press; Perry *et al.*, 2001). We have also incorporated a more objective measure of high school aptitude as a covariate in our analyses, namely students' actual high school percent, calculated by averaging students' final grades in their college entrance courses (e.g., Hall, Hladkyj, Perry, and Ruthig, 2004; Ruthig, Perry, Hall, and Hladkyj, 2004). Thus, by incorporating a measure of high school aptitude, whether self-reported or actual grades, we have been able to distinguish achievement differences in college due to academic control perceptions from those due to prior aptitude in high school.

ACADEMIC CONTROL AND OTHER INDIVIDUAL DIFFERENCES

Although academic control has a variety of positive benefits for college students, the consequences are not always straightforward because other individual differences among students may actually enhance or nullify the effects of academic control. Within our own research program, we have examined differences in the emotional and cognitive experiences of students in relation to their perceptions of control to determine how they jointly impact scholastic development. Ruthig *et al.* (2005), for example, explored whether certain achievement-related emotions, namely enjoyment, boredom, and anxiety, moderated the effects of academic control on scholastic performance and persistence. At the start of the academic year, students were identified as having either low or high academic control and low or high levels of learning-related enjoyment, boredom, and anxiety. An academic control (low/high control) × learning emotion (low/high emotion) 2 × 2 factorial design was used to examine the effects on students' introductory psychology course grade, overall cumulative GPA, and cumulative course withdrawal.

Positive emotions appeared to "enable" academic control to increase students' course grades and GPAs and decrease their course withdrawal. Conversely, negative emotions seem to "disengage" the positive impact of perceived control. Specifically, high-control students who reported high levels of course enjoyment (or low levels of course boredom or anxiety), had the highest final psychology course grade, cumulative GPA, and lowest attrition rates. However, among students with low enjoyment, having high control did not significantly impact their academic development, such that low- and high-control students had similar achievement and attrition levels. Similarly, for students with high boredom or anxiety, high control did not enhance academic achievement or persistence, meaning that low- and high-control students again had comparable levels of achievement and attrition. These findings indicate that various negative emotional states (e.g., high boredom, high anxiety, low enjoyment) can eliminate the advantageous effect of high academic control. Thus, it is in combination with more favorable emotional experiences in the classroom, either stronger positive emotions or weaker negative emotions, that students' perceptions of academic control foster achievement striving, performance, and persistence in their courses.

In keeping with our phenomenological focus on academic control, we have also examined perceptions of academic success as an important student difference, which potentially can modify the effects of academic control on scholastic performance. Weiner's attribution theory (1985, 1995) asserts that subjective evaluations of academic performance outcomes are an important precursor to causal search, which in turn, has a significant effect on students' perceptions of controllability concerning their course grades. Schönwetter *et al.* (1993) found that students' perceptions of success interacted with their academic control so that students with high control/high success had the highest level of achievement out of the four possible combinations of perceived control, (low/high) and success (low/high). Interestingly, students with low control and high perceived success demonstrated the poorest academic performance, followed by students with high control and low perceived success. These seemingly counterintuitive findings may be explained by the fact that low-control/high-success students believe that, although they are successful, they do not have control over academic outcomes. In contrast, high-control/low-success students believe they have control, yet see themselves as unsuccessful. These findings indicate that, similar to research on academic control and emotions, perceived control and success can interact to predict achievement, thereby providing a valuable perspective on the role of academic control in relation to other individual difference variables. Hence, it is often not adequate to examine academic control or perceptions of success alone when attempting to determine academic achievement. Rather, perceptions of both control and success are necessary for optimal academic performance.

Self-regulation is another individual difference among college students that has been considered in combination with academic control. Defining self-regulation as preoccupation with failure or persistent focusing on negative events, Perry *et al.* (2001) found that students with both high preoccupation with failure and high academic control obtained better course grades than students with low preoccupation with failure, regardless of their control level. Although being preoccupied with failure would appear negative at first glance, high-control, high-failure-preoccupied students outperformed the other three groups by two full letter grades in their introductory psychology course. When paired with a sense of control over academic outcomes, students with high failure preoccupation are able to give sufficient attention to monitoring and assessing the causes of failure, and thus more likely to prevent the recurrence of failure. Again, this research highlights the importance of evaluating the benefits of perceived academic control in the context of other individual differences, in this case, involving students' self-regulatory capacity to maintain their focus on and overcome academic failure experiences.

The academic control by failure preoccupation findings from Perry *et al.* (2001) were replicated and extended in a three-year longitudinal study designed to examine the generalizability of this interaction

501

(Perry *et al.*, in press). A similar interaction pattern was found for grade point average (GPA) and voluntary course withdrawal across three academic years. That is, high academic control, high failure-preoccupied students had better GPAs and had dropped fewer courses after three years than the other three groups. These results provide stronger and consistent support for how self-regulation variables such as failure preoccupation can interact with academic control to affect college students' achievement and persistence over a prolonged period.

The empirical evidence presented so far highlights the importance of academic control in the scholastic development of college students. Student differences in control perceptions, often interacting with other academic factors, can translate into significant disparities in learning-related cognitions, emotions, motivation, and performance. Consequently, our analysis of the academic development of college students would not be complete without including a central contextual determinant of classroom settings, namely quality of instruction. Both logic and empirical evidence suggest that teaching is very important to the motivation and performance of college students, yet social cognition researchers often omit instructional variables from their studies. In most studies, teaching is simply assumed to be a random background variable and the focus is primarily on student attributes as predictors of learning and performance (cf., Aspinwall and Taylor, 1992; Pascarella and Terenzini, 1991). In the next section, we explore the consequences of this association between academic control and the quality of college instruction.

ACADEMIC CONTROL AND QUALITY OF INSTRUCTION

In response to increasing attrition in postsecondary institutions, stakeholders argue that the panacea for failing students — and any other plight afflicting higher education today — is "to have the professors teach better"! This commonly held "one size fits all" effective-teaching remedy is supported, in part, by extensive research during the past 80 years showing that students do benefit from effective college teaching (cf., Feldman, 1998; Marsh and Dunkin, 1992; McKeachie, 1997; Murray, 1991; Perry and Smart, 1997). While this evidence is supportive, it is incomplete because research also shows that certain students do not profit from effective instruction, notably those low in perceived academic control (Perry, 1991). A profile of learned helplessness (low motivation, negative affect, and poor performance), characteristic of failure-prone students, can occur despite the presence of effective instruction. Simply put, the students most in need of enriched educational opportunities (e.g., effective teaching) are least likely to profit from them.

Faculty members are concerned not just with teaching more effectively, but with how certain teaching methods affect students differently, specifically with which methods are most effective for certain types of students (Perry, 1997). When meeting a class for the first time, college instructors are often confronted with pronounced differences between students. Race, gender, age, social class, ethnicity, and religion are but a few overt signs of that diversity, augmented by less apparent, but equally important differences in intelligence, motivation, impulsivity, and boredom. Alongside enthusiastic, determined, and responsible students sit apathetic, bored, and failure-prone students, intermingled with still others possessing various attributes of the first two groups. Not surprisingly, this complex diversity represents a fundamental challenge for college instructors who must ensure that learning opportunities are optimized for all students. This issue highlights the differential impact that a certain teaching method can have in relation to specific attributes that vary between students, generally referred to as an aptitude-treatment interaction (Cronbach and Snow, 1977). This section deals with this aptitude-treatment interaction in terms of academic control and effective teaching in college classrooms.

EFFECTIVE TEACHING IN COLLEGE CLASSROOMS

It has long been recognized by classroom instructors, students, and policymakers alike that some teaching methods are more effective in promoting learning and performance. The common wisdom that "teaching makes a difference in college classrooms" is supported by correlational and causal evidence from laboratory and quasi-experimental studies dating back over 80 years. The correlational evidence consistently reveals that specific college teaching behaviors associated with lecturing, such as organization, knowledge, clarity, and expressiveness, are directly related to better student performance. In a prototypical study, Sullivan and Skanes (1974) randomly assigned students and instructors to multiple sections of an introductory psychology course at the beginning of year, and at the end of year students evaluated their instructors on a standard questionnaire. Student ratings were moderately correlated with course grades based on tests prepared by instructors from all sections.

The student ratings/final grades correlation was .42 for all instructors combined, and .60 for senior instructors.

Meta-analytic reviews of multi-section validity studies (e.g., Cohen, 1981, 1983; Feldman, 1989) show that specific college teaching behaviors, defined in terms of student ratings, are significantly correlated with end-of-term final grades. Instructor organization, for example, defined by items such as "presents and organizes course material" and "plans class activities in detail," is correlated .55 with end-of-course final grades. This means that roughly 30% of the achievement variance in final grades in explained by instructor organization. Instructor clarity, denoted by such items as "makes good use of examples of illustrations" and "synthesizes and summarizes the material" is correlated .51 with final grades, and consequently accounts for 25% of the variance in course grades. Student ratings of instructor interaction, feedback, stimulation, and elocution are correlated .45, .29, .38, and .35 respectively with final grades. Clearly then, empirical evidence from correlational studies supports the position that teaching does make a difference to scholastic attainment in college classrooms.

To put these teaching behaviors/final grades correlations in perspective, consider construct validity studies in other research domains. In a comprehensive review of more than 125 meta-analytic validity studies, Meyer *et al.* (2001) analyzed 800 samples using multi-method assessment procedures. In Table 1T1 of their study, they present small and large correlations between well-established variables in the health domain: aspirin and reduced risk of death by heart attack, $r(22,071) = .02$; antihypertensive medication and reduced risk of stroke, $r(59,086) = .03$; calcium intake and bone mass in premenopausal women, $r(2,493) = .08$; gender and weight for U.S. adults, $r(16,950) = .26$; weight and height for U.S. adults, $r(16,948) = .44$.

In another set of analyses, Meyer *et al.* (2001, Table 2)T2 report validity coefficients for various types of physical and psychological tests, including: fecal occult blood test screening and reduced death from colorectal cancer, $r(329,642) = .01$; ultrasound examinations and successful pregnancy, $r(16,227) = .01$; decreased bone density and hip-fracture risk in women, $r(20,849) = .25$; mammogram results and breast cancer detection after two years, $r(192,009) = .27$; extraversion and subjective well-being, $r(10,364) = .17$; Graduate Record Exam (quantitative) performance and graduate GPA, $r(5,186) = .22$; neuroticism and decreased subjective well-being, $r(9,777) = .27$; information processing speed and reasoning ability, $r(4,026) = .55$.

In relative terms, the teaching behaviors/final grades correlations compare favorably to those involving commonly known psychological and medical tests in other areas of research. Correlations between .20 and .55 for teaching behaviors (e.g., instructor organization or clarity) and final grades are similar to correlations involving GRE/GPA (.22), mammogram/breast cancer (.27), weight/height (.44), and information processing/reasoning (.55), and are substantially higher than widely-accepted correlations for aspirin intake/reduced heart attacks (.02), blood pressure medication/reduced risk of stroke (.03), and extraversion/well-being (.17). Furthermore, teaching behavior correlations between .20 and .55 are statistically meaningful according to Cohen (1988) who considers correlation coefficients below .10 of little interest, but between .10 and .20 as small, .20 and .40 as moderate, and above .40 as large. In practical terms, this means that college teaching behaviors such as instructor organization or instructor clarity can explain roughly 25% of final grades in a course, and have an effect size that is of the same magnitude as widely recognized associations between intelligence tests and performance (e.g., GRE/GPA = .22) and height and weight (.44).

ACADEMIC CONTROL AND EFFECTIVE TEACHING

We turn now to how instructional treatments in relation to academic control affect the scholastic development of college students. Instructional treatment is broadly defined here as a systematic application of pedagogical methods and procedures to facilitate learning and performance which would include lecture-related teaching behaviors, course structures, grading standards, and curriculum design, though all may not occur in a single teaching episode, nor be used by a specific instructor. We focus on lecturing because it has been the subject of extensive empirical investigation that shows it is typically comprised of several discrete teaching behaviors, namely expressiveness, organization, clarity, etc. (cf., Perry and Smart, 1997). Our interest is in instructor expressiveness as a teaching behavior because it is a key element of the lecture method and has received detailed scrutiny in both laboratory and field settings (e.g., Murray, 1991, 2001; Perry, Abrami, and Leventhal, 1979; Perry, Leventhal, and Abrami, 1979).

Our analysis of the relation between academic control and college teaching takes an aptitude-treatment interaction approach (cf., Cronbach and Snow, 1977) in which the quality of college instruction interacts with either transient or stable academic control. In a series of analog studies of the college classroom (cf., Perry, 1991), teaching effectiveness was examined in terms of the lecture method which is made up of specific teaching behaviors such as instructor expressiveness, organization, and clarity (cf., Feldman, 1989; Murray, 2001), recognizing that college teaching encompasses a variety of teaching methods. Transient academic control is deemed to be a component of perceived academic control determined by the college classroom, as opposed to the student, the result of episodic events which create low- and high-control learning environments. Low-control classrooms are those which are infused with unpredictable, noncontingent associations between students' achievement-striving behaviors and subsequent performance outcomes, creating a helpless orientation in students. High-control classrooms are those which involve contingent relations between achievement behavior and performance, thereby encouraging a mastery orientation in students. Stable academic control is an attribute of students which they bring to the classroom separately from the transient control aspects of the classroom setting.

The laboratory analog is an improvement over correlational studies of college teaching which have not systematically manipulated the quality of teaching directly and which have not tested cause-effect relations between teaching and learning. It is also an improvement over studies in the social cognition literature which have virtually ignored the role of teaching variables in exploring academic motivation and achievement-striving. Based on previous research using this classroom analog (Perry, Abrami, and Leventhal, 1979; Perry, Leventhal, and Abrami, 1979), we paired either transient or stable academic control (low, high) with videotape lectures varying in the quality of instruction (ineffective, effective) within a 2×2 factorial design.

In one study, transient academic control was manipulated using falsified test performance results prior to the videotape lecture to create either a transient low-control (unpredictable failure feedback), or high-control (predictable failure feedback) experience for students (Perry and Dickens, 1984). Aside from the transient control main effect, a transient control $\times$ instructional quality interaction emerged. Not unexpectedly, transient high-control students who received effective instruction performed better on the post-lecture test compared to their low-control counterparts who received ineffective instruction. Converting the performance of high-control students to a percentage scale reveals that their achievement is 12% better with the effective, compared to the ineffective instructor, which translates into almost a one and a half letter grade difference. More interestingly, however, low-control students did not do any better with the effective instructor than with the ineffective instructor.

In subsequent research, we found that this interaction was not limited to a brief, single-lecture episode, but extended to a second lecture one week later (Perry and Magnusson, 1987). After students participated in the first lecture, they returned to the laboratory a week later to view a second videotape lecture and to take a test on the lecture material. In both Lecture 1 and Lecture 2, transient high-control students performed better following effective instruction, compared to ineffective instruction, whereas low-control students did no better following effective instruction. The basic form of the transient academic control × instructional quality (aptitude-treatment) interaction has been consistently replicated in other studies as well (Perry and Dickens, 1987; Perry, Magnusson, Parsonson, and Dickens, 1986) and is seen in Figure 1.F1 Consistent with the research literature on college teaching, the effective instructor produced more learning than the ineffective instructor, but only for transient high-control students. For transient low-control students, having effective instruction produces no better performance than having ineffective instruction. Consequently, students who are at risk and failure prone (low control) do not benefit from enriched learning experiences (effective instruction).

In extending these transient academic control × instructional quality interaction findings, Magnusson and Perry (1989) paired

Figure 1: Academic control × instruction interaction effect, adapted from Perry and Magnusson (1987). Transient control assessed: low academic control = noncontingent feedback; high academic control = contingent feedback.

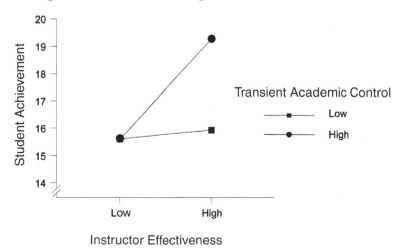

507

stable academic control with quality of instruction (ineffective, effective). Stable academic control was measured in terms of locus of control (internal, external), wherein internal locus implies stable, high academic control and external locus reflect stable, low academic control. The aptitude-treatment interaction previously found for transient academic control was replicated for stable academic control and instructional quality as well. Internal-locus (high-control) students learned more from the effective compared to the ineffective instructor, even when they experienced a temporary loss of control. External-locus (low-control) students, however, did not perform better following effective instruction. Once more, those students most at risk were least likely to benefit from optimal (effective teaching) learning conditions.

Taken together, these simulated classroom laboratory studies indicate that student differences in experiencing *transient* low and high academic control have important implications for the effectiveness of classroom instruction. If such experiences are inherent to low-control situations, the first year of college being a prime example, then good teaching facilitates performance only in students who have a temporary increase in their sense of control. Good teaching, however, is of no avail to students who experience a temporary loss of control: they performed equally poorly whether they received effective or ineffective instruction. This same pattern of results was replicated for *stable* academic control, as well, in which high-control students did better after receiving effective instruction, yet their low-control counterparts did not. Paradoxically then, and contrary to common wisdom, students who are most in need of academic assistance are *least* likely to benefit from effective teaching.

WHEN GOOD TEACHING FAILS: PRIMARY AND SECONDARY ACADEMIC CONTROL

To this point, we have argued that both academic control and effective instruction can greatly enhance college students' academic development. Unfortunately, effective teaching can fail to foster achievement striving for either low-control students or students who experience temporary, environmentally-induced losses of control. What then keeps such students from simply giving up and withdrawing from college altogether? A possible explanation is that some low-control students possess certain cognitive capabilities that allow them to avoid feeling completely helpless in low-control learning environments and to persist in their academic endeavors. One such cognitive factor that has become a major focus in our own research is *secondary* academic control, a type of perceived control which is distinct from the traditional concept of academic control discussed thus far, namely *primary* academic control. In general, primary control refers to attempts by students to directly influence outcomes in academic settings, such as performance on achievement tests. In contrast, secondary control involves attempts by students to adjust to academic challenges involving failure, noncontingent feedback, lack of information, or unpredictability (Rothbaum *et al.*, 1982).

To maintain a sense of control within low-control achievement settings, some students resort to secondary control beliefs and strategies involving the cognitive reconstrual of negative learning experiences. Having failed a test, for example, secondary control strategies may include focusing on the positive aspects of the experience (e.g., "My performance helped me see where I can improve"), downgrading its importance (e.g., "The test is only worth 20% of my grade"), or downward social comparisons (e.g., "At least I did better than some of the other students"). Conversely, primary control involves attempts to modify external outcomes to attain or regain desired goals (Heckhausen and Schulz, 1998; Rothbaum *et al.*, 1982). For example, if the desired goal is to pass an exam, primary control strategies may include taking lecture notes, asking the instructor for assistance, or participating in a study group.

Hladkyj, Pelletier, Drewniak, and Perry (1998) designed a measure of secondary academic control to assess students' attempts to adjust to the many control-eroding episodes experienced during their first year of college, a typically low-control transition period. This measure was derived from Rothbaum *et al.*'s (1982) two-process model of perceived control where, in addition to primary control, individuals may maintain an overall sense of control by reinterpreting uncontrollable events to make them less negative. Using this conceptual model, Hladkyj, Pelletier, *et al.* devised a 7-item Likert-style measure of secondary control (e.g., "When bad things happen to me, I make an intentional effort to understand how they fit into the rest of my life") which was positively correlated with elaborative learning ($r = .36$), self-monitoring ($r = .18$), intrinsic academic motivation ($r = .19$), course enjoyment ($r = .24$), feelings of success ($r = .14$), and end-of-year feelings of adjustment to college ($r = .16$). Although the magnitudes of some of the effect sizes are relatively small, they indicate a systematic involvement of secondary control in supporting greater academic engagement and adjustment to the college experience.

Subsequent research (e.g., Hladkyj, Perry, and Pelletier, 2000; Hladkyj, Taylor, Pelletier, and Perry, 1999) involved both examining how this new measure corresponds with students' adjustment to their first year of college and how it relates to a more domain-specific measure of secondary academic control. In a multi-sample study involving data obtained from 3,973 introductory psychology students from five separate cohorts (1996, 1997, 1998, 2000, and 2001), higher levels of secondary control were associated with greater academic mastery ($r = .31–.36$), metacognitive engagement ($r = .32–.44$), and adjustment to college ($r = .12–.16$), and was positively correlated with a domain-specific measure of secondary academic control ($r = .32–.38$) across three different samples of first-year college students (Hladkyj, Perry, Hall, Ruthig, and Pekrun, 2003).

Together, this research suggests that secondary control protects students from threats to their primary academic control, but not without some cost. Specifically, when faced with excessive failure during their first year of college, high secondary-control students exhibited a mastery orientation in their achievement-related cognitions, emotions, and strategies, similar to high primary-control students, yet their course grades were no different from low secondary-control students. Thus, by changing their *internal* reality, secondary control may limit students' effectiveness to influence the *external* situation to their favor. Moreover, other research (Hall, Perry, Ruthig, Hladkyj, and Chipperfield, 2005; Hall et al., in press) indicates that there is virtually no relation between secondary control and achievement in terms of final grades ($r = −.08$ to $.01$) or GPA ($r = −.07$), suggesting that having greater secondary control is not advantageous in terms of academic performance.

Given that primary or secondary control can alleviate the negative effects of feeling out of control, is it more beneficial to perceive oneself as having high levels of *both* types of academic control? Hall, Perry, Ruthig, Hladkyj, et al. (2005) found that it is indeed optimal to have high levels of both types of academic control. Specifically, unsuccessful students with high primary and high secondary control had higher cumulative GPAs, lower course attrition, higher expected academic success, lower stress, and more positive learning-related affect (i.e., pride, happiness, anger) compared to students with high primary but low secondary control. In fact, the combination of high primary and low secondary control may actually put students at risk academically if they are initially unsuccessful in their first year of college. Hall, Perry, Ruthig, Hladkyj, and Chipperfield (in press) explain that the positive consequences of relying only on primary control may be limited to successful students, and do not occur among students experiencing repeated failure. These findings for secondary control provide further evidence of the importance of investigating the effect of (primary) academic control on achievement with respect to other individual difference variables (see Academic Control and Other Individual Differences). Fortunately, high primary-/low secondary-control students who are initially unsuccessful in college tend to benefit academically from Attributional Retraining, a cognitive intervention technique which is aimed at changing students' maladaptive attributions for their academic performance (e.g., Hall et al., in press). This intervention strategy is discussed in detail in a subsequent section of this paper.

Further research by Hall, Hladkyj, Ruthig, Pekrun, and Perry (2002) provides an explanation for why students with high levels of both primary and secondary control are more successful than their counterparts who have different combinations of primary and secondary control. Hall, Hladkyj, Ruthig, et al. posit that students who are high in both types of control are in the enviable position of maximizing their sense of control if they are able to "switch" their emphasis from one type of control to the other as necessary. For instance, in failure situations when primary control is low, if these students are able to switch over to rely more on secondary control strategies, then they would retain or regain a sense of control in the situation. Thus, having high levels of both types of academic control allow students to retain their overall sense of control if they can switch their control orientations as they negotiate their way through the many challenges presented in the college setting (e.g., Hall, Hladkyj, Chipperfield, and Perry, 2002; Hall, Hladkyj, Chipperfield, and Stupnisky, 2003).

Based on this body of research showing academic control to be a considerable asset for academic adjustment and performance in the context of higher education, it follows that increasing perceptions of control in low-control students should produce consequent favorable outcomes. To assist in the ongoing effort to increase perceptions of academic control and achievement in college students, motivational researchers have developed a control-enhancing instructional treatment, referred to as Attributional Retraining, which consistently results in improved academic motivation and performance for low-control students. Unlike traditional teaching methods involving quality of instruction, this remedial psychotherapeutic treatment based on Weiner's attribution theory (1985, 1995) represents an effective means of improving academic development in these otherwise disadvantaged students by encouraging them to reflect on the controllable nature of failure experiences. The following section provides an overview of previous and recent research on attributional retraining in college students, and discusses in greater detail how this treatment is administered and how it interacts with student differences in academic control to impact academic achievement.

ATTRIBUTIONAL RETRAINING: A CONTROL-ENHANCING INSTRUCTIONAL TREATMENT

To this point in our discussion, we have focused on the first set of research questions posed at the start of this chapter: whether perceived academic control, as an individual difference, directly affects achievement motivation and scholastic performance; and, whether the effects of academic control vary depending on other individual differences and the quality of instruction in college classrooms. As we have seen, the empirical answer to these questions is unequivocally affirmative. Despite the abundance of positive empirical findings demonstrating the efficacy of certain teaching methods, the evidence presented here consistently shows that what is deemed to be effective instruction is not beneficial to all students (Perry, 1991, 2003). Specifically, students who have lower academic control do poorly, despite receiving high-quality instruction (see Figure 1). Ironically then, it is the most vulnerable college students who do not benefit from enriched instructional treatments. If traditional teaching methods like lecturing are not effective for certain students such as those low in academic control, then other, more effective instructional treatments must be considered.

For over 15 years, we have examined an educational treatment intervention designed to enhance perceived academic control based on Weiner's attribution theory (1985, 1995), referred to as *Attributional Retraining (AR)*. The AR intervention modifies dysfunctional causal attributions for academic performance to attributions that are more conducive to achievement motivation and performance. Specifically, AR is a control-enhancing teaching method that replaces dysfunctional attributions for success and failure with functional attributions, and as such, complements traditional teaching methods such as lecturing. The relation between academic control and college instruction is examined in the following sections in terms of AR which is intended primarily for low-control students. In addressing this academic control-AR combination, we view AR as a type of instructional treatment in keeping with other aptitude-treatment interactions described earlier involving academic control-instructional quality interactions.

As discussed in previous sections, the first research question concerning academic control-instructional quality interactions was addressed by examining the effectiveness of lecturing (treatment) for low- and high-control students (aptitude) and was tested using an academic control × quality of lecturing interaction (Perry, 1997). This aptitude-treatment interaction is confirmed if high-control students performed better when receiving effective, as opposed to ineffective instruction and low-control students show no comparable improvement following effective instruction. However, in addressing our second research question involving an instructional treatment specifically intended to enhance academic control in low-control students, a different pattern of findings would be expected. That is, following the control-enhancing AR treatment, low-control students should perform better compared to their low-control/no-AR treatment counterparts, without similar treatment gains occurring for high-control students. The remainder of this section explores the effectiveness of AR techniques in college classrooms and whether this control-enhancing AR instructional treatment can be of benefit to low-control students.

ATTRIBUTIONAL RETRAINING: AN OVERVIEW

Research consistently shows that effective instruction in higher education positively influences student development with respect to achievement, emotions, and motivation (Perry and Smart, 1997). However, this research also indicates that a pattern of low perceived control, negative affect, and poor performance characteristic of failure-prone students can occur despite the presence of high-quality teaching, as seen in Figure 1 (see Perry, 1991, 2003, for reviews). Research on achievement motivation accounts for these developments in terms of maladaptive attributions for academic performance made by college students. Specifically, Weiner's attribution theory of achievement motivation (1985, 1995) suggests that the reasons that students use to explain academic outcomes can significantly influence subsequent learning-related emotions and cognitions, and in turn, achievement-striving behaviors (see An Attributional Framework for Perceived Control in College Classrooms section above). According to Weiner, causal attributions for poor performance to uncontrollable or stable causes, such as lack of ability or task difficulty, engender disengagement

513

and a sense of hopelessness because these factors cannot be changed and are expected to continue to negatively affect one's performance. In contrast, failure attributions made to controllable or unstable factors, such as lack of effort or unfamiliarity, foster feelings of hope and persistence in students by generating perceptions of control over academic performance.

Over the past 30 years, research based on Weiner's attribution theory (1985, 1995) has consistently demonstrated the effectiveness of attributional interventions in helping individuals deal with failure. More specifically, ongoing research has concerned the development and evaluation of a psychotherapeutic cognitive treatment, referred to as Attributional Retraining (AR), which assists individuals by encouraging controllable and unstable attributions (e.g., effort, strategy) primarily for negative experiences. The benefits of AR techniques for improving performance are well known and have been illustrated in a variety of domains involving personal development and achievement. In terms of psychological and physical health outcomes, attributional retraining has been found to be effective in the areas of group counseling (Green-Emrich and Altmaier, 1991; see Försterling, 1986, for review), health and aging (Weinberg, 2001), as well as the clinical treatment of psychosomatic disorders (i.e., Kaaya, Goldberg, and Gask, 1992; Morriss and Gask, 2002; see Garcia-Campayo, Sanz Carrillo, Larrubia, and Monton, 1997, for review). AR has also been found to correspond with better performance in achievement settings involving athletic competition (Miserandino, 1998; Sinnott and Biddle, 1998), persuasion (Anderson, 1983; Miller, Brickman and Bolen, 1975), and job satisfaction (Curtis, 1992).

In an academic achievement context, research examining the effectiveness of attributional retraining techniques has provided considerable empirical support for the use of this remedial intervention to improve student development at all levels of the education system. In elementary school classrooms, AR has been found to be an effective means of reducing aggressive behavior (Hudley *et al.*, 1998), improving social skills (Aydin, 1988; see also Carlyon, 1997), and increasing learning strategy use (Borkowski, Weyhing, and Carr, 1988; Borkowski, Weyhing, and Turner, 1986; Ho and McMurtrie, 1991). AR techniques have also been shown to improve problem solving, motivation, self-esteem, and academic achievement in elementary school students (Andrews and Debus, 1978; Craske, 1985, 1988; Dweck, 1975; Heller, 2003; Heller and Ziegler, 1996; Miller *et al.*, 1975; Okolo, 1992; Schunk, 1983; Ziegler and Heller, 2000; see also Heller, 1999). Research exploring the benefits of attributional retraining for high school students is encouraging, with AR treatments resulting in greater perceptions of control in depressed adolescents (Dieser and Ruddell, 2002), as well as improved self-esteem and academic performance (den Boer, Meertens, Kok, and Van Knippenberg, 1989).

In addition to AR studies with younger students, attributional retraining researchers have focused extensively on college students and their scholastic development, particularly the transition from high school to college. The bulk of research on AR in higher education has been directed toward improving students' academic development in terms of motivation and performance, as is the mandate of course instructors and academic administrators alike. Research aimed at facilitating overall career development has also found AR techniques to be effective in increasing students' perceptions of control concerning career-related decision making (Luzzo, Funk, and Strang, 1996) as well as career exploration (Luzzo, James, and Luna, 1996). Because enriched learning interventions are periodically ineffective for low-control college students (Perry, 1991), motivational researchers have focused on AR treatments which can compliment traditional classroom teaching practices by enhancing students' perceptions of control over their academic achievement, and in turn, their academic career.

Previous reviews of research on attributional retraining in college students have repeatedly underscored the effective nature of the AR treatment in improving academic motivation and performance in low-control college students (Försterling, 1985; Menec and Perry, 1995; Perry, Hechter, Menec, and Weinberg, 1993; Wilson, Damian, and Sheldon, 2002). The following section provides an overview of findings from previous research on AR and achievement in college students, highlighting the results of classic studies as well as recent research from our laboratory.

ATTRIBUTIONAL RETRAINING IN THE COLLEGE CLASSROOM

Given the substantial differences between college and high school settings with respect to appropriate study strategies, note-taking, time-management, autonomy, etc., the extent to which academic success is controllable may not be immediately evident to first-year college students. In order to circumvent feelings of guilt that, according to Weiner's theory, can result from internal and controllable attributions for having failed, these students may choose maladaptive reasons for failing to absolve themselves of academic responsibility (i.e., attributions to test difficulty, or the professor), rather than directly alleviating feelings of guilt by exercising control over their learning activities. Thus, first-year students, particularly those having a low-control or helpless orientation, are considered to be "at risk" of developing motivational deficits due to dysfunctional attribution patterns. However, as freshman college students' attributions for academic failure are more malleable during this transition phase (Perry *et al.*, 1993), these students are well suited to benefit from attributional retraining.

To provide a conceptual framework for the following review of research on attributional retraining and academic achievement in college students, a chronological overview of AR research from classic studies such as Wilson and Linville (1982) to recent research by our laboratory is provided in Table 1. This table presents the specific intervention format employed in each study in terms of the induction technique employed (e.g., videotape) and the subsequent "consolidation exercise" intended to help students understand the attributional information. Observed improvements on various measures of academic performance (e.g., lecture-based exams, final course grades, GPA) as well as the specific student risk groups found to improve most following the AR treatment are outlined as well. For example, the study conducted by Perry and Penner (1990) is described in Table 1 as including an AR treatment consisting of a videotape presentation (AR induction) and aptitude/achievement tests (AR consolidation) and as improving lecture-based test scores (outcome) for students with an external locus of control (risk condition). This table provides a useful overview of the sections below which describe in greater detail the impact of AR treatments on academic motivation and performance in college students, and particularly those students predisposed to academic failure due to control-related factors.

EARLY ATTRIBUTIONAL RETRAINING (AR) RESEARCH

Försterling (1985) classified attributional retraining methods in terms of informational approaches, operant methods, vicarious learning methods such as persuasion, and indirect communication. In early research with children, repeated exposures to face-to-face AR techniques, such as verbal performance feedback, have typically been employed in order to ensure the induction of AR information (e.g., Dweck, 1975; Miller *et al.*, 1975; Schunk, 1983). For the most part, however, only informational methods, usually involving written

Table 1: Chronological Overview of Methods and Achievement Outcomes in AR Research in College Students

AR induction	AR consolidation	Outcome	Risk conditions
Wilson and Linville (1982, 1985)			
Written report and video	Aptitude test, anagram task, and reason analysis	GPA*, GRE*	Concern over course performance; low course exam scores
Jesse and Gregory (1986–87)			
GPA video	Written information on attributions	Stable GPA in second term	N/A
Noel et al. (1987)			
Video	Written summary	Final grade*	N/A
Van Overwalle et al. (1989); Van Overwalle and De Metsenaere (1990)			
List performance attributions and video interviews	Written and verbal reports	Exam score*	Low course exam scores
Perry and Penner (1990)			
8 minute video	Aptitude test and achievement test	Achievement test*	External locus of control
Menece et al. (1994)			
1. 1 or 2 video sessions	Achievement test	Achievement test*	Low aptitude test scores
2. 1 or 2 video sessions	Achievement test	Achievement test*	Low aptitude test scores, external locus of control
Perry and Struthers (1994)			
Written handout	• None	None	Low perceived success
8 minute video	• None	None	
	• Group discussion	Final grade*	
Hunter and Perry (1996)			
8 minute video	• None	None	Low high school grades
	• Aptitude test	Final grade*	
	• Achievement test	None	
	• Group discussion	None	

(Continued)

Table 1: (*Continued*)

AR induction	AR consolidation	Outcome	Risk conditions
Struthers and Perry (1996)			
8 minute video	Group discussion	Final grade*	Uncontrollable attributions
Pelletier et al. (1999)			
8 minute video	Aptitude test	Final grade*	Performance-orientation
Haynes et al. (2003)			
Written handout	• Written assignment	Final grade	High optimism, low perceived success; low optimism, high perceived success
Newall et al. (2003)			
Written handout	• Written assignment	Final grade*	Low academic control and low desire for control
Hall et al. (2004)			
8 minute video	• Aptitude test	Final grade and GPA*	N/A
	• Written assignment	Final grade and GPA*	
Hall et al. (in press)			
8 minute video	• Aptitude test	None	Low course exam scores, high primary control, low secondary control
	• Written assignment	Final grade*	
Ruthig et al. (2004)			
Written handout	• None	GPA*	High optimism
8 minute video	• None	GPA*	
	• Group discussion	GPA*	
Stupinsky et al. (2004)			
8 minute video	• Aptitude test	Exam score*	N/A

Note: * = Increase.

information or staged videotaped interviews, have been employed in studies with college students. In contrast to research with younger samples, studies on AR in college students have largely used these more abstract induction methods in order to capitalize on students' level of education and because these techniques are more efficient and can be administered en masse in larger college classrooms. As such, an AR intervention provided to college students typically consists of a videotaped discussion between graduate students or with a professor discussing the benefits of controllable or unstable attributions for failure, followed by an activity allowing students to personally elaborate on the information, either in a concrete fashion (e.g., by completing a difficult aptitude test) or in a more abstract manner (e.g., small group discussion; see Table 1). Researchers utilizing such attributional retraining techniques have shown modest, yet consistent, improvements in academic motivation and the performance of college students (Perry *et al.*, 1993).

As presented in Table 1, an early study by Wilson and Linville (1982) found male first-year students increased their GRE and GPA performance as a result of videotaped interviews in which senior students described how low grades, being *unstable* in nature, often improve significantly after the first semester. Wilson and Linville (1985) presented failure as unstable, as opposed to controllable, arguing that attributing failure to a lack of effort may give rise to feelings of guilt which would inhibit future achievement striving. Weiner (1988) supports this approach, noting that encouraging students to adopt unstable attributions for poor performance should result in increases in expectancies of future success similar to the promotion of controllable attributions.

Block and Lanning (1984) undertook a secondary analysis of Wilson and Linville's data and found evidence contradicting their claims in that the GPAs of students who withdrew from college were actually higher than those of remaining students. They also noted that the improvements resulting from the intervention could be explained by regression toward the mean, among other factors. However, Wilson and Linville (1985) replicated their initial findings after considering these arguments, effectively illustrating the benefits of AR for motivation and performance in students. These results were also replicated by Van Overwalle *et al.* (1989) and Van Overwalle and De Metsenaere (1990) who used a videotape intervention to present academic success as a product of *controllable* achievement striving behaviors. The videotape consisted of students presenting reasons for their failure such as lack of peer cooperation, lack of effort, or ineffective study strategy, and then describing attempts to prevent failure in the future. Exposure to the intervention resulted in higher GPA scores at the end of the academic year.

In a review of attributional retraining techniques administered to college students, Perry *et al.* (1993) identify two studies showing that the inclusion of a written handout in addition to a videotape intervention is effective as well. Jesse and Gregory (1986–87) gave students AR in both handout and videotape formats, presenting GPA as an unstable phenomenon which generally improves over time. Students exposed to the intervention maintained stable GPA scores throughout the academic year, whereas students who did not receive the intervention experienced a decline in their second term GPA scores. Noel, Forsyth, and Kelley (1987) also used the combination of both the videotape and written AR formats. After viewing the videotape depicting poor performance as unstable and receiving a handout summarizing the main points of the videotape, students showed marked improvements in exam scores and final course grades. Thus, attributional retraining interventions in which failure is presented as either controllable or unstable have shown positive results in college students with respect to both course-specific and cumulative measures of academic performance.

ASSISTING LOW-CONTROL COLLEGE STUDENTS

Despite the generally effective nature of attributional retraining (AR) in the college classroom, continuing research has been directed toward students who are most likely to benefit from an AR intervention, namely low-control students at risk of academic failure. As discussed in previous sections, individual differences in students' perceptions of control have important implications for performance in the classroom. Specifically, students lacking perceived academic control exhibit lower academic motivation, more negative emotions, diminished persistence, and poorer achievement (Perry *et al.*, 2001, in press; Schönwetter *et al.*, 1993). Our research also indicates that, although quality of instruction is largely beneficial for college student learning and performance (Perry, Leventhal, and Abrami, 1979; Perry and Smart, 1997; Perry and Williams, 1979), low-control students are least likely to benefit from effective classroom instruction (Magnusson and Perry, 1989; Perry and Dickens, 1984, 1987; Perry and Magnusson, 1987; Perry *et al.*, 1986). As such, ongoing research in our laboratory has focused on how students' perceptions of control interact with not only other individual differences and quality of instruction, but also instructional treatments involving AR techniques.

For instance, Perry and Penner (1990) administered AR using a videotape presentation in which a male psychology professor presented ability as unstable and encouraged students to attribute poor performance to effort (see Table 1). Contrary to Wilson and Linville (1985), Perry and Penner suggested that, in fact, external locus of control students do perceive effort as a salient explanation for performance following attributional retraining, thus allowing for increased confidence, motivation, and subsequent achievement striving (see Weiner, 1985). This premise was supported by findings showing significant improvements in students' performance on a homework assignment and achievement test following the intervention. This study is noteworthy because it was one of the first to demonstrate the effectiveness of attributional retraining primarily for low-control students, in this case as defined by an external locus of control.

This stable academic control × attributional retraining (aptitude-treatment) interaction presented in Figure 2F2 has been replicated repeatedly in subsequent research by this laboratory on providing AR to low-control students. Consistent with Perry and Penner (1990), our research has since demonstrated that, although high-control students perform well and generally do not benefit from the AR treatment, low-control students improve significantly following the intervention. However, in the absence of attributional retraining, low-

Figure 2: Academic control × attributional retraining interaction effect, adapted from Perry and Penner (1990). Stable control assessed: low academic control = external locus; high academic control = internal locus.

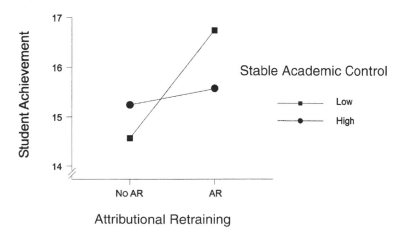

521

control students perform more poorly than their high-control counter-parts and risk more serious long-term academic failure experiences.

For instance, research conducted under similar laboratory conditions by Menec *et al.* (1994) showed significant improvements on a lecture-based achievement test following the first AR session in which the videotaped intervention depicted a student discussing how poor academic performance was the result of ineffective study strategies and a lack of effort. In keeping with Perry and Penner's (1990) focus on control-related risk factors, Menec *et al.* found that such improvements were evident only for students who had performed poorly on a pre-lecture GRE-type aptitude test, and further, for low-achieving individuals having an external locus of control. Thus, this study also found the positive impact of attributional retraining primarily to be observed for low-control students, assessed in this study using multiple academic risk factors related to academic control including poor test performance and an external locus of control. Although this study also addressed the potential for increased academic performance as a result of multiple AR sessions, the results showed no further increase in performance when two additional AR sessions were administered after the first session. As such, these results served to further highlight the effectiveness of brief AR interventions in college student populations — a finding replicated repeatedly in research conducted since the classic work of Wilson and Linville (1982). See Wilson *et al.* (2002) for an elaborated discussion concerning the efficacy of brief attributional treatments for college student populations.

Following from Menec *et al.* (1994), a longitudinal field study by Struthers and Perry (1996) also utilizing a more complex classification of low-control students, showed that an AR treatment involving a group discussion resulted in higher grades in a psychology course for college students who initially used uncontrollable and unstable attributions for academic failure. However, despite increases in motivation and hope after AR for students with a stable/uncontrollable attributional style, similar improvements in performance were not found for these students. Pelletier, Hladkyj, Moszynski, and Perry (1999) also examined other groups of students that could benefit from attributional retraining, in this case, involving the completion of an aptitude test to allow students to more deeply reflect on the attributional content of the videotape presentation (see AR Consolidation Techniques below). Students were classified as at-risk based on previous goal orientation research showing that performance-oriented college students, who study course material primarily to achieve success and make ability attributions (see Atkinson and Feather, 1966; Covington, 1993) are likely to feel helpless and perform poorly after academic failure experiences. For students enrolled in a one-year psychology course, the AR intervention produced significant improvements in final course grades only for low-control students.

MATCHING AR TREATMENTS TO LOW-CONTROL STUDENTS

Ongoing research in attributional retraining has also involved the manipulation of AR procedures in order to determine which techniques are best suited for specific groups of low-control college students. For instance, Perry and Struthers (1994) contrasted several AR procedures in a longitudinal field study in order to find the most effective intervention technique for students reporting low levels of perceived success in college at the beginning of the academic year (see Table 1). As discussed earlier, perceived success is an important precursor for perceived academic control in college students (Schönwetter et al., 1993) and represents an intriguing avenue for investigating aptitude-treatment interactions in AR research. Attributional retraining was administered in three formats: written handout only, videotape only, and videotape and small group discussion. The videotape depicted two graduate students discussing how adopting controllable explanations for poor performance following a difficult exam contributed to increased motivation and performance on subsequent tests. Results indicated that only students low in perceived success did better on in-class psychology tests and psychology final grades at the end of the year, and only in the videotape plus discussion condition.

Other student risk factors related to academic control described in earlier sections of this chapter have also been assessed in combination with AR intervention techniques. Hunter and Perry (1996) contrasted various AR techniques in attempting to find an effective intervention format for students having poor high school grades. Compared were four attributional retraining procedures: videotape only, videotape and aptitude test, videotape and achievement test, and videotape and small group discussion. The results showed marked improvements in psychology final grades only for students with poor high school grades following the videotape and aptitude test condition (see Table 1). Similarly, based on earlier research showing infrequent use of elaborate learning strategies to predispose college students to academic failure (Hladkyj, Hunter, Maw, and Perry, 1998), Hall et al. (2004) compared two AR procedures in an effort to establish an intervention technique most appropriate for these low-elaborating students. Specifically, we compared the effectiveness of the videotape and aptitude test condition used in Hunter and Perry (1996) with a videotape and AR-related writing assignment condition. Findings indicated that, for students who infrequently used elaborate learning strategies, both AR techniques were effective in improving psychology final grades. Surprisingly, both AR techniques also proved effective in increasing final course grades for high-elaborating students who were not at risk of academic failure (see Underlying AR Processes section below).

More recent studies have also involved the administration of AR procedures to students who are demotivated and failing because of overly-confident control beliefs. In a longitudinal field study, Ruthig *et al.* (2004) explored the effectiveness of the three AR techniques developed by Perry and Struthers (1994) for freshman college students who were potentially failure prone due to overly optimistic beliefs about success. Ruthig *et al.* found that all AR methods resulted in higher cumulative GPAs, lower test anxiety, and decreased course attrition for overly optimistic students. Hall, Chipperfield, Perry, Pekrun, and Schönwetter (2001) compared two AR treatment methods, involving either an aptitude test or a writing assignment, for unsuccessful students who had a maladaptive combination of primary- and secondary-control beliefs. These students were unusual in that they had failed, but had high primary-control beliefs (e.g., effort, persistence) coupled with low secondary-control beliefs (e.g., reinterpretation of failure in a positive way). They found that only after the writing AR treatment were significant improvements in end-of-year course performance observed. These findings were replicated in a large-scale study by Hall *et al.* (in press) which showed an increase of approximately 10% or one full letter grade (i.e., D to C) in these students' course performance over the academic year following the writing-based AR intervention.

In sum, a major research focus in the literature has involved efforts to find appropriate attributional retraining methods for specific groups of students deemed to be prone to academic failure because of control-related factors (cf., Perry *et al.*, 1993; Menec *et al.*, 1994), as students' academic performance can be influenced by both the method of attributional retraining and student characteristics. Our research has found that AR can be particularly effective for certain students, namely those who are academically at risk of failure due to both dispositional and situational factors such as poor performance (Hunter and Perry, 1996; Menec *et al.*, 1994), maladaptive perceptions of control (Hall *et al.*, in press; Perry and Penner, 1990), low perceptions of success (Perry and Struthers, 1994), having performance goals as opposed to learning goals (Pelletier *et al.*, 1999), and overly optimistic beliefs (Ruthig *et al.*, 2004). In addition, this research demonstrates how the overall effectiveness of AR techniques may be improved by the explicit manipulation of treatment methods in order to find the most effective approach for specific types of low-control students (e.g., Hall *et al.*, 2001; Hall *et al.*, 2004; Hunter and Perry, 1996; Perry and Struthers, 1994; Ruthig *et al.*, 2004). However, it is through examining the specific components of the attributional retraining treatment that the processes presumed to underlie the effectiveness of this intervention may be more fully explored.

AR CONSOLIDATION TECHNIQUES

In attributional retraining research involving college students, the procedure typically consists of a videotaped "treatment" followed by a consolidation exercise intended to facilitate the cognitive integration of the attributional principles presented in the videotape. When contrasting the findings of research conducted by Perry and Struthers (1994) and Hunter and Perry (1996) with Jesse and Gregory (1986–87), Menec *et al.* (1994), Van Overwalle and De Metsenaere (1990), Van Overwalle *et al.* (1989), and Wilson and Linville (1982, 1985), inconsistent results concerning the effectiveness of the videotape-only attributional retraining condition are evident. The former studies indicate that videotape-only attributional retraining does not lead to significant improvements in academic performance. However, neither Perry and Struthers nor Hunter and Perry required students to engage in any further activities following the attributional retraining videotape, whereas studies showing the videotape-only technique to be effective do indicate that some form of consolidation exercise was included (see Table 1).

For instance, both Perry and Penner (1990) and Menec *et al.* (1994) note that following the videotape presentation, the completion of either an achievement or GRE-type exam was included to allow students to put the attributional information presented in the videotape into practice (see Table 1). Wilson and Linville (1982, 1985) also indicate that immediately following attributional retraining, students were required to complete both an anagram task and GRE-type exam. In addition, these authors required half of the students to record as many reasons as possible for why grades improve following the first year of college. Similarly, the studies conducted by Van Overwalle *et al.* (1989) and Van Overwalle and De Metsenaere (1990) had participants describe in writing what they perceived to be the important aspects of the attributional retraining session and to discuss their comments with others in their experimental group. Such written accounts are similar in nature to the small group discussions employed in both Perry and Struthers (1994) and Hunter and Perry (1996) in that both activities require students to reflect on the attributional process in a meaningful way.

These studies clearly demonstrate that attributional retraining interventions require some sort of consolidation activity to be effective in which students are given an opportunity to either reflect about or act upon the information presented. Perry and Struthers (1994) suggest that such activities augment the influence of the intervention by encouraging students to actively reflect on and consolidate the attributional information with their existing achievement-related perceptions. In an earlier study in which attributions for academic performance were manipulated, Perry and Magnusson (1989) also noted that a lack of significant findings was most likely the result of not allowing students an opportunity for cognitive restructuring following the intervention.

Research on cooperative learning and academic achievement (i.e., group discussion; see Slavin, 1996, for review) suggests that cognitive elaboration processes may, in fact, be responsible for the effectiveness of such post-videotape exercises. Further to this point, Hall *et al.* (2004) suggest that consolidation activities facilitate the impact of attributional retraining by encouraging greater elaborative processing of the information presented. Similar to explanations such as cognitive restructuring or consolidation (Perry and Magnusson, 1989; Perry and Struthers, 1994), *elaborative learning* involves the construction of meaningful cognitive interconnections between new and previously learned information, and is revealed in attempts to explain personal experience according to a new conceptual framework (Entwistle, 2000; Pintrich, Smith, and McKeachie, 1989). As such, our most recent research suggests that consolidation activities facilitate a greater understanding of the attributional process through elaborative mechanisms which allow students to relate their own life experiences to attribution theory, either through abstract thinking or more practical means.

IMPLICATIONS AND FUTURE DIRECTIONS

The significance of perceived control in human discourse is recognized by social scientists and laypersons alike when discussing personal relationships, job success, academic performance, or physical and psychological health. Simply put, people who believe that they have greater control over life's challenges seem to enjoy more of life's benefits, a reality reinforced by several decades of research evidence. In our attempts to understand the complexities of perceived control and the scholastic development of college students, our paradigm of choice has been social cognition, notably Weiner's (1985, 1995) attribution theory which provides a powerful explanatory framework for understanding perceived control in achievement settings.

From our research, it is clear that perceived academic control can have both short-term and long-term consequences for college students' scholastic development based on evidence from both laboratory and field studies. In seeking to optimize internal validity, laboratory studies afford strong experimental control in which subjects are randomly assigned to experimental conditions and independent variables are systematically manipulated. In our laboratory studies, perceived academic control was experimentally manipulated using attribution theory principles, either through failure/success feedback (Menec et al., 1994), attributional inductions (Perry and Magnusson, 1989), or attributional retraining (Perry and Penner, 1990), or it was measured as a dependent variable (Perry et al., 1984). In our field studies, perceived control was manipulated with attributional retraining and was measured using questionnaires (Perry et al., 2001; Ruthig et al., 2004). In seeking to maximize external validity, the field studies complement the laboratory studies by observing the effects of perceived academic control in actual classroom conditions. AR has consistently been found in these field trials to increase perceptions of control in low-control students and to improve their scholastic performance.

Our research shows that, in times of academic uncertainty, such as the transition from high school into college, higher perceptions of control are beneficial to first-year students' scholastic development. Students who have a higher sense of academic control are better equipped to conquer the challenges of the first year of college likely because they believe the onus is on them to invest more effort to adjust their study strategies, and to seek their instructor's assistance as required. These high-control students generally experience more positive emotions and fewer negative emotions, such as shame, anxiety, and boredom than their low-control counterparts (Perry et al., 2001; Schönwetter et al., 1993). Students with higher academic control also tend to be more motivated to learn, putting more effort into academic tasks and persisting in their college courses to a greater extent than students with less academic control (Ruthig *et al.*, 2002) and to engage in more active learning, self-monitoring, and cognitive elaboration (Cassidy and Eachus, 2000; Perry *et al.*, 2001).

These positive academic-related emotional, cognitive, and motivational outcomes experienced by high-control students put them at a distinct advantage over their low-control counterparts in terms of achievement performance, ranging from higher introductory psychology course grades (Perry *et al.*, 2001), to cumulative GPAs (Hall, Perry, Ruthig, Hladkyj, and Chipperfield, 2005; Ruthig *et al.*, 2001), to persistence in first-year courses (Ruthig *et al.*, 2005; Perry *et al.*, in press). In contrast, students with a lower sense of academic control often feel completely overwhelmed when faced with the daunting challenges of first-year college, unable to make the connection between their own efforts and strategies and subsequent academic outcomes. Thus, having a sense of academic control is instrumental to surpassing the challenges of first-year college and can mean the difference between a mastery and helpless orientation in their scholastic development (e.g., Skinner, 1996; Thompson *et al.*, 1993).

EARLY IDENTIFICATION OF ACADEMIC CONTROL DIFFERENCES

An early identification of students' level of academic control is advantageous in assisting them to make the transition from high school into college because normally effective instruction often can be ineffective for low-control students (Magnusson and Perry, 1989; Perry and Dickens, 1984). The discussion method of instruction, for example, may be quite suitable for high-control students because of its open-ended structure, but less suitable for low-control students for the same reason. Alternately, the lecture method may appeal to low-control students because of its highly structured and predictable nature, but not to high-control students because of the lack of autonomy. Therefore, instructors may want to tailor their teaching methods early in the academic year to better accommodate students with differing levels of control.

Aside from the opportunity to adjust teaching methods to meet the learning-related needs of low-control students, early identification of students' level of academic control would enable instructors to provide intervention techniques to bolster students' sense of control. Research has repeatedly shown that providing low-control students with attributional retraining early in the academic year results in better performance on homework assignments, achievement tests (Menec et al., 1994; Perry and Penner, 1990), and final course grades by the end of that academic year (Pelletier et al., 1999; Struthers and Perry, 1996). Consequently, modifying classroom instruction methods to incorporate AR techniques can serve to enhance the adjustment of low-control students to their first year of college. Thus, assessing students' level of academic control early in the school year, perhaps after receiving feedback on their first test or assignment, would allow for the opportunity to identify the particular needs of each student and maximize their likelihood of success during this critical transition period.

ACADEMIC CONTROL AND OTHER STUDENT DIFFERENCES

Although clearly positive, the consequences of academic control are not always as straightforward as initially thought. Instead, academic control often interacts with other individual differences between students to affect both the short-term (e.g., course grades) and long-term (e.g., GPA three years later) achievement of college students. Failure preoccupation, for example, enhances the effects of academic control (Perry et al., 2001, in press), so that students with high academic control who are preoccupied with failure outperform high-control students who are less preoccupied with failure. In addition, various academic emotions appear to moderate the effects of academic control. Higher levels of positive emotions, such as course enjoyment, or lower levels of negative emotions, such as course boredom or anxiety, tend to maximize the effects of high academic control on students' final course grades, cumulative GPA, and course attrition (Ruthig et al., 2005). Conversely, low levels of positive emotions and high levels of negative emotions tend to nullify the effects of high academic control on achievement and attrition outcomes.

Evidently, knowing more about students' emotional states is critical to fully appreciate the role of academic control in persistence and achievement in college. Thus, further research focusing on the interactive effects of academic control and other commonly-experienced academic emotions such as pride (e.g., in achievement), hope (e.g., to succeed academically), shame (e.g., for poor performance), and guilt (e.g., for lack of effort) is needed to provide greater insight into how emotions enhance or impede the effects of academic control on achievement. Based on our own research, greater levels of positive emotions like pride or hope and lower levels of negative emotions like shame or guilt would likely maximize the benefits of high academic control. Conversely, lower levels of pride or hope and greater levels of guilt or shame would likely diminish the positive consequences of academic control.

Aside from learning-related emotions and failure preoccupation, perceived success is another major student difference that can modify the effects of academic control on scholastic performance. When paired with high academic control, perceptions of success are associated with greater achievement, yet when paired with low academic control, these same perceptions of success are associated with worse levels of achievement than having low perceived success (Schönwetter *et al.*, 1993). These findings are attributed to the fact that low-control/high-success students believe that, although they are successful, they do not have control over their academic outcomes. Thus, perceptions of success appear to only be adaptive if that success is believed to be within one's control.

The same may also be true of future expectations of success. Research by Ruthig *et al.* (2004), for example, explored the effects of high optimism on first-year students' GPA, test anxiety, and attrition, and drew similar conclusions. That is, highly optimistic students were thought to be at-risk academically if they did not have control perceptions in keeping with their optimistic expectations (e.g., "I expect to achieve an A+ in this course and my achievement depends on my own hard work"). Currently, we are testing this assumption in a study in which highly optimistic students were randomly assigned to either an AR or no-AR condition and their pre- and post-treatment perceptions of control were examined along with their year-end academic outcomes (Ruthig, Hladkyj, Hall, and Haynes, 2003; see Underlying AR Processes section below). These findings, in combination with the results of Ruthig *et al.* (2004), show that high-optimism students who received AR developed increased perceptions of control and consequently obtained better grades than their no-AR counterparts. These preliminary findings support the notion that optimistic expectations are only adaptive among first-year students if they believe that making those positive expectations a reality is within their own control.

Although these recent studies provide some support, additional research is needed to confirm that both perceived success and positive future expectations are adaptive only when accompanied by perceptions of academic control. Future academic control research needs to consider additional student differences such as failure preoccupation, emotions, and current and future success expectations, which have been shown to interact with control perceptions to differentially affect students' scholastic achievement and persistence.

ACADEMIC CONTROL AND STUDENT HEALTH

Because the physical and psychological health of college students can potentially have serious academic consequences, health factors must be taken into account when considering students' scholastic development. In this connection, some of our recent findings indicate that academic control measured at the beginning of the first year of college significantly predicts health outcomes, with higher levels of control corresponding to better self-reported physical health and psychological well-being five months later (Ruthig et al., 2002). Other research shows that the advantages of having both primary and secondary academic control extend beyond academic achievement into student health. Among female college students, for example, those who were proficient in both primary- and secondary-control strategies reported the best physical health and psychological well-being compared to students in three other groups who were deficient in either primary- or secondary-control strategies, or both (Hall, Chipperfield, Clifton, Ruthig, and Perry, 2002). These results can be explained, in part, by the fact that high-primary/high-secondary control students appear to switch between primary- and secondary-control beliefs when necessary in response to success and failure experiences.

This explanation is supported in a follow-up study by Hall, Hladkyj, Chipperfield, and Perry et al. (2002) which revealed that, among high-primary/high-secondary control students, those who were also capable of switching from primary to secondary control in failure situations reported the lowest occurrence of headaches, appetite loss, weight gain, indigestion, muscle tension, and fatigue. Thus, being able to switch between primary and secondary control as needed bolsters students' physical and psychological health, in addition to their motivation and academic performance (Hall, Hladkyj, Ruthig, et al., 2002). Finally, additional recent research suggests that gender and perceived stress may moderate the effects of perceived control on student health (Hall, Chipperfield, Perry, Ruthig, and Götz, 2005). Although primary control related to better self-reported health among male students, and secondary control related to better health mainly among female students, the health benefits of both control approaches were largely due to their positive effects on students' perceptions of stress.

Future research can contribute to our preliminary academic control and student health findings in several ways. For instance, the study by Hall, Chipperfield *et al.* (2005) emphasized the importance of assessing the impact of primary and secondary control on more objective measures of physical health, such as the number of classes missed due to illness and number of physician visits, as well as the frequency of observable health risk behaviors (e.g., smoking, drinking, unprotected sex, drug use, etc.). In addition to more subjective measures of perceived health, these objective health measures would provide a more comprehensive representation of student health outcomes. It would also be useful for future research to examine long-term effects of perceived control on student health, over the course of a year or longer, to determine whether the benefits of control extend beyond the five-month duration assessed in our preliminary research. Finally, these health-related findings are encouraging in that percep-tions of academic control are largely malleable. They suggest that increasing students' primary and secondary academic control through attribution-based AR treatments can enhance their physical health and psychological well-being, along with their academic motivation and achievement, and in doing so, potentially forestall the progression of more serious future health problems for low-control students. These recommendations underline the need to gain greater insight into the impact of primary and secondary academic control in the physical and psychological well-being of college students, as high-lighted in our preliminary findings.

ACADEMIC CONTROL AND ATTRIBUTIONAL RETRAINING

Based on the rapidly expanding literature on attributional retraining in a higher education context, several promising areas for future research are apparent. Consistent with these previous studies, ongoing research in our laboratory on AR in college students is directed toward three main issues: (a) identifying other low-control student groups, (b) speci-fying the cognitive and motivational processes underlying the effec-tiveness of AR, and (c) administering AR treatments on a larger scale. Findings discussed below highlight the need for future research in each of these areas to further our understanding of how these techniques work, for whom they are best suited, and how they can be improved to benefit specific groups of low-control students.

IDENTIFICATION OF STUDENT RISK FACTORS

Recent research has found that examining combinations of control-related risk factors will enable the identification of students most at risk of academic failure and in greater need of attributional retraining. Such research is not new to attributional retraining researchers as exemplified by Menec *et al.* (Study 2, 1994) who defined at-risk students as having not only an external locus of control, but also poor performance on a GRE-type exam. In Pelletier *et al.* (1999), students were deemed to be at risk not only according to their goal orientation, but also in terms of failure-avoidance. Hall, Perry, Ruthig, Hladkyj, and Chipperfield (2005) also outlined how maladaptive perceptions of control involving high primary control and low secondary control predispose initially unsuccessful students to more serious deficits in end-of-year academic performance.

In a similar vein, recent research by Newall, Haynes, Hladkyj, and Chipperfield (2003) assessed the utility of a writing-based AR treatment for students differing in their perceptions of academic control and their desire for control over academic outcomes. As discussed earlier in this chapter (see Desire for Control section), some students have congruent perceptions of academic control and desire for control (i.e., high or low in both), but other students may feel in control yet not value it (high control/little desire), or conversely, they may desire a sense of control that they do not possess (low control/high desire). Following an AR treatment, significant improvements in course performance were found only for students who were either high or low in *both* academic control and desire for control. Further, this study found that AR was not effective for students who were "mismatched" on these factors, that is, those who did not value the control they felt they had, or those who wanted more academic control than they felt they had.

Recent research has also examined the manner in which perceptions of academic success and feelings of optimism interact with AR to improve academic achievement in college students. Haynes, Ruthig, Newall, and Perry (2003) found that, following the administration of a writing-based AR treatment similar to that used in Newall *et al.* (2003) and Hall *et al.* (in press), course grades increased only for students with mismatched levels of optimism and perceived success. Specifically, AR was effective for students who were not optimistic but perceived themselves as successful, or did not feel successful but were optimistic, whereas it was *not* beneficial for students already feeling both successful and optimistic (i.e., "non-risk" students) or feeling neither successful nor optimistic (i.e., helpless students). Taken together, these findings suggest that by exploring how specific combinations of control-related student characteristics interact with attributional retraining to influence performance, we can obtain greater insight into what types of student dispositions are most beneficial or risky for academic development, and how AR can be used to help those students most at risk of failing during their first year of college.

Underlying AR Processes

Although the process of attributional change presumed to occur in college students following AR treatments has been assessed in previous research (Hall *et al.*, in press; Luzzo, James, and Luna, 1996; Menec *et al.*, 1994; Noel *et al.*, 1987; Perry and Penner, 1990), studies are needed that examine why AR treatments are effective for low-control students. For example, a recent study by Stupnisky, Perry, Hall, and Haynes (2004) used structural equation modelling to assess the attributional, cognitive, and emotional consequences of attributional retraining in first-year college students as proposed in Weiner's (1985) attributional model. This research showed that for first-year college students who received attributional retraining, administered using the videotape and aptitude test format employed in Pelletier *et al.* (1999), the predicted mediational path was observed from first- to second-semester performance through controllable attributions (effort), perceptions of responsibility, and feelings of hope. In contrast, this attributional sequence was not found for students who did not receive AR, for whom previous performance was found to correspond instead to uncontrollable attributions (ability).

Underlying AR processes were also investigated by Perry, Hall, Newall, Haynes, and Stupnisky (2003) who explored how both low- and high-elaborating students could benefit from a writing-based AR treatment. To examine this issue more closely, the AR presentation was followed by either a writing exercise asking students to elaborate on the attributional information in an abstract manner (e.g., summarization, personal examples; see Entwistle, 2000) or on the emotional impact of an academic failure experience (Pennebaker, 1997). High-elaborating students showed the greatest improvement in course performance and motivation when administered the writing exercise including specific

534

questions of an abstract nature, whereas low-elaborating students benefitted most when encouraged to elaborate more generally on their failure-related emotions.

Similarly, findings from Ruthig *et al.* (2003) indicate that control- and stress-related processes may underlie the effectiveness of AR for overly optimistic students, as found in Ruthig *et al.* (2004). The AR treatment encouraged more attributions to controllable causes (effort) and fewer attributions to uncontrollable causes (luck, instructor, test difficulty) in these overly optimistic students, and also increased perceptions of control and reduced feelings of stress by the end of the academic year. Hall *et al.* (in press) also explored changes in academic control resulting from AR in the context of Rothbaum *et al.*'s (1982) dual-process model of control. For freshman students with low test scores who relied on primary control to the exclusion of secondary control, higher perceptions of secondary control (e.g., finding the "silver lining") were found, along with lower uncontrollable attributions, following a writing-based AR treatment. In sum, these studies highlight the importance of exploring how processes involving perceived control, attributions, elaboration, and stress enable AR to improve the academic motivation and performance of low-control college students.

LARGE-SCALE AR ADMINISTRATION

By making attributional retraining techniques more user-friendly and efficient to administer, the large-scale application of brief yet effective AR treatments in the college classroom is quickly becoming a reality. Our research shows that AR involving consolidation exercises which are independently completed and administered en masse (e.g., writing assignment, aptitude test) are effective in improving academic performance in college students: reporting poor high school grades (Hunter and Perry, 1996); having a performance as opposed to mastery orientation (Pelletier *et al.*, 1999); relying on primary relative to secondary control in failure situations (Hall *et al.*, 2001; Hall *et al.*, in press), and other recently identified risk combinations (Haynes *et al.*, 2003; Newall *et al.*, 2003). Although previous AR research in laboratory settings has shown group discussion consolidation activities to be of benefit to certain groups of low-control students (Perry and Struthers, 1994; Struthers and Perry, 1996), large college classrooms make it difficult for instructors to adequately monitor the content and direction and group discussions, ensure equal and motivated student participation, and minimize factors such as noise level, unequal group sizes, and gender-heterogeneity within groups (Slavin, 1996).

In contrast, AR consolidation activities that are completed more independently allow students to elaborate on the AR message in an efficient, yet highly personal manner, while minimizing the negative effects of group dynamics. For example, psychological processes involving social comparison and self-presentation (Tesser and Campbell, 1983) may render discussion consolidation techniques ineffective for some students when administered in actual intact classrooms because of students' concerns about discussing personal failure experiences in the presence of their peers (Hladkyj *et al.*, 1998; Weiner, Graham, Taylor, and Meyer, 1984). The administration of individually-oriented consolidation treatments also avoids difficulties posed by attempting to externally regulate an unstructured classroom discussion, and requires much less direct instructor supervision. Furthermore, due to the development of web-based research technologies, AR treatments could also be administered entirely over the Internet. Online AR methods allow this intervention to be provided not only to traditional college students, but also to other student groups who are often overlooked, including rural, mature, physically disabled, and deaf students. In this connection, computer-based AR methods have been found to promote mathematics skill development in children with learning disabilities (Okolo, 1992).

Preliminary research on the use of Internet-based AR techniques to facilitate career decision making in college students is also encouraging (Tompkins-Bjorkman, 2002). For more information on AR and career uncertainty in college students, see Luzzo, Funk, and Strang (1996) and Luzzo, James, and Luna (1996). Moreover, our own preliminary research shows that a web-based AR session requiring students to read attributional information and complete an online aptitude test results in significantly higher subsequent test scores and final course grades for first-year students (Hall, Perry, Ruthig, Haynes, and Stupnisky, 2005). As such, AR techniques involving independently-completed consolidation exercises hold considerable promise for use in actual as well as virtual classroom settings by allowing large numbers of students to reflect on the attributional process in a structured yet meaningful way, while at the same time reducing distractions and instructor supervision.

In terms of assisting students on an individual basis, attributional retraining techniques could be implemented by peer counselors and academic advisors who regularly come into contact with college students who are demotivated, performing poorly, and are tempted to withdraw from a course or their academic program. By providing academic counselors with an understanding of Weiner's attribution theory (1985, 1995) so that they could encourage students to make controllable and unstable attributions for poor performance, these counselors would assist students in adjusting to the college environment, particularly during their first year. However, considering that many students in need of academic support do not seek professional assistance, another important potential application of AR in the college classroom involves the training of course instructors. Menec and Perry (1995) provide details for training college instructors to incorporate AR techniques into everyday classroom activities to assist the academic development of students who would otherwise perform poorly (see also Schönwetter *et al.*, 2001).

In terms of enhancing the efficacy of existing AR administration methods for college students, previous research suggests that including additional training modules alongside the standard attributional retraining session may improve its effectiveness. For instance, the findings of Hall *et al.* (2004) highlight the potential applicability of elaboration training in the college classroom (see Stark, Mandl, Gruber, and Renkl, 2002, for review). The results of this study suggest that by encouraging elaborative learning through explicit instruction, low-elaborating students may benefit from AR in not only course-specific but also overall first-year performance.

As done in previous AR research with college students (Van Overwalle and De Metsenaere, 1990) and elementary school students (Borkowski *et al.*, 1986, 1988; Miranda, Villaescusa, and Vidal Abarca, 1997; see also Pearl, 1985, for a review), strategy training based on a domain-specific skill set can also be incorporated into the attributional retraining intervention. For example, following the motivational AR treatment, students can be provided an opportunity to learn the skills and behaviors required to succeed in a given course (e.g., memorization techniques for a biology course) or in college more generally (e.g., essay writing, study techniques). Finally, for students already investing considerable effort or those with overly inflated perceptions of academic (primary) control (Hall *et al.*, in press), an AR treatment encouraging students to also consider secondary-control strategies, such as adopting more realistic expectations or finding the "silver lining" (see Weisz, Thurber, Sweeney, Proffitt, and LeGagnoux,

1997), may also be an effective tool in facilitating the impact of attributional retraining in the college classroom.

SUMMARY OF RESEARCH ON ACADEMIC CONTROL IN HIGHER EDUCATION

Overall, our research on academic control has shown that a high level of control over educational experiences benefits students in several ways, over and above the predictive validity of traditional scholastic indicators, such as student aptitude. From enhancing their emotions, cognitions, and achievement motivation (Perry *et al.*, 2001; Schönwetter *et al.*, 1993), to improving their course grades and GPA (Hall, Perry, Ruthig, Hladkyj, and Chipperfield, 2005; Hall *et al.*, in press), to increasing their persistence as reflected in fewer courses dropped (Ruthig *et al.*, 2001, 2002), academic control provides students with the resources to overcome various educational obstacles. These findings also highlight the sustainability of the benefits of academic control over time, as evidenced by longitudinal research showing positive effects of academic control lasting up to three years (Perry *et al.*, in press). In addition to these main effects of academic control on student development, we have found that students' academic control also interacts with other individual difference variables involving academic emotions (Ruthig *et al.*, 2005), perceived success (Schönwetter *et al.*, 1993), and self-regulation (Perry *et al.*, 2001, in press) to predict performance outcomes. Previous laboratory analog studies of college classrooms demonstrate how classroom factors involving instructor effectiveness mediate the influence of academic control on scholastic development (Magnusson and Perry, 1989; Perry and Dickens, 1984, 1987; Perry and Magnusson, 1987; Perry *et al.*, 1986). Finally, our recent research suggests that by utilizing a dual-process model of perceived control, consisting of both primary and secondary academic control, we can gain a better understanding of how students adjust to failure experiences encountered during their first academic year (Hall, Hladkyj, Ruthig, *et al.*, 2002; Hall, Perry, Ruthig, Hladkyj, and Chipperfield, 2005).

A major focus in our research has been to design attributional retraining (AR) procedures to assist low-control students (cf., Perry *et al.*, 1993; Menec *et al.*, 1994). We have found that AR techniques can be particularly effective for students who are failure prone due to both dispositional and situational factors such as an external locus of control

(Menec *et al.*, 1994; Perry and Penner, 1990), maladaptive primary-/secondary-control beliefs (Hall *et al.*, in press), overly optimistic beliefs (Ruthig *et al.*, 2004), low perceptions of success (Perry and Struthers, 1994), infrequent use of elaborative learning strategies (Hall *et al.*, in press), reliance on performance goals as opposed to learning goals (Pelletier *et al.*, 1999), as well as poor academic performance (Hunter and Perry, 1996; Menec *et al.*, 1994). This research also shows how the overall effectiveness of AR techniques may be improved by the explicit manipulation of treatment methods in order to identify which AR procedures work best for different types of low-control students (e.g., Hall *et al.*, 2001, 2004; Hunter and Perry, 1996; Perry and Struthers, 1994; Ruthig *et al.*, 2004). These studies highlight the importance of providing not only AR information to students, but also of giving them the opportunity to elaborate on this information in a meaningful way through consolidation exercises which can be adapted to optimize the scholastic development of low-control students.

In having demonstrated the importance of academic control as an individual difference in college students and of attributional retraining as a viable instructional method for enhancing academic control, our next priority is to identify the underlying processes contributing to these findings. Notably, this requires a strong conceptual framework to guide the analysis of the underlying processes and a balance of methodological approaches involving both laboratory and field trials. In combination with our existing findings, these new studies should enable academic control differences between college students to be more clearly delineated, both for research and classroom purposes. In so doing, they would enable the efficacy of attributional retraining techniques to be subject to further development and improvement. As a consequence, failure-prone students would be more quickly identified by classroom instructors, before the students drop courses or withdraw from college altogether, and would be able to benefit from attributional retraining techniques applied in the classroom or offered more widely in university student-support programs.

REFERENCES

Anastasi, A. (1988). *Psychological Testing*. New York, NY: Macmillan.

Anderson, C.A. (1983). Motivational and performance deficits in interpersonal settings: The effect of attributional style. *Journal of Personality and Social Psychology* 45: 1136–1147.

Andrews, G.R., and Debus, R.L. (1978). Persistence and the causal perception of failure: Modifying cognitive attributions. *Journal of Educational Psychology* 70: 154–166.

Ashenfelter, O., and Krueger, A. (1994). Estimates of the economic returns to schooling from a new sample of twins. *American Economic Review* 84: 1157–1173.

Aspinwall, L.G., and Taylor, S.E. (1992). Modelling cognitive adaptation: A longitudinal investigation of the impact of individual differences and coping on college adjustment and performance. *Journal of Personality and Social Psychology* 83: 989–1003.

Atkinson J.W., and Feather, N.T. (1966) (eds.), *A Theory of Achievement Motivation*. New York, NY: Wiley.

Aydin, G. (1988). The remediation of children's helpless explanatory style and related unpopularity. *Cognitive Therapy and Research* 12: 155–165.

Bandura, A. (1977). Self-efficacy: Toward a unifying theory of behavioral change. *Psychological Review* 84: 191–215.

Bandura, A. (1997). *Self-efficacy: The Exercise of Control*. Englewood Cliffs, NJ: Prentice Hall.

Barling, J., and Snipelisky, B. (1983). Assessing the determinants of children's academic self-efficacy beliefs: A replication. *Cognitive Therapy and Research* 7: 371–376.

Bess, J.L. (1973). Integrating faculty and student life cycles. *Review of Educational Research* 43: 377–403.

Block, J., and Lanning, K. (1984). Attribution therapy requestioned: A secondary analysis of the Wilson-Linville study. *Journal of Personality and Social Psychology* 46: 705–708.

Borkowski, J.G., Weyhing, R.S., and Carr, M. (1988). Effects of attributional retraining on strategy-based reading comprehension in learning-disabled students. *Journal of Educational Psychology* 80: 46–53.

Borkowski, J.G., Weyhing, R.S., and Turner, L.A. (1986). Attributional retraining and the teaching of strategies. *Exceptional Children* 53: 130–137.

Britton, B.K., and Tesser, A. (1991). Effects of time-management practices on college grades. *Journal of Educational Psychology* 83: 405–410.

Burger, J.M. (1989). Negative reactions to increases in perceived personal control. *Journal of Personality and Social Psychology* 56: 246–256.

Burger, J.M. (1995). Need for control and self-esteem: Two routes to a high desire for control. In M.H. Kernis (ed.), *Efficacy, Agency, and Self-esteem* (pp. 217–233). New York, NY: Plenum Press.

Burger, J.M., and Cooper, H.M. (1979). The desirability of control. *Motivation and Emotion* 3: 381–393.

Canadian Association of University Teachers. (2003). *CAUT Almanac of Post-secondary Education in Canada*. Ottawa, ON: Author.

Carlyon, W.D. (1997). Attribution retraining: Implications for its integration into prescriptive social skills training. *School Psychology Review* 26: 61–73.

Cassidy, S., and Eachus, P. (2000). Learning style, academic belief systems, self-report student proficiency, and academic achievement in higher education. *Educational Psychology: An International Journal of Experimental Educational Psychology* 20: 307–322.

Chipperfield, J.G. (1993). Perceived barriers in coping with health problems: A twelve-year longitudinal study of survival among elderly individuals. *Journal of Aging and Health* 5: 123–139.

Chipperfield, J.G., and Greenslade, L. (1999). Perceived control as a buffer in the use of health care services. *Journal of Gerontology: Psychological Sciences* 54B: P146–P154.

Clifton, R.A. (2000, May). *Post-secondary Education in Canada: 1960 to 2000: The Best Years We Have Ever Had*. Paper presented at the annual meeting of the Canadian Society for the Study of Higher Education, Edmonton, AB.

Clifton, R.A., and Roberts, L.W. (1992). *Authority in Classrooms*. Scarborough, ON: Prentice Hall.

Cohen, J. (1988). *Statistical Power for the Behavioral Sciences* (2nd ed). Hillsdale, NJ: Erlbaum.

Cohen, P.A. (1981). Student ratings of instruction and student achievement: A meta-analysis of multisection validity studies. *Review of Educational Research* 51: 281–309.

Cohen, P.A. (1983). Comment on a selective review of the validity of student ratings of teaching. *Journal of Higher Education* 54: 448–458.

Covington, M.V. (1992). *Making the Grade: A Self-worth Perspective on Motivation and School Reform*. New York, NY: Cambridge University Press.

Covington, M.V. (1993). A motivational analysis of academic life in college. In J.C. Smart (ed.), *Higher Education: Handbook of Theory and Research* (Vol. 7, pp. 61–101). New York, NY: Agathon Press.

Craske, M.L. (1985). Improving persistence through observational learning and attribution retraining. *British Journal of Educational Psychology* 55: 138–147.

Craske, M.L. (1988). Learned helplessness, self-worth motivation and attribution retraining for primary school children. *British Journal of Educational Psychology* 58: 152–164.

Creech, S.K., Carpenter, S., and Davis, E.J. (1994). The direct economic impact of Texas' appropriations to higher education. *The Review of Higher Education* 17, 125–141.

Cronbach, L.J., and Snow, R.E. (1977). *Aptitudes and Instructional Methods: A Handbook for Research on Interactions*. Oxford, England: Irvington.

Curtis, K.A. (1992). Altering beliefs about the importance of strategy: An attributional intervention. *Journal of Applied Social Psychology* 22: 953–972.

DasGupta, B. (1992). Perceived control and examination stress. *Psychology: A Journal of Human Behavior* 29: 31–34.

DeCharms, R. (1968). *Personal Causation: The Internal Affective Determinants of Behavior*. New York, NY: Plenum.

Deci, E.L., and Ryan, R.M. (1985). *Intrinsic Motivation and Self-determination in Human Behavior*. New York, NY: Plenum.

den Boer, D.J., Meertens, R., Kok, G., and Van Knippenberg, A. (1989). Measurements effects in reattribution research. *European Journal of Social Psychology* 19: 553–559.

Desruisseaux, P. (1998). US trails 22 nations in high school completion. *The Chronicle of Higher Education*, December 4, A45.

541

Dev, P.C. (1998). Intrinsic motivation and the student with learning disabilities, *Journal of Research and Development in Education* 31: 98–108.

Dicintio, M.J., and Gee, S. (1999). Control is the key: Unlocking the motivation of at-risk students. *Psychology in the Schools* 36: 231–237.

Dieser, R.B., and Ruddell, E. (2002). Effects of attribution retraining during therapeutic recreation on attributions and explanatory styles of adolescents with depression. *Therapeutic Recreation Journal* 36: 35–47.

Dweck, C.S. (1975). The role of expectations and attributions in the alleviation of learned helplessness. *Journal of Personality and Social Psychology* 31: 674–685.

Eaton, S.B., and Bean, J.P. (1995). An approach/avoidance behavior model of college student attrition. *Research in Higher Education* 36: 617–645.

Edmonds, H.K. (2003). Grade retention and children's academic self-efficacy and use of self-protective strategies. *Dissertation Abstracts International Section A: Humanities and Social Sciences* 63: 11-A.

El-Hindi, A.E., and Childers, K.D. (1996, January). *Exploring Metacognitive Awareness and Perceived Attributions for Academic Success and Failure: A study of at-risk college students.* Paper presented at the Southwest Educational Research Association annual meeting, New Orleans, LA.

Entwistle, N. (2000). Approaches to studying and levels of understanding: The influences of teaching and assessment. In J.C. Smart (ed.), *Higher Education: Handbook of Theory and Research* (Vol. 15, pp. 156–218). New York, NY: Agathon Press.

Eysenck, H.J. (1997). Personality and experimental psychology: The unification of psychology and the possibility of a paradigm. *Journal of Personality and Social Psychology* 73: 1224–1237.

Feldman, K. (1989). The association between student ratings of specific instructional dimensions and student achievement: Refining and extending the synthesis of data from multisection validity studies. *Research in Higher Education* 30: 583–645.

Feldman, K.A. (1998). Reflections on the study of effective college teaching and student ratings: One continuing question and two unresolved issues. In J.C. Smart (ed.), *Higher Education: Handbook of Theory and Research* (Vol. 13, pp. 35–74). New York, NY: Agathon.

Folkman, S. (1984). Personal control and stress and coping processes: A theoretical analysis. *Journal of Personality and Social Psychology* 46: 839–852.

Försterling, F. (1985). Attributional retraining: A review. *Psychological Bulletin* 98: 495–512.

Försterling, F. (1986). Attributional conceptions in clinical psychology. *American Psychologist* 41: 275–285.

Furio, B.J. (1987). The relationship between instructor behaviors and student perceptions of control in the classroom. *Dissertation Abstracts International* 47(8-A): 2798.

Garber, J., and Seligman, M.E.P. (1980) (eds.), *Human Helplessness: Theory and Applications.* New York, NY: Academic Press.

Garcia-Campayo, J., Sanz Carrillo, C., Larrubia, J., and Monton, C. (1997). Reattribution revisited: A critical appraisal. *European Journal of Psychiatry* 11: 5–10.

Geraghty, M. (1996, July 19). More students quitting college before sophomore year, data show. *The Chronicle of Higher Education* A35–A36.

Glass, D.C., and Singer, J. (1971). *Urban Stress.* New York, NY: Academic Press.

Green-Emrich, A., and Altmaier, E.M. (1991). Attributional retraining as a structured group counselling intervention. *Journal of Counselling and Development* 69: 351–355.

Hall, N.C., Chipperfield, J.G., Clifton, R.A., Ruthig, J.C., and Perry, R.P. (2002, April). *Primary Control, Secondary Control, and Gender: Empirical Links to Health and College Students' Academic Development*. Paper presented at the American Educational Research Association annual meeting, New Orleans, LA.

Hall, N.C., Chipperfield, J.G., Perry, R.P., Pekrun, R.H., and Schönwetter, D. (2001, April). *Attributional Retraining, Perceived Control, and Failure: Assisting at-risk Students Through Writing*. Paper presented at the American Educational Research Association annual meeting, Seattle, WA.

Hall, N.C., Chipperfield, J.G., Perry, R.P., Ruthig, J.C., and Götz, T. (2005). *Primary and Secondary Control in Academic Development: Gender-specific Implications for Stress and Self-rated Health in College Students*. Manuscript under review.

Hall, N.C., Hladkyj, S., Chipperfield, J.G., and Perry, R.P. (2002, June). *Primary, Secondary, and Action Control Strategies: Health Implications of College Students' "switching capacity."* Paper presented at the Canadian Psychological Association annual convention, Vancouver, BC.

Hall, N.C., Hladkyj, S., Chipperfield, J.G., and Stupnisky, R.H. (2003, May). *Perceived Control and Self-regulation: A Structural Equation Modelling Approach*. Paper presented at the Western Psychological Association annual convention, Vancouver, BC.

Hall, N.C., Hladkyj, S., Perry, R.P., and Ruthig, J.C. (2004). The role of attributional retraining and elaborative learning in college students' academic development. *Journal of Social Psychology* 144: 591–612.

Hall, N.C., Hladkyj, S., Ruthig, J.C., Pekrun, R., and Perry, R.P. (2002, April). *The Role of Action Control in Moderating Primary versus Secondary Control Strategy Use in College Students*. Paper presented at the American Educational Research Association annual meeting, New Orleans, LA.

Hall, N.C., Perry, R.P., Chipperfield, J.G., Clifton, R.A., and Haynes, T.L. (in press). Enhancing primary and secondary control in at-risk college students through writing-based attributional retraining. *Journal of Social and Clinical Psychology*.

Hall, N.C., Perry, R.P., Ruthig, J.C., Haynes, T.L., and Stupnisky, R.H. (2005, April). *Internet-based Attributional Retraining: Longitudinal Effects on Academic Achievement in College Students*. Paper presented at the American Educational Research Association annual meeting, Montreal, PQ.

Hall, N.C., Perry, R.P., Ruthig, J.C., Hladkyj, S., and Chipperfield, J.G. (2005). *Primary and Secondary Control in Achievement Settings: A Longitudinal Field Study of Academic Motivation, Emotions, and Performance*. Manuscript under review.

Harackiewicz, J.M., Barron, K.E., Tauer, J.M., and Elliot, A.J. (2002). Predicting success in college: A longitudinal study of achievement goals and ability measures as predictors of interest and performance from freshman year through graduation. *Journal of Educational Psychology* 94: 562–575.

Haynes, T., Ruthig, J.C., Newall, N.E., and Perry, R.P. (2003, May). *Attributional Retraining, Dispositional Optimism, and Success: Effects on Academic Achievement*. Paper presented at the Western Psychological Association annual convention, Vancouver, BC.

Heckhausen, J., and Schulz, R. (1998). Developmental regulation in adulthood: Selection and compensation via primary and secondary control. In J. Heckhausen and C.S. Dweck (eds.), *Motivation and Self-regulation Across the Life Span* (pp. 50–77). New York, NY: Cambridge University Press.

543

Heller, K.A. (1999). Individual (learning and motivational) needs versus instructional conditions of gifted education. *High Ability Studies* 10: 9–21.

Heller, K.A. (2003). Attributional retraining as an attempt to reduce gender-specific problems in mathematics and the sciences. *Gifted and Talented* 7: 15–21.

Heller, K.A., and Ziegler, A. (1996). Gender differences in mathematics and the natural sciences: Can attributional retraining improve the performance of gifted females? *Gifted Child Quarterly* 40: 200–210.

Hladkyj, S., Hunter, A.J., Maw, J., and Perry, R.P. (1998, April). *Attributional Retraining and Elaborative Learning in the College Classroom*. Paper presented at the American Educational Research Association annual meeting, San Diego, CA.

Hladkyj, S., Pelletier, S.T., Drewniak, E.P., and Perry, R.P. (1998, April). *Evidence for the Role of Secondary Control in Students' Adaptation to College*. Paper presented at the American Educational Research Association annual meeting, San Diego, CA.

Hladkyj, S., Perry, R.P., Hall, N.C., Ruthig, J.C., and Pekrun, R. (2003, April). *The Emplotment of Unpredictable Experience: A Multi-sample Study of Secondary Control in College Student Motivation*. Paper presented at the American Educational Research Association annual meeting, Chicago, IL.

Hladkyj, S., Perry, R.P., and Pelletier, S.T. (2000, April). *Narrative Emplotment and the Creation of Meaning: Links to Student Emotion, Cognition, and Motivation*. Paper presented at the American Education Research Association annual meeting, New Orleans, LA.

Hladkyj, S., Taylor, J.R., Pelletier, S.T., and Perry, R.P. (1999, April). *Narrative Emplotment: Meaning and Value in Unpredictable Experience and its Role in Student Motivation*. Paper presented at the American Educational Research Association annual meeting, Montreal, PQ.

Ho, R., and McMurtrie, J. (1991). Attributional feedback and underachieving children: Differential effects on causal attributions, success expectancies, and learning processes. *Australian Journal of Psychology* 43: 93–100.

House, J.D. (1995). Noncognitive predictors of achievement in introductory college mathematics. *Journal of College Student Development* 36: 171–181.

Hudley, C., Britsch, B., Wakefield, W.D., Smith, T., Demorat, M., and Cho, S.-J. (1998). An attribution retraining program to reduce aggression in elementary school students. *Psychology in the Schools* 35: 271–282.

Hunter, A.J., and Perry, R.P. (1996, August). *Attributional Retraining: Identifying at-risk Students before Admission to University*. Paper presented at the XXVI International Congress of Psychology, Montreal, PQ.

Jesse, D.M., and Gregory, W.L. (1986–87). A comparison of three attributional approaches to maintaining first year college GPA. *Educational Research Quarterly* 11: 12–25.

Kaaya, S., Goldberg, D., and Gask, L. (1992). Management of somatic presentations of psychiatric illness in general medical settings: Evaluation of a new training course for general practitioners. *Medical Education* 26: 138–144.

Kuhl, J. (1985). Volitional mediators of cognition-behavior consistency: Self-regulatory processes and action versus state orientation. In J. Kuhl and J. Beckmann (eds.), *Action Control: From Cognition to Behavior* (pp. 101–128). Berlin: Springer Verlag.

Langer, E.J. (1989). Minding matters: The consequences of mindlessness-mindfulness. *Advances in Experimental Social Psychology* 22: 137–173.

Leondari, A., and Gialamas, V. (2000). Relations between self-esteem, perceived control, possible selves, and academic achievement in adolescents. *Psychology: The Journal of the Hellenic Psychological Society* 7: 267–277.

Leslie, L.L., and Slaughter, S.A. (1992). Higher education and regional economic development. In W.E. Becker and R. Lewis (eds.), *The Economics of American Higher Education*. Boston, MA: Kluwer Academic Publishers.

Luzzo, D.A., Funk, D.P., and Strang, J. (1996). Attributional retraining increases career decision-making self-efficacy. *Career Development Quarterly* 44: 378–386.

Luzzo, D.A., James, T., and Luna, M. (1996). Effects of attributional retraining on the career beliefs and career exploration behavior of college students. *Journal of Counselling Psychology* 43: 415–422.

Magnusson, J.-L., and Perry, R.P. (1989). Stable and transient determinants of students' perceived control: Consequences for instruction in the college classroom. *Journal of Educational Psychology* 81: 362–370.

Marsh, H.W., and Dunkin, M. (1992). Students' evaluations of university teaching; A multidimensional perspective. In J.C. Smart (ed.), *Higher Education: Handbook of Theory and Research* (Vol. 8, pp. 143–233). New York, NY: Agathon.

McKeachie, W.J. (1997). Student ratings: The validity of use. *American Psychologist* 52: 1218–1225.

Menec, V.H., and Perry, R.P. (1995). Disciplinary differences in perceptions of success: Modifying misperceptions with attributional retraining. In N. Hativa and M. Marincovich (eds.), *Disciplinary Differences in Teaching and Learning in Higher Education*. San Francisco, CA: Jossey-Bass.

Menec, V.H., Perry, R.P., Struthers, C.W., Schönwetter, D.J., Hechter, F.J., and Eichholz, B.L. (1994). Assisting at-risk college students with attributional retraining and effective teaching. *Journal of Applied Social Psychology* 24: 675–701.

Menges, R.J., and Associates (eds.) (1999). *Faculty in New Jobs*. San Francisco, CA: Jossey-Bass.

Meyer, G.J., Finn, S.E., Eyde, L.D., Kay, G.G., Moreland, K.L., Dies, R.R., Eisman, E.J., Kubiszyn, T.W., and Reed, G.M. (2001). Psychological testing and psychological assessment: A review of evidence and issues. In A.E. Kazdin (ed.), *Methodological Issues and Strategies in Clinical Research* (Vol. 3, pp. 265–345). Washington, DC: American Psychological Association.

Miller, C., Mulvey, P., and Martin, N. (1995). What do twins studies reveal about the economic returns to education? A comparison of Australian and U.S. findings. *American Economic Review* 3: 586–599.

Miller, R.L., Brickman P., and Bolen, D. (1975). Attribution versus persuasion as a means for modifying behavior. *Journal of Personality and Social Psychology* 31: 430–441.

Miranda, A., Villaescusa, M.I., and Vidal-Abarca, E. (1997). Is attribution retraining necessary? Use of self-regulation procedures for enhancing the reading comprehension strategies of children with learning disabilities. *Journal of Learning Disabilities* 30: 503–512.

Miserandino, M. (1998). Attributional retraining as a method of improving athletic performance. *Journal of Sport Behavior* 21: 286–297.

Morriss, R.K., and Gask, L. (2002). Treatment of patients with somatized mental disorder: Effects of reattribution training on outcomes under the direct control of the family doctor. *Psychosomatics: Journal of Consultation Liasion Psychiatry* 43: 394–399.

Murphy, K.M., and Welch, F. (1992). Wages of college graduates. In W.E. Becker and D.R. Lewis (eds.), *The Economics of American Higher Education* (pp. 121–140). Boston, MA: Kluwer Academic Publishers.

Murray, H.G. (1991). Effective teaching behaviors in the college classroom. In J.C. Smart (ed.), *Higher Education: Handbook of Theory and Research* (Vol. 7, pp. 135–172). New York, NY: Agathon.

Murray, H.G. (2001). Low-inference teaching behaviors and college teaching effectiveness: Recent developments and controversies. In J.C. Smart (ed.), *Higher Education: Handbook of Theory and Research* (Vol. 16, pp. 239–272). New York, NY: Agathon.

Musher-Eizenman, D.R., Nesselroade, J.R., and Schmitz, B. (2002). Perceived control and academic performance: A comparison of high- and low-performing children on within-person change patterns. *International Journal of Behavioral Development* 26: 540–547.

National Center for Educational Statistics. (2004, August 22). *Enrollment in Degree-granting Institutions* [On-line]. Available: http://nces.ed.gov/pubs2002 /proj2012/ch_2.asp

Newall, N.E., Haynes, T., Hladkyj, S., and Chipperfield, J.G. (2003, May). *Academic Achievement: Effects of Attributional Retraining, Perceived Control and Desire for Control*. Paper presented at the Western Psychological Association annual convention, Vancouver, BC.

Noel, J.G., Forsyth, D.R., and Kelley, K.N. (1987). Improving performance of failing students by overcoming their self-serving attributional biases. *Basic and Applied Psychology* 8: 151–162.

Okolo, C. (1992). The effects of computer-based attribution retraining on the attributions, persistence, and mathematics computation of students with learning disabilities. *Journal of Learning Disabilities* 25: 327–334.

Pascarella, E.T., and Terenzini, P.T. (1991). *College Affects Students: Findings and Insights from Twenty Years of Research*. San Francisco, CA: Jossey-Bass.

Paulsen M. B. (1998). Recent research on the economics of attending college: Returns on investments and responsiveness to price. *Research in Higher Education* 39: 471–489.

Pearl, R. (1985). Cognitive-behavioral interventions for increasing motivation. *Journal of Abnormal Child Psychology* 13: 443–454.

Pelletier, S.T., Hladkyj, S., Moszynski, S.L., and Perry, R.P. (1999, August). *Goal Orientation and Perceived Control: Delineating Prerequisites for Sustained Motivation with an Attributional Retraining Context*. Paper presented at the American Psychological Association annual meeting, Boston, MA.

Pennebaker, J.W. (1997). Writing about emotional experiences as a therapeutic process. *Psychological Science* 8: 162–166.

Perry, R.P. (1991). Perceived control in college students: Implications for instruction in higher education. In J.C. Smart (ed.), *Higher Education: Handbook of Theory and Research* (Vol. 7, pp. 1–56). New York, NY: Agathon Press.

Perry, R.P. (1997). Teaching effectively: Which students? What methods? In R.P. Perry and J.C. Smart (eds.), *Effective Teaching in Higher Education: Research and Practice* (pp. 154–168). New York, NY: Agathon.

Perry, R.P. (2003). Perceived (academic) control and causal thinking in achievement settings. *Canadian Psychologist* 44: 312–331.

Perry, R.P., Abrami, P.C., and Leventhal, L. (1979). Educational seduction: The effect of instructor expressiveness and lecture content on student ratings and achievement. *Journal of Educational Psychology* 71: 109–116.

Perry, R.P., Clifton, R.A., Menec, V.H., Struthers, C.W., and Menges, R.J. (2000). Faculty in transition: A longitudinal analysis of perceived control and type of institution in the research productivity of newly hired faculty. *Research in Higher Education* 41: 165–194.

Perry, R.P., and Dickens, W.J. (1984). Perceived control in the college classroom: The effect of response outcome contingency training and instructor expressiveness on students' attributions and achievement. *Journal of Educational Psychology* 76: 966–981.

Perry, R.P., and Dickens, W.J. (1987). Perceived control and instruction in the college classroom: Some implications for student achievement. *Research in Higher Education* 27: 291–310.

Perry, R.P., Hechter, F.J., Menec, V.H., and Weinberg, L. (1993). Enhancing achievement motivation and performance in college students: An attributional retraining perspective. *Research in Higher Education* 34: 687–720.

Perry, R.P., Hall, N.C., Newall, N.E., Haynes, T.L., and Stupnisky, R.H. (2003, May). *Attributional Retraining and Elaboration: Differential Treatment Effects in College Students*. Paper presented at the Western Psychological Association annual convention, Vancouver, BC.

Perry, R.P., Hladkyj, S., and Pekrun, R.H. (1988, April). *Action-control and Perceived Control in the Academic Achievement of College Students: A Longitudinal Analysis*. Paper presented at the American Educational Research Association annual meeting, San Diego, CA.

Perry, R.P., Hladkyj, S., Pekrun, R., and Pelletier, S. (2001). Academic control and action control in the achievement of college students: A longitudinal field study. *Journal of Educational Psychology* 93: 776–789.

Perry, R.P., Leventhal, L., and Abrami, P.C. (1979). An observational learning procedure for improving university instruction. *Improving University Teaching* 5: 240–248.

Perry, R.P., and Magnusson, J.-L. (1987). Effective instruction and students perceptions of control in the college classroom: Multiple-lectures effects. *Journal of Educational Psychology* 79: 453–460.

Perry, R.P., and Magnusson, J.-L. (1989). Causal attributions and perceived performance: Consequences for college students' achievement and perceived control in different instructional conditions. *Journal of Educational Psychology* 81: 164–172.

Perry, R.P., Magnusson, J.-L., Parsonson, K., and Dickens, W.J. (1986). Perceived control in the college classroom: Limitations in instructor expressiveness due to noncontingent outcomes and lecture content. *Journal of Educational Psychology* 78: 96–107.

Perry, R.P., Menec, V.H., Struthers, C.W., Hechter, F.J., Schönwetter, D.J., and Menges, R.J. (1997). Faculty in transition: A longitudinal analysis of the role of perceived control and type of institutions in adjustment to postsecondary institutions. *Research in Higher Education* 38: 519–556.

Perry, R.P., and Penner, K.S. (1990). Enhancing academic achievement in college students through attributional retraining and instruction. *Journal of Educational Psychology* 82: 262–271.

547

Perry, R.P., and Smart, J.C. (eds.) (1997). *Effective Teaching in Higher Education: Research and Practice*. New York, NY: Agathon.

Perry, R.P., and Struthers, C.W. (1994, April). *Attributional Retraining in the College Classroom: Some Cause for Optimism*. Paper presented at the American Educational Research Association, New Orleans, LA.

Perry, R.P., and Williams, R.G. (1979). Videotape instruction. The impact of teacher characteristics on student ratings and achievement. In A.M. Sullivan (ed.), *Experimental Research in Videotaped Instruction*. St. Johns, NF: Memorial University Press.

Perry, R.P., Hladkyj, S., Pekrun, R.H., Clifton, R.C., and Chipperfield, J.G. (in press). Perceived academic control and failure in college students: A three-year study of scholastic attainment. *Research in Higher Education*.

Pintrich, P.R., Smith, D.A., and McKeachie, W.J. (1989). *A Manual for the Use of the Motivated Strategies for Learning Questionnaire*. Ann Arbor, MI: National Center for Research to Improve Postsecondary Teaching and Learning, School of Education, University of Michigan.

Reed, J.G. (1981). Dropping a college course: Factors influencing students' withdrawal decisions. *Journal of Educational Psychology* 73: 376–385.

Robbins, S.B., Lauver, K., Davis, H.L., Davis, D., Langley, R., and Carlstrom, A. (2004). Do psychosocial and study skill factors predict college outcomes? A meta-analysis. *Psychological Bulletin* 130: 261–288.

Rodin, J. (1986). Health, control, and aging. In M.M. Baltes and P.B. Baltes (eds.), *Aging and the Psychology of Control* (pp. 139–165). Hillsdale, NJ: Erbaum.

Ross, C.E., and Broh, B.A. (2000). The roles of self-esteem and the sense of perceived control in the academic achievement process. *Sociology of Education* 73: 270–284.

Rothbaum, F., Weisz, J., and Snyder, S. (1982). Changing the world and changing the self: A two-process model of perceived control. *Journal of Personality and Social Psychology* 42: 5–37.

Rotter, J.B. (1966). Generalized expectancies for internal versus external control of reinforcement. *Psychological Monographs* 80: 1–28.

Rotter, J.B. (1975). Some problems and misconceptions related to the construct of internal versus external control of reinforcement. *Journal of Consulting and Clinical Psychology* 43: 56–67.

Ruthig, J.C., Hladkyj, S., Hall, N.C., and Haynes, T.L. (2003, May). *Attributional Retraining: Longitudinal Effects on Optimistic Students' Perceived Control and Stress*. Paper presented at the Western Psychological Association annual convention, Vancouver, BC.

Ruthig, J.C., Hladkyj, S., Hall, N.C., Pekrun, R., and Perry, R.P. (2002, April). *Profiling Voluntary Course Withdrawal Among College Students: A Longitudinal Study with Motivational Implications*. Paper presented at the American Educational Research Association annual meeting, New Orleans, LA.

Ruthig, J.C., Hladkyj, S., Perry, R.P., Clifton, R.A., and Pekrun, R. (2001, April). *Academic Emotions and Perceived Control: Effects on Achievement and Voluntary Course Withdrawal*. Paper presented at the American Educational Research Association annual meeting, Seattle, WA.

Ruthig, J.C., Perry, R.P., Hall, N.C., and Hladkyj, S. (2004). Optimism and attributional retraining: Longitudinal effects on academic achievement, test anxiety, and voluntary course withdrawal. *Journal of Applied Social Psychology* 34: 709–730.

Ruthig, J.C., Perry, R.P., Hladkyj, S., Hall, N.C., Pekrun, R., and Chipperfield, J.G. (2005). *A Longitudinal Analysis of Perceived Control and Emotions in an Academic Setting*. Manuscript under review.

Schönwetter, D.J., Perry, R.P., and Struthers, C.W. (1993). Students' perceptions of control and success in the college classroom: Affects and achievement in different instruction conditions. *Journal of Experimental Education* 61: 227–246.

Schönwetter, D., Walker, L.J., Hladkyj, S., Perry, R.P., Ruthig (Kobylak), J.C., and Hall, N.C. (2001, April). *Facilitating the Academic Development of High-risk Freshmen Students Through a Deliberate Teaching Strategy*. Paper presented at the American Educational Research Association annual meeting, Seattle, WA.

Schulz, R., and Heckhausen, J. (1996). A life span model of successful aging. *American Psychologist* 51: 702–714.

Schunk, D.H. (1983). Ability versus effort attributional feedback: Differential effects on self-efficacy and achievement. *Journal of Educational Psychology* 75: 848–856.

Seligman, M.E.P. (1975). *Helplessness: On Depression, Development, and Death*. San Francisco, CA: Freeman.

Shapiro, D.H., Schwartz, C.E., and Astin, J.A. (1996). Controlling ourselves, controlling our world. *American Psychologist* 51: 1213–1230.

Sinnott, K., and Biddle, S. (1998). Changes in attributions, perceptions of success and intrinsic motivation after attributional retraining in children's sport. *International Journal of Adolescence and Youth* 7: 137–144.

Skinner, E.A. (1996). A guide to constructs of control. *Journal of Personality and Social Psychology* 71: 549–570.

Skinner, E.A., Connell, J.P., and Zimmer-Gembeck, M.J. (1998). Individual differences and the development of perceived control. *Monographs of the Society for Research in Child Development* 63: 1–220.

Skinner, E.A., Wellborn, J.G., and Connell, J.P. (1990). What it takes to do well in school and whether I've got it: A process model of perceived control and children's engagement and achievement in school. *Journal of Educational Psychology* 82: 22–32.

Slavin, R.E. (1996). Research on cooperative learning and achievement: What we know, what we need to know. *Contemporary Educational Psychology* 21: 43–69.

Smart, J.C. (1986). College effects on occupational status attainment. *Research in Higher Education* 24: 73–95.

Smart, J.C. (1988). College influences on graduates' income levels. *Research in Higher Education* 29(1): 4–59.

Smart, J.C. (1990). A causal model of faculty turnover intentions. *Research in Higher Education* 31(5): 405–424.

Sokoloff, H. (2004, March 6). Why aren't men going to university? *National Post*, pp. RB1, RB2.

Stark, R., Mandl, H., Gruber, H., and Renkl, A. (2002). Conditions and effects of example elaboration. *Learning and Instruction* 12: 39–60.

Stipek, D.J., and Weisz, J.R. (1981). Perceived control and academic achievement. *Review of Educational Research* 51: 101–138.

Struthers, C.W., and Perry, R.P. (1996). Attributional style, attributional retraining, and inoculation against motivational deficits. *Social Psychology of Education* 1: 171–187.

Stupnisky, R.H., Perry, R.P., Hall, N.C., and Haynes, T.L. (2004, April). *Individual Differences in Attributional Retraining: A Longitudinal Study.* Paper presented at the Western Psychological Association annual meeting. Phoenix, AZ.

Sullivan, A.M., and Skanes, G.R. (1974). Validity of student evaluation of teaching and the characteristics of successful instructors. *Journal of Educational Psychology* 66: 584–590.

Tesser, A., and Campbell, J. (1983). Self-definition and self-evaluation maintenance. In J. Suls and A.G. Greenwald (eds.), *Psychological Perspectives on the Self* (Vol. 2). Hillsdale, NJ: Erlbaum.

Tompkins-Bjorkman, A.B. (2002). Internet-based attributional retraining and career decision making. *Dissertation Abstracts International Section B: Sciences and Engineering* 63(11-B): 5540.

Thompson, S.C., Sobolew-Shubin, A., Galbraith, M.E., Schwankovsky, L., and Cruzen, D. (1993). Maintaining perceptions of control: Findings perceived control in low control circumstances. *Journal of Personality and Social Psychology* 64: 293–304.

Van Overwalle, F. (1989). Structure of freshmen's causal attributions for exam performance. *Journal of Educational Psychology* 81: 400–407.

Van Overwalle, F. (1997). Dispositional attributions require the joint application of the methods of difference and agreement. *Personality and Social Psychology Bulletin* 23: 974–980.

Van Overwalle, F., and De Metsenaere, M. (1990). The effects of attribution-based intervention and study strategy training on academic achievement in college freshmen. *British Journal of Educational Psychology* 60: 299–311.

Van Overwalle, F., Segebarth, K., and Goldchstein, M. (1989). Improving performance of freshman through attributional testimonies from fellow students. *British Journal of Educational Psychology* 59: 75–85.

Weary, G., Gleicher, F., and Marsh, K.L. (eds.) (1993). *Control Motivation and Social Cognition.* New York, NY: Springer-Verlag.

Weinberg, L.E. (2001). The effects of attributional retraining, age, and perceived control on health-related cognitions: A longitudinal field study of older adults attending geriatric day hospitals. *Dissertation Abstracts International Section A: Humanities and Social Sciences* 61(7-A): 2865.

Weiner, B. (1980). A cognitive (attribution)–emotion–action model of motivated behavior: An analysis of judgments of help-giving. *Journal of Personality and Social Psychology* 39: 186–200.

Weiner, B. (1985). An attributional theory of achievement motivation and emotion. *Psychological Review* 92: 548–573.

Weiner, B. (1986). *An Attributional Theory of Motivation and Emotions.* New York, NY: Springer-Verlag.

Weiner, B. (1988). Attribution theory and attributional therapy: Some theoretical observations and suggestions. *British Journal of Clinical Psychology* 27: 93–104.

Weiner, B. (1995). *Judgments of Responsibility: A Foundation for a Theory of Social Conduct.* New York, NY: Guilford Press.

Weiner, B., Graham, S., Taylor, S.E., and Meyer, W.U. (1984). Social cognition in the classroom. *Educational Psychologist* 18: 109–124.

Weisz, J.R., Thurber, C.A., Sweeney, L., Proffitt, V.D., and LeGagnoux, G.L. (1997). Brief treatment of mild-to-moderate child depression using primary and secondary control enhancement training. *Journal of Consulting and Clinical Psychology* 65:703–707.

White, R.W. (1959). Motivation reconsidered: The concept of competence. *Psychological Review* 66: 297–333.

Wiggins, J.S. (1996). *The Five-factor Model of Personality.* New York, NY: Guilford Press.

Wilson, T.D., Damiani, M., and Shelton, N. (2002). Improving the academic performance of college students with brief attributional interventions. In J. Aronson (ed.), *Improving Academic Achievement: Impact of Psychological Factors on Education* (pp. 88–108). San Diego, CA: Academic Press.

Wilson, T.D., and Linville, P.W. (1982). Improving the academic performance of college freshmen: Attributional therapy revisited. *Journal of Personality and Social Psychology* 42: 367–376.

Wilson, T.D., and Linville, P.W. (1985). Improving the performance of college freshmen with attributional techniques. *Journal of Personality and Social Psychology* 49: 287–293.

Wise, S.L. (1994). Understanding self-adapted testing: The perceived control hypothesis. *Applied Measurement in Education* 7: 15–24.

Wise, S.L., Roos, L.R., Leland, V., Oats, R.G., and McCrann, T.O. (1996). The development and validation of a scale measuring desire for control on examinations. *Educational and Psychological Measurement* 56: 710–718.

Wise, S.L., Roos, L.L., Plake, B.S., and Nebelsick-Gullett, L.J. (1994). The relationship between examinee anxiety and preference for self-adapted testing. *Applied Measurement in Education* 7: 81–91.

Wortman, C.B., and Brehm, J.W. (1975). Responses to uncontrollable outcomes: An integration of reactance theory and the learned helplessness model. In L. Berkowitz (ed.), *Advances in Experimental Social Psychology* (Vol. 8, pp. 277–336). New York, NY: Academic Press.

Yajima, H., Sato, J., and Arai, K., (1996). The relationship between motives for science, perceived control, achievement anxiety, and self-regulation in junior high school students. *Psychologia: An International Journal of Psychology in the Orient* 39: 248–254.

Yamauchi, H., Kumagai, Y., and Kawasaki, Y. (1999). Perceived control, autonomy, and self-regulated learning strategies among Japanese high school students. *Psychological Reports* 85: 779–798.

Yan, W., and Gaier, E.L. (1991, April). *Causal Attributions for College Success and Failure: An American-Asian Comparison.* Paper presented at the American Educational Research Association annual meeting, Chicago, IL.

Ziegler, A., and Heller, K.A. (2000). Effects of an attribution retraining with female students gifted in physics. *Journal for the Education of the Gifted* 23: 217–243.

13. EMOTIONS IN STUDENTS' SCHOLASTIC DEVELOPMENT

Reinhard Pekrun

University of Munich
pekrun@edupsy.uni-muenchen.de

Abstract

Emotions are of critical importance for college students' academic performance, personality development, and health. With few exceptions such as research on test anxiety, however, students' emotions have been neglected by higher education research. In this chapter, the available evidence is reviewed, and theoretical considerations on the relevance of emotions for students' scholastic development are presented. The chapter features occurrence and base rates of student emotions in academic settings; the development of instruments assessing these emotions; their impact on academic learning and performance; their individual and social antecedents; as well as implications for emotion regulation, therapy, and educational classroom practices at college and university. In closing, directions for future research are outlined

Key Words: Emotion, affect, enjoyment, pride, anxiety, anger, shame, boredom, motivation, learning strategies, academic achievement, classroom instruction, college environment

Emotions are ubiquitous in academic settings at college and university. Academic learning and achievement are of fundamental importance for students' educational careers, determining their current life situation as well as future educational and occupational opportunities. Important objects or events, however, tend to instigate emotional reactions (Scherer, Schorr and Johnstone, 2001). By implication, achievement-related emotions are frequent, pervasive, manifold, and often intense in situations at college and university. The social nature of many academic situations further contributes to the emotional character of university settings. Social emotions likely play a major role in these settings as well, in addition to achievement emotions (Weiner, in press; see Table 1T1 for examples of students' achievement-related and social academic emotions).

R.P. Perry and J.C. Smart (eds.), The Scholarship of Teaching and Learning in Higher Education: An Evidence-Based Perspective, 553–610.

Table 1: The Domain of Academic Emotions: Examples

		Positive	Negative
Activity-related		Enjoyment	Boredom
Outcome-related	Prospective	Anticipatory Joy Hope	Hopelessness Anxiety
	Retrospective	Joy Satisfaction Pride Relief	Sadness Disappointment Shame/Guilt
Social		Gratitude Empathy Admiration Sympathy/Love	Anger Jealousy/Envy Contempt Antipathy/Hate

Adding to their relevance, emotions are functionally important for students' study-related and social behavior, adaptation to college, and academic success. Positive emotions like enjoyment of learning can help to envision goals and challenges, open the mind to creative problem-solving, and lay the groundwork for individual self-regulation (Ashby, Isen & Turken, 1999; Isen, 1999; Pekrun, Goetz, Titz, & Perry, 2002a). Maladaptive emotions like excessive anxiety, hopelessness, or boredom, on the other hand, are detrimental to academic success, induce students to drop out of college, and impact negatively on both psychological and physical health (Zeidner, 1998, in press). In the sizable numbers of attempted and committed suicides among college students (Westefeld, Homaifar, Spotts, Furr, Rage, and Werth, 2005), emotional problems related to failures in individual academic agency probably play a major role.

Due to their relevance for engagement and scholastic development, students' emotions are important for college instructors as well. Instructors face a formidable task when they first encounter the eager students arraigned before them at the beginning of an academic year. Not only must they inculcate the knowledge and analytic tools of their disciplines, but they must also inspire a passion for the discipline and an excitement about learning. Of these goals, passion and excitement are the most elusive because college instructors receive little or no training in the principles of affect and learning. If they succeed in inspiring excitement about the course content, the motivational benefits will extend far beyond the course, stimulating a commitment to the discipline, and a persistence to an educational career at college more generally. If they fail, however, the ensuing negative emotions (such as anxiety or boredom) can quickly undermine motivation and the will to remain in the course and in university.

Despite the clear relevance of students' emotions, however, emotions have been neglected by higher education research, and by educational research more generally, with few exceptions (Pekrun and Frese, 1992; Schutz and Lanehart, 2002; see the literature search in Pekrun, Goetz, Titz, and Perry, 2002b). On a theoretical level, the achievement emotions of pride and shame were regarded as central to the instigation of achievement-directed motivation and behavior in traditional achievement motivation theories (see Atkinson, 1964; Heckhausen, 1991). Empirically, however, emotions were not studied as phenomena in their own right by classical achievement motivation research. Rather, they were regarded as being no more than subcomponents of global, summary constructs of achievement motives, with the exception of test anxiety that was often equated with the fear of failure motive (Atkinson, 1964). Also, the recent boom of emotion research in basic disciplines of psychology (like personality and social psychology), and in the neurosciences, was just ignored by the mainstream of educational research.

There are two notable exceptions to this inattention to achievement-related emotions. One is research on students' test anxiety which originated in the 1930s (e.g., Brown, 1938; Stengel, 1936), started to flourish in the 1950s, and has continued to be a highly active field of research since then (Zeidner, 1998, 2007). Whereas achievement emotions other than anxiety attracted few researchers, test anxiety has been analyzed in more than 1,000 empirical studies to date (Zeidner, 1998; Pekrun et al., 2002b). The second exception is research on the attributional antecedents of emotions following success and failure, largely originating in Bernard Weiner's attributional theory of achievement motivation and emotion (Weiner, 1985, in press).

As a consequence of neglecting emotional processes, we still lack cumulative empirical knowledge on college students' emotions. Over the past ten years, there has been a slow, but discernable increase in the number of studies dealing with students' emotions, as evidenced in three recent special issues and one edited volume on this topic (Efklides and Volet, 2005; Linnenbrink, 2006; Schutz and Pekrun, in press; Schutz and Lanehart, 2002). These studies have produced initial findings on a number of emotions. To date, however, this evidence is still too scant to warrant firm conclusions, research on test anxiety being the predominant exception. As for students' emotions in postsecondary settings, the situation is even worse, since the bulk of extant studies has been conducted with upper elementary, middle and high school students. For example, of the 27 studies on relationships between students' achievement goals and their emotions cited by Linnenbrink and Pintrich (2002), only five pertained to samples of college and university students.

Studies on emotions in K-12 students have produced important insights into the mechanisms of academic emotions, but these results cannot easily be generalized to higher education settings, for two reasons. First, college students are young adults who are in a developmental phase that differs from childhood and adolescence. Second, these students represent a select part of the student population, being of higher intellectual ability, on an average, and having a more positive personal history of academic accomplishments than their peers not going to college (which, paradoxically, puts them at considerable risk when being confronted with the challenging academic environment of a university; Perry, 1991).

The reader who is familiar with psychological research on emotions might be tempted to argue that most of the available experimental evidence on human moods and emotions has been gained using college students as participants, such that there should be plenty of evidence on students' emotions. However, there are clear limits as to the generalizability of this experimental evidence to students' real-life academic emotions. First, experimental research on emotion is often faced with problems of ecological validity, one reason being the ethical constraints on inducing more intense emotions in the laboratory, as opposed to positive or negative mood as typically used in many experiments (e.g., Forgas and Vargas, 2000). Second, most of the evidence from experimental emotion research pertains to fundamental mechanisms of human emotion, but does not relate to learning and achievement as being situated in academic contexts.

By implication, much of the present chapter will be a call for empirical research, rather than a review of cumulative evidence that can be used for deriving validated practical recommendations. In the following sections, I will first discuss the occurrence of emotions in academic settings at college and university. Second, the assessment of students' emotions will be addressed. Test anxiety questionnaires and the Achievement Emotions Questionnaire (AEQ; Pekrun et al., 2002b; Pekrun, Goetz, and Perry, 2005) will be cited as examples how to measure academic emotions. In the third section, I will address the functional relevance of students' emotions for their academic learning

556

and achievement. Next, antecedents and development of students' emotions will be considered, as well as aspects of coping, emotion regulation, and therapy. In concluding, I will discuss implications for educational practice and future research on higher education.

OCCURRENCE OF EMOTIONS IN ACADEMIC SETTINGS: EXPLORATORY FINDINGS

As noted at the outset, From a theoretical perspective, given the importance of academic agency in college students' scholarly development, situations of learning and performance can be assumed to frequently induce intense emotions. Empirically, however, there is a lack of evidence on the occurrence, frequency, and intensity of different emotions as experienced by university students in academic settings. Test anxiety is a unique exception, as this emotion has consistently been found to be experienced by many students before and during test taking at college and university (Zeidner, 1998).

In our own research, we conducted a number of exploratory studies to analyze the diversity of emotions as experienced by K – 12 and university students. Four of these studies related to emotional experiences in academic situations of attending class, studying, and taking test and exams at university (Pekrun, 1992a; Molfenter, 1999; Spangler, Pekrun, Kramer, and Hofmann, 2002; Titz, 2001). These studies used semi-structured interviews and questionnaires to explore college students' emotions and the cognitive, behavioral, and situational processes functioning as antecedents or effects of emotions. In each of these interviews and questionnaires, students were asked a series of fixed questions and could give open-ended answers, thus providing qualitative narratives of emotional episodes. Video-stimulated recall and psychophysiological analyses were also used in some of this research in order to facilitate and validate respondents' self-reports.

In the first study (Pekrun, 1992a), students recalled typical academic episodes from their autobiographical memories and reported the affective processes experienced within these episodes. The other three studies (Molfenter, 1999; Spangler et al., 2002; Titz, 2001) used a situated approach in which emotions were assessed immediately after situations of attending class, studying, or taking a test. Students' descriptions of emotional episodes were recorded, transcribed, and analyzed in both qualitative and quantitative ways.

As expected, the results of all four studies showed that students experience a wide variety of emotions in academic settings. There was no major human emotion that was not reported in the students' narratives, disgust being an exception. Anxiety proved to be the emotion that was reported most frequenty, accounting for 15–27% of all emotional episodes reported in the four studies. Anxiety was mentioned with regard to all three types of academic situations (attending class, studying, and taking tests and exams). This prevalence of anxiety corroborates the importance of test anxiety research. Also, the anxiety problems reported by many students imply that they are faced with a "workplace" at college and university that can pose a serious threat to their psychological health. Achievement pressure and expectancies of failure were reported as major determinants of anxiety, indicating that a reduction of excessive demands and an increase in opportunities for success might benefit students' psychological health.

However, our findings on relative frequencies also imply that the vast majority of emotions reported pertained to emotion categories other than anxiety. Overall, positive emotions were mentioned no less frequently than negative emotions. Enjoyment, satisfaction, hope, pride, and relief were reported as being experienced frequently in academic settings, as were anger, shame, and boredom. Furthermore, there were many accounts of less frequently experienced emotions, including hopelessness as well as social emotions like gratitude, admiration, contempt, and envy.

The relative frequencies of emotions differed across the three types of academic situations specified. In the classroom setting and during studying, positive emotions typically accounted for slightly more than 50% of the emotions reported, whereas negative emotions outweighed positive emotions when taking tests and exams. Typically, attending class and studying involves less pressure for achievement and more autonomy for self-regulation than writing an exam, which may explain these differential frequencies.

The findings or our exploratory research thus confirm assumptions on the diversity of emotions experienced by college students in academic settings. However, there may be limits to the generalizability of these findings. First, emotions that are experienced less intensely may be underreported in any self-report assessment of emotions that relies on the availability of emotional episodes in situational or long-term memories. Also, culturally defined rules of reporting about emotions may play a role, perhaps implying that emotions like contempt or envy are experienced more often than acknowledged by the participants of self-report studies. Furthermore, our studies used samples of German university students, thus pertaining to emotions as experienced at German universities. Higher education institutions share many features across countries, but there are differences as well, thus limiting the cross-cultural generalizability of findings. The German higher education system is about to undergo major change, but as of to date, the German and North American university systems still differ in a number of aspects that are likely important for students' emotions. For example, most study programs and courses are less structured in the German than in the North American systems to date, implying that more self-regulation is expected from students in German universities. Second, there still is less high-stakes testing in the German system, and course exams are typically less frequent.

By implication, whereas conclusions on the diversity of academic emotions experienced by college students likely are generalizable, more specific findings on relative frequences and situational antecedents of distinct emotions may partially be culture-specific. More exploratory and base-rate research on the emotions experienced by higher education students in different countries is clearly warranted.

ASSESSMENT OF STUDENTS' ACADEMIC EMOTIONS

Exploratory research can be used to investigate the occurrence and phenomenology of students' emotions, but more rigorous quantitative methodology is needed to get more precise evidence on functions, antecedents and development of these emotions. Measurement instruments are a necessary prerequisite to apply quantitative methods. To date, many self-report instruments assessing students' test anxiety are available. As for emotions other than anxiety, however, there still remains a lack of suitable measures. In this section, I begin by discussing conceptual and methodological issues. I will then address test anxiety measurement and a newly constructed instrument assessing a diversity of students' academic emotions (Achievement Emotions Questionnaire, AEQ; Pekrun et al., 2002b; Pekrun, Goetz, and Perry, 2005).

CONCEPTUAL ISSUES AND WAYS TO ASSESS EMOTIONS

There seems to be consensus today that emotions should be conceptualized as multi-component processes comprising emotion-specific subjective feelings (affective component), cognitions (cognitive component), motivational tendencies (motivational component), peripheral physiological processes (physiological component), as well

559

as expressive behavior (expressive component; see Kleinginna and Kleinginna, 1981; Scherer, 1984, 2000). Typical components of students' anxiety experienced before an exam, for example, would be uneasy, nervous feelings; appraisals of threat of failure and lack of own competencies; motivation to escape the situation; physiological activation; and anxious facial expression. Whereas other components need not always be present when an emotion is instigated, the affective component is at the core of the concept of emotion. From a neuropsychological perspective, this component comprises an activation of subcortical structures of the brain (e.g., the amygdala in anxiety), as well as feedback loops between subcortical and cortical structures that make it possible to experience an emotion as a subjective feeling state (Damasio, 2004).

The diversity of emotion components implies that there may be many ways to assess emotions, including self-report, neuroimaging methods (e.g., fMRI), analysis of peripheral physiological processes, and observation of nonverbal behavior like facial, gestural and postural expression or the prosodic features of verbal speech. With the exception of self-report instruments, all of these methods are still under-used by educational research to date. For example, while video-based research on classroom interaction flourishes, this research has yet to attempt to analyze the emotional processes that characterize interactions between instructors and students. This could be done by adapting methods developed in emotion research (e.g., the Facial Action Coding System, FACS; Ekman and Rosenberg, 1997) for use in classroom observation. Similarly, neuroimaging methods could be employed to analyze brain indicators of students' emotional reactions when confronted with academic tasks, and an assessment of peripheral physiological processes could be used to analyze students' emotional activation in academic settings (recording of heart rate, skin resistance, cortisol levels, etc.; see e.g. Spangler et al., 2002).

ASSESSMENT OF TEST ANXIETY

Since test anxiety has been the one emotion that has attracted educational researchers' interest universally, the development of instruments assessing this emotion has made significant progress over the past seven decades, making it amenable to scientific investigation (Pekrun, Goetz, Perry, Kramer, and Hochstadt, 2004; Zeidner, 1998). Self-report instruments are the most frequently used method, including interviews, think-aloud protocols, single-item rating scales, or questionnaire scales asking students to report about their anxiety experienced prior to, during, or after exams. Among these instruments, multi-item questionnaire scales became most popular since they are easy to administer and proved to show good psychometric qualities (Hodapp and Benson, 1997; Zeidner, 1998). Questionnaire scales can be used to assess students' momentary emotional reactions to exams (*state* test anxiety), as well as their habitual tendency to react, typically, by experiencing anxiety when being confronted with tests or exams (*trait* test anxiety).

The first questionnaire assessing students' test anxiety was developed by C. H. Brown at the University of Chicago in the 1930s (Brown, 1938), but this instrument did not gain widespread acceptance. In contrast, G. Mandler's and S. B. Sarason's Test Anxiety Questionnaire (TAQ; Mandler and Sarason, 1952) became the progenitor of many of the questionnaires assessing test anxiety that were developed over the past five decades. The TAQ was a uni-dimensional instrument resting on the assumption that test anxiety is a homogenous, one-dimensional phenomenon. Progress as to dimensionality was made when Liebert and Morris (1967) proposed to distinguish affective and physiological components of test anxiety (called *emotionality* by them) from cognitive components (called *worry* by these authors). Since 1967, test anxiety measurement has further refined the worry-emotionality distinction. Examples of current instruments that can be used with university students are the *Test Anxiety Inventory* (TAI; Spielberger, 1980), the *Reactions to Test* instrument (Sarason, 1984), the integrative test anxiety scale proposed by Hodapp and Benson (1997), and the test anxiety scale of the *Achievement Emotions Questionnaire* (Pekrun et al., 2002b) discussed below.

Today, most of the available test anxiety scales possess good psychometric properties. Coefficients of internal reliability typically are above Alpha = .85. Structural validity is ensured by use of confirmatory factor analysis (e.g., Hodapp and Benson, 1997), and external construct validity by correlations with measures of academic learning and performance (Zeidner, 1998).

The sophistication achieved in the measurement of test anxiety was instrumental for the success of test anxiety research in analyzing this emotion. However, there also are problems that remain to be solved. Specifically, there seems to be no agreement between test anxiety researchers as to the precise nature of the multidimensionality of the construct. Whereas all of the major instruments available to date assess affective-physiological components as well as the worry component of test anxiety, there is dispute as to which additional components should be included in the construct (lack of self-confidence, task-irrelevant thinking, manifest behaviors, etc.; Zeidner, 1998).

A second major problem is that test anxiety research disregarded other emotions experienced in exam situations, and, therefore, ignored problems of discriminant validity, in spite of early calls for making test anxiety measurement more specific (Nicholls, 1976). Items measuring cognitive components of test anxiety, for example, often pertain to exam-related worries that are typical not only of anxiety, but of hopelessness and despair as well (e.g., items like "Before taking a test, I worry about failure"; Sarason, 1984). Typically, these items do not differentiate between worries in anxiety (defined by subjective uncertainty of threatening failure) and worries in hopelessness (characterized by subjective certainty of failure; Pekrun et al., 2004). Also, many items tapping the physiological components of test anxiety assess physiological activation that is characteristic for other activating emotions such as anger or shame as well. It may thus be that current test anxiety instruments still measure "more than they denote" (Nicholls, 1976) by implicitly assessing other negative emotions as well. Future research on the assessment of achievement emotions like test anxiety should pay more attention to issues of discriminant validity, in addition to internal structural validity that has been emphasized over the past decades.

ASSESSMENT OF DIVERSE ACADEMIC EMOTIONS: THE ACHIEVEMENT EMOTIONS QUESTIONNAIRE (AEQ)

Whereas the measurement of test anxiety made systematic progress over the past fifty years, measures for students' academic emotions other than test anxiety, and for other achievement emotions more generally, are still largely lacking. Based on the findings of our exploratory research cited above, we therefore constructed a multi-dimensional instrument measuring a variety of major academic emotions, including test anxiety, but also assessing other achievement emotions (Achievement Emotions Questionnaire, AEQ; Pekrun, Goetz et al., 2002b; Pekrun, Goetz, and Perry, 2005)[1].

The AEQ is a self-report instrument assessing college students' achievement emotions. It measures a number of discrete emotions for each of the three main categories of academic situations, that is,

---

[1] The Achievement Emotions Questionnaire was first published under the name "Academic Emotions Questionnaire" (Pekrun et al., 2002b).

attending class, studying, and writing tests and exams. These situations differ in terms of functions and social structures, implying that emotions regarding these situations can differ as well. For example, enjoyment of classroom instruction may be different from enjoying the challenge of an exam – some students may be excited when going to class, others when writing exams. Therefore, the AEQ provides separate scales for class-related, learning-related, and test-related emotions.

The AEQ assesses students' typical, individual emotional reactions in academic situations (*trait* academic emotions). Instructions require respondents to indicate how they feel, typically, in these situations. However, by employing alternative instructions, the AEQ can also be used to measure emotions experienced in single courses (*course-specific* emotions), or at specific points of time when attending class, studying, or taking a test (*state* academic emotions).

In its current version, the AEQ can be used to assess eight different class-related emotions, eight learning-related emotions, and eight test emotions (see Table 2). The selection of these emotions was based on criteria of frequency and theoretical relevance (Pekrun et al., 2002b). The class-related emotion scales include 80 items and measure emotions by instructing students to report how they feel during, before, or after being in class. The emotions assessed by these scales include class-related enjoyment (sample item: "I enjoy being in class"), hope ("I am full of hope"), pride ("I am proud of myself"), anger ("I feel anger welling up in me"), anxiety ("I feel nervous in class"), shame ("I feel ashamed"), hopelessness ("I feel hopeless"), and boredom ("I get bored"). The learning-related emotion scales consist of 75 items assessing the same set of emotions in situations of studying. The instruction for these scales require respondents to report how they feel during, before, or after studying. The eight test emotions scales include 77 items pertaining to test-related enjoyment, hope, pride, relief, anger, anxiety, shame, and hopelessness. Instructions ask respondents to indicate how they feel during, before or after taking tests and exams.[2]

Within each section, the items are ordered in three blocks assessing emotional experiences before, during, and after being in academic situations addressed by the section. For example, the section

---

[2] The test emotions section of the instrument has been published under the name "Test Emotions Questionnaire" (TEQ; Pekrun et al., 2004). The Test Emotions Questionnaire is an integral part of the AEQ.

Table 2: Achievement Emotions Questionnaire (AEQ): Scales and Reliabilities[a]

	Scales					
	Class-Related Emotions		Learning-Related Emotions		Test Emotions	
Emotions	α	Items	α	Items	α	Items
Enjoyment	.85	10	.78	10	.78	10
Hope	.79	8	.77	6	.80	8
Pride	.82	9	.75	6	.86	10
Relief	–[b]	–	–	–	.77	6
Anger	.86	9	.86	9	.86	10
Anxiety	.86	12	.84	11	.92	12
Hopelessness	.89	11	.86	11	.87	10
Shame	.90	10	.90	11	.92	11
Boredom	.93	11	.92	11	–[c]	–

[a] Coefficients for English version of the AEQ. [b] Relief scale for test emotions only. [c] Boredom scale for class-related and learning-related emotions only.

on test emotions contains three blocks of items pertaining to emotions experienced before, during, and after taking tests. Sequencing items this way is in line with principles of situation-reaction inventories (Endler and Okada, 1975) and is intended to help respondents in accessing their emotional memories.

The construct definitions underlying the AEQ use the consensual multi-component definition of "emotion" cited above. The items of each of the scales pertain to affective, cognitive, physiological/expressive, and motivational components of the emotion to be measured. This is in line with the state of the art in test anxiety measurement, but extends test anxiety assessment in two important ways. Whereas current test anxiety measures assess affective, physiological and cognitive components of anxiety, they neglect the motivational component. Items pertaining to this component were part of G. Mandlers' and S. B. Sarason's (1952) Test Anxiety Questionnaire, but were dropped in test anxiety measurement later on. Second, an effort was made to construct items that ensure discriminant content validity of scales measuring different discrete emotions, including a differentiation between test anxiety and closely neighboring emotions like test-related shame and hopelessness.

The reliabilities of the AEQ scales range from adequate to very good (Alpha = .75 to .93, with Alpha > .80 for 18 of the 24 scales).

The structural validity of the AEQ scales has been tested by confirmatory factor analysis (e.g., Pekrun et al., 2004). As to external validity, the AEQ has been shown to be predictive for college students' academic achievement, course enrollment, and dropout rates. Also, achievement emotions as assessed by the AEQ relate to components of students' learning processes such as study interest, achievement goals, intrinsic and extrinsic motivation to learn, cognitive and metacognitive strategies of learning, the investment of study effort, and the self-regulation of academic learning (Goetz, 2004; Goetz, Pekrun, Hall, and Haag, 2006; Kleine, Goetz, Pekrun, and Hall, 2005; Molfenter, 1999; Pekrun, Elliot, and Maier, 2006; Pekrun et al., 2002a, b; Pekrun et al., 2004; Perry, Hladkyi, Pekrun, and Pelletier, 2001; Perry, Hladkyj, Pekrun, Clifton, and Chipperfield, 2005; Spangler et al., 2002; Titz, 2001). Gender, social feedback, teachers' instructional behavior, and the composition and social climate of classrooms have been shown to be further important correlates of the achievement emotions assessed by the AEQ (e.g., Frenzel, Pekrun, and Goetz, in press; Pekrun, 2000; Pekrun, Frenzel, Goetz, and Perry, 2006).

In sum, college students' emotions and their components can be assessed by means of diverse measures including self-report, behavioral observation, neuroimaging, and physiological analysis. Standardized self-report scales have beeen used most often to date, and have proven to be a reliable, valid, and cost-effective way of measuring students' achievement emotions. Traditionally, these measures addressed students' test anxiety. Future research should develop instruments assessing academic emotions other than anxiety as well, as is done by the Achievement Emotions Questionnaire described above. Also, research on assessment should explore alternative ways to assess students' emotions, including the measurement of emotional processes that are less well represented in conscious awareness than the explicit emotional experiences typically targeted by self-report instruments.

FUNCTIONS OF EMOTIONS FOR COLLEGE STUDENTS' ACADEMIC LEARNING AND ACHIEVEMENT

In experimental research, mood and emotions have been found to influence a wide range of cognitive processes, including attention, memory storage and retrieval, social judgment, decision making, convergent problem solving, and creative thinking (Lewis and Haviland-Jones, 2000). Much of this research has focused on the effects of positive vs. negative mood, without differentiating more specific, discrete mood states and emotions. Three important, cumulative findings of this research pertaining to attentional processes, memory, and problem solving are the following. First, as addressed by the resource allocation model proposed by Ellis and Ashbrook (1988), emotions typically consume *cognitive resources* by focusing attention on the object of the emotion. The resource allocation model was originally formulated for negative emotions, but the assumptions of the model can be extended to positive emotions as well (Pekrun, 1992b; for empirical evidence, see Meinhardt and Pekrun, 2003). Consumption of cognitive resources for task-irrelevant purposes implies that less resources are available for task completion. For example, a student preparing for an exam and being afraid of failing may focus on worrying about failure, which distracts attention away from the learning task at hand.

Second, mood can enhance *mood-congruent memory processes* by mechanisms of state-dependent learning and mood-congruent recall (e.g., Levine and Burgess, 1997). Mood-congruent recall implies that positive mood can facilitate the retrieval of positive self- and task-related information, whereas negative mood sustanins the retrieval of negative information. Positive mood, for example, can foster positive self-appraisals, thus benefitting motivation to learn (e.g., Olafson and Ferraro, 2001). Mood-congruent memory processes can thus contribute to positive cycles of positive mood, enhanced motivation, and improved task performance, and to vicious circles of negative mood, reduced motivation, and failure.

Third, positive and negative mood have been shown to influence *cognitive problem solving*. Specifically, the experimental evidence implies that positive mood can be beneficial for flexible, creative, and holistic ways of solving problems, and for a reliance on gener-alized, heuristic knowledge structures. Negative mood, on the other hand, can help more focused, detail-oriented and analytical ways of thinking. A number of theoretical explanations have been proffered for these findings. For example, in mood-as-information approaches, it is assumed that positive affective states signal that "all is well", whereas negative states imply that something is going wrong (e.g., Bless, Clore, Schwarz, Golisano, Rabe, and Wölk, 1996). "All is well" conditions imply safety and the discretion to creatively explore the environment, broaden one's cognitive horizon, and build new actions (as addressed by Fredrickson's, 2001, "broaden-and-build" metaphor of the effects of positive emotions). In contrast, if there are problems threatening well-being and agency, it may be wise to focus on these problems in analytical, cognitively cautious ways. Furthermore, it has been argued that positive emotions can increase brain dopamine levels, thereby facilitating flexible thinking (Ashby, Isen and Turken, 1999), and that negative mood can induce motivation for "mood repair" (e.g., Schaller and Cialdini, 1990) that can enhance effortful task performance, which may also help to explain why negative mood can have positive effects on performance at analytical tasks requiring effort.

However, while experimental research has proved valuable in unravelling some of the basic mechanisms of human mood and emotions, it is open to question as to whether the findings of this research are generalizable to real-life field settings outside the laboratory, and to the more intense emotions experienced in these settings. It may be that different mechanisms are operating under natural conditions, or that these mechanisms interact in different ways. For example, in traditional experimental mood research, it has often been stated that positive emotions can be detrimental to task motivation and cognitive performance (see Aspinwall, 1998). Layperson's everyday experiences, as well as more recent empirical evidence, however, indicate that positive emotions, typically, exert positive effects on performance in academic and work-related settings (see below). Laboratory research is confined by methodological and ethical constraints, implying that it may be useful for generating hypotheses, but that it cannot replace a more ecologically valid analysis of college students real-life emotions.

In the following sections, the available evidence on the effects of college students' achievement emotions on their academic learning and achievement is discussed. To date, this evidence mainly referes to the effects of test anxiety. However, a limited number of studies reported here have begun to address the effects of emotions other than anxiety as well. Based on the evidence from these studies, a generalized theoretical framework addressing the cognitive and motivational effects of students' achievement-related emotions is outlined.

EFFECTS OF TEST ANXIETY

The effects of test anxiety on, and correlations with, academic learning and performance have been analyzed in several hundreds of studies. Many of these studies dealt with test anxiety experienced in college classrooms. Four types of investigations are most prominent. In *group comparison studies*, the cognitive performance of low and high test anxious students was compared. In experimental *test anxiety induction studies*, anxiety and neutral mood were induced by announcing an experimental task as being ego threatening (e.g., by delivering social comparison information on performance) or non-threatening. In *cross-sectional field studies*, students' test anxiety was correlated with variables of their learning and academic achievement. Finally, in *longitudinal field studies*, the predictive or cross-lagged relations between test anxiety, on the one hand, and academic achievement, on the other, were analyzed. Whereas group comparison, anxiety induction, and cross-sectional studies have been conducted frequently, longitudinal studies on test anxiety are still scarce to date, and most of these studies pertained to students of K – 12 classrooms (Zeidner, 1998).

In experimental *group comparison* and *anxiety induction* studies, test anxiety was found to impair performance on complex or difficult tasks that demand cognitive resources (e.g., difficult intelligence test items). Performance on easy, less complex, and repetitive tasks need not suffer, or is even enhanced. Several accounts have been offered for this finding. In *interference* and *attentional deficit* models of test anxiety (e.g., Wine, 1971), it is assumed that anxiety produces task-irrelevant thinking that reduces on-task attention, and, therefore, interferes with performance on tasks requiring cognitive resources in terms of working memory capacity. The assumptions of these models are in line with postulates of the resource allocation model cited above (Ellis and Ashbrook, 1988). An extension of interference models is Eysenck's *processing efficiency* model assuming that anxiety can reduce the efficiency of cognitive processing due to the working memory load imposed by anxiety (Eysenck, 1997). Finally, an alternative hypothesis is put forward by *skills-deficit models* (Zeidner, 1998). Skills-deficit models hypothesize that test anxious students suffer from a lack of competence in the first place, implying an increased probability of failure complex or difficult tasks, as well as increased anxiety induced by appraisals of these deficits.

These different models can be regarded as being complementary rather than mutually exclusive. Empirically, test anxiety has been shown to be accompanied by task-irrelevant thinking distracting attention away from cognitive tasks, and the available evidence also shows that low-ability students are more prone to experience exam-related anxiety. Furthermore, it seems reasonable to assume that competence, anxiety, and performance are often linked by reciprocal causation over time: Lack of competence can induce anxiety of failure, anxiety can impair the quality of learning and performance, and poor-quality learning leads to a lack of competence.

In line with experimental findings on the detrimental effects of test anxiety on cognitively demanding tasks, *cross-sectional field studies* have shown that self-report measures of test anxiety correlate moderately negatively with college students' academic performance. The results of meta-analyses imply that, typically, 5 to 10% of the variance in students' achievement scores is explained by self-reported anxiety (Hembree, 1988; Zeidner, 1998). Correlations are higher for test anxiety than for students' general anxiety, as measures of general anxiety do not specifically pertain to the academic domain.

However, caution should be exerted in interpreting these correlations in causal ways, for at least two reasons. First, it might be that relations between test anxiety and achievement are primarily caused by effects of academic success and failure on the development of students' anxiety, rather than by effects of anxiety on students' academic performance. The *longitudinal evidence* available to date suggests that test anxiety and students' academic achievement are linked by reciprocal causation across schoolyears, but this evidence also seems to suggest that achievement effects on anxiety are stronger than effects of anxiety on achievement (Meece, Wigfield, and Eccles, 1990; Pekrun, 1992c; Schnabel, 1998). These longitudinal findings pertain to upper elementary, middle, and high school students, but the basic pattern of results is likely generalizable to college students as well.

Second, correlations with performance variables have not been uniformly negative across studies. Zero and positive correlations have sometimes been found, pointing to the complexity of anxiety-achievement relationships. Also, between-subject correlations are sample statistics that cannot be generalized to each and every individual student (Schmitz and Skinner, 1993). Detrimental and beneficial effects of anxiety on performance may be balanced differently in different individuals. In general, anxiety likely has deleterious effects in many students, but it may induce motivation to study harder, and thus facilitate overall performance, in those who are more resilient to the devastating aspects of anxiety (Pekrun and Hofmann, 1996).

Furthermore, for getting a more complete description of the effects of test anxiety on college students' academic agency, it would be necessary to take the motivational effects of anxiety into account as well, beyond its effects on cognitive performance. It is noteworthy that so many studies have analyzed the relations between test anxiety and performance, whereas only few studies are available that analyzed effects on students' motivation. The findings of these studies imply that test anxiety relates negatively to students' interest and intrinsic motivation (e.g., Pekrun et al., 2004). However, they also indicate that test anxiety can relate positively to students' extrinsic academic motivation. Specifically, test anxiety has been found to relate positively to students' motivation to invest effort in order to avoid failures (failure-avoidance motivation). Thus, the overall effects of test anxiety on academic motivation appear to be quite variable.

From an educator's perspective, however, any benefits of anxiety in resilient, highly motivated students are certainly outweighed by the negative effects of anxiety on performance, interest, and intrinsic motivation in the vast majority of students. Despite differences in relative maturity and competencies for self-regulation, the available evidence implies that this is no less true for college students than for K – 12 students (Hembree, 1988; Zeidner, 1998). Also, beyond effects on academic learning, test anxiety can have severe consequences for college students' long-term psychological well-being, social adaptation, and physical health (Zeidner, 1998), thus indicating an urgent need to ameliorate students' fear of failing in their academic careers.

EFFECTS OF STUDENTS' ANGER, SHAME, BOREDOM, AND HOPELESSNESS

Few studies have addressed college students' negative emotions other than anxiety, in spite of theoretical accounts that emotions like shame, hopelessness, or boredom can be no less deleterious than anxiety has been shown to be (e.g., Metalsky, Halberstadt, and Abramson, 1987). *Anger* and *shame* are two frequently experienced *activating* negative emotions implying physiological arousal, being similar to anxiety in this respect. *Boredom* and *hopelessness*, on the other hand, are two *deactivating* emotions that, typically, are characterized by reduced levels of physiological activation.

Anger is an emotion that can be induced by many kinds of academic situations blocking students' goal attainment or well-being. Anger relating to academic settings is experienced frequently by college students (Pekrun, 1992a), but has rarely been studied empirically. The few studies available seem to suggest that overall correlations between self-reported anger and academic performance are zero to moderately negative in K – 12 and college student populations (Boekaerts, 1993; Pekrun et al., 2004; Stratton, 1927; Titz, 2001). Students' anger has been shown to be positively correlated with task-irrelevant thinking (Pekrun et al., 2004) and lack of motivation ("a-motivation"; Assor, Kaplan, Kanat-Maymon, and Roth, 2005), and negatively with measures

570

of academic self-efficacy, primary academic control, interest, and self-regulation of learning (Pekrun, Goetz, Titz et al., 2002b; Pekrun, Goetz, Perry et al., 2004).

However, as with anxiety, the underlying pattern of functional mechanisms may be complex and imply more than just negative effects. For example, in a study with undergraduate students reported by Lane, Whyte, Terry, and Nevill (2005), depressed mood interacted with anger experienced before an academic exam such that anger was related to *improved* performance in students who did not feel depressed (see also Lane, Terry, Beedle, Curry, and Clark, 2001, for related evidence on facilitating vs. debilitating effects of anger in schoolchildren). Likely, anger is detrimental for motivation and performance under many conditions, but can translate into increased task motivation when expectancies for agency and success are favorable.

The emotion of *shame* is at the core of negative feelings of self-worth, often implying devastating, pervasive feelings of self-debasement (Covington and Beery, 1976; Covington and Omelich, 1981). As noted, achievement-related shame had been postulated to be central to achievement motivaton (specifically, to the fear of failure motive; Heckhausen, 1991). Similar to anxiety and anger, students' achievement-related shame as measured by the AEQ shame scales tends to show negative overall correlations with academic achievement (Pekrun et al., 2004; Titz, 2001), and with overall self-reported effort. However, as with anxiety and anger, shame seems to exert motivational effects that can be variable. In studies with undergraduate college students, Turner and Schallert (2001) showed that students experiencing shame following negative exam feedback increased their motivation when continuing to be committed to academic goals and holding positive expectancies to reach these goals (see also Thompson, Altmann, and Davidson, 2004).

Boredom and *hopelessness* can be assumed to differ from anxiety, anger, and shame by reducing both intrinsic and extrinsic motivation, and being detrimental for any kind of cognitive performance (with rare exceptions of indirect benefits produced by efficient coping with these emotions). In spite of the frequency of academic boredom experienced by students, this emotion has received scant attention, as has the less frequent, but devastating emotion of achievement-related hopelessness. Boredom at work was researched early as being induced by monotonous assembly-line work (e.g., Wyatt, 1930), and was discussed as being experienced by gifted K – 12 students in recent years, but has been neglected in research on college students.

In our own studies using the AEQ boredom scales, boredom correlated negatively with indicators of motivation (Pekrun et al., 2002b; Titz, 2001). Correlations with academic achievement, however, were more ambiguous. Likely, boredom has negative effects on achievement, but can itself be induced by either low or high achievement, implying reciprocal causation and curvilinear relations instead of unidirectional, linear effects. Hopelessness, on the other hand, showed uniformly negative correlations with measures of motivation, study behavior, and academic achievement (Pekrun et al., 2004; Titz, 2001).

EFFECTS OF POSITIVE EMOTIONS: WHERE IS THE "POSITIVE PSYCHOLOGY" OF COLLEGE STUDENTS' AFFECT?

In many traditional approaches to the functions of human emotions, it was assumed that positive emotions are maladaptive by inducing unrealistic appraisals, fostering superficial information processing, and reducing motivation to pursuit challenging goals (Aspinwall, 1998; Pekrun, Goetz, Titz, and Perry, 2002a). Much of the available experimental, laboratory-based evidence seems to support such a view. For example, experimental research has shown that positive mood can (a) lead to illusionary probability estimates for favorable outcomes and an underestimation of the probability of failure, due to mood-congruent retrieval of positive outcome-related probability information; (b) induce relaxation and undermine effortful action by signalling that everything is going well, making effort expenditure unnecessary; (c) induce motivation to maintain pleasant mood by avoiding negative thoughts and neglecting cautionary prevention of future adversities; and (d) reduce cognitive resources needed for task purposes.

As aptly summarized by Aspinwall (1998, p. 7), traditional experimental approaches to positive emotions thus imply that "our primary goal is to feel good, and feeling good makes us lazy thinkers who are oblivious to potentially useful negative information and unresponsive to meaningful variations in information and situation". However, educators' experiences as well as more recent experimental evidence contradict views that positive emotions are uniformly detrimental for motivation and cognitive performance. Specifically, as noted above, experimental research has shown that positive mood can enhance divergent thinking and flexible problem solving, thus facilitating many kinds of cognitive performance. Also, experimental evidence suggests that positive mood can enhance elaborate processing of information when the goal is to solve a problem (as is typical for academic situations), rather than just to maintain present positive mood (Aspinwall, 1998).

Empirical evidence on the effects of students' positive emotions as experienced at college and university is scarce, but supports the view that positive emotions can enhance academic learning and performance. Specifically, enjoyment of learning was consistently found to be positively correlated with K – 12 and college students' academic performance (Pekrun et al., 20002b). Furthermore, in research with the AEQ enjoyment, hope, and pride scales, we found that all three of these positive emotions correlated positively with study interest, effort at studying, elaboration of learning material, and self-regulation of learning, thus corroborating that these emotions can be beneficial for college students' academic agency (Pekrun et al., 2002a, b). However, as with the correlational evidence on negative emotions cited above, caution should be exerted in interpreting these relationships in causal ways – effects of academic success on students' positive emotions may be no less important in producing such correlations than any beneficial effects of positive emotions.

TOWARDS A GENERAL THEORETICAL FRAMEWORK OF THE COGNITIVE AND MOTIVATIONAL EFFECTS OF COLLEGE STUDENTS' EMOTIONS

How can we make sense of the available evidence and the multitude of – sometimes contradictory – theoretical approaches on the performance effects of mood and emotions? As outlined in more detail elsewhere (Pekrun, 1992b, 2006; Pekrun et al., 2002a, b), it would seem insufficient to simply distinguish positive vs. negative affect for doing so, or to assume uniformly positive or negative effects for specific emotions. Rather, more differentiated conceptions of emotions and their functional mechanisms are called for. In terms of categorizing emotions, it is helpful to adopt two traditional dimensions describing affect in order to classify college students' achievement-related emotions: *valence* and *activation*. These two dimensions can be viewed as being orthogonal, thus rendering a two-dimensional descriptive space (often conceptualized as a circumplex model of affective states; see Feldman Barrett and Russell, 1998). For the sake of conceptual simplicity, this space can conveniently be subdivided in four basic categories of achievement emotions (Table 3). (1) *activating positive* emotions like enjoyment of learning, hope for success, and pride experienced after mastery and performance; (2) *deactivating*

Table 3: A 2 × 2 (Valence × Activation) Taxonomy of Achievement Emotions

	Positive	Negative
Activating	Joy, Enjoyment	Anger
	Hope	Anxiety
	Pride	Shame, Guilt
Deactivating	Satisfaction	Sadness, Hopelessness
	Relief	Disappointment
	Relaxation	Boredom

positive emotions like relief and relaxation; (3) *activating negative* emotions such as anger, anxiety, shame, and guilt; and (4) *deactivating negative* emotions, prototypical examples being sadness, hopelessness, and boredom.

Concerning the functional mechanisms of emotions, primary mechanisms important for academic learning and achievement likely are (a) emotion-induced consumption or preservation of cognitive resources; (b) intrinsic and extrinsic motivation to learn and perform; (c) the use of cognitive learning strategies; and (d) self- vs. external regulation of learning, including the use of meta-cognitive, meta-emotional, and meta-motivational strategies. Emotions of the four categories described above can be assumed to affect these mechanisms, as well as resulting academic achievement, in the following ways.

(1) Cognitive resources. The experimental evidence cited above seems to imply that any emotion consumes cognitive resources by distracting attention away from the task at hand. However, in interpreting this evidence, the ecological validity of the experimental settings of mood research has to be considered. In these settings, mood induction procedures have been used that focus participants' attention on emotion-arousing stimuli (pictures, life events etc.), implying that less attention was available for a secondary, different task. This situation is similar to academic situations in which a student experiences emotions focused on objects or events that are separate from the learning task at hand, like anxious worries about an upcoming exam. However, if the emotion is focused on the learning task itself, the situation may be quite different. In this type of emotion arousal, attention would not be distracted, but directed towards on-task efforts. A prototypical example for such an emotion is enjoyment of learning activities. Enjoyment of ongoing action can induce flow experiences which imply focusing attention on the action, and to become immersed, subjectively, with

the activity to such an extent that even the monitoring of time and of the borders between self and environment diminish in subjective consciousness (Csikszentmihalyi and Csikszentmihalyi, 1988).

Based on these considerations, it can be assumed that emotions reduce the availability of cognitive resources available for task purposes, with the exception of positive emotions focusing attention on the task at hand.[3] These positive emotions can be called *task-intrinsic* emotions, since they relate to inherent properties of the task material or to the activity of dealing with the material (Pekrun et al., 2002b). In contrast, emotions focusing on aspects of the setting, other persons, the self, the future etc., can be regarded as *task-extrinsic* emotions distracting attention away from learning and task completion.

Motivation, interest and effort. Emotions serve adaptation by instigating, modulating or reducing emotion-specific motivational impulses underlying adaptive behavior. Academic emotions, and achievement emotions more generally, are no exception to this rule. Academic emotions can induce and modulate motivation and motivation-based effort by shaping students' goals and intentions. This process can be facilitated by mood-congruent recall of motivationally relevant information (e.g., positive self- and task-related information in a positive mood, threat-related information in an anxious mood, and aggression-related information in an angry mood; Levine and Burgess, 1997). From this perspective, positive activating emotions like enjoyment of learning can generally enhance academic motivation and effort, whereas negative deactivating emotions like hopelessness and boredom should be detrimental. Furthermore, enjoyment of learning can contribute positively to the development of students' interest in learning material (Krapp, 2005). Boredom and hopelessness, on the other hand, can be assumed to be deleterious for interest development since they are incompatible with enjoyment.

The motivational effects of deactivating positive emotions and activating negative emotions, however, are likely more complex. As argued by Pekrun et al. (2002a, b), relief and relaxation may reduce situational motivation, but they may also serve as reinforcers for the long-term investment of effort. Similarly, anger, anxiety, and shame

---

[3] Whereas enjoyment of learning should focus attention on the learning task, the situation may be more difficult for other positive emotions like hope or pride having both task-related and task-irrelevant reference objects. For example, social-comparison pride may focus attention on having defeated others, thus distracting attention. Mastery pride, on the other hand, may focus attention on task-related progress, thus preserving tast-focused attention. For different kinds of hope, similar arguments can be made.

can be assumed to exert ambivalent effects. The evidence cited above is clearly in line with this view. Specifically, whereas all three emotions can reduce intrinsic motivation and interest because they tend to be incompatible with enjoyment, they can produce strong extrinsic motivation to cope with the aversive events that caused them. For example, anger can produce motivation to overcome obstacles, and anxiety, as well as shame, can strengthen motivation to avoid failure. The overall effects on total motivation and effort may depend on the situation-dependent, often person-specific balance of these different mechanisms (Pekrun and Hofmann, 1996).

Cognitive learning strategies. The available experimental evidence on mood and problem solving cited above suggests that positive emotions enhance the use of creative, flexible ways of learning like elaboration and organization of learning material or critical thinking. Negative emotions, on the other hand, should sustain more rigid, detail-oriented learning, like in simple rehearsal of learning material. However, for deactivating positive and negative emotions, these effects may be less pronounced. Deactivating emotions like relaxation or boredom may produce shallow information processing rather than any more intensive use of learning strategies.

Meta-strategies and self-regulation of learning. Self-regulation of learning includes the use of meta-cognitive, meta-motivational, and meta-emotional strategies (Wolters, 2003) making it possible to adopt goals, monitor and regulate learning activities, and evaluate their results in flexible ways, such that learning activities can be adapted to the demands of academic tasks. An application of these strategies presupposes cognitive flexibility. Therefore, it can be assumed that positive emotions foster self-regulation and the implied use of meta-strategies. Negative emotions, on the other hand, can motivate the individual to rely on external guidance. The correlational evidence provided by Pekrun et al. (2002b) is in line with these assumptions (positive correlations for academic enjoyment and hope with college students' perceived self-regulation of learning, and for anxiety with external, instructor-provided regulation of learning). However, the reverse causal direction may also play a role in producing such correlations (instigation of enjoyment by self-regulated learning, and arousal of anxiety by external directions for learning).

Academic achievement. Since many different mechanisms can contribute to the functional effects of emotions, the overall effects of students' emotions on their academic achievement are inevitably complex, and may depend on the interplay between different mechanisms, as well as between these mechanisms and task demands. Nevertheless, it seems to be possible to derive assumptions on net effects from the above considerations.

Due to their positive effects on interest, motivation, use of flexible learning strategies, and self-regulation, *positive activating* emotions probably are beneficial to college students' overall academic agency in their scholastic development. Specifically, this may be true for task-intrinsic emotions like enjoyment of learning that focus attention on academic tasks, thereby inducing states of flow. In contrast, the attention-distracting and motivation-reducing effects of *negative deactivating* emotions like boredom and hopelessness likely imply that these emotions are simply detrimental. The correlational evidence cited above is in line with these assumptions.

For *positive deactivating* and *negative activating* emotions, effects may be diverse and may, in part, depend on task demands and individual propensities. For emotions of these two groups, it is assumed that they distract attention, reduce momentary interest and intrinsic motivation, and do not foster flexible, self-regulated learning. On the other hand, there may also be positive motivational effects (long-term beneficial effects in positive deactivating emotions, effects on extrinsic motivation in negative activating emotions). Also, negative activating emotions may facilitate the use of rigid learning strategies and a reliance on external regulation, which may be beneficial for achievement under conditions of teacher-centered instruction and exams that focus on rote memory performance. For positive deactivating emotions, there is no substantial evidence to validate assumptions and draw any firm conclusions. For the negative activating emotions of anger, anxiety, and shame, however, the evidence outlined above clearly indicates that, on an average, the deleterious effects on academic achievement outweigh any potential benefits.

In sum, theoretical assumptions, the evidence produced by experimental studies, and the findings of field studies imply that emotions can have profound effects on college students' academic learning and achievement, suggesting that administrators and instructors should pay attention to students' emotions. Most likely, the effects of students' enjoyment of learning are clearly beneficial, and the impact of their hopelessness and boredom detrimental. The effects of emotions like anger, anxiety, or shame are more complex, but in the average college student, negative overall effects will be typical for these emotions as well.

INDIVIDUAL AND SOCIAL DETERMINANTS
OF STUDENTS' EMOTIONS

Given the relevance of emotions for student learning and achievement, their determinants should be analyzed as well, such that evidence-based recommendations on fostering these emotions can be derived. Generally, emotions can be caused or modulated by numerous individual factors including cognitive appraisals, situational perceptions, biologically prepared emotion schemata, neurohormonal processes, and sensory feedback from facial, gestural and postural expression (Lewis and Haviland-Jones, 2000). Among all of these factors, however, cognitive appraisals probably play a major role in the emotions experienced by college students in academic settings. In contrast to emotions aroused in phylogenetically older and more constrained situations (e.g., physiological need fulfillment, or interactions between caregiver and child), emotions in academic situations pertain to culturally defined demands in settings that are a recent product of civilization. In settings of this kind, the individual has to learn how to adapt to situational demands while preserving individual autonomy, which inevitably is a process guided by appraisals.

This may be especially true in college and university settings, since the transition from high school to college often implies that one has to break with habits developed during childhood and adolescence. Typically, this transition implies challenges to adapt to new academic demands, to leave one's home, move to a new city and live on one's own, and to create new friendships and social networks. All of these changes make it necessary to appraise new situations and to re-appraise one's personal strengths and weaknesses, and these appraisals certainly play a major role in the emotions college students experience.

In line with such considerations, most theories on the determinants of students' emotions focus on the emotional relevance of self- and task-related appraisals, and on the importance of situational factors shaping students' emotions by mediating their appraisals. In this section, I discuss theoretical approaches and empirical evidence pertaining to the individual determinants of students' emotions, and to their instructional and social determinants. Based on this discussion, I outline basic assumptions of a recent control-value theory of achievement emotions that makes an attempt to integrate hypotheses from expectancy-value and attributional approaches to achievement emotions, including the emotions experienced by students at college and university (Pekrun, 2000, 2006; Pekrun et al., 2002b).

INDIVIDUAL DETERMINANTS

Research on the individual determinants of students' emotions has focused on the antecedents of test anxiety, on the causal attributional antecedents of emotions following success and failure, and on the role of achievement goals for students' positive vs. negative affect. Beyond these three specific research agendas, studies are rare, with few exceptions pertaining to the antecedents of activity-related academic emotions like enjoyment of learning and boredom.

Test anxiety. Test anxiety is a prospective emotion relating to threat of failure in an upcoming or ongoing exam. Therefore, threat-related appraisals have been regarded as main proximal determinants by many authors. Specifically, the *transactional stress model* provided by R. S. Lazarus has often been used as a frame of reference to explain test anxiety (Lazarus and Folkman, 1984, 1987). In the different variants of this model, *stress* is defined as any situation implying demands that tax or exceed the individual's resources. In a *primary appraisal* of the situation, an evaluation in terms of potential threat, challenge, harm, or benefit implied by the situation is made. This appraisal pertains to the evaluation of the situation or its outcomes as being subjectively relevant to the individuals' needs and goals. In a *secondary appraisal*, possibilities to cope with the situation are explored cognitively. Depending on the combined result of the two appraisals, different emotions can be aroused. In the case of threat and insufficient perceived control over the threatening event, anxiety is assumed to be instigated.

Lazarus' analysis implies that achievement-related anxiety is aroused when two conditions are met. First, there has to be an anticipation of failure that can happen and is sufficiently important to the individual to imply subjective threat. Second, the individual has to doubt whether it will be possible to control the situation such that failure is avoided. In an *expectancy-value model* of test anxiety, and of anxiety more generally, I have made an attempt to reconceptualize these two assumptions in more precise, mathematically formulated ways (Pekrun, 1984, 1992c). In this model, it is assumed that test anxiety is a function of (a) the expectancy of failure (specifically, the subjective probability of failure), and (b) the subjective value of failure. Both components are assumed to be necessary for test anxiety to be instigated (if one is sure that failure can't happen, there is no need to be afraid of an exam; the same applies if one doesn't care). The expectancy of failure is postulated to depend on situation-outcome expectancies (Bolles, 1972; Heckhausen, 1991) that failure will result from the situation if no counteraction is undertaken, and on action-related expectancies that suitable actions, such as sustained effort in preparing for an exam, can be performed and will prevent failure. Anxiety is assumed to be a curvilinear function of expectancy, being replaced by hopelessness if failure is subjectively certain. The subjective value of failure is seen to be a function of both the intrinsic importance of achievement per se, and of its extrinsic, instrumental relevance in terms of producing further outcomes. For example, failing an exam may be threatening for a student because failure is inherently negative for him or her, because positive outcomes like the students' career prospects are compromised, and because negative consequences like contempt by peers can result (for the formalized versions of these assumptions, see Pekrun, 1984; and for a conceptual discussion, Pekrun, 1992c).

Typically, situational appraisals of these kinds are based on objective characteristics of the setting (e.g., the relative difficulty of exam material), but they are also influenced by individual expectancy-related and value-related beliefs. These beliefs can take "irrational" forms (Ellis, 1962) implying that failures are appraised has being probable in spite of high individual ability, or as undermining self-worth and peer recognition even if pertaining to unimportant fields of achievement. Irrational beliefs can make students highly vulnerable to experience anxiety and related negative achievement emotions, like shame and hopelessness ("I am not allowed to fail – if I fail, I am a worthless person").

The available empirical evidence is in line with these assumptions. Specifically, test anxiety has been found to correlate positively with students' expectancies of failure, and negatively with their self-concepts of ability, academic self-efficacy expectations, and academic control beliefs (Hembree, 1988; Pekrun et al., 2004; Zeidner, 1998). Also, in research on linkages between achievement goals and test anxiety, it has consistently been found that students' performance avoidance goals (implying high subjective relevance of failure) relate positively to their test anxiety scores (see Linnenbrink and Pintrich, 2002).

Attributional determinants of achievement emotions. Extending the perspective beyond the single emotion of test anxiety, B. Weiner (1985) proposed an attributional approach to the appraisal antecedents of achievement emotions following success and failure. In Weiner's theory, causal attributions of success and failure in achievement settings are held to be the primary determinants of many of these emotions. More specifically, it is assumed that achievevement outcomes are first evaluated subjectively as success or failure. This outcome

580

appraisal immediately leads to "primitive", cognitively less elaborated, attribution-independent emotions, namely, happiness following success, and frustration and sadness following failure (Weiner, 1985, p. 560). Following outcome appraisal and the immediate emotional reaction, causal ascriptions are sought that lead to cognitively more differentiated, attribution-dependent emotions.

Three dimensions of causal attributions are assumed to play a key role in determining attribution-dependent emotions: (a) the perceived *locus* of causes (differentiating internal vs. external causes of achievement, such as ability and effort vs. environmental circumstances or chance); (b) the perceived *controllability* of causes (differentiating, for example, subjectively controllable effort from uncontrollable ability); and (c) the perceived *stability* of causes (differentiating, for example, stable ability from unstable chance). *Pride* is assumed to be linked to the locus dimension, being aroused by attributions of achievement to internal causes. *Shame, guilt, gratitude,* and *anger* are deemed to be depend on both the locus and the controllability of causes. Weiner assumes that shame and guilt are instigated by failure that is attributed to internal, controllable causes (like lack of effort), and gratitude and anger by attributions of success to external causes that are under control by others (gratitude), or of failure to such causes (anger).

Weiner's attributional theory thus focusses primarily on retrospective emotions following success and failure that occur to the student, in line with the retrospective nature of causal attributions seeking to explain the causes of experienced success and failure. However, some predictions for prospective, future-related emotions are made as well. Specifically, hopefulness and hopelessness are assumed to be linked to attributions of success and failure, respectively, to stable causes (like stable ability, or lack of ability). Furthermore, Weiner (in press) recently extended his theory by also speculating about the causal attributional antecedents of "moral" emotions like envy, scorn, sympathy, admiration, regret, and "Schadenfreude".

Much of the evidence on the validity of these assumptions was gained by scenario studies asking students how they, or others, might react to success and failure. In such studies, participants' subjective theories about links between achievement outcomes, attributions, and emotions following achievement are tested. Findings support the congruence between attributional theory and students' subjective theories. However, there also are experimental and field studies with samples of college students corroborating the validity of many of Weiner's assumptions (Heckhausen, 1991).

In addition, other approaches to the affective relevance of causal attributions have also found evidence that attributions can play a role in students' emotional reactions. Specifically, studies on the *reformulated helplessness and hopelessness theories* of depression have found that college students' emotions can be explained, in part, by their attributional styles. In this research tradition, the perceived *globality* of causes (i.e., their degree of generalization across situations) is held to be an additional important dimension of causal attributions (e.g., Metalsky et al., 1987).

Achievement goals as determinants of positive vs. negative affect. A few studies have analyzed relations between students' achievement goals and their positive vs. negative affect experienced at college and university (see Linnenbrink and Pintrich, 2002; Pekrun et al., 2006). Most of these studies used the dichotomous model of achievement goals differentiating between mastery goals (pertaining to competence as judged by mastery and intraindividual standards) and performance goals (pertaining to competence as defined by social comparison norms). The findings of studies using dichotomous conceptions of goals, as well as dichotomous conceptions of positive vs. negative affect, are inconsistent, with the exception of a positive relations between mastery goals and positive affect.

As argued by Pekrun et al. (2006), this lack of consistency may have been due to insufficient differentiation between different types of goals, and between different emotions. Specifically, as to goals, approach goals and avoidance goals may have quite different effects on students' emotions. In the two studies reported by these authors, U.S. and German undergraduate college students' achievement goals were assessed early in the semester, and their course-related achievement emotions later in the semester. Mastery approach goals were positive predictors of course-related enjoyment of learning, hope, and pride, and negative predictors of boredom and anger. Performance-approach goals were positive predictors of pride, whereas performance-avoidance goals were positive predictors of anxiety, hopelessness, and shame. These findings corroborate that value-related cognitions like students' self-set goals can be important for their emotions.

Determinants of activity-related emotions (enjoyment and boredom). Activity-related emotions have been neglected by cognitive approaches to students' emotions. The limited evidence on these emotions seems to imply that positive self-evaluations of competence, as well as task-

582

related goals and interest in academic tasks, are positively related to enjoyment of learning (Pekrun et al., 2002a). However, causal relations were not clear in these studies, and they pertained primarily to K – 12 students. Similarly, evidence on college students' boredom is largely lacking. Studies by Vodanovich, Weddle, and Piotrowski (1997) and Watt and Vodanovich (1999) imply that boredom is related to students' external work values and reduced educational involvement.

In sum, theories on achievement emotions, as well as related empirical evidence, imply that failure expectancies and perceived lack of competence are primary determinants of college students' test anxiety, and that causal attributions of achievement are important antecedents of emotions following success and failure. Also, there is evidence that students' achievement goals can be important determinants of their emotions. Beyond these three specific bodies of research, however, the evidence on individual determinants of college students' emotions is to scarce to allow generalizable conclusions.

CLASSROOM INSTRUCTION AND SOCIAL ENVIRONMENTS

Within programs of empirical research on psychological phenomena, research questions are often addressed sequentially. As a first step, the relevance of the phenomenon has to be shown such that the scientific community can be convinced that related research should be acknowledged and funded. Typically, the next step involves a refinement of concepts and assessment, and an analysis of internal structures and individual determinants of the phenomenon. Contextual antecedents, however, are often adressed last in psychologically oriented research. It seems that research on students' emotions is no exception to this rule. The classroom and social antecedents of college students' emotions have been neglected even more than other aspects of their affective life. Again, research on students' test anxiety is an exception. A number of consistent findings on the relevance of task demands and students' social environments for students' anxiety emerged from this research. The following summary is based on the excellent overview given by Zeidner (1998), who also provides a detailed list of references to relevant studies.

Instruction and learning environments. Lack of structure and clarity have been found to relate positively to students' test anxiety. Also, excessively high task demands can contribute to achievement-related anxiety. The effects of these factors are likely mediated by students' expectancies of failure (Pekrun, 1992c).

Format of exams. With exams as well, lack of structure and transparency has been shown to contribute to students' anxiety. Findings imply that important factors are clarity concerning the demands, materials and procedures of exams, and concerning the standards used for grading. Furthermore, the format of items has also been found to be relevant, with open-ended formats inducing more anxiety than multiple-choice formats. Open-ended formats require more working memory capacity which may be less available in states of anxiety due to the consumption of cognitive resources by worrying and task-irrelevant thinking, thus inducing more threat and debilitating performance in anxious students. The use of multiple-choice formats can reduce these effects. The availability of external aids (books, computers etc.) for solving items has also been shown to be a factor that can reduce working memory load and the threat of failure. Finally, giving students the choice between items, relaxing time constraints, and giving them second chances in terms of retaking tests, has been found to reduce test anxiety, presumably so because perceived control is enhanced, thereby alleviating expectancies of failure under these conditions.

Expectancies, feedback, consequences of achievement, and competition in the classroom. High achievement expectancies from significant others, negative feedback after achievement, and negative consequences of failure have been shown to correlate positively with students' test anxiety. Also, between-individuals competition in classrooms is positively related to students' test anxiety, probably because competition reduces expectancies for success, and increases the importance of avoiding failure. In contrast, in K – 12 research, social support by parents and teachers, and a cooperative classroom climate, have been found to be uncorrelated with students' test anxiety scores (Hembree, 1988). This surprising lack of correlation may be due to coercive components of teachers' and parents' efforts to support students which can counteract beneficial effects of support per se. An second explanation would be negative feedback loops between support and anxiety implying that social support alleviates anxiety (negative effect of support on anxiety), but that anxiety provokes support in the first place (positive effect of anxiety on support), thus yielding an overall zero correlation.

THE CONTROL-VALUE THEORY OF ACHIEVEMENT EMOTIONS: AN INTEGRATIVE APPROACH TO THE INDIVIDUAL AND SOCIAL DETERMINANTS OF COLLEGE STUDENTS' EMOTIONS

The assumptions of different approaches to the determinants and effects of students' emotions seem to be largely complementary, rather than being contradictory or mutually exclusive. It should thus be possible to create more integrative frameworks helping to interpret extant empirical findings, and to derive practical recommendations. I have attempted to do so by proposing a control-value theory of achievement emotions that aims to integrate assumptions from expectancy-value (Pekrun, 1992c; Turner and Schallert, 2001) and attributional (Weiner, 1985) approaches to emotions (Pekrun, 2000, 2006; Pekrun et al., 2002b), The theory pertains to both the individual and the social determinants of students' emotions. In its most recent version, the theory also addresses the effects of achievement goals on students' emotions (Pekrun et al., 2006).

Control and value determinants of achievement emotions. Students' control-related and value-related appraisals are assumed to be the most important proximal determinants of their achievement emotions. *Control appraisals* pertain to the perceived controllability of achievement-related actions and outcomes. The controllability of causes of achievement as addressed by B. Weiner's theory is assumed to be relevant by contributing to perceived control over actions and outcomes, as are the locus and the stability of causes. Appraisals of control, or of factors contributing to control, are seen as being implied by causal expectations (self-efficacy expectations and outcome expectancies), causal attributions of achievement, and students' competence appraisals (e.g., academic self-concepts of ability). *Value appraisals* relate to the subjective importance of achievement activities and their outcomes. Value appraisals are part of students' subject matter interest, and of their achievement goals implying the desire to attain success or to avoid failure.

Different kinds of control and value appraisals are assumed to instigate different kinds of emotions. For *outcome emotions*, expectancies and attributions are held to be important. More specifically, causal expectancies implying perceptions of control are assumed to influence prospective outcome emotions like hope, anticipatory enjoyment, anxiety, and hopelessness, and causal attributions retrospective outcome emotions like pride and shame.

Prospective, outcome-related *enjoyment* and *hopelessness* are seen to be triggered when there is high perceived control (enjoyment), or a complete lack of perceived control (hopelessness). *Hope* and *anxiety* are assumed to be instigated when there is some medium amount of perceived control, the attentional focus being on the positive valences of anticipated success in the case of hope, and on the negative valences of anticipated failure in the case of anxiety.

As to retrospective outcome emotions induced by the experience of success or failure, *joy* and *sadness* about achievement outcomes are seen as immediately following perceived success and failure, without any more elaborate cognitive mediation (in line with B. Weiner's assumptions cited above). In contrast, *disappointment* and *relief* are assumed to depend on appraisals of the match between previous expectations and the actual outcome, disappointment being induced when anticipated success did not occur, and relief when anticipated failure did not occur. Emotions like pride, shame, gratitude, and anger, are seen to be induced by attributions of success and failure as being caused by oneself or other persons, respectively. In contrast to B. Weiner's assumptions on shame, gratitude, and anger, the perceived controllability of success and failure *themselves* is assumed to be of critical importance for these emotions, rather than the controllability of the *causes* of success and failure (Pekrun, 2006).

Finally, achievement-related *activity emotions* are also assumed to depend on appraisals of control and values. Activity emotions have been neglected by previous theories of achievement emotions, in spite of their importance for students' learning and academic agency. *Enjoyment* of achievement activities (e.g., enjoyment of learning) is seen to depend on a combination of positive competence appraisals, and positive appraisals of the intrinsic qualities of the action (e.g., studying) and its objects (e.g., learning material). *Anger* and *frustration* are assumed to be instigated when the incentive values of the activity are negative (e.g., when studying difficult problems takes too much effort experienced as being aversive). *Boredom* is assumed to be experienced when the activity lacks any incentive values.

Implications I. Subconscious appraisals and habitualized achievement emotions. The control-value theory does not imply that students' achievement emotions are always mediated by concious appraisals. Rather, it is assumed that recurring appraisal-based induction of emotions can habitualize over time. When academic experiences are repeated over and over again, appraisals and the induction of emotions can become routinized to the extent that there is no longer any conscious mediation of emotions, or no longer any cognitive mediation at all (Pekrun, 1988; Reisenzein, 2001).

Implications II. Goals and achievement emotions. In a recent extension of the theory presented by Pekrun et al. (2006), it is assumed that students' achievement goals influence their emotions by mediating their control- and value-related appraisals. Specifically, we assume that mastery approach goals focus attention on controllability and positive values of achievement activities, thus fostering positive activity emotions like enjoyment of learning, and reducing negative activity emotions such as boredom. In contrast, performance-approach goals should focus attention on positive outcome-related appraisals, and performance-avoidance goals on negative outcome-related appraisal, thus facilitating positive or negative outcome emotions. As noted above, these predictions on the effects of goals on emotions were largely supported in the studies reported by Pekrun et al. (2006), although the presumed mediational role of appraisals still awaits an empirical test.

Implications III. Instructional and social antecedents of achievement emotions. The theory implies that environmental factors shaping students' academic perceived control and academic values are influencing their emotions as well. It is assumed that the following factors may be especially important.

(1) Cognitive quality of learning environments and tasks. The cognitive quality of classroom instruction and assignments should have positive effects on college students' perceived competence and control, and of their valuing of instruction and academic contents, thus positively influencing their emotions. The relative difficulty of instruction and task demands should be important as well. Difficulty can be assumed to influence control, and the match between task demands and students' competences can influence the subjective value of tasks. If demands are too high or too low, the incentive value of tasks may be reduced to the extent that boredom is experienced.

(2) Motivational quality of learning environments and tasks. Professors and peers deliver direct messages conveying academic values, as well as more indirect messages implied by their behavior. Two ways of inducing emotionally relevant values in indirect ways may be most important. First, if instruction, learning environments and assignments are shaped such that they meet the needs of students, positive

activity-related emotions should be fostered. For example, learning environments that support cooperative student learning should help students to fulfill needs for social relatedness, thus making learning in such environments subjectively more valuable (Krapp, 2005). Second, professor's own enthusiasm in dealing with academic material can facilitate students' adoption of academic values. Observational learning and emotional contagion may be primary mechanisms mediating the effects of teachers' enthusiasm on students' values (Hatfield, Cacioppo, and Rapson, 1994).

(3) Support of autonomy and self-regulated learning. Learning environments supporting students' self-regulated learning can be assumed to increase their sense of control. In addition, meeting needs for autonomy, such environments can increase academic values. However, these beneficial effects probably depend on the match between students' competence and individual need for academic autonomy, on the one hand, and the affordance of these environments, on the other. In case of a mismatch, loss of control and negative emotions may result.

(4) Achievement goal structures and achievement expectations. Academic achievement can be defined by standards of individual mastery pertaining to absolute criteria or intraindividual competence gain, by normative standards based on competitive social comparison between students, or by standards pertaining to cooperative group performance instead of individual performance. These different standards imply individualistic (mastery), competitive (normative), or cooperative goal structures in the classroom. Goal structures can be assumed to influence students' emotions in two ways. First, to the extent that these structures are adopted by students, they influence their achievement goals and any emotions mediated by their goals as outlined above. Second, goal structures and grading practices determine students' relative opportunities for experiencing success and perceiving control, thus influencing expectancy-dependent emotions. Specifically, competitive goal structures imply, by definition, that some students experience success, whereas others have to experience failure (negative linkage between the success of different individuals; Johnson and Johnson, 1974). It can be assumed that students' average achievement expectancies are lower under these conditions, such that average values of negative prospective outcome emotions like anxiety and hopelessness are increased. Similarly, the demands implied by

excessively high achievement expectancies of significant others can be assumed to lead to lowered expectancies on the side of the student, and to all of the negative emotions resulting from reduced subjective control.

(5) *Feedback and consequences of achievement.* Cumulative success is assumed to strengthen students' perceived control, and cumulative failure is assumed to undermine subjective control. In systems involving frequent testing, test feedback is likely one primary mechanism determining students' outcome-related achievement emotions. In addition, the perceived consequences of success and failure are important as well, since consequences affect the extrinsic, instrumental values of achievement outcomes. Positive outcome emotions like hope for success can be increased if a student appraises academic success to produce beneficial long-term outcomes (e.g., in terms of future occupational chances), and perceives sufficient contingencies between own efforts, success, and these outcomes. Negative outcomes of academic failure, on the other hand, may increase students' achievement-related anxiety and hopelessness.

Implications IV. Reciprocal causation of antecedents, emotions, and effects. The assumptions of the control-value theory imply that environmental antecedents, individual antecedents, students' achievement emotions, and their academic learning and performance are linked by reciprocal causation (Figure 1).F1 As outlined above, classroom instruction is assumed to affect individual goals and appraisals mediating students' achievement emotions. These emotions, in turn, are assumed to influence learning and achievement, as described in the above section on functions of emotions. Students' emotions and their emotion-dependent achievement, however, can feed back on individual and environmental determinants. Specifically, emotions can influence goal adoption, control appraisals, and value appraisals, by way of emotion-dependent cognitive processes like mood-congruent recall of task information. Furthermore, students' emotion-dependent academic behaviors and achievement can influence classroom instruction and the wider social context including parents, peers, and partners. For example, lack of effort, disruptive student behavior, and poor achievement caused by students' boredom can affect professors' engagement negatively, whereas engaged students can fuel the enthusiasm experienced by professors.

589

Figure 1: Basic assumptions of the control-value theory of achievement emotions.

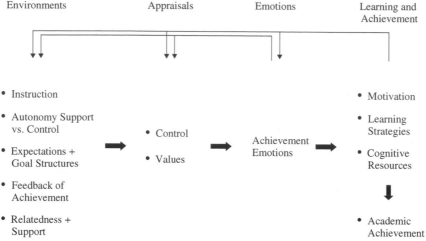

Determinants, emotions, and effects can thus be linked by feedback loops over time. These feedback loops can take different forms. Considering professors' enthusiasm, once again, enthusiasm and students' enjoyment of instruction can be linked by *positive feedback loops*. Over the semester, instructors' enthusiasm enhances students' enjoyment, enjoyment has positive effects on subsequent achievement on course tests, and students' achievement in turn impacts positively on instructors' enthusiasm. Similarly, positive feedback loops would be implied if achievement pressure in the classroom increases students' anxiety, anxiety leads to academic failure, and failure motivates professors to increase the pressure on their students. Beneficial and vicious circles of these kinds may be most typical for students' achievement emotions. However, more complex mechanisms may play role as well, also including *negative feedback loops*. For example, if a mismatch between task demands and competence increases a students' anger, but anger fuels the students' effort to raise his or her competences such that the mismatch gets reduced, relative demands, the emotion of anger, and achievement may be linked by a negative feedback loop over time.

Reciprocal effects of emotions, their determinants, and their effects have barely been addressed by educational research to date. However, any more complete account of classroom reality would have to take these more complex dynamics of students' emotions into account (also see Turner and Waugh, in press).

EMOTION REGULATION, COPING, AND THERAPY

As argued to this point, positive emotions like pride or joyful relaxation after success can be pleasant and facilitative, but they can also be situationally detrimental for further effortful processing of information. Similarly, negative emotions like anger, anxiety, or shame can be helpful for tackling tasks by focusing attention and enhancing motivation to invest effort, but they can also be quite deleterious for learning and general well-being. Thus, while pleasant emotions are beneficial and unpleasant emotions detrimental under many conditions, any emotion can become an obstacle for goal attainment. If emotions impede higher-order goals, attempts to regulate them can be undertaken. Regulation of negative emotions, and of stress situations which are taxing or exceeding individual capabilities, is called *coping* in the emotions literature (Zeidner and Endler, 1996). Emotion regulation and coping can be used by the individual student, but in case of more severe emotional problems, regulation by professional therapists can be sought after (*therapy* of academic emotions). Finally, college instructors and administrators can also make an attempt to influence students' emotional situation in beneficial ways. In this section, evidence on coping, emotion regulation and therapy is discussed. Implications for educational classroom practices are addressed in the next section.

EMOTION REGULATION AND COPING WITH TEST ANXIETY

Emotion regulation serves higher-order goals like physical or psychological well-being, academic achievement, and the maintenance of social relations. Typically, but not always, emotion regulation implies strengthening or maintaining positive emotions, and preventing or decreasing negative emotions. Basic components of regulation are *recognition and understanding* of one's own emotions, *managing* one's own emotions by inducing, increasing, decreasing, or preventing them, and *using* these emotions for action and goal attainment (e.g., for studying). Beyond regulatory competencies pertaining to one's own emotions, emotional competencies more generally also comprise abilities to recognize, understand, manage, and use the emotions of others. Cognitive competencies to regulate one's own and others' emotions have become popular under the label of *emotional intelligence* (Matthews, Zeidner, and Roberts, 2002).

To date, little is known about students' regulation of their emotions at college and university. The only major exception is

591

students' coping with their test anxiety, and with the exam stress causing test anxiety. Coping with anxiety has been addressed by Lazarus' transactional stress model cited above (Lazarus and Folkman, 1984, 1987). In this model, appraisals of threat as implied by situations taxing or exceeding one's own capabilities are assumed to induce test anxiety, and anxiety is thought to lead to attempts to regulate this emotion or the stress that caused it. After Lazarus had proposed his model, many taxonomies of coping with negative emotions, and with test anxiety more specifically, have been proposed. Basic to most of these conceptions is a differentiation of problem-oriented, emotion-oriented, and avoidant coping (Rost and Schermer, 1987; Zeidner and Endler, 1996).

Problem-oriented coping implies active attempts to change the situation that causes subjective stress and negative emotions. In exam-related situations, problem-oriented coping would imply to employ cognitive, metacognitive, and resource-oriented strategies of learning and problem solving, both in the preparatory phase and during the exam itself. Problem-oriented coping with exams can have side effects of increasing situational anxiety, since dealing with the exam material can arouse thoughts focusing on the upcoming exam (Bolger, 1990). On the long run, however, the beneficial effects of preparing and raising one's competencies likely outweigh these negative situational effects in most students. Improved preparation can prevent exam failure and lead to better grades, thus serving academic goals, but also alleviating anxiety pertaining to future exams.

Emotion-oriented coping aims at directly changing unpleasant emotions, including any attempts to actively modify the symptoms or antecedents of these emotions. Typical strategies are (a) anxiety reduction by consumption of alcohol, nicotine, or medical drugs, or by using relaxation techniques; (b) reduction of emotional tension by simply accepting anxiety and the possibility of failure ("secondary control"; Morling and Evered, 2006; Rothbaum et al., 1982); (c) induction of positive emotions that are incompatible with anxiety (e.g., by using humor, music, or emotional support from others); and (d) a cognitive reinterpretation of the situation as more controllable or less important. Many of these strategies are in fact effective in reducing negative emotions. Some of them, however, clearly have negative side effects in terms of reduced achievement or health.

Avoidance-oriented coping implies escaping the situation behaviorally or mentally. Examples of strategies to avoid being confronted with test situations include (a) a search for mental distraction by focusing attention on task-irrelevant contents and reducing on-task effort; (b) procrastination, prolongued phases of recess, and precocious termination of preparing; and (c) absentism in classes and on exams, and dropping out of study programs and college. Like emotion-oriented coping, these strategies can lead to a reduction of situational anxiety. However, the side effects can be severe. First, avoidance of consciously experienced anxiety can lead to an increase of less conscious emotional arousal on a physiological level that can be detrimental (see Spanger, Pekrun, Kramer and Hofmann, 2002). Also, while immediately decreasing situational anxiety, neglecting to prepare for an exam can increase anxiety experienced later upon noticing the lack of preparation. Second, all of these strategies can clearly be detrimental for students' learning, achievement, and future career prospects.

Most of the coping literature used these or related concepts to describe coping strategies. All too often ignored, however, was that specific strategies can be classified into more than one of three categories cited. Classifying strategies may depend on the observer's perspective. For example, as seen from the perspective of stress reduction, relaxation techniques would imply emotion-oriented coping. However, to the extent that reduction of emotional tension helps academic agency, relaxation can also be regarded as problem-oriented coping. Contemporary measurement instruments of coping using traditional classifications thus run the danger of assessing behavioral surface structures of students' attempts to cope with stress, while missing deeper structures of functional equivalence.

A second problem in much of the existing literature is the simplistic assumption that problem-oriented coping should be adaptive, and emotion-oriented as well as avoidance-oriented coping maladaptive since they don't change the stress-inducing situation. First, different criteria can be used to judge adaptation (is it more important to increase achievement, or to live a life free of excessive anxiety?). Second, the employment of any strategy can have side effects that themselves can be either adaptive or maladaptive, and need not be congruent to the main effects the strategy produces. For example, while persistent, time-consuming academic studying can raise academic achievement and reduce exam stress, it can also cause a break-up of friendships, implying that problem-oriented coping need not always be adaptive. Conversely, caution should also be exerted in regarding emotion-oriented or avoidance strategies as maladaptive by default. In the waiting phase after an exam, for example, it can be quite functional to simply reduce any thoughts about the exam or the upcoming announcement of exam results. Any attempts at problem-oriented coping would be futile in this situation, since exam results can't be changed after the fact. Also, an emotion-driven dropping out of a program of studies that does not match individual needs and capabilities can be a blessing for a student's future development.

Therapy of Test Anxiety

Individual test anxiety can be successfully treated today. Some types of test anxiety treatment are among the most successful psychological therapies available, effect sizes being above $d = 1$ (Hembree, 1988). Similar to the various kinds of individual coping strategies, different ways of treating test anxiety focus on different manifestations and antecedents of this emotion, including affective-physiological symptoms (emotion-oriented therapy), cognitive appraisals (cognitive therapy), and competence deficits caused by lack of strategies for learning and problem-solving (skills training). In this section, basic features of the three types of therapy are briefly outlined. A more detailed review of test anxiety treatment, however, is beyond the scope of this chapter (see the summary in Zeidner, 1998).

Emotion-oriented ways of treating students' anxiety include anxiety induction (e.g., flooding), biofeedback procedures, relaxation techniques (e.g., progressive muscle relaxation; Jacobson, 1938), and systematic desensitization. *Cognitive therapies* aim to modify anxiety-inducing control beliefs, value beliefs, and styles of self-related thinking. Examples are cognitive-attentional training, cognitive restructuring therapy, and stress-inoculation training. *Study-skills training* teaches students to understand and use task-oriented strategies of learning and problem-solving enabling them to be academically successful, thus alleviating their anxiety. Finally, *multimodal therapies* integrate different procedures, thus making it possible to address different symptoms and antecedents of students' anxiety within one treatment.

Cognitive and multimodal therapy proved to be especially effective, concerning both the reduction of test anxiety, and the improvement of academic performance. With learners having deficits of learning strategies, study-skills training also turned out to be successful. Therapies focusing exclusively on emotion-oriented procedures, however, are successful in terms of reducing anxiety, but are less effective as to students' academic improvement. These kinds of therapy typically address the affective and physiological components of anxiety, but do not directly modify the cognitive components of anxiety that are primarily responsible for the performance-debilitating effects of students' anxiety.

IMPLICATIONS FOR HIGHER EDUCATION PRACTICE AND RESEARCH

This chapter set out to provide a summary review of research on student emotions in higher education. As is described throughout the sections of this review, there is cumulative evidence on the nature, assessment, effects, development, and treatment of just one major emotion experienced by students at college and university, namely, their test anxiety. By implication, concerning test anxiety, a number of practical recommendations for educational practices in higher education institutions can be derived. As for emotions other than anxiety, research is just beginning to accumulate knowledge that might help to develop a more complete account of students' emotions, and to construct more comprehensive guidelines for fostering these emotions in college classroom settings. By necessity, the research reviewed in this chapter implies that research is needed first on other emotions than anxiety, and that evidence-based practical recommendations are largely confined to dealing with students' anxiety up to date.

IMPLICATIONS FOR EDUCATIONAL PRACTICE IN HIGHER EDUCATION

While students' achievement emotions may quite often be deeply rooted in pre-college experiences, the college environment provides new settings and challenges that, likely, can change students' emotional approaches to learning and achievement in fundamental ways. Situational demands for more self-regulation at college, for example, pose new tasks for students' self-development. Also, the community of college students within classrooms and across the campus provides new reference groups for evaluating own abilities, and fresh experiences that can drastically differ from any previous experiences at high school.

It is educators' and administrators' responsibility to shape these college environments, and the classroom learning environments embedded in them, such that students' learning, performance, academic development, and physical as well as psychological health are fostered. Regarding the question as to how to foster students' adaptive emotions and prevent or reduce maladaptive emotions, however, practical recommendations remain largely speculative to date, due to the lack of educational intervention research targeting student emotions.

Theoretically, it can be assumed that educational practices intended to foster adaptive emotions can refer to different components and antecedents of emotions, much as different treatment practices pertaining to test anxiety do (see above). For example, while announcements of specific grading practices can be suited to change students' emotion-inducing expectancies, teachers' own emotions can model the affective and expressive components of students' emotions by way of emotional contagion. Assumptions on suitable practices can be inferred from the above discusssion on instructional and social determinants of emotions, and a limited number of more firmly based recommendations can be derived from test anxiety studies.

Shaping learning environments, classroom instruction, and assignments. Increasing the *cognitive quality* of tasks and classroom instruction can be speculated to influence college students' enjoyment of learning positively. As noted, this can likewise be assumed for providing tasks and learning assignments that imply a fine-tuned match between task demands, on the one hand, and students' competencies and prior knowledge, on the other, thus preventing boredom produced by demands that are too high or too low. Furthermore, shaping learning environments such that they meet students' needs for social relatedness, in addition to meeting their needs for competence and cognitive quality, can also be assumed to have beneficial effects.

Creating learning environments that involve the need to *self-regulate learning* (individually or in cooperative group work) can also be beneficial. As argued above, if there is a sufficient match between situational affordances and students' competencies to self-regulate their learning, enjoyment probably can be increased, for at least two reasons. First, students are given the chance to fulfill needs for autonomy. Second, provided there is sufficient match, students can select and organize learning material such that their individual interests are met, and that enjoyment-arousing mastery is benefitted. In case of a mismatch between situational demands and students' competencies, however, maladpative emotions will likely be induced in addition to, or instead of, adaptive emotions.

Beyond structural properties of learning environments and tasks, displaying *emotional enthusiasm* might be one primary mechanism suited to prevent boredom in classrooms, and to induce situational enjoyment that can generalize into more general enjoyment of academic learning. However, emotional enthusiasm probably needs to be enacted such that true emotions are displayed, since fake emotions can be recognized from subtle cues indicating incomplete or distorted facial expression, which would probably undermine any positive modeling effects.

Shaping exams, grading practices, and the consequences of achievement. As implied by the above-cited evidence on the determinants of test anxiety, structuring *exams and grading practices* in beneficial ways can be one of the most important means to foster students' emotions. However, due to occasionally complex and ambivalent effects, this may not be an easy task. As to the reduction of test anxiety, research has shown that any measures that increase perceived control, decrease the importance of failure, or decrease the impact of anxiety on performance, can be beneficial. Judging from the empirical evidence cited above, this seems to be true for (a) making demands transparent by clearly structuring materials and procedures, (b) giving students a choice between tasks, (c) giving them second chances, (d) providing external aids, and (e) using closed item formats easing working memory load. However, some of these measures may have negative side effects. For example, using highly structured material may benefit anxious students, but may impede performance in less anxious students. Also, using multiple-choice items only may reduce anxiety, but may preclude the use of item formats that are better suitable to assess competences for creative problem-solving.

As to grading practices and the classroom goal structures created by them, competitive practices based on social comparison norms probably increase average levels of student's anxiety, shame, and hopelessness by limiting chances for success and raising the visibility and social importance of academic success and failure (by increasing the value of achievement, competition might also increase positive emotions if success is experienced; Frenzel, Pekrun, and Goetz, in press). Grading based on social comparison may be needed for purposes of placement and selection, implying that goals of fostering student emotions, on the one hand, and producing usable information on student achievement, on the other, may be in conflict. However, to the extent that assessments aim to serve teaching and learning rather than being used for external purposes, criterion-oriented grading pertaining to mastery of the learning material probably is more recomendable than the normative practices prevailing in today's college classrooms.

Finally, as to the consequences of achievement that make success and failure important for instrumental, future-oriented reasons, it might prove helpful to provide contingencies implying that individual academic effort does in fact benefit the student's future prospects. Effort-outcome contingencies of this type can probably increase perceived control, thus strengthening positive future-related academic emotions, and reducing negative emotions. A lack of contingency, on the other hand, likely implies reduced subjective control and an increase of negative prospective emotions like anxiety or hopelessness. Typically, these contingencies are beyond the control of professors and administrators in higher education, but should be addressed by individuals and organizations shaping a society's job market (e.g., the business industry hiring college graduates, and politicians defining legal rules of making contracts and regulating the economy).

Directions for Future Research

Given the clear importance of many of the emotions experienced by college students, more research on these emotions is overdue. Some of the pressing concerns that research should attempt to tackle in the upcoming years are the following (see Pekrun and Schutz, in press).

Integrating theoretical approaches and research traditions. To date, many disciplines of psychology and education are characterized by a prevalence of mini-theories addressing isolated phenomena, and by related research traditions working in relative isolation. Emotion research is no exception to this rule. For example, experimental research addressing the effects of positive and negative mood on cognitive performance is in a disintegrated state to date that makes if difficult, for researchers and practitioners alike, to draw any generalizable conclusions. In order to build cumulative knowledge and lay the foundations for integrating empirical findings, it seems necessary to construct more integrative theories by identifying common assumptions of existing approaches, combining these assumptions, and extend assumptions so that gaps between emotion research and neighboring fields (like motivation) can be bridged. The control-value theory of achievement emotions outlined above represents one attempt to do so.

Concepts of emotion. At present, the boundaries of the concept of "emotion" still remain unclear. While there is consensus that anxiety, anger, or joy are basic emotions that belong to this conceptual category, this is less clear for a number of other phenomena. For example, interest has variously been seen as an emotion, as an amalgam of values and emotion (more specifically, enjoyment), or as a construct different from emotion. Defining the conceptual relations betweens students' interest and their emotions, however, is a necessary precondition for conceptualizing their functional relations (is students' interest part of the domain of emotions, or does it function as a determinant or an effect of emotions?).

Also, should emotions be seen as separate from students' mood, or is mood just one subcategory of emotion? In social psychological theories, mood and emotions are often seen as distinct entities, the boundaries being defined by intensity (high vs. low) and object focus (emotions having a clear focus, mood having a less clear or no focus). Since both of these differences seem to imply dimensional distinctions rather than categorical differentiation, it might be more fruitful to see mood vs. emotion as bipolar ends of a conceptual continuum, rather than as a categorical distinction between qualitatively different phenomena. This latter view has been used in the present chapter (moods and emotions as belonging to the same category of processes), but to date this issue seems far from being settled in mood and emotion research.

Mapping the domain of students' emotions: Dimensions, categories, and taxonomies. There is disagreement on how students' emotions, and human emotions more generally, should best be classified. Dimensional approaches focus on the common denominators of emotions and distinguish emotions along common dimensions. A prototypical example is the circumplex model of affect using the dimensions of activation and valence (Feldman Barrett and Russell, 1998). In contrast, categorical approaches focus on the specific, discrete qualities of different emotions. Among the many specific implications of this debate is whether the affective consequences of students' achievement goals should be defined in terms of positive vs. negative affect (e.g., Linnenbrink and Pintrich, 2002), or in terms of discrete achievement emotions like enjoyment, hope, anger, anxiety, etc. (Pekrun et al., 2006). These different approaches also differ in terms of the taxonomies of student emotions that might be based on them.

Mixed-method research strategies: I. Analyzing emotions from idiographic and nomothetic perspectives. In field-based educational research on emotion, inferences about the within-person functions and antecedents of college students' emotions are often derived from interindividual correlations of variables (e.g., inferences on the causal role of test anxiety for performance are often deduced from correlations of test anxiety scores with subsequent academic performance).

Such inferences may be quite misleading, since it may happen that an interindividual correlation between two variables does not represent the intraindividual relation between these two variables in any single individual under study. Generally, interindividual and intraindividual correlations of variables are statistically independent, such that any inferences of this type may be unwarranted (see Robinson, 1950; Schmitz and Skinner, 1993).

Rather than relying on interindividual correlations, future research should take care to make use of strategies analyzing the psychological functions of emotions within individuals first, before drawing any population-oriented conclusions. Such an approach would imply to first use *idiographic*, intraindividual analysis, then analyze the distributions of intraindividual functions across individuals, and, finally, draw *nomothetic* conclusions on more general mechanisms of functioning, on condition that there is sufficient homogeneity of idiographic findings across individuals (for empirical examples, see Pekrun and Hofmann, 1996; Schmitz and Perels, 2006; Schmitz and Skinner, 1993).

Mixed-method research strategies: II. Integrating qualitative and quantitative methodology. As can be seen from the chapters of a recent edited volume on emotions in education (Schutz and Pekrun, in press), educational research on emotion uses both qualitative and quantitative approaches today. However, rarely both approaches are combined such that use is made of the benefits of each of them. Also, the limitations of both types of approaches are rarely fully acknowledged. For example, while qualitative evidence may well be used to generate hypotheses on college students' emotions, it is less suited to test these hypotheses in more precise ways. Conversely, while quantitative evidence is needed to test a priori hypotheses, it often needs added qualitative insights to explain findings, especially in the case of anomalies. Future investigations of college students' emotions should make use of systematically combining both types of approaches.

Baserates, phenomenology, and components of student emotions. As noted at the outset, there is a clear lack of exploratory research into the occurrence and phenomenology of college students' emotions. Such research seems necessary to judge the relative importance of different emotions as experienced by different students, and in different types of academic situations. Also, it would be important to explore if there are differences between the emotions found in college classrooms and the emotions experienced by students in other educational settings, such as K – 12 classrooms or settings of business education.

In addition, phenomenological evidence is needed for generating more comprehensive conceptions of the contents and functions of student emotions, beyond assumptions that can deductively be derived from existing theories. Finally, we also need more qualitative and quantitative evidence on the structural relations between the different components of student emotions. To date, it is clear that different component processes of emotions are, typically, loosely coupled instead of showing deterministic relations, but the precise mechanisms of reciprocal relations between components, and the degree to which components can be predicted from information about other components, are still largely unclear.

Evidence on baserates and structures can have far-reaching consequences for assessment, treatment, and educational practice. For example, if components of emotions strongly influence each other, modifying one component can produce spill-over effects such that the other component is changed as well. If influences are weak, effects of treatments or educational practice would be more circumscribed. For example, if cognitive treatment indirectly changes physiological emotion components as well, it might well be suited to foster students' emotion-dependent health. If the effects are confined to cognitive components of emotions, other methods would have to be used instead of, or in addition to, cognitive therapy.

Assessment and modeling of student emotions. As noted in the section on assessment, different methodologies to assess human emotions are available to date, but most of these methodologies have not yet systematically been applied to college students' emotions. Specifically, this pertains to neuropsychological methods of mental imaging, and to observational procedures of assessing emotions in academic situations like classroom interaction. As to self-report methods, many instruments are available to assess students' test anxiety, but there is a clear lack of multidimensional instruments measuring a broader range of emotions (the Achievement Emotions Questionnaire discussed above being an exception). A specific, important deficit is the lack of real-time indicators of emotions being able to assess their dynamics over time (EEG methods are an exception; e.g., Meinhardt and Pekrun, 2003). Since instruments are lacking, it also is open to question which types of indicators (self-report, physiological, observational, etc.) might be best suited to assess specific aspects of college students' emotions.

Emotions are processes that unfold over time. Therefore, beyond static measures of students' trait or state emotions, methods to assess and model the dynamics of these emotions, and the multidirectional linkages between the implied component processes, would be needed to get more fine-grained descriptions of emotions and their functional properties. Experiments can deliver evidence on no more than isolated segments of these dynamical, multidirectional relationships. Many non-experimental approaches (e.g., structural equations modeling based on field studies), on the other hand, have difficulties of disentangling the multiplicity of causal effects often operating simultaneously in the dynamics of emotions. It is a challenge for future research on student emotions is to develop or adapt dynamic modeling procedures that are better suited to model real-time emotional processes.

Effects of student emotions on learning, achievement, social relations, personality development, and overall health. As outlined in the preceding sections, evidence on the consequences of college students' emotions is largely lacking, with the exception of knowledge about the performance effects of test anxiety. However, even for test anxiety, two research deficits should be noted. First, the bulk of test anxiety research focused on the effects of anxiety on academic learning and performance. Far less evidence has been accumulated as to the consequences of students' anxiety for their social relationships, for their long-term identity formation and personality development, and for their health. Second, as noted, most empirical studies have used unidirectional designs analyzing the performance effects of students' anxiety. There is a clear need for more longitudinal investigations analyzing the reciprocal linkages between emotions (including anxiety), on the one hand, and students' academic learning and performance, on the other.

Determinants, development, and regulation of student emotions. As with the effects of college students' emotions, evidence on individual determinants, social and classroom antecedents, development, and regulation of these emotions is largely confined to test anxiety to date, with the exception of studies on the attributional antecedents of emotions following success and failure. More research on cognitive as well as non-cognitive individual determinants is needed, including research on the precise mechanisms linking appraisals and emotions (Reisenzein), on the genetical and physiological foundations of achievement emotions, and on the interactions between different types of determinants. Similarly, research should systematically analyze how different learning environments, types of classroom instruction, academic tasks, and behaviors of significant others influence students' emotions. Finally, coping research should address emotions other than anxiety as well, and students' regulation of their emotions, as well as the role of their emotional competences and emotional intelligence, should be analyzed.

The role of higher education systems and institutions in their socio-cultural and historical context. Higher education institutions are among the oldest institutions of our societies. To my knowledge, however, no attempt has yet been made to situate perspectives on college students' emotions in the larger socio-cultural and historical context that shapes higher education institutions and the learning environments these institutions provide. Also, in contrast to international assessments of K – 12 education (e.g., OECD, 2004), empirical evidence implying international and cross-cultural comparisons of students' emotional situations across higher education systems of different countries seems to be largely lacking to date. Contextual knowledge on cross-cultural differences and similarities across the centuries, and across different nations, might prove helpful for planning long-term institutional trans-formation such that it takes retrospective accounts of possible change into account, while at the same being embedded in future-oriented perspectives.

Intervention research: Need for evidence-based knowledge on therapy, prevention, and "emotionally sound" college environments. To date, we lack knowledge about effective treatment for college students' problems with negative academic emotions, with the exception of test anxiety therapy. Furthermore, there also is a lack of knowledge on ways to prevent maladaptive emotions, even for test anxiety (Zeidner, 1998). Finally, evidence is needed how higher education institutions and their learning environments can be shaped such that college students' emotions are fostered and influenced in "emotionally sound" (Astleitner, 2000) ways. Researchers should conduct intervention studies exploring ways to do so. This may not be an easy task, as can be seen from the obstables that recent K – 12 intervention studies targeting students' emotions have encountered (e.g., Glaeser-Zikuda, Fuss, Laukenmann, Metz, and Randler, 2005). However, in order to lay the foundations for transferring the insights of emotion research into educational practice, and to do so in empirically based ways, there is no alternative to intervention research directly addressing the impact of change.

CONCLUSION

In the concluding chapter of their 2000 *Handbook of Self-Regulation* that covered the state of the art in research on self-regulation, Boekaerts, Pintrich and Zeidner (2000, p. 754) posed the question, "How should we deal with emotions or affect?". The review provided by the present chapter has shown that research on college students' academic agency takes no exception in not yet being able to answer this question. Rather, it seems that higher education research has not even begun to search for systematical, evidence-based answers to questions about college students' emotions, research on students' test anxiety being an exception.

Theoretical considerations and the few evidence that is available, however, suggest that the emotions experienced in academic settings are critical to college students' scholastic development, as described in this chapter. This pertains to students' motivation to learn, use of learning strategies, and self-regulation of learning underlying their acquisition of knowledge. Furthermore, beyond their functions for knowledge building and performance, emotions likely are no less important for college students' long-term persistence and dropout behavior in pursuing their academic careers, and for their overall personality development, social behavior, and physical as well as psychological health.

By implication, higher education research would be well advised to pay more attention to the affective sides of students' scholastic development. With the advent of broader conceptions of human psychological functioning replacing an exclusive focus on cognitive processes by including neuropsychological, emotion-oriented, and socio-cultural perspectives as well, chances may in fact have increased that researchers start analyzing the emotional aspects of students' learning and achievement, and of their personality development and well-being more generally.

In conclusion, it should be noted that similar arguments can be made for the emotions experienced by instructors, professors, and administrators in higher education institutions. To date, next to nothing is known about professors' emotions experienced in classroom teaching, and the role these emotions play in the quality of their teaching, their professional development, and their well-being, burnout, and physical health (for emotions in K – 12 teachers, see Schutz and Pekrun, in press). Future research should analyze college students' emotions, but it should also extend perspectives to include the emotions experienced by professors and administrators as well.

REFERENCES

Ashby, F.G., Isen, A.M., and Turken, A.U. (1999). A neuropsychological theory of positive affect and its influence on cognition. *Psychological Review* 106: 529–550.

Aspinwall, L. (1998). Rethinking the role of positive affect in self-regulation. *Motivation and Emotion* 22: 1–32.

Assor, A., Kaplan, H., Kanat-Maymon, Y., and Roth, G. (2005). Directly controlling teacher behaviors as predictors of poor motivation and engagement in girls and boys: The role of anger and anxiety. *Learning and Instruction* 15: 397–413.

Astleitner, H. (2000). Designing emotionally sound instruction: The FEASP-approach. *Instructional Science* 28: 169–198.

Atkinson, J.W. (1964). *An Introduction to Motivation*. Princeton, NJ: Van Nostrand.

Bless, H., Clore, G.L., Schwarz, N., Golisano, V., Rabe, C., and Wölk, M. (1996). Mood and the use of scripts: Does a happy mood really lead to mindlessness? *Journal of Personality and Social Psychology* 71: 665–679.

Boekaerts, M. (1993). Anger in relation to school learning. *Learning and Instruction* 3: 269–280.

Boekaerts, M., Pintrich, P., and Zeidner, M. (2000) (eds.), *Handbook of Self-regulation*. San Diego: Academic Press.

Bolger, N. (1990). Coping as a personality process: A prospective study. *Journal of Personality and Social Psychology* 59: 525–537.

Bolles, R.C. (1972). Reinforcement, expectancy, and learning. *Psychological Review* 79: 394–409.

Brown, C.H. (1938). Emotional reactions before examinations: II. Results of a question-naire. *Journal of Psychology* 5: 11–26.

Covington, M.V., and Beery, R.G. (1976). *Self-worth and School Learning*. Oxford, UK: Holt, Rinehart and Winston.

Covington, M.V., and Omelich, C.L. (1981). As failures mount: Affective and cognitive consequences of ability demotion in the classroom. *Journal of Educational Psychology* 73: 796–808.

Csikszentmihalyi, M., and Csikszentmihalyi, I.S. (1988) (eds.), *Optimal Experience: Psychological Studies of Flow in Consciousness*. New York: Cambridge University Press.

Damasio, A.R. (2004). Emotions and feelings: A neurobiological perspective. In A.S.R. Manstead, N. Frijda and A. Fischer (eds.), *Feelings and Emotions* (pp. 49–57). Cambridge, UK: Cambridge University Press.

Efklides, A., and Volet, S. (2005) (eds.), Special Issue: Feelings and emotions in the learning process. *Learning and Instruction* 15: 377–515.

Ekman, P., and Rosenberg, E.L. (1997) (eds.), *What the Face Reveals: Basic and Applied Studies of Spontaneous Expression using the Facial Action Coding System (FACS)*. New York, NY: Oxford University Press.

Ellis, A. (1962). *Reason and Emotion in Psychotherapy*. New York: Lyle Stuart.

Ellis, H.C., and Ashbrook, P.W. (1988). Resource allocation model of the effect of depressed mood states on memory. In K. Fiedler and J. Forgas (eds.), *Affect, Cognition, and Social Behavior*. Toronto, Canada: Hogrefe International.

Endler, N., and Okada, M. (1975). A multidimensional measure of trait anxiety: The S-R Inventory of General Trait Anxiousness. *Journal of Consulting and Clinical Psychology* 43: 319–329.

Eysenck, M.W. (1997). *Anxiety and Cognition.* Hove, East Sussex, UK: Psychology Press.

Feldman Barrett, L., and Russell, J.A. (1998). Independence and bipolarity in the structure of current affect. *Journal of Personality and Social Psychology* 74: 967–984.

Forgas, J.P., and Vargas, P.T. (2000). The effects of mood on social judgment and reasoning. In M. Lewis and J.M. Haviland-Jones (eds.), *Handbook of Emotions* (2nd edition, pp. 350–381). New York: Guilford Press.

Fredrickson, B.L. (2001). The role of positive emotions in positive psychology: The broaden-and-build theory of positive emotions. *American Psychologist* 56: 218–226.

Frenzel, A.C., Pekrun, R., and Goetz, T. (in press). Perceived learning environment and students' emotional experiences: A multi-level analysis of mathematics classrooms. *Learning and Instruction.*

Glaeser-Zikuda, M., Fuss, S., Laukenmann, M., Metz, K., and Randler, C. (2005). Promoting students' emotions and achievement – Instructional design and evaluation of the ECOLE-approach. *Learning and Instruction* 15: 481–495.

Goetz, T. (2004). *Emotionales Erleben und selbstreguliertes Lernen bei Schülern im Fach Mathematik* [Students emotions and self-regulated learning in mathematics]. Munich, Germany: Utz.

Goetz, T., Pekrun, R., Hall, N., and Haag, L. (2006). Academic emotions from a socio-cognitive perspective: Antecedents and domain specificity of students' affect in the context of Latin instruction. *British Journal of Educational Psychology.*

Heckhausen, H. (1991). *Motivation and Action.* New York: Springer.

Hembree, R. (1988). Correlates, causes, effects, and treatment of test anxiety. *Review of Educational Research* 58: 47–77.

Hatfield, E., Cacioppo, J.T., and Rapson, R.L. (1994). *Emotional Contagion.* New York: Cambridge University Press.

Hodapp, V., and Benson, J. (1997). The multidimensionality of test anxiety: a test of different models. *Anxiety, Stress and Coping* 10: 219–244.

Isen, A.M. (1999). Positive affect. In T. Dalgleish and M. Power (eds.), *Handbook of Cognition and Emotion* (pp. 521–539). New York, NY: Wiley.

Jacobson, E. (1938). *Progressive Relaxation.* Chicago: University of Chicago Press.

Johnson, D.W., and Johnson, R.T. (1974). Instructional goal structure: Cooperative, competitive or individualistic. *Review of Educational Research* 4: 213–240.

Kleine, M., Goetz, T., Pekrun, R. and Hall, N. (2005). The structure of students' emotions experienced during a mathematical achievement test. *International Reviews on Mathematical Education* 37: 221–225.

Kleinginna, P.R., and Kleinginna, A.M. (1981). A categorized list of emotion definitions, with suggestions for a consensual definition. *Motivation and Emotion* 5: 345–379.

Krapp, A. (2005). Basic needs and the development of interest and intrinsic motivational orientations. *Learning and Instruction* 15: 381–395.

Lane, A.M., Terry, P.C., Beedle, C.J., Curry, D.A., and Clark, N. (2001). Mood and performance: Test of a conceptual model with a focus on depressed mood. *Psychology of Sport and Exercise* 2: 157–172.

Lane, A.M., Whyte, G.P., Terry, P.C., and Nevill, A.M. (2005). Mood, self-set goals and examination performance: The moderating effect of depressed mood. *Personality and Individual Differences* 39: 143–153.

Lazarus, R.S., and Folkman, S. (1987). Transactional theory and research on emotions and coping. *European Journal of Personality* 1: 141–169.

Lazarus, R.S., and Folkman, S. (1984). *Stress, Appraisal, and Coping*. New York: Springer.

Levine, L.J., and Burgess, S.L. (1997). Beyond general arousal: Effect of specific emotions on memory. *Social Cognition* 15: 157–181.

Lewis, M., and Haviland-Jones, J.M. (2000) (eds.), *Handbook of Emotions*. New York: Guilford Press.

Liebert, R.M., and Morris, L.W. (1967). Cognitive and emotional components of test anxiety : A distinction and some initial data. *Psychological Reports* 20: 975–978.

Linnenbrink, E.A. (2006) (ed.). Emotion research in education: Theoretical and methodological perspectives on the integration of affect, motivation, and cognition [Special issue]. *Educational Psychology Review*. 18(1):

Linnenbrink, E.A., and Pintrich, P.R. (2002). Achievement goal theory and affect: An asymmetrical bidirectional model. *Educational Psychologist* 37: 69–78.

Mandler, G., and Sarason, S.B. (1952). A study of anxiety and learning. *Journal of Abnormal and Social Psychology* 47: 166–173.

Matthews, G., Zeidner, M., and Roberts, R.D. (2002). *Emotional Intelligence: Science and Myth*. Cambridge, MA: MIT Press.

Meece, J.L., Wigfield, A., and Eccles, J.S. (1990). Predictors of math anxiety and its influence on young adolescents course enrollment intentions and performance in mathematics. *Journal of Educational Psychology* 82: 60–70.

Meinhardt, J., and Pekrun, R. (2003). Attentional resource allocation to emotional events: An ERP study. *Cognition and Emotion* 17: 477–500.

Metalsky, G.I., Halberstadt, L.J., and Abramson, L.Y. (1987). Vulnerability to depressive mood reactions: Toward a more powerful test of the diathesis-stress and causal mediation components of the reformulated theory of depression. *Journal of Personality and Social Psychology* 52: 386–393.

Molfenter, S. (1999). *Prüfungsemotionen bei Studierenden* [Test emotions in university students]. Unpublished dissertation. University of Regensburg, Institute of Psychology.

Morling, B., and Evered, S. (2006). Secondary control reviewed and defined. *Psychological Bulletin* 13: 269–296.

Nicholls, J.G. (1976). When a scale measures more than its name denotes: The case of the Test Anxiety Scale for Children. *Journal of Consulting and Clinical Psychology* 44: 976–985.

Olafson, K.M., and Ferraro, F.R. (2001). Effects of emotional state on lexical decision performance. *Brain and Cognition* 45: 15–20.

Organization for Economic Co-operation and Development (OECD). (2004). *Learning for Tomorrow's World – First Results from PISA 2003*. Paris: OECD Publications.

Pekrun, R. (1984). An expectancy-value model of anxiety. *Advances in Test Anxiety Research* 3: 53–72.

Pekrun, R. (1992a). Kognition und Emotion in studienbezogenen Lern- und Leistungssituationen: Explorative Analysen (Cognition and emotion in academic situations of learning and achievement: Exploratory analysis). *Unterrichtswissenschaft* 20: 308–324.

Pekrun, R. (1992b). The impact of emotions on learning and achievement: Towards a theory of cognitive/motivational mediators. *Applied Psychology* 41: 359–376.

607

Pekrun, R. (1992c). The expectancy-value theory of anxiety: Overview and implications. In D.G. Forgays, T. Sosnowski and K. Wrzesniewski (eds.), *Anxiety: Recent Developments in Self-appraisal, Psychophysiological and Health Research* (pp. 23–41). Washington, DC: Hemisphere.

Pekrun, R. (2000). A social cognitive, control-value theory of achievement emotions. In J. Heckhausen (ed.), *Motivational Psychology of Human Development* (pp. 143–163). Oxford, UK: Elsevier.

Pekrun, R. (2006). The control-value theory of achievement emotions: Assumptions, corollaries and implications for educational research and practice. *Educational Psychology Review* 18: 315–341.

Pekrun, R., Elliot, A.J., and Maier, M.A. (2006). Achievement goals and discrete achievement emotions: A theoretical model and prospective test. *Journal of Educational Psychology* 98: 583–597.

Pekrun, R., Frenzel, A., Goetz, T., and Perry, R.P. (2006, April). *Control-value Theory of Academic Emotions: How Classroom and Individual Factors Shape Students' Affect.* Paper presented at the annual meeting of the American Educational Research Association, San Francisco, CA.

Pekrun, R., and Frese, M. (1992). Emotions in work and achievement. In C.L. Cooper and I.T. Robertson (eds.), *International Review of Industrial and Organizational Psychology* (Vol. 7, pp. 153–200). Chichester, UK: Wiley.

Pekrun, R., Goetz, T., Perry, R.P., Kramer, K., and Hochstadt, M. (2004). Beyond test anxiety: Development and validation of the Test Emotions Questionnaire (TEQ). *Anxiety, Stress and Coping* 17: 287–316.

Pekrun, R., Goetz, T., and Perry, R.P. (2005). *Achievement Emotions Questionnaire (AEQ). User's manual.* Department of Psychology, University of Munich.

Pekrun, R., Goetz, T., Titz, W., and Perry, R.P. (2002a). Positive emotions in education. In E. Frydenberg (ed.), *Beyond Coping: Meeting Goals, Visions, and Challenges* (pp. 149–174). Oxford, UK: Elsevier.

Pekrun, R., Götz, T., Titz, W., and Perry, R.P. (2002b). Academic emotions in students' self-regulated learning and achievement: A program of quantitative and qualitative research. *Educational Psychologist* 37: 91–106.

Pekrun, R., and Hofmann, H. (1996, April). *Affective and Motivational Processes: Contrasting Interindividual and Intraindividual Perspectives.* Paper presented at the annual meeting of the American Educational Research Association, New York.

Pekrun, R., and Schutz, P.A. (in press). Where do we go from here? Implications and future directions for inquiry on emotions in education. In P.A. Schutz and R. Pekrun (eds.), *Emotions in Education.* San Diego, CA: Academic Press.

Perry, R.P. (1991). Perceived control in college students: Implications for instruction in higher education. In J. Smart (ed.), *Higher Education: Handbook of Theory and Research* (Vol. 7, pp. 1–56). New York: Agathon.

Perry, R.P., Hladkyj, S., Pekrun, R.H., Clifton, R.A., and Chipperfield, J.G. (2005). Perceived academic control and failure in college students: A three-year study of scholastic attainment. *Research in Higher Education* 46: 535–569.

Perry, R.P., Hladkyi, S., Pekrun, R., and Pelletier, S. (2001). Academic control and action control in college students: A longitudinal study of self-regulation. *Journal of Educational Psychology* 93: 776–789.

Reisenzein, R. (2001). Appraisal processes conceptualized from a schema-theoretic perspective. In K.R. Scherer, A. Schorr and T. Johnstone (eds.), *Appraisal Processes in Emotion* (pp. 187–201). Oxford, UK: Oxford University Press.

Robinson, W.S. (1950). Ecological correlations and the behavior of individuals. *American Sociological Review* 15: 351–356.

Rost, D.H., and Schermer, F.J. (1987). Emotion and cognition in coping with test anxiety. *Communication and Cognition* 20: 225–244.

Rothbaum, F., Weisz, J.R., and Snyder, S.S. (1982). Changing the world and changing the self: A two process model of perceived control. *Journal of Personality and Social Psychology* 42: 5–37.

Sarason, I.G. (1984). Stress, anxiety, and cognitive interference: Reactions to tests. *Journal of Personality and Social Psychology* 44: 929–938.

Schaller, M., and Cialdini, R.B. (1990). Happiness, sadness, and helping: A motivational integration. In R. Sorrentino and E.T. Higgins (eds.), *Handbook of Motivation and Cognition: Foundations of Social Behavior* (Vol. 2, pp. 265–296). New York: Guilford Press.

Scherer, K.R. (1984). On the nature and function of emotion: A component process approach. In K.R. Scherer and P. Ekman (eds.), *Approaches to Emotion* (pp. 293–317). Hillsdale, NJ: Erlbaum.

Scherer, K.R. (2000). Emotions as episodes of subsystems synchronization driven by nonlinear appraisal processes. In I. Granic and M.D. Lewis (eds.), *Emotion, Development, and Self-organization: Dynamic Systems Approaches to Emotional Development* (pp. 70–99). New York: Cambridge University Press.

Scherer, K.R., Schorr, A., and Johnstone, T. (2001) (eds.), *Appraisal Processes in Emotion*. Oxford, UK: Oxford University Press.

Schmitz, B., and Perels, F. (2006, April). *Studying Homework Behavior from the Perspective of Self-regulated Learning Using Learning Diaries*. Paper presented at the annual meeting of the American Educational Research Association, San Francisco, CA.

Schmitz, B., and Skinner, E. (1993). Perceived control, effort, and academic performance: Interindividual, intraindividual, and multivariate time series analyses. *Journal of Personality and Social Psychology* 64: 1010–1028.

Schnabel, K. (1998). *Prüfungsangst und schulisches Lernen* (Test anxiety and academic). Münster, Germany: Waxmann.

Spangler, G., Pekrun, R., Kramer, K., and Hofmann, H. (2002). Students' emotions, physiological reactions, and coping in academic exams. *Anxiety, Stress and Coping* 15: 413–432.

Schutz, P.A., and Lanehart, S.L. (2002) (eds.), Emotions in education [Special issue]. *Educational Psychologist* 37(2).

Schutz, P.A., and Pekrun, R. (in press) (eds.), *Emotions in Education*. San Diego, CA: Academic Press.

Spielberger, C.D. (1980). *Test Anxiety Inventory: Preliminary Professional Manual*. Palo Alto, CA: Consulting Psychologist Press.

Stengel, E. (1936). Prüfungsangst und Prüfungsneurose [Exam anxiety and exam neurosis]. *Zeitschrift für psychoanalytische Pädagogik* 10: 300–320.

Stratton, G.M. (1927). Anger and fear: Their probable relation to each other, to intellectual work, and to primogeniture. *American Journal of Psychology* 39: 125–140.

Thompson, T., Altmann, R., and Davidson, J. (2004). Shame proneness and achievement behavior. *Personality and Individual Differences* 36: 613–627.

Titz, W. (2001). *Emotionen von Studierenden in Lernsituationen* (university students' emotions at learning). Münster: Waxmann.

Turner, J.E., and Schallert, D.L. (2001). Expectancy-value relationships of shame reactions and shame resiliency. *Journal of Educational Psychology* 93: 320–329.

Turner, J.E., and Waugh, R.M. (in press). A dynamical systems perspective regarding students' learning processes: Shame reactions and emergent self-organizations. In P.A. Schutz and R. Pekrun (eds.), *Emotions in Education*. San Diego, CA: Academic Press.

Vodanovich, S.J., Weddle, C., and Piotrowoski, C. (1997). The relationship between boredom proneness and internal and external work values. *Social Behavior and Personality* 25: 259–264.

Watt, J.D., and Vodanovich, S.J. (1999). Boredom proneness and psychosocial development. *Journal of Psychology: Interdisciplinary and Applied* 133: 303–314.

Weiner, B. (1985). An attributional theory of achievement motivation and emotion. *Psychological Review* 92: 548–573.

Weiner, B. (in press). Examining emotional diversity on the classroom: An attribution theorist considers the moral emotions. In P. Schutz and R. Pekrun (eds.), *Emotions in Education*. San Diego: Academic Press.

Westefeld, J.S., Homaifar, B., Spotts, J., Furr, S., Range, L., and Werth, J.L. (2005). Perceptions concerning college student suicide: Data from our universities. *Suicide and Life Threatening Behavior* 35: 640–645.

Wine, J.D. (1971). Test anxiety and the direction of attention. *Psychological Bulletin* 76: 92–104.

Wolters, C.A. (2003). Regulation of motivation: Evaluating an underemphasized aspect of self-regulated learning. *Educational Psychologist* 38: 189–205.

Wyatt, S. (1930). The problem of monotony and boredom in industrial work. *Industrielle Psychotechnik* 7: 114–123.

Zeidner, M. (1998). *Test Anxiety: The State of the Art*. New York: Plenum.

Zeidner, M. (in press). Test anxiety in educational contexts: What I have learned so far. In P. Schutz and R. Pekrun (eds.), *Emotions in Education*. San Diego: Academic Press.

Zeidner, M., and Endler, N. (1996) (eds.), *Handbook of Coping: Theory, Research, Applications*. New York: Wiley.

14. CONTEXTUAL DETERMINANTS OF MOTIVATION AND HELP SEEKING IN THE COLLEGE CLASSROOM

Akane Zusho[†], Stuart A. Karabenick[‡], Christina Rhee Bonney[†], and Brian C. Sims[§]

[†]*Fordham University*
zusho@fordham.edu
[‡]*University of Michigan*
[§]*North Carolina A & T University*

Abstract

This chapter reviews the extant literature on college students' help seeking and motivation to learn. Specific attention is paid to how classroom contextual factors (e.g., instructional climate, teacher support and caring) are believed to influence college students' patterns of motivation and willingness to seek help. In terms of help seeking, a distinction is made between proactive (e.g., instrumental) and generally maladaptive forms of help seeking (e.g., executive). Emphasis is placed on the importance of developing learners who learn to seek help when needed. Motivation in this chapter is defined primarily in terms of achievement goal theory. To this end, discussions focus on college students' endorsement of multiple achievement goals and which goals (i.e., mastery-approach, mastery-avoidance, performance-approach, and performance-avoidance) have been found to be related to course achievement. The chapter concludes with implications for practice and a discussion of future research in the areas of motivation and self-regulated learning

Key Words: Help Seeking; Motivation; Achievement Goal Theory; Classroom Context

What are characteristics of a good college student? Typically, instructors appreciate most those students who focus on learning and understanding the course material; students who are effortful even

[*]Manuscript prepared for *The Scholarship of Teaching and Learning in Higher Education: An Evidence-Based Perspective (2007)*, R. Perry and J. Smart (Eds.) Please address all correspondence to Akane Zusho, Graduate School of Education, Fordham University, 113 West 60th Street, New York, NY 10023. Telephone – (212)-636-7256; E-mail: zusho@fordham.edu.

R.P. Perry and J.C. Smart (eds.), The Scholarship of Teaching and Learning in Higher Education: An Evidence-Based Perspective, 611–659.
© 2007 *Springer.*

in the face of difficulties, who seek help when confused, and above all, those students who can manage their time effectively. Indeed, the research on motivation and self-regulated learning demonstrates that students who exhibit such characteristics are often rewarded with higher grades and better learning outcomes (see Pintrich & Zusho, this volume). In other words, successful completion of college often depends on the ability to motivate and regulate one's learning.

The overall aim of this chapter is to review this research and to draw upon our own studies, which present further evidence regarding contextual determinants of college student achievement. We begin by providing a brief overview of the overarching theoretical framework, including a definition of terms. From here we proceed to discuss three main issues: (1) the motivation of college students, (2) college students' patterns of help seeking, and (3) classroom factors that facilitate or undermine student motivation and help seeking. We conclude with a discussion of future research in these areas and implications for policy and practice.

In an effort to distinguish this chapter's contributions from that of Pintrich & Zusho (this volume), emphasis is placed on theoretical and empirical developments that have taken place since the publication of that chapter. First, for self-regulated learning, processes related to behavioral regulation, specifically help seeking, are highlighted. Second, in terms of motivation, more attention is paid to the multiple goals perspective of achievement goal theory. Finally, an expanded discussion of how classroom contextual factors influence college students' motivation and self-regulatory processes is offered.

THEORETICAL APPROACHES TO THE STUDY OF MOTIVATION AND SELF-REGULATED LEARNING

Contemporary research in motivation and self-regulated learning is primarily social-cognitive in nature, with an emphasis on the role of students' beliefs, perceptions, and strategies (Weiner, 1990; Pintrich & Schunk, 2002). To this end, motivation and self-regulated learning are assumed to be discernable through students' reports of their beliefs and strategies as well as through behaviors such as choice of activities, level and quality of task engagement, persistence, and performance. This approach also underscores the multi-dimensional nature of such processes, and examines how motivation and strategy use are influenced by broader cultural and contextual factors. In other words, emphasis is placed on the *process* of learning, and on understanding the factors, both personal and contextual, that influence how an individual approaches, engages in, and responds to achievement-related situations. In contrast to earlier research, motivation is no longer considered to be a dispositional trait, with some students being "more" or "less" motivated. Rather, student motivation is assumed to be situated and changeable as a function of instructions, tasks, and activities that take place in a classroom (Bonney, Kempler, Zusho, Coppola, & Pintrich, 2005).

Figure 1 presents our general model of achievement motivation and learning that forms the basis of this chapter. Briefly, the model depicts the influence of classroom contextual factors on students' subsequent motivational and self-regulatory processes, and how these factors, in turn, ultimately produce outcomes such as choice, effort, persistence, and performance. In line with the social-cognitive perspective of motivation, this model also assumes that the relations between the various constructs are reciprocal, that is, they can mutually influence one another.

OUTCOMES

In terms of outcomes of learning, a distinction can be made between "meaningful" and "superficial" learning outcomes. With widespread concerns about the quality of education in the U.S., an increasing number of studies are being directed toward uncovering

Figure 1: A General Model for Student Motivation and Self-Regulated Learning in the College Classroom.

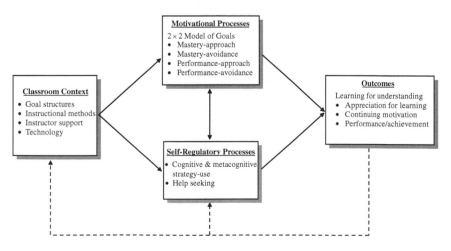

mechanisms of learning for understanding (Bransford, Brown, and Cocking, 2000). This emphasis on understanding can be contrasted to previous approaches concerned with the acquisition and transmission of knowledge. Rather than focusing on memorization and rote learning, this new science of learning stresses more the application and transformation of knowledge. With these developments, issues of motivation and self-regulation have taken center stage; authentic learning tasks with real-world applications and the development of higher-order and metacognitive skills are now believed to be critical to the learning process. For these reasons, motivation and indices of self-regulation can be considered important learning outcomes in their own right; however, for the purposes of this chapter, we examine how motivation and self-regulatory processes influence traditional measures of achievement (i.e., grades, exam scores), and measures of continuing motivation (i.e., choice, persistence, effort) (Maehr & Braskamp, 1986).

MOTIVATION

As reviewed in Pintrich and Zusho (this volume) and elsewhere (Eccles, Wigfield, & Schiefele, 1998), theories of motivation typically address questions such as "Can I do this task?", "Do I want to do this task? and Why?" Expectancy constructs such as self-efficacy and perceptions of competence typically are related to the former question whereas value constructs such as task-value and achievement goals are often associated with the latter questions. While we do not deny the importance of expectancy constructs in influencing learning outcomes (indeed, self-efficacy is often found to be among the strongest, if not the strongest, predictor of achievement) (see Schunk & Pajares, 2005), given space constraints and the undeniable popularity of goal theory within the achievement motivation paradigm, we focus on motivation in this chapter primarily in terms of achievement goals.

Typically, achievement goals are defined both in terms of the reasons underlying task engagement and the standards by which individuals measure their progress toward goal attainment. As we discuss in detail subsequently, contemporary research in this area distinguishes between four types of achievement goals, namely mastery-approach, mastery-avoidance, performance-approach, and performance-avoidance goals (called the 2×2 model of achievement goals) (Elliot, 1999; Elliot & McGregor, 2001; Pintrich, 2000).

Briefly, mastery-approach goals represent a focus on learning and understanding the course material whereas mastery-avoidance goals represent a focus on the avoidance of incomplete mastery of the material. Performance-approach goals (also called self-enhancing or relative ability goals) are generally defined as goals oriented toward outperforming others, whereas performance-avoidance goals represent a focus on not looking incompetent relative to others (see Table 1).

Table 1: The 2 × 2 Model of Achievement Goals

	Approach Focus	Avoidance Focus
Mastery Goal Orientation	• Focus on mastering task, learning, understanding • Use standards of self-improvement, progress, deep understanding of the task • Also called learning, task, or task-involved goals	• Focus on avoiding misunderstanding, not learning or mastering task • Use standards of not being wrong, doing it incorrectly relative to task
Performance Goal Orientation	• Focus on being superior, besting others, being the best at task, being the smartest • Use of normative standards such as getting the best or highest grades, being the top performer in class • Also called ego-involved goal, performance goal, relative ability goal, self-enhancing ego orientation	• Focus on mastering task, learning, understanding • Use normative standards of not getting worst grades, being lowest performer in class • Also called performance goal, ego-involved goal, self-defeating ego orientation

SELF-REGULATION AND HELP SEEKING

Many theoretical models of self-regulation have been proposed (see Boekaerts, Pintrich, & Zeidner, 2000); nevertheless, most models assume self-regulation to be an active, constructive process whereby learners set goals for their learning and then attempt to monitor, regulate, and control their learning in the service of those goals. Said differently, students are believed to be self-regulated to the extent that they participate actively in monitoring, regulating, and controlling their thinking, motivation, behavior, and the context(s) in which they learn (see Pintrich, 2000; Pintrich & Zusho, this volume).

More often than not, indices of self-regulation focus on the regulation of cognition, and assess the various cognitive and metacognitive strategies that students report using. In this chapter, we highlight another important type of self-regulation, namely behavioral self-regulation. Of primary interest is help seeking, which has received increasing attention because of its important role in the learning process (Karabenick & Newman, 2006). Help seeking is considered a behavioral self-regulated learning strategy that students employ as they would cognitive and metacognitive strategies (e.g., rehearsal or planning) (Karabenick, 1998; Pintrich & Zusho, 2002). However, seeking help is also a social-interactive process with self-relevant implications not shared by other forms of self-regulation. Among these are risks to self worth because of what seeking help can imply about a learner's abilities. In part, such concerns derive from the pejorative identification of help seeking with dependency in Western (primarily North American) societies (e.g., Fischer & Torney, 1976; Sears, Maccoby, & Levin, 1957). Given the negative implications of dependency, early research examined the personal and situational determinants of threats to self-worth (e.g., Covington, 1992). For example, early research indicated that college students lower in self-esteem view seeking help to be more threatening (Karabenick & Knapp, 1991), and students generally are more reluctant to seek help in public or on tasks diagnostic of highly valued abilities (Nadler, Fisher, & Depaulo, 1983). It is not surprising, therefore, that many college students fail to seek needed help, considering it an admission of defeat, embarrassing, and something to be avoided whenever possible. Increasing the likelihood that such students will obtain the help they need is an important reason for focusing on the person and situation influences on the help-seeking process.

Recent theoretical and empirical advances have shifted attention to the strategic benefits of help seeking that highlights the costs of not seeking it, because of the advantages that doing so affords the learner. Nelson-Le Gall's focus on students' reasons for seeking help provided the seminal conceptual shift that initiated the recognition of help seeking as an adaptive form of self-regulation (e.g., Nelson-Le Gall, 1981, 1985; Nelson-Le Gall, Gumerman & Scott-Jones, 1983). The analysis identified "instrumental" help seeking as that designed to obtain just enough assistance to overcome difficulties when learning, for example, by asking for hints or explanations. There is now substantial evidence that more resourceful and proactive learners, those who generally employ other learning strategies, are more likely to seek instrumental help when needed (Karabenick, 1998; Karabenick & Knapp, 1991; Karabenick & Newman, 2006; Zimmerman & Martinez-Pons, 1990). For those students, seeking help is considered preferable to stoically maintaining their independence and learning less, performing poorly, or even failing as a consequence. By contrast, "executive" help seeking is defined as that motivated by work avoidance goals and considered unnecessary, for example, students asking classmates for answers to an Introductory Psychology homework assignment. Help seeking undertaken for this purpose is unlikely to increase understanding or decrease subsequent dependency. In contrast, executive help seeking describes the form that many would consider it appropriate to discourage. Thus, explicating the reasons why students seek help was the turning point in understanding its adaptive significance.

CONTEXTUAL INFLUENCES

Reflected in familiar comments such as "my students are just not motivated," a common misconception of the research on motivation and self-regulated learning is that they are traits of the learner; students either have it or they don't. While one cannot deny the influence of personality on such processes, contemporary research on motivation and self-regulated learning clearly demonstrates that the context in which a student learns may be just as important a determinant of his/her motivation, cognition, and achievement-related behaviors (Hickey, 1997).

For example, goal theorists suggest that teachers' behavior and discourse often communicate to students their beliefs about the purposes of achievement, and may influence the goals, achievement-related behaviors, cognitions, and affect that students will adopt in that class (Turner, Meyer, Midgley, & Patrick, 2003; Ames, 1992). This may take place in the form of classroom- or school-level policies that make mastery or performance goals salient to students, or it could be direct messages from the teachers that convey goal-related emphases (Kaplan, Middleton, Urdan, & Midgley, 2002). These communications may have an influence on students' subsequent personal goal adoption, and other motivation- and achievement-related outcomes. Thus, investigating contextual influences on students' motivation is vital to the application of empirical research to teacher practice and represents a core assumption of our theoretical approach.

COLLEGE STUDENT MOTIVATION AND HELP SEEKING: A PROGRAM OF RESEARCH

In reviewing the extant research on college students' motivation and help seeking, it is important to note that we draw heavily from data that we have gathered over the past 10 years with other members of the College Research Group at the University of Michigan, notably Paul Pintrich and Bill McKeachie. Thus, before we proceed further with our review, it is worthwhile to explain the details of our project. In particular, we present data from two large-scale projects focused on understanding motivational and self-regulatory processes in the college classroom. One project was conducted in Introductory Chemistry classrooms, the other in Introductory Psychology classrooms. The participants for the Chemistry study were 458 undergraduate students at a selective Midwestern university with an average ACT score of 27 and Carnegie classification of University Research I. The 740 participants for the second study were recruited from thirteen introductory psychology classes at a large Midwestern comprehensive university with an average ACT score of 21 classified as University Masters I. For reasons of background and subject domain, these two studies thus represent two distinct populations of college students.

The general procedures for both studies were fairly similar; students completed surveys on their motivation, use of self-regulated learning strategies, and patterns of help seeking, at multiple time points throughout the semester. Achievement measures included students' exam and quiz grades, obtained with student consent from the instructor at the end of the semester. In addition to these student measures, the psychology study was supplemented with teacher questionnaires, augmented by classroom observations. In what follows, we supplement our reviews of the research with the findings from these two studies.

THE MOTIVATION AND GOAL ORIENTATIONS OF COLLEGE STUDENTS

The history of achievement goal theory is not long, but is nevertheless complex (for an excellent review, we direct the reader to Elliot, 2005). Its original tenets are, perhaps, most clearly outlined in the work of Carol Dweck (Dweck & Elliott, 1983; Dweck & Leggett, 1988) and John Nicholls (Nicholls 1984). This early work (now referred to as the *normative* or traditional perspective) largely focused on documenting the beneficial effects of goals focused on learning and understanding (i.e., mastery, learning, task-focused goals) over goals focused on the demonstration of competence (i.e., performance, ego-focused goals). In contrast to this earlier work, recent theoretical conceptualizations have placed more emphasis on two related issues. First, is the bifurcation of mastery and performance goals into its approach and avoidance components and the second is the issue of multiple goal adoption. We consider these developments in this section by reviewing first the 2×2 achievement goal framework and second, the pursuit of multiple goals and its relation to indices of SRL and learning. In doing so, we provide empirical data addressing the kinds of goals college students report adopting, and how the pursuit of such goals influences their learning.

THE STRUCTURE AND VALIDITY OF THE 2×2 FRAMEWORK

There is emerging evidence to suggest that college students do indeed distinguish between the four goal constructs. Elliot & McGregor (2001), for example, relying on a sample of (mostly female) introductory psychology college students, demonstrated that it is possible to obtain four separate factors in both exploratory and confirmatory factor analyses of items assessing the four goal orientations. Our research group, too, has conducted similar analyses on comparable samples of college students (Rhee, Zusho, & Pintrich, 2005). Figure 2 displays the results of confirmatory factor analyses. The top model was derived from data on college chemistry students; the bottom model was based on analyses on introductory psychology students. The models are very

Figure 2: Results of CFAs on goal orientation items *Note*. Data based on sample of college chemistry students; $\chi^2(21) = 48$, $N = 461$; NFI = .98; NNFI = .98; CFI = .99; RMSEA = .05 *Note*. Data based on sample of college psychology students; $\chi^2(14) = 49$, $N = 461$; NFI = .98; NNFI = .97; CFI = .98; RMSEA = .06.

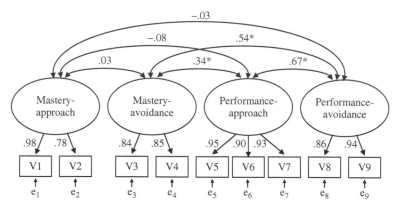

Note. Data based on sample of college chemistry students; χ^2 (21)=48, N=461; NFI=.98; NNFI=.98; CFI=.99; RMSEA=.05

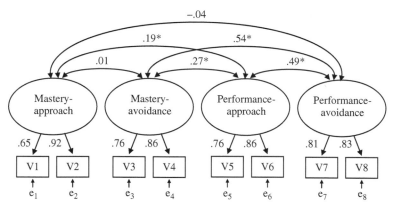

Note. Data based on sample of college psychology students; χ^2 (14)=49, N=461; NFI=.98; NNFI=.97; CFI=.98; RMSEA=.06

similar, especially considering differences in the subject matter and differing characteristics of students in the two samples.

We then used confirmatory factor analyses to test the extent to which the hypothesized model (in this case the 2×2 model of goals) fit the data, as well as a set of alternative models, determining best fits according to goodness-of-fit indices, such as the normed fit index (NFI), non-normed fit index (NNFI), and comparative fit index (CFI), and the root-mean-square error of approximation (RMSEA) (Raykov,

Tomer, & Nesselroade, 1991). According to Hu and Bentler (1995), fit indices above .95 and misfit indices below .06 are considered acceptable.

Six models were compared (see Figure 3): (1) the 2×2 model; (2) trichotomous model A, in which performance-approach and performance-avoidance goal items load separately on their own latent variables, while mastery-approach and mastery-avoidance

Figure 3: a. 2×2 model b. Trichotomous model A c. Trichotomous model B d. Trichotomous model C e. Mastery – Performance model f. Approach – Avoidance model.

a. 2×2 model

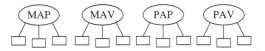

b. Trichotomous model A

c. Trichotomous model B

d. Trichotomous model C

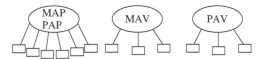

e. Mastery – Performance model

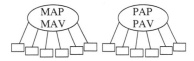

f. Approach – Avoidance model

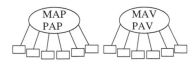

items load together on the same latent variable; (3) trichotomous model B, in which mastery-approach and performance-approach items load on respective latent variables, and mastery-avoidance and performance-avoidance goal items load together on one latent variable; (4) trichotomous model C, in which mastery-avoidance and performance-avoidance items load on separate latent variables, and mastery-approach and performance-approach items load together on a third variable; (5) a mastery-performance model, in which mastery-approach and mastery-avoidance goal items load together on one latent variable, while performance-approach and performance-avoidance items load together on the other variable; and (6) an approach-avoidance model, in which mastery-approach and performance-approach goal items load together on one latent variable, and mastery-avoidance and performance-avoidance items load together on another.

Considering the fit indices across the two samples, the 2×2 model was found to provide an excellent fit to the data, and what is more, was the best fit when compared to the five alternative models specified above. Together with the findings of reliability analyses (Cronbach alphas for the four goals ranged from .84 to .90 for the chemistry study and .78 to .86 for the psychology study), these data suggest that the four achievement goals are indeed reliable and empirically distinct.

Nevertheless, it is important to keep in mind that while CFAs can help to establish a scale's reliability, it does not necessarily follow that distinct and reliable goal constructs, as confirmed by CFAs, are valid or necessarily stable across time. The CFAs utilized in this study and others (e.g., Elliot & McGregor, 2001), merely separate constructs that are reliably different from each other, but do not necessarily test whether all items being evaluated validly assess college students' goals in a class. Therefore, such analyses cannot speak, for instance, to whether mastery-avoidance goals are in fact a common goal adopted by students, or for that matter, how the mastery-avoidance goal construct is distinct from purported related constructs such as fear of failure or anxiety unless such constructs are also included in factor analyses. For that we turn to additional evidence.

Do college students report using the four goals? Results of studies typically suggest variations in the mean-level endorsement of the four goal orientations. Such variations are often attributed to contextual factors including those discussed in subsequent sections of this chapter. Nevertheless, it is possible to discern general trends in the average endorsement of the four goals across studies.

As a rule, college students report endorsing mastery-approach goals more than the other three goal orientations. For example, the average scores for mastery-approach goals were found to be the highest in our own research (see Figure 4). Elliot & McGregor (2001) also found the mean scores of mastery-approach goals to exceed that of the other three goals. There is also some evidence to suggest that the variance in mastery-approach goals is more constrained in comparison to the other goals. In sum, these findings suggest that for whatever reason, college students are more likely to state that they adopt goals focused on learning and understanding with greater frequency and consistency than the other achievement goals.

When it comes to the other three goals, there is less of a consistent pattern across studies. In order of decreasing popularity, the participants in Elliot & McGregor's study reported endorsing performance-approach goals, performance-avoidance goals, and mastery-avoidance goals. On the other hand, we found students to report, on average, fairly comparable levels of mastery-avoidance and performance-approach goals, and performance-avoidance goals to be the least popular among the four goals.

The effects of the four goals on learning. Of course, examining average goal endorsement provides only a limited understanding of college students' motivation and learning. In fact, one could very well argue that what is more important is not whether college students endorse these goals but *how* these goals actually influence or predict their outcomes of learning. By and large, researchers have focused on outcomes such as achievement (i.e., exam or final course grades),

Figure 4: Average Goal Endorsement by Chemistry and Psychology College Students.

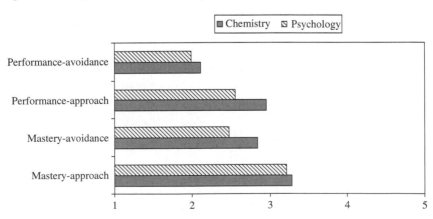

positive affect, (e.g., interest, intrinsic motivation, enjoyment, free choice), negative affect (e.g., anxiety, test anxiety, threat construals), and cognitive (e.g., rehearsal, organization, elaboration) and metacognitive strategy-use.

Studies typically find benefits of pursuing a mastery-approach goal, particularly in terms of its role in fostering interest in academics (e.g., Harackiewicz, Barron, Tauer, Carter, & Elliot, 2000) and the use of deeper-processing cognitive and metacognitive strategies (Pintrich & De Groot, 1990). For example, in both the Chemistry and Psychology studies, we found mastery-approach goals to be a significant positive predictor of interest and students' self-reported use of cognitive (i.e., rehearsal, organization, elaboration) and metacognitive strategies (Rhee et al., 2005). We also found mastery-approach goals to be a significant predictor of course performance ($\beta = .13$, $p < .05$) in Chemistry classrooms, after controlling for prior achievement, gender, and course type (i.e., inorganic vs. organic chemistry).

While findings of mastery-approach goals predicting interest are commonplace, it should be noted that mastery-approach goals are rarely found to actually predict achievement. Apart from our finding, which we largely attribute to the efforts being made at the time by the Chemistry department to increase student engagement and to use criterion-referenced evaluation, we are aware of only one other published study on college students that has found a positive relation between mastery-approach goals and achievement (Church, Elliot, & Gable, 2001). This may be because the majority of studies that survey college students' goal orientations to date have been conducted in classrooms emphasizing normative grading standards (e.g., Elliot & Church, 1997; Elliot & McGregor, 1999, 2001; Elliot, McGregor & Gable, 1999; Harackiewicz et al., 2002; Harackiewicz et al., 2000; McGregor & Elliot, 2002), thus underscoring how contextual factors can influence students' goal endorsement.

There is also almost unequivocal evidence to suggest that the endorsement of performance-avoidance goals is inimical to learning. We have found, as have others, that college students who report a focus on not looking incompetent relative to others have higher levels of anxiety, and lower levels of both interest and achievement (Church et al., 2001; Elliot & Church, 1997; Elliot & McGregor, 1999, 2001; Rhee et al., 2005; Skaalvik, 1997).

In short, the research on mastery-approach and performance-avoidance goals have been fairly consistent; in line with the traditional or normative perspective, the pursuit of mastery-approach goals has been demonstrated to be largely positive, while the adoption of performance-avoidance goals has been shown to be detrimental to most important outcomes of learning. On the other hand, the findings concerning performance-approach and mastery-avoidance goals have been somewhat more uneven. Such findings may seem puzzling at first, but it is important to keep in mind that both of these goals are believed to represent a hybrid of both potentially positive (i.e., the approach and/or mastery components) and negative (i.e., the avoidance and/or performance components) motivations. To this end, it may be reasonable to expect these goals to predict both positive and negative outcomes.

In terms of the research on mastery-avoidance goals, Elliot & McGregor (2001) found mastery-avoidance goals to positively predict anxiety (both worry and emotionality components) as well as the subsequent adoption of mastery-approach, mastery-avoidance, and performance-approach goals. In our own research we, too, have found mastery-avoidance goals to positively predict measures of anxiety and strategy-use but negatively predict course performance (Rhee et al., 2005). Taken together, these findings suggest that students who adopt such goals are typically more anxious, and report using more cognitive and metacognitive strategies, but that this does not necessarily translate to higher levels of achievement.

Whereas the mastery-avoidance goal construct has received only limited attention in the literature, much has been made of the role of performance-approach goals in influencing learning outcomes of late. Based on mounting evidence suggesting a link between performance-approach goals and enhanced achievement, a question was raised as to whether the pursuit of goals focused on outperforming others could, under certain circumstances, be considered adaptive (Harackiewicz, Barron, Pintrich, Elliot, & Thrash, 2002).

When considering the approach and avoidance dimensions of performance goals, there is, indeed, support for the claim that the detrimental effects of performance goals are generally more observed when students pursue performance-*avoidance* goals. As reported earlier, in our own research, performance-avoidance goals were found to predict higher levels of anxiety and lower levels of achievement, as well as use of superficial learning strategies, or worse yet, to be unrelated to the use of any cognitive and metacognitive strategies. In contrast, the pursuit of a performance-approach goal, where students are focused on besting others or demonstrating their competence to others, was not found to be related to any negative outcomes. As in previous research, we did not find any links between performance-approach goals and both course-related and test-related anxiety levels (Rhee et al., 2005)

We nevertheless believe that the current research does not provide overwhelming evidence to support the notion that performance-approach goals are necessarily *good* for achievement. While we did find a positive main effect of performance-approach goals on course performance, we believe this finding to represent a classical suppression effect given that the zero-order correlation between performance-approach goals and achievement was close to zero. In fact, since we determined performance-avoidance goals to be the main suppressor, we believe the only claim that can be made from this finding is that students who adopt "approach" goals generally do better than students who adopt "avoidance" goals. It is important to note that this suppression effect has been found in other studies as well (Elliot & McGregor, 1999; Elliot et al, 1999). For example, Elliot and McGregor (1999) reported a modest zero-order correlation between exam performance and performance-approach goals ($r = .09$), but a positive standardized regression weight for performance-approach goals on exam performance ($\beta = .24$). Similarly, Elliot et al (1999) also report minimal zero-order correlations between exam performance and performance-approach goals ($r = .08$) but report performance-approach goals to positively predict students' exam performance in regression analyses ($\beta = .17$).

So are performance goals adaptive? The results from this study do not particularly support nor discount such a claim. Rather, the strongest statement we can make based on our data and others is that the consequences are much worse for those students who pursue performance-avoidance goals than those who pursue performance-approach goals. We must acknowledge, however, that in stating thus, it does not necessarily follow that performance-approach goals are indeed *adaptive*. Given the fact that competition is, for better or for worse, still valued in our society, we would instead argue that the pursuit of approach-related goals at the *individual* level, whether mastery- or performance-oriented in nature, is probably better than the pursuit of avoidance-related personal goals. That said, it is not our intention to recommend to teachers that performance goals should be emphasized in their classrooms. In fact, we suspect that in comparison to a mastery goal structure, a performance-oriented classroom would still be more likely to foster the endorsement of avoidance goals, thereby underscoring the importance of mastery-oriented practices. Thus, the distinction here is between performance goals at the individual and classroom level, and it would be important for future research to examine this difference more closely.

THE PURSUIT OF MULTIPLE GOALS

Two main issues distinguish the contemporary research in achievement goal theory from the normative or traditional perspective. The first is, as mentioned above, the assumption that performance goals are not always detrimental to learning. The second concerns the adoption of multiple goal orientations. The notion that individuals often pursue multiple goals is certainly not a new one and has long been accepted among those who research goals in general (e.g., Ford, 1992; Pervin, 1989). However, much of the early work in the field of achievement goal theory characterized students as being *either* mastery- or performance-oriented; very little was said about the possibility of students endorsing varying levels of both of these goals (for exception see Dweck & Elliott, 1983). Thus, one of the hallmarks of the multiple goals perspective of achievement goal theory, which subsumes the work on the 2 × 2 goal framework, is that individuals can embrace varying levels of both mastery and performance goals (see Harackiewicz, Barron, Pintrich, Elliot, & Thrash, 2002). More particularly, it is assumed that students who endorse the approach forms of both mastery- and performance-goals might display the most adaptive patterns of motivation and achievement. From this perspective, one would expect to find positive intercorrelations among the achievement goal constructs, especially among those goals that share either a valence or definitional component.

Barron and Harackiewicz (2001) have proffered several hypotheses to explain how multiple goal adoption might function. First, the *additive* hypothesis proposes that mastery and performance-approach goals could each have a positive effect on certain outcomes. Within an empirical study, this hypothesis would be supported if one observed a main effect for both mastery and performance goals on adaptive outcomes, such as achievement or interest. Second, the *interactive* hypothesis suggests that students high in both mastery and performance goals would display the most adaptive patterns of learning and motivation to the extent that these students would benefit from the positive effects of both of these goals. This hypothesis would be supported if one found significant interaction effects between these two goals on positive outcome measures, such that the combination of high mastery-approach and performance-approach goals would exhibit more adaptive outcomes above those of additive effect. The third hypothesis, called the *specialized* hypothesis predicts that mastery and performance goals each have independent effects on different adaptive outcomes. For example, mastery goals may be a better predictor of interest, while performance goals may be a better predictor of achievement.

Indeed, these comprehensive hypotheses have been influential in providing a theoretical framework for work on multiple goals. Nevertheless, it is important to note that in proposing these hypotheses, the authors were assuming that the endorsement of a performance goal where students are focused on besting others (i.e., performance-approach goals) is not necessarily detrimental to learning outcomes. More importantly, they did not consider the role of avoidance goals. Rather, their hypotheses refer mainly to the simultaneous adoption of mastery-approach and performance-approach goals. Accordingly, it should be worthwhile for future research to consider what the implications of their hypotheses are for avoidance goals.

At present, there are varying degrees of support for each of the proposed hypotheses. Generally speaking, although not always consistent, we found, more often than not, more than one goal to be a significant predictor of an outcome. In line with our predictions, we typically found goals that shared a dimension to predict an outcome similarly. For example, we found performance-avoidance and mastery-avoidance goals to be positive predictors of anxiety; we also found mastery-approach and mastery-avoidance goals to be associated with reported increases in use of deeper-processing cognitive strategies. Such findings might suggest that when considering both approach and avoidance goals, the distinction between the additive and specialized hypotheses may not be as important.

Despite the straightforward nature of the theoretical assumption that the concomitant adoption of mastery-approach and performance-approach goals should be most adaptive, our research does not provide strong support for the interactive hypothesis. Across the chemistry and psychology studies, we investigated interactions between goals that shared the valence dimension (i.e., mastery-approach x performance-approach; mastery-avoidance x performance-avoidance), and found no significant interaction effects. However, we relied mainly on hierarchical regression analyses. Future research would benefit from conducting more person-centered analyses (e.g., cluster analysis) to investigate this general hypothesis.

COLLEGE STUDENTS' HELP SEEKING

College students frequently seek help when encountering difficulties with comprehension or poor performance, which can range from asking a classmate for an assignment due the next day to attending remedial sessions prior to an exam. Models of the help-seeking process propose a number of stages and decision points that determine how learners cope with difficulties, which may or may not result in students seeking help (Gross & McMullen, 1983; Nelson-Le Gall, 1981; Newman, 1998). Although varying in certain details, the models share common elements, including: (a) the occurrence of a precipitating event (e.g., receiving an exam grade), (b) determining if a problem exists, (c) determining whether help is needed, (d) assessment of the costs and benefits of seeking and not seeking help, (e) the decision to seek or not seek help, (f) identification of helping resources (e.g., teachers, other students), (g) deciding on the type of help to ask for, (h) planning ways to solicit that help, (i) obtaining help, and (j) processing the help received. There is no presumption that these events occur in sequence, or even that learners are mindful of the steps involved. In that respect, the help-seeking process is a prime example of a blend of automatic and controlled cognitive processing and related emotions (e.g., Barone, Maddux, & Snyder, 1997; Hassan, Uleman, & Bargh, 2005). For example, the first conscious experience could be deciding whether to seek help, and the choice of helpers (e.g., teachers or other students) could occur prior to or after weighing the costs and benefits of doing so.

HELP-SEEKING NEED, BEHAVIOR, AND INTENTIONS

Before discussing the research findings, it is important to explicate why knowing the level of learners' need for help is critical for understanding the help-seeking process (Karabenick, 1996). For example, consider whether students ask questions in class. Not asking questions may mean: (a) that students have no need to because (hopefully) they comprehend the lecture or the assigned reading, (b) they understand very little and need to ask but cannot formulate a reasonable question, or (c) they understand enough to formulate a question but perceive the instructor to be unresponsive to questions or even punitive when students do so (Karabenick & Sharma, 1994). When students do ask, we could infer a lack of comprehension—and therefore need—but that is not definitive because students may have asked questions for other reasons, possibly to be ingratiating.

Research on help seeking has dealt with the issue of need in a number of ways: manipulating need by controlling performance levels (e.g., Newman, 2000), making reasonable inferences based on naturally occurring performance levels, or self-reported level of need. As an example of inferred and self-reported need, Karabenick & Knapp (1988b) found the incidence of academic-related help seeking by college students to be a curvilinear (inverted-U) function of academic performance. Students in the C− to B+ range of performance reported the highest rates of help seeking whereas those at the high and low ends of the performance continuum reported the lowest levels. Because students' self-reported need for help was a monotonic inverse of academic performance, it was inferred that high performing students did not seek help because doing so was unnecessary, mid-level performing students apparently were both above some threshold level of need and sufficiently motivated to seek help, whereas very low performers needed help but were apparently not appropriately motivated to seek it.

Help-seeking research has also made extensive use of behavioral intentions, that is, students' reported likelihood of seeking help contingent on the need for help. With this approach, the level of need is effectively controlled for as learners report what they would do *if* they needed help. Evidence indicates that such need-contingent self-reports are equivalent to asking students whether they would seek help (not contingent on need) and statistically controlling for their reported level of need for help (Karabenick & Knapp, 1991). As surmised in the Karabenick and Knapp study described above, for example, high performing students reported low levels of help seeking because they didn't need to; however, such students generally indicate they would be more likely to seek help when necessary than would poorer performing students.

It is therefore important whether studies of help seeking are based on asking students whether they did seek help, would seek help, or asking whether they would if necessary. For example, evidence indicates that students who report they would seek help when needed are also more likely to self-regulate in other ways (i.e., use cognitive and metacognitive strategies)—better students are also more likely to seek needed help (Karabenick & Knapp, 1991). More self-regulating students are not more likely to actually seek help, however, because employing those strategies decreases their need for help. As discussed above, even direct observations of whether college students seek help may not be as informative as it might seem in the absence of need-related information. To compound matters, whereas some college student help seeking may be observable, for example as question asking in classrooms, most help-seeking interaction probably occur in non-classroom settings. Self-reports may be problematic (e.g., Schwartz, 1999) but nevertheless especially useful when examining college student help seeking, and of these, likelihood estimates that control for need levels are especially informative and the most widely used in field research.

HELP-SEEKING GOALS

As discussed earlier, help seeking traditionally signified dependency and therefore was believed to be incompatible with achievement (Beller, 1957; Winterbottom, 1958), until the shift to a strategic view of help seeking that began with Nelson-Le Gall's distinction between instrumental and executive help-seeking goals. Similarly, Nadler (1983, 1998) proposed distinctions between achievement-motivated behavior that fosters independence and that which perpetuates dependency (Nadler, 1983). The link between achievement motivation and help seeking has also been analyzed within achievement attribution theory (e.g., Weiner, 1974). According to this approach, help seeking should be more likely for learners who believe they are generally capable but lack specific knowledge or skills, and that failure is due to lack of effort. By contrast, lower rates of help seeking would be expected for learners with internal, stable beliefs about their lack of ability and that outcomes are a function of luck or others' arbitrary actions (Ames & Lau, 1983).

More recently, Butler (1998) has identified three help-seeking orientations, which have implications for how students cope with learning and performance difficulties. As with instrumental help-seeking goals, students with an autonomous help-seeking orientation are focused on understanding and increased competency. By contrast, the concern of those with an ability-focused help-seeking orientation is in not appearing incompetent. Such learners take fewer risks to acquire the help they need. An expedient orientation is similar to Nelson-Le Gall's goal of executive help seeking, with students lightening their own burden by taking advantage of others. Among Butler's important contributions are the implications of each orientation for when and how help seeking is expressed. Each orientation implies a different resolution regarding help seeking—whether or not and how to seek help. For example, depending on the circumstances, students with an autonomous orientation may not seek help if that option is believed to increase understandings that would ultimately be more beneficial, and those with an ability orientation may cheat if that can mask their inadequacies.

Help seeking can also be characterized by whether it is adaptive, an assessment that builds on the help-seeking models described earlier. Similar to Nelson-Le Gall's instrumental goal and Butler's autonomous orientation, an adaptive help seeker begins by accurately assessing that help is necessary (i.e., good metacognitive calibration), then formulates an appropriate request for help, understands the best help resources available, designs strategies for successful requests, and productively processes the help received, that is, increases their understanding and mastery of the material or the ability to solve problems when future difficulties arise (Newman, 1994, 1998). Newman's adaptive model provides yet another version of the strategic perspective that views help seeking from a self-regulatory perspective.

As with other self-regulated learning strategies, most recent research on help seeking has been conducted within the framework of achievement goal theory, which includes personal goal orientations and students' perceptions of the classroom achievement goal structure (e.g., Midgley, 2002), to which we now turn. Although much of this research has focused on elementary and middle school students, conclusions based on younger learners, and grade- and age-related trends, provides the foundation for understanding the help seeking of college students.

HELP SEEKING AND ACHIEVEMENT GOAL ORIENTATIONS

Associations between achievement goal orientations and help-seeking are now well understood (Arbreton, 1993, 1998; Butler & Neuman, 1995; Karabenick, 2003; Newman, 1991, 1994; Ryan, Hicks, & Midgley, 1997; Ryan & Pintrich, 1997, 1998). Studies have consistently shown that mastery approach goal orientation levels are directly related to instrumental/adaptive help-seeking, and inversely related to help-seeking threat, help-seeking avoidance, and expedient or executive help seeking. Consistently as well, both performance-approach and avoidance, as well as mastery-avoidance goal orientations are generally directly related to help-seeking threat, help-seeking avoidance, and a preference for expedient help seeking goals. However, performance goal orientations and instrumental help seeking tend to be unrelated (Arbreton, 1993; Karabenick, 2003; Ryan & Pintrich, 1997). Similarly, in the study of college students reported in this chapter (see Karabenick, 2004), seeking need-contingent autonomous help from teachers (designated an approach help-seeking pattern) was directly related to mastery-approach goal orientation levels. By contrast an avoidance pattern, which consisted of experiencing help seeking as threatening, intentions to avoid seeking needed help, and the preference for executive help, was related to levels of mastery-avoidance, performance-approach, and performance-avoidance achievement goal orientations. Thus, relations between achievement goal orientations and help seeking are similar for college students and younger learners.

In a companion study, Karabenick (2003) used cluster analysis and identified four homogeneous student groups. These groups were characterized as follows: (a) strategic/adaptive students who were likely to seek needed help from their teachers; (b) strategic/adaptive students who preferred to approach other students for help; (c) non-strategic students who were low in their tendencies to seek help; and (d) help-seeking avoidant or expedient help seekers. Strategic/adaptive students who preferred asking teachers for help were more adaptively motivated, had higher mastery approach achievement goal levels, used cognitive strategies related to performance, and had higher levels of performance. By contrast, help seeking avoidant students were more anxious, performed more poorly, and had higher mastery-avoidance, performance-approach, and performance-avoidance achievement goal orientations. These results are consistent with those based on variable-centered analyses (e.g., factor analysis) and indicate how person-centered approaches using cluster, or more recently latent class analysis (see Niemivirta, 2002), show promise in identifying characteristic ways that college students seek help.

SEEKING HELP FROM FORMAL AND INFORMAL RESOURCES

Depending on their circumstances, learners have a variety of helping resources available to them, which research has generally divided into formal and informal categories (Knapp & Karabenick, 1988; Karabenick & Knapp, 1988b). Formal help denotes professionals or individuals with authority or in institutionally defined roles, such as teachers and academic advisors. Informal sources are not in those roles such as class members or other peers. In an examination of the incidence of formal and informal academic help seeking among college students, Knapp & Karabenick (1988) surveyed students in general psychology courses to determine the extent of their need for assistance in that course. If students indicated a need for help, they were asked if they had sought help, and from whom from a list of possible help sources. Formal sources included their course professor, student tutors and various official support centers. Informal sources were friends or other students. Student self-reports indicated that informal sources of help were contacted more frequently than formal sources.

Evidence generally suggests that college students tend to under-utilize academic support services (Karabenick & Knapp, 1988b; Abrams & Jernigan, 1984). One reason is that such services often require scheduled appointments and have scheduled meeting times or other formal arrangements; whereas informal sources are more accessible. For this reason many academic support programs attempt to make formal help services as informal and accessible as possible, including providing online assistance (see subsequent discussion of computers and information rich contexts). In a typical example, the Sweetland Writing Center, an academic support program at the University of Michigan offers email submission of writing assignment drafts, which allows tutors to quickly assess and give feedback on writing assignments.

Alexitch (2006) examined formal (i.e., institutionally-provided) helping resources in higher education contexts that provide guidance, direction, and strategies to help students succeed. These sources include faculty, academic advisors, career counsellors, and program advisors. At issue is what academic advisors and faculty could do to meet the needs of students by providing effective help. Alexitch suggests strategies for reaching students with a variety of advising goals, as well as those who avoid advising entirely.

One important reason why students approach each other for help rather than instructors or advisors involves reduced evaluation-based threat. Grayson, Miller, and Clark (1998) interviewed students about their experiences with seeking advice from instructors and found that students were concerned with how their instructors viewed them (a form of help-seeking threat). In response, many support programs now enlist the help of college students in the role of peer advisors—undergraduate students who are trained to advise, tutor and even counsel other students. Peer advisors often share many experiences with students (e.g., living arrangements, knowledge of campus life) and are typically similar in age to those that they help. Because peers can play important roles in student adjustment (Thomas, 2000), peer advisors are thought to be especially effective in helping students.

Collins and Sims (2006) examined college orientation and other transition programs that make available to students valuable resources and on-campus support. The underlying purpose is to give students the skills and motivation to ask for help rather than fail in isolation. The authors discuss implications of the help-seeking literature for these programs. According to Collins and Sims, an important route to students' willingness to ask for help is their understanding of the reasons for and means of doing so. As noted earlier, it would also be important that support service personnel be able to identify the various forms of help seeking and have an awareness of the kinds of obstacles that may make it less likely students will ask for help. Collins and Sims describe a specific high school to college transition program that, evidence suggests, accomplishes many of these objectives, which includes building self-regulated learning skills.

CLASSROOM INFLUENCES ON STUDENT MOTIVATION AND HELP SEEKING

One of the important assumptions of our theoretical model is that motivational and self-regulatory processes are heavily dependent upon characteristics of the learning context. To this end, we examine, in this section, the role of classroom contextual factors, beginning with a discussion on the measurement of context, followed by a general overview of our research findings in this area, concluding with a review of the research on the relations between contextual measures and help seeking.

MEASUREMENT OF CLASSROOM CONTEXT

One of the greatest challenges facing the research on classroom context is the operationalization and measurement of "context". Figure 5 depicts a general conceptualization of this area of research. As a first level of organization, we distinguish between "subjective" and "objective" measures of the classroom environment. Subjective measures include the use of self-report surveys and interviews, while objective measures primarily refer to classroom observations. The goal, here, is the triangulation of data; it is believed that use of these varied

635

Figure 5: Measurement of Classrom Context.

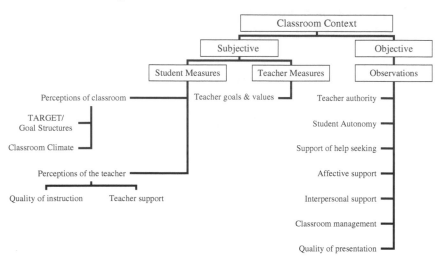

approaches can serve to verify the accuracy of subjective measures and provide a richer portrait of classroom processes (Ryan, Gheen, & Midgley, 1998; Urdan, Midgley, and Anderman, 1998).

Turner and Meyer (2000) discuss the advantages and disadvantages of self-reports, observations, and interview protocols in classroom context research. Self-reports such as surveys and questionnaires are often used to measure students' and teachers' beliefs, behaviors, strategies, and affect. As such, the individual's perception is what is important in drawing conclusions about the situation or context. Observation methods assume that the teachers' behaviors and discourse have a direct influence on student outcomes; therefore, these studies may use behavior checklists for identifying target behaviors that occur during a given period. Observation methods may also utilize more narrative systems, or the use of running records in which detailed descriptions of classroom occurrences are recorded for subsequent analysis. Finally, interview methods can range from highly structured interviews with predetermined questions, to unstructured formats in which the subjects are simply asked to tell their stories with few prompts from the interviewer.

In general, classroom contextual measures (be it subjective or objective; classroom-focused or teacher-focused) typically provide evidence regarding two general categories of classroom or instructional context: climate and structure (Ames, 1992; Linnenbrink & Pintrich, 2001; Turner & Meyer, 2000). Classroom climate refers to the affective tone or mood of the classroom (Linnenbrink & Pintrich, 2001) and also encompasses teacher expectations, beliefs and feedback (Turner & Meyer, 2000). Apart from the climate literature from decades ago (e.g., Moos, 1978; Trickett & Moos, 1973) there is relatively little research actually examining classroom climate.

By contrast, classroom structure has received much of the attention. Linnenbrink & Pintrich (2001) refer to classroom structure as the routines, rules, tasks, and evaluations that a teacher establishes. Goal theorists frequently refer to the TARGET framework – six dimensions originally identified by Epstein (1989) of teacher practices that influence the classroom goal structure (Ames, 1992; Patrick, Anderman, Ryan, Edelin, & Midgley, 2001; Pintrich & Schunk, 2002; Maehr & Midgley, 1996): classroom *task* or learning activity design; distribution of *authority* between teachers and students; *recognition* by way of rewards and incentives; students' abilities and opportunities to work with others in *groups*; the methods of *evaluation* for assessing student learning; and the allotment of *time* for allowing students to complete work, including the pace of instruction and the appropriateness of students' workload.

Research suggests that depending on teachers' instructional practices regarding these six dimensions in their classroom, students may perceive the goal structure to be more or less mastery- or performance-oriented (Ames, 1992; Maehr & Midgley, 1996; Patrick et al., 2001; Pintrich & Schunk, 2002). For example, teachers may emphasize competition by congratulating high achieving students in front of the class, communicating to students that they should demonstrate their own ability and outperform their classmates (i.e., a performance goal structure). Teachers can stress understanding and personal improvement by recognizing students for their effort or by encouraging students to help one another (i.e., a mastery goal structure). These structural characteristics represent features of the classroom that are evident not only to students, but to observers as well. To this end, contextual measures of classroom structure are typically assessed through student self-reports and classroom observations.

Empirical findings of studies that examine the influence of students' perceptions of the goal structure on various student outcomes generally follow a similar pattern to early goal research in that perceptions of mastery goal structures lead to positive outcomes, whereas perceptions of performance goal structures lead to negative outcomes. Stipek and her colleagues found that particular instructional practices consistent with mastery goal emphases such as focusing on learning and understanding, encouraging risk-taking and self-confidence among students, and cultivating an enjoyment of mathematics, were related to positive motivation in upper-elementary mathematics classrooms (Stipek et al., 1998). Ames and Archer (1988) found that when students perceived a mastery goal structure in their classroom, they were more likely to report using adaptive learning strategies, take risks with challenging tasks, report higher enjoyment of class, and believe that success was due to effort. Perceptions of mastery goal structures has also been linked to such adaptive outcomes as increased likelihood to seek help, to be discussed in greater detail subsequently (Karabenick, 2004; Ryan et al., 1998), and decreased likelihood of self-handicapping behavior (Midgley & Urdan, 2001).

In contrast, perceptions of a performance goal structure in the classroom have been linked to negative outcomes. Perceived performance goal structures tend to focus on normative ability comparisons, in which failure is often attributed to an "uncontrollable" locus such as lack of ability, rather than a more "controllable" factor such as effort. Making such failure attributions may lead students to avoid taking risks or pursuing challenging tasks. Turner et al. (2003) suggest that classrooms in which performance goals are perceived to be emphasized are more likely to view mistakes as related to lower ability, which would lead to negative affect for failure. Students perceiving a performance goal structure are less likely to seek help (Karabenick, 2004; Ryan et al., 1998), more likely to use self-handicapping strategies (Midgley & Urdan, 2001), and more likely to rate their competence as lower (Stipek & Daniels, 1988). Finally, Church et al. (2001) found that perceptions of performance goal structures were associated with the use of harsh evaluation standards (part of the TARGET framework), which was more likely to lead the student to not only adopt performance-avoidance goals but also possibly even inhibit mastery goal adoption.

Despite these negative outcomes associated with performance goal structures, Ames and Archer (1988) found that, with younger aged children, it was the degree to which students perceived a mastery climate that was predictive of students' subsequent behaviors and beliefs. "This suggests that the presence of performance cues may not inhibit some aspects of achievement behavior when mastery cues are salient" (p. 265). Therefore, they suggested not necessarily discouraging performance goals in the classroom, but simply encouraging mastery goals might be sufficient for adaptive outcomes. This argument would be consistent with the multiple goals framework of achievement goal theory that proposes that simultaneously adopting both mastery and performance goals might be most beneficial for student outcomes (Barron & Harackiewicz, 2001). Turner et al. (2003) suggested that a classroom environment that "emphasizes both mastery goals, including support for effort and value for learning, and performance goals, or support for high achievement, would be expected to support students' approach behaviors" (p. 361). Their findings were consistent with this hypothesis, in that a high-mastery/high-performance pattern facilitated an adaptive motivational pattern within the perceived classroom goal structure. In another study, Turner and her colleagues found that perceptions of a performance goal structure were unrelated to students' reports of avoidance behaviors, which further lends credence to Ames and Archer (1988) suggestion that a focus on reducing a performance goal structure may not be necessary when fostering a mastery goal structure (Turner et al., 2002). However, these studies were with younger students, and the results may not generalize to college students populations.

The vast majority of studies that investigate the role of classroom goal structure use only the mastery/performance dichotomy. A limited number of studies assess perceptions of both classroom performance-approach and classroom performance-avoidance goal structures; however, in most of these studies, the performance-approach and performance-avoidance scales were either collapsed to a single classroom performance scale (Karabenick, Zusho, & Kempler, 2005), classroom performance-avoidance items were dropped from analyses (Wolters, 2004), or perceptions of classroom performance-avoidance goal structures were not found to vary significantly between classrooms; thus not warranting its use as a classroom-level variable in subsequent analyses (Kaplan, Gheen, & Midgley, 2002). It is important to note however, that in Karabenick et al.'s (2005) study to be described subsequently in greater detail, although exploratory factor analyses indicated that students did not differentiate between classroom performance-approach and classroom performance-avoidance goals, HLM analyses conducted with the classroom performance goals treated separately indicate that perceived classroom performance-approach and classroom performance-avoidance goals differentially predict college students' help-seeking avoidance. Therefore, results of factor analysis may not be the only criterion for determining the importance of the approach-avoidance distinction in students' perceptions of their college classroom context, which we examine now in greater detail.

THE COLLEGE CLASSROOM CONTEXT

Because most of the empirical work examining these aspects of classroom context has focused on elementary and middle school classrooms, less is known about college classrooms. The college classroom has traditionally been overlooked for two reasons. First, there is an assumption that the interpersonal context in the college classroom is less important than it is for younger children because of the developmental maturity of the students. College classrooms do not have the same social factors that have been shown to influence students early in school (Wentzel, 1997). Second, the traditional image of the college classroom is arguably not one of classroom at all, but rather a large lecture hall with a professor lecturing and students taking notes and very little interaction between students. However, our data challenges this notion of the college classroom context, indicating high levels of student interaction, efforts at interpersonal connection and support on the part of instructors, and varying levels of classroom structure and climate.

Given the challenges inherent in the measurement of context, we were careful to obtain numerous indices, both subjective and objective, of the college classroom environment (see Table 2). In terms of subjective measures, we collected students' perceptions of classroom goal structure, as well as measures of climate such as teacher support of questioning and teacher caring. As for our objective measures, classroom observations were conducted across 13 introductory psychology classrooms. In all, classes were rated along eight dimensions.

Focusing first on the student perception measures, students' mean perceptions of the goal structure and climate at two time points are presented in Figure 6. Several patterns can be discerned here. We detect a statistically significant difference in most of the ratings across time, with students' average ratings at Time 1 exceeding their ratings at Time 2. This difference is most apparent for classroom mastery; perhaps given impending final exams, students were generally found to report that their classroom was less mastery-focused at the end of the semester than at the beginning of the semester. Nevertheless, the general pattern of findings are encouraging; the college students sampled as part of this study typically reported that their classrooms were mastery-focused, and that their instructors encouraged the asking of questions and were generally caring. Correlational analyses further indicated that students who perceived their classroom to be mastery-oriented

Table 2: Contextual Measures

Variables:	Definition	Sample Items
Classroom Perceptions:		
Classroom mastery emphasis	Student's perception that class goal is oriented toward learning and understanding material, and improving skills	In this course, it's important to understand the work, not just memorize it.
Classroom performance emphasis	Student's perception that class goal is focused on besting others, competition for top grades, and demonstrating ability	In this course, it's important to show how smart you are compared to others.
Teacher support of questioning	Student's perception that instructor is willing to answer questions about course material	The instructor provides sufficient time for students to ask questions.
Teacher caring	Student's perception that instructor respects and cares about students and wants to help them learn	The instructor likes to help me learn.
Classroom Observations:		
Teacher as authority	The amount of control the teacher retained over the content and pace of the class, content of lectures/presentations, and types of questions asked to the class	
Student autonomy	The amount of choice and control the students had in determining the pace of the class, the types of activities and work done for the course	
Support of help seeking	How much the teacher supported students questions and their responsiveness to student requests for help or clarification of ideas	
Motivational support for learning	Instructor attempts to motivate students by increasing their interest in the topic (e.g., connect it to their experiences), suggest its utility and importance, and increase efficacy for learning	
Affective support	The extent to which teachers created emotional support for students in general versus a stressful and uncomfortable classroom environment	
Interpersonal support	The interest that teachers showed in students, their lives, and attempts to build some relationships with them	
Classroom management/ discipline	The direction that teachers had over class procedures and whether students talked, acted out, or were paying attention	
Quality of presentation	The instructors' content knowledge and organization of class time	

Figure 6: Average Perceptions of Goal Structure and Climate by Introductory Psychology College Students

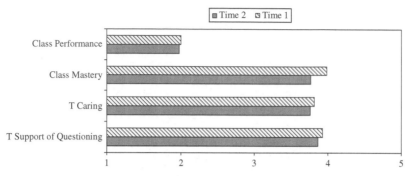

Note: N≈720. Rated on a 5-point scale. T caring = Teacher caring; T support of questioning = Teacher support of Questioning; Difference between Time 1 and Time 2 classroom mastery measure significant at the *p* < .001 level; Differences between Time 1 and Time 2 T caring and T Support of Questioning measures significant at the *p* < .05 level; T1 and T2 class room performance, *ns*

($r = .08$, $p < .05$) and their instructors to be supportive of questioning ($r = .17$, $p < .01$) and caring ($r = .16$, $p < .01$) also received higher grades at the end of the semester. In addition, an inverse relationship between classroom performance emphasis and achievement was found ($r = -.21$, $p < .01$), suggesting that students who perceived their classroom to be performance-oriented were more likely to obtain lower grades.

Similar findings were obtained with the classroom observational measures. The average ratings (on a 5-point scale) of the eight dimensions are presented in Figure 7. Subsequent correlational analyses indicated substantial covariation between the classroom rating dimensions, some of which were found to be statistically significant despite the very low power ($df = 11$). An exploratory factor analysis was conducted to determine whether the dimensions could be treated more parsimoniously; based on this analysis, two scales were constructed by averaging (i.e., unit weighting) the rating dimensions with salient loadings. One labeled "Support" combined Interpersonal Support, Motivational Support, Help-Seeking Support, and Teacher Authority (reverse coded). This dimension summarizes the interpersonal-affective features of the class. The other, labeled "Quality," combined Class Management, Quality of Presentation and Student Autonomy. Because it cross-loaded on both, Affective Support was not included in either scale. Although descriptively related ($r = .30$), the derived indices were substantially (and statistically) independent to suggest they could relate

Figure 7: Average Ratings of Classroom Observation Dimensions.

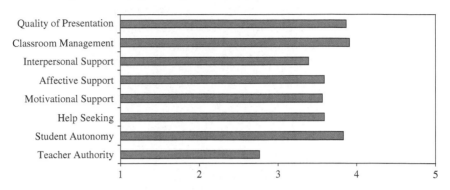

differently to the way students perceived classroom goals and to their motivation and help-seeking orientations.

CLASSROOM CONTEXT AND STUDENT MOTIVATION

While much research has been conducted investigating the influence of classroom context on students' personal goals, it is generally assumed, although rarely studied, that personal goal orientations influence perceptions of classroom goal structures. For example, students with a performance goal orientation may be more sensitive to competition cues in the classroom, causing them to perceive a performance goal structure in the classroom. This relation completes the dynamic cycle of reciprocal influence between personal orientations and perceived contextual goals.

We systematically examined the reciprocal influences of goal orientations and their respective perceived classroom goals with a two-wave longitudinal design. Specifically, mastery-approach, performance-approach, and performance-avoidance goals were assessed at the beginning and end of a single semester in large college classes. A structural model then permitted estimating the direct effects of: a) changes in personal goal orientations over time as a function of classroom perceptions at Time 1, b) changes in perceived goal structure as a function of personal goals at Time 1, and c) differences in the magnitude of these effects. Separate models were estimated for each achievement goal dimension. The design also permitted estimating associations between goal orientations and perceived structure at each time point and the stability of goal orientations and perceived goals structure over time.

Figure 8 presents results of separate structural equation models for each achievement goal orientation and context in the form of perceived achievement goal structure. In each case, fit indices were acceptable (e.g., CFI > .90 and RMSEA < .06), with standardized coefficients shown. Clearly, mastery, performance-approach and performance-avoid personal goal orientations were closely associated with their respective perceived classroom goal structures both at the beginning (T_1) and the end of the term (T_2). Without additional evidence, however, the extent of reciprocal influence is not determinable. The cross-lagged paths (i.e., goal orientations at T_1 to perceived goal structure at T_2 and perceived goal structure at T_1 to goal orientation at T_2) provide such evidence for directional influence.

As shown in Figure 8, in the case of mastery goals, there is no evidence to support influences in either direction. For performance-approach goals, however, evidence suggests that students' perceptions of a classroom performance-approach goal at T_1 influenced the adoption of personal performance-approach goals at T_2, but not the obverse. And for performance-avoidance goals, both cross-lagged paths were statistically significant, indicating that students' perceptions of a classroom performance-avoidance goal structure at T_1 predicted personal performance-avoidance goals at T_2, and also that students' personal performance-avoidance goals at T_1 positively predicted perceptions of classroom performance-avoidance goals at T_2. The present study contributes to the expanding body of evidence on the effects of classroom context (Turner et al., 2002; Urdan, 1997; Volet & Jarvela, 2001). For college students, the effect is present only for performance-avoidance but not mastery or performance-approach goals, which is consistent with previously-reported hierarchical analyses that found no evidence for the effects of perceived classroom mastery goal structure (Karabenick, 2004).

CONTEXTUAL INFLUENCES ON HELP SEEKING

Achievement goal structure. In addition to students' personal goal orientations, there is now considerable evidence that help seeking is influenced by goals emphasized in the learning context. Most of the research to date involves young learners' perceptions of their classes' achievement goal structure (Ames & Archer, 1988; Church, Elliot, & Gable, 2001; Midgley, 2002; Urdan et al., 2002). Studies using appropriate hierarchical modeling procedures (i.e., HLM) have examined students' collective perceptions to assess the effects of between

Figure 8: Results of SEM analysis of personal achievement goal orientations and perceived classroom goal structures with statistically significant paths indicated (*).

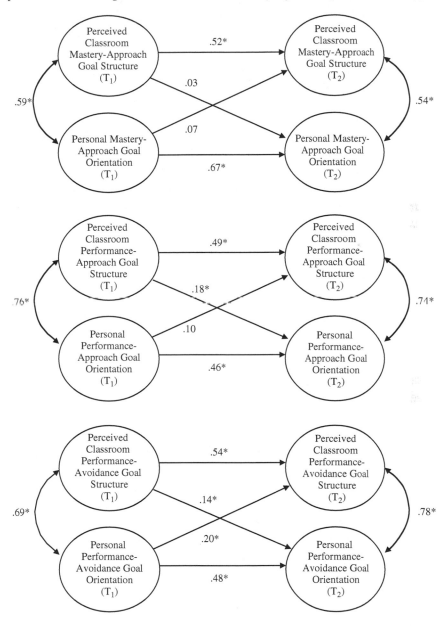

classroom differences. Turner, Midgley, Meyer, Gheen, Anderman, Kang, and Patrick (2002) reported that students in elementary school classes they judged, collectively, as more mastery focused were less likely to report they would avoid seeking needed help (as well as other avoidance behaviors). However, there was no relation between the classes' perceived degree of emphasis on ability (i.e., performance goal structure) and elementary students' reluctance to seek help (Urdan & Midgley, 2003).

With somewhat older middle school students, Ryan, Gheen, and Midgley (1998) also found the association between perceived mastery and intentions to seek needed help. In addition, help seeking avoidance was higher in classes that students perceived, collectively, as more performance focused, which the authors attributed to greater emphasis on evaluation in middle schools. Similarly, in a study of high school as well as middle school students, Karabenick, Zusho, & Kempler (2005) also reported that between classroom differences in perceived mastery goal structure (as well as their perceptions of the degree of academic press) were directly related to the likelihood that students would seek autonomous/instrumental help from their teachers. In addition, reluctance to seek needed help was directly related to students' (collective) perceptions of their classes' emphasis on performance avoidance goal structure (i.e., avoiding revealing the lack of ability) but not performance approach goal structure (i.e., desire to demonstrate high ability). Thus, both perceived mastery and performance classroom emphasis influence the help-seeking tendencies of middle and high school students. For college students, however, there is not evidence for the differential effect of differences in class and teacher emphasis on mastery. Whereas Karabenick (2004) found that perceptions of psychology classes as more performance avoidance focused were more likely to engage in a pattern of help-seeking avoidance, there was no detectable influence of perceived differences between classes in perceived emphasis on mastery.

Taken together, therefore, there is clear evidence for the increasing effects on the avoidance of help seeking of students' perceptions of their classes' emphasis on performance as they progress through the grades, and decreasing influence of perceived mastery goal structures. This pattern reflects the increasing focus on evaluation that begins in middle school. With respect to instruction in college classes, these results should not be interpreted to indicate that a focus on learning and improvement is unimportant. Rather, they suggest that students are particularly sensitive to teaching practices and related features of instruction that foreground lack of ability and normative judgments— a focus on avoiding performing worse than others. And apparently, students can, collectively, perceive differences between classes in the relative degree of emphasis on performance-avoidance goals. Students in high performance-avoidance classes are less likely to seek the help they need as a consequence.

Perceived teacher support. In addition to perceptions of the achievement goal structure of classes, there is also evidence that students' perceptions of teacher support influence whether and how they seek or avoid seeking help. In a large study of middle and high school students ($N > 14,000$), classes in which teachers were perceived as more supportive (a composite measure that combines perceived teacher support for student collaboration and student questioning, teacher fairness and respect and caring) were also more likely to indicate they would seek adaptive help when necessary and less likely to avoid seeking needed help (Karabenick et al., 2005). Effects of perceived support of student questioning—one of the components of teacher support—have also been found for college students (Karabenick & Sharma, 1994). Using structural equation modeling (i.e., SEM) with classroom ($N = 67$) as the level of analysis, there was evidence that students' perceived teacher support of questioning had an indirect influence on the likelihood that students would ask questions. Specifically, perceived teacher support had a direct effect on whether students had a question to ask (which directly predicted their intentions to ask questions) and inversely influenced their inhibition to ask questions, which in turn predicted (inversely) students' intentions to ask questions. Thus college students in classes that, collectively, perceived their teachers as more supportive were more likely to have questions, less inhibited to ask them, and thus more likely to ask questions when necessary.

Analyses of the support of questioning scale in that study also pointed to two practices that were particularly important in students' judgments of whether their instructors were supportive: providing students with the opportunity to ask questions (e.g., wait time), and how elaborate were teachers' responses to questions. Of lesser or no importance were whether teachers instructed students to ask questions or told them questions were important, rewarded them (or not) for asking, or responded emotionally (positively or negatively) when questions were asked. Thus teachers demonstrate their commitment to student questioning by allowing themselves to be interrupted when presenting material and by taking the time to provide extended and elaborative responses to questions that are asked.

Help seeking in and by groups. Despite the voluminous collaborative learning literature, and although typically part of the collaborative

647

process, help seeking has generally not been isolated for examination in studies of group performance. Recently, however, Webb, Ing, Kersting, and Nemer (2006) reanalyzed studies of small group collaboration in classrooms to focus on relationships between giving and receiving help, subsequent activity that processes the help received, and learning outcomes. Among their conclusions were: (a) that negative group process (e.g., put-downs, insults) was linked to reduced help seeking, and (b) help seeking in groups is influenced by the classroom culture within which collaboration occurs; that is, it would be difficult for facilitative collaboration in general, and help seeking in particular, to flourish in otherwise performance-focused learning contexts. Therefore, consistent with previously cited studies of classroom context (e.g., Karabenick, 2004; Ryan et al., 1998; Turner et al., 2002), help seeking when collaborating is more likely when the overall instructional context emphasizes understanding rather just correct answers, that fosters communication and the acceptability of error, and that encourages sharing of ideas (Cobb, Wood, & Yackel, 1993; Wood, Cobb, & Yackel, 1991). There are other strategies for increasing students' ability and willingness to ask questions in groups, such as reciprocal questioning (King, 1992, 1999) and other practices that reduce the risks of help seeking (Schoenfeld, 1987). Further, the overall classroom context and collaborative experiences are likely to be mutually reinforcing rather than isolated and discontinuous, and features of both determine whether that reciprocity facilitates or impedes adaptive help seeking.

In addition to help seeking by individuals within groups is that of groups seeking assistance from an external source, a frequent necessity in organizational settings as well as schools (Sandoval & Lee, 2006), which if not utilized effectively can have disastrous consequences (e.g., the Challenger space shuttle tragedy described by Capers & Lipton, 1993). The likely resource in K-12 school settings is of course the classroom teacher; additional sources of help are college students in work groups (Volet & Ang, 1998). As with any group decision, whether and in what form to seek help involves many of the within-group processes discussed above, which include students' individual experiences and intentions to seek help. We could predict that groups of students all of whom tend to seek adaptive help individually should be similarly likely when in groups. Groups of students with avoidance tendencies should likewise reflect individual help seeking tendencies. The consequences for groups with mixed approaches to help seeking would be more difficult to predict, and as noted above, characteristics of the learning context would also matter.

These predictions were tested in an experimental analog of group help seeking in the classroom, Karabenick and Newman (2004) assigned college students, pre-assessed for their individual differences to avoid help seeking, were assigned to dyads instructed to solve difficult word problems, which resulted in failure experiences. Pairs of students performed either under mastery or performance achievement goal conditions during which they could ask for assistance from an external source. In general, help seeking was more prevalent under mastery achievement goal conditions, which stressed the importance of learning and improvement, than under performance goal conditions that emphasized ability and competition with other dyads. Results were that both the achievement goal conditions and individual tendencies to avoid seeking help interacted to determine the incidence of group help seeking. Most intriguing was that dyads in which both members were classified as high in help-seeking threat asked for just as much help under performance as under mastery achievement goal conditions. When one dyad member was high in threat, however, group help seeking was less frequent under performance than under mastery conditions. This suggested that, when conditions emphasized that performance was diagnostic of ability, the threat posed by students who sought help as individuals was mitigated when shared with similarly threatened others (e.g., Amoroso & Walters, 1969). The frequency of group help seeking, as well as discourse analysis of the dyads as they performed the task, provided support for a diffusion of threat model of collaborative help seeking. Further studies of this phenomenon are warranted given how often collaborative learning is employed in higher education instructional settings, which would predict that highly threatened students working collaboratively would be more likely to ask their instructors or other outside sources for help than the students would when working alone.

FUTURE DIRECTIONS FOR RESEARCH

Although the research reviewed in this chapter represents a promising start, studies in the fields of motivation and self-regulated learning remain inherently biased toward K-12 students and classrooms. We believe this is due, in part, to the faulty assumption that students who attend college represent the privileged few, and generally only those who are "motivated" attend college. However, with more and more jobs requiring a college education or beyond, it is clear that college is increasingly viewed by many no longer as a luxury but as a necessity. For this reason, further studies on this population certainly seemed warranted. We thus present in this section our recommendations for future research in the areas of motivation, self-regulated learning, and context.

In terms of motivation, achievement goal theory is predicated on the assumption that when it comes to learning outcomes, mastery and performance goals (regardless of valence) are important determinants of learning outcomes. Accordingly, most studies on achievement goals ask participants to indicate their level of agreement to statements believed to assess these predefined goals. Researchers rarely ask students to report, in an open-ended fashion, the goals that they set for a specific course or task. As a result, an important question remains as to whether or not college students would spontaneously report endorsing such goals. Despite the attention performance-approach goals have received in the literature, strong evidence does not exist that students generally set and pursue such goals (Brophy, 2005). For example, to what extent will students actually admit that their goal is to impress the teacher, or to not look dumb in front of other students? Emerging evidence also seems to suggest that those students who do report adopting performance goals do so for various reasons, which often are at odds with researchers' interpretations of these goals (Urdan & Mestas, 2006).

Karabenick and Woolley (2006) have extended concerns about researchers' interpretations of performance goal scores more broadly to motivation-related assessment in general. At issue is whether items used to assess such constructs as goal orientations or classroom context convey intended meanings to respondents. Coding of content elicited through cognitive interviewing procedures (similar to cognitive pretesting) revealed that many middle school students interpreted and responded to numerous scale items at variance with researchers' assumptions. Such evidence raises questions about the interpretations of scores derived from motivation-related scales, notwithstanding other psychometric evidence of scale reliability and validity. Although some of the middle school students' misinterpretations can be explained by the limited vocabulary of younger children, it nevertheless suggests that research with college students employ similar procedures to assess what these authors term cognitive validity, as a way to ensure the construct validity of motivation-related scales used in this domain of research. Such questions represent important lines for future research in this area of inquiry.

Another promising avenue of research is the influence of information and computer technologies (ICT) on learning. From Power-Point presentations to interactive software, the use of technology is becoming increasingly evident in the college classroom. For example, it is often difficult to estimate the impact of ICT on help seeking. Access to information from archival sources (Wikipedia, Google), from other individuals, and from intelligent systems has dramatically altered the help-seeking landscape (Keefer & Karabenick, 1998). Computer-mediated communication (CMC) provides a seemingly unlimited supply of individuals and virtual communities that are potential sources of assistance and information, and the cost (time, effort) of seeking help via CMC is dramatically decreased. In addition to decreased cost, CMC contexts can facilitate help seeking as a function of real or perceived anonymity and by the reduction or elimination of social status cues that may be threatening (Karabenick & Knapp, 1988b). The ubiquity of course management systems (e.g., Blackboard) in higher education has accelerated the formal use of CMC.

Furthermore, automated learning systems have been a feature of the educational landscape for some time, and more sophisticated and intelligent interactive learning environments (ILEs) that respond to changing learner characteristics are increasingly available. Among the most recent innovations are intelligent tutoring systems that use performance information not only to adjust task difficulty (as in adaptive testing) but also to adjust to learner responses and provide online tutoring and help. Recent innovations are based on comprehensive models of the help-seeking process (Aleven, McLaren, & Koedinger, 2006; Aleven, Stahl, Schworm, Fischer, & Wallace, 2003). With these systems, not only is the help offered context dependent, learners can also select different types of help (e.g., answers or hints). Although presently used primarily in mathematics by younger learners, successful implementation of the cognitive tutor paradigm will undoubtedly become increasingly available to college students and in multiple content domains.

One consequence of work with CMC and ILEs is that, increasingly, intelligent help systems pose conceptual challenges regarding the definition of help seeking itself (Keefer & Karabenick, 1998). If we assume that help seeking is a social-interactive process, then how do we classify obtaining "help" from intelligent systems? One resolution is to focus on whether the system is implicitly social. This comes from the definition of social influences, which is typically whether the "others" influencing behavior are real, imagined, or implied. In other words, it may not matter whether those "others" are present at the time learners opt to receive artificial help but rather whether traces of that act—what is potentially disclose—would be subject to social influences. In that regard, ILEs raise the issue of how college students, as well as younger learners, construe seeking help from artificial sources, that is, whether ILEs alter the very identification of such actions as help seeking when they solicit help from artificial sources (Keefer & Karabenick, 1998; Vallacher & Wegner, 1987). In addition, what becomes critical to understand when creating more optimal motivational contexts for college students, as well as younger learners, are the broader motivation-related characteristics and consequences of learning contexts in which artificial systems are situated (Schofield, 1995). Whether learning occurs in a mastery- versus performance-focused instructional setting may be just as important when seeking help from cognitive tutors in ILEs as it is when asking professors for help after class. Further research is needed to examine ILEs in relation to the motivational contexts in which they are situated.

CONCLUSION

We began this chapter with an overview of our guiding theoretical framework. Among the key assumptions of this framework is the idea that motivation and self-regulated learning are not, as is commonly perceived, traits of the learner. Rather, we assume that these processes can be influenced by the instructor. The tasks she assigns and the manner in which she evaluates them, the climate she establishes in the classroom, how supportive and caring she is perceived by her students, all can have a profound influence on the goals students adopt toward their learning, and whether and for what reason(s) students seek help. In general, research underscores the importance of creating a mastery-oriented learning environment. How such an environment is created and maintained particularly in the college classroom context remains an important question for future research.

REFERENCES

Abrams, H., and Jernigan, L. (1984). Academic support services and the success of high-risk students. *American Educational Research Journal* 21: 261–274.

Arbreton, A. (1993). *When Getting Help Is Helpful: Developmental, Cognitive, and Motivational Influences on Students' Academic Help Seeking.* Unpublished doctoral dissertation, University of Michigan, Ann Arbor.

Arbreton, A. (1998). Student goal orientation and help-seeking strategy use. In S.A. Karabenick (ed.), *Strategic Help Seeking: Implications for Learning and Teaching* (pp. 95–116). Mahwah, NJ: Erlbaum.

Aleven, V., McLaren, B.M., and Koedinger, K.R. (2006). Toward computer-based tutoring of help-seeking skills. In S.A. Karabenick and R.S. Newman (eds.), *Help Seeking in Academic Settings: Goals, Groups, and Contexts* (pp. 259–296). Mahwah, NJ: Lawrence Erlbaum Associates.

Aleven, V., Stahl, E., Schworm, S., Fischer, F., and Wallace, R.M. (2003). Help seeking and help design in interactive learning environments. *Review of Educational Research* 73(2): 277–320.

Alexitch, L.R. (2006). Help seeking and the role of academic advising in higher education. In S.A. Karabenick and R.S. Newman (eds.), *Help Seeking in Academic Settings: Groups, Goals, and Contexts* (pp. 175–202). Mahwah, NJ: Erlbaum.

Ames, C. (1992). Classrooms: Goals, structures, and student motivation. *Journal of Educational Psychology* 84(3): 261–271.

Ames, C., and Archer, J. (1988). Achievement goals in the classroom: Students' learning strategies and motivation processes. *Journal of Educational Psychology* 80: 260–267.

Amoroso, D., and Walters, R. (1969). Effects of anxiety and socially mediated anxiety reduction on paired-associate learning. *Journal of Personality and Social Psychology* 11: 388–396.

Barron, K.E., and Harackiewicz, J.M. (2001). Achievement goals and optimal motivation: Testing multiple goal models. *Journal of Personality & Social Psychology* 80(5): 706–722.

Barone, D.F., Maddux, J.E., and Snyder, C.R. (1997). *Social Cognitive Psychology: History and Current Domains.* New York: Plenum Press.

Beller, E. (1957). Dependency and autonomous achievement striving related to orality and anality in early childhood. *Child Development* 28: 287–315.

Boekaerts, M., Pintrich, P.R., and Zeidner, M. (eds.). (2000). *Handbook of Self-regulation.* San Diego, CA, US: Academic Press.

Bonney, C.R., Kempler, T.M., Zusho, A., Coppola, B.P., and Pintrich, P.R. (2005). Student learning in science classrooms: What role does motivation play? In S. Alsop (ed.), *Beyond Cartesian Dualism: Encountering Affect in the Teaching and Learning of Science* (Vol. 29, pp. 83–97). Dordrecht, Netherlands: Springer.

Bransford, J.D., Brown, A.L., and Cocking, R.R. (eds.). (2000). *How People Learn: Brain, Mind, Experience and School.* Washington, DC: National Academy Press.

Brophy, J. (2005). Goal theorists should move on from performance goals. *Educational Psychologist* 40(3): 167–176.

Butler, R. (1998). Determinants of help seeking: Relations between perceived reasons for classroom help-avoidance and help-seeking behaviors in an experimental context. *Journal of Educational Psychology* 90: 630–644.

Butler, R., and Neuman, O. (1995) Effects of task and ego achievement goals on help-seeking behaviors and attitudes. *Journal of Educational Psychology* 87: 261–271.

Capers, B., and Lipton, C. (1993). Hubble error: Time, money and millionths of an inch. *Academy of Management Executive* 7(4): 41–57.

Church, M.A., Elliot, A.J., and Gable, S.L. (2001). Perceptions of classroom environment, achievement goals, and achievement outcomes. *Journal of Educational Psychology* 93: 43–54.

Cobb, P., Wood, T., and Yackel, E. (1993). Discourse, mathematical thinking, and classroom practice. In E.A. Forman, N. Minick and C.A. Stone (eds.), *Contexts for learning: Sociocultural dynamics in children's development* (pp. 91–119). New York, NY: Oxford University Press.

Collins, W., and Sims, B.C. (2006). Help seeking and the role of academic advising in higher education. In S.A. Karabenick and R.S.Newman (eds.), *Help Seeking in Academic Settings: Groups, Goals, and Contexts* (pp. 203–223). Mahwah, NJ: Erlbaum.

Covington, M.V. (1992). Making the grade: *A Self-worth Perspective on Motivation and School Reform*. Cambridge, MA: Cambridge University Press.

Dweck, C.S., and Elliott, E.S. (1983). Achievement motivation. In E.M. Heatherington (ed.), *Handbook of Child Psychology: Social and Personality Development* (Vol. 4, pp. 643–691). New York: John Wiley & Sons, Inc.

Dweck, C.S., and Leggett, E.L. (1988). A social-cognitive approach to motivation and personality. *Psychological Review* 95(2): 256–273.

Eccles, J.S., Wigfield, A., and Schiefele, U. (1998). Motivation to succeed. In N. Eisenberg (ed.), *Handbook of Child Psychology* (5th edition, Vol. 3, pp. 1017–1094). New York: Wiley.

Elliot, A.J. (1999). Approach and avoidance motivation and achievement goals. *Educational Psychologist* 34: 169–189.

Elliot, A.J. (2005). A conceptual history of the achievement goal construct. In A.J. Elliot and C.S. Dweck (eds.), *Handbook of Competence and Motivation* (pp. 52–72). New York: Guilford.

Elliot, A.J., and Church, M.A. (1997). A hierarchical model of approach and avoidance achievement motivation. *Journal of Personality and Social Psychology* 72(1): 218–232.

Elliot, A.J., and McGregor, H.A. (1999). Test anxiety and the hierarchical model of approach and avoidance achievement motivation. *Journal of Personality & Social Psychology* 76(4): 628–644.

Elliot, A.J., and McGregor, H.A. (2001). A 2 × 2 achievement goal framework. *Journal of Personality and Social Psychology* 80: 501–519.

Elliot, A.J., McGregor, H.A., and Gable, S. (1999). Achievement goals, study strategies, and exam performance: A mediational analysis. *Journal of Educational Psychology* 91(3): 549–563.

Fischer, P.L., and Torney, J.V. (1976). Influence of children's stories on dependency: A sex-typed behavior. *Developmental Psychology* 12(5): 489–490.

Ford, M.E. (1992). *Motivating Humans: Goals, Emotions, and Personal Agency Beliefs*. Thousand Oaks, CA: Sage Publications Inc.

Grayson, A., Miller, H., and Clark, D.D. (1998). Identifying barriers to help seeking: A qualitative analysis of students' preparedness to seek help from tutors. *British Journal of Guidance and Counseling* 26: 237–253.

Gross, A.A., and McMullen, P.A. (1983). Models of the help seeking process. In B.M. DePaulo, A. Nadler, and J.D. Fisher (eds.), *New Directions in Helping: Vol. 2. Help Seeking* (pp. 45–70). San Diego, CA: Academic Press.

Harackiewicz, J.M., Barron, K.E., Pintrich, P.R., Elliot, A.J., and Thrash, T.M. (2002). Revision of achievement goal theory: Necessary and illuminating. *Journal of Educational Psychology* 94(3): 638–645.

Harackiewicz, J.M., Barron, K.E., Tauer, J.M., Carter, S.M., and Elliot, A.J. (2000). Short-term and long-term consequences of achievement goals: Predicting interest and performance over time. *Journal of Educational Psychology* 92(2): 316–330.

Harackiewicz, J.M., Barron, K.E., Tauer, J.M., and Elliot, A.J. (2002). Predicting success in college: A longitudinal study of achievement goals and ability measures as predictors of interest and performance from freshman year through graduation. *Journal of Educational Psychology* 94: 562–575.

Hassan, R.R, Uleman, J.S., and Bargh, J.A. (eds.) (2005). *The New Unconscious*. New York: Oxford University Press.

Hickey, D.T. (1997). Motivation and contemporary socio-constructivist instructional perspectives. *Educational Psychologist* 32(3): 175–193.

Hu, L., and Bentler, P.M. (1995). Evaluating model fit. In R. H. Hoyle (ed.), *Structural Equation Modeling: Concepts, Issues, and Applications*. Thousand Oaks, CA: Sage.

Kaplan, A., Gheen, M., and Midgley, C. (2002). Classroom goal structure and student disruptive behaviour. *British Journal of Educational Psychology* 72: 191–211.

Kaplan, A., Middleton, M.J., Urdan, T., and Midgley, C. (2002). Achievement goals and goal structures. In C. Midgley (ed.), *Goals, Goal Structures, and Patterns of Adaptive Learning* (pp. 21–53). Mahwah, NJ: Lawrence Erlbaum Associates.

Karabenick, S.A. (1996). Social influences on metacognition: Effects of colearner questioning on comprehension monitoring. *Journal of Educational Psychology* 88(4): 689–703.

Karabenick, S.A. (2003). Help seeking in large college classes: A person-centered approach. *Contemporary Educational Psychology* 28: 37–58.

Karabenick, S.A. (2004). Perceived achievement goal structure and college student help seeking. *Journal of Educational Psychology* 96: 569–581.

Karabenick, S.A. (ed.). (1998). *Strategic Help Seeking: Implications for Learning and Teaching*. Mahwah, NJ: Erlbaum.

Karabenick, S.A., and Knapp, J.R. (1988b). Help Seeking and Need for Academic Assistance.*Journal of Educational Psychology* 80(3): 406–408.

Karabenick, S.A., and Knapp, J.R. (1991). Relationship of academic help seeking to the use of learning strategies and other instrumental achievement behavior in college students. *Journal of Educational Psychology* 83(2): 221–230.

Karabenick, S.A., and Newman, R.S. (2004, April).*Should We Seek Help: An Unexplored Aspect of Group Collaboration*. Annual meeting of the American Educational Research Association, San Diego, CA.

Karabenick, S.A., and Newman, R.S. (eds.). (2006). *Help Seeking in Academic Settings: Goals, Groups, and Contexts*. Mahwah, NJ: Erlbaum.

Karabenick, S.A., and Sharma, R. (1994). Perceived teacher support of student questioning in the college classroom: Its relation to student characteristics and role in the classroom questioning process. *Journal of Educational Psychology* 86: 90–103.

Karabenick, S.A., and Woolley, M.E. (2006, April). *Cognitive Validity and the Construct Validity of Motivation-related Assessments.* Presented as part of a symposium: at the annual meeting of the American Educational Research Association, San Francisco, CA.

Karabenick, S.A., Zusho, A., and Kempler, T.M. (2005, August). *Help Seeking and Perceived Classroom Context.* Paper presented at the biennial meeting of the European Association for Research on Learning and Instruction. Nicosia, Cyprus.

Keefer, J.A., and Karabenick, S.A. (1998). Help seeking in the information age. In S.A. Karabenick (ed.), *Strategic Help Seeking: Implications for Learning and Teaching* (pp. 219–250). Mahwah, NJ: Erlbaum.

King, A. (1992). Facilitating elaborative learning through guided student-generated questioning. *Educational Psychologist, 27,* 111–126.

King, A. (1999). Discourse patterns for mediating peer learning. In A.M.O'Donnell and A. King (eds.) *Cognitive Perspectives on Peer Learning* (pp. 87–116). Mahwah, NJ: Erlbaum.

Knapp, J.R., and Karabenick, S.A. (1988). Incidence of formal and informal academic help-seeking in higher education. *Journal of College Student Development* 29(3): 223–227.

Linnenbrink, E., and Pintrich, P.R. (2001). Multiple goals, multiple contexts: The dynamic interplay between personal goals and contextual goal stresses. In S. Volet and S. Jarvela (eds.), *Motivation in Learning Contexts: Theoretical Advances and Methodological Implications* (pp.251–269). Amsterdam: Elsevier Science.

Maehr, M.L., and Braskamp, L.A. (1986). *The Motivation Factor: A Theory of Personal Investment.* Lexington, MA: Lexington Books.

Maehr, M.L., and Midgley, C. (1996). *Transforming School Cultures.* Boulder, CO: Westview.

Midgley, C. (ed.). (2002). *Goals, Goal Structures, and Patterns of Adaptive Learning.* Mahwah, NJ: Erlbaum.

Midgley, C., and Urdan, T. (2001). Academic self-handicapping and performance goals: A further examination. *Contemporary Educational Psychology* 26: 61–75.

McGregor, H.A., and Elliot, A.J. (2002). Achievement goals as predictors of achiement-relevant processes prior to task engagement. *Journal of Educational Psychology* 94(2): 381–395.

Moos, R.H. (1978). A typology of junior high and high school classrooms. *American Educational Research Journal* 15(1): 53–66.

Nadler, A. (1983). Personal characteristics and help-seeking. In B. M. DePaulo, A. Nadler, and J.D. Fisher (eds.), *New Directions in Helping (Vol. 2): Help Seeking* (pp. 303–340). New York: Academic Press.

Nadler, A. (1998). Relationship, esteem, and achievement perspectives on autonomous and dependent help seeking. In S.A. Karabenick (ed.), *Strategic Help Seeking: Implications for Learning and Teaching* (pp. 61–93). Mahwah, NJ: Erlbaum.

Nadler, A., Fisher, J.D., and DePaulo, B.M. (eds.). (1983). *New Directions in Helping. Vol. 3: Applied Perspectives on Help-seeking and Receiving.* New York: Academic Press.

Nelson-Le Gall, S. (1981). Help-seeking: An understudied problem-solving skill in children. *Developmental Review* 1(3): 224–246.

Nelson-le Gall, S.A. (1985). Motive-outcome matching and outcome foreseeability: Effects on attribution of intentionality and moral judgments. *Developmental Psychology* 21(2): 332–337.

Nelson-Le Gall, S., Gumerman, R.A., and Scott-Jones, D. (1983). Instrumental help-seeking and everyday problem-solving: A developmental perspective. *New Directions in Helping* (Vol. 2, pp. 265–283). New York: Academic Press.

Newman, R.S. (1991). Goals and self-regulated learning: What motivates children to seek academic help? In M.L. Maehr and P.R. Pintrich (eds.), *Advances in Motivation and Achievement* (Vol. 7, pp. 151–183). Greenwich, CT: JAI Press.

Newman, R.S. (1994). Adaptive help seeking: A strategy of self-regulated learning. In D.H. Schunk and B.J.Zimmerman (eds.), *Self-regulation of Learning and Performance: Issues and Educational Applications* (pp. 283–301). Mahwah, NJ: Erlbaum.

Newman, R.S. (1998). Adaptive help seeking: A role of social interaction in self-regulated learning. In S.A. Karabenick (ed.), *Strategic Help Seeking: Implications for Learning and Teaching* (pp. 13–37). Mahwah, NJ: Erlbaum.

Newman, R.S. (2000). Social influences on the development of children's adaptive help seeking: The role of parents, teachers, and peers. *Developmental Review* 20: 350–404.

Nicholls, J.G. (1984). Achievement motivation: Conceptions of ability, subjective experience, task choice, and performance. *Psychological Review* 91(3): 328–346.

Niemivirta, M. (2002). Individual differences and developmental trends in motivation: Integrating person-centered and variable-centered methods. In P.R. Pintrich and M.L. Maehr (eds.), *Advances in Motivation and Achievement: New Directions in Measures and Methods* (Vol.12, pp. 241–275). Amsterdam: Elsevier.

Patrick, H., Anderman, L.H., Ryan, A.M., Edelin, K.C., and Midgley, C. (2001). Teachers' communication of goal orientations in four fifth-grade classrooms. *The Elementary School Journal* 102: 35–58.

Pervin, L.A. (ed.). (1989). *Goal Concepts in Personality and Social Psychology*. Hillsdale, NJ, US: Lawrence Erlbaum Associates, Inc.

Pintrich, P.R. (2000). An achievement goal theory perspective on issues in motivation terminology, theory, and research. *Contemporary Educational Psychology* 25: 92–104.

Pintrich, P.R., and De Groot, E.V. (1990). Motivational and self-regulated learning components of classroom academic performance. *Journal of Educational Psychology* 82: 33–40.

Pintrich, P.R., and Schunk, D.H. (2002). *Motivation in Education: Theory, Research, and Applications* (2nd edition). Upper Saddle River, NJ: Merrill Prentice Hall.

Pintrich, P.R., and Zusho, A (this volume).Student learning and self-regulated learning in the college classroom. In R. Perry and J. Smart (eds.), *The Scholarship of Teaching and Learning in Higher Education: An Evidence-Based Perspective*. London: Springer.

Pintrich, P.R., and Zusho, A. (2002). The development of academic self-regulation: The role of cognitive and motivational factors. In A. Wigfield and J.S. Eccles (eds.), *Development of Achievement Motivation* (pp. 250–284). San Diego: Academic Press.

Raykov, T., Tomer, A., and Nesselroade, J.R. (1991). Reporting structural equation modeling results in Psychology and Aging: Some proposed guidelines. *Psychology and Aging* 6: 499–503.

Rhee, C.K., Zusho, A., and Pintrich, P.R. (2005). *Multiple Goals, Multiple Hypotheses: Reexamining the 2 × 2 Achievement Goal Framework in Introductory Chemistry and Psychology Classes*. Poster presented at the American Educational Research Association, Montreal, Canada.

Ryan, A.M., and Pintrich, P.R. (1997). "Should I ask for help?" The role of motivation and attitudes in adolescents' help seeking in math class. *Journal of Educational Psychology* 89: 329–341.

Ryan, A.M., and Pintrich, P.R. (1998). Achievement and social motivational influences on help seeking in the classroom. In S.A. Karabenick (ed.), *Strategic Help Seeking: Implications for Learning and Teaching* (pp. 117–139). Mahwah, NJ: Erlbaum.

Ryan, A.M., Hicks, L., and Midgley, C. (1997). Social goals, academic goals, and avoiding help in the classroom. *Journal of Early Adolescence* 17: 152–171.

Ryan, A., Gheen, M., and Midgley, C. (1998). Why do some students avoid asking for help? An examination of the interplay among students' academic efficacy, teachers' social-emotional role, and classroom goal structure. *Journal of Educational Psychology* 90: 528–535.

Sandoval, B.A., and Lee, F. (2006). When is seeking help appropriate? Now norms affect help seeking in organizations. In S.A. Karabenick and R.S. Newman (eds.), *Help Seeking in Academic Settings: Groups, Goals, and Contexts* (pp. 151–173). Mahwah, NJ: Erlbaum.

Schoenfeld, A.H. (1987). What's all the fuss about metacognition? In A.H. Schoenfeld (ed.), *Cognitive science and mathematics education* (pp.189–215). Mahwah, NJ: Earlbaum Associates.

Schofield, J.W. (1995). *Computers and Classroom Culture*. Cambridge, MA: Cambridge University Press.

Schwartz, N. (1999). Self-reports: How the questions shape the answers. *American Psychologist* 54: 93–105.

Schunk, D.H., and Pajares, F. (2005). Competence perceptions and academic functioning. In A.J. Elliott and C.S. Dweck (eds.), *Handbook of Competence and Motivation* (pp. 85–104). New York: Guilford.

Sears, R.R., Maccoby, E.E., and Levin, H. (1957). *Patterns of Child Rearing*. Oxford, England: Row, Peterson.

Skaalvik, E.M. (1997). Self-enhancing and self-defeating ego orientation: Relations with task and avoidance orientation, achievement, self-perceptions, and anxiety. *Journal of Educational Psychology* 89(1): 71–81.

Stipek, D.J., and Daniels, D.H. (1988). Declining perceptions of competence: A consequence of changes in the child or in the educational environment? *Journal of Educational Psychology* 80: 352–356.

Stipek, D.J., Salmon, J.N., Givvin, K.B., Kazemi, E., Saxe, G., and MacGyvers, V.L. (1998). The value (and convergence) of practices suggested by motivation research and promoted by mathematics education reformers. *Journal for Research in Mathematics Education* 29: 465–488.

Thomas, S.L. (2000). Ties that bind: A social network approach to understanding student integration and persistence. *Journal of Higher Education* 71: 591–615.

Trickett, E.J., and Moos, R.H. (1973). Social environment of junior high and high school classrooms. *Journal of Educational Psychology* 65(1): 93–102.

Turner, J.C., and Meyer, D.K. (2000). Studying and understanding the instructional contexts of classrooms: Using our past to forge our future. *Educational Psychologist* 35(2): 69–85.

Turner, J.C., Meyer, D.K., Midgley, C., and Patrick, H. (2003). Teacher discourse and sixth graders' reported affect and achievement behaviors in two high-mastery/high-performance mathematics classrooms. *Elementary School Journal* 103(4): 357–382.

Turner, J.C., Midgley, C., Meyer, D.K., Gheen, M., Anderman, E.M., Kang, Y., and Patrick, H. (2002). The classroom environment and students' reports of avoidance strategies in mathematics: A multimethod study. *Journal of Educational Psychology* 94: 88–106.

Urdan, T. (1997). Achievement goal theory: Past results, future directions. In M.L. Maehr and P.R. Pintrich (eds.), *Advances in Motivation and Achievement* (Vol. 10, pp. 99–142). Greenwich, CT: JAI Press, Inc.

Urdan, T., and Mestas, M. (2006). The goals behind performance goals. *Journal of Educational Psychology* 98: 354–365.

Urdan, T., and Midgley, C. (2003). Changes in the perceived classroom goal structure and pattern of adaptive learning during early adolescence. *Contemporary Educational Psychology* 28(4): 524–551.

Urdan, T., Midgley, C., and Anderman, E.M. (1998). The role of classroom goal structure in students' use of self-handicapping strategies. *American Educational Research Journal* 35(1): 101–122.

Urdan, T., Ryan, A.M., Anderman, E.M., and Gheen, M.H. (2002). Goals, goal structures, and avoidance behaviors. In C. Midgley (ed.), *Goals, Goal Structures, and Patterns of Adaptive Learning* (pp. 55–84). Mahwah, NJ: Erlbaum.

Vallacher, R.R., and Wegner, D.M. (1987). What do people think they're doing? Action identification and human behavior. *Psychological Review* 94: 3–15.

Volet, S.E., and Ang, G. (1998). Culturally mixed groups on international campuses: An opportunity for intercultural learning. *Higher Education Research & Development* 17(1): 5–23.

Volet, S., and Jarvela, S. (eds.), *Motivation in Learning Contexts: Theoretical Advances and Methodological Implications*. Amsterdam: Elsevier Science.

Webb, N.M., Ing, M., Kersting, N., and Nemer, M.N. (2006) Help seeking in cooperative learning groups. In S.A. Karabenick and R.S. Newman (eds.), *Help Seeking in Academic Settings: Goals, Groups, and Contexts* (pp. 45–88). Mahwah, NJ: Lawrence Erlbaum Associates.

Weiner, B. (1974). *Achievement Motivation and Attribution Theory*. Morristown, NJ: General Learning Press.

Weiner, B. (1990). History of motivational research in education. *Journal of Educational Psychology* 82: 616–622.

Wentzel, K.R. (1997). Student motivation in middle school: The role of perceived pedagogical caring. *Journal of Educational Psychology* 89: 411–419.

Winterbottom, M. (1958). The relationship of need for achievement to learning experiences in independence and mastery. In J.A.Atkinson (ed.), *Motives in Fantasy, Action and Society*. Princeton, NJ: Van Nostrand.

Wolters, C.A. (2004). Advancing achievement goal theory: using goal structures and goal orientations to predict students' motivation, cognition, and achievement. *Journal of Educational Psychology* 96(2): 236–250.

Wood, T., Cobb, P., and Yackel. E. (1991). Change in teaching mathematics: A case study. *American Educational Research Journal* 28: 587–616.

Zimmerman, B.J., and Martinez-Pons, M. (1990). Student differences in self-regulated learning: Relating grade, sex, and giftedness to self-efficacy and strategy use. *Journal of Educational Psychology* 82: 51–59.

15. A Motivational Analysis of Academic Life in College

Martin V. Covington

University of California, Berkeley
cov@berkely.edu

Key Words: Intrinsic motivation; extrinsic motivation, grades; instruction, fear of failure; self-worth dynamics; college students

> The curriculum does not matter. If it did matter, we could not do anything
> about it. If we could do something about it, we would not know what to do.
> —Carnegie Foundation for the Advancement of Teaching, 1977

INTRODUCTION

Of course the curriculum matters; but yes, admittedly, we do not always know what alterations to make if we could. One reason is our imperfect understanding of the very processes of change that we hope to initiate in our students, encouraging changes from novice to expert and shedding an emotional dependency on authority so they may become independent learners. Although recently there has been a dramatic upturn nationwide in the commitment of university faculty to the enhancement of creative and independent thinking at the undergraduate level (Carnegie Foundation for the Advancement of Teaching, 1989), the particular educational policies and practices that best promote these goals are not always clear.

We are at a particular handicap when it comes to understanding the part that *motivation* plays in the process of growing up educated, and how best to respond to those who advocate that the highest goal of university life is to instill a "love of learning" and a willingness to

R.P. Perry and J.C. Smart (eds.), The Scholarship of Teaching and Learning in Higher Education: An Evidence-Based Perspective, 661–729.
© 2007 Springer.

continue learning over a lifetime. Peter Drucker puts it this way: "We know nothing about motivation. All we can do is write books about it." Drucker is correct to the extent that knowing *how* to motivate individuals is not the same as knowing *what* is motivation. As a concept, motivation can be more easily described in terms of its observable effects (e.g., persistence, purposeful action) than it is to define. But leaving aside various definitional issues (see Covington, 1992), and here is where Drucker is misled, we do in fact know at least *something* about how to motivate individuals to higher effort and about those conditions that encourage a love of learning. The essence of our knowledge is that a willingness to continue learning depends heavily on the individual's reasons (motives) for learning in the first instance.

The overall purpose of this chapter is to explore the implications of this proposition for policy and practice at the university and college level. In the first section, we will review what is known about motivation, what factors affect it, and how it in turn enters into and influences the larger achievement process. This considerable body of evidence is organized around the traditional view of *motives-as-drives*, internal needs or states that impel individuals to action. This perspective views motivation as residing largely within the individual, and treats these internal factors as an enabling device—a means to an end, with the end inevitably being improved status, better test performance, or a higher grade point average. This drive perspective dominates popular thinking whenever schools are admonished to motivate (drive) students to do better in response to those highly publicized comparisons of achievement scores, especially in science and mathematics, among students from the leading industrial nations, a contest which puts American students dead last. As one politician confided to Stanford education professor, Michael Kirst (1990), "I just want the little buggers to work harder." Presumably by increasing the rewards for being industrious and threatening sufficient punishments if effort is not forthcoming, schools can arouse otherwise indifferent students to renewed action. This same mentality regarding the motivating properties of rewards and punishments also prevails at the college level albeit in more sophisticated and less crudely expressed forms.

In the second section, we will consider more promising directions for enhancing achievement motivation among undergraduate students, an undertaking that is best conceived of in terms of an alternative metaphor: *motives-as-goals*. Researchers in this tradition assume that all actions are given meaning, direction, and purpose by the goals individuals seek out, and that the quality and intensity of behavior will change as these goals change. Considered from this perspective, motivation is a unique human resource to be encouraged for its own sake, not simply a means to increased school achievement. The topic of motivational change invariably raises the question of the extent to which motives are the property of individuals or of the circumstances in which individuals find themselves, a point to be considered later.

MOTIVES AS DRIVES

Educational decisions depend ultimately on answering three classic questions: *what* is worth knowing (curriculum issues)? *how* do we best impart this preferred knowledge (instructional issues)? and, finally, the question that puts students at the heart of the educational enterprise: *why*, or for what reasons, do students learn? The question of *why* provides us with the necessary motivational dimension. *Why*, for example, does Alice, a sophomore transfer student who must work long hours in the school cafeteria as part of her financial aid package, still find time to organize a Young Socialists Club on campus, compete for the lead in the school play, and have enough energy left over to maintain a 4.0 grade point average? And why does Ted who could do anything well, given his extraordinary intellectual gifts, appear content with choosing only those courses that offer him the most units for the least amount of work. To be sure, Alice's reasons (motives) for her extraordinary accomplishments may be far from positive—perhaps she is attempting to outperform others for fear that she might not prove worthy of perfection. In this case, keeping busy has the virtue of making one feel important and if Alice can't quite manage to do it all, then the implicit assumption is that she must be doing something significant. Similarly, Ted's lack of involvement may not be as aimless as appearances suggest. Rather it may stem from a basically healthy search for alternative, nontraditional means of self expression. In any event, it is natural to describe these different behaviors as *driven*, with Alice compelled to aggrandize her status even at the risk of exhaustion and Ted seeking to connect with a lifestyle worthy of his talents.

The view of motives-as-drives had its origins beginning in the first decades of the present century (e.g., Woodworth, 1918, for review see also Bolles, 1967; Weiner, 1972, 1990) in laboratory and animal research which stressed physiological needs as the most important instigators of behavior. Simply put, organisms become aroused (motivated), and then goal-directed in an effort to reduce a physiological imbalance, typically represented by states of hunger or thirst, in order to return the body to a state of equilibrium (homeostasis). As valuable as this need-reduction view was for initiating research on motivation, its limitations became increasingly apparent when applied to human beings. The fact is that humans do not act solely to reduce stress, but will on occasion actually seek out stimulation, something any African safari guide or amusement park operator will tell us. More than anything, humans are active explorers and manipulators of their environment. This common sense observation eventually led researchers to postulate the existence of the so-called *stimulus motives* (Harlow, 1953; Hebb, 1961). These motives, like basic tissue needs, are likely unlearned, but their particular expression is conditioned heavily by social rules and conventions. It is easy to imagine that the ultimate expression of the need to control, explore, and manipulate is reflected in those processes required to land a new job, to decipher the meaning of the Dead Sea Scrolls, or to corner silver trading on the Chicago Commodities Exchange. These behaviors are thought to reflect *learned drives* or psychological motives, including a need for power, belongingness, and achievement. The term *drive* is applicable here because individuals often seem driven, even compelled by an internal state or demand for action; and *learned* because the strength and direction of such behavior is controlled to a great extent by custom.

NEED ACHIEVEMENT THEORY

The most important of the earlier learned-drive approaches to achievement motivation, and still enormously influential today, was developed by John Atkinson (1957, 1964) and his long-time colleague David McClelland (1958, 1961), beginning in the late 1950s. This theory holds that the need for achievement is the consequence of a conflict between two opposing forces: the desire to *approach* success and a fear of failure which results in a disposition (or motive) to *avoid* situations that are likely to devalue the individual. These twin motives were described largely in emotional terms with the anticipation of *pride* characterizing the approach motive and the anticipation of *shame* at failing, character-izing the avoidance motive. In essence, for Atkinson and McClelland the answer to the question of *why* individuals choose certain jobs and not others, or why they pursue tasks with more or less vigor, depended on the quality of the feelings that accompany success and failure.

Atkinson argued that individuals differ markedly in the degree to which they are characterized by these opposing motives. For instance, for those persons whose optimism, or hope for success, outweighs a fear of failure, the conflict is minimal and is typically resolved in a positive direction; by contrast, things are resolved in an opposite fashion for those persons for whom fear overpowers hope. These latter individuals, or *failure acceptors*, as they have recently been described (Covington and Omelich, 1991), are unwilling to volunteer their ideas in class, enter the achievement arena only reluctantly, and prefer either the easy course assignment because the probability of failure is low, or the exceedingly difficult task because they will not feel too badly if they fail at something for which so few others could be expected to succeed (Atkinson and Litwin, 1960; Lewin, Dembo, Festinger, and Sears, 1944; Moulton, 1965). By comparison, success-oriented persons prefer neither the easy nor the difficult assignment, but rather those tasks of intermediate difficulty for which the likelihood of success is exquisitely balanced off against the probability of failure, thus ensuring themselves enough successes to sustain future hope, yet without cheapening the rewards of success by too easy a victory.

Besides focusing on internal states, Atkinson's theory also exemplifies another important feature of the concept of motives-as-drives in that motives are viewed largely as an enabling factor, with the overriding objective being success at the chosen task. Another aspect of the motives-as-drives tradition is reflected in a decidedly entrepreneurial spirit which according to McClelland (1961, 1965) involves competing with standards of excellence, if not directly with other individuals, which amounts to a contest to outdo one's adversaries (Combs, 1957; Greenberg, 1932). This competitive element, not to be confused with striving to overcome one's own limitations or seeking out knowledge for its own sake, reflects what Nicholls (1989) and others (Ames, 1981, 1984; Ames and Ames, 1984; Dweck, 1986) have called an *ego-involved* or *performance* (as opposed to *learning*) mentality. For ego-involved students, noteworthy performance is a way to enhance one's status, commonly one's intellectual or ability standing, and usually at the expense of others. Thus intrinsic reasons for learning are largely missing from the need achievement tradition.

Over the years the need achievement model has evolved in several distinctive ways. First, Atkinson and McClelland have more fully developed their views on how approach and avoidance motives interact with other related motives, including the need for social approval and for power (Veroff and Veroff, 1972; Winter, 1973). The resulting *dynamics of action* model (Atkinson, 1981; McClelland, 1980,

1985) suggests that many motives operate simultaneously and on a moment-to-moment basis within the same individual, a perspective that allows for more dynamic predictions that can be measured in terms of the *percentage* of time that, say, success-oriented individuals spend on various tasks compared with earlier predictions which recognized only all-or-nothing choices among tasks.

Second, Nuttin and Lens (Nuttin, 1984; Nuttin and Lens, 1985) have infused the need achievement model with a decidedly goal-directed orientation in which they argue that the individual's perceptions of the future, especially subjective notions of time, form the fundamental motivational space within which all human beings operate. Success-oriented individuals aspire to more complex, distant goals than do failure-threatened individuals (DeVolder and Lens, 1982) and they are more likely to divide the task of achieving those goals into small steps of intermediate difficulty, like stepping stones, so that the chances of ultimate success are maximized. Raynor (1969, 1970) has characterized these kinds of plans as *partially contingent pathways*, meaning that success at one step creates the opportunity to move to the next, but failure does not necessarily preclude advancement. This is because success-oriented persons create backup plans in case their initial strategies fall short. And they also entertain alternative goals if the original objective becomes impossible such as becoming a paramedic instead of a physician, or working as a paralegal rather than as an attorney.

This research holds important implications for both educational theory and practice. For one thing, it suggests that the ability to plan may be an essential part of what we speak of as motivation; indeed, it may be that *motives* are actually just *plans* but by a different name. For another thing, the research of Nuttin and Lens along with that of others (Findley and Cooper, 1983; Skinner, Wellborn, and Connell, 1990; Stipik and Weiss, 1981) makes the point that believing oneself to be in personal control of events is central to all noteworthy accomplishments. In this connection, Pintrich and his colleagues (Eccles, 1983; Pintrich, 1988, 1989, 1990; Pintrich and De Groot, 1990) have identified several factors essential to task involvement that are linked to the effective regulation of plans and to realistic goal setting: (1) An expectancy factor that includes beliefs about one's ability to perform well; (2) a value factor that includes the reasons for being involved, what we have called motives; and, (3) an emotional component, "How do I feel about this task?"

The legacy of Atkinson's need achievement model is clearly evident in these most recent developments in motivation theory.

ATTRIBUTION THEORY

Beginning in the early 1970s a significant reinterpretation of Atkinson's model was offered by Bernard Weiner and his colleagues (Weiner et al., 1971; Weiner, 1972, 1974) guided by the principles of attribution theory which are based on the proposition that the way individuals perceive the causes of their successes and failures influences their subsequent achievement. According to Weiner, the important difference between success-oriented and failure-threatened individuals is not so much variations in emotional reaction (pride vs. shame) as the differences in their cognitions. Failure-prone persons tend to attribute their failures to inadequate ability and their successes to external factors such as luck, chance, or mood. By comparison, success-oriented persons typically ascribe their failures to insufficient effort since they believe themselves to be capable enough; and, by extension, they attribute their successes to a combination of skill (ability) and diligence. This latter attributional pattern promotes a highly positive interpretation of achievement outcomes: Success inspires greater confidence in one's ability and promotes a sense of control, whereas failure merely signals the need to try harder (Man and Hrabal, 1988). On the other hand, failure-prone individuals find themselves in a "no-win" situation: Failure implies that success is unlikely, and not worth pursuing; and, on those infrequent occasions when success does occur, it is discounted as the result of forces outside one's ability to control.

The weight of accumulated evidence supports these attributional differences between success-oriented and failure-prone persons (Arkin, Detchon, and Maruyama, 1982; Leppin, Schwarzer, Belz, Jerusalem, and Quast, 1987; Meyer, 1970; Weiner and Kukla, 1970, Experiment 4; Weiner et al., 1971; Weiner, Heckhausen, Meyer, and Cook, 1972). The findings are especially compelling for the predominance of low-ability attributions among failure-prone students (Covington and Omelich, 1979a).

This cognitive reinterpretation of Atkinson's need achievement model prompted a subtle, but important, shift in the focus of motivational research from the question of *why* to one of *how*—that is, how individuals interpret events like failure—and also suggests that what is most important to future achievement is the meaning that individuals

667

Figure 1: Attribution model of achievement motivation (Source: Adapted from Covington, 1989).

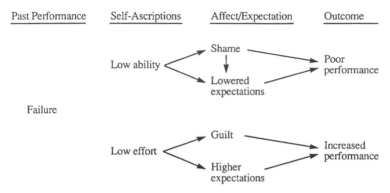

attribute to their failures (and successes) and not simply the frequency of their occurrence.

These different attributional patterns are thought to enter into the achievement process in the ways portrayed in Figure 1.F1

First, consider the plight of failure-threatened students (upper portion of Figure 1). Students who interpret failure as caused by insufficient ability are likely to: (1) experience shame (low ability → shame), shame being an ability-linked emotion (Covington and Omelich, 1984a); and, (2) reduce their expectations for future success (low ability → lowered expectation). Lowered expectations occur because among adults, at least, ability is typically perceived to be a fixed, immutable factor, and because ability is also believed to be the preemptive cause of academic success. In short, if someone is not very smart, he or she can only do so well despite having tried hard (Harari and Covington, 1981). The presence of shame eventually inhibits achievement via the expectancy linkage (shame → low expectation → poor performance) because shame triggers renewed self-doubts about one's ability whenever students begin studying again (Covington and Omelich, 1990). According to Figure 1, lower expectations perse also undercut future performance, a lineage that depends largely on the fact that self-doubting students persist less in their work on a problem (Battle, 1965).

Now consider the achievement dynamics of success-oriented persons (lower portion of Figure 1). Individuals who interpret failure as caused primarily by insufficient effort experience feelings of guilt for not having tried hard enough, guilt being an effort-linked emotion (Covington and Omelich, 1984a). In moderation, feelings of guilt mobilize further effort (Hoffman, 1982; Wicker, Payne, and Morgan, 1983), especially among bright individuals who often feel keenly the responsibility associated with brilliance (guilt → increased performance) (Weiner and Kukla, 1970). Also because effort level is perceived of as modifiable, expectations for future success remains high among success-oriented students even in the face of failure because they believe that success is within their grasp if only they try harder. Such optimism (increased expectations) guarantees a measure of persistence which eventually pays off in the form of higher achievement (low effort → higher expectations → improved performance).

From this overall analysis we now see why failure can drive some individuals to renewed effort and others to despair, depending on the prevailing self-perceived causes of failure. Also it is clear why some individuals reject success despite the fact that it is so sought after. When success is seen as due to external factors beyond one's control— the generosity of an instructor, luck, or the help of others—doing well adds little to one's confidence that success can be repeated.

Cognitive theorists have focused principally on the role of effort in the dynamics portrayed in Figure 1, and as a consequence, several important effort-related linkages have been well established. First, as already noted, if individuals do not exert enough effort in a failing cause, they are more likely to remain optimistic since one can always try harder the next time (Fontaine, 1974; McMahan, 1973; Meyer, 1970; Rosenbaum, 1972; Valle, 1974; Weiner et al., 1972). Second, trying hard mitigates feelings of guilt (for not trying), thereby reinforcing the value of effort (Brown and Weiner, 1984). Third, and perhaps of greatest significance, it is widely accepted that student effort is modifiable through the actions of teachers. For example, many teachers believe that the greater the rewards offered, the harder students will try and that distributing rewards on a competitive basis is the most effective means to drive students to greater effort. Although these particular beliefs are largely misplaced (a point to be discussed later), it is clearly the case that teachers do value effort. They reward least those students who succeed without trying and punish most those who fail for lack of trying (Covington and Omelich, 1979b; Eswara, 1972; Rest, Nierenberg, Weiner, and Heckhausen, 1973; Weiner and Kukla, 1970). For this reason, according to cognitive theorists, students should come to value effort as a major if not the main source of personal worth, and to the extent that students disregard this work ethic, they will experience chagrin and rejection by others.

But it is also clear, abundantly so, that students do not always respond as expected to this dominant work ethic. Many students postpone assignments and generally act in ways contrary to their own best interests insofar as getting high grades are concerned. But why should this be if teachers generously reward trying hard, and are quick to punish inactivity?

There is more afoot here than can be accounted for easily by cognitive reinforcement mechanisms alone. For example, despite the evidence cited above, attributing a prior failure to inadequate effort does not guarantee that a student will remain optimistic about his or her future chances. Such inaction may also reflect the fact that the student has become demoralized and has given up. In effect, the explanations people harbor for their successes and failures are not necessarily synonymous with their reasons for achieving or not achieving. In short, attributions are no simple substitute for the concept of motivation.

SELF-WORTH THEORY

The self-worth theory of achievement motivation (Covington, 1984a, 1984b, 1985b, 1992; Covington and Beery, 1976) attempts to create a theoretical rapport between the cognitive tradition with its emphasis on self-perceptions of causality, especially effort attributions, and the drive theory formulations of Atkinson's earlier need achievement model, along with research on the topics of fear-of-failure and defensive dynamics (e.g., Birney, Burdick, and Teevan, 1969; Snyder et al., 1976). Self-worth theory holds that the search for self-acceptance is the highest priority among humans and that in schools (at least as presently constituted) self-acceptance typically becomes equated with the ability to achieve competitively. In effect, individuals come to believe themselves only as worthy as their accomplishments competitively defined. Thus individuals may approach success (in Atkinson's terms) not only to benefit from the social and personal rewards of high accomplishment, but also to aggrandize their reputations for high ability. And, if success become unlikely, as is typically the case when rewards are distributed on a competitive basis—with the greatest number going to those who perform best—then the first priority is to avoid failure, or at least avoid the implications of failure that one is incompetent.

Self-worth theory stresses those aspects of personal worth that are tied to a sense of competency and those feelings of worthlessness arising out of disclosures of incompetency. A growing body of evidence under-scores the importance of ability perceptions among college students as the most salient aspect of their academic self-definition. As only one example, Covington and Omelich (1984a) asked students to analyze retrospectively any one of their courses from a previous semester. Students rated their ability to deal with the subject matter in the course, estimated how hard they had worked, and judged how much positive self-regard they enjoyed as a student. They also reported the course grade they received. By far the most important contributor to feelings of self-regard were self-estimates of ability, a factor which accounted for more than 50% of the variance. The actual grade received in the course proved to be a distant second as a contributor to feelings of worthiness. And, of lesser importance still was the amount of effort expended. Although those students who worked harder did in fact feel slightly more worthy, hard work was no substitute for a reputation of brilliance when it came to defining academic self-worth. The importance of ability status has also been corroborated in several related studies. For instance, Brown and Weiner (1984) concluded that college students prefer to achieve because of ability rather than effort. Moreover, among those studies that permit estimates of the relative contributions of ability and effort to a sense of worth, ability cognitions accounted for most of the variation in shame (Covington and Omelich, 1984a; Weiner and Kukla, 1970). Finally, analyses of actual college test-taking experiences indicated that ability cognitions were the dominant factor affecting pride and shame reactions as well as actual achievement level (Covington and Omelich, 1979a, 1981, 1982).

The cognitive model stresses those aspects of worthiness associated with hard work, whereas self-worth theory stresses those aspects associated with feelings of competency. But are these two sources of worth necessarily incompatible? Cannot students achieve via hard work and in the process also increase their sense of competency and feelings of control over events? Yes, possibly, but it is unlikely—at least not if the rewards for learning are distributed on a competitive basis where failure is the most frequent outcome. Under competitive conditions learning becomes an ability game: The fewer the rewards available the more they come to depend on ability. And in the circum-stance, effort becomes a threat because if one tries hard and fails anyway, then explanations for failure go to low ability. But, try or not, teachers still reward effort and students are expected to comply with this work ethic. Herein lies the dilemma for students: To try hard and fail leads to shame and feelings of worthlessness; but not trying leads to feelings of guilt and teacher punishment.

A number of studies using different methodologies have confirmed this effort dilemma for college students. For example, we collected a number of self-report measures from students over several successive midterm examinations and subjected these data to multivariate path analysis (Covington & Omelich, 1981). For those students who experienced failure (i.e., falling below their competitively derived aspirations), shame not only followed directly from diminutions in self-perceived ability status, but most important from the standpoint of an effort dilemma, the reciprocal linkage between degree of effort expended and feelings of competency (high effort → low ability) increased in saliency as failures accumulated from one midterm to the next. This means that the more individuals study as a response to having failed previously, the more likely it is that any future failures will be interpreted by them and others as a matter of incompetency.

Several companion studies (Covington and Omelich, 1979b; Covington, Spratt, and Omelich, 1980) which employed a role-playing methodology further illustrate this effort dilemma. Students rated the degree of shame they would expect (hypothetically) if they had failed a test under several different circumstances. Those failures that elicited the greatest shame were preceded by high effort (study), whereas those failures that elicited lesser degrees of shame were associated with little or no study preparation. These same students were then asked to assume the role of teachers and punish hypothetical students under each of the same conditions of failure. As "teachers" these subjects now assigned the *greatest* degree of punishment to precisely those failures that previously had offered them (as students) the greatest emotional protection from diminished self-perceptions of ability (i.e., failure without effort); and, conversely, these "teachers" punished far less those failures that triggered the greatest sense of shame among students (i.e., failure after trying hard). Excuses served to moderate this conflict of classroom values. "Teachers" punished least of all those low-effort failures in which lack of study was blamed on illness, exactly the same condition (low-effort/excuse) that elicited the least shame among students. Also alleged explanations for why studying hard did not paid off—in this case, because the test emphasized material not studied by the student—resulted in substantial reductions in both teacher punishment and student shame. This series of studies not only illuminates the motivational dynamics involved when students face the threat of failure, but also indicates how students can avoid the threat: By not trying or at least trying but with excuses available. As Covington and Beery (1976) have observed:

> Thus there emerges from this complex interplay among students, peers, and teacher a "winning" formula in the anticipation of failure that is designed to avoid personal humiliation and shame on the one hand and to minimize teacher punishment on the other: try, or at least *appear* to try, but not too energetically and with excuses handy. It is difficult to imagine a strategy better calculated to sabotage the pursuit of personal excellence. (p.84)

Failure-avoiding Strategies

Over the last two decades researchers have investigated a number of defensive ploys which college students use in attempts to avoid failure. These self-serving tactics are intended to shift the presumed causes of failure from internal (ability) factors to external causes beyond the individual's control or responsibility; in effect, they work by obscuring the causes of failure which calls to mind Nietzsche's celebrated remark that, "Those who know they are profound strive for clarity. Those who would like to seem profound to the crowd strive for obscurity." These latter tactics can be divided into two groups.

First, consider those ploys described collectively as "self-handicapping" strategies (Berglas and Jones, 1978; Tucker, Vuchinich, and Sobell, 1981); self-handicapping because ironically enough they set up the very failures that individuals are attempting to avoid, but at least they are failures "with honor," that is, readily explained, if not always excused. Perhaps the most celebrated and certainly the most frequently employed self-handicapping strategy is procrastination (Silver and Sabini, 1981, 1982). Some observers estimate that a near-majority of college students procrastinate on a regular basis (Rothblum, Solomon, and Murakami, 1986; Solomon and Rothblum, 1984) while other more pessimistic estimates run as high as 90 percent (Ellis and Kraus, 1977). By postponing study for a test or work on a term paper until the very last minute, students can argue that their performance is not representative of what they could really do, if they had only "not run out of time." An additional benefit of procrastination is that if the student should do well despite having studied only briefly, then a reputation for brilliance will be enhanced. Students have also been known to take on so many tasks that they cannot give sufficient time to any one of them. This variation on the procrastination theme not only allows students to score points for being energetic, but being busy makes one feel important despite the mediocre performances that are likely to result.

Another self-handicapping strategy involves setting one's academic goals so high, say, hoping to maintain a perfect grade point average while carrying a double major, that failure is virtually guaranteed, but a failure that would befall most every other student as well. "If I cannot succeed," the implied argument runs, "then the problem is in the goal, not in me." This reasoning depends on being able to convince oneself that failed tasks are inherently difficult, a mental sleight of hand that appears easily accomplished if we can judge from the research of Bennett and Holmes (as reported in Snyder, 1984). These investigations gave college students a vocabulary test. One-half of the students were told, falsely, that they had failed, while the remaining students were given no feedback at all. A significantly greater percentage of the first group estimated that their friends had also failed the test. From a self-worth perspective these results are to be expected because, indeed, "misery loves company," and the more the better, since the failure of the many obscures the failure of the individual.

Another tactic involves admitting to a minor or nonthreatening handicap such as test-taking anxiety, while avoiding disclosure of a greater real or imagined weakness—in this case, incompetency. The test-anxious student is the perfect blameless victim. Anxiety is real enough and does, in fact, disrupt learning so the affliction is credible; also everyone has experienced anxiety to some degree and as a result the sufferer can convert imagined scorn at being disclosed as stupid into instant sympathy and concern. All in all, the temptation is too great for some students not to use the symptoms of anxiety to personal advantage. For example, when Smith, Snyder, and Handelsman (1982) gave test-anxious subjects legitimate reason to report symptoms of anxiety following a test, they did so more often than another group of equally anxious individuals who were given no permission. By contrast, low test-anxious students reported no more feelings of anxiety whether or not they were given permission to do so. Thus anxiety symptoms among anxious individuals may or may not appear depending upon circumstances and on their potential for self-justification.

Researchers have also documented the use of failure-avoiding strategies in numerous situations outside formal academic settings whenever one's reputation for ability is at stake, whether ability be musical aptitude and the failure to perform well in a public piano recital (Covington, 1982) or physical prowess and the failure to maintain a competitive edge in high school wrestling competition (Burton and Martens, 1986).

A second cluster of failure-avoiding tactics, unlike self-handicapping strategies, seemingly accents the positive by attempting to guarantee success, but success not so much for the sake intrinsic satisfaction as a way to avoid failure. The premier case is that of the *overstriver* (Beery et al., 1975; Covington and Beery, 1976). We will consider overstrivers in more detail in the next section. Meantime, suffice it to say that in terms of Atkinson's need achievement model overstrivers reflect simultaneously a desire to approach success largely for its high status value and a desire to avoid failure given the implication that one is not worthy of perfection. As we will see, this hybrid quality of hope and fear can drive some individuals to extraordinary accomplishments.

Another technique for ensuring success is to set one's academic aspirations low enough so as to avoid outright failure by means of what Birney et al. (1969) refer to as the *confirming interval*. The confirming interval is that range between the highest test score or grade one can reasonably hope to achieve and the lowest acceptable outcome. Students often manipulate the lower bounds of this range, raising it on occasion when they feel confident of outcomes and lowering it in anticipation of a particularly difficult exam. This latter maneuver can protect them from experiencing feelings of failure despite the fact that at best their performances may be only mediocre. Indeed, chronic low-goal setting often leads to a prolonged state of mediocrity where success is defined only by not losing.

Covington (1992) has summarized the lessons to be learned from this collection of defensive strategies and the fact of their universality and pervasiveness. "Humans stop at little; lying, cheating, even failing is not too high a price to pay. Yet, in the process failure-threatened students become their own worst enemies. No matter how adroitly they maneuver, they still harbor doubts about their ability because they are unwilling to test the limits by trying their hardest. They fear that they *might* be inadequate, but what they fear most is finding out" (pp. 88–89).

Individual Student Differences

The self-worth dynamics described so far do not apply equally to all students. Individuals enter college already disposed to deal with academic stress in various distinctive ways and to protect, or if

675

necessary, to salvage a belief in themselves, especially those individuals who have tied their sense of worth to competitive excellence. This process of coping is not uniform nor are the outcomes identical, but rather it results in an almost endless variety of adaptation and maladaptation. How are we to make sense of such complexity? One response of the social scientist is to identify the fewest, most salient dimensions along which all students can be located and then aggregate them in clusters with each student type reflecting (hopefully) different styles of coping.

The development of student typologies in higher education has become something of a cottage industry with a long and distinguished history. One of the first major typologies was that developed by Clark and Trow (1960, 1966) who differentiated students in terms of their subculture membership—vocational, collegiate, nonconformist, and the like (for a critique, see Ellis, Parelius, and Parelius, 1971; Peterson, 1965; Warren, 1968). Other typologies have followed, most notably the classification schema created by Holland and his colleagues (Holland, 1966, 1973; Osipow, Ashby, and Wall, 1966; Folsom, 1969) which was intended to reflect broad occupational choices among students, including enterprising, artistic, and intellectual (investigative) types. Yet other approaches have been rooted more firmly in traditional personality research as represented by the Omnibus Personality Inventory which was used by its developers, Heist and Yonge (1968), and others (Elton, 1967; Korn, 1968) to study changes in student coping styles over the course of their college careers. Katchadourian and Boli (1985) have rightly pointed out that most of these typologies are based on a phenomenological approach in which student types are defined either by institutional or group membership, or informally by the students themselves. This means that student types are not always defined in terms of a common set of dimensions so that, for example, nonconformists might describe themselves in terms of the social causes they espouse while intellectually oriented individuals might locate themselves around different philosophical positions.

My approach to typology development, like that of Katchadourian and Boli (1985) who studied careerism and intellectualism among college students, is more analytical. Katchadourian and Boli explicitly classified students on two dimensions, one reflecting a preference/nonpreference for career preparation and the other a preference/nonpreference for an intellectual life of discovery. Thus the four types of students resulting from this 2 × 2 matrix were based on an interplay of careerism and intellectualism variables and nothing else. I, too, catalogued students on two, independent dimensions, those of *approach* and *avoidance*, dynamic poles which served as the bedrock of Atkinson's need achievement model.

As originally proposed, Atkinson's theory featured a two-dimensional quadripolar model of the kind presented in Figure 2.F2 Individuals could be placed either high or low on either an approach or on a failure-avoiding dimension.

They could also be located high on *both* dimensions. This two-dimensional approach had the advantage of allowing for conflicting motivational tendencies represented by those individuals located high on both dimensions, that is, driven simultaneously by hope and fear (Student A). Also, students could remain seemingly indifferent to achievement events as reflected by the relative absence of *both* hope and fear (Student D).

However, despite the heuristic value of Atkinson's quadripolar model, few researchers have maintained the distinction of two independent dimensions (for exceptions, see Atkinson and Litwin, 1960; Feather, 1965). Instead, most have adopted a unidimensional,

Figure 2: Quadripolar model of need achievement.

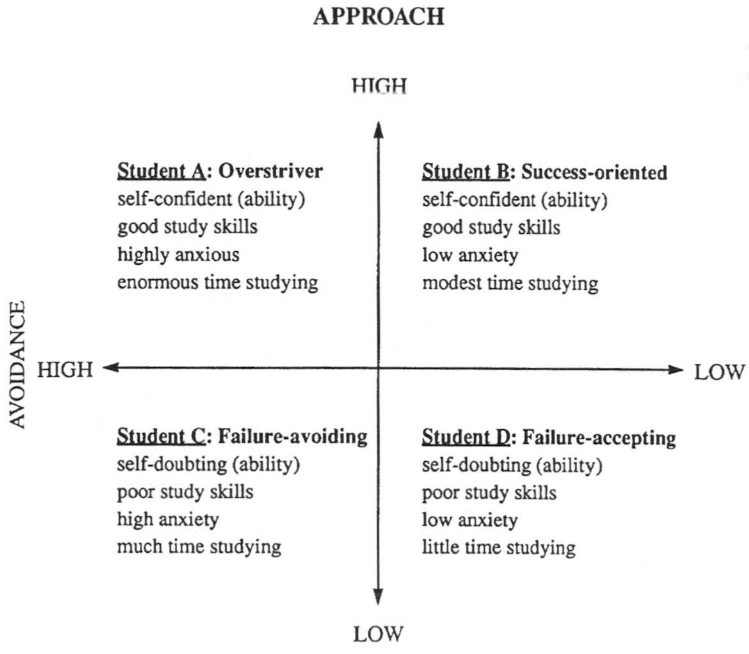

APPROACH

HIGH

Student A: Overstriver
self-confident (ability)
good study skills
highly anxious
enormous time studying

Student B: Success-oriented
self-confident (ability)
good study skills
low anxiety
modest time studying

AVOIDANCE   HIGH ← ——————————————————————— → LOW

Student C: Failure-avoiding
self-doubting (ability)
poor study skills
high anxiety
much time studying

Student D: Failure-accepting
self-doubting (ability)
poor study skills
low anxiety
little time studying

LOW

bipolar interpretation of achievement motivation in which approach and avoidance tendencies represent extreme polar opposites on only one dimension (e.g., Feather, 1961, 1963; Littig, 1963; Litwin, 1966; Moulton, 1965). By this reckoning approach and avoidance tendencies become blended within the same person so that everyone can be placed somewhere along a single continuum, differing only in relative amounts of hope and fear. Not only does this procedure confound the two approach and avoidance elements of the original model in unknown ways, and disregard the possibility of conflicting tendencies, but it also creates an awkwardness when trying to describe those persons for whom approach and avoidance tendencies balance off equally— the presumed zero point midway between high avoidance and high approach. Is a complete absence of motivation best represented by the resultant canceling of two extreme motives? Probably not. A bipolar model leaves no room for genuine indifference.

In an effort to reestablish Atkinson's original quadripolar model, we analyzed the learning characteristics and achievement styles of some 400 Berkeley undergraduates (Covington and Omelich, 1991) employing a newly developed battery of achievement motive measures which including self-ratings of perceived ability, proneness to anxiety arousal, and the quality of one's study habits and skills. A series of stepwise discriminant analyses confirmed Atkinson's original quadripolar model. Four distinct groups emerged, separated one from the other along two independent axes, one labeled approach and the other, avoidance. First, these data confirmed the classic distinction between success-oriented and failure-avoiding persons as behaviorally distinct (students B and C, respectively: see Figure 2). Success-oriented students rated themselves markedly higher on general ability than did failure avoiders, exhibited far less anxiety about their schoolwork, and harbored few fears of being unmasked as incompetent. Moreover, success-oriented individuals exhibited superior study skills, although they often spent less time preparing for tests than did many failure-avoiding students. Second, two hybrid groups also emerged: students high in both approach and avoidance tendencies (Student A), or *overstrivers*; and students low in both approach and avoidance tendencies (Student D), or *failure-acceptors* as we have called them (Covington and Omelich, 1985).

In self-worth terms, overstrivers attempt to avoid failure by succeeding! Although a seemingly clever response to academic threat, this strategy is basically defensive and eventually can prove self-defeating. Basically, overstrivers are conflicted over the prospects for success. On the one hand, success is sought after because it reassures them, but on the other, it perpetuates fear because overstrivers know they cannot succeed indefinitely, test-after-test, since their goal is not merely excellence, but perfection. Consistent with this self-worth interpretation, overstrivers were found to combine behaviors associated with both pure-approach and pure-avoidance tendencies (see Figure 2). As to the approach dimension, overstrivers possessed superior study strategies, persisted in their work (but to a fault), and gave themselves high marks for ability. As to avoidance tendencies, overstrivers were unsure of their claims on brilliance, and as a result experience considerable anxiety whenever they studied for a test.

From a self-worth perspective, failure-accepting students are those individuals who have given up the struggle to maintain a sense of worth via ability, and because of repeated failures in school, have become convinced to a certainty of their incompetency. We will consider shortly the causal dynamics involved in this progression from defensive failure-avoidance to failure-acceptance. Failure-accepting individuals combine those behaviors and beliefs associated with both low-approach and low-avoidance tendencies. The relative absence of approach tendencies in this group was associated with a life of self-derogation where ability is concerned and with inferior study skills, while the relative absence of avoidance tendencies was associated with a pervasive lack of achievement affect (see also Covington and Omelich, 1985). This group expressed neither much pride in their successes, nor much shame in their failures. It appears that these students have resigned themselves to mediocrity as a way of life. Naturally, other interpretations of inaction are always possible, if only because of the inherent difficulty of explaining a negative event (in this case the relative absence of behavior). It is also possible that these individuals have simply chosen not to participate in what they perceive to be a useless contest, and have sought other alternative sources of personal satisfaction such as self-discovery or the pursuit of socially meaningful achievements (Roberts and Covington, 1991).

INTEGRATION

Recapping so far, we began with a review of research on the concept of achievement motivation organized around the metaphor of motives-as-drives. In the process we considered three successive waves of theory development—the need achievement model, a cognitive reinterpretation of need achievement, and then the marriage of these two approaches according to the tenets of self-worth theory. But how do these many factors—cognitive, motivational, and affective—all interact and play themselves out, causally, in real-life college classrooms? For answers we must look beyond the results of isolated correlational studies that merely establish simple associations between variables taken two at a time. Nor can we rely only on experimental laboratory studies conducted under artificial conditions. In the last analysis, we must investigate multiple variables operating simultaneously as they influence one another and impact jointly on distant achievement outcomes over extended periods of time and for the same persons.

To this end, a series of multivariate achievement studies was conducted at Berkeley in college classrooms. The time frames involved extended over meaningful periods in the academic life of students, ranging from an analysis of a single study/test cycle (Covington & Omelich, 1981) to investigations of several successive midterm examinations in the same course (Covington and Omelich, 1979a, 1984b, 1988; Covington, Omelich, and Schwarzer, 1986). In all cases, we ask several basic questions: Do emotional, cognitive, and motivational factors combine lawfully to influence achievement? And do different types of students respond differently to the challenges and threats inherent in college achievement?

The results of one representative study from our laboratory are reported here in some detail, supplemented by the work of other American as well as European investigators whose findings complement and extend this research. This particular study (Covington and Omelich, 1988) tracked 432 Berkeley undergraduates enrolled in an introductory psychology course over three midterm tests during which time some 200 observations were made per student. Among other things, these students were asked to rate the amount of anxiety they were experiencing at various points in the course, attribute reasons for their successes and failures following each test, indicate how frequently their study was compromised by intrusive worries, describe the sources of this worry, and judge their ability to handle the subject matter following each study session and each test. The general model around which this massive data set was organized is presented in Figure 3.F3

The horizontal dimension includes a temporal, stagewise sequence through which antecedent factors from each of three different psychological domains play out their respective roles in the achievement process. First, consider the domain of motives. Depending on their dominant motivational orientation (some combination of approach and

Figure 3: Interactive model of achievement dynamics: Motivational, cognitive, and emotional components.

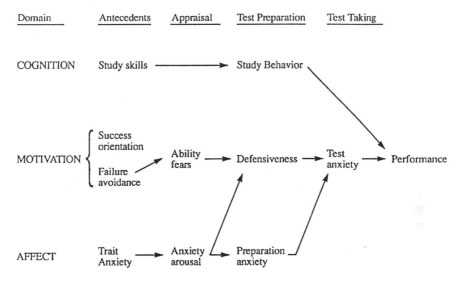

avoidance tendencies), students will be more or less concerned about their ability status, an issue that becomes especially salient for some students during the first few class meetings when they learn about the course requirements (appraisal stage). Students who believe the course to be within their intellectual capabilities are likely to view it as a challenge, whereas those who doubt their ability to succeed (e.g., failure-avoiders) will likely become threatened. According to theory, for this latter group perceptions of threat in turn trigger varying degrees of defensiveness as students prepare for each successive test (preparation stage). Similarly, those antecedent factors associated with the *cognitive* domain, such as the quality of one's study skills, also contribute to feelings of threat and challenge, with good study habits likely to offset the presence of threat (Tobias, 1985, 1986). Finally, regarding the emotional domain, anxiety aroused during the appraisal stage, will interfere with subsequent study and also eventually disrupt the recall of what was originally learned (anxiety → poor study → poor performance).

Not only do these three time-ordered strands exert a forward-reaching influence individually on a common outcome (in this case, test performance), but they also are likely to interact among themselves as students progress from one stage of the model to the next. These interactions can take many forms. Sometimes the relationship may be *compensatory* as when, for example, good study habits (cognitive strand) offset the negative influence of anxiety (emotional strand) on performance. Other times the relationship among domains may be *additive* or even *multiplicative*. For instance, for some students the presence of anxiety, far from disrupting achievement, may actually mobilize them to study harder than ever.

Having provided the general rationale for the various time-ordered linkages we investigated, it remains only to say that the data were analyzed according to multiple prediction procedures (Anderson and Evans, 1974) in which the numerous (multiple) kinds of information gathered at each stage in the model were used to predict eventual scores on achievement tests. There are several advantages to this approach. First, not only was a longitudinal perspective created, but, second, we were able to investigate the *relative* importance of various factors as predictors of test outcome, say, emotions versus cognitions (worries), at any point in the study/test cycle. Third, because we proposed a testable model in advance of actual data collection, we were justified in interpreting the results of the multiple prediction analysis in causal terms. Thus the arrows in Figure 3 imply cause-and-effect relationships as well as the direction of influence.

Failure-avoiding Students.

Prior research indicated that failure-avoiding students feel inadequately prepared (Covington and Omelich, 1988), harbor considerable doubts about their ability to succeed (Laux and Glanzmann, 1987; Salamé, 1984; Schmalt, 1982), and experience excessive achievement anxiety (Carver and Scheier, 1988; Hagtvet, 1984). This portrait was confirmed in all aspects by the Berkeley data. But how does this failure-avoiding legacy of fear and doubt enter into the achievement process itself?

During the appraisal stage various apprehensions were magnified out of all proportion for failure-avoiders (compared with the self-reports of success-oriented students), especially those worries associated with being revealed as incompetent and of not doing well enough to stay in school. These ability-linked doubts reverberated in a forward-reaching cascade (from left to right) across the entire model. Worries not only lingered, but intensified during the test preparation stage especially as the first test grew closer, and became manifest as defensively oriented thoughts that diverted the attention of failure-avoiding students from the study task at hand. They hoped, for example, that there would be no test ("I wish the test would somehow go away"), they externalized blame in anticipation of failure ("If I had a better teacher, I might do better"), and they sought relief from anxiety by minimizing the importance of any projected failure ("This course is less important than I originally thought"). Not surprisingly, such thoughts were accompanied by emotional tension and occasionally physiological reactions (upset stomach, dizziness) which in turn added their own unique contribution to the disruption of effective study.

Through this confection of denial, subterfuge and magical thinking we can sense the quiet desperation that serves as a seedbed for the many classic failure-avoiding strategies catalogued earlier, including procrastination and irrationally high goal-setting. As a consequence, failure-avoiding students find themselves largely unprepared even though on average they spent as much or more time studying (or at least going through the motions) as did success-oriented students.

In the final test-taking stage fears of incompetency were triggered anew, sometimes by seeing other students finishing the test early ("I'm so slow, I must really be dumb") or by the obsessive rehearsing of past failures, which recalls to mind a classic definition of anxiety: "The interest paid on trouble before it is due." Unlike mild emotional responses whose arousal depends on cues largely incidental to test-taking such as merely walking into an examination room, the kinds of reactions of which I speak here do not lose their potency once the test begins, but rather continue to preoccupy students even after the test is over in the form of self-criticism and rebuke.

Overall these dynamics place failure-avoiding students in harm's way for two reasons: They learn relatively less to begin with; then, what little they do learn is recalled only imperfectly—they forget the most basic facts and sometimes cannot even remember the questions they are trying to answer. Ironically enough, some failure-avoiding students appear deliberately, and repeatedly, to put themselves in jeopardy. Reagan (1991) studied a select group of community college students who continued to enroll for coursework, semester after semester, despite a record of failing grades. For these students, the majority of whom were identified as failure-avoiding, the noxious gauntlet of repeated failure was more than offset by the sense of self-importance and prestige afforded them by being enrolled in a college level course of study. Needless to say, it was their status as college students, and not their grades, that formed the basis for their projected public image.

Overstriving Students

Although overstrivers share much in common with other failure-prone students that is negative, they do possess certain redeeming qualities; namely, superior study skills and high ability despite their relentless self-doubts. As a result, rather than disrupting their study, anxiety acted to focus their considerable study skills. Overstrivers spent more time studying by far than any other type of student investigated; they were the first to begin studying sometimes weeks before the exam, and the last to stop often just before the instructor threatens to withhold the test unless they put away their notes. Basically this slavish devotion to study, which is more to be pitied than admired, occurs because overstrivers have no choice but to succeed. They dare not procrastinate, nor can they settle for less than perfection because they are betting on success, not on excused failure, as the way to prove their worth.

Eventually, however, the defensively driven character of such meticulous, excessive study catches up with overstrivers. As tension mounts during the test-taking stage, they suffer a massive failure to recall what they had spent so much time overlearning. The student who justifiably laments, "but I knew it cold before the exam," is likely an overstriver. Several hours after the first midterm was administered, all students in the Berkeley sample were invited back to retake parts of the test (Covington and Omelich, 1987a). It was overstrivers (those individuals who combined high anxiety and good study habits) who improved most on retesting, presumably due to the dissipation of a temporary blockage of otherwise superior mental functioning. This "anxiety-blockage" phenomenon is likely heightened by the fact that the presence of anxiety discourages deep-level processing during original learning, and favors instead superficial rote memorization. Information stored in such a mindless fashion is more subject to forgetting later since it was not organized around memorable principles and concepts in the first place (Covington, 1985c).

Failure-accepting Students

I have characterized failure-acceptors as individuals who have given up the struggle to define their worth in terms of competitive achievement via high ability, and as a consequence have become dispirited and apathetic. Although, as mentioned earlier, such indifference is potentially subject to many interpretations, the results of the Berkeley

study are consistent with the notion of a general state of resig-
nation. Not only are these undergraduates relatively lacking in the
proper study skills, but they also studied far less than did other
groups, and reported low levels of anxiety and worry at all stages
of the study/test cycle (Covington and Omelich, 1985). This pattern
parallels findings from the literature on learned helplessness which
has been described as the loss of hope or the will to act that accom-
panies a belief that no matter how hard one tries, failure is the
inevitable outcome (Abramson, Seligman, and Teasdale, 1978; Coyne
and Lazarus, 1980; Miller and Norman, 1979; Seligman, 1975). Interestingly, it has been shown that the trigger for such despair is not
the fact that trying hard does not work, that is, a noncontingent
relationship between effort and outcome, but rather the fact that
despair follows from the personal implication that one is incompetent
(Covington, 1985a). Thus the phenomenon of learned helplessness
becomes yet another instance of the larger self-worth legacy whenever
individuals anchor their sense of worth to ability status and to competitive achievement. Feelings of incompetency give rise to task-irrelevant
worry about ability which in turn interferes with effective information
processing (Carver, 1979; Kuhl, 1981, 1984; Lavelle, Metalsky, and
Coyne, 1979).

Success-oriented Students

Success-oriented students are especially intriguing for the fact that
the measures included in the Berkeley study did a relatively poor
job of predicting the test scores of these students. It appears that
the dynamics that uniquely describe success-oriented students were
not well represented in the model presented in Figure 3. Even self-
estimates of ability, a highly salient factor among all the failure-prone
groups, was only marginally related to the achievement of success-
oriented individuals. It is likely that in a competitive climate, ability
factors become exaggerated for those individuals who are already self-
doubting, whereas self-confident individuals continued learning for its
own sake, a goal for which variations in perceived ability are less importance to success (Roberts and Covington, 1991). In any event, there
is mounting evidence that success-oriented individuals can accommodate to a wide range of achievement conditions, and still do a
uniformly superior job. For instance, in an attempt to minimize test-
taking anxiety, Covington and Omelich (1987b) arranged a set of test
items so that either the easier items were presented first, assuming that

students would be encouraged by their initial successes, or hard items presented first on the grounds that failure at a difficult task would hold fewer implications for ability and therefore render the remainder of the test less threatening. Not only did success-oriented students perform equally well under all item orders (including a random order of difficulty), but their performances were invariably superior to those of either failure-avoiders, overstrivers, or failure-acceptors. Also regarding the matter of uniform superiority, we know that the performance of intrinsically motivated students is less influenced by the presence of tangible rewards, because these individuals are already performing at their best, and are less likely to suffer a performance decrement if tangible rewards are withdrawn (Harackiewicz and Manderlink, 1984; Harackiewicz, Abrahams, and Wageman, 1987).

We can draw several broad conclusions from the Berkeley data. First, the achievement process is best viewed as a complex interaction of numerous factors—self-protective cognitions, emotions, and motivational dispositions—whose relationships to one another and ultimately to achievement outcomes (test performance) change as individual students move progressively through different stages of the study/test cycle. These relationships also vary lawfully depending on the kinds of students under observation.

Second, this study also clarified the relationship between the so-called *skill-deficit* and *retrieval-deficit* theories of anxiety which provide quite different explanations for the general finding of a negative correlation between measures of test anxiety, on the one hand, and achievement test scores on the other (Schwarzer, Seipp, and Schwarzer, 1989; Seipp, 1991; Seipp and Schwarzer, 1990). The retrieval-deficit position holds that anxiety interferes with the recall of information during test taking when students must remember, or retrieve, what they learned earlier (Deffenbacher, 1977, 1986; Liebert and Morris, 1967; Mandler and Sarason, 1952). By contrast, skill-deficit proponents argue that poor performance is largely the result of inadequate study, and that test-anxious individuals actually have little to retrieve (Culler and Holahan, 1980). By this reckoning, anxious feelings are merely a noncausal byproduct of recognizing that one is unprepared and likely to fail. Some researchers have treated the skill-deficit and retrieval-deficit positions as incompatible (e.g., Kirkland and Hollandsworth, 1980). But we now know that both kinds of deficiencies can operate to varying degrees within the same individual depending on the type of students involved. Both deficits are present among failure-avoiding students; overstrivers are relatively more handicapped by the failure to retrieve, while failure-acceptors suffer most heavily during the acquisition phase of the study/test cycle.

These findings hold considerable implications for the treatment of test anxiety. According to this analysis, no single therapeutic intervention will be equally effective for all students. This point has not always been fully appreciated by university-based counseling and guidance centers. Until a closer match is created between the choice of therapy and the particular sources of disruption, the record of therapeutic intervention will remain spotty (Hembree, 1988). Naveh-Benjamin (1985) convincingly demonstrated this point when he deliberately matched and mismatched different kinds of students with different therapeutic interventions. He provided relaxation therapy for anxious students who already possessed good study skills (akin to our overstrivers) and for anxious skill-deficient students he provided study practice. With these proper matches, both groups improved their school work. But not so for two identical comparison groups to whom Naveh-Benjamin gave the same treatments but in the reverse order.

Third, and finally, we can now appreciate why some researchers have found little or no correspondence between academic performance and the possession of good study skills (e.g., Schuman, Walsh, Olson, and Etheridge, 1985). Students do not always prepare adequately, even though they may know how, because effort is potentially threatening to their sense of worth. Clearly, knowing how best to study is a highly important ingredient for success in college, but this knowledge can only benefit students fully if the prevailing achievement context is nonthreatening.

REPEATED FAILURES

The student typology presented in Figure 2 must retain a measure of fluidity. The boundaries between groups are intended to be semipermeable, reflecting the fact that in real life students are often in flux and transition. Sometimes fearful students reverse course and become more success-oriented as the result of counseling, while other students may change precipitously and in a negative direction when a single failure forces an overstriver to give up all pretense of being successful.

Researchers in both the United States and Europe have begun investigating the processes by which otherwise able college students become increasingly discouraged about their ability to succeed, a dynamic that is inevitably triggered by repeated academic failure (for a review, see Stiensmeier-Pelster and Schürmann, 1990). In a second wave of analysis of the Berkeley data base described above, Covington and Omelich (1990) followed the fortunes of those undergraduates who failed (i.e., fell short of their grade goals) on several successive midterms. Following each disappointment, these students were asked to rate their chances for success the next time, to estimate their ability to succeed, and to judge the importance of ability as a factor in doing well. They also rated the degree of shame they felt at having failed and attributed various causes to their failures, including bad luck, insufficient effort, and instructor indifference.

Following the first failure, students typically registered surprise, especially if failure was unexpected, a finding consistent with the work of Schwarzer and his colleagues (Schwarzer, Jerusalem, and Schwarzer, 1983; Schwarzer, Jerusalem, and Stiksrud, 1984) who tracked German high school students over a two-year period. For some of the Berkeley students, typically those who were success-oriented, surprise was mixed with a resolve to do better the next time (which they usually did). But for other students, feelings of shame dominated their reactions to failure, particularly among those who rated themselves low in ability to begin with. A greater tendency to blame others for their failures was also detected among these students as they began preparing for the second examination. As one failure followed another, feelings of shame continued unabated and often intensified, driven by a progressive decrease in the students' self-perceived levels of ability. Most destructive by far was the fact that as self-estimates of ability dwindled, estimates of the importance of ability as a causal factor in attaining success increased. Thus these hapless students believed themselves deficient, increasingly so, in the very factor—ability—that was becoming more and more important in their minds. Again, these dynamics were most obvious among those students who initially held themselves in the lowest self-regard.

The key to resisting this slide into despondency appears to be the extent to which the individuals' suspicions of incompetency crystallize to a certainty. To the degree that students remain uncertain about their ability status, they will continue to strive and in some cases can be driven to extraordinary achievements in an effort to reduce uncertainty in a positive direction (Coopersmith, 1967). Maintaining a state of uncertainty regarding one's ability in the face of repeated failures depends in turn on how credibile are the excuses one gives for failure. Insuring that excuses are credible in the eyes of others is an exceedingly complex undertaking which requires that explanations "fit the constraints of reason" (Heider, 1958); that is, they must not only appear logical (free of egotistic reasoning) but excuse-givers must also be convinced themselves that others will agree with these inflated views of their ability, a condition referred to as *ego-centrism* (Jones and Nisbett, 1971).

Covington and Omelich (1978) investigated the conditions under which college students are most likely to act in an egotistic fashion. Egotism was defined as rating one's own ability higher than the ability of others under identical circumstances of failure. The results indicated that students overestimate their own ability compared with their estimates of the ability of others whenever logical excuses are available to explain their own poor performance (such as having failed due to illness) even though everyone had exactly the same excuse! Also in these situations students believed outsiders would agree with their over-stated self-estimates thus closing the circle of self-deception. It is only when low ability was a compelling expla-nation for failure (when, for instance, the student tried hard and failed anyway) that these undergraduates moderated their inflated views of self and brought them more in line with those they attributed to others.

This study supports the view that individuals tend to aggrandize their ability status whenever reason permits. It is in this sense (of Self-worth theory) that the need for self-justification can be said to be the primary psychological reality and rational considerations secondary and supportive, or as Reuven Bar-Levav puts it, "In general, people are led by their feelings, and then they unknowingly invent rationalizations to explain their actions or decisions to themselves and to justify them to others."

Another revealing aspect of this experiment concerns the presence of pervasive sex differences. The findings as just described apply to male students both high and low in self-perceptions of ability as well as to high self-confident females. However, compared with these three groups, women with low self-confidence underestimated their ability status in all conditions of failure, whether their estimates were justified or not, and believed that observers would agree with these excessively pessimistic views. Far from aggrandizing ability, then, these women denigrated their talents beyond what was ratio-nally indicated. The defensive tendency reported among males is scarcely surprising given the consistent evidence that males are more likely to tie their sense of worth to ability, especially their ability to compete for and hold jobs (Snyder, Stephan, and Rosenfeld, 1976;

Streufert and Streufert, 1969; Wolosin, Sherman, and Till, 1973). By contrast there is considerable evidence that many females view the struggle for intellectual status as less role appropriate (Dweck, Davidson, Nelson, and Enna, 1978; Nicholls, 1975; Stephan, Rosenfield and Stephan, 1976). This suggests that women may be more vulnerable to the dynamics of learned helplessness and more quickly give up the struggle to maintain a positive self-image based on ability.

DIRECTIONS FOR CHANGE: MOTIVES AS GOALS

This self-worth perspective on motivation and college academics is troubling. Basically it portrays college classrooms as battlefields where the rules favor sabotage, lackluster effort, and self-deception. Naturally, it can be properly argued that this accounting is far too pessimistic, and that on balance American universities and colleges approximate the more idealized view of schools as places where "teachers gladly teach and students gladly learn." No reasonable person would contend that these disturbing dynamics are solely the product of a system of higher education gone awry. From the larger perspective, these failures are as much or more a consequence of the processes and risks of growing up in an increasingly dangerous and unforgiving world as they are the result of misappropriated educational policy. Still, according to self-worth theory, certain aspects of academic life do represent potential threats to learners and to the development of the talent necessary for America's economic, political, and social survival. What are these sources of peril? And in what directions might we find relief? First, we should note that we are not dealing simply with a matter of inadequate motivation. According to self-worth theory, poor performance is as much the result of being *overmotivated*, but for the wrong reasons, as it is of not being motivated at all. The real threat to learning occurs whenever the individual's sense of worth becomes tied to the ability to achieve competitively. If pride in success and shame in failure depend largely on self-perceptions of ability, then students' involvement in learning will last only for as long as they continue to succeed as a means to aggrandize ability. But once failure threatens a self-image of competency, with its legacy of shame and anger, students will likely withdraw from learning.

By this analysis, the best solutions require changing the reasons for learning, not simply intensifying motivation driven out of a competitive climate. This does not mean that we should stop rewarding noteworthy achievements or no longer withold rewards when students work beneath their capacity. To argue otherwise would fly in the face of a world dominated by contingent incentives. Boggiano points to the pervasiveness of such contingencies when she observes that "If you sell enough items then you will receive a commission; if you succeed on the GRE then you will be admitted to graduate school; if you publish enough research then you will receive tenure" (Boggiano and Pittman, in press).

What I am arguing for is an alternative basis for rewarding behavior, one that shifts the payoff away from being competitive to becoming competent. Gardner (1961) makes this same point when he proposes that we measure excellence, not as a comparison among individuals, but rather as a comparison "... between myself at my best and myself at my worst. It is this latter comparison which enables me to assert that I am being true to the best that is in me—or forces me to confess that I am not" (p. 128).

Another way to envision this transformation is to set aside the dominant metaphor of *motives-as-drives* in favor of *motives-as-goals*—incentives that draw, not drive, individuals toward action (Covington, 1992; Bolles, 1967). Clearly, the distinction between drives and goals is elusive and the concepts somewhat overlapping. For instance, we could just as well describe Alice's compulsive behavior in our earlier example, not as driven, but as goal-oriented—with the dubious goal of aggrandizing her own importance by outdoing others. Yet goals and drives are not the same, and in the difference lie several advantages favoring the concept of goals for educators. First, goals are more malleable than the kinds of deeply rooted inclinations of which drive theory speaks, and by rewarding some goals and not others, instructors can change the reasons students learn, which is to say, change their motives. Second, goal-setting stands as a practical surrogate for motives. We need not await final definitions of the kind Drucker found missing in his appraisal of motivation research before we take steps to solve more immediate problems that are basically motivational in nature. Third, goals (as contrasted to drives) become educational objectives in their own right; thus, motives are not merely the handmaidens to higher achievement, but also give meaning and purpose to achievement.

What goals are worth encouraging? They are scarcely new; but they are honored more in the breach than in the observance because educators rarely arrange reward contingencies in ways that favor them directly. The first goal is that of self-mastery, becoming the best one can be; the second, defined by Nicholls (1989) as a commitment to solving society's problems, involves helping others. The third goal concerns the expression of creativity and the satisfaction of curiosity. How might we arrange learning so these positive reasons are promoted systematically? Several broad guidelines have emerged from the research literature over the past years. Three are considered here.

ENGAGING TASKS

College assignments themselves must be worthy of sustained curiosity, and challenge the highest levels of thought and creativity of which students are presently capable. What task characteristics promote these positive ends (Malone, 1981)?

First, tasks are engaging to the degree they feature multiple goals that unfold progressively as work proceeds. Diggory (1966) describes the enormous staying power of such self-initiated complexity:

> If [the individual] chooses an activity he never attempted before, his first attempts will be purely exploratory...[but] once this exploration ends and he begins a more or less systematic attempt to produce something, he very likely will set implicit or explicit aspirations for his successive attempts.... Now he tries to produce a result that is as good as the last one, but quicker. Next he may disregard time altogether and try to improve the product. Later he may concentrate on the smoothness of the project and attempt to swing elegantly through a well-ordered and efficient routine. He may discover and invent new processes or adapt new materials or new methods of work. To the casual uninterested observer this may all seem repetitive and dull, but the operator, the worker, may be intensely interested because he never has exactly the same goals on two successive trials.... (p.125–126)

This passage also conveys something of the tremendous need for humans to improve themselves, to do things better, or at least differently, a disposition which is taken full advantage of by the college instructor in physics who announces to her students (upon their having developed an efficient solar cell), "Now I want you to make it cheaper," "smaller," and so forth. The civil engineering professor also turns this human potential to advantage when he identifies, one by one, the various negative consequences of his students' decision to dam the upper Nile basin as a way to convert the Egyptian desert to productive farmlands—severe erosion of the Nile delta and rising salt levels in the Mediterranean basin—all unforeseen, but not unpredictable consequences if his students had but paid closer attention to the supplementary readings on oceanographics, biology, and atmospheric physics. The professor's next assignment to his students is to correct the problems that they themselves have created.

Second, tasks are engaging of creativity to the extent they challenge preconceived notions, require students to detect familiar forms in unfamiliar settings, and to be puzzled by the obvious. Science curricula provide especially rich opportunities for identifying and rewarding creative styles of thought, ranging from practicing the art of problem discovery to becoming sensitized to the dynamics of serendipity, the ability to find something of value when you are looking for something else (Shapiro, 1986). Then there are opportunities to practice the skills involved in conceiving of and modifying unlikely, far-fetched, but potentially useful ideas (Covington, 1986) such as the unlikely notion of moving ships *over* the water, not through the water (Hovercraft). Introducing controversies and staging debates that require students to take sides or to entertain unpopular or fanciful perspectives are excellent methods to keep students sufficiently challenged to remain open and receptive to further learning.

Third, intrinsic task involvement is enhanced by the social reinforcers that accompany cooperative learning. Not only can all players win when learning becomes a cooperative venture (Ames, 1981; Harris and Covington, 1989; Slavin, 1983, 1984), but learning takes place in a social context where most meaningful adult work occurs anyway, and also becomes part of what Lave (1988) calls *authentic activities* where learners become apprentices who hone the skills of their craft through group collaboration and social interaction. Consider the field of mathematics. Shoenfeld (1989) argues for the teaching of mathematics as basically an empirical, group-defined discipline, one consisting of data and mutual discovery and sharing much like biology and physics. From such a vantage point learning mathematics becomes a group enterprise in which truth becomes "that for which the majority of the community believes it has compelling arguments. In mathematics truth is socially negotiated, as it is in science" (p. 9).

Finally, tasks are inherently self-absorbing to the extent they allow the student to exercise control over the degree of challenge. The quintessential, everyday example is the game of tag (Eifferman, 1974). Here players adjust the risks of being caught as well as the chances of catching others by altering the distance they stay away from whoever is it, in the first instance, and deciding whom to chase, in the second instance. The drama and excitement generated by the manageable challenges of playing tag need not be limited only to young players, nor need they function merely for recreational purposes, but also lie at the heart of what has been called *serious games* (Abt 1971/1987; Covington, 1992).

PROVIDING SUFFICIENT REINFORCERS

Arranging exciting learning opportunities is a necessary first step in shifting the reasons for learning in more positive directions, but more is needed. Students must also be rewarded for their efforts at self-mastery, for preparing to help others, and for problem discovery. The kinds of rewards associated with these intrinsic reasons for learning have a special motivating property: their absolute nature. These rewards do not depend on how many others succeed or fail, but rather on the kinds of tasks chosen—with the greatest number of rewards going to the realistic goal setter—and on whether or not one's performance meets or surpasses the prevailing (or absolute) standards of excellence. In short, these rewards are plentiful and open to all.

A number of grading schema have been developed to accommodate absolute standards (for reviews, see Block, 1977, 1984; Block and Burns, 1976; Kulik, Kulik, and Cohen, 1979; Kulik, Kulik, and Shwalb, 1982), the most sophisticated being a *grade-choice arrangement* (Covington, 1989). Here students work for any grade they wish and stop whenever they have accumulated sufficient credit, so many points needed for an A, so many points for a B, and so forth. Points are awarded depending on how many tasks the individual undertakes, the complexity of these assignments, and the quality of work performed.

Motivationally speaking, a number of benefits derive from the use of absolute grading systems. For one thing, the presence of absolute standards is known to encourage perceptions of fairness in grading (Covington and Omelich, 1984b). For another, they also enhance perceptions of personal control over events because students know what they must do and how well they must perform for a given grade (Ames, Ames, and Felker, 1980; Crockenberg, Bryant, and Wilce, 1976; Williams et al., 1976). It is this positive covariation between the amount of work expended by students and the rewards (grades) attained that forestalls feelings of learned helplessness. In this connection, a sense of personal control and autonomy has been linked to increased task engagement. In a study involving 10 college courses including three English classes, three biology classes, and four social science classes, Garcia and Pintrich (1991) found that those courses rated highest on an autonomy dimension by students (e.g., "Students can negotiate with the instructor over the nature of the course requirements") were also judged highest for eliciting intrinsic task involvement. Moreover, feelings of task engagement increased as the year progressed among those courses rated in the highest quartile for autonomy, while self-perceptions of engagement actually declined in the same period among the lowest quartile classes.

However, for all the potential advantages of absolute grading systems, several issues remain. One concerns the sheer frequency of rewards. There is considerable evidence that the reinforcing value of rewards depends on their scarcity; that is, the fewer the rewards the more sought after they become (for a review, see Covington, 1992). What, then, will happen when rewards are made freely available? Will not their value be cheapened? No, not necessarily. Scarcity becomes valuable largely in those situations where students are playing an ability game. The fewer the rewards, the more ability becomes a factor in attaining them and in turn the more their attainment signals high ability. By contrast, when rewards are distributed on an absolute merit basis, especially for work performed on inherently satisfying tasks, pride in accomplishment comes to depend more on how hard one worked and on whether or not learners believe themselves to have measured up favorably to the instructor's standards. This phenomenon was demonstrated in a study conducted by Covington and Jacoby (1983) in which several hundred introductory psychology students completed various work projects for their grade. These projects required that students create their own solutions to contemporary issues, dilemmas, and puzzles within the field of psychology including devising an explanation for the *moon illusion* (the fact that the moon appears larger on the horizon than at its zenith) and designing toys to help accelerate young children through various intellectual stages of development. All projects were graded in absolute terms, but the level of standards employed varied. One group was always given full credit as long as they met a minimum standard, whereas a second group was required to meet increasingly stringent standards of excellence depending on the grade they sought (i.e., grade-choice arrangement). Those students who received full credit for a minimal effort produced inferior products, were less satisfied with their final course grade, and felt themselves less deserving than those other students who had worked much harder. Moroever, for students in this latter group course satisfaction was undiminished despite the fact that a disproportionate number of their classmates also received the same high grades. In short, when much is demanded of students and much given by them in response, especially in response to meaningful problems, students tend to feel satisfied no matter how many others also achieve at or above the same grade level.

SUCCESS-ORIENTED ASSESSMENT

When competitive-based grades are used as motivators to arouse or goad students to greater effort then task engagement, even performance itself, is likely to suffer, especially among failure-prone students (Covington, 1992; Deci, 1975; Deci and Ryan, 1987; Goldberg, 1965). These students tend to give up in the face of poor grades because they interpret failure as the result of inability for which they believe there is no remedy. At the same time, rewarding failure-prone students with higher grades than they expect, as a positive incentive, is likely to be met with disbelief if not suspicion because they do not expect to succeed, and when they do succeed, success is typically attributed to factors beyond their control such as luck.

By contrast, when grades are treated as a source of information or feedback (as in absolute merit systems) they can take on intrinsic properties. Students come to seek out information, and even respond well to negative feedback as long as it provides a constructive basis for self-improvement (Butler and Nisan, 1986). In this connection, one of the most promising forms of assessment involves performance-based appraisals. For the reader unfamiliar with them, performance-based assessments are best explained by example (Frederiksen and Collins, 1989). Consider the concept of *verbal aptitude*, which traditionally is assessed by administering verbal analogies or tests of vocabulary skill. In performance terms, however, verbal aptitude might be defined as the ability to formulate and express arguments in meaningful contexts such as requiring students to develop arguments favoring their side of the law in a small claims court action. Such tasks are reminiscent of those described earlier as *authentic activities* with the addition that, following work on the assignment, students are provided sample answers (feedback) of varying quality, ranging from "exemplary" or "acceptable" to "incomplete" so that it becomes clear to students just how a particular performance is being judged and how they can improve. Hopefully, performance-based testing will encourage students to become their own critics, to notice what is distinctive about their own work, and what is still missing and needs to be accomplished (Levin, 1990). At its most profound, the assessment function becomes an integral part of the instructional process itself (deLange Jzn, 1987).

A DILEMMA RESOLVED

Motivationally speaking, these guidelines for change emphasize a task-focused approach, not an ability-focused approach to learning, with assessment procedures designed to maximize the achievement of *all* students. But this vision of the educational mission and particularly the nontraditional role and function of testing and grades is at funda-mental odds with the purpose of schooling as a selection device for identifying those students most capable of further learning. Many educators stress the predictive role of grades as imperfect, yet useful, indices of how efficiently a person will learn similar material on future occasions. They also argue that competitive sorting provides an orderly way to distribute individuals proportionately across the available jobs in our society, some of which are more attractive than others (for a critique, see Deutsch, 1975, 1979). Competitive grading has long been the primary mechanism for assigning talent according to job demands and availability, a reality which has infuriated many educational reformers, among them Campbell (1974) who points out that the whole frantic scramble to win over others is essential for the kinds of institutions that our schools have become, "bargain-basement personnel screening agencies for business and government" (p. 145–146). Campbell's remark perhaps more than any other lays bare the fundamental incompatibility of the mission confronting all of education: Schools—elementary, secondary, and post-secondary alike—are not only places of learning, but also places for sorting out those capable of learning the most. And teachers are caught in the middle. When teachers view their primary job to maximize the academic potential of each student, they recognize hard work and reward persistence on task. But when they are asked to recommend those students who are most suitable for highly prestigious jobs, it is ability not dedication that becomes the dominant criteria (Kaplan and Swant, 1973). Naturally, this selection function is not lost on students. Little wonder that so many of them define their worth in terms of their ability to compete successfully.

The vital question becomes how can institutions of higher learning balance the seemingly incompatible goals of intrinsic task engagement and learning for its own sake against the demands for externally regulated talent selection? I believe the key to resolving this dilemma is the fact that for students at least the paramount issue regarding their own feelings of well being is not so much a matter of the presence of competitive pressure, even severe pressure, as it is a perceived lack of opportunities for instrinsic satisfaction. Meaningful academic work appears to be the critical factor for mitigating the otherwise abrasive gauntlet of competition. Our anecdotal evidence suggests that when students succeed at valued tasks over which they have some choice and control, and can gain the respect of their peers and coworkers, and the admiration of their mentors, then final course grades even those that are computed competitively are far less important in determining the perceived value of a course than for those students who are also judged competitively, but who have little opportunity to satisfy intrinsic interests and curiosities. The experience of Berkeley undergraduates indicates that intrinsic satisfaction comes largely from opportunities to work in field placements, or to volunteer for community service in conjunction with regular course offerings, and the opportunity to produce things of value in classes including creating needed educational material such as new bibliographies or instructional manuals (Promoting Student Success at Berkeley, 1991).

It may seem improbable that individuals can actively pursue intrinsic goals in institutions that also rank order their output publicly and competitively. But we know they can. At present the best evidence on this point comes from research with children. Ames and Archer (1987) observed elementary school youngsters who perceived themselves either to be in a mastery-oriented classroom—striving for the sake of self-improvement through effort—or in classrooms dominated by a performance-orientation—striving to do better than someone else by reason of ability. These researchers also observed classroom combinations of both performance- and mastery-orientations. As long as mastery goals were in evidence, the presence of competition did not diminish intrinsic task engagement. Students still explained their successes and failures in terms of variations in effort expended—a decidedly task-oriented attribute; they also used sophisticated planing strategies in their work, and chose problems where "you can learn a lot of new things but will also have some difficulty and make many mistakes." Also, it appears that the use of competitive or norm-based feedback which establishes one's rank order status in the larger group is at times actually sought out by students and can actually benefit learning especially in the early stages of work on a task as long as other forms of feedback are also available, including samples of work reflecting various absolute levels of quality and information about different styles of thinking or permissable approaches to the problem (Butler, in press).

These findings are central to the process of educational reform at all levels, because if striving for personal excellence requires the virtual absence of competitive comparisons, then change would be impossible. This line of reasoning suggests an important future research agenda: Asking the question of how much or how little an emphasis must be placed on a mastery or merit-based orientation, and for what kinds of students, in order to offset the inevitable press of competition. Perhaps far fewer and less radical changes are needed to tip the classroom balance in favor of spontaneity, involvement, and creativity than was once thought. Yet the answers will likely be complex. For example, will reducing competition actually rob some students of their will to achieve? This query is especially relevant for overstrivers whose reasons for succeeding may actually depend on the presence of a threat to their worth. Although educators are in no position presently to answer these kinds of questions fully, at least they are the proper questions to ask when it comes to reshaping the educational experience of our youth.

CONCLUSIONS

The reader may well ask if there is anything particularly new about the motivational guidelines proposed here since virtually all the examples are standard teaching practice at the post-secondary level. For instance, project-oriented courses (those that feature authentic tasks) are much in evidence on university and college campuses especially in the professional schools and in the applied arts and sciences including architecture and engineering. Similarly, opportunities already abound for students to participate in fieldwork which allow them to integrate theory and practice as well as to clarify career objectives. Nor is there much that is new about the educational philosophy underlying these recommendations that draw heavily on the notion of *reflective inquiry* first made popular by John Dewey (1916, 1963) in the early part of this century and developed more fully by Hullfish and Smith (1961) and by Pratte (1988).

What *is* new, however, is that these familiar teaching practices that evolved mostly through trial-and-error experimentation are now being legitimized within a network of empirically grounded, conceptually based theories. Theory helps teachers recognize what is profound about the commonplace; it tells them when they are on the right track, when they are not, and what corrections may be needed. Moreover, current motivation theory is quite sophisticated. No longer are investigators content with searching for simple correspondences between variables, say, demonstrating that as anxiety level increases, academic performance tends to decrease. These discoveries were a good start, but now we know that such general relationships are controlled by moderator variables including the reasons for learning and the causal attributions that students make. Until relatively recent times notions of achievement motivation were so poorly defined and their linkage to classroom success and failure so imperfectly delineated as to provide little in the way of guidance to educators who have been vexed by a host of puzzles. But all that has begun to change. For instance, instructors may wonder, if high achievement enhances one's status, then why is there only a marginal relationship between GPA and satisfaction as a student? We now know the answer is that the relationship between self-acceptance and academic performance depends on the reasons students learn, some of which can be self-defeating and dissatisfying, such as achieving to avoid feelings of inferiority. As a second example, why should otherwise highly successful students be devastated after only *one* failure; should not one's accumulated successes count for more than that? No, not always, especially if one is driven to succeed out of a fear of failing. Here even an isolated failure confirms what overstrivers have feared all along, that they are unworthy of perfection. And third, why should some failure-threatened students perform best when the odds of failing are greatest? Should not a hopeless cause increase their despair? From a self-worth perspective, there is no puzzle here. Vying against long odds permits threatened students to perform at their best because failing at an exceedingly difficult task holds few implications for ability. Similarly, why should students with low self-confidence reject success when it occurs? Because they fear the implied obligation that success must be repeated, and they doubt their ability to do so. Finally, why should failure devastate some individuals and mobilize others to greater action? From an attributional perspective, the answer is clear. Failure affects individuals differently depending on their causal explanations, with success-oriented individuals believing failure to be reversible through renewed effort, while failure-threatened students see increased effort as a waste of time.

As a group, these examples illustrate that the relationship between motives and performance is complex; and at times, the predictions of motivation theory are counterintuitive, but lawful nonetheless. It is this lawfulness that permits educators to begin redressing those conditions described by the Carnegie Foundation for the Advancement of Teaching whose quote opens this chapter. Leaving aside the issue of whether or not we can do anything to improve schooling—resistance to reform being what is—at least we have a surer and growing grasp on what we should do if we could.

REFERENCES

Abramson, L.Y., Seligman, M.E.P., and Teasdale, J.D. (1978). Learned helplessness in humans: Critique and reformulation. *Journal of Abnormal Psychology* 87: 49–74.

Abt, C.C. (1971/1987). *Serious Games*. New York: Lanham.

Ames, C. (1981). Competitive versus cooperative reward structures: The influence of individual and group performance factors on achievement attributions and affect. *American Educational Research Journal* 18: 273–388.

Ames, C. (1984). Achievement attributions and self-instructions under competitive and individualistic goal structure. *Journal of Educational Psychology* 76: 478–487.

Ames, C., and Ames, R. (1984). Systems of student and teacher motivation: Toward a qualitative definition. *Journal of Educational Psychology* 76: 535–556.

Ames, C., Ames, R., and Felker, D. (1980). Effects of self-concept on children's causal attributions and self-reinforcement. *Journal of Educational Psychology* 71: 613–619.

Ames, C., and Archer, J. (1987). Mothers' beliefs about the role of ability and effort in school learning. *Journal of Educational Psychology* 79: 409–414.

Anderson, J.G., and Evans, F.B. (1974). Causal models in educational research: Recursive models. *American Education Research Journal* 11: 29–39.

Arkin, R.M., Detchon, C.S., and Maruyama, G. M. (1982). Roles of attribution, affect, and cognitive interference in test anxiety. *Journal of Personality and Social Psychology* 43: 1111–1124.

Atkinson, J.W. (1957). Motivational determinants of risk-taking behavior. *Psychological Review* 64: 359–372.

Atkinson, J.W. (1964). *An Introduction to Motivation*. Princeton, NJ: Van Nostrand.

Atkinson, J.W. (1981). Studying personality in the context of an advanced motivational psychology. *American Psychologist* 36: 117–128.

Atkinson, J.W., and Litwin, G.H. (1960). Achievement motive and test anxiety conceived as motive to approach success and motive to avoid failure. *Journal of Abnormal and Social Psychology* 60: 52–63.

Barnard, J.W., Zimbardo, P.G., and Sarason, S.B. (1968). Teachers' ratings of student personality traits as they relate to IQ and social desirability. *Journal of Educational Psychology* 59: 128–132.

Battle, E.S (1965). Motivational determinants of academic task persistence. *Journal of Personality and Social Psychology* 2: 209–218.

Beery, R.G. (1975). Fear of failure in the student experience. *Personnel and Guidance Journal* 54: 190–203.

Berglas, S., and Jones, E. (1978). Drug choice as a self-handicapping strategy in response to noncontingent success. *Journal of Personality and Social Psychology* 36: 405–417.

Birney, R.C., Burdick, H., and Teevan, R.C. (1969). *Fear of Failure*. New York: Van Nostrand.

Block, J.H. (1977). Motivation, evaluation, and mastery learning. *UCLA Educator* 12: 31–37.

Block, J.H. (1984). Making school learning activities more playlike: Flow and mastery learning. *The Elementary School Journal* 85: 65–75.

Block, J.H., and Burns, R.B. (1976). Mastery learning. In L.S. Schulman (ed.), *Review of Research in Education*. Itasca, IL: Peacock.

Boggiano, A.K., and Pittman, T.S. (eds.), (in press). *Achievement and Motivation: A Social-Development Perspective*. New York: Cambridge University Press.

Bolles, R.C. (1967). *Theory of Motivation*. New York: Harper and Row.

Brown, J., and Weiner, B. (1984). Affective consequences of ability versus effort ascriptions: Controversies, resolutions, and quandaries. *Journal of Educational Psychology* 76: 146–158.

Burton, D., and Martens, R. (1986). Pinned by their own goals: An exploratory investigation into why kids drop out of wrestling. *Journal of Sport Psychology* 8: 1983–1997.

Butler, R. (in press). What young people want to know when: Effects of mastery and ability goals on interest in different kinds of social comparisons. *Journal of Personality and Social Psychology*.

Butler, R., and Nisan, M. (1986). Effects of no feedback, task-related comments, and grade on intrinsic instruction and performance. *Journal of Educational Psychology* 78: 210–216.

Campbell, D.N. (1974, October). On being number one: Competition in education. *Phi Delta Kappan* 143–146.

Carnegie Foundation for the Advancement of Teaching. (1977). *Missions of the College Curriculum: A Contemporary Review with Suggestions*. San Francisco: Jossey-Bass.

Carnegie Foundation for the Advancement of Teaching. (1989). *The Condition of the Professoriate: Attitudes and Trends*. New York: The Carnegie Corporation.

Carse, J.P. (1986). *Finite and Infinite Games*. New York: Ballantine.

Carver, C.S. (1979). A cybernetic model of self-attention processes. *Journal of Personality and Social Psychology* 37: 1251–1281.

Carver, C.S., and Scheier, M.F. (1988). A control-process perspective on anxiety. *Anxiety Research* 1: 17–22.

Clark, B.R., and Trow, M. (1960). Determinants of college student subcultures. Unpublished paper, Center for the Study of Higher Education, Berkeley.

Clark, B.R., and Trow, M. (1966). Determinants of the sub-cultures of college students—The organizational context. In T.M. Newcomb and E. Wilson (eds.), *College Peer Groups*. Chicago: Adeline.

Combs, A.W. (1957). The myth of competition. *Childhood Education*. Washington, DC: Association for Childhood Education International.

Coopersmith, S. (1967). *The Antecedents of Self-Esteem*. San Francisco: Freeman.

Covington, M.V. (1982, August). Musical chairs: Who drops out of music instruction and why? Proceedings of the National Symposium on the Applications of Psychology to the Teaching and Learning of Music: The Ann Arbor Symposium. Session III: Motivation and Creativity. Ann Arbor: University of Michigan.

Covington, M.V. (1984a). Motivated cognitions. In S.G. Paris, G.M. Olson, and H.W. Stevenson (eds.), *Learning and Motivation in the Classroom*. Hillsdale, NJ: Erlbaum.

Covington, M.V. (1984b). The motive for self-worth. In R. Ames and C. Ames (eds.), *Research on Motivation in Education* (Vol. 1). New York: Academic Press.

Covington, M.V. (1985a). Anatomy of failure-induced anxiety: The role of cognitive mediators. In R. Schwarzer (ed.), *Self-Related Cognitions in Anxiety and Motivation*. Hillsdale, NJ: Erlbaum.

Covington, M.V. (1985b). The role of self-processes in applied social psychology. *Journal of the Theory of Social Behavior* 15: 355–389.

Covington, M.V. (1985c). The effects of multiple-testing opportunities on rote and conceptual learning and retention. *Human learning* 4: 57–72.

703

Covington, M.V. (1986). Instruction in problem solving and planning. In S.L. Friedman, E.K. Scholnick and R.R. Cocking (eds.), *Intelligence and Exceptionality*. Norwood, NJ: Ablex.

Covington, M.V. (1989). Self-esteem and failure in school: Analysis and policy implications. In A.M. Mecca, N.J. Smelser, and J. Vasconcellos (eds.), *The Social Importance of Self-Esteem*. Berkeley: University of California.

Covington, M.V. (1992). *Making the Grade: A Self-Worth Perspective on Motivation and School Reform*. New York: Cambridge.

Covington, M.V., and Beery, R.G. (1976). *Self-Worth and School Learning*. New York: Holt, Rinehart and Winston.

Covington, M.V., and Jacoby, K.E. (1983). *Productive Thinking and Course Satisfaction as a Function of an Independence-conformity Dimension*. Paper presented at the meeting of the American Psychological Association, Montreal.

Covington, M.V., and Omelich, C.L. (1978). *Sex Differences in Self-aggrandizing Tendencies*. Unpublished manuscript, Department of Psychology, University of California, Berkeley.

Covington, M.V., and Omelich, C.L. (1979a). Are causal attributions causal? A path analysis of the cognitive model of achievement motivation. *Journal of Personality and Social Psychology* 37: 1487–1504.

Covington, M.V., and Omelich, C.L. (1979b). Effort: The double-edged sword in school achievement. *Journal of Educational Psychology* 71: 169–182.

Covington, M.V., and Omelich, C.L. (1981). As failures mount: Affective and cognitive consequences of ability demotion in the classroom. *Journal of Educational Psychology* 73: 796–808.

Covington, M.V., and Omelich, C.L. (1982). Achievement anxiety, performance, and behavioral instruction: A cost/benefits analysis. In R. Schwarzer, H.M. van der Ploeg and C.D. Spielberger (eds.), *Advances in Test Anxiety Research* (Vol. 1). Hillsdale, NJ: Erlbaum.

Covington, M.V., and Omelich, C.L. (1984a). Controversies or consistencies? A reply to Brown and Weiner. *Journal of Educational Psychology* 76: 159–168.

Covington, M.V., and Omelich, C.L. (1984b). Task-oriented versus competitive learning structures: Motivational and performance consequences. *Journal of Educational Psychology* 76: 1038–1050.

Covington, M.V., and Omelich, C.L. (1985). Ability and effort valuation among failure-avoiding and failure-accepting students. *Journal of Educational Psychology* 77: 446–459.

Covington, M.V., and Omelich, C.L. (1987a). "I knew it cold before the exam": A test of the anxiety-blockage hypothesis. *Journal of Educational Psychology* 79: 393–400.

Covington, M.V., and Omelich, C.L. (1987b). Item difficulty and test performance among high-anxious and low-anxious students. In R. Schwarzer, H.M. van der Ploeg and C.D. Spielberger (eds.), *Advances in Test Anxiety Research* (Vol. 5). Hillsdale, NJ: Erlbaum.

Covington, M.V., and Omelich, C.L. (1988). Achievement dynamics: The interaction of motives, cognitions and emotions over time. *Anxiety Journal* 1: 165–183.

Covington, M.V., and Omelich, C.L. (1990). *The Second Time Around: Coping with Repeated Failures*. Unpublished manuscript, Department of Psychology, University of California, Berkeley.

Covington, M.V., and Omelich, C.L. (1991). Need achievement revisited: Verification of Atkinson's original 2 × 2 model. In C.D. Spielberger, I.G. Sarason, Z. Kulcsár and G.L. Van Heck (eds.), *Stress and Emotion: Anxiety, Anger, and Curiosity* (Vol. 14). Washington, DC: Hemisphere.

Covington, M.V., Omelich, C.L., and Schwarzer, R. (1986). Anxiety, aspirations, and self-concept in the achievement process: A longitudinal model with latent variables. *Motivation and Emotion* 10: 71–88.

Covington, M.V., Spratt, M.F., and Omelich, C.L. (1980). Is effort enough, or does diligence count too? Student and teacher reactions to effort stability in failure. *Journal of Educational Psychology* 72: 717–729.

Coyne, J.C., and Lazarus, R.S. (1980). Cognitive style, stress perception, and coping. In I.L. Kutash and L.B. Schlesinger (eds.), *Handbook on Stress and Anxiety*. San Francisco: Jossey-Bass.

Crockenberg, S., Bryant, B., and Wilce, L. (1976). The effects of cooperatively and competitively structured learning environments on inter and intrapersonal behavior. *Child Development* 47: 386–396.

Culler, R.E., and Holahan, C.J. (1980). Test anxiety and academic performance: The effects of study-related behaviors. *Journal of Educational Psychology* 72: 16–20.

Csikszentmihalyi, M. (1975). *Beyond Boredom and Anxiety*. San Francisco: Jossey-Bass.

de Lange Jzn, J. (1987). *Mathematics, Insight and Meaning*. Vakgroep Onderzoek Wiskundeonderwijs en Onderwijscomputercentrum, Rikjsuniversiteit Utrecht.

De Volder, M., and Lens, W. (1982). Academic achievement and future time perspective as a cognitive-motivational concept. *Journal of Personality and Social Psychology* 42: 566–571.

Deci, E.L. (1975). *Intrinsic Motivation*. New York: Plenum.

Deci, E.L., and Ryan, R.M. (1987). The support of autonomy and the control of behavior. *Journal of Personality and Social Psychology* 53: 1024–1037.

Deffenbacher, J.L. (1977). Relationship of worry and emotionality to performance on the Miller Analogies Test. *Journal of Educational Psychology* 69: 191–195.

Deffenbacher, J.L. (1986). Cognitive and physiological components of test anxiety in real-life exams. *Cognitive Therapy and Research* 10: 635–644.

Deutsch, M. (1975). Equity, equality, and need. *Journal of Social Issues* 31: 137–149.

Deutsch, M. (1979). Education and distributive justice. *American Psychologist* 34: 391–401.

Dewey, J. (1916). *Democracy and Education*. New York: Macmillan.

Dewey, J. (1963). *Experience and Education*. New York: Collier. (Original work published 1938)

Diggory, J.C. (1966). *Self-evaluation: Concepts and Studies*. New York: Wiley.

Dweck, C.S. (1986). Motivational processes affecting learning. *American Psychologist* 41: 1040–1048.

Dweck, C.S., Davidson, W., Nelson, S., and Enna, B. (1978). Sex differences in learned helplessness: II. The contingencies of evaluative feedback in the classroom and III. An experimental analysis. *Developmental Psychology* 14: 268–276.

Eccles, J. (1983). Expectancies, values and academic behaviors. In J.T. Spence (ed.), *Achievement and Achievement Motives*. San Francisco: Freeman.

Eifferman, R.R. (1974). It's child's play. In L. M. Shears and E. M. Bower (eds.), *Games in Education and Development*. Springfield, IL: Charles C. Thomas.

Ellis, A., and Kraus, W.J. (1977). *Overcoming Procrastination*. New York: Institute for Rational Living.

Ellis, R.A., Parelius, R.J., and Parelius, A.P. (1971). The collegiate scholar: education for elite status. *Sociology of Education* 44: 27–58.

Elton, C. F. (1967). Male career role and vocational choice: Their prediction with personality and aptitude variables. *Journal of Counseling Psychology* 14(2): 99–105.

Eswara, H.S. (1972). Administration of reward and punishment in relation to ability, effort, and performance. *Journal of Social Psychology* 87: 139–140.

Feather, N.T. (1961). The relationship of persistence at a task to expectation of success and achievement-related motives. *Journal of Abnormal and Social Psychology* 63: 552–561.

Feather, N.T. (1963). Persistence at a difficult task with an alternative task of intermediate difficulty. *Journal of Abnormal and Social Psychology* 66: 604–609.

Feather, N. T. (1965). The relationship of expectation of success to Achievement and test anxiety. *Journal of Personality and Social Psychology* 1: 118–126.

Findley, M.J., and Cooper, H.M. (1983). Locus of control and academic achievement: A literature review. *Journal of Personality and Social Psychology* 44: 419–427.

Folsom, C.H., Jr. (1969). An investigation of Holland's theory of vocational choice. *Journal of Counseling Psychology* 16(3): 260–266.

Fontaine, G. (1974). Social comparison and some determinants of expected personal control and expected performance in a novel task situation. *Journal of Personality and Social Psychology* 29: 487–496.

Frederiksen, N., and Collins, J.R. (1989). A systems approach to educational testing. *Educational Researcher* 18(9): 27–32.

Garcia, T., and Pintrich, P.R. (1991). *The Effects of Autonomy on Motivation, Use of Learning Strategies and Performance in the College Classroom*. Paper presented at the annual meetings of the American Educational Research Association, San Francisco.

Gardner, J.W. (1961). *Excellence: Can We Be Equal and Excellent Too?* New York: Harper and Row.

Goldberg, L.R. (1965). Grades as motivants. *Psychology in the Schools* 2: 17–24.

Greenberg, P. J. (1932). Competition in children: An experimental study. *American Journal of Psychology* 44: 221–250.

Hagtvet, K.A. (1984). Fear of failure, worry and emotionality: Their suggestive causal relationships to mathematical performance and state anxiety. In H.M. van der Ploeg, R. Schwarzer and C.D. Spielberger (eds.), *Advances in Test Anxiety Research*, Vol. 3. Hillsdale, NJ: Erlbaum.

Harackiewicz, J.M., Abrahams, S., and Wageman, R. (1987). Performance evaluation and intrinsic motivation: The effects of evaluative focus, rewards, and achievement orientation. *Journal of Personality and Social Psychology* 53: 1015–1023.

Harackiewicz, J.M., and Manderlink, G. (1984). A process analysis of the effects of performance-contingent rewards on intrinsic motivation. *Journal of Experimental Social Psychology* 20: 531–551.

Harari, O., and Covington, M.V. (1981). Reactions to achievement behavior from a teacher and student perspective: A developmental analysis. *American Educational Research Journal* 18: 15–28.

Harlow, J.F. (1953). Mice, monkeys, men, and motives. *Psychological Review, 60*, 23–32.

Harris, A.M., and Covington, M.V. (1989). *Cooperative Team Failure: A Double Threat for the Low Performer?* Unpublished manuscript, Department of Psychology, University of California at Berkeley.

Hebb, D.O. (1961). Distinctive features of learning in the higher mammal. In J.F. Delafresnaye (ed.), *Brain Mechanisms and Learning.* London: Oxford University Press.

Heider, F. (1958). *The Psychology of Interpersonal Relations.* New York: Wiley.

Hembree, R. (1988). Correlates, causes, effects, and treatment of test anxiety. *Review of Educational Research* 58: 47–77.

Heist, P.A., and Yonge, G. (1968). *Manual for the Omnibus Personality Inventory, Form F.* New York: Psychological Corporation.

Hoffman, M.L. (1982). Development of prosocial motivation: Empathy and guilt. In N. Eisenberg-Borg (ed.), *Development of Prosocial Behavior.* New York: Academic Press.

Holland, J.L. (1966). *Psychology of Vocational Choice.* Waltham, MA: Blaisdell.

Holland, J.L. (1973). *Making Vocational Choices: A Theory of Careers.* Englewood Cliffs, NJ: Prentice-Hall.

Hullfish, G., and Smith, P. (1961). *Reflective Thinking: The Method of Education.* New York: Dodd, Mead.

Jones, E.E., and Nisbett, R.E. (1971). The actor and the observer: Divergent perceptions of the causes of behavior. In E.E. Jones, D.E. Kanouse, H.H. Kelley, R.E. Nisbett, S. Valins and B. Weiner (eds.), *Attribution: Perceiving the Causes of Behavior.* Morristown, NJ: General Learning Press.

Kaplan, R.M., and Swant, S.G. (1973). Reward characteristics in appraisal of achievement behavior. *Representative Research in Social Psychology* 4: 11–17.

Katchadourian, H.A., and Boli, J. (1985). *Careerism and Intellectualism Among College Students.* San Francisco: Jossey-Bass.

Kirkland, K., and Hollandsworth, J. (1980). Effective test taking: Skills-acquisition versus anxiety-reduction techniques. *Journal of Counseling and Clinical Psychology* 48: 431–439.

Kirst, M. (1990, March). *Stanford Magazine* p. 110.

Korn, H.A. (1968). Differences in student responses to the curriculum. In J. Katz and Associates (eds.), *No time for youth: Growth and Constraint in College Students.* San Francisco: Jossey-Bass.

Kuhl: J. (1981). Motivational and functional helplessness: The moderating effect of action versus state orientation. *Journal of Personality and Social Psychology* 40: 155–170.

Kuhl, J. (1984). Volitional aspecte of achievement motivation and learned helplessness: Toward a comprehensive theory of action-control. In B.A. Maher (ed.), *Progress in Experimental Personality Research* (Vol. 13). New York: Academic Press.

Kulik, J.A., Kulik, C.C., and Cohen, P.A. (1979). A meta-analysis of outcome studies of Keller's personalized system of instruction. *American Psychologist* 34: 307–318.

Kulik, C.C., Kulik, J.A., and Shwalb, B.J. (1982). Programmed instruction in secondary education: A meta-analysis of evaluation findings. *The Journal of Educational Research* 75: 307–318.

Laux, L., and Glanzmann, P. (1987). A self-presentational view of test anxiety. In R. Schwarzer, H.M. van der Ploeg, and C.D. Spielberger (eds.), *Advances in Test Anxiety Research* (Vol. 5). Hillsdale, NJ: Erlbaum.

Lave, J. (1988). *Cognition in Practice*. Boston: Cambridge.

Lavelle, T.L., Metalsky, G.I., and Coyne, J.C. (1979). Learned helplessness, test anxiety, and acknowledgement of contingencies. *Journal of Abnormal Psychology* 88: 381–387.

Leppin, A., Schwarzer, R., Belz, D., Jerusalem, M., and Quast, H. -H. (1987). Causal attribution patterns of high and low test-anxious students. In R. Schwarzer, H.M. van der Ploeg and C.D. Spielberger (eds.), *Advances in Test Anxiety Research* (Vol. 5). Hillsdale, NJ: Erlbaum.

Levin, B.B. (1990). Portfolio assessment: Implications for the communication of effort and ability in alternative forms of assessment. Unpublished paper, School of Education, University of California at Berkeley.

Lewin, K., Dembo, T., Festinger, L., and Sears, P. (1944). Level of aspiration. In J. McV. Hunt (ed.), *Personality and the Behavior Disorders* (Vol. 1). New York: Ronald.

Liebert, R.M., and Morris, L.W. (1967). Cognitive and emotional components of test anxiety: A distinction and some initial data. *Psychological Reports* 20: 975–978.

Litwin, L.W. (1963). Effects of motivation on probability preference. *Journal of Personality* 31: 417–427.

Littig, G.H. (1966). Achievement motivation, expectancy of success, and risk-taking behavior. In J.W. Atkinson and N.T. Feather (eds.), *A Theory of Achievement Motivation*. New York: Wiley.

Malone, T.W. (1981). Toward a theory of intrinsically motivating instruction. *Cognitive Science* 4: 333–369.

Man, F., and Hrabal, V. (1988). Self-concept of ability, social consequences anxiety, and attribution as correlates of action control. In F. Halisch and J.H.L. van den Bercken (eds.), *Achievement and Task Mtivation*. Lisse, The Netherlands: Swets and Zeitlinger/Erlbaum.

Mandler, G., and Sarason, S. (1952). A study of anxiety and learning. *Journal of Abnormal and Social Psychology* 47: 166–173.

McClelland, D.C. (1958). Methods of measurement human motivation. In J.W. Atkinson (ed.), *Motives in Fantasy, Action, and Society*. Princeton, NJ: Van Nostrand.

McClelland, D.C. (1961). *The Achieving Society*. Princeton, NJ.

McClelland, D.C. (1965). Toward a theory of motive acquisition. *American Psychologist* 20: 321–333.

McClelland, D.C. (1980). Motive dispositions: The merits of operant and respondent measures. In L. Wheeler (ed.), *Review of Personality and Social Psychology* (Vol. 1). Beverly Hills, CA: Sage.

McClelland, D.C. (1985). How motives, skills, and values determine what people do. *American Psychologist* 40: 812–825.

McMahan, I.D. (1973). Relationships between causal attributions and expectancy of success. *Journal of Personality and Social Psychology* 28: 108–114.

Meyer, W.U. (1970). Selbstverantwortlichkeit und leistungs. Unpublished doctoral dissertation, Ruhr Universität, Bochum, Germany.

Miller, I.W., and Norman, W.H. (1979). Learned helplessness in humans: a review and attribution-theory model. *Psychological Bulletin* 86: 93–118.

Moulton, R.W. (1965). Effects of success and failure on level of aspiration as related to achievement motives. *Journal of Personality and Social Psychology* 1: 399–406.

Naveh-Benjamin, M. (1985). A comparison of training programs intended for different types of test-anxious students. Paper presented at symposium on information processing and motivation, American Psychological Association, Los Angeles.

Nicholls, J.G. (1975). Causal attributions and other achievement-related cognitions: Effects of task outcome, attainment values, and sex. *Journal of Personality and Social Psychology* 31: 379–389.

Nicholls, J.G. (1989). *The Competitive Ethos and Democratic Education*. Cambridge: Harvard University Press.

Nuttin, J. (1984). *Motivation, Planning and Action: A Relational Theory of Behavior Dynamics*. Hillsdale, NJ: Erlbaum.

Nuttin, J., and Lens, W. (1985). *Future Time Perspective and Motivation: Theory and Research Method*. Hillsdale, NJ: Erlbaum.

Osipow, S.H., Ashby, J.D., and Wall, H.W. (1966). Personality types and vocational choice: A test of Holland's theory. *Personnel and Guidance Journal* 45: 37–42.

Peterson, R.E. (1965). On a typology of college students. Research Bulletin, RB-65–9. Princeton, NJ: Educational Testing Service.

Pintrich, P.R. (1988). A process-oriented view of student motivation and cognition. In J.S. Stark and L. Mets (eds.), *Improving Teaching and Learning Through Research* New Directions for Institutional Research, 57. San Francisco: Jossey-Bass.

Pintrich, P.R. (1989). The dynamic interplay of student motivation and cognition in the college classroom. In C. Ames and M. Maehr (eds.), *Advances in Motivation and Achievement* (Vol. 6). Greenwich, CT: JAI Press.

Pintrich, P.R., and De Groot, E.V. (1990). Motivational and self-regulated learning components of classroom academic performance. *Journal of Educational Psychology* 82: 33–40.

Pratte, R. (1988). *The Civic Imperative: Examining the Need for Civic Education*. New York: Teachers College Press.

Promoting student success at Berkeley: Guidelines for the future. (1991). (Report of the Commission on Responses to a Changing Student Body). Berkeley: University of California.

Raynor, J.O. (1969). Future orientation and motivation of immediate activity: An elaboration of the theory of achievement motivation. *Psychological Review* 76: 606–610.

Raynor, J.O. (1970). Relationships between achievement-related motives, future orientation, and academic performance. *Journal of Personality and Social Psychology* 15: 28–33.

Reagan, D. (1991). *The Academic Dismissal Student and the Self-worth Theory of Achievement Motivation*. Unpublished doctoral dissertation, {NAME OF UNIVERSITY}.

Rest, S., Nierenberg, R., Weiner, B., and Heckhausen, H. (1973). Further evidence concerning the effects of perceptions of effort and ability on achievement evaluation. *Journal of Personality and Social Psychology* 28: 187–191.

Roberts, B., and Covington, M. V. (1991). *The Myth of Hermes*. Unpublished manuscript, Institute of Personality Assessment and Research, University of California, Berkeley.

Rosenbaum, R.M. (1972). *A Dimensional Analysis of the Perceived causes of Success and Failure*. Unpublished doctoral dissertation, University of California, Los Angeles.

709

Rothblum, E.D., Solomon, L.J., and Murakami, J. (1986). Affective, cognitive and behavioral differences between high and low procrastinators. *Journal of Counseling Psychology* 33: 387–394.

Salamé, R. (1984). Test anxiety: Its determinants, manifestations and consequences. In H.M. van der Ploeg, R. Schwarzer and C.D. Spielberger (eds.), *Advances in Test Anxiety Research* (Vol. 3) Hillsdale, NJ: Erlbaum.

Schmalt, H.D. (1982). Two concepts of fear of failure motivation. In R. Schwarzer, H.M. van der Ploeg and C.D. Spielberger (eds.), *Advances in Test Anxiety Research* (Vol. 1). Lisse: Swets and Zeitlinger.

Schoenfeld, A.H. (1989). Reflections on doing and teaching mathematics. Paper presented at a conference, Mathematical Thinking and Problem Solving, Berkeley.

Schuman, H., Walsh, E., Olson, C., and Etheridge, B. (1985). Effort and reward: The assumption that college grades are affected by quantity of study. *Social Forces* 63: 945–966.

Schwarzer, R., Jerusalem, M., and Schwarzer, C. (1983). Self-related and situation-related cognitions in test anxiety and helplessness: A longitudinal analysis with structural equations. In R. Schwarzer, H.M. van der Ploeg and C.D. Spielberger (eds.), *Advances in Anxiety Research* (Vol. 2). Hillsdale, NJ: Erlbaum.

Schwarzer, R., Jerusalem, M., and Stiksrud, A. (1984). The developmental relationship between test anxiety and helplessness. In H.M. van der Ploeg, R. Schwarzer, and C.D. Spielberger (eds.), *Advances in Test Anxiety Research* (Vol. 3). Hillsdale, NJ: Erlbaum.

Schwarzer, R., Seipp, B., and Schwarzer, C. (1989). Mathematics performance and anxiety: A meta-analysis. In R. Schwarzer, H.M. van der Ploeg and C.D. Spielberger (eds.), *Advances in Test Anxiety Research* (Vol. 6). Lisse, Netherlands: Swets and Zeitlinger.

Seipp, B. (1991). Anxiety and academic performance: A meta-analysis of findings. *Anxiety Journal* 4: 27–42.

Seipp, B., and Schwarzer, C. (1990, July). Anxiety and academic achievement: A meta-analysis of findings. Paper presented at the 11th International Conference of the Society for Test Anxiety Research (STAR), Berlin.

Seligman, M.E.P. (1975). *Helplessness: On Depression, Development, and Death.* San Francisco: Freeman.

Shapiro, G. (1986). *A Skeleton in the Darkroom: Stories of Serendipity in Science.* New York: Harper and Row.

Silver, M., and Sabini, J. (1981). Procrastinating. *Journal for the Theory of Social Behavior* 11: 207–221.

Silver, M., and Sabini, J. (1982, January). When it's not really procrastination. *Psychology Today* 16: 39–42.

Skinner, E.A., Wellborn, J.G., and Connell, J.P. (1990). What it takes to do well in school and whether I've got it: A process model of perceived control and children's engagement and achievement in school. *Journal of Educational Psychology* 82: 22–32.

Slavin, R.E. (1983). When does cooperative learning increase student achievement? *Psychological Bulletin* 94: 429–445.

Slavin, R.E. (1984). Students motivating students to excel: Cooperative incentives, cooperative tasks, and student achievement. *The Elementary School Journal* 85: 53–64.

Smith, T.W., Snyder, C.R., and Handelsman, M.M. (1982). On the self-serving function of an academic wooden leg: Test anxiety as a self-handicapping strategy. *Journal of Personality and Social Psychology* 42: 314–321.

Snyder, C.R. (1984, September). Excuses, excuses: They sometimes actually work—to relieve the burden of blame. *Psychology Today* 18: 50–55.

Snyder, M.L., Stephan, W.G., and Rosenfeld, C. (1976). Egotism and attribution. *Journal of Personality and Social Psychology* 33: 435–441.

Solomon, L.J., and Rothblum, E.D. (1984). Academic procrastination: Frequency and cognitive-behavioral correlates. *Journal of Counseling Psychology* 31: 503–509.

Stiensmeier-Pelster, J., and Schürmann, M. (1990). Performance deficits following failure: Integrating motivational and functional aspect of learned helplessness. *Anxiety Research* 2(3): 211–222.

Stipiek, D.J., and Weisz, J.R. (1981). Perceived personal control and academic achievement. *Review of Educational Research* 51: 101–137.

Streufert, S., and Streufert, S.C. (1969). Effects of conceptual structure, failure, and success on attribution of causality and interpersonal attitudes. *Journal of Personality and Social Psychology* 11: 138–247.

Tobias, S. (1985). Test anxiety: Interference, defective skills, and cognitive capacity. *Educational Psychologist* 20: 135–142.

Tobias, S. (1986). Anxiety and cognitive processing of instruction. In R. Schwarzer (ed.), *Self-Related Cognitions in Anxiety and Motivation*. Hillsdale, NJ: Erlbaum.

Topman, R.M., and Jansen, T. (1984) "I really can't do it, anyway": The treatment of test anxiety. In H.M. van der Ploeg, R. Schwarzer and C.D. Spielberger (eds.), *Advances in Test Anxiety Research* (Vol. 3). Hillsdale, NJ: Erlbaum.

Tucker, J.A., Vuchinich, R.E., and Sobell, M.B. (1981). Alcohol consumption as a self-handicapping strategy. *Journal of Abnormal Psychology* 90: 220–230.

Valle, V.A. (1974). *Attributions of Stability as a Mediator in the Changing of Expectations*. Unpublished doctoral dissertation, University of Pittsburgh.

Veroff, J., and Veroff, J.B. (1972). Reconsideration of a measure of power motivation. *Psychological Bulletin* 78: 279–291.

Warren, J.R. (1968). Student perceptions of college subcultures. *American Educational Research Journal* 5: 213–232.

Weiner, B. (1972). *Theories of Motivation: From Mechanism to Cognition*. Chicago: Markham.

Weiner, B. (1974). *Achievement Motivation and Attribution Theory*. Morristown, NJ: General Learning Press.

Weiner, B. (1990). History of motivational research in education. *Journal of Educational Psychology* 82: 616–622.

Weiner, B., Frieze, L., Kukla, A., Reed, L., Rest, S., and Rosenbaum, R. (1971). Perceiving the causes of success and failure. In E.E. Jones, D.E. Kanouse, H.H. Kelley, R.E. Nisbett, S. Valins and B. Weiner (eds.), *Attribution: Perceiving the Causes of Behavior*. Morristown, NJ: General Learning Press.

Weiner, B., Heckhausen, H., Meyer, W., and Cook, R. (1972). Causal ascriptions and achievement behavior: A conceptual analysis of effect and reanalysis of locus of control. *Journal of Personality and Social Psychology* 21: 239–248.

Weiner, B., and Kukla, A. (1970). An attributional analysis of achievement motivation. *Journal of Personality and Social Psychology* 15: 1–20.

711

Wicker, F.W., Payne, G.C., and Morgan, R.D. (1983). Participant descriptions of guilt and shame. *Motivation and Emotion* 7: 25–39.

Williams, J.P. (1976). Individual differences in achievement test presentation and evaluation anxiety. Unpublished doctoral dissertation, University of Illinois at Urbana-Champaign.

Winter, D.G. (1973). *The Power Motive*. New York: The Free Press.

Wolosin, R.J., Sherman, S.J., and Till, A. (1973). Effects of cooperation and competition on responsibility attribution after success and failure. *Journal of Experimental Social Psychology* 15: 1–20.

Woodworth, R.S. (1918). *Dynamic Psychology*. New York: Columbia University Press.

UPDATE ON EDUCATIONAL POLICY, PRACTICE, AND RESEARCH FROM A SELF-WORTH PERSPECTIVE

Martin V. Covington
University of California, Berkeley
pcomeau@berkeley.edu

Abstract

This article summarizes research developments on the Berkeley campus since 1993 regarding an exploration of the relationship between intrinsic and extrinsic motivation in the college classroom. A number of nested, systematically-sequenced experiments are reported which in the aggregate lead to the broad conclusion that intrinsic, or learning goals, are not necessarily incompatible with performance goals, but rather can be mutually-reinforcing when (1) students are attaining their grade goals; (2) when what they are studying is of personal interest; and (3) when the dominant reasons for learning are task oriented, not self-aggrandizing or failure avoidant. The educational policy implications of these findings are discussed for issues of college instructional design, the mission of campus counseling as well as professional teacher training

Key Words: Intrinsic motivation; extrinsic motivation, grades; instruction, fear of failure; self-worth dynamics; college

INTRODUCTION

I ended my 1993 chapter on a sobering note, namely, that the self-worth perspective on the dynamics of college achievement was troubling at best. Basically, it portrays college classrooms as battlegrounds where students struggle to maintain a sense of personal worth in a contest with other students in which the rules of engagement favor lackluster effort, sabotage, and self-deception. The inevitable casualty is not only the quality of academic achievement, but also the will to continue learning. Some students manage to excel, despite these rules of engagement, but our emphasis has been on those who do not excel, and why.

To backfill briefly, self-worth theory (Beery, 1975; Covington, 1992, 1998; Covington & Beery, 1976) alleges that all individuals strive to establish and protect a sense of personal worth and acceptance by others, an objective which depends on one's ability to achieve socially-valued goals. For many students the test of their worth is positive,

713

that is, success-oriented in nature, defined by such laudable goals as achieving personal mastery over events, the pursuit of intellectual inquiries, and the betterment of one's ability to help others. These goals carry their own intrinsic rewards. The rewards are inherent in the actions themselves, and hence are unlimited—everyone can improve themselves, help others, or satisfy their curiosities. Other students, however, equate their worth with achievement outcomes for purposes of aggrandizing their ability status. This dynamic can be represented by the equation: P (performance)=A (ability)=W (worth) (Beery, 1975). Students who adopt this formula inevitably become preoccupied with avoiding failure because typically in school the struggle for high grades is a competitive affair in which only a few can win. Most of these students must console themselves with the dubious satisfaction of either avoiding failure, or in the event of actually failing, of at least avoiding the implications of their failures—that they are incompetent, and hence unworthy. Ironically, the excuses these students generate to protect their threatened ability status tend to create the very failures they are attempting to avoid. For example, when students procrastinate or choose to take an overwhelming course load, they virtually insure failure, but failure that reflects little on their ability because so few others could do any better under the circumstances (Covington & Omelich, 1979; Thompson, 1996).

THE WILL TO LEARN

The main thrust of much of the research conducted under the auspices of the Berkeley Teaching/Learning Project in the decade since publication of the 1993 chapter has been to address the policy implications of these fear-driven dynamics in students for purposes of encouraging educational change in post-secondary institutions. Our research has focused on arguably the most cherished of all educational objectives: intrinsic motivation, or the will to learn. Our initial question was whether intrinsic objectives such as subject-matter appreciation can coexist to any degree, let alone flourish, in the face of competing loyalties involving the dominance of extrinsic incentives and goals such as grades, which according to self-worth theory have the power to determine one's sense of worth as a person. We were not alone in this interest nor with these concerns. Numerous observers in higher education have emphasized the significance of intrinsic engagement, not merely as a by-product of successful achievement, but as a fundamental educational objective in its own right. Some have even despaired of the prospects of ever encouraging intrinsic values in situations seemingly controlled by tangible extrinsic rewards (Kohn, 1993).

Our investigations began with an examination of the widely-held belief—indeed, virtually an article of faith approximating the status of an illuminated truth, that the pursuit of grades and the valuing of what one is learning are necessarily incompatible goals, if not actually antagonistic. More particularly, as typically couched in the contemporary research literature, the assumption is that the offering of extrinsic, tangible rewards (e.g., gold stars, praise, and grades) undercuts intrinsic reasons for learning. Several explanations have been offered for the alleged negative effects of rewards. One explanation is that it is the very nature of the extrinsic reward—being basically unrelated, or extrinsic to the task at hand which distracts the learner, and draws attention away from the inherent benefits of learning (Condry & Chambers, 1978). As a result it is feared that learning may become merely the means to an end, that is, a way to get rewards, and that when these rewards are no longer available, the willingness to learn will suffer. A second, interpretation, that of the 'overjustification effect' asserts that by rewarding students, say, with praise, for pursuing what already interests them, that is, overjustifying their interests—then, paradoxically, these interests may actually be discouraged (Lepper, Greene, & Nisbett, 1973).

INITIAL RESEARCH STEPS

As a first step in our deliberations, we conducted a number of informal interviews with Berkeley undergraduates (Covington, 1999). These data provided us with unmistakable evidence that much of what students learn is acquired out of personal interest and not simply for the sake of grades. It seemed that intrinsic motivation was alive, and if not completely well, at least surviving! But most important to our inquiries was that, although our informants did confirm having feelings of conflict regarding the goals of achieving good grades and of caring about learning, these were not necessarily feelings of incompatibility. The conflict arises, they suggested, largely because of the demands of academic life leave scant room to pursue either goal fully, let along both simultaneously. Given the pressures of school work in the face of often overwhelming personal and financial demands, students must often choose between concentrating their studies on what they guess will be tested in opposition to exploring what may be the personal value of their studies. Clearly, such prioritizing is a problem, but not the same problem implied by incompatibility which sounds insurmountable from the perspective of encouraging caring about learning.

REINTERPRETATIONS

Based on these and other observations, we became convinced that the incompatibility of processes implied by the classic intrinsic motive/extrinsic reward dichotomy was not only overblown but misplaced as well. It focused on the wrong culprit which leads to unnecessarily pessimistic judgments about the prospects for encouraging intrinsic values in schools, and jeopardizes the hopes for true educational reform. We concluded that it was not so much the extrinsic nature of these grade rewards as their scarcity and implied negativity that is the root cause of the threat to learning for its own sake (Covington, 2000; Covington & Müeller, 2001). First, consider scarcity. High grades are typically a scarce commodity in college owing to prevailing competitive grading policies in which only a few can win. The struggle to outperform others for a limited supply of grade rewards, and the defensive tactics induced by the fear of failing undercut the enjoyment of what one is learning. Second, consider the incentive value of grades. Given their scarcity, grades can act as negative reinforcers. These are not the kinds of grade payoffs associated with achieving something positive, such as pride on completing a difficult assignment, but payoffs for avoiding something abrasive, as in the case of students studying to avoid failing. When students are encouraged to approach success as the preeminent reason for achieving, they become engaged in the material, and tangible rewards become an added incentive. By contrast, if learners are motivated to avoid failure, the pursuit of intrinsic values is the first victim. Here the lure of grades, far from being an inducement to learning, becomes a threat if one does not learn.

In short, the more appropriate dichotomy for setting the issue straight is not an intrinsic/extrinsic distinction, but rather the distinction between approach/avoidant motivation (Covington, 2000; Covington & Elliot, 2001). To our way of thinking (Covington & Müeller, 2001), this analysis clarifies the true role of extrinsic incentives in the achievement process. Extrinsic payoffs such as social recognition, grades, or money stand neutral with respect to their effects on achievement until associated with either approach or avoidance goals. In effect, extrinsic payoffs can advance a love of learning, if they serve to reinforce positive, task-focused reasons for learning as when the purpose is, say, to satisfy one's curiosity. Conversely, extrinsic payoffs

716

interfere with caring about learning when such rewards are sought after in conditions of scarcity for self-aggrandizing reasons or are being withheld by an instructor as a means of compliance and control.

By assuming that a positive and additive relationship can exist between intrinsic motivation and extrinsic rewards, our understanding was extended in several important ways (Covington, 2002). First, it allowed us to make sense of common observations which defy an exclusively negative view of extrinsic rewards. For example, it is plainly clear that even blatantly tangible payoffs like money, can actually promote personal engagement (e.g., the monetary award allowing the aspiring actor to work in summer stock theatre). The influence of extrinsic rewards depends on the purposes they serve, as in the positive instance in which money provides further opportunities for creative self-expression.

Second, given the preeminence of a grade focus among many college students, we were surprised that little attention had been given by researchers to the effects of success and failure on intrinsic task engagement. We assumed that being successful in one's studies would promote emotions such as pride and enjoyment; whereas by contrast, falling short of one's grade goals would either intensify one's concentration on studying to the exclusion of appreciation, or divert attention to the protection of one's sense of worth.

Third, we reasoned that it may not be the offering of tangible rewards that undercuts personal task engagement as much as it is the absence of the kinds of payoffs that encourage and recognize the importance of being involved in and caring about what one is learning.

In summary, we now had in hand a tentative explanation for why a dominant grade focus among students does not necessarily preclude the valuing of what is being learned. The pursue of high grades and valuing learning are not necessarily incompatible goals as long as certain conditions prevail: (1) when students are attaining their grade goals, (2) when what they are studying is of personal interest, and (3) when the dominant reasons for learning are task-oriented, not self-aggrandizing or failure avoidant.

FURTHER RESEARCH

This proposition lead to a direct test of the plausibility of our arguments in the form of a role playing scenario in which a group of some 400 undergraduate students were directed to imagine themselves beginning work on a final assignment in a hypothetical course (Covington, 2002).

The conditions under which this imagined event took place were varied along two dimensions: first, whether students had succeeded grade-wise on several highly similar prior assignments, or had consistently received disappointing grades; and second, whether the subject-matter was personally meaningful or not. These two conditions were crossed so that all students responded to each of the four possible combinations in a within-subjects, repeated-measure design. One between-subject factor was also introduced consisting of type of respondent, either success-oriented or failure-avoiding students. For all four scenarios, students rated the degree to which they would likely appreciate and value what they had learned from working on this last assignment.

The results were not always anticipated nor easily explained by conventional views of the incompatible nature of grade-striving and caring goals. First, as to the expected outcomes, the effect of prior success or failure was significant at both levels of interest: Doing well at one's studies was associated with increased valuing of what one is learning, irrespective of degree of interest. Also, the effect of interest level was significant for both levels of grade-goal attainment. Basically, people enjoy learning more about what interests them than about topics of little interest, irrespective of grade received.

Not so obvious, however, was the presence of a significant inter-action: Appreciation for what was being learned was far greater in a failed, but task-interested cause than when students had been succeeding, grade-wise, but with content that held little interest. In effect, it appears that personal interest can trump even failure when it comes to subject-matter appreciation! Another aspect of the data was also intriguing in light of the predictions of the 'overjustification' hypothesis which state that the offering of tangible rewards for what is already engaging for students would undercut further interest. Yet, contrary to this expectation, it was a combination of achieving one's grade goals, that is, being rewarded for work on a topic of high interest that led to the greatest degree of subject-matter appreciation among the four conditions. Our informants were not at all surprised by this outcome. It made perfect sense to them. For example, students reported, anecdotally, that doing well at what interests them creates pride in accomplishment which in turn sustains their enthusiasm for learning more. Others suggested that succeeding, grade-wise, reduces their worries about failing so they feel freer to explore what interests them. Such explanations suggest that the concerns represented by the 'overjustification' hypothesis may be exaggerated.

Now, what of the reactions of success-oriented and failure-avoidant students? The respective dynamics of these two groups proved to be virtually parallel and varied only by degree. Both groups responded positively to having succeeded, except that success-oriented students were more appreciative of what they had learned. Likewise, appreciation levels of both groups were adversely affected by disappointing grades, but failure-oriented students were more impacted. Most importantly, these data suggest that all students possess a capacity for intrinsic engagement to one degree or another, irrespective of the extent to which they may be driven by failure-avoidant tendencies.

Finally, we followed up on the intriguing possibility that subject-matter appreciation can survive even disappointing grades. We put the question to our informants by asking them to recall a time, if any, when they felt they had learned something of value, despite having received a disappointing course grade. They then rated the intensity of their disappointment and indicated why they believed they received this grade. Quite apart from variations in the individual circumstances of these experiences, students generally gave three reasons for the undiminished value of their learning. First, students cited the critical role of teachers as models of enthusiasm for their discipline. Teacher enthusiasm encourages positive student attitudes toward the subject-matter, a finding that compliments of the work of Perry and his colleagues (Perry & Dickens, 1984; Perry & Magnusson, 1987). Second, students value learning, irrespective of grade outcomes, when it is germane to their life goals and career ambitions. Third, disappointing grades are offset when instructors reinforced intrinsic reasons for learning which is typically achieved by such techniques as allowing students the opportunity to explain why what they are learning is important to them or by permitting students to chose work assignments consistent with their interests.

POLICY AND PRACTICE

Several implications for educational policy and practice followed from these collective findings:

First, if the causes of diminished appreciation for learning can be attributed to the high-stakes meaning of grades as conveyors of a sense of worth combined with their relative scarcity, then access to good grades need be made available to all students as long as they satisfy the standards of workmanship required by an instructor.

719

Second, if appreciation depends as much on the perceive social and personal value of academic tasks as on how well one is doing, grade-wise, then students should be allowed considerable freedom to create their own personal challenges.

Third, if it is not the offering of tangible rewards that undercuts task appreciation as much as it is the absence of those kinds of payoffs that encourage the importance of being involved, then these latter kinds of incentives should be provided students as a matter of policy.

The next phase of our research program was to convert these propositions into workable instructional strategies whose effects could be evaluated in actual classroom settings.

SCARCE VS. PLENTIFUL REWARDS

Under conditions of scarcity, students will scramble for higher grades, at least for a time, but inevitably for many students achievement levels will degrade due in part to the adoption of failure-avoidant strategies such as procrastination (Covington & Omelich, 1981). Our response to this situation was to experiment with substituting new rules of engagement which provided students with the possibility of an abundance of grade payoffs. For this purpose, we explored a novel use of a mastery-learning paradigm which we referred to as a 'grade-choice arrangement.' Under this system students are encouraged to work for any grade they choose by amassing grade credits (i.e., so many points for an A, a B, etc) with the requirement that the higher the grade to which they aspire, the better they must perform and/or the more they must accomplish. Quality of work was assessed against absolute, criterion referenced benchmarks. Thus, students still must compete— not against one another for a limited supply of rewards, but against the standards of excellence set by the instructor.

Although to date we have not made direct, experimental comparisons between competitively-based courses and those in which we have introduced a 'grade-choice' arrangement, the within-class response of students subjected to this latter grading scheme has been uniformly positive. Of particular interest are the ratings reflecting the extent to which students experienced feelings of task engagement at various points in these courses. Both the frequency and intensity of such incidents were substantial, and often unprecedented in the prior experience of many students. In other studies, students were asked to make retrospective comparisons between their experiences under 'grade-choice' arrangements and those encountered in other courses in which they had been recently enrolled which featured competitive grading. The actual grades received in these comparison courses were controlled so that retrospective ratings were more likely to reflect the effects of the different grading policies per se, on intrinsic motivation. The 'grade-choice' arrangement proved superior on several counts. First, students judged that the presence of absolute standards made more explicit the relationship between the amount and quality of academic work required for various grade-level payoffs, thereby creating a heightened sense of fairness as well as a reduction in the ambiguity regarding grading policies. Second, students reported reduced anxiety over grades as they worked on assignments. Third, students reported a greater willingness to cooperate with fellow students in studying and greater enjoyment and pride in group work because they were not in competition.

PERSONALLY MEANINGFUL ASSIGNMENTS

The motivational value of being personally interested in one's learning is widely recognized. Our present findings regarding the redemptive value of working on meaningful assignments even in the face of disappointing grades underscores the potency of such personal meaning. Yet the relation between task interest and grading remains complex. Take, for example, the overjustification hypothesis. According to the logic of this proposition, instructors might avoid discouraging student's already established interests by simply not rewarding them—in effect, leaving well enough alone! This seems reasonable as long as interest is high. In this case, personal interest carries the motivational burden. But what of those cases where initial interest is low or non-existent? Our data suggests that in these situations, even successful achievement does little to promote task engagement. Good grades are no guarantee of task engagement. We explored several strategies for avoiding this impasse. One consisted of giving students the opportunity to always be working on an interesting task! If the task was not of personal interest initially, students had the option of turning this 'boring task into an interesting one' (Sansome, 1986). In one study, students were presented with a standard essay assignment that was rated by a prior subsample of students as dull and lackluster. Half the students were then asked to complete this form of the assignment, while the other half was given the option of altering various superficial aspects of the assignment in order to enhance its personal interest or novel value before beginning work. Despite the fact that as a group these latter

721

'altered' problems were subsequently rated by our research staff as more difficult to solve than the standard form, the 'interest-generating' group rated their work as more satisfying. Moreover, knowing that their work would eventually be graded was less of a distraction as they worked.

REWARDING INTRINSIC INVESTMENT

If it is true that the offering of tangible rewards is less the cause of the decline of task engagement than is the failure to reward one's intrinsic investment of time and energy, then more of these payoffs should be offered students. And perhaps these payoffs can even count as part of one's grade! If, so this might go a long way toward reducing the conflict of priorities between grade goals and caring about learning of which students routinely complain. Basically, this strategy would involve rewarding the processes by which learning occurs, not just rewarding the quality of the end-products of learning such as test performances. Our undergraduate informants have identified a variety of such rewards which one student characterized as 'surplus learning,' that is, knowledge acquired above and beyond grade-driven considerations, including discovery of the unexpected, the serendipitous combining of unlikely thoughts in creative ways, and feelings of being poised to learn more.

In a series of studies (Covington, 2002), we explored the effects of providing students with a small proportion of the total course credits available if they provide a thoughtful addendum to their regular assignments which might include reflections on their thought processes as they worked or a consideration of what they found interesting about what they were learning. But, could genuine appreciation be nurtured when extrinsic payoffs are involved? Our evidence suggests that it can. Our informants conceded that without a tangible payoff in the form of extra grade credit—modest as it was, they would likely have paid little attention to sources of personal satisfaction as they worked. Yet, once they became sensitized to these personal, inner experiences, the fact that they were paid initially was generally discounted as a distraction. And, eventually, even when this extra-credit option did not apply, retrospective ratings of personal involvement in these particular assignments remained high. This kind of tangible recognition by instructors takes on a disproportionate importance, far beyond its modest contribution to final grades, by elevating intrinsic task appreciation and personal involvement in learning to a favored instructional priority.

OUTREACH AND CONSULTATION

The most recent phase of our ongoing research and development efforts involved the creation of a dialogue with Berkeley students, teaching staff, and administrators for ways to enhance of the quality of undergraduate teaching and learning across the entire campus, irrespective of discipline or department. This work was made possible by my appointment in 2001 as the Berkeley Presidential Chair in Undergraduate Education. The project has proceeded in close collaboration with Dr. Linda von Hoene, Director of the Graduate Student Instructor Teaching and Resource Center, and with Learning Skills Counselor Nic Voge of the Student Learning Center. The entry point for this outreach effort is to inform these campus groups about the importance of the concept of *motivation* as a fundamental element both in the planning and teaching of courses as well as for thinking about one's role as a learner. Particular attention is being paid to working with the teachers, students, and the staff in large-enrollment, lower division classes because our data indicate that once freshmen enter college, they experience a substantial decline in their commitment to learning for its own sake, far below the levels of task engagement they enjoyed in high school (Covington & Dray, 2001).

Our consulting work has revealed an additional source of conflict beyond the self-worth dynamics of fear which magnifies the difficulties confronting any outreach efforts. This involves a mismatch between instructors and students regarding their perceived roles and responsibilities. In brief, students tend to assume that their task as learners is simply to absorb information and instructors are expected to provide that information in a clear, simple, and accessible manner. Additionally, students expect instructors to provide the motivational impetus for learning by presenting information in entertaining, enjoyable, and memorable ways. Overall, this is a decidedly passive mind-set.

By contrast, instructors assume (rightly so) that it is students who are ultimately responsible for their own learning and meaning-making. Instructors typicallly champion intellectual independence of thought and action as the ultimate goal of a college education. Yet, not withstanding these noble expectations, instructors can easily become unwitting co-dependents in reinforcing student passivity in several ways. First, instructors often assume that inspired problem-solving and innovative thought occur more or less automatically once sufficient factual information is provided students. Second, instructors are sometimes convinced that they must 'cover all the material,' often by means of a rapid-fire, stenographically-challenging presentation of facts and figures which is at odds with instruction in higher-level cognitive functioning, like problem-solving, which typically requires extensive practice, time and patience. Third, instructors often favor the assessment of skills associated with the memorizing of facts and the application of routine formulas because such lower-level mental functioning is more easily, reliably, and efficiently measured. Each of these beliefs and practices reinforces the view in the minds of students that learning is merely a matter of the transmittal of information, not its transformation for greater purpose, which further reinforces the role of students as passively absorbent sponges.

How might these dynamics be corrected? This is the question that animates much of our current outreach activities with a variety of campus audiences (Covington, 2004). Basically, the answer involves altering the relationship between students and instructors by recasting their roles and reapportioning their responsibilities in ways that are mutually supportive. Typically, the first consulting step is to clarify the causes of this impasse in the respective roles of students and instructors. This is where motivational perspectives, like self-worth theory, come into their own. They provide explanations for otherwise inexplicable, even infuriating behaviors like the passive, apparently indifferent mind set of students in situations which instructors believe should arouse the highest levels of effort and inquiry or the actions of students who appear to set up the very failures which they fear through the use of procrastination or by holding themselves to unattainable standards. Understanding the root causes of these frustrating puzzles clarifies the directions in which solutions can be sought.

These strategies for change need be packaged and presented in different forms with different emphases depending on the three audiences involved—instructors, Graduate Student Instructors, and students.

INSTRUCTORS

Instructors need take the lead in negotiating a learning contract—so to speak, among all the stake-holders, one that favors active intellectual inquiry among students, not passive acquiescence, and which features direct guidance by instructors to make intellectual risk-taking safer as well as more rewarding for students. In many instances, this involves overhauling course policy. But recognizing the need for change is not a easy proposition. Instructors can be resistant to such fundamental change, not only because real changes require time and effort—commodities always in short supply, but also because the same self-worth dynamics that animates students has its counterpart among teachers. Instructors are especially vulnerable to being rejected by students because they care so deeply about their disciplines and the values that typify the examined life. This is why the dismissive or indifferent gestures of students wound so deeply, and why instructors complain with such anger about their students disregard for the gifts of learning.

There is wide-spread agreement among instructors, in theory at least, regarding the value of being intrinsically invested in one's learning. Yet, in practice, these values are often honored more in the breach than in the observance. Our research suggests several reasons for this. First, concepts like motivation are viewed by many instructors as mysterious and elusive, hence unlikely to contribute significantly to tangible performance goals. Second, it is sometimes argued that because of the highly selected nature of Berkeley students, everyone is already motivated to learn. Third, there is also the belief that intrinsic engagement is itself a byproduct of doing well academically, and therefore, makes no direct contribution to the pursuit of academic goals. Fourth, some instructors feel it is beyond their expertise to encourage these motivational goals. These concerns are legitimate, but largely misguided. Indeed, the major effort of our outreach program is to allay these concerns and encourage a more accurate and constructive vision of the motivational basis of the teaching and learning process. Our message includes the points that the instructional principles which control the motivational climate of classrooms are lawful, well-documented, and accessible to all teachers; that although Berkeley students are, indeed, motivated, but often motivated—even overmotivated, for fear-driven reasons which undercut both the acquisition and appreciation of subject-matter knowledge; and that being intrinsically-engaged contributes directly to academic goals.

GRADUATE STUDENT INSTRUCTORS (GSIs)

The most underappreciated players in the teaching/learning process are the GSIs who typically constitute the instructional 'back-bone' of most large-enrollment, lower-division introductory courses. Underappreciated, perhaps, but not overlooked, at least not recently. In the past few years, this teaching underclass has become the center of a firestorm of public resentment amidst nation-wide charges that faculty, especially in elite, research-oriented universities, are abandoning their teaching responsibilities to these novices, and that with rare exception they are being abandoned to their fate—'sink or swim,' without proper teacher training (McClay, 2005).

Based on our own observations and extensive interviews, we have concluded that GSIs are, in fact, 'the beleaguered players in the middle.' On the one hand, GSIs are seen by their students as potential protectors—both interpreters and buffers between themselves and course demands as well as knowledgeable guides to learning. On the other hand, GSIs are often seen by instructors as their surrogates in matters of administering course policy, maintaining the teaching infrastructure, and of course assigning course grades. The nature of this auxiliary role makes GSIs responsible for so much, but with so little power over teaching decisions. Rarely are GSIs the co-architects of course policy, nor are they always consulted by instructors in these matters. Moreover, their situation is made even more precarious by the fact that they are very much students themselves—often only one or two years beyond their own undergraduate careers. Still, they are considered subject-matter experts by their students as well as seasoned teachers. However, typically they know little about the art of teaching. As a result GSIs are often fearful of having their ignorance exposed to their students, of having their relatively unsure grasp of their discipline challenged by mere undergraduates, and frightened over thoughts of losing control of their classroom. The full intensity of this fear of failing, and the resulting humiliation, can be best appreciated when considering its magnification through the lens of self-worth theory.

Much is being done currently to prepare beginning GSIs for their teaching duties, largely through the leadership of the Berkeley GSI Teaching and Resource Center. Our joint contributions to this campus-wide effort involve, among other programs, conferences for instructors who employ large numbers of GSIs in their teaching duties. Here the emphasis is on exploring ways for instructors to carry out their professional obligation as teaching mentors for GSIs. Also, of special interest are seminars for advanced GSIs who themselves will be going on the Ph.D. job market within a year. Today, successful job candidates are expected to provide teaching portfolios and evidence of a sophisticated understanding of the dynamics of teaching and learning. In our seminar, participants design courses they are likely to teach as beginning faculty with particular attention paid to establishing the motivational rationale behind their creations.

STUDENTS

Students are the central players—some would say, clients, in the educational drama. In the end, it is students who must take up the lessons of learning and internalize them in ways that create understanding and personal meaning. This often requires that students take on responsibilities for learning that are not always thought to be theirs, and for this reason reluctance may trump resolve. In short, inviting students to approach success does not insure that they will always accept the invitation, especially among those who are failure-threatened or who are already demoralized. Yet, in the last analysis, it is students who must do the 'heavy-lifting' when it comes to offsetting the academic self-doubts that affect many of them. According to self-worth theory, it is the misguided tests by which fear-driven students define their worth—measured in terms of aggrandizing their ability status by outperforming others, that must be examined. The teaching staff can, and should, be catalyses for such positive change, but the chemistry is up to students.

From our perspective, students need come to grips with the implications of the fateful self-worth formulation presented in my 1993 chapter: $P = A = W$. Students need to assess the extent to which their achievement behavior is dominated by this formula, and if found complicit, reconsider the narrow, often fleeting pay-offs associated with winning over others, and create other personal equations in which, for example, grades are thought to be the by-products of learning, not an end in itself, and learning for the rights reasons—for the sake of self-improvement, to prepare to help others, or for the satisfaction of personal interest. Perhaps the most hopeful observation regarding this struggle comes from students themselves. It will be recalled that our students asserted that ultimately the matter boils down not so much to a conflict between the goals of sheer achievement vs. appreciation for learning as to the need to prioritize these goals. From this perspective our task as educators is to help students redress these priorities in favor of caring about what they are achieving.

REFERENCES

Beery, R.G. (1975). Fear of failure in the student experience. *Personnel Guidance Journal* 54: 190–203.

Condry, J.D., and Chambers, J. (1978). Intrinsic motivation and the process of learning. In M.R. Lepper and D. Greene (eds.), *The Hidden Costs of Reward: New Perspectives on the Psychology of Human Motivation*. Hillsdale, NJ: Lawrence Erlbaum Associates, Inc.

Covington, M.V. (1992), *Making the Grade: A Self-Worth Perspective on Motivation and School Reform*. New York, NY: Cambridge University Press.

Covington, M.V. (1998), *The Will to Learn: A Guide for Motivating Young People*. New York, NY: Cambridge Press.

Covington, M.V. (1999). Caring about learning: The nature and nurturing of subject-matter appreciation. *Educational Psychologist* 34: 127–136.

Covington, M.V. (2000). Intrinsic versus extrinsic motivation in schools: A reconciliation. *Current Directions in Psychological Science* 9: 22–25.

Covington, M.V. (2002). Rewards and intrinsic motivation: A needs-based developmental perspective. In T. Urdan, and F. Pajares (eds.), *Motivation of Adolescents* (pp. 169–192). New York, NY: Academic Press.

Covington, M.V. (2004). Self-worth theory goes to college: Or do our motivation theories motivate? In D. McInerney (ed.). Big Theories Revisited.

Covington, M.V., and Beery, R.G. (1976). *Self-Worth and School Learning*. New York, NY: Holt, Rinehart & Winston.

Covington, M.V., and Dray, E. (2001). The developmental course of achievement motivation: A need-based approach. In A. Wigfield and P. Eccles (eds.), *Development of Achievement Motivation* (pp. 33–56). New York, NY: Academic Press.

Covington, M.V., and Elliot, A.J. (eds.) (2001). Special issue of *Educational Psychological Review*. New York, NY: Plenum Press. (Published Issue lists Elliot as first author, an error that was subsequently acknowledged in journal erratum.).

Covington, M.V., and Müeller, K.J. (2001). Intrinsic versus extrinsic motivation: An approach/avoidance reformulation. In M.V. Covington and A.J. Elliott (eds.), Special issue of *Educational Psychology Review* (pp. 111–130). New York, NY: Plenum Press.

Covington, M.V., and Omelich. C.L. (1979). Effort: The double-edged sword in school achievement. *Journal of Educational Psychology* 71: 169–182.

Covington, M.V., and Omelich, C.L. (1981). As failures mount: Affective and cognitive consequences of ability demotion in the classroom. *Journal of Educational Psychology* 73: 796–808.

Kohn, A. (1993). *Punished by Rewards*. New York, NY: Houghton Mifflin.

Lepper, M.R., Greene, D., and Nisbett, R.E. (1973). Undermining children's intrinsic interest with extrinsic reward: A test of the "overjustification" hypothesis. *Journal of Personality & Social Psychology* 28: 129–137.

McClay, W.M. (2005) Teaching the teachers. *Wall Street Journal*, October 28.

Perry, R.P., and Dickens, W.J. (1984). Perceived control in the college classroom: Response-outcome contingency training and instructor expressiveness effects on student achievement and causal attributions. *Journal of Educational Psychology* 76: 966–981.

Perry, R.P., and Magnusson, J.-L. (1987). Effective instruction and students' perceptions of control in the college classroom: Multiple-lectures effect. *Journal of Educational Psychology* 79: 453–460.

Thompson, T. (1996). Self-worth protection in achievement behavior: A review and implications for counselling. *Australian Psychologist* 31: 41–51.

16. STUDENT MOTIVATION AND SELF-REGULATED LEARNING IN THE COLLEGE CLASSROOM

Paul R. Pintrich* and Akane Zusho[†]

*The University of Michigan
[†]Fordham University
zusho@fordham.edu

Key Words: Achievement goal theory, academic motivation and achievement, goal theory, intrinsic motivation, achievement striving

College student motivation is a persistent and persuasive problem for faculty and staff at all levels of postsecondary education. Faculty at community colleges, comprehensive universities, small liberal arts colleges, and private and public research universities all bemoan the lack of student motivation. The questions that college faculty and staff raise include: why don't the students seem to care about their work, why don't they seem more interested in the disciplinary content of the courses, why do they only care about their grades but not learning, why don't they try very hard, why don't they study very much, why do they procrastinate and try to study for an exam at the last minute, or try to write a paper the day before it is due, why can't they be more organized and plan their work better, and why don't they learn or perform very well. All of these issues can be partially explained by a motivation and self-regulation perspective on student learning in the college classroom. Of course, there are other models of college student cognition and learning that are relevant, but in this chapter we will focus on motivational and self-regulatory constructs. The purpose of this chapter is to provide an overview of current research on college student motivation and self-regulated learning that should provide some insights into these general problems.

Given the scope and page limitations of this chapter, we cannot review all the different theoretical models and all the research literature on the topic. In fact, we do not think a review of all the different theories

R.P. Perry and J.C. Smart (eds.), The Scholarship of Teaching and Learning in Higher Education: An Evidence-Based Perspective, 731–810.
© 2007 *Springer.*

and models is that helpful at this point in the development of our understanding of college student motivation and self-regulation. Accordingly, we organize our chapter around some general constructs that cut across different theoretical models; we hope that the model will then provide a conceptual framework that is useful for higher education researchers, college faculty, and college administrators and staff. In addition, we will propose some first-order principles or generalizations about motivation and learning based on empirical studies from our research program at Michigan as well as other studies. These generalizations should be useful in guiding future research as well as practice. The model explicitly focuses on college student motivation and self-regulation regarding academic learning, not motivation for non-academic activities (e.g., relationships, friendships, athletics, careers). Finally, the model is best applied to the college classroom or course level, not college in general, as there are other models that attempt to explain how college attendance influences a host of student outcomes including motivation and learning (see Pascarella and Terenzini, 1991).

This focus on the college classroom level has both theoretical and practical value. First, most of the current research on student motivation and self-regulation at the college and precollegiate levels has been at the classroom level and therefore is very relevant for developing a model of academic motivation and learning. More importantly, most academic student learning is situated in a college classroom or course context that includes not just the time spent in the actual classroom itself, but also the time spent outside formal class time working on the specific course tasks and assignments. Finally, a classroom level focus is the most meaningful and pragmatic for college instructors and our own teaching. We cannot change or easily influence factors outside our classroom (such as the institutional and community norms and structures, the attitudes and beliefs of the students' friends and roommates, or the students' family background and beliefs), but we can change and control what we do in our own classrooms. Of course, we are always operating under constraints in our classrooms, such as class size, time, and curriculum demands; nevertheless, we still have more control over our own classrooms than other aspects of the college environment. Accordingly, we have focused this chapter on the college classroom context and students' motivational beliefs and self-regulation in relation to various classroom and course features.

Before we discuss our general model, a description of two students who show differing patterns of motivation and self-regulation may help to ground the model in the realities of college student learning.

Both Mike and Lyndsay were good students in high school, but both are having some difficulties in college. Mike studies in the same way for all his classes, even though they differ greatly in terms of their requirements (papers, exams, lab reports) and the nature of instruction (discussion, lectures, small group work). He doesn't think much about his goals for different classes, he just wants to get good grades such as an A or a B in all his courses. He studies by reading the course material over and over and when he studies for an exam, he concentrates on memorizing important terms and ideas. He finds some of his classes interesting, but others are fairly boring to him. He spends much more time on those classes where he likes the content, and as the term progresses, he finds it harder and harder to do the work in the boring classes. It always seems that when he sets aside time to work on those classes, his roommates ask him to go out with them; and he usually goes, instead of studying. He tends to wait until the week of an exam or the week a paper is due to start working on it and often feels rushed and realizes that he did not do his best work. In some of his classes his grades are fine, but in others he is getting C's or lower. When he thinks about why he does not do well in those classes, he thinks that he lacks the ability to do well in those classes — and they are boring anyway. He rarely asks other students or the instructors for help. He just keeps on working and studying the way he did in high school, since it worked for him then — although he does worry about his ability to succeed in college, since it is much harder than high school. Mike is not a terrible student. He does try to do his work and he does study, just as most college students do, but he is not as successful as he could be if he were more self-regulating.

Lyndsay approaches the same courses differently. She, too, wants to get good grades; but she also wants to learn and understand the material. She knows she will be able to use the course material in other classes and in her career, so she focuses not just on grades but on understanding. In addition, she thinks about how the courses are different and realizes that different tasks like exams and papers require different approaches to studying and learning. In some classes, where the exams test for recall, she does spend some time memorizing the important terms. However, in all her classes, when she reads the material, she tries to paraphrase it, write summaries, or make outlines of the text. This helps her see the connections between the lectures and the readings. Also, when she is studying, she gives herself mini-quizzes on the material and these self-tests help her to monitor her understanding. When she finds that she can't get 100% of the questions

733

correct on her own quizzes, she goes back over the material and figures out what she did not understand. She also tries to keep a regular study schedule and plans her work by the week and month, so that she is not starting a paper the week it is due. Of course, when an exam is coming up or a paper is due, she concentrates on that course, but she usually feels prepared since she is not doing the work at the last minute. Of course, she finds some of the course material boring, but she makes sure she spends more time on those courses since she knows it is harder for her to concentrate on that material. She often studies with her friends. They work together, and then go out for a pizza after several hours of studying. She thinks of these pizza breaks as a reward for her studying. She also incorporates her friends into her study routine, which helps her regulate her studying and keep focused on her task, rather than having her friends be a distraction that takes her away from school work as in Mike's case. In the long run, Lyndsay will be much more successful than Mike. She may struggle with the transition to college, as do most college students, but she is using all her cognitive and motivational resources to try to become more self-regulating and a better student.

Our general model can capture some of the important differences between Mike's and Lyndsay's approaches to learning. We will first describe the general model and the components and then we will discuss the relations among the different components of the model. We will refer to the examples of Lyndsay and Mike throughout the chapter, to help the reader understand the different aspects of the model in concrete terms.

Figure 1F1 displays the model of student academic motivation and self-regulation in the college classroom that serves to organize this chapter. There are five major components in the model. First, there are student personal characteristics such as age, gender, and ethnicity (labeled A, in Figure 1) which are related to student motivation, self-regulation, and outcomes. There also are contextual factors (B) that include various features of the classroom environment (e.g., the different tasks that Mike and Lyndsay confront in their courses). These two factors are assumed to influence the operation of the motivational (C) and self-regulatory processes (D), the next two main components in the model. The motivational processes (C) reflect the internal thoughts and emotions that students have about themselves in relation to the context and their perceptions of that context. Both Mike and Lyndsay have goals for their learning. They think about how boring the courses are, they worry about doing well, and they wonder if they

Figure 1: A general model for student motivation and self-regulated learning in the college classroom.

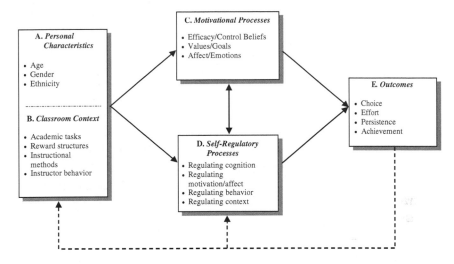

have the capabilities to succeed. Self-regulatory processes (D) include the internal strategies and processes that students can use to monitor, control, and regulate themselves. Both Mike and Lyndsay use a number of different strategies for studying and learning. The fifth factor in the model includes various student outcomes such as choice, effort, persistence, and actual achievement (E). Lyndsay and Mike make different choices about how to use their time and have different outcomes in terms of effort, persistence, and achievement.

It is important to note that although the general model is presented in a linear format with the direction of influence described as flowing from the classroom context and personal characteristics to motivation and self-regulatory processes to outcomes, this is only for ease of presentation in this chapter. Given that the model reflects a social cognitive perspective, it is assumed that all the relations between components in the model are reciprocal (Pintrich, 2000c; Zimmerman, 2000). College students' actual behavior and outcomes provide feedback to them that influences their motivation and self-regulation (dotted line flowing from box E to boxes C and D). For example, it has been shown in numerous studies that students' level of achievement (and the grades they receive) will influence their beliefs about their competence as well as their motivation in general (Bandura, 1986; Pintrich and Schunk, 1996; Weiner, 1986).

In the same fashion, college student behavior in the class will influence the instructor's behavior (a contextual factor, dotted line from box E to B). For example, students who are actively engaged in class discussion may influence the instructor's choice of teaching strategies (e.g., a move away from lecture to more discussion). Finally, college students do have some *a priori* motivational beliefs about themselves and the course, before they even come to the first several classes, which can influence their perceptions of the college classroom context and their subsequent beliefs and behavior. Accordingly, the model represents an attempt to describe a dynamic and interacting system of the major components of classroom context, personal characteristics, motivation, self-regulation, and behavior.

It also should be noted that the model does not have a direct path from personal characteristics (A) or classroom contextual factors (B) to student out-comes (E). This reflects our assumption that the effects of personal and contextual factors on student outcomes (E) are mediated through the motivational (C) and self-regulatory processes (D). For example, it is not that females and males are inherently different in some ways that lead them to achieve at different levels (E). The model assumes that males and females might have different patterns of motivation (C) and self-regulation (D) which in turn lead to different outcomes. The same argument can be made for ethnic differences or even age-developmental differences. The key issue is understanding the psychological mediators of motivation, cognition, and self-regulation (C and D) and how they may be linked to personal characteristics (A) and the outcomes (E). In the same manner, the models assumes that classroom contextual factors (B) have their effects on outcomes (E) through their effects on student motivation (C) and self-regulation (D). This student mediating model also offers hope for educators as motivation (C) and self-regulation (D) are assumed to be changeable and malleable, whereas student characteristics (A) like gender and ethnicity are not changeable.

STUDENT OUTCOMES (E)

In describing the model in more detail, it is easiest to start with the out-come component (E) on the far right side of Figure 1. These are behaviors that all college instructors would deem important. In addition, psychological models of motivation and self-regulation attempt to explain the development of these outcomes.

Motivational theories (C) are concerned with why individuals choose one activity over another, whether it be the day-to-day decisions regarding the choice of working on a task or relaxing, or the more momentous and serious choices regarding career, marriage, and family.

Self-regulation research (D) focuses on the different strategies that can be used to approach these goals or choices. In the achievement context of a college classroom, choice behaviors include students' choosing to work on the course material and study instead of watching television or talking with friends or roommates. Mike often chooses to go out with his friends instead of studying, while Lyndsay incorporates her friends into her studying patterns, thereby satisfying both the social goal of being with peers as well as the academic goal of studying. In addition, many faculty members would take as evidence of motivated behavior students' choice to take another course in their discipline, a choice to major in the discipline, or even to go on to graduate school in the discipline. In fact, many faculty members state explicitly that these latter types of choice behavior are some of the most important outcomes of their introductory classes. These choice behaviors are good exemplars of motivated behavior.

A second aspect of motivated behavior that psychological research has examined is the students' level of activity or involvement in a task. We would assume that students are motivated when they put forth a great deal of effort for our courses, from not falling asleep to more active engagement in the course. Behavioral indicators of this involvement could include taking detailed notes, asking good questions in class, being willing to take risks in class in terms of stating ideas or opinions, coming after class to office hours to discuss in more detail the ideas presented in class, discussing the ideas from the course with classmates or friends outside of class time, spending a reasonable amount of time studying and preparing for class or exams, spending more time on our course than on other activities, and seeking out additional or new information from the library or other sources that goes beyond what is presented in class. Lyndsay clearly spends more time and effort on her school work than Mike.

Besides these behavioral indicators, there are more covert or unobservable aspects of engagement which include cognitive engagement and processing, such as thinking deeply about the material, using various cognitive strategies to learn the material in a more disciplined and thoughtful manner, seeking to understand the material (not just memorize it), and integrating the new material with previously-held conceptions of the content. Lyndsay tries to use these deeper strategies, while Mike seems to rely mainly on memorization. All of these cognitive processes are crucial for deeper understanding and learning. Some of these cognitive processes will be discussed in more detail in the section on self-regulatory processes (D), but not all of

737

them. A detailed discussion of all the various aspects of cognition that play a role in student learning is beyond the scope of this chapter. Nevertheless, it is important to note that it is not enough for students to be engaged in the course only behaviorally; they also must be cognitively engaged in order for true learning and understanding to occur.

The third general aspect of motivated behavior that has been examined in most motivational theories is persistence. If individuals persist at a task, even in the face of difficulty, boredom, or fatigue, we usually say they are motivated to do that task. Persistence is easily observable in general, although college faculty might not normally have access to the situations where the issue of persistence most readily arises for students. In precollegiate classrooms, teachers do have more opportunities to observe students actually working on course tasks during class time. It is common for teachers in precollegiate classrooms to comment on the students' willingness to persist and try hard on the class work. In contrast, college faculty often do not have the chance to see how the students work and study for their class.

However, casual observations of undergraduates studying in the library or conversations with students about their workload quickly reveal that the issue of persistence is an important one for most college students. For example, persistence is important when students confront a difficult task, whether it is working through calculus problems, balancing equations in chemistry, understanding conservative and Marxist economic theories, or applying deconstructionist theory to the interpretation of a novel; most college students will confront some tasks that are difficult for them, given their prior knowledge and skills. Students' willingness to persist in the face of these individually-defined difficult tasks is a good exemplar of motivated behavior. In addition, given their prior interests and selected majors, students may see some course material as boring or unimportant to them. Again, being able to persist at these tasks is an important feature of motivated behavior, which Lyndsay exhibits in contrast to Mike. Finally, students often have many competing demands on their time (i.e., school work, employment, social activities) and are often tired due to being involved in so many activities. In the face of this potential overexertion and fatigue, students who overcome their lassitude and continue to persist at their school work would be considered motivated.

Finally, the last outcome is student academic performance or achievement. This can be indexed by grades in the course or overall GPA. For most faculty, performance involves what the students have learned in the course including their understanding of new ideas, new theories, and new models as well as new skills (i.e., writing) or ways of thinking (i.e., critical thinking, scientific thinking, mathematical thinking). Of course, a key issue is how to assess these understandings and skills. Faculty assume that the assignments, exams, papers, and other tasks and activities that students engage in during the course should reflect these desired outcomes. However, it often is difficult, albeit not impossible, to assess these outcomes using standard multiple choice format examinations. Accordingly, there may be a need for diversity in assessment procedures in order to measure learning and understanding. In any event, student performance and achievement on all the different types of course assessments are partially a function of motivational and self-regulatory processes. Of course, they also are influenced heavily by the students cognition and prior knowledge, but we will focus on the role of motivation (C) and self-regulation (D) in this chapter. We turn now to a discussion of self-regulatory processes.

THE ROLE OF SELF-REGULATORY PROCESSES (D)

There are many different models of motivation and self-regulated learning that propose different constructs and mechanisms, but they do share some basic assumptions about learning and regulation. One common assumption might be called the active, constructive assumption, which follows from a general cognitive perspective. That is, all the models view learners as active, constructive participants in the learning process. Learners are assumed to actively construct their own meanings, goals, and strategies from the information available in the "external" environment as well as information in their own minds (the "internal" environment). College students are not just passive recipients of information from professors, parents, or other adults, but rather active, constructive meaning-makers as they go about learning. Accordingly, giving the "perfect" lecture does not necessarily mean that the students in the course will understand the material in the expected manner. The students will create their own meaning from this lecture, and part of their meaning will perhaps reflect the appropriate disciplinary knowledge, but other parts may be based on the students' own prior knowledge and misconceptions that they had when they came to the lecture hall.

A second, related assumption is the potential for control assumption. All the models assume that learners can potentially monitor, control, and regulate certain aspects of their own cognition, motivation, and behavior as well as some features of their environments. This assumption does not mean that college students will or can

739

monitor and control their cognition, motivation, or behavior at all times or in all contexts, only that some monitoring, control, and regulation is possible. All of the models recognize that there are biological, developmental, contextual, and individual difference constraints that can impede or interfere with individual efforts at regulation.

In addition, it is clear that college students can most readily control or regulate their own personal goals for learning and understanding. There are obviously higher-order goals or standards that are defined externally by the college course (e.g., in an English course students need to write a certain way to get a good grade), or by the university (e.g., a certain GPA is what it takes to get on the Dean's List), or by society at large (e.g., the standards and requirements to become a medical doctor). These goals and standards are not readily controllable by the individual college student, but rather represent aspects of the context to which the students have to respond and adapt as they attempt to regulate their own behavior. Accordingly, to some extent, some aspects of the external environment do control or guide an individual college students' regulatory behavior. The important issue for the model discussed in this chapter is how individual college students respond to these external demands or goal stresses.

A third general assumption that is made in these models of self-regulated learning — as in all general models of regulation stretching back to Miller, Galanter, and Pribram (1960) — is the goal, criterion, or standard assumption. All models of regulation assume that there is some type of criterion or standard (also called goals, reference value) against which comparisons are made in order to assess whether the process should continue as is or if some type of change is necessary. The common sense example is the thermostat operation for the heating and cooling of a house. Once a desired temperature is set (the goal, criterion, standard), the thermostat monitors the temperature of the house (monitoring process) and then turns on or off the heating or air conditioning units (control and regulation processes) in order to reach and maintain the standard. In a parallel manner, the general example for learning assumes that individuals can set personal standards or goals to strive for in their learning, monitor their progress towards these goals, and then adapt and regulate their cognition, motivation, and behavior in order to reach their goals. Mike and Lyndsay both have goals of getting good grades and they both do study. However, Lyndsay also has a goal of learning and understanding, which leads her to engage the material in a deeper manner.

A fourth general assumption of most of the models of motivation and self-regulated learning is that motivational beliefs and self-regulatory activities are mediators between personal and contextual characteristics and actual achievement or performance. That is, it is not just individuals' cultural, demographic, or personality characteristics that influence achievement and learning directly, nor just the contextual characteristics of the classroom environment that shape achievement (see Figure 1), but the individuals' motivation and self-regulation of their cognition, motivation, and behavior that mediate the relations between the person, context, and eventual achievement. Given this assumption, we do not include a direct path from personal characteristics (A) and classroom context (B) to outcomes (E) in Figure 1. Most models of self-regulation assume that self-regulatory activities (D) are directly linked to outcomes (E) such as achievement and performance, although much of the research examines self-regulatory activities as outcomes in their own right.

Given these assumptions, a general working definition of self-regulated learning is that it is an active, constructive process whereby learners set goals for their learning and then attempt to monitor, regulate, and control their cognition, motivation, and behavior, guided and constrained by their goals and the contextual features in the environment. These self-regulatory activities can mediate the relations between individuals and the context and their overall achievement. This definition is similar to other models of self-regulated learning (e.g., Butler and Winne, 1995; Zimmerman, 1989, 1998a, b; 2000). Although this definition is relatively simple, the remainder of this section outlines in more detail the various processes and areas of regulation and their application to learning and achievement in the academic domain, which reveals the complexity and diversity of the processes of self-regulated learning.

PHASES OF SELF-REGULATION

Figure 2F2 displays a simple four-phase model of self-regulated learning. The four phases are processes that many models of regulation and self-regulation share (e.g., Zimmerman, 1998a, b; 2000) and reflect goal-setting, monitoring, control and regulation, and self-reflection processes. These phases are suggested as a heuristic to organize our thinking and research on self-regulated learning.

Figure 2: Four phase model of self-regulated learning.

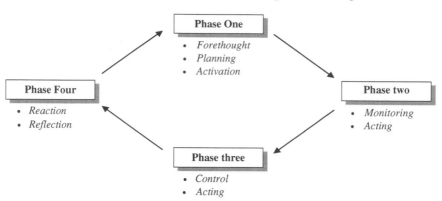

Of course, not all academic learning follows these phases, as there are many occasions for students to learn academic material in more tacit or implicit or unintentional ways, without self-regulating their learning in such an explicit manner as suggested in the model. There are many cases where students study, learn, and think without much intentional or explicit goal-setting, monitoring, or attempt to control their cognition and learning. In fact, in some cases, it is important for college students to have automatized certain types of cognitive processing (e.g., basic reading skills). If students are spending most of their cognitive resources on decoding and understanding the words in a textbook, there are fewer cognitive resources left over for deeper thinking about the text material. The distinctions between consciousness and intentional, controlled or self-regulated learning in contrast to more unconscious, automatic processing or learning are still being debated in the research and represent important directions for future research. Nevertheless, there are occasions when students can bring their cognition and learning under conscious, explicit, and intentional control and the model in this chapter helps outlines the various processes involved when students do attempt to regulate their own learning.

Phase 1 involves planning and goal-setting as well as activation of perceptions and knowledge of the task and context and the self in relation to the task. For example, as Lyndsay begins a study session, she might ask herself questions such as, "what are my goals for the next three hours, what do I want to focus on as I read this course material, what do I already know about this topic?". The first two questions help frame Lyndsay's goals for her study session. These goals can then serve as the criteria she uses to help regulate her behavior. As she approaches the goals, she can note that she is making progress towards them and continue doing what she is doing. On the other hand, if she notes that she has not been focusing on what she set as her goals, she can adjust or change her studying to help her refocus her learning (as Lyndsay does when she goes back over material she does not understand). The last question involves the activation of prior knowledge. Prior knowledge has a huge effect on new learning, and thinking about what one already knows and how it relates to what he or she will study is a good regulatory strategy.

As the student actually starts to engage in the task, she is obviously doing certain activities and engaging in various cognitive processes (attending, comparing, analyzing, thinking, etc.). However, Phase 2 also concerns various monitoring processes that represent metacognitive awareness of different aspects of the self and task or context. For example, as she reads her textbook, Lyndsay might begin to think that she does not understand all that she is reading. This type of awareness is called metacognitive because it is "above" or about cognition. The student is basically monitoring her reading comprehension to see if she is understanding what she is reading. This type of metacognitive monitoring of learning is a very important self-regulatory process. Self-regulation depends heavily on students' monitoring what they are doing and thinking and then adjusting their behavior and cognition accordingly. The little self-quizzes that Lyndsay gives herself reflects this type of active monitoring of comprehension and understanding.

Phase 3 involves efforts to control and regulate different aspects of the self or task and context. As the student performs the task but also monitors her learning, she may come to realize that she is not understanding as much of the text as she had hoped (as Lyndsay comes to realize). One outcome of this metacognitive monitoring from Phase 2 is a decision to go back and repair her comprehension, for example, by rereading the whole text, by going back over certain parts of the text, by drawing a diagram of some of the relations between the ideas, or by taking notes on parts of the text. All of these strategies are designed to help the student regulate or control her reading comprehension, to bring her closer to the goals that she set for herself at the beginning of the task. These control and regulation processes can take place anytime during the task and help to change the behavior or cognition to make it more adaptive in terms of obtaining the goal for the task.

Finally, Phase 4 represents various kinds of reactions and reflections on the self and the task or context after the task is completed. This type of reaction often has to do with the types of attributions a student makes regarding the causes of his or her success or failure. For example, if a student thinks he was successful on a test, he can attribute it to his own high ability or effort, or he can attribute it to other factors such as good luck, the ease of the test, or another's help (such as the instructor) and many other factors. In the same way, if a student fails an exam, he can attribute it to the lack of ability (as did Mike in our earlier example) or effort on his part, bad luck, the difficulty of the task, lack of help from others, and countless other factors. The type and the nature of attribution the student makes has profound implications for future attempts at the task, future expectancies for the task, and general motivation and achievement (Pintrich and Schunk, 1996; Weiner, 1986). In general, if students attribute success to stable causes (such as high ability), they will expect to succeed in the future. In the same manner, students who attribute failure to unstable causes (such as lack of effort) will at least believe they can change the outcome in the future (Weiner, 1986). In research on college students, Perry and his colleagues (Perry, 1991; Perry and Dickens, 1988; Perry and Magnusson, 1989; Perry and Penner, 1990) have shown that students who believe they have some control over their own behavior achieve better than those who don't think they have much control. These types of reactions feed into the previous phases, especially Phase 1, and become part of the knowledge that individuals bring with them to the next task.

The four phases represent a general time-ordered sequence that individuals would go through as they perform a task, but there is no strong assumption that the phases are hierarchically or linearly structured such that earlier phases must always occur before later phases. In most models of self-regulated learning, the processes of monitoring, control, and reaction can be ongoing simultaneously and dynamically as the individual progresses through the task, with the goals and plans being changed or updated based on the feedback from theseprocesses. In fact, Pintrich, Wolters, and Baxter (2000) suggest that much of the empirical work on monitoring (Phase 2) and control/regulation (Phase 3) shows little separation of these processes in terms of people's experiences as revealed by data from self-report questionnaries or think-aloud protocols. These four phases of self-regulation can be applied to four general areas of self-regulation. Table 1T1 show how the four phases can be applied to four areas of self-regulation.

Table 1: Phases and Areas for Self-regulated Learning

	AREAS FOR REGULATION			
Phases	Cognition	Motivation/Affect	Behavior	Context
1) Forethought, Planning, and Activation	1) Target goal setting 2) Prior content knowledge activation 3) Metacognitive knowledge activation	1) Goal orientation adoption 2) Efficacy judgments 3) Ease of learning judgments (EOLs), Perceptions of task difficulty 4) Task value activation 5) Interest activation	1) Time and effort planning 2) Planning for self-observations of behavior	1) Perceptions of task 2) Perceptions of context
2) Monitoring	1) Metacognitive awareness and monitoring of cognition (JOLs)	1) Awareness and monitoring of motivation and affect	1) Awareness and monitoring of effort, time use, need for help	1) Monitoring changing task and context conditions
3) Control	1) Selection and adaptation of cognitive strategies for learning, thinking	1) Selection and adaptation of strategies for managing motivation and affect	1) Increase/decrease effort 2) Persist, give up 3) Help-seeking behavior	1) Change or re-negotiate task 2) Change or leave context
4) Reaction and Reflection	1) Cognitive judgments 2) Attributions	1) Affective reactions 2) Attributions	1) Choice behavior	1) Evaluation of task 2) Evaluation of context

AREAS OF SELF-REGULATION

The four columns in Table 1 represent different areas for regulation that an individual learner can attempt to monitor, control, and regulate. The first three columns of cognition, motivation/affect, and behavior reflect the traditional tripartite division of different areas of psychological functioning (Snow, Corno, and Jackson, 1996). As Snow et al. (1996) note, the boundaries between these areas may be fuzzy, but there is utility in discussing them separately, particularly since much of traditional psychological research has focused on the different areas in isolation from the others.

These first three areas in the columns in Table 1 represent aspects of the individual's own cognition, motivation/affect, and behavior that he or she can attempt to control and regulate. These attempts to control or regulate are "self-regulated" in that the individual is focused on trying to control or regulate his or her own cognition, motivation, and behavior. Of course, other individuals in the environment (such as instructors, peers, or parents) can try to "other" regulate an individual's cognition, motivation, or behavior as well, by directing or guiding the individual in terms of what, how, and when to do a task. More generally, other task and contextual features (e.g., task characteristics, feedback systems, evaluation structures) can facilitate or constrain an individual's attempts to self-regulate his or her learning.

The cognitive column in Table 1 concerns the different cognitive strategies that individuals may use to learn and perform a task as well as the metacognitive strategies individuals may use to control and regulate their cognition. Mike and Lyndsay both used a number of different cognitive and metacognitive strategies when they studied for their courses. In addition, both content knowledge and strategic knowledge are included in the cognitive column. The motivation and affect column (second column in Table 1) concerns the activation and control of various motivational beliefs that individuals may have about themselves in relation to the task, such as self-efficacy beliefs, goal orientation, and values for the task. In addition, interest or liking of the task would be included in this column as well as positive and negative affective reactions to the self or task. Finally, any strategies that individuals may use to control and regulate their motivation and affect would be included in this column. The behavior column (third column in Table 1) reflects the general effort the individual may exert on the task as well as persistence, help-seeking, and choice behaviors.

The fourth column in Table 1, context, represents various aspects of the task environment or general classroom or cultural context where the learning is taking place. Individuals do try to monitor and control their environment to some extent, and in fact, in some models of intelligence (e.g., Sternberg, 1985), attempts to selectively control and change the context are seen as very adaptable. In the same manner, in this model, it is assumed that individual attempts to monitor and control the environment is an important aspect of self-regulated learning. This area of contextual features is omitted from some models of self-regulation, as it reflects context, not the self or aspects of the individual, and in those models attempts to control the context are not considered part of self-regulation (see Boekaerts, Pintrich and Zeidner, 2000 for other models of self-regulation).

This general description of the rows and columns of Table 1 provides an overview of how the different phases of regulation relate to different areas for regulation. The next section describes in more detail the cells in the Table, organized by column.

REGULATION OF COGNITION

Table 1 displays the four general phases of self-regulation that can occur; within the first column for cognition, there are four cells going down the cognitive column that represent how these different phases may be applied to various aspects of cognition. Each of these four cells is discussed separately for rhetorical and logical reasons, including ease of presentation — although, as noted above, the phases may overlap or occur simultaneously with multiple interactions among the different processes and components. There is no strong assumption of a simple linear, static process with separable non-interacting components.

Cognitive planning and activation. At the intersection of the row for Phase 1 and the column for cognition in Table 1, there are three general types of planning or activation, 1) target goal setting, 2) activation of relevant prior content knowledge, and 3) activation of metacognitive knowledge. Target goal setting involves the setting of task-specific goals which can be used to guide cognition in general and monitoring in particular (Harackiewicz, Barron, and Elliot, 1998; Pintrich et al., 2000; Pressley and Afflerbach, 1995; Schunk, 1994; Zimmerman, 1989; Zimmerman and Martinez-Pons, 1986, 1988). As noted above, the goal acts as a criterion against which to assess, monitor, and guide cognition, just as the temperature setting of a thermostat guides the operation of the thermostat and heating/cooling system. Of course, goal-setting is most often assumed to occur before starting a task, but goal-setting can actually occur at any point during performance. Learners may begin a task by setting specific goals for learning, goals for time use, and goals for eventual performance, but all of these can be adjusted and changed at any time during task performance as a function of monitoring, control, and reflection processes. Lyndsay set goals of both getting good grades and of understanding, while Mike only set a general goal of getting good grades.

The second aspect of forethought and planning involves the activation of relevant prior content knowledge. At some level, this process of activation of prior knowledge can and does happen automatically and without conscious thought. That is, as college students approach a task in a particular domain, for example, mathematics, some aspects of their knowledge about mathematics will be activated automatically and quickly without conscious control. This type of process would not be considered self-regulatory and involves general cognitive processing, as it is not under the explicit control of the learner. At the same time, college students who are more self-regulating can actively search their memory for relevant prior knowledge before they actually begin performing the task (Alexander, Schallert, and Hare, 1991; Flavell, 1979; Pintrich et al., 2000).

The third entry in the upper left-most cell in Table 1, the activation of metacognitive knowledge, includes the activation of knowledge about cognitive tasks and cognitive strategies and seems to be useful for learning (Pintrich et al., 2000; Schneider and Pressley, 1997). Again, as with prior content knowledge, this activation can be rather automatic, stimulated by individual, task, or contextual features or it can be more controlled and conscious. Metacognitive task knowledge includes knowledge about how task variations can influence cognition. For example, if more information is provided in a question or a test, then it will generally be more easily solved than when little information is provided. Most students come to understand this general idea and it becomes part of their metacognitive knowledge about task features. Other examples include knowing that some tasks, or the goals for the task, are more or less difficult, such as trying to remember the gist of a story versus remembering the story verbatim (Flavell, 1979).

Knowledge of strategy variables includes all the knowledge individuals can acquire about various procedures and strategies for cognition including memorizing, thinking, reasoning, problem solving, planning, studying, reading, writing, etc.. This is the area that has seen the most research and is probably the most familiar category of metacognitive knowledge. Knowledge that rehearsal strategies can help in recalling a telephone number, or that organizational and elaboration strategies can help in the memory and comprehension of text information, are examples of strategy knowledge.

Metacognitive knowledge has been broken down further into declarative, procedural, and conditional metacognitive knowledge (Alexander et al., 1991; Paris, Lipson, and Wixson, 1983; Schraw and Moshman, 1995). Declarative knowledge of cognition is the knowledge of the "what" of cognition and includes knowledge of the different cognitive strategies (such as rehearsal or elaboration) that can be used for learning. Procedural knowledge includes knowing how to perform and use the various cognitive strategies. It may not be enough to know that there are elaboration strategies like summarizing and paraphrasing; it is important to know how to use these strategies effectively. Finally, conditional knowledge includes knowing when and why to use the various cognitive strategies. For example, elaboration strategies may be appropriate in some contexts for some types of tasks (learning from text); other strategies such as rehearsal may be more appropriate for different tasks or different goals (trying to remember a telephone number). This type of conditional knowledge is important for the flexible and adaptive use of various cognitive strategies. It seems that Lyndsay has much more conditional knowledge than Mike and tries to adjust her strategy use to fit the different demands of the courses and tasks. This is much more reflective of a self-regulating learner and helps her perform better than Mike.

Cognitive monitoring. The second cell down the cognitive column in Table 1 includes metacognitive monitoring processes. Cognitive monitoring involves the awareness and monitoring of various aspects of cognition and is an important component of what is classically labeled metacognition (Brown, Bransford, Campione, and Ferrara, 1983; Flavell, 1979; Koriat and Goldsmith, 1996; Pintrich et al., 2000; Schneider and Pressley, 1997). In contrast to metacognitive knowledge (discussed in the previous section), which is more static and "statable" (individuals can tell whether they know it or not), metacognitive judgments and monitoring are more dynamic and process-oriented and reflect metacognitive awareness and ongoing metacognitive activities individuals may engage in as they perform a task.

One type of metacognitive judgment or monitoring activity involves judgments of learning (JOLs) and comprehension monitoring (Nelson and Narens, 1990; Pintrich et al., 2000). These judgments may manifest themselves in a number of activities, such as individuals

749

becoming aware that they do not understand something they just read or heard, or becoming aware that they are reading too quickly or slowly given the text and their goals. Judgments of learning also would be made as students actively monitor their reading comprehension by asking themselves questions. Lyndsay does seem to make these judgments by using self-quizzes, while Mike seem to just plow on in his studying, without much metacognitive awareness. Judgments of learning also could be made when students try to decide whether they are ready to take a test on the material they have just read and studied or in a memory experiment as they try to judge whether they have learned the target words (Nelson and Narens, 1990). Pressley and Afflerbach (1995) provide a detailed listing of monitoring activities that individuals can engage in while reading. In the classroom context, besides reading comprehension or memory judgments, JOLs could involve students making judgments of their comprehension of a lecture as the instructor is delivering it or checking whether they could recall the lecture information for a test at a later point in time.

Cognitive control and regulation. Cognitive control and regulation includes the types of cognitive and metacognitive activities that individuals engage in to adapt and change their cognition. In most models of metacognition and self-regulated learning, control and regulation activities are assumed to be dependent on, or at least strongly related to, metacognitive monitoring activities, although metacognitive control and monitoring are conceived as separate processes (Butler and Winne, 1995; Nelson and Narens, 1990; Pintrich et al., 2000; Zimmerman, 1989, 1994). That is, it is assumed that attempts to control, regulate, and change cognition should be related to cognitive monitoring activities that provide information about the relative discrepancy between a goal and current progress towards that goal. For example, if a student is reading a textbook with the goal of understanding (not just finishing the reading assignment), then as the student monitors his or her comprehension, this monitoring process can provide the student with information about the need to change reading strategies. Lyndsay does this by going back over the material she does not understand, based on her answers to her self-quizzes.

One of the central aspects of the control and regulation of cognition is the actual selection and use of various cognitive strategies for memory, learning, reasoning, problem solving, and thinking. Numerous studies have shown that the selection of appropriate cognitive strategies can have a positive influence on learning and performance. An important aspect of selection is adapting or selecting strategies that fit the task requirements or course requirements. To use a tool metaphor, there are different cognitive tools for different cognitive tasks and the important issue is selecting when to use what cognitive tool or strategy for what type of academic task. These cognitive strategies range from the simple memory strategies very young children through adults use to help them remember (Schneider and Pressley, 1997) to sophisticated strategies that individuals have for reading (Pressley and Afflerbach, 1995), mathematics (Schoenfeld, 1992), writing (Bereiter and Scardamalia, 1987), problem solving, and reasoning (see Baron, 1994; Nisbett, 1993). Although the use of various strategies is probably deemed more "cognitive" than metacognitive, the decision to use them is an aspect of metacognitive control and regulation as is the decision to stop using them or to switch from one strategy type to another.

In research on self-regulated learning, the various cognitive and learning strategies that individuals use to help them understand and learn the material would be placed in this cell. For example, many researchers have investigated the various rehearsal, elaboration, and organizational strategies that learners can use to control their cognition and learning (cf., Pintrich and De Groot, 1990; Pintrich, Marx and Boyle, 1993; Pressley and Afflerbach, 1995; Schneider and Pressley, 1997; Weinstein and Mayer, 1986; Zimmerman and Martinez-Pons, 1986). These strategies include using imagery to help encode information on a memory task, as well as imagery to help visualize correct implementation of a strategy (e.g., visualization in sports activities as well as academic ones, cf., Zimmerman, 1998a). The use of mnemonics would be included in this cell, as well as various strategies like paraphrasing, summarizing, outlining, networking, constructing tree diagrams, and note-taking (see Weinstein and Mayer, 1986). Mike seems to rely on basic rehearsal and memorizing strategies, which can be helpful when the exams test for simple recall of information. However, he may have more difficulty when he is required to synthesize or analyze information, as in essay exams or in papers. Lyndsay, in contrast, uses a number of different strategies for summarizing and organizing the information and this seems to help her learn in a more meaningful manner as well as lead to better performance.

Cognitive reaction and reflection. The processes of reaction and reflection involve learners' judgments and evaluations of their performance on the task as well as their attributions for performance. As Zimmerman (1998b) has pointed out, good self-regulators evaluate their performance in comparison to learners who avoid self-evaluation

751

or are not aware of the importance of self-evaluation in terms of the goals set for the task. In addition, it appears that good self-regulators are more likely to make adaptive attributions for their performance (Zimmerman, 1998b). Adaptive attributions are generally seen as making attributions to low effort or poor strategy use, not to a lack of general ability (e.g., "I did poorly because I'm stupid or dumb") in the face of failure (Weiner, 1986; Zimmerman and Kitsantas, 1997). These adaptive attributions have been linked to deeper cognitive processing and better learning and achievement (Pintrich and Schrauben, 1992) as well as a host of adaptive motivational beliefs and behaviors such as positive affect, positive efficacy and expectancy judgments, persistence, and effort (Weiner, 1986).

In the case of our two students, Lyndsay makes a much more adaptive attribution for her doing poorly in some courses. She attributes it to her lack of expertise in studying and seeks help from her professors and more successful peers to learn how to study more adaptively. Lyndsay knows that one can improve or change how to study and this attribution leads her to expect to do better in the future as well as search for ways to actually improve her studying. Mike, in contrast, attributes his poor performance to his lack of ability; he begins to doubt his ability to do well and does not expect to do as well in the future. Given that he thinks it is a question of general ability, and most people think that general ability is not changeable, he is not motivated to try new ways of learning or studying.

REGULATION OF MOTIVATION AND AFFECT

Just as learners can regulate their cognition, they can regulate their motivation and affect (the second column in Table 1 and the four cells down the second column). However, less research has been done on how students can regulate their motivation and affect than on regulation of cognition, including all the research on metacognition and academic learning by cognitive and educational psychologists. The area of motivational regulation has been discussed more by personality, motivational, and social psychologists (e.g., Kuhl, 1984; 1985), not educational psychologists (see Boekaerts, 1993; Corno, 1989; 1993; Garcia, McCann, Turner, and Roska, 1998 for exceptions), but this trend is changing as research on learning and self-regulation recognizes the importance of motivation in general and attempts to regulate motivation in the classroom (Wolters, 1998).

Regulation of motivation and affect would include attempts to regulate the various motivational beliefs that have been discussed in the achievement motivation literature (see Pintrich and Schunk, 1996; Wolters, 1998), such as goal orientation (purposes for doing task), self-efficacy (judgments of competence to perform a task), task value beliefs (beliefs about the importance, utility, and relevance of the task) and personal interest in the task (liking the content area or domain). Kuhl (1984, 1985) as well as Corno (1989, 1993) discuss, under the label of volitional control, various strategies that individuals might use to control their motivation. In their more global construct of volitional control they also include strategies for emotion control, as does Boekaerts (1993), which includes coping strategies for adapting to negative affect and emotions such as anxiety and fear.

Motivational planning and activation. In terms of the phases in Table 1, planning and activation of motivation (first cell in the second column in Table 1) would involve judgments of efficacy as well as the activation of various motivational beliefs about value and interest. In terms of self-efficacy judgments, Bandura (1997) and Schunk (1989, 1991, 1994) have shown that individuals' judgments of their capabilities to perform a task have consequences for affect, effort, persistence, performance, and learning. Of course, once a learner begins a task, self-efficacy judgments can be adjusted based on actual performance and feed-back as well as the individual's attempts to actively regulate or change his efficacy judgments (Bandura, 1997).

In the cognitive research on memory, individuals can make determinations as to the difficulty level of the task, such as how hard it will be to remember or learn the material, or, in the Nelson and Narens (1990) framework, what they call ease of learning judgments (EOL). These EOL judgments draw on both metacognitive knowledge of the task and metacognitive knowledge of the self in terms of past performance on the task. In the classroom context, students might make these EOL judgments as the instructor introduces a lesson or assigns a worksheet, project, or paper. These EOL judgments are similar to self-efficacy judgments, although the emphasis is on the task rather than the self. In this sense, EOL judgments and self-efficacy judgments reflect the task difficulty perceptions and self-competence perceptions from expectancy-value models (e.g., Eccles, 1983).

Along with judgments of competence, learners also have perceptions of the value and interest the task or content area has for them. In expectancy-value models (Eccles, 1983; Wigfield, 1994; Wigfield and Eccles, 1992), task value beliefs include perceptions of the relevance, utility, and importance of the task. If students believe that the task is relevant or important for their future goals or generally useful for them (e.g., "Chemistry is important because I want to be a doctor"; "Math is useful because I need it to be a smart consumer"), then they are more likely to be engaged in the task as well as to choose to engage in the task in the future (Wigfield, 1994; Wigfield and Eccles, 1992). Lyndsay believes that what she is learning in different courses may be useful for her in her future career, even if she doesn't like all of the content. In terms of a model of self-regulated learning, it seems likely that these beliefs can be activated early on, either consciously or automatically and unconsciously, as the student approaches or is introduced to the task by instructors or others. In addition, in the current model of self-regulated learning, it is assumed that students can attempt to regulate or control these value beliefs (e.g., Wolters, 1998).

Besides value beliefs, learners also have perceptions of their personal interest in the task or in the content domain of the task (e.g., liking and positive affect towards math, history, science, etc.). Both Mike and Lyndsay find some of their courses boring or uninteresting, so they would have less personal interest in these courses. The research on personal interest suggests that it is a stable and enduring characteristic of an individual, but that the level of interest can be activated and may vary according to situational and contextual features, which are collectively labeled the psychological state of interest (Krapp, Hidi, and Renninger, 1992; Schiefele, 1991). Most importantly, this work suggests that interest is course- or domain-specific or even topic-specific, so it is important to keep in mind that interest and value can vary by course. Students are not interested in courses generally, at a very global level, but the different courses and even topics within a course will activate different interest beliefs. In addition, this research has shown that interest is related to increased learning, persistence, and effort. Mike shows much less persistence and effort in those courses that he finds less interesting — a common pattern for many college students. Although the research on interest has been pursued both from an expectancy-value framework (Wigfield, 1994; Wigfield and Eccles, 1992) and through intrinsic motivation or needs-based models (see Deci and Ryan, 1985; Renninger, Hidi, and Krapp, 1992), it seems clear that interest can be activated by task and contextual features and that learners also can try to control and regulate it (Sansone, Weir, Harpster, and Morgan, 1992; Wolters, 1998).

Finally, just as interest can be a positive anticipatory affect, learners also can anticipate other more negative affects such as anxiety or fear. This may also include the activation of implicit motives such as the need for achievement or the need for power (Pintrich & Schunk, 1996). These implicit motives can also generate affect that the college student has to cope with in dealing with different tasks. In the academic learning domain, test anxiety would be the most common form of anxiety and the most researched in terms of its links with learning, performance, and achievement (Hembree, 1988; Hill and Wigfield, 1984; Wigfield and Eccles, 1989; Zeidner, 1998). Students who anticipate being anxious on tests and who worry about doing poorly even before they begin the test can set in motion a downward spiral of maladaptive cognitions, emotions, and behaviors that lead them to do poorly on the exam (Bandura, 1997; Zeidner, 1998). In this way, these anticipatory affects such as anxiety or fear can influence the subsequent learning process and certainly set up conditions that require active and adaptive self-regulation of cognition, motivation, and behavior.

Motivational monitoring. In terms of monitoring motivation and affect (the second cell in the second column in Table 1), there has not been as much research on how individuals explicitly monitor their motivation and affect as there has been on metacognitive monitoring, but it is implied in the research on how students can control and regulate their motivation and affect. That is, as in the cognitive research, it can be assumed that in order for individuals to try to control their efficacy, value, interest, or anxiety, they would have to be aware of these beliefs and affects, and monitor them at some level. In fact, paralleling the cognitive strategy intervention research (Pressley and Woloshyn, 1995), research on interventions to improve motivation often focus on helping students become aware of their own motivation so they can adapt it to the task and contextual demands. For example, research on self-efficacy focuses first on having individuals become aware of their own efficacy levels and self-doubts and then on changing their efficacy judgments to make them more realistic and adaptive (Bandura, 1997). Research on attributional retraining usually attempts to help individuals become aware of their maladaptive attributional patterns and then change them (Foersterling, 1985; Peterson, Maier, and Seligman, 1993). In the test anxiety research, besides attempts to change the environmental conditions that increase anxiety, there are a host of suggested coping strategies that individuals can adopt that include monitoring both the emotionality (negative affect) and cognitive (negative self-thoughts and doubts) components of anxiety (Hill and Wigfield, 1984; Tryon, 1980; Zeidner, 1998). In all these cases, the monitoring of motivation and affect is an important prelude to attempts to control and regulate motivation and affect.

Motivational control and regulation. The third cell in the second column in Table 1 represents attempts to control motivation. There are many different strategies that individuals can use to control their motivation and affect — not as many, perhaps, as have been discussed by cognitive researchers investigating strategies to control cognition, but still a fair number. Kuhl (1984, 1985), Corno (1989, 1993), and Boekaerts (1993; Boekaerts and Niemivirta, 2000) all have discussed various strategies for motivation and emotion control, including how to cope with negative emotions.

These strategies include attempts to control self-efficacy through the use of positive self-talk (e.g., "I know I can do this task"; see Bandura, 1997). Students also can attempt to increase their extrinsic motivation for the task by promising themselves extrinsic rewards or making certain appealing activities (taking a nap, watching TV, talking with friends, etc.) contingent on completing an academic task (Wolters, 1998; called self-consequenting in Zimmerman and Martinez-Pons, 1986; and incentive escalation in Kuhl, 1984). Lyndsay does this when she goes out with friends after a study session. Wolters (1998) found that college students would intentionally try to evoke extrinsic goals such as getting good grades to help them maintain their motivation. Students also can try to increase their intrinsic motivation for a task by trying to make it more interesting (e.g., "make it into a game", Sansone, et al., 1992; Wolters, 1998) or to maintain a more mastery-oriented focus on learning (Wolters, 1998). Finally, Wolters (1998) also found that students would try to increase the task value of an academic task by attempting to make it more relevant or useful to them or their careers, experiences, or lives. In all these cases, students are attempting to change or control their motivation in order to complete a task that might be boring or difficult. Lyndsay seems much more successful at attempting to control her motivation than Mike, especially in the case of boring courses.

In other cases, students may use a self-affirmation strategy whereby they decrease the value of a task in order to protect their self-worth, especially if they have done poorly on the task (Garcia and Pintrich, 1994). For example, students who fail on an academic task might try to affirm their self-worth by saying it doesn't matter to them, that school is not that important compared to other aspects of their lives that they value more. Steele (1988, 1997) has suggested that self-affirmation and dis-identification with school (devaluing of school in comparison to other domains) might help explain the discrepancy between African American students' achievement and their self-esteem.

In addition, there are strategies students can use to try to control their emotions that might differ from those that they use to control their efficacy or value (Boekaerts, 1993; Boekaerts and Niemivirta, 2000; Corno, 1989, 1993; Kuhl, 1984, 1985; Wolters, 1998). Self-talk strategies to control negative affect and anxiety (e.g., "don't worry about grades now", "don't think about that last question, move on to the next question") have been noted by anxiety researchers (Hill and Wigfield, 1984; Zeidner, 1998). Students also may invoke negative affects such as shame or guilt to motivate them to persist at a task (Corno, 1989; Wolters, 1998). Defensive pessimism is another motivational strategy that students can use to actually harness negative affect and anxiety about doing poorly in order to motivate them to increase their effort and perform better (Garcia and Pintrich, 1994; Norem and Cantor, 1986). Self-handicapping, in contrast to defensive pessimism, involves the decrease of effort (little or no studying) or procrastination (only cramming for an exam, writing a paper at the very end of the deadline) in order to protect self-worth by attributing the likely poor outcome to low effort, not to low ability (Baumeister and Scher, 1988; Berglas, 1985; Garcia and Pintrich, 1994; Midgley, Arunkumar, and Urdan, 1996).

Motivational reaction and reflection. The last cell in the second column in Table 1 concerns reaction and reflections about motivation. After the students have completed a task, they may have emotional reactions to the outcome (e.g., happiness at success, dismay at failure) as well as reflecting on the reasons for the outcome, that is, making attributions for the outcome (Weiner, 1986). According to attribution theory, the types of attributions that students make for their success and failure can lead to the experience of more complicated emotions like pride, anger, shame, and guilt (Weiner, 1986; 1995). As students reflect on the reasons for their performance, both the quality of the attributions and the quality of the emotions experienced are important outcomes of the self-regulation process. Individuals can actively control the types of attributions they make in order to protect their self-worth and motivation for future tasks. Many of the common attributional biases identified by social psychologists (Fiske and Taylor, 1991) may be used rather automatically (e.g., the fundamental attribution error, the actor-observer bias), but they could also be more intentional strategies used to protect self-worth (e.g., the self-serving or hedonic bias; the self-centered bias, see Fiske and Taylor, 1991; Pintrich and

Schunk, 1996). Mike begins to have doubts about his ability and does not seem as hopeful as Lyndsay, who takes a more active approach to her poor performances.

In fact, much of the attributional retraining literature is focused on helping individuals change their attributions or attributional style in order to develop more adaptive cognitive, motivational, affective, and behavioral reactions to life events (Peterson, et al., 1993; Foersterling, 1985). Finally, these reflections and reactions can lead to changes in the future levels of self-efficacy, expectancy for future success, and value and interest (Pintrich and Schunk, 1996; Weiner, 1986; 1995). In this sense, these potential changes in efficacy, value, and interest from phase four flow back into phase one and become the "entry" level motivational beliefs that students bring with them to new tasks.

REGULATION OF BEHAVIOR

Regulation of behavior is an aspect of self-regulation that involves individuals attempts to control their own overt behavior (the third column in Table 1). Since this does not explicitly involve attempts to control and regulate the personal self, some models of regulation would not include it as an aspect of "self" regulation but would just label it behavioral control. In contrast, the framework in Table 1 follows the triadic model of social cognition (Bandura, 1986; Zimmerman, 1989) where behavior is an aspect of the person, albeit not the internal "self" that is represented by cognition, motivation, and affect. Nevertheless, individuals can observe their own behavior, monitor it, and attempt to control and regulate it and as such these activities can be considered self-regulatory for the individual.

Behavioral planning and activation. The first cell in the third column of Table 1 includes behavioral planning. Models of intentions, intentional planning, and planned behavior (e.g., Ajzen, 1988; 1991; Gollwitzer, 1996) have shown that the formation of intentions is linked to subsequent behavior in a number of different domains. In the academic learning domain, time and effort planning or management would be the kind of activities that could be placed in this cell in Table 1. Time management involves the making of schedules for studying and allocating time for different activities, which is a classic aspect of most learning and study skills courses (see Hofer, Yu, and Pintrich, 1998; McKeachie, Pintrich, and Lin, 1985; Pintrich, McKeachie, and Lin, 1987; Simpson, Hynd, Nist, and Burrell, 1997). Zimmerman and Martinez-Pons (1986) have shown that self-regulating learners and high achievers do engage in time management activities. In addition, Zimmerman (1998a) has discussed the fact that not only students but expert writers, musicians, and athletes also engage in time management activities. As part of time management, students also may make decisions and form intentions about how they will allocate their effort and the intensity of their work. For example, students might plan to study regularly one or two hours a night during the semester, but during midterms or finals intend to increase their effort and time spent studying. Lyndsay is a much more planned time and study manager than Mike, who seems to study when he has time, but also is susceptible to distractions such as friends pulling him away from his studies.

Zimmerman (1998a, 2000) also has discussed how individuals can observe their own behavior through various methods and then use this information to control and regulate their behavior. For example, writers can record how many pages of text they produce in a day and record this information over weeks, months, and years (Zimmerman, 1998b). In order to enact these self-observational methods, some planning must be involved in order to organize the behavioral record-keeping. Many learning strategy programs also suggest some form of behavioral observation and record-keeping in terms of studying in order to provide useful information for future attempts to change learning and study habits. Again, the implementation of these self-observational methods requires some planning and the intention to actual implement them during learning activities.

Behavioral monitoring. In Phase 2 (the second cell in the third column in Table 1), students can monitor their time management and effort levels and attempt to adjust their effort to fit the task. For example, in Phase 1, students may plan to spend only two hours reading two textbook chapters for the course, but once they begin reading, they might realize that the task is more difficult than they foresaw and that it will take either more time or more concentrated effort to understand each chapter. They might also realize that although they set aside two hours for reading the chapters in the library, they spent one hour of that time talking with friends who were studying with them. Of course, this type of monitoring should lead to an attempt to control or regulate their effort (e.g., set aside more time, don't study with friends; the next cell in Table 1). This type of monitoring behavior is often helped by formal procedures for self-observation (e.g., keeping logs of study time, diaries of activities, record-keeping, etc.) or self-experimentation (Zimmerman, 1998a, 2000). All of these activities will help students become aware of and monitor their own behavior, thus gaining information that they can use to actually control or regulate their behavior. Lyndsay seems much more aware of her studying behavior and monitors it much better than Mike does.

Behavioral control and regulation. Strategies for actual behavioral control and regulation are important aspects of self-regulated learning (cell 3 in the third column in Table 1). As noted in the previous section, students may regulate the time and effort they expend studying two textbook chapters based on their monitoring of their behavior and the difficulty of the task. If the task is harder than they originally thought, they may increase their effort, depending on their goals, or they may decrease effort if the task is perceived as too difficult. Another aspect of behavioral control includes general persistence, which is also a classic measure used in achievement motivation studies as an indicator of motivation. Students may exhort themselves to persist through self-talk ("keep trying, you'll get it") or they may give up if the task is too difficult, again depending on their goals and monitoring activities. Mike seems much more likely to give up and not put forth as much effort, compared to Lyndsay.

The motivational strategies mentioned earlier, such as defensive pessimism and self-handicapping, included attempts to control anxiety and self-worth but also had direct implications for an increase in effort (defensive pessimism) or decrease in effort (self-handicapping). As such, these strategies are also relevant to behavioral control efforts. One aspect of self-handicapping is procrastination, which is certainly behavioral in nature — putting off studying for an exam or writing a paper until the last minute. Of course, since effort and persistence are two of the most common indicators of motivation, most of the motivational strategies mentioned in the earlier section will have direct implications for the behaviors of effort and persistence. Mike does tend to procrastinate and begin studying or writing papers close to their due dates, while Lyndsay takes a much more planned and regulated approach to her work by pacing her work and trying to prepare before the due dates.

Another behavioral strategy that can be very helpful for learning is help-seeking. It appears that good students and good self-regulators know when, why, and from whom to seek help (Karabenick and Sharma, 1994; Nelson LeGall, 1981; 1985; Newman, 1991, 1994, 1998a, b; Ryan and Pintrich, 1997). Lyndsay is a very good help-seeker and seeks out professors and other students who are doing well to help her improve her studying. Mike, in contrast, doesn't seek help and it is not clear that he is aware that he should ask for help. Help-seeking is listed here as a behavioral strategy because it involves the person's own behavior, but it also involves contextual control because it necessarily involves the procurement of help from others in the environment and as such is also a social interaction (Ryan and Pintrich, 1997). Help-seeking can be a dependent strategy for students who are seeking the correct answer without much work or who wish to complete the task quickly without much understanding or learning. In terms of this goal of learning and understanding, dependent help-seeking would be a generally maladaptive strategy, in contrast to adaptive help-seeking where the individual is focused on learning and is only seeking help in order to overcome a particularly difficult aspect of the task.

Behavioral reaction and reflection. Reflection is a more cognitive process (cell four in the third column in Table 1) and so there may be no "behavioral" reflection per se, but just as with forethought, the cognitions an individual has about behavior can be classified in this cell. For example, reflections on actual behavior in terms of effort expended or time spent on task can be important aspects of self-regulated learning. Just as students can make judgments or reflect on their cognitive processing or motivation, they can make judgements about their behaviors. They may decide that procrastinating in studying for an exam may not be the most adaptive behavior for academic achievement. In the future, they may decide to make a different choice in terms of their effort and time management. Certainly, in terms of reaction, the main behavior is choice. Students can decide not only to change their future time and effort management efforts, but they also may make choices about what classes to take in the future (at least, for high school and college students), or more broadly, what general course of study they will follow. This kind of choice behavior results in the selection of different contexts and leads us into the last column in Table 1.

It is important to note that while persistence is usually considered a good example of motivated behavior, more recent research on self-regulation and self-regulated learning (e.g., Zimmerman, 2000; Zimmerman and Schunk, 1989) suggests that students also have to be able to regulate their own behavior in order to be successful. In the case of persistence, "blind and willful" persistence on a difficult task that goes on too long without the student seeking help from others may not be the most adaptive coping strategy. If the student gives up too easily on a difficult task, that is not representative of adaptive or motivated behavior — but neither is the continual putting forth of more effort, when the student does not have the knowledge or skills to eventually succeed. Accordingly, help-seeking behavior can be an important self-regulatory strategy when the task is beyond the students' level of competence (Karabenick and Knapp, 1991). In the same way, just trying harder on a "boring" task may not be the most helpful strategy. There are strategies available to regulate motivation and reactions to the task to make it more interesting (e.g., Sansone, et al., 1992). Accordingly, the research on these strategies for self-regulation of effort and persistence suggests that it is not just overall persistence that is important, but persistence that is adapted to the nature of the task (e.g., difficulty, interestingness) and coordinated with the individual's own capabilities (e.g., knowledge and cognitive skills, motivation, and fatigue levels).

REGULATION OF CONTEXT

As noted above, regulation of context (last column on the right-hand side of Table 1) includes the individual's attempts to monitor, control, and regulate the context as an important aspect of self-regulated learning because the focus is on the personal self or individual who is engaged in these activities. Given that it is the active, personal self who is attempting to monitor, control, and regulate the context, it seems important to include these activities in a model of self-regulated learning.

Contextual planning and activation. The first cell in the last column of Table I includes college students' perceptions of the task and context. In a college class-room context, these perceptions may be about the nature of the tasks in terms of the norms for completing the task (e.g., the format to be used, the procedures to be used to do the task such as whether working with others is permitted or is considered cheating, etc.) as well as general knowledge about the types of tasks and classroom practices for grading in the course (Blumenfeld, Mergendoller, and Swarthout, 1987; Doyle, 1983).

In addition, perceptions of the college classroom norms and classroom climate are important aspects of college students' knowledge activation of contextual information. For example, when college students enter a classroom, they may activate knowledge about general norms or perceive certain norms (talking is not allowed, working with others is cheating, the faculty member always has the correct answer, students are not allowed much autonomy or control, etc.) which can influence their approach to the classroom and their general learning. Other aspects of the college classroom climate such as instructor warmth and enthusiasm as well as equity and fairness for all students (e.g., no bias on basis of gender or ethnicity) can be important perceptions or beliefs that are activated when students come into a classroom (Pintrich and Schunk, 1996). Of course, these perceptions can be veridical and actually represent the classroom dynamics, but there is also the possibility that the students can misperceive the classroom context because they are activating stereotypes without reflecting on the actual nature of the classroom. For example, there may be occasions when females accurately perceive a male math faculty member to be biased against females in math, but there also can be cases where this is a more stereotypical perception that is not reflected in the instructor's behavior. In any case, these perceptions, veridical or not, offer opportunities for monitoring and regulation of the context.

Contextual monitoring. Just as students can and should monitor their cognition, motivation, and behavior, they also can and should monitor the task and contextual features of the classroom (cell 2 in the last column in Table 1). In classrooms, just as in work and social situations, individuals are not free to do as they please; they are involved in a social system with various opportunities and constraints operating that shape and influence their behavior. If students are unaware of the opportunities and constraints that are operating, then they will be less likely to be able to function well in the classroom. Awareness and monitoring of the classroom rules, grading practices, task requirements, reward structures and general instructor behavior are all important for students to do well in the classroom. For example, students need to be aware of the different grading practices and how different tasks will be evaluated and scored for grades. For example, if they are not aware that "original" thinking is important in a paper (as opposed to summarizing other material from books or journal articles), then they will be less likely to adjust their behavior to be in line with these requirements. In college classrooms, entering freshmen often have difficulty in their first courses because they are not monitoring or adjusting their perceptions of the course requirements to the levels expected by the faculty. Many college learning strategy or study skills courses attempt to help students become aware of these differences and adjust their strategy use and behavior accordingly (Hofer et al., 1998; Simpson et al., 1997). Mike seems to rely on a memorization-only strategy, which may not be what is required in some of his courses. He is having difficulty in understanding some of the new contextual norms. Lyndsay also might be having some difficulties in figuring out these norms, but she seeks

763

out the professor and other students to help her determine how to do better in her courses.

Contextual control and regulation. Of course, as with cognition, motivation, and behavior, contextual monitoring processes are intimately linked to efforts to control and regulate the tasks and context (third cell in the last column in Table 1). In comparison to control and regulation of cognition, motivation, and behavior, control of the tasks or context may be more difficult because they are not always under direct control of the individual learner. However, even models of general intelligence (e.g., the contextual sub-theory, see Sternberg, 1985), often include attempts to shape, adapt, or control the environment as one aspect of intelligent behavior. Models of volitional control usually include a term labeled environmental control, which refers to attempts to control or structure the environment in ways that will facilitate goals and task completion (Corno, 1989; 1993; Kuhl, 1984, 1985). In terms of self-regulated learning, most models include strategies to shape or control or structure the learning environment as important strategies for self-regulation (Zimmerman, 1998a).

In the traditional classroom context, the instructor controls most of the aspects of the tasks and context and therefore there may be little opportunity for students to engage in contextual control and regulation. However, students often may attempt to negotiate the task requirements "downward" ("Can we write 10 pages instead of 20?", "Can we use our books and notes on the exam?", etc.) to make them simpler and easier for them to perform (Doyle, 1983). This kind of task negotiation has probably been experienced by all instructors from elementary through graduate school faculty and does represent one attempt by students to control and regulate the task and contextual environment even in classrooms with high levels of instructor control.

In postsecondary settings, students have much more freedom to structure their environment in terms of their learning. Much of the learning that goes on takes place outside the college lecture hall or classroom, and students have to be able to control and regulate their study environment. Monitoring of their study environment for distractions (music, TV, talkative friends or peers) and then attempts to control or regulate their study environment to make them more conducive for studying (removing distractions, having an organized and specific place for studying) can facilitate learning; this seems to be an important part of self-regulated learning (Hofer et al., 1998; Zimmerman, 1998a). Zimmerman (1998a) also discusses how writers, athletes, and musicians attempt to exert contextual control over their environment by structuring it in ways that facilitate their learning and performance. Lyndsay does attempt to control some aspects of her context by studying with her friends, thereby making them less likely to ask her to go out to socialize and take her away from her studies. Mike tends to be controlled by the environment, rather than controlling it, as he lets his friends talk him out of studying in order to go out with them.

Contextual reaction and reflection. Finally, in terms of contextual reaction and reflection (the last cell in the last column in Table 1), students can make general evaluations of the task or classroom environment. These evaluations can be made on the basis of general enjoyment and comfort as well as more cognitive criteria regarding learning and achievement. In some of the more student-centered class-rooms, there is time set aside for occasional reflection on what is working in the classroom and what is not working in terms of both student and faculty reactions (Brown, 1997). As with cognition and motivation, these evaluations can feed back into Phase 1 components when the student approaches a new task.

In summary, this four phase by four areas for regulation in Table 1 represents a general framework for conceptualizing self-regulated learning in the academic domain. It provides a taxonomy of the different processes and components that can be involved in self-regulated learning. The format of the taxonomy also allows for the integration of much of the research on self-regulated learning that has spawned a diversity of terms and constructs, but organized it in such a manner that the similarities and differences can be seen easily. As researchers traverse the different areas of self-regulated learning, the taxonomy allows them to locate their own efforts within this topography as well as to spy under-explored territories in need of further investigation and examination. The next section of this chapter turns to how different motivational beliefs (C in Figure 1) are linked to these self-regulatory processes (D in Figure 1) and to actual achievement (E in Figure 1).

THE ROLE OF MOTIVATIONAL BELIEFS (C)

The second process component in the model in Figure 1 is students' motivational beliefs (C). Although there are many models of motivation that may be relevant to student learning (see Heckhausen, 1991; Weiner, 1992, for reviews of different motivational theories), a general expectancy-value model serves as a useful framework for analyzing the research on motivational components (Pintrich, 1988a, b, 1989, 1994; Pintrich and Schunk, 1996). Three general components seem to be important in these different models: a) beliefs about one's ability or skill to perform the task (expectancy components), b) beliefs about the importance and value of the task (value components), and c) feelings about the self, or emotional reactions to the task (affective components). These three general components are assumed to interact with one another and, in turn, to influence the outcomes (E) in Figure 1 as well as the self-regulatory processes (D) outlined in the previous section. In this section, we outline the nature of the motivational beliefs and how they are related to both self-regulation and student outcomes.

EXPECTANCY COMPONENTS

Expectancy components are college students' "answer" to the question: "Can I do this task?". If students believe that they have some control over their skills and the task environment and that they have confidence in their ability to perform the necessary skills, they are more likely to choose to do the task, more likely to be involved in self-regulatory activities, and more likely to persist at the task. Various constructs have been proposed by different motivational theorists; they can be categorized as expectancy components. The main distinction is between how much control one believes one has in the situation and perceptions of efficacy to accomplish the task in that situation. Of course, these beliefs are correlated empirically, but most models do propose separate constructs for control beliefs and efficacy beliefs.

Control beliefs. A number of constructs and theories have been proposed about the role of control beliefs for motivational dynamics. For example, early work on locus of control (e.g., Lefcourt, 1976; Rotter, 1966) found that students who believed that they were in control of their behavior and could influence the environment (an internal locus of control) tended to achieve at higher levels. Deci (1975) and de Charms (1968) discussed perceptions of control in terms of students' belief in self-determination. De Charms (1968) coined the terms "origins" and "pawns" to describe students who believed they were able to control their actions and students who believed that others controlled their behavior. Connell (1985) suggested that control beliefs have three aspects: an internal source, an external source (or powerful others), and an unknown source. Students who believe in internal sources of control are assumed to perform better than students who believe powerful others (e.g., faculty, parents) are responsible for their success or failure and better than those students who don't know who or what is responsible for the outcomes. In the college classroom, Perry and his colleagues (e.g., Perry, 1991; Perry and Dickens, 1988; Perry and Magnusson, 1989; Perry and Penner, 1990) have shown that students' beliefs about how their personal attributes influence the environment — which they label "perceived control" — are related to achievement and to aspects of the classroom environment (e.g., instructor feedback).

In self-efficacy theory, outcome expectations refer to individuals' beliefs concerning their ability to influence outcomes, that is, their belief that the environment is responsive to their actions, which is different from self-efficacy (the belief that one can do the task; see Bandura, 1986; Schunk, 1985). This belief that outcomes are contingent on their behavior leads individuals to have higher expectations for success and should lead to more persistence. When individuals do not perceive a contingency between their behavior and outcomes, this can lead to passivity, anxiety, lack of effort, and lower achievement, often labeled learned helplessness (cf., Abramson, Seligman, and Teasdale, 1978). Learned helplessness is usually seen as a stable pattern of attributing many events to uncontrollable causes, which leaves the individual believing that there is no opportunity for change that is under their control. These individuals do not believe they can "do anything" that will make a difference and that the environment or situation is basically not responsive to their actions.

The overriding message of all these models is that a general pattern of perception of internal control results in positive outcomes (i.e., more cognitive engagement, higher achievement, higher self-esteem), while sustained perceptions of external or unknown control result in negative outcomes (lower achievement, lack of effort, passivity, anxiety). Reviews of research in this area are somewhat conflicting, however (cf., Findley and Cooper, 1983; Stipek and Weisz, 1981) and some have argued that it is better to accept responsibility for positive outcomes (an internal locus of control) and deny responsibility for negative or failure outcomes (an external locus of control, see Harter, 1985). Part of the difficulty in interpreting this literature is the different ages of the samples and the use of different definitions of the construct of control, different instruments to measure the construct, and different outcomes measures in the numerous studies. In particular, the construct of internal locus of control confounds three dimensions of locus (internal vs. external), controllability (controllable vs. uncontrollable), and stability (stable vs. unstable). Attributional theory proposes that these three dimensions can be separated conceptually and empirically and that they have different influences on behavior (Weiner, 1986).

Attributional theory proposes that the causal attributions an individual makes for success or failure mediates future expectancies, not the actual success or failure event. A large number of studies have shown that individuals who tend to attribute success to internal and stable causes like ability or aptitude will tend to expect to succeed in the future. In contrast, individuals who attribute their success to external or unstable causes (i.e., ease of the task, luck) will not expect to do well in the future. For failure situations, the positive motivational pattern consists not of an internal locus of control, but rather of attributing failure to external and unstable causes (difficult task, lack of effort, bad luck) and the negative motivational pattern consists of attributing failure to internal and stable causes (e.g., ability, skill). Lyndsay and Mike show different attributional patterns to explain their failures, with Lyndsay having a much more adaptive pattern. This general attributional approach has been applied to numerous situations and the motivational dynamics seem to be remarkably robust and similar (Weiner, 1986).

It should also be noted that in an attributional analysis, the important dimension linked to future expectancies (beliefs that one will do well in the future) is stability, not locus (Weiner, 1986). That is, it is how stable you believe a cause is that is linked to future expectancies (i.e., the belief that your ability or effort to do the task is stable over time, not whether you believe it is internal or external to you). Attributional theory generally takes a situational view of these attributions and beliefs, but some researchers have suggested that individuals have relatively consistent attributional patterns across domains and tasks that function somewhat like personality traits (e.g., Fincham and Cain, 1986; Peterson, et al., 1993). These attributional patterns seem to predict individuals' performance over time. For example, if college students consistently attributed their success to their own skill and ability as learners, then it would be predicted that they would continually expect success in future classes. In contrast, if students consistently attribute success to other causes (e.g., the instructors are excellent, the material is easy, luck), then their expectations might not be as high for future classes.

Individuals' beliefs about the causes of events can be changed through feedback and other environmental manipulations to facilitate the adoption of positive control and attributional beliefs. For example, some research on attributional retraining in achievement situations (e.g., Foersterling, 1985; Perry and Penner, 1990) suggests that teaching individuals to make appropriate attributions for failure on school tasks (e.g., effort attributions instead of ability attributions) can facilitate future achievement. Of course, a variety of issues must be considered in attributional retraining, including the specification of which attributional patterns are actually dysfunctional, the relative accuracy of the new attributional pattern, and the issue of only attempting to change a motivational component instead of the cognitive skill that also may be important for performance (cf., Blumenfeld, Pintrich, Meece, and Wessels, 1982; Weiner, 1986).

In summary, individuals' beliefs about the contingency between their behaviors and their performance in a situation are linked to student outcomes (E) and self-regulation (D) in Figure 1. In a classroom context, this means that college students' motivational beliefs about the linkage between their studying and self-regulated learning behavior and their achievement will influence their actual studying behavior. For example, if students believe that no matter how hard they study, they will not be able to do well on a chemistry test because they simply lack the aptitude to master the material, then they will be less likely to actually study for the test (the case of Mike). In the same fashion, if students believe that their effort in studying can make a difference, regardless of their actual aptitude for the material, then they will be more likely to study the material (the case of Lyndsay). Accordingly, these beliefs about control and contingency have motivational force because they influence future behavior.

Self-efficacy beliefs. In contrast to control beliefs, self-efficacy concerns students' beliefs about their ability just to do the task, not the linkage between their doing it and the outcome. Self-efficacy has been defined as individuals' beliefs about their performance capabilities in a particular domain (Bandura, 1982, 1986; Schunk, 1985). The construct of self-efficacy includes individuals' judgments about their ability to accomplish certain goals or tasks by their actions in specific situations (Schunk, 1985). This approach implies a relatively situational or domain specific construct rather than a global personality trait. In an achievement context, it includes college students' confidence in their cognitive skills to perform the academic task. Mike starts to doubt his self-efficacy for college work, while Lyndsay seems to believe that she can learn and improve. Continuing the example from chemistry, a college student might have confidence in her capability (a high self-efficacy belief) to learn the material for the chemistry test (i.e., "I can learn this material on stoichiometry") and consequently exert more effort in studying. At the same time, if the student believes that the grading curve in the class is so difficult and that her studying won't make much difference in her grade for the exam (a low control belief) she might not study as much. Accordingly, self-efficacy and control beliefs are separate constructs, albeit they are usually positively correlated empirically. Moreover, they may combine and interact with each other to influence student self-regulation and outcomes.

One issue in most motivational theories regarding self-efficacy and control beliefs concerns the domain or situational specificity of the beliefs. As noted above, self-efficacy theory generally assumes a situation specific view. That is, individuals' judgment of their efficacy for a task is a function of the task and situational characteristics operating at the time (difficulty, feedback, norms, comparisons with others, etc.) as well as their past experience and prior beliefs about the task and their current beliefs and feelings as they work on the task. However, there may be generalized efficacy beliefs that extend beyond the specific situation and influence motivated behavior. Accordingly, college students could have efficacy beliefs not just for a specific exam in chemistry, but also for chemistry in general, for natural science courses in contrast to social science or humanities courses, or for learning and school work in general. An important direction for future research will be to examine the domain generality of both self-efficacy and control beliefs. Nevertheless, it has been shown in many studies in many different domains, including the achievement domain, that college students' self-efficacy beliefs (or, in more collo-quial terms, their self-confidence in their capabilities to do a task) are strongly related to the outcomes in Figure 1 (E) including their choice of activities, their level of engagement, and their willingness to persist at a task (Bandura, 1986; Pintrich and Schrauben, 1992; Schunk, 1985).

In our own research at Michigan, we have examined the role of self-efficacy beliefs and college student self-regulated learning and achievement in the college classroom. We have been involved in research in college classrooms since 1982 and have collected data on over 4,000 students from a variety of disciplines and courses including mathematics, biology, chemistry, English literature, English composition, sociology, and psychology (see Garcia and Pintrich, 1994, 1996; Pintrich, 1988a, b, 1989; 1999; Pintrich and Garcia, 1991, 1993; Pintrich, Smith, Garcia, and McKeachie, 1993; VanderStoep, Pintrich, and Fagerlin, 1996). In addition, these studies have been carried out at Research I institutions like Michigan, but also at comprehensive universities, small liberal arts colleges, and community colleges, increasing the generalizability of our findings. These studies have been correlational in design and used the Motivated Strategies for Learning Questionnaire (MSLQ, Pintrich et al., 1993) to assess student motivation and self-regulated learning in the classroom. We have used other measures such as student grades on course assignments (papers, midterms, final exams, quizzes, lab projects) as well as their final course grade as measures of achievement outcomes.

The MSLQ is a self-report instrument designed to measure student motivation and self-regulated learning in classroom contexts. The items and scales from the MSLQ focus on motivation and self-regulation at the course level. That is, college students are asked about their motivation and self-regulation for a specific course. It is not task or assignment specific (e.g., midterm exams, papers), nor is it more global with items about their motivation or self-regulation for college in general. In these correlational studies, we have assessed motivation and self-regulation at the beginning of the semester (a few weeks after the start of class) and then again at the end of the term, and in some studies we have used the MSLQ at three time points over the course of a 15-week semester. This type of design allows us to examine the relative role of different motivational beliefs over time within the course and how these beliefs predict various achievement outcomes.

In terms of self-efficacy beliefs, our results are very consistent over time and are in line with more experimental studies of self-efficacy (Bandura, 1997). Self-efficacy is one of the strongest positive predictors of actual achievement in the course, accounting for 9% to 25% of the variance in grades (an outcome, E in Figure 1), depending on the study and the other predictors entered in the regression (Pintrich, 1999). College students who believe they are able to do the coursework and learn the material are much more likely to do well in the course. Moreover, in these studies, self-efficacy remains a significant predictor of final achievement, albeit accounting for less total variance, even when previous knowledge (as indexed by performance on earlier tests) or general ability (as indexed by SAT scores) are entered into the equations in these studies.

Finally, in all of these studies, we also find that self-efficacy is a significant positive predictor of student self-regulation (D in Figure 1) and cognitive engagement in the course. College students who are confident of their capabilities to learn and do the coursework are more likely to report using more elaboration and organizational cognitive strategies (D in Figure 1). These strategies involve deeper cognitive processing of the course material, where students try to paraphrase the material, summarize it in their own words, or make outlines or concept maps of the concepts, in comparison to just trying to memorize the material. Lyndsay uses these strategies; Mike does not. In addition, college students who are higher in their self-efficacy for learning also are much more likely to be metacognitive, trying to regulate their learning by monitoring and controlling their cognition as they learn. In our studies, we have measures of these cognitive and self-regulatory strategies at the start of the course and at the end of the course, and self-efficacy remains a significant predictor of cognitive and self-regulatory strategy use at the end of the course, even when the earlier measure of cognition is included as a predictor along with self-efficacy. Accordingly, positive self-efficacy beliefs (C in Figure 1) can boost cognitive and self-regulatory strategy use (D in Figure 1) over the course of a semester.

In summary, our first generalization about the role of motivational beliefs in self-regulated learning emphasizes the importance of self-efficacy beliefs.

Generalization 1 – *Self-efficacy beliefs are positively related to adaptive cognitive and self-regulatory strategy use as well as to actual achievement in the college classroom.*

Accordingly, college students who feel capable and confident about their abilities to do the coursework are much more likely to be cognitively engaged, to try hard, to persist, and to do well in the course (C predicts outcomes E in Figure 1 as well as self-regulation D processes). In fact, the strength of the relations between self-efficacy and these different outcomes in our research as well as others' (Bandura, 1997; Pintrich and Schunk, 1996; Schunk, 1991) suggests that self-efficacy is one of the best and most powerful motivational predictors of learning and achievement. Given the strength of the relations, research on the motivational aspects of college student learning and performance needs to include self-efficacy as an important mediator between classroom contextual and personal factors and student outcomes. In terms of pedagogical implications, this generalization suggests that faculty need to be aware of how different aspects of the classroom environment can facilitate or constrain self-efficacy beliefs. More discussion of this issue will follow in the section on classroom context factors.

VALUE COMPONENTS

Value components of the model incorporate individuals' goals for engaging in a task as well as their beliefs about the importance, utility, or interest of a task. Essentially, these components concern the question: Why am I doing this task? In more colloquial terms, value components concern whether students "care" about the task and the nature of that concern (see opening paragraph regarding faculty concerns that students do not care about, or are not interested in, course material). These components should be related to self-regulatory activities as well as to outcomes such as the choice of activities, effort, and persistence (Eccles, 1983; Pintrich, 1999). Although there are a variety of different conceptualizations of value, two basic components seem relevant; goal orientation and task value.

Goal orientation. All motivational theories posit some type of goal, purpose, or intentionality to human behavior, although these goals may range from relatively accessible and conscious goals as in attribution theory to relatively inaccessible and unconscious goals as in psychodynamic theories (Zukier, 1986). In recent cognitive reformulations of achievement motivation theory, goals are assumed to be cognitive representations of the different purposes students may adopt in different achievement situations (Dweck and Elliott, 1983; Dweck and Leggett, 1988; Ford, 1992).

In current achievement motivation research, two general classes of goals have been discussed under various names such as target goals and purpose goals (e.g., Harackiewicz et al., 1998; Harackiewicz and Sansone, 1991), or task specific goals and goal orientations (e.g., Garcia and Pintrich, 1994; Pintrich and Schunk, 1996; Wolters, Yu, and Pintrich, 1996; Zimmerman and Kitsantas, 1997). The general distinction between these two classes of goals is that target and task specific goals represent the specific outcome the individual is attempting to accomplish. In academic learning contexts, it would be represented by goals such as "wanting to get a 85% out of 100% correct on a quiz" or "trying to get an A on a midterm exam", etc.. These goals are specific to a task and are most similar to the goals discussed by Locke and Latham (1990) for workers in an organizational context such as "wanting to make 10 more widgets an hour" or to "sell 5 more cars in the next week."

In contrast, purpose goals or goal orientations reflect the more general reasons why individuals perform a task; these goals are related more to the research on achievement motivation (Elliot, 1997; Urdan,

1997). Here, it is a matter of the individual's general orientation (or "schema" or "theory") for approaching the task, doing the task, and evaluating performance on the task (Ames, 1992; Dweck and Leggett, 1988; Pintrich, 2000a, b, c). In this case, purpose goals or goal orientations refer to why individuals want to get 85% out of 100%, why they want to get an A, or why they want to make more widgets or sell more cars, as well as the standards or criteria (85%, an A) they will use to evaluate their progress towards the goal. Given the focus of our own work, we will limit our discussion to the role of goal orientation in learning and achievement in this chapter.

Several different models of goal orientation have been advanced by different achievement motivation researchers (cf., Ames, 1992; Dweck and Leggett, 1988; Harackiewicz et al., 1998; Maehr and Midgley, 1991; Nicholls, 1984; Pintrich, 1989; Wolters et al., 1996). These models vary somewhat in their definition of goal orientation and the use of different labels for similar constructs. They also differ on the proposed number of goal orientations and the role of approach and avoidance forms of the different goals. Finally, they also differ on the degree to which an individual's goal orientations are more personal, based in somewhat stable individual differences, or the degree to which an individual's goal orientations are more situated or sensitive to the context and a function of the contextual features of the environment. Most of the models assume that goal orientations are a function of both individual differences and contextual factors, but the relative emphasis along this continuum does vary between the different models. Much of this research also assumes that classrooms and other contexts (e.g., business or work settings; laboratory conditions in an experiment) can be characterized in terms of their goal orientations (see Ford, Smith, Weissbein, Gully, and Salas, 1998 for an application of goal orientation theory to a work setting), but for the purposes of this chapter the focus will be on individuals' personal goal orientation.

Most models propose two general goal orientations that concern the reasons or purposes individuals are pursuing when approaching and engaging in a task. In Dweck's model, the two goal orientations are labeled learning and performance goals (Dweck and Leggett, 1988), with learning goals reflecting a focus on increasing competence and performance goals involving either the avoidance of negative judgments of competence or attainment of positive judgments of competence. Ames (1992) labels them mastery and performance goals with mastery goals orienting learners to "developing new skills, trying to understand their work, improving their level of competence, or achieving a sense of mastery based on self-referenced standards" (Ames, 1992, p. 262). In contrast, performance goals orient learners to focus on their ability and self-worth, to determine their ability in reference to besting other students in competitions, surpassing others in achievements or grades, and to receiving public recognition for their superior performance (Ames, 1992). Harackiewicz and Elliot and their colleagues (e.g., Elliot, 1997; Elliot and Church, 1997; Elliot and Harackiewicz, 1996; Harackiewicz et al., 1998) have labeled them mastery and performance goals as well. Nicholls (1984) has used the terms task-involved and ego-involved for similar constructs (see Pintrich, 2000c for a review). In our own work, we have focused on mastery and performance goals and will use these labels in our discussion in this chapter.

In the literature on mastery and performance goals, the general theoretical assumption has been that mastery goals foster a host of adaptive motivational, cognitive, and achievement outcomes, while performance goals generate less adaptive or even maladaptive outcomes. Moreover, this assumption has been supported in a large number of empirical studies on goals and achievement processes (Ames, 1992; Dweck and Leggett, 1988; Pintrich, 2000c; Pintrich and Schunk, 1996), in particular the positive predictions for mastery goals. The logic of the argument is that when students are focused on trying to learn and understand the material and trying to improve their performance relative to their own past performance, this orientation will help them maintain their self-efficacy in the face of failure, ward off negative affect such as anxiety, lessen the probability that they will have distracting thoughts, and free up cognitive capacity and allow for more cognitive engagement and achievement. Lyndsay adopts a mastery goal of learning and understanding and certainly shows this adaptive pattern of outcomes. In contrast, when students are concerned about trying to be the best, to get higher grades than others, and to do well compared to others under a performance goal, it is possible that this orientation will result in more negative affect or anxiety, or increase the possibility of distracting and irrelevant thoughts (e.g., worrying about how others are doing, rather than focusing on the task), and that this will diminish cognitive capacity, task engagement, and performance.

In our own empirical research at Michigan, we have found similar patterns in our data with college students. Mastery goals have been positively related to cognitive strategy use and self-regulation as well as performance. These studies have shown that college students who report higher levels of mastery goals are more likely to use elaboration and organizational strategies as well as to be more metacognitive and regulating (as shown by Lyndsay), with mastery goals accounting for up to 16% of the variance in these outcomes. College students who adopted mastery goals and tried to focus on learning also tended to achieve at higher levels in terms of grades, albeit the variance accounted for was lower (only about 4%). These relations are not as strong as those for self-efficacy, but they were still statistically reliable across a number of samples and studies.

In terms of performance goals, we have not measured them on the MSLQ as they are traditionally defined in terms of outperforming others and trying to get the highest grades relative to peers. In contrast, we have assessed students' focus on general extrinsic goals for doing their coursework such as wanting to get good grades in general (both Lyndsay and Mike had this type of goal) and wanting to do well to satisfy parents and other adults. Using this measure of extrinsic goal orientation, we generally find that it is unrelated to, or is negatively related to, the use of cognitive strategies and self-regulation in college students. That is, students who are focused on grades, not learning, are less likely to be cognitively engaged and self-regulating (as was the case with Mike). In contrast, for performance, we do find some positive relations between an extrinsic goal orientation and grades, with extrinsic goal orientation accounting for 4% of the variance in some studies. In this case, it appears that students who have set a goal of getting good grades do get somewhat better actual grades than other students. Nevertheless, the results for extrinsic goals are not as stable or reliable as those for mastery goals.

More recently, some empirical evidence has emerged to indicate that performance goals are not necessarily maladaptive for all outcomes (Harackiewicz et al., 1998; Pintrich, 2000a, b, c). In this research, performance goals — the competitive urge or goal (where students are trying to approach the goal of doing better than others), seems to be positively related to actual performance at least in terms of final course grade (Harackiewicz, et al., 1998). In addition, these studies seem to show that there is not necessarily a decrement in cognitive engagement or self-regulation as a function of adopting a performance goal (Pintrich, 2000a, b, c). Finally, studies with younger students in junior high classrooms also have shown that students high in approach performance goals and high in mastery goals are not more anxious, do not experience more negative affect, and are equally motivated as those low in approach performance goals and high in mastery (Pintrich, 2000b). This recent research is leading to some reconceptualization of the general theoretical assumption that mastery goals are adaptive and performance goals are maladaptive, but there is still a need for much more research on the stability of these findings for performance goals.

In summary, the research on goal orientation suggests that at this point in time only one stable generalization is valid. Our second generalization is:

Generalization 2 – *Mastery goals are positively related to adaptive cognitive and self-regulatory strategy use as well as actual achievement in the college classroom.* Students who adopt a mastery goal and focus on learning, understanding, and self-improvement are much more likely to use adaptive cognitive and self-regulatory strategies as well as to achieve better results (C predicts outcomes in E, in Figure 1, as well as self-regulation processes D). Accordingly, classroom contexts that foster the adoption of mastery goals by students should facilitate motivation and learning. For example, college classrooms that encourage students to adopt goals of learning and understanding through the reward and evaluation structures (i.e., how grades are assigned, how tasks are graded and evaluated), rather than just getting good grades or competing with other college students, should foster a mastery goal orientation.

Task value. Goal orientation can refer to students' goals for a specific task (a midterm exam) as well as their general orientation to a course or a field. In the same way, students' task value beliefs can be fairly specific or more general. Three components of task value have been proposed by Eccles (1983) as important in achievement dynamics: the individual's perception of the importance of the task, their personal interest in the task (similar to intrinsic interest in intrinsic motivation theory), and their perception of the utility value of the task for future goals. These three value components may be rather parallel in children and college students, but can vary significantly in adults (Wlodkowski, 1988).

The perceived importance of a task, the importance component of task value, refers to the individuals' perception of the task's importance or salience for them. It is related to a general goal orientation, but importance could vary according to goal orientation. An individual's orientation may guide the general direction of behavior, while value may relate to the level of involvement. For example, some college students may believe that success in a particular course is very important (or unimportant) to them, regardless of their intrinsic or extrinsic goals. That is, the students may see success in the course as learning the material or getting a good grade, but they still may attach differential importance to these goals. Importance should be related to the individuals' persistence at a task as well as choice of a task.

Student interest in the task is another aspect of task value. Interest is assumed to be an individual's general attitude or liking of the task that is somewhat stable over time and a function of personal characteristics. In an educational setting, this includes the individual's interest in the course content and reactions to the other characteristics of the course, such as the instructor (cf., Wlodkowski, 1988). Both Lyndsay and Mike find some of their classes interesting and others less interesting (or even boring). Personal interest in the task is partially a function of individuals' preferences as well as aspects of the task (e.g., Malone and Lepper, 1987). However, personal interest should not be confused with situational interest, which can be generated by simple environmental features (e.g., an interesting lecture, a fascinating speaker, a dramatic film) but which are not long-lasting and do not necessarily inculcate stable personal interest (Hidi, 1990). Schiefele (1991) has shown that students' personal interest in the material being studied is related to their level of involvement in terms of the use of cognitive strategies as well as actual performance. There is a current revival in research on the role of interest in learning (see Renninger, Hidi, and Krapp, 1992).

In contrast to the means or process motivational dynamic of interest, utility value refers to the ends or instrumental motivation of the student (Eccles, 1983). Utility value is determined by the individual's perception of the task's usefulness for them. For students this may include beliefs that the course will be useful for them immediately in some way (e.g., help them cope with college), in their major (e.g., they need this information for upper level courses), or their career and life in general (e.g., this will help them somehow in graduate school). At a task level, student may perceive different course assignments (e.g., essay and multiple choice exams, term papers, lab activities, class discussion) as more or less useful and decide to become more or less cognitively engaged in the tasks. Lyndsay does try to see how the course material may be useful to her, even if she does not find it very interesting.

Although these three components of task value can be separated, conceptually, in our work at Michigan with the MSLQ they have tended to factor together into one scale, which we have labeled task value. In our work with college students, task value is positively related to self-reports of cognitive strategy use including elaboration, organizational, and metacognitive strategies (Pintrich, 1999; Pintrich and Garcia, 1991; 1993). In these studies, task value accounted for between 3% to 36% of the variance in these different measures of cognitive engagement and self-regulation (C in Figure 1 predicts self-regulation process D). In addition, task value also was positively related to performance in these studies, albeit much less strongly. The general strength of the relation between task value and self-regulation was weaker than the relation between self-efficacy and self-regulation, but the positive association was still statistically reliable across studies. In other words, students who valued the course believed it was important to them and who were interested in the course material were more likely to be cognitive engaged and self-regulating as well as achieving at higher levels. These findings lead us to the next generalization.

Generalization 3 – *Higher levels of task value are associated with adaptive cognitive outcomes, such as higher levels of self-regulatory strategy use as well as higher levels of achievement.* This generalization may not be surprising, but it is important to formulate because constructs like value, utility, and interest are often considered to be unrelated to cognitive outcomes or achievement, and to be important non-cognitive outcomes. It is of course important to foster value, utility, and interest as outcomes in their own right, but the generalization suggests that by facilitating the development of task value in the college classroom, an important byproduct will be more cognitive engagement, self-regulation, and achievement (C predicts both E outcomes in Figure 1 and self-regulation processes, D). For example, the use of materials (e.g., tasks, texts, articles, chapter) that are meaningful and interesting to college students can foster increased levels of task value. In addition, class activities (demonstrations, small group activities) that are useful, interesting, and meaningful to college students will facilitate the development of task value beliefs.

AFFECTIVE COMPONENTS

Affective components include students' emotional reactions to the task and their performance (i.e., anxiety, pride, shame) and their more emotional needs in terms of self-worth or self-esteem, affiliation, self-actualization (cf., Covington and Beery, 1976; Veroff and Veroff, 1980). Affective components address the basic question, how does the task make me feel? There is considerably less research on the affective components, except for student anxiety.

Anxiety. There is a long history of research on test anxiety and its general negative relationship to academic performance (Covington, 1992; Zeidner, 1998). Test anxiety is one of the most consistent

779

individual difference variables that can be linked to detrimental performance in achievement situations (Hill and Wigfield, 1984). The basic model assumes that test anxiety is a negative reaction to a testing situation that includes both a "cognitive" worry component and a more emotional response (Liebert and Morris, 1967). The worry component consists of negative thoughts about performance while taking the exam (e.g., "I can't do this problem. That means I'm going to flunk; what will I do then?") which interfere with the students' ability to actually activate the appropriate knowledge and skills to do well on the test. These "self-perturbing ideations" (Bandura, 1986) can build up over the course of the exam and spiral out of control as time elapses, which then creates more anxiety about finishing in time. The emotional component involves more visceral reactions (e.g., sweaty palms, upset stomach) that also can interfere with performance.

In our own research program, we have examined the role of the worry component of test anxiety in the college classroom. Our results generally show a small relation between student's responses on the MSLQ items on test anxiety and their reports of strategy use, such as rehearsal, elaboration, or organizational strategies (correlations are in the range of .03 to .15, but include both low negative and low positive correlations). For metacognitive strategies, the correlations again are low (.07 to .17), but in the negative direction (Pintrich and Garcia, 1993; Pintrich et al., 1993). Given that there may be curvilinear relations between test anxiety and these cognitive and self-regulatory processes, the linear correlation estimates may not adequately capture the nature of the relations.

Zeidner (1998), in his review of the research on test anxiety and information processing, notes that anxiety generally has a detrimental effect on all phases of cognitive processing (see Figure 2).F2 In the planning and encoding phase, people experiencing high levels of anxiety have difficulty attending to and encoding appropriate information about the task. In terms of actual cognitive processes while doing the task, high levels of anxiety lead to less concentration on the task, difficulties in the efficient use of working memory, more superficial processing and less in-depth processing, and problems in using metacognitive regulatory processes to control learning (Zeidner, 1998). Of course, these difficulties in cognitive processing and self-regulation will usually result in less learning and lower levels of performance.

In summary, test anxiety is generally not adaptive and gives us **Generalization 4** – *High levels of test anxiety are generally not adaptive* *and usually lead to less adaptive cognitive processing, self-regulation and lower levels of achievement.*

This generalization is based on a great deal of both experimental and correlational work as reviewed by Zeidner (1998). Of course, Zeidner (1998) notes that there may be occasions when some aspects of anxiety lead to some facilitating effects for learning and performance. For example, Garcia and Pintrich (1994) have suggested that some students, called defensive pessimists (Norem and Cantor, 1986), can use their anxiety about doing poorly to motivate themselves to try harder and study more, leading to better achievement. The harnessing of anxiety for motivational purposes is one example of a self-regulating motivational strategy that students might use to regulate their learning.

Nevertheless, in the case of test anxiety, which is specific to testing situations, the generalization still holds that students who are very anxious about doing well do have more difficulties in cognitive processing and do not learn or perform as well as might be expected. One implication is that faculty need to be aware of the role of test anxiety in reducing performance and should try to reduce the potential debilitating effects in their own classroom.

Other affective reactions. Besides anxiety, other affective reactions can influence choice and persistence behavior. Weiner (1986), in his attributional analysis of emotion, has suggested that certain types of emotions (e.g., anger, pity, shame, pride, guilt) are dependent on the types of attributions individuals make for their successes and failures. For example, this research suggests that an instructor will tend to feel pity for a student who did poorly on a exam because of some uncontrollable reason (e.g., death in family) and would be more likely to help that student in the future. In contrast, a instructor is more likely to feel anger at a student who did poorly through a simple lack of effort and be less willing to help that student in the future. In general, an attributional analysis of motivation and emotion repeatedly has been shown to be helpful in understanding achievement dynamics (Weiner, 1986) and there is a need for much more research on these other affective reactions in the college classroom.

Emotional needs. The issue of an individual's emotional needs (e.g., need for affiliation, power, self-worth, self-esteem, self-actualization) is related to the motivational construct of goal orientation, although the needs component is assumed to be less cognitive, more affective and, perhaps, less accessible to the individual. Many models of emotional needs have been proposed (e.g., Veroff and Veroff, 1980; Wlodkowski, 1988), but the need for self-worth or self-esteem seems particularly relevant. Research on student learning shows that self-esteem or sense of self-worth has often been implicated in models of school performance (e.g., Covington, 1992; Covington and Beery, 1976). Covington (1992) has suggested that individuals are always motivated to establish, maintain, and promote a positive self-image. Given that this hedonic bias is assumed to be operating at all times, individuals may develop a variety of coping strategies to maintain self-worth but, at the same time, these coping strategies may actually be self-defeating.

Covington and his colleagues (e.g., Covington, 1984; Covington and Beery, 1976; Covington and Omelich, 1979a,b) have documented how several of these strategies can have debilitating effects on student performance. Many of these poor coping strategies hinge on the role of effort and the fact that effort can be a double-edged sword (Covington and Omelich, 1979a). Students who try harder will increase the probability of their success, but also increase their risk of having to make an ability attribution for failure, followed by a drop in expectancy for success and self-worth (Covington, 1992).

There are several classic failure-avoiding tactics that demonstrate the power of the motive to maintain a sense of self-worth. One strategy is to choose easy tasks. As Covington (1992) notes, individuals may choose tasks that insure success although the tasks do not really test the individuals' actual skill level. College students may choose this strategy by continually electing "easy" courses or deciding upon "easy" majors. A second failure-avoiding strategy involves procrastination. For example, a college student who does not prepare for a test because of lack of time can, if successful, attribute it to superior aptitude. On the other hand, this type of procrastination maintains an individual's sense of self-worth because, if it is not successful, the student can attribute the failure to lack of study time, not poor skill. Of course, this type of effort-avoiding strategy increases the probability of failure over time which will result in lowered perceptions of self-worth, so it is ultimately self-defeating.

In summary, although less researched, affective components can influence students' motivated behavior. Moreover, as the analysis of the self-worth motive shows (Covington, 1992), the affective components can interact with other more cognitive motivational beliefs (i.e., attributions) as well as self-regulatory strategies (management of effort) to influence achievement. However, we do not offer any generalizations for these components given that they have not been subject to the same level of empirical testing as the other motivational components.

THE ROLE OF PERSONAL CHARACTERISTICS (A)

There are many different personal characteristics that college students bring with them to the college classroom. Of course, there are important personality differences (e.g., the Big Five personality traits) or more trait-like differences in implicit motives such as the need for achievement (Snow et al., 1996). In this chapter, due to space considerations, we will note just three of the main personal differences — age, gender, and ethnicity (see A in Figure 1). These personal characteristics can have a major effect on the motivational and self-regulatory processes as well as outcomes as indexed by mean level differences in these variables. At the same time, and perhaps more importantly, these personal characteristics may moderate the relations between motivation (C in Figure 1) and outcomes (E in Figure 1), or motivation and self-regulation (D), or self-regulation (D) and outcomes (E).

AGE

Generally stated, important age-developmental differences in motivational beliefs and self-regulatory processes develop over the course of the life-span (Eccles, Wigfield, & Schiefele, 1998; Pintrich and Schunk, 1996). The overall trend is in line with general developmental assumptions that both motivational and self-regulatory processes become more differentiated with age and that individuals become more capable of self-regulation with age. Most of the work that has explicitly focused on developmental differences has been concerned with age-related changes that occur before college, particularly in elementary and secondary school-age samples. The research with college students has not been explicitly developmental and has rarely used longitudinal designs that are needed to estimate developmental changes over the course of college, rather than simple cross-sectional designs.

In our own work on college student motivation, we have used relatively homogeneous samples with age ranges between 17 and 25, not a large span, for examining developmental differences. Moreover, we have not used longitudinal designs but have focused on student motivation within specific college classroom contexts, which of course change over the years in college. However, within our studies, we have collected short-term longitudinal data within a course for a semester or over a year-long course (e.g., two-semester calculus course, two-semester chemistry course). These designs have used two or three waves of data collection on student motivation, providing some estimates of how student motivation changes over the length of a course.

In all of our studies that have used multiple waves of data, the results have been fairly consistent, with various motivational beliefs decreasing over the course of the semester or year. Average levels of self-efficacy and task value, in particular, show reliable drops over time within a course. This may be expected as, at the beginning of the course, most students may have relatively high perceptions of self-efficacy, but as the course progresses and they receive feedback on their work, and there is the inevitable distribution of grades, then some students will lower their efficacy perceptions, resulting in a lower overall average. In the same manner, task value may be somewhat higher at the beginning of a course, as students report that they are interested in the course material and think that it will be important and useful to them. However, as the course progresses, some of the students come to find that some of the material is less than interesting, important, or useful to them. These students then rate the course lower and the overall average for the course decreases.

The results for use of self-regulatory strategies have been less consistent in our research, but given their generally positive relation with motivational beliefs, they would be expected to decrease as well within a course, over a semester. On the other hand, as students develop expertise in the use of self-regulatory strategies in the college context, one could expect that they would become more proficient in the used of various self-regulatory strategies. First year college students often may not even know very much about the different self-regulatory strategies that are available to them (e.g., Mike's case) or, even if they are able to use some self-regulatory strategies (e.g., Lyndsay's case), they still have to adjust and adapt their use to the college context. Accordingly, over the course of a four- or five-year college career, students will become more adept at self-regulating their cognition, motivation, behavior, and their context.

Of course, as we have worked with college faculty in our research, they generally find these decreases in motivation over the semester discouraging, and to some extent the drops in motivation are disappointing. However, it is important to recall that these are average decreases over all students, and that, given the variance in ratings, there are also some students who report increases in their motivation over time. Accordingly, it seems more important to consider the potential role of age as a moderator of the relations between motivation and self-regulation, rather than the average mean level differences that occur as a function of age. This also reminds us of the importance of aptitude-treatment interactions (ATIs) in which different students perceive, react to, and learn differentially in different college classroom contexts. That is, some students might be motivated in a classroom context that is structured a certain way or involves a certain type of material, while other students in the exact same course are less motivated and may even be bored by it. As in our two examples, both Lyndsay and Mike were bored by some of their classes, but it is likely that other students found those classes very interesting.

In terms of age as a moderator, within the age range of the traditional 17- to 25-year-old college student, it is unlikely that there will be many differences in the relations between motivation and self-regulation as a function of age. However, there is a need for research on potential age moderators effects, even within this traditional college group. More importantly, if one considers non-traditional college students who are over 25, then there may some important moderating effects. For example, these non-traditional students may have much higher levels of task value for their school work (C in Figure 1), be more focused on learning and not grades (C in Figure 1), and be much more willing to engage in the important types of self-regulatory activities (D, in Figure 1) focused on academic tasks, given they may be less distracted by other social activities in comparison to more traditionally-aged college students. In this case, the second and third generalizations regarding mastery goals and task value may not be as strong for these older students, essentially because there is little variance in mastery goals or task value in older college students. In the same manner, self-efficacy may not work in line with the first generalization given that older college students may be less confident of their academic skills, yet still self-regulate quite well. Research is needed on these types of moderator effects of age with diverse samples.

In summary, age may be an important personal characteristic that can change the nature of the student motivation and self-regulation in college classrooms. Certainly, students who have been in college longer and are older, even if they are within the traditional 17- to 25-year-old group, should be able to self-regulate better than new college students. To some extent, third and fourth year college students who are still enrolled in college have learned "the game" and have a repertoire of self-regulatory strategies that they can use to adapt to college demands. New college students often have to learn how to adapt their "high school" cognitive strategies and regulation processes to fit the increased demands in college (as is the case for both Mike and Lyndsay). Moreover, there are many high school students who have been "other-regulated" by parents or high school teachers and now find they have to self-regulate in the absence of these supports. There will be an age-related developmental progression in how students learn to cope and self-regulate their cognition, motivation, and behavior as they enter and progress through college. In addition, research is needed on the potential moderator effects of non-traditional aged college students on the general relations proposed between motivation and self-regulation.

GENDER

Researchers have contended for many years that males and females possess varied academic strengths, that males and females differ in mathematical and verbal skills and that these different capabilities, in turn, partially account for the disparities in achievement levels between the sexes in certain academic domains (Maccoby and Jacklin, 1974). While such views are still pervasive in popular culture, recent research on gender differences in academic achievement and motivation would suggest otherwise.

First, the explanation concerning varied cognitive abilities between males and females has been called into question. There is very little evidence to support the notion that males and females possess different academic aptitudes. Researchers generally have found no gender differences in mathematical and verbal abilities. Moreover, when they did find differences, as in the case of spatial ability, they found that the differences were limited to specific types of tasks — in this case, mental rotation (Linn and Petersen, 1985).

Second, the statement that a gender-related achievement gap exists is apparently no longer accurate. Recent meta-analytic reviews of the research in this area have reported minimal, if any, gender differences in academic achievement (Hyde, Fennema, and Lamon, 1990; Linn and Hyde, 1989). Studies examining gender differences in mathematics generally discredit the notion of male superiority in mathematics. In fact, in some cases, females were found to outperform males on tests of mathematical ability (cf., Eisenberg, Martin, and Fabes, 1996). Similar findings were found in other academic domains. Hyde and Linn (1988), for example, maintain that sex-related differences in language competence, if they ever truly existed, certainly no longer exist.

This is not to say, however, that there are absolutely no gender-related differences. While there may be no variation between males and females in actual achievement levels, there are certainly differences in other outcome variables, namely choice and persistence (E in Figure 1). The percentage of females who choose to pursue natural science and/or mathematics majors in college, although increasing, is still modest at best, particularly in the fields of physical science and engineering. Moreover, while females comprise approximately half of the graduates who receive baccalaureates in life sciences and mathematics, less than one-fifth of all doctoral degrees in these fields are awarded to women (Rayman and Brett, 1995). Accordingly, women remain severely underrepresented in the fields of science, engineering, and mathematics.

The interesting question, of course, is why? If it is the case that women and men obtain comparable achievement test scores, then why do not more women pursue careers in science and mathematics? Motivational theorists generally explain this finding in terms of self-efficacy theory. Researchers have found that females generally have lower perceptions of competence (i.e., self-efficacy) than males in subjects such as mathematics and science, even when their actual performance is just as high, if not higher, than males' (Eccles, 1983; Meece and Eccles, 1993). That is, females are generally less confident that they can perform well on mathematics and science tasks. Researchers have also found that such disparities in self-efficacy levels are not limited to adolescents and college-aged women; gender related differences in self-efficacy beliefs have been found even among early elementary age girls (Entwisle and Baker, 1983; Frey and Ruble, 1987; Phillips and Zimmerman, 1990). Thus, it is believed that females' low self-perceptions of their competence influences, or rather deters them their pursuit of science-related career trajectories. After all, why would any student pursue a career in an area where she believed that she did not have the competence to learn or to do well in the academic domains related to that career?

Nevertheless, such findings should not imply that nothing can be done to counter this female fatalism. Lenney (1977), for example, suggests that this gender difference in self-efficacy levels may be influenced by certain contextual variables. In his review of the research, he concluded that variables such as the provision of clear and objective evaluative feedback, the sex-typing of academic tasks, and the emphasis on social comparison moderate the gender difference in self-confidence levels. In addition, some researchers have posited that perhaps the mean level differences in students' ratings of their efficacy beliefs are really a manifestation of response bias. Investigators believe that males have a tendency to over-inflate their ratings of confidence levels while females have a tendency toward modesty (Pajares and Graham, 1999; Wigfield, Eccles, MacIver, Reuman, and Midgley, 1991).

In addition to the research on self-efficacy beliefs, there is some limited evidence to suggest that females show comparatively lower levels of other components of motivation (C in Figure 1) than males. The research on attributions, for example, suggests that girls have a tendency to make maladaptive attributions. Numerous studies have demonstrated that females display decreased achievement strivings, especially under failure conditions, and often blame themselves (i.e., make internal causal attributions) for poor academic performance (in our two cases, Mike shows this debilitating pattern more than Lyndsay does). Even in situations where they are successful, researchers have found that females more often attribute their success to external and/or unstable causes. In contrast, males generally have been found to make more adaptive attributions, often attributing their performance to lack of effort or bad luck and even showing improvements in performance after failure (Dweck and Reppucci, 1973; Meece, Parsons, Kaczala, Goff, and Futterman, 1982). At the same time, however, Eccles and her colleagues caution against making such generalizations about the attributional styles of males and females, as studies often employed different methodologies when measuring attributions. Correspondingly, more recent research findings contradict the claim that females make maladaptive attributions. Roberts (1991), for instance, found that women in her study on gender differences in responsiveness to evaluations were not more self-disparaging in response to negative feedback.

Thus, the research on gender differences in motivational beliefs to date has proved somewhat inconclusive, with the possible exception that females generally tend to have lower self-perceptions of their academic ability. The research examining differences by gender of students' self-regulatory processes (D, in Figure 1) has been even more inconsistent. First, there are very few studies on self-regulation that have specifically sought to test whether these processes vary by gender. Additionally, what few studies that do exist on this topic have focused on students in middle school grades or younger (Ablard and Lipschultz, 1998; Anderman and Young, 1994; Nolen, 1988; Zimmerman and Martinez-Pons, 1990). At present, we do not know of any study that has found conclusive evidence that gender differences exist in college students' self-regulated learning. Even in our own studies at Michigan, although we have at times found mean level differences, these differences were never consistent across studies and we believe were not indicative of any systematic pattern. Of those studies that focused on younger pre-collegiate students, however, researchers generally have found mixed results. Some researchers report that females display higher levels of self-regulated learning (e.g., Zimmerman and Martinez-Pons, 1990) while others contend that females are no more likely than males to self-regulate their learning (e.g., Meece and Jones, 1996). Clearly, more research is needed before definitive conclusions can be drawn about how gender might possibly moderate the relations between motivational and self-regulatory processes and the various outcome measures. On the other hand, if one were to speculate based on the stereotype that girls are more diligent note-takers and generally more studious, it would not be entirely unreasonable to expect females to display more self-regulatory behavior than males.

ETHNICITY

Despite having emerged primarily from research on White, middle-class youths, most current models of psychology generally make assumptions about the applicability of psychological research and generalizations to students from various cultures, contexts, and ethnicities. The models of self-regulation and motivation are certainly no exception. Unfortunately, however, very little research has been done to test these assumptions. The dearth of studies examining ethnic differences in students' motivational (C, in Figure 1) and self-regulatory processes (D, in Figure 1) is especially troublesome as the need for such research is quite apparent. As the ethnic minority enrollment continues to increase on college campuses across the country, college instructors are constantly confronted with issues concerning how to teach these students better. Consequently, it is imperative that our models of learning and motivation address potential variation according to ethnicity.

Similar to the research on gender differences, studies examining group differences in motivation and self-regulated learning generally address the following two questions. First, are there mean level differences across various ethnic groups in their levels of academic performance, motivation, and self-regulated learning? Second, do the relations between these various constructs differ across minority group students? That is, do we need to modify our general models of self-regulated learning and motivation to accommodate ethnic differences? Or, can we conclude that our models can be generalized more or less and that the constructs operate similarly among the various ethnic groups?

In terms of the first question, pronounced ethnic differences in mean achievement levels (E in Figure 1) have been found. In comparison to students from other ethnic minority groups and, in certain cases, Caucasian students, Asian American students have attained a relatively high level of academic success. Not only do they outperform other minority students on standardized test measures, the percentage of Asian American students who continue on to post-secondary education is greater than either African American or Hispanic students (Hsia and Peng, 1998). In contrast, researchers have found that African American and Hispanic students display the lowest levels of academic achievement and performance (e.g., Graham, 1994).

Motivational theorists have largely accounted for these disparities in achievement levels by suggesting that a) Asian American students have higher levels of achievement motivation and that b) African Americans, in contrast, are generally amotivated toward academic goals. As Graham (1994) points out in her review of African American achievement motivation, traditional research on this subpopulation intimated that African American students' low achievement levels can be attributed not to deficits in cognitive abilities, but rather their low expectations for future success as well as their low academic self-concept. The exact opposite has been said for Asian Americans. Researchers on Asian-Americans have suggested that these students are more likely to make effort attributions, to believe in the importance of education, as well as have high expectations for academic success (Hess, Chang, and McDevitt, 1987; Holloway, Kashiwagi, Hess, and Azuma, 1986; Stevenson and Lee, 1990).

However, recent research on both of these populations suggest that such explanations are too simplistic. Graham (1994), for example, found no evidence that African Americans display lower expectancies for success, nor did she find support for the notion that African American students have lower concepts of their academic ability. In fact, she states that the vast majority of studies report African American students to have higher expectations for success as well as higher self-concept beliefs. Similarly, the research on Asian Americans has also proved to be somewhat inconclusive. Studies on causal attributions have found that Asian Americans are prone to make internal and stable attributions especially in the face of failure which, according to attribution theory, should make one more susceptible toward learned helplessness and should not, by any means, lead to increased achievement levels. The research examining Asian-American self-efficacy beliefs has been equally troublesome. Numerous researchers have documented Asians and Asian American students' comparatively lower levels of self-efficacy and self-concepts of ability, even though their actual achievement test scores were often higher than non-Asians (Eaton and Dembo, 1997; Stigler, Smith, and Mao, 1985; Whang and Hancock, 1994).

Such findings bring us to our second question regarding how widely we can generalize our model to other populations. These studies certainly suggest that specific motivational constructs, like attributions and self-efficacy (C, in Figure 1), might not operate in a similar fashion for Asian American and African American students. More specifically, these findings imply that the magnitude of the relationships between these motivational variables and outcomes (E, in Figure 1) may not be as great for these two ethnic groups as it may be for Caucasian students. For example, the relationship between self-efficacy and achievement for both Asian American and African American students seems to be an inverse one, albeit in different directions. African American students have higher perceptions of their competence yet lower achievement test scores. Asian-American students, on the hand, have lower perceptions of their competence and higher achievement levels. In both cases, researchers have attempted to explain this discrepancy in terms of task value beliefs. Numerous researchers (e.g., Steele, 1997; Fordam and Ogbu, 1986; Graham, Taylor, and Hudley, 1998) suggest that in the case of African-American students, repeated school failures have led these students to devalue education and therefore self-efficacy beliefs do not come into play as much as it does for other students. In a similar fashion, Eaton and Dembo (1997) have proposed that Asian American students focus less on their situational perceptions of competence (i.e., self-efficacy) and more on the importance of successfully completing an academic task (i.e. value).

Another plausible explanation for this discrepancy is calibration — that is, the extent to which students' ratings of their motivational beliefs accurately reflect their true level of motivation. Similar to the research on gender differences in self-efficacy beliefs, there is evidence to suggest that African-Americans generally over-estimate their ability to perform an academic task while Asian-Americans may underestimate their ability. Given our model of self-regulation, which relies on monitoring of cognition and performance for regulatory efforts, if students are not calibrated then they will be less likely to seek to regulate and repair their cognition or behavior. More concretely, if some college students, such as African Americans, believe they are doing well and yet are not achieving at the appropriate level, they may be less likely to attempt to regulate their behavior. These students would not put forth more effort to change their cognition or behavior in order to improve their performance. In the long run, this lack of calibration, monitoring, and regulation would lead to lowered levels of performance and achievement.

In addition to the above research, a select group of researchers has proposed alternative models that focus more on the influence of social factors on the relations between the various motivational constructs. Steele and his colleagues, for example, have demonstrated how stereo-types can have deleterious effects on African American college students' academic achievement (Steele and Aronson, 1995; Steele, 1997). Steele's model rests on the notion of stereotype threat: he argues that in any evaluative situation, as a result of widespread negative stereotypes about the academic competence of African Americans, these students confront the threat of potentially being judged according to the stereotype as well as the threat of possibly fulfilling the stereotype. He further contends that this threat can interfere with students' cognitive processes, thus resulting in lower achievement levels. In support, Steele found in his series of empirical studies with college students that African American students indeed performed relatively poorly in comparison to a matched sample of European American college students, when they were told that a test was diagnostic of their true academic capabilities (Steele and Aronson, 1995).

In addition, the recent work of Shih and her colleagues extends the stereotype vulnerability framework by not only applying the model to another cultural group, but also by examining the potential effects of "positive" stereotypes on subsequent achievement. Interest-ingly, their research findings suggest that the mere activation of a "positive" stereotype (i.e., Asian Americans possess superior mathe-matical abilities) can serve to heighten Asian American college students scores on standardized measures of mathematics achievement (Shih, Pittinsky, and Ambady, 1999).

Finally, in terms of ethnic differences in self-regulated learning variables, there are very few studies that have examined how the process of self-regulated learning might be moderated by ethnicity. In terms of strategy use, however, there is some evidence to suggest that Asian-Americans have a tendency to employ what researchers have called surface-processing strategies when studying (i.e., memorization and rehearsal), rather than deep-processing strategies like metacognitive strategies (Marton, Dall'Alba, and Kun, 1996). However, such claims run counter to the assertion that the use of deep-processing strategies should lead to the highest levels of achievement.

In summary, there are potential age, gender, and ethnicity differences in both mean levels of motivation (C) and self-regulation (D), and more importantly potential moderator effects of these personal characteristics on the relations between motivation and self-regulation. There is a clear need for much more research on how these personal characteristics facilitate the development of motivation and self-regulation. In addition, it is important to consider how these personal characteristics might conditionalize the four generalizations offered in this chapter. At this point, it seems that these four generalizations can be taken as applying to all groups of college students, but there is a need for much more research on how age, gender, or ethnic differences may change the nature of these generalizations.

THE ROLE OF CLASSROOM CONTEXTUAL FACTORS (B)

A multitude of classroom contextual factors (B in Figure 1) may influence student motivation (C) and self-regulation (D) in the college classroom. However, four general factors can have a dramatic effect in these two areas: the nature of the task, the reward and goal structure of the classroom, the instructional methods, and the instructor's behavior. At the same time, there is not as much empirical research on how these classroom contextual factors (B) may influence student motivation (C) and self-regulation (D). One limitation of the model of motivation and self-regulation presented in this chapter is that it tends to concentrate on the individual college student, and not give enough consideration to how the context can situate motivation and self-regulation. There is a clear need for more research on how different aspects of the college classroom influence college student motivation and learning. Accordingly, this section on classroom contextual factors is not as detailed as the previous sections, but it does provide a sketch of potential relations and many directions for future research efforts.

NATURE OF ACADEMIC TASKS

Classroom research on teaching often focuses on what the instructor says and does in class and how that can have an influence on student motivation. However, the types of tasks that students are asked to complete also can have a dramatic influence. The academic tasks that students confront in the college classroom include multiple choice and essay exams, library research papers, expository essay papers, solution of problem sets, performing and writing up results from experiments, reading a text and discussing it in class, and other variations on assignments and assessment tasks. It has become an important assumption of research in cognitive psychology (cf., Brown, Bransford, Ferrara, and Campione, 1983; Crooks, 1988; Doyle, 1983) that the features of these different tasks (B in Figure 1) help to organize and guide students' cognition (D). For example, multiple choice tests that require only recognition of the course material often do not lead to deeper levels of cognitive processing in comparison to essay exams that require not only recall of information but also transformation of the information. In the same fashion, features of the academic tasks (B) may influence student motivation (C).

Two important components of tasks are content and product (Blumenfeld, Mergendoller, and Swarthout, 1987). Content refers to the actual course content that is embedded in the task. For example, two courses could cover the same basic material and concepts, but in one class students read secondary sources (e.g., a standard textbook) and in the other course they read primary sources (e.g., original writings in the field). The nature of these two types of readings could influence motivation in several ways. First, the primary source material may be written in a more engaging style and be more interesting to students, thereby fostering personal interest on the part of students which could lead to more motivated behavior (Garner, Brown, Sanders, and Menke, 1992). On the other hand, the primary source material may be much more difficult for students to read in contrast to the standard textbook, which could result in lower self-efficacy perceptions for understanding the course material and less-motivated behavior. This simple example suggests that how the content is structured and organized in terms of both its difficulty level and interest can influence student motivation.

The product dimension of academic tasks involves what the students actually have to produce to complete the assignment or task. For example, tasks where students have some choice over what they do (e.g., choosing topics for research papers, choice of essays on exams) may foster higher control beliefs because students actually do have some personal control over the assignment. Of course, the difficulty level of the cognitive activities that students must carry out to complete the product can influence students' self-efficacy beliefs and interest levels. A too difficult task may elicit low self-efficacy beliefs and high anxiety, a too easy task may engender feelings of boredom, not interest. Accordingly, the key is to develop tasks that are within the range of most students' capabilities, but are still challenging to them (Pintrich and Schunk, 1996). Other features of exams (type of questions, time allowed to complete it) can increase test anxiety and have detrimental features on motivated behavior. Although these examples follow from theoretical predictions, there is very little empirical research on the role of academic tasks in college classrooms and there is a need for more research on tasks and their links to student motivation and cognition.

REWARD AND GOAL STRUCTURES

The academic tasks that students confront in college classrooms are embedded in a larger classroom context that includes the overall reward and goal structures of the classroom. Reward structure refers to how "rewards" (i.e., grades) are distributed among students. The goal structure refers to how the different tasks are designed to be accomplished by the students (e.g., alone, cooperatively). These two structures may be related to one another in practice, but theoretically they can be orthogonal (Good and Brophy, 1987). Reward structures can be independent (grades are assigned based only on an individual's performance in relation to some standard or criteria, not on other students' performance), cooperative (grades are linked to other students' performance because a group of students have done a project or paper together and they all get the same grade for the one product), or competitive (grading on some type of curve where grades are assigned based on a "zero-sum game" which limits the number of high grades, where higher scores by some students automatically mean other students receive lower grades). Some research suggests that competitive reward structures have a detrimental influence on students' motivation by increasing anxiety and lowering students' self-efficacy and self-worth beliefs (Ames, 1992; Covington, 1992; Johnson and Johnson, 1974; Slavin, 1983).

However, research on the use of rewards in general, not just in competitive structures, has become very controversial again. There have been meta-analyses by Cameron and Pierce (1994) and Eisenberger and Cameron (1996, 1998) that suggest that rewards have few detrimental effects. In contrast, Deci, Koestner, and Ryan (1999), in another meta-analysis that re-analyzed the same studies, suggest that rewards can have detrimental effects on students' intrinsic motivation.

The controversy has spawned a new edited book (Sansone and Harack-iewicz, 2000) where various authors discuss the issues related to the use of rewards and their effects on student motivation and learning. The issues are complicated and it does not appear that any simple generalization like "rewards are good/rewards are bad" can be made, based on the research, although rewards that convey information to students about their capabilities seem to foster positive outcomes (Pintrich & Schunk, 1996). It is more important to note that activities and their accompanying rewards can have multiple effects on both the intrinsic and extrinsic motivation of students and that future research should attempt to understand the relations between contextual factors like rewards and both college student motivational and cognitive processes.

In terms of the goal structure of the classroom, again the structure can be individualistic, cooperative, or competitive in terms of how students are organized to accomplish the tasks. Most college classrooms are probably individualistic, where students basically work by themselves to master and understand the material. There may be occasions when college students are asked to cooperate formally (lab partners, writing groups, or formal study groups). Of course, students often cooperate informally in studying for exams. Students also may compete with one another in class discussion, competing for the floor and the presenting of ideas in the discussion. The evidence is overwhelmingly in favor of having students work together cooperatively to accomplish the tasks, because of increased self-efficacy and interest, lower anxiety, more cognitive engagement, and generally better performance (Ames, 1984, 1992; Covington, 1992; Slavin, 1983). Of course not all tasks can be done in a cooperative manner, but the evidence suggests that, if possible, instructors should provide opportunities in class for cooperative work or encourage students to work together outside class. It also should be noted that some of the research suggests that the most beneficial arrangement is to have students work together on the task (a cooperative goal structure), but to maintain an individualized reward structure where individual students are held accountable for their own work. For example, students may study together for a test, but they all are graded independently. Even more important, the research (Pintrich & Schunk, 1996) suggests that if students are put into groups to work together on a project (cooperative goal structure), they should still be required to produce a separate write-up or paper that is then graded independently (individualized reward structure). This allows students to work together, but still requires individual accountability which helps avoids the problem of "free riders" (students who do not contribute to the group).

INSTRUCTIONAL METHODS AND INSTRUCTOR BEHAVIOR

The general instructional methods that can be used in the college classroom (e.g., lectures, discussions, recitations, lab activities, simulations, etc.) may influence student motivation (see McKeachie, 1986; Perry, 1991), but research seems to be moving beyond simple comparisons of the relative effectiveness of these different methods, to focus on how the "quality" of these methods influences different cognitive and motivational processes and in turn how these processes mediate achievement (Murray, 1991; Perry, 1991). For example, it may be that student-centered discussions generally promote more student involvement and motivation than lectures (McKeachie, 1986), but it seems clear that lectures that are delivered in an interesting and stimulating manner can also increase student motivation. The key to understanding the relative effects of these different instructional strategies is to begin to examine how they may influence different components of students' motivational beliefs. Discussion methods do allow students more "control" over the class in terms of the pace and the "content" presented and therefore might be expected to facilitate motivation by increasing students' control beliefs. On the other hand, interesting and stimulating lectures could facilitate motivation by activating students' situational and personal interest in the subject. Accordingly, a consideration of the different components of motivation and how they might be related to different features of the classroom context suggests that there may be multiple pathways to the same general goal of facilitating student motivation. The instructional methods set the context and constraints that allow for more or fewer opportunities for certain motivating events to occur, but the actual occurrence of these events is a function of the instructor and the students' behaviors.

This general focus on the quality and process of the actual instructional context highlights the importance of instructor behavior. It seems clear that the ways in which the different instructional methods are used and implemented by the instructor can have dramatic effects on student motivation. For example, if small cooperative groups are used and implemented in the classroom in an unstructured, disorganized, "anything goes" manner, it is likely that not only actual student learning will suffer, but student motivation in terms of interest and selfefficacy will be diminished. Moreover, research on different instructor characteristics (e.g., clarity, organization, enthusiasm, rapport, expressiveness, etc.) has shown that these features are related to students' ratings as well as their actual learning, cognition, and motivation (see Feldman, 1989; Murray, 1991, Perry, 1991). For example, Perry and Penner (1990) found that instructor expressiveness (physical movement, eye contact, voice inflection and humor) had a positive influence on students' learning and motivation. Moreover, instructor expressiveness interacted with the control beliefs of students with expressiveness showing a larger effect for external locus of control students. There is still much research to be done, but this type of research that attempts to link different features of instructor behavior to different cognitive and motivational outcomes will have the most benefit for our understanding of college teaching and learning.

At the same time, the research will have to take into consideration that these instructor behaviors are embedded in classroom context that includes different task, goal, and reward structures as well as different instructional methods which may moderate the direct effects of instructor behaviors. Clearly, what will emerge from this type of research is a much more complex picture of how the classroom context can influence student motivation (see McKeachie, 1990), but it also will be a much more realistic view that eschews simplistic answers and "pat" solutions to the problems of teaching and student motivation.

CONCLUSION

Student motivation and self-regulation both have important roles to play in college student learning and achievement. The four generalizations offered in this chapter serve as good first principles for understanding how student motivation can facilitate or constrain self-regulated learning and achievement in the college classroom. Students who feel efficacious about their ability to learn and to do the work are more likely to be engaged and to do better. Likewise, students who are focused on learning, mastery, and self-improvement are more likely to be involved in learning and perform better. Finally, a third facilitating factor of engagement and achievement is task value with students who think the material is interesting, important, and useful more likely to be engaged and learning. A constraining factor on engagement and learning is test anxiety with higher levels of test anxiety interfering or impeding cognitive engagement, learning, and achievement.

These generalizations seem to apply to all groups of students, but there is a clear need for more research on how different personal characteristics may moderate or delimit how these four principles can be generalized. Finally, classroom context factors can certainly influence student motivation and cognition. Moreover, the classroom context factors discussed here are inherently open to manipulation and change, offering hope to faculty members who want to make improvements in their classrooms and in the nature of their instruction to facilitate student motivation and learning. Much research remains to be done, but the general model offered here should provide a conceptual framework for future research as well as practice.

REFERENCES

Ablard, K.E., and Lipschultz, R.E. (1998). Self-regulated learning in high achieving students: Relations to advanced reasoning, achievement goals, and gender. *Journal of Educational Psychology* 90(1): 94–101.

Abramson, L., Seligman, M., and Teasdale, J. (1978). Learned helplessness in humans: A critique and reformulation. *Journal of Abnormal Psychology* 87: 49–74.

Ajzen, I. (1988). *Attitudes, Personality, and Behavior*. Chicago: Dorsey Press.

Ajzen, I. (1991). A theory of planned behavior. *Organizational Behavior and Human Decision Processes 50*: 179–211.

Alexander, P., Schallert, D., and Hare, V. (1991). Coming to terms: How researchers in learning and literacy talk about knowledge. *Review of Educational Research 61*: 315–343.

Ames, C. (1984). Competitive, cooperative, and individualistic goal structures: A cognitive-motivational analysis. In R. Ames and C. Ames (eds.). *Research on Motivation in Education* (Vol. 1, pp. 177–207). New York: Academic Press.

Ames, C. (1992). Classrooms: Goals, structures, and student motivation. *Journal of Educational Psychology 84*: 261–271.

Anderman, E., and Young, A. (1994). Motivation and strategy use in science: Individual differences and classroom effects. *Journal of Research in Science Teaching 31*: 811–831.

Bandura, A. (1982). Self-efficacy mechanisms in human agency. *American Psychologist 37*: 122–147.

Bandura, A. (1986). *Social Foundations of Thought and Action: A Social Cognitive Theory*. Engle-wood Cliffs, NJ: Prentice Hall.

Bandura, A. (1997). *Self-efficacy: The Exercise of Control*. New York: W.H. Freeman.

Baron, J. (1994). *Thinking and Deciding*. New York: Cambridge University Press.

Baumeister, R.F., and Scher, S.J. (1988). Self-defeating behavior patterns among normal individuals: Review and analysis of common self-destructive tendencies. *Psychological Bulletin 104*: 3–22.

Bereiter, C., and Scardamalia, M. (1987). *The Psychology of Written Composition*. Hillsdale, NJ: Lawrence Erlbaum Associates.

Berglas, S. (1985). Self-handicapping and self-handicappers: A cognitive/attributional model of interpersonal self-protective behavior. In R. Hogan and W.H. Jones (eds.), *Perspectives in Personality: Theory, Measurement, and Interpersonal Dynamics* (pp. 235–270). Greenwich, CT: JAI Press.

Blumenfeld, P., Pintrich, P.R., Meece, J., and Wessels, K. (1982). The formation and role of self-perceptions of ability in the elementary classroom. *Elementary School Journal 82*: 401–420.

Blumenfeld, P., Mergendoller, J., and Swarthout, D. (1987). Task as a heuristic for understanding student learning and motivation. *Journal of Curriculum Studies 19*: 135–148.

Boekaerts, M. (1993). Being concerned with well-being and with learning. *Educational Psychologist 28*: 148–167.

Boekaerts, M., and Niemivirta, M. (2000). Self-regulated learning: Finding a balance between learning goals and ego-protective goals. In M. Boekaerts, P.R. Pintrich, and M. Zeidner (eds.), *Handbook of Self-regulation: Theory, Research, and Applications*, (pp. 417–450). San Diego, CA: Academic Press.

Boekaerts, M., Pintrich, P.R., and Zeidner, M. (2000). *Handbook of Self-regulation*. San Diego, CA: Academic Press.

Brown, A.L. (1997). Transforming schools into communities of thinking and learning about serious matters. *American Psychologist* 52: 399–413.

Brown, A.L., Bransford, J.D., Ferrara, R.A., and Campione, J.C. (1983). Learning, remembering, and understanding. In J.H. Flavell and E.M. Markman (eds.), *Handbook of Child Psychology: Cognitive development* (Vol. 3, pp. 77–166). New York: Wiley.

Butler, D.L., and Winne, P.H. (1995). Feedback and self-regulated learning: A theoretical synthesis. *Review of Educational Research* 65: 245–281.

Cameron, J., and Pierce, W. (1994). Reinforcement, reward, and intrinsic motivation: A meta-analysis. *Review of Educational Research* 64: 363–423.

Connell, J.P. (1985). A new multidimensional measure of children's perceptions of control. *Child Development* 56: 1018–1041.

Corno, L. (1989). Self-regulated learning: A volitional analysis. In B.J. Zimmerman and D.H. Schunk, (eds.), *Self-regulated Learning and Academic Achievement: Theory, Research and Practice* (pp. 111–141). New York: Springer-Verlag.

Corno, L. (1993). The best-laid plans: Modern conceptions of volition and educational research. *Educational Researcher* 22: 14–22.

Covington, M.V. (1992). *Making the Grade: A Self-worth Perspective on Motivation and School Reform*. Cambridge: Cambridge University Press.

Covington, M. (1984). The motive for self-worth. In R. Ames and C. Ames (eds.), *Research on Motivation in Education* (Vol. 1, pp. 77–113). New York: Academic Press.

Covington, M., and Beery, R. (1976). *Self-worth and School Learning*. New York: Holt, Rinehart and Winston.

Covington, M.V., and Omelich, C.L. (1979a). Are causal attributions causal? A path analysis of the cognitive model of achievement motivation. *Journal of Personality and Social Psychology* 37: 1487–1504.

Covington, M.V., and Omelich, C.L. (1979b). Effort: The double-edged sword in school achievement. *Journal of Educational Psychology* 71: 169–182.

Crooks, T. (1988). The impact of classroom evaluation practices on students. *Review of Educational Research* 58: 438–481.

Deci, E.L. (1975). *Intrinsic Motivation*. New York: Plenum.

Deci, E.L. Koestner, R., and Ryan, R.M. (1999). A meta-analytic review of experiments examining the effects of extrinsic rewards on intrinsic motivation. *Psychological Bulletin* 125: 627–668.

Deci, E.L., and Ryan, R.M. (1985). *Intrinsic Motivation and Self-determination in Human Behavior*. New York: Plenum.

de Charms, R. (1968). *Personal Causation: The Internal Affective Determinants of Behavior*. New York: Academic Press.

Doyle, W. (1983). Academic work. *Review of Educational Research* 53: 159–199.

Dweck, C.S., and Elliott, E.S. (1983). Achievement motivation. In P.H. Mussen (Series Ed.,) and E.M. Hetherington (Vol. ed.) *Handbook of Child Psychology: Vol 4. Socialization, Personality, and Social Development*. (4th edition, pp. 643–691). New York: Wiley.

Dweck, C.S., and Leggett, E.L. (1988). A social-cognitive approach to motivation and personality. *Psychological Review* 95: 256–273.

Dweck, C., and Repucci, N. (1973). Learned helplessness and reinforcement responsibility in children. *Journal of Personality and Social Psychology 25*: 109–116.

Eaton, M.J., and Dembo, M.H. (1997). Differences in the motivational beliefs of Asian American and Non-Asian students. *Journal of Educational Psychology 89*(3): 433–440.

Eccles, J.S. (1983). Expectancies, values, and academic behaviors. In J.T. Spence (ed.), *Achievement and Achievement Motives* (pp. 75–146). San Francisco: Freeman.

Eccles, J.S., Wigfield, A., and Schiefele, U. (1998). Motivation to succeed. In W. Damon (Series Ed.,) and N. Eisenberg (Vol. ed.) *Handbook of Child Psychology: Vol 3. Social, Emotional, and Personality Development.* (5th edition, pp. 1017–1095). New York: Wiley.

Eisenberg, N., Martin, C.L., and Fabes, R.A. (1996). Gender development and gender effects. In D.C. Berliner and R.C. Calfee (eds.), *Handbook of Educational Psychology.* New York: Simon and Schuster Macmillan.

Eisenberger, R., and Cameron, J. (1996). Detrimental effects of reward: Reality or myth? *American Psychologist 51*: 1153–1166.

Eisenberger, R., and Cameron, J. (1998). Reward, intrinsic interest, and creativity: New findings, *American Psychologist 53*: 676–679.

Elliot, A.J. (1997). Integrating the "classic" and "contemporary" approaches to achievement motivation: A hierarchical model of approach and avoidance achievement motivation. In M.L. Maehr and P.R. Pintrich (eds.), *Advances in Motivation and Achievement.* (Vol. 10, pp. 143–179). Greenwich, CT: JAI Press.

Elliot, A.J., and Church, M. (1997). A hierarchical model of approach and avoidance achievement motivation. *Journal of Personality and Social Psychology 72*: 218–232.

Elliot, A.J., and Harackiewicz, J.M. (1996). Approach and avoidance achievement goals and intrinsic motivation: A mediational analysis. *Journal of Personality and Social Psychology 70*: 461–475.

Entwisle, D.R., and Baker, D.P. (1983). Gender and young children's expectations for performance in arithmetic. *Developmental Psychology 19*: 200–209.

Feldman, K. (1989). The association between student ratings of specific instructional dimensions and student achievement: Refining and extending the synthesis of data from multisection validity studies. *Research in Higher Education 30*: 583–645.

Fincham, F.D. and Cain, K.M. (1986). Learned helplessness in humans: A developmental analysis. *Developmental Review 6*: 301–333.

Findley, M., and Cooper, H. (1983). Locus of control and academic achievement: A review of the literature. *Journal of Personality and Social Psychology 44*: 419–427.

Fiske, S., and Taylor, S. (1991). *Social Cognition.* New York: McGraw-Hill.

Flavell, J.H. (1979). Metacognition and cognitive monitoring: A new area of cognitive-developmental inquiry. *American Psychologist 34*: 906–911.

Foersterling, F. (1985). Attributional retraining: A review. *Psychological Bulletin 98*: 495–512.

Ford, J.K., Smith, E.M., Weissbein, D.A., Gully, S.M., Salas, E. (1998). Relationships of goal orientation, metacognitive activity, and practice strategies with learning outcomes and transfer. *Journal of Applied Psychology 83*: 218–233.

Ford, M. (1992). *Motivating Humans: Goals, Emotions, and Personal Agency Beliefs.* Newbury Park, CA: Sage Publications.

Fordham, S., and Ogbu, J. (1986). Black students' school success: Coping with the burden of "acting white". *Urban Review 18*: 176–206.

Frey, K., and Ruble, D.N. (1987). What children say about classroom performance: Sex and grade differences in perceived competence. *Child Development* 58: 1066–1078.

Garcia, T., McCann, E., Turner, J., and Roska, L. (1998). Modeling the mediating role of volition in the learning process. *Contemporary Educational Psychology* 23: 392–418.

Garcia, T., and Pintrich, P.R. (1994). Regulating motivation and cognition in the classroom: The role of self-schemas and self-regulatory strategies. In D.H. Schunk and B.J. Zimmerman (eds.), *Self-regulation of Learning and Performance: Issues and Educational Applications* (pp. 127–153). Hillsdale, NJ: Lawrence Erlbaum Associates.

Garcia, T., and Pintrich, P.R. (1996). Assessing students' motivation and learning strategies in the classroom context: The Motivated Strategies for Learning Questionnaire. In M. Birenbaum (ed). *Alternatives in Assessment of Achievements, Learning Processes, and Prior Knowledge* (pp. 319–339). Boston, MA: Kluwer Academic Publishers.

Garner, R., Brown, R., Sanders, S., and Menke, D. (1992). "Seductive details" and learning from text. In K.A. Renninger, S. Hidi, and A, Krapp (eds.), *The Role of Interest in Learning and Development* (pp. 239–254). Hillsdale, NJ: Lawrence Erlbaum Associates.

Gollwitzer, P. (1996). The volitional benefits of planning. In P. Gollwitzer and J. Bargh (eds.), *The Psychology of Action: Linking Cognition and Motivation to Behavior* (pp. 287–312). New York: Guilford Press.

Good, T., and Brophy, J. (1987). *Looking in Classrooms.* New York: Harper and Row.

Graham, S. (1994). Motivation in African Americans. *Review of Educational Research* 64: 55–117.

Graham, S., Taylor, A., and Hudley, C. (1998). Exploring achievement values among ethnic minority early adolescents. *Journal of Educational Psychology* 90: 606–620.

Harackiewicz, J.M., Barron, K.E., and Elliot, A.J. (1998). Rethinking achievement goals: When are they adaptive for college students and why? *Educational Psychologist* 33: 1–21.

Harackiewicz, J.M., and Sansone, C. (1991). Goals and intrinsic motivation: You can get there from here. In M.L. Maehr and P.R. Pintrich (eds.), *Advances in Motivation and Achievement: Goals and Self-regulation* (Vol. 7, pp. 21–49). Greenwich, CT: JAI Press.

Harter, S. (1985). Competence as a dimension of self-evaluation: Toward a comprehensive model of self-worth. In R. Leary (ed.), *The Development of the Self* (pp. 95–121). New York: Academic Press.

Heckhausen, H. (1991). *Motivation and Action.* New York: Springer Verlag.

Hembree, R. (1988). Correlates, causes, effects and treatment of test anxiety. *Review of Educational Research* 58: 47–77.

Hess, R.D., Chang, C.M., and McDevitt, T.M. (1987). Cultural variations in family beliefs about children's performance in mathematics: Comparisons among People's Republic of China, Chinese-American, and Caucasian-American families. *Journal of Educational Psychology* 79(2): 179–188.

Hidi, S. (1990). Interest and its contribution as a mental resource for learning. *Review of Educational Research* 60: 549–571.

Hill, K., and Wigfield, A. (1984). Test anxiety: A major educational problem and what can be done about it. *Elementary School Journal* 85: 105–126.

Hofer, B., Yu, S., and Pintrich, P.R. (1998). Teaching college students to be self-regulated learners. In D.H. Schunk and B.J. Zimmerman (eds.), *Self-regulated Learning: From Teaching to Self-reflective Practice* (pp. 57–85). New York: Guilford Press.

Holloway, S.D., Kashiwagi, K., Hess, R.D., and Azuma, H. (1986). Causal attributions by Japanese and American mothers and children about performance in mathematics. *International Journal of Psychology* 21: 269–286.

Hsia, J., and Peng, S.S. (1998). Academic achievement and performance. In L. C. Lee and N. W. S. Zane (Eds.), *Handbook of Asian American Psychology*. Thousand Oaks: Sage.

Hyde, J.S., Fennema, E., and Lamon, S.J. (1990). Gender differences in mathematics performance: A meta-analysis. *Psychological Bulletin* 107: 139–155.

Hyde, J.S. and Linn, M.C. (1988). Gender differences in verbal ability: A meta-analysis. *Psychological Bulletin* 104: 53–69.

Johnson, D., and Johnson, R. Instructional goal structure: Cooperative, competitive, or individualistic. *Review of Educational Research* 44: 213–240.

Karabenick, S., and Knapp, J.R. (1991). Relationship of academic help seeking to the use of learning strategies and other instrumental achievement behavior in college students. *Journal of Educational Psychology* 83: 221–230.

Karabenick, S., and Sharma, R. (1994). Seeking academic assistance as a strategic learning resource. In P.R. Pintrich, D.R. Brown, and C.E. Weinstein (eds.), *Student Motivation, Cognition, and Learning: Essays in Honor of Wilbert J. McKeachie* (pp. 189–211). Hillsdale, NJ: Lawrence Erlbaum Associates.

Koriat, A., and Goldsmith, M. (1996). Monitoring and control processes in the strategic regulation of memory accuracy. *Psychological Review 103*: 490–517.

Krapp, A., Hidi, S., and Renninger, K.A. (1992). Interest, learning and development. In K.A. Renninger, S. Hidi, and A. Krapp (eds.), *The Role of Interest in Learning and Development* (pp. 3–25). Hillsdale, NJ: Lawrence Erlbaum Associates.

Kuhl, J. (1984). Volitional aspects of achievement motivation and learned helplessness: Toward a comprehensive theory of action control. In B. Maher and W. Maher (Eds.), *Progress in Experimental Personality Research*. (Vol. 13, pp. 99–171). New York: Academic Press.

Kuhl, J. (1985). Volitional mediators of cognition-behavior consistency: Self-regulatory processes and action versus state orientation. In J. Kuhl and J. Beckman (eds.), *Action Control: From Cognition to Behavior* (pp. 101–128). Berlin: Springer-Verlag.

Lefcourt, H. (1976). *Locus of Control: Current Trends in Theory Research*. Hillsdale, NJ: Erlbaum.

Lenney, E. (1975). Women's self-confidence in achievement settings. *Psychological Bulletin 84*: 1–13.

Liebert, R., and Morris, L. (1967). Cognitive and emotional components of test anxiety: A distinction and some initial data. *Psychological Reports 20*: 975–978.

Linn, M.C., and Hyde, J. S. (1989). Gender, mathematics, and science. *Educational Researcher 18*: 17–19, 22–27.

Linn, M.C., and Petersen, A.C. (1985). Emergence and characterization of sex differences in spatial ability: A meta-analysis. *Child Development 56*: 1479–1498.

Locke, E.A., and Latham, G.P. (1990). *A Theory of Goal Setting and Task Performance*. Engle-wood Cliffs, NJ: Prentice Hall.

Maccoby, E.E., and Jacklin, C.N. (1974). *The Psychology of Sex Differences*. Stanford, CA: Stanford University Press.

Maehr, M.L., and Midgley, C. (1991). Enhancing student motivation: A school-wide approach. *Educational Psychologist 26*: 399–427.

Malone, T., and Lepper, M. (1987). Making learning fun: A taxonomy of intrinsic motivations for learning. In R. Snow and M. Farr, (eds.), *Aptitude, Learning, and Instruction: Vol. 3. Cognitive and Affective Process Analyses* (pp. 223–253). Hillsdale, NJ: Erlbaum.

Marton, F., Dall'Alba, G., and Kun, T.L. (1996). Memorizing and understanding: The keys to a paradox? In D. Watkins and J. Biggs (eds.), *The Chinese Learner: Cultural, Psychological, and Contextual Influence*. Hong Kong: Comparative Education Research Centre, The Australian Council for Educational Research Ltd.

McKeachie, W.J. (1986). *Teaching Tips: A Guidebook for the Beginning College Teacher*. Lexington, MA: Heath.

McKeachie, W.J. (1990). Research on college teaching: The historical background. *Journal of Educational Psychology 82*: 189–200.

McKeachie, W.J., Pintrich, P.R., and Lin, Y.G. (1985). Teaching learning strategies. *Educational Psychologist 20*: 153–160.

Meece, J., Parsons, J., Kaczala, C., Goff, S., and Futterman, R. (1982). Sex differences in math achievement: Toward a model of academic choice. *Psychological Bulletin 91*: 324–348.

Meece., J., and Eccles, J. (1993). Introduction: Recent trends in research on gender and education. *Educational Psychologist 28*: 313–319.

Meece, J.L., and Jones, M.G. (1996). Gender differences in motivation and strategy use in science: Are girls rote learners? *Journal of Research in Science Teaching 33*(4): 393–406.

Midgley, C., Arunkumar, R., and Urdan, T. (1996). "If I don't do well tomorrow, there's a reason": Predictors of adolescents' use of academic self-handicapping strategies. *Journal of Educational Psychology 88*: 423–434.

Miller, G., Galanter, E., and Pribram, K. (1960). *Plans and the Structure of Behavior*. New York: Holt.

Murray, H. (1991). Effective teaching behaviors in the college classroom. In J. Smart (ed.), *Higher Education: Handbook of Theory and Research* (Vol. 7, pp. 135–172). New York: Agathon Press.

Nelson, T., and Narens, L. (1990). Metamemory: A theoretical framework and new findings. In G. Bower (ed.), *The Psychology of Learning and Motivation* (Vol. 26, pp. 125–141). New York: Academic Press.

Nelson-Le Gall, S. (1981). Help-seeking: An understudied problem solving skill in children. *Developmental Review 1*: 224–246.

Nelson-Le Gall, S. (1985). Help-seeking behavior in learning. *Review of Research in Education* (Vol. 12, pp. 55–90). Washington DC: American Educational Research Association.

Newman, R. (1991). Goals and self-regulated learning: What motivates children to seek academic help? In M.L. Maehr and P.R. Pintrich (eds.), *Advances in Motivation and Achievement: Goals and Self-regulatory Processes* (Vol. 7, pp. 151–183). Greenwich, CT: JAI Press.

Newman, R. (1994). Adaptive help-seeking: A strategy of self-regulated learning. In D.H. Schunk and B.J. Zimmerman (eds.), *Self-regulation of Learning and Performance:*

Issues and Educational Applications (pp. 283–301). Hillsdale, NJ: Lawrence Erlbaum Associates.

Newman, R. (1998a). Adaptive help-seeking: A role of social interaction in self-regulated learning. In S. Karabenick (ed.), *Strategic Help-seeking: Implications for Learning and Teaching* (pp. 13–37). Hillsdale, NJ: Lawrence Erlbaum Associates.

Newman, R. (1998b). Students' help-seeking during problem solving: Influences of personal and contextual goals. *Journal of Educational Psychology 90*: 644–658.

Nicholls, J. (1984). Achievement motivation: Conceptions of ability, subjective experience, task choice, and performance. *Psychological Review 91*: 328–346.

Nisbett, R. (1993). *Rules for Reasoning*. Hillsdale, NJ: Lawrence Erlbaum Associates.

Nolen, S.B. (1988). Reasons for studying: Motivational orientations and study strategies. *Cognition and Instruction 5*: 269–287.

Norem, J.K., and Cantor, N. (1986). Defensive pessimism: Harnessing anxiety as motivation. *Journal of Personality and Social Psychology 51*: 1208–1217.

Pajares, F., and Graham, L. (1999). Self-efficacy, motivation constructs, and mathematics performance of entering middle school students. *Contemporary Educational Psychology 24*: 124–139.

Paris, S.G., Lipson, M.Y., and Wixson K.K. (1983). Becoming a strategic reader. *Contemporary Educational Psychology 8*: 293–316.

Pascarella, E., and Terenzini, P. (1991). *How College Affects Students*. San Francisco, CA: Jossey-Bass.

Perry, R. (1991). Perceived control in college students: Implications for instruction in higher education. In J. Smart (ed.), *Higher Education: Handbook of Theory and Research* (Vol. 7, pp. 1–56). New York: Agathon Press.

Perry, R., and Dickens, W. (1988). Perceived control and instruction in the college classroom: Some implications for student achievement. *Research in Higher Education 27*: 291–310.

Perry, R., and Magnusson, J-L. (1989). Causal attributions and perceived performance: Consequences for college students' achievement and perceived control in different instructional conditions. *Journal of Educational Psychology 81*: 164–172.

Perry, P., and Penner, K. (1990). Enhancing academic achievement in college students through attributional retraining and instruction. *Journal of Educational Psychology 82*: 262–271.

Peterson, C., Maier, S., and Seligman, M. (1993). *Learned Helplessness: A Theory for the Age of Personal Control*. New York: Oxford University Press.

Phillips, D., and Zimmerman, B.J. (1990). The developmental course of perceived competence and incompetence among competent children. In R. Sternberg and J. Kolligian (eds.), *Competence Considered*. New Haven, CT: Yale University Press.

Pintrich, P.R. (1988a). A process-oriented view of student motivation and cognition. In J.S. Stark and L. Mets (eds.). *Improving Teaching and Learning Through Research*. Vol. 57. *New directions for institutional research* (pp. 55–70). San Francisco: Jossey-Bass.

Pintrich, P.R. (1988b). Student learning and college teaching. In R.E. Young and K.E. Eble (eds.), *College Teaching and Learning: Preparing for New Commitments*. Vol. 33. *New Directions for Teaching and Learning* (pp. 71–86). San Francisco: Jossey-Bass.

Pintrich, P.R. (1989). The dynamic interplay of student motivation and cognition in the college classroom. In C. Ames and M.L. Maehr (eds.), *Advances in Motivation and*

Achievement: Motivation-Enhancing Environments (Vol. 6, pp. 117–160). Greenwich, CT: JAI Press.

Pintrich, P.R. (1994). Student motivation in the college classroom. In K. Prichard and R.M. Sawyer (eds.), *Handbook of College Teaching: Theory and Applications* (pp. 23–43). Westport, CT: Greenwood Press.

Pintrich, P.R. (1999). The role of motivation in promoting and sustaining self-regulated learning. *International Journal of Educational Research 31*: 459–470.

Pintrich, P.R. (2000a). An achievement goal theory perspective on issues in motivation terminology, theory, and research. *Contemporary Educational Psychology 25*: 92–104.

Pintrich, P.R. (2000b). Multiple goals, multiple pathways: The role of goal orientation in learning and achievement. *Journal of Educational Psychology 92*: 544–555.

Pintrich. P.R. (2000c). The role of goal orientation in self-regulated learning. In M. Boekaerts, P.R. Pintrich, and M. Zeidner (eds.), *Handbook of Self-regulation: Theory, Research, and Applications* (pp. 451–502). San Diego, CA: Academic Press.

Pintrich, P.R., and De Groot, E.V. (1990). Motivational and self-regulated learning components of classroom academic performance. *Journal of Educational Psychology 82*: 33–40.

Pintrich, P.R., and Garcia, T. (1991). Student goal orientation and self-regulation in the college classroom. In M.L. Maehr and P.R. Pintrich (eds.), *Advances in Motivation and Achievement: Goals and Self-regulatory Processes* (Vol. 7, pp. 371–402). Greenwich, CT: JAI Press.

Pintrich, P.R., and Garcia, T. (1993). Intraindividual differences in students' motivation and self-regulated learning. *Zeitschrift fur Padagogische Psychologie 7*: 99–187.

Pintrich, P.R., Marx, R., and Boyle, R. (1993). Beyond cold conceptual change: The role of motivational beliefs and classroom contextual factors in the process of conceptual change. *Review of Educational Research 63*(2): 167–199.

Pintrich, P.R., McKeachie, W., and Lin, Y-G. (1987). Teaching a course in learning to learn. *Teaching of Psychology 14*: 81–86.

Pintrich, P.R., Smith, D., Garcia, T., and McKeachie, W. (1993). Predictive validity and reliability of the Motivated Strategies for Learning Questionnaire (MSLQ). *Educational and Psychological Measurement 53*: 801–813.

Pintrich, P.R., and Schrauben, B. (1992). Students' motivational beliefs and their cognitive engagement in classroom tasks. In D. Schunk and J. Meece (eds.), *Student Perceptions in the Classroom: Causes and Consequences* (pp. 149–183). Hillsdale, NJ: Erlbaum.

Pintrich, P.R., and Schunk, D.H. (1996). *Motivation in Education: Theory, Research and Applications*. Englewood Cliffs, NJ: Prentice Hall Merrill.

Pintrich, P.R., Wolters, C., and Baxter, G. (2000). Assessing metacognition and self-regulated learning. In G. Schraw and J. Impara (eds.). *Issues in the Measurement of Metacognition*. Lincoln, NE: Buros Institute of Mental Measurements.

Pressley, M., and Afflerbach, P. (1995). *Verbal Protocols of Reading: The Nature of Constructively Responsive Reading*. Hillsdale, NJ: Lawrence Erlbaum Associates.

Pressley, M., and Woloshyn, V. (1995). *Cognitive Strategy Instruction that Really Improves Children's Academic Performance*. Cambridge, MA: Brookline Books.

Rayman, P., and Brett, B. (1995). Women science majors: What makes a difference in persistence after graduation? *The Journal of Higher Education 66*(4): 388–415.

Renninger, K.A., Hidi, S., and Krapp, A. (1992). *The Role of Interest in Learning and Development*. Hillsdale, NJ: Erlbaum.

Roberts, T.-A. (1991). Gender and the influence of evaluations on self-assessments in achievement settings. *Psychological Bulletin* 109(2): 297–308.

Rotter, J. B. (1966). Generalized expectancies for internal versus external control reinforcement. *Psychological Monographs 80*: 1–28.

Ryan, A., and Pintrich, P.R. (1997). "Should I ask for help?" The role of motivation and attitudes in adolescents' help seeking in math class. *Journal of Educational Psychology* 89: 329–341.

Sansone, C., and Harackiewicz, J. (2000). *Intrinsic and Extrinsic Motivation: The Search for Optimal Motivation and Performance.* San Diego, CA: Academic Press.

Sansone, C., Weir, C., Harpster, L., and Morgan, C. (1992). Once a boring task, always a boring task? The role of interest as a self-regulatory mechanism. *Journal of Personality and Social Psychology 63*: 379–390.

Schiefele, U. (1991). Interest, learning, and motivation. *Educational Psychologist 26*: 299–323.

Schneider, W., and Pressley, M. (1997). *Memory Development between 2 and 20.* Mahwah, NJ: Lawrence Erlbaum Associates.

Schoenfeld, A. (1992). Learning to think mathematically: Problem solving, metacognition, and sense making in mathematics. In D. Grouws (ed.), *Handbook of Research on Mathematics Teaching and Learning* (pp. 334–370). New York: Macmillan.

Schraw, G., and Moshman, D. (1995). Metacognitive theories. *Educational Psychology Review 7*: 351–371.

Schunk, D. (1985). Self-efficacy and school learning. *Psychology in the Schools 22*: 208–223.

Schunk, D.H. (1989). Social cognitive theory and self-regulated learning. In B.J. Zimmerman and D.H. Schunk (eds.), *Self-regulated Learning and Academic Achievement: Theory, Research, and Practice* (pp. 83–110). New York: Springer-Verlag.

Schunk, D.H. (1991). Self-efficacy and academic motivation. *Educational Psychologist* 26: 207–231.

Schunk, D.H. (1994). Self-regulation of self-efficacy and attributions in academic settings. In D. H. Schunk and B. J. Zimmerman (eds.), *Self-regulation of Learning and Performance: Issues and Educational Applications* (pp. 75–99). Hillsdale, NJ: Lawrence Erlbaum Associates.

Shih, M., Pittinsky, T.L., and Ambady, N. (1999). Stereotype susceptibility: Identity salience and shifts in quantitative performance. *Psychological Science 10*(1): 80–83.

Simpson, M., Hynd, C., Nist, S., and Burrell, K. (1997). College academic assistance programs and practices. *Educational Psychology Review 9*: 39–87.

Slavin, R. (1983). *Cooperative Learning.* New York: Longman.

Snow, R., Corno, L., and Jackson, D. (1996). Individual differences in affective and conative functions. In D. Berliner and R. Calfee (eds.), *Handbook of Educational Psychology* (pp. 243–310). New York: Macmillan.

Steele, C.M. (1988). The psychology of self-affirmation: Sustaining the integrity of the self. *Advances in Experimental Social Psychology 21*: 261–302.

Steele, C.M. (1997). A threat in the air: How stereotypes shape intellectual identity and performance. *American Psychologist 52*: 613–629.

Steele, C. M., and Aronson, J. (1995). Stereotype threat and the intellectual test performance of African Americans. *Journal of Personality and Social Psychology* 69(5): 797–811.

Sternberg, R. (1985). *Beyond IQ: A Triarchic Theory of Intelligence.* New York: Cambridge University Press.

Stevenson, H. W., and Lee, S.-Y. (1990). *Contexts of Achievement* (Vol. 55). Chicago: The University of Chicago Press.

Stigler, J. W., Smith, S., and Mao, L.-W. (1985). The self-perception of competence by Chinese children. *Child Development* 56: 1259–1270.

Stipek, D., and Weisz, J. (1981). Perceived personal control and academic achievement. *Review of Educational Research* 51: 101–137.

Tryon, G. (1980). The measurement and treatment of test anxiety. *Review of Educational Research* 50: 343–372.

Urdan, T. (1997). Achievement goal theory: Past results, future directions. In M.L. Maehr and P.R. Pintrich (eds.), *Advances in Motivation and Achievement* (Vol. 10, pp. 99–141). Greenwich, CT: JAI Press.

VanderStoep, S. W., Pintrich, P.R., and Fagerlin, A. (1996). Disciplinary differences in self-regulated learning in college students. *Contemporary Educational Psychology* 21: 345–362.

Veroff, J., and Veroff, J.B. (1980). *Social Incentives: A Life-span Developmental Approach.* New York: Academic Press.

Weiner, B. (1986). *An Attributional Theory of Motivation and Emotion.* New York: Springer-Verlag.

Weiner, B. (1992). *Human Motivation: Metaphors, Theories, and Research.* Newbury Park, CA: Sage Publications.

Weiner, B. (1995). *Judgments of Responsibility: A Foundation for a Theory of Social Conduct.* New York: Guilford Press.

Weinstein, C.E., and Mayer, R. (1986). The teaching of learning strategies. In M. Wittrock (ed.) *Handbook of Research on Teaching and Learning* (pp. 315–327). New York: Macmillan.

Whang, P.A., and Hancock, G.R. (1994). Motivation and mathematics achievement: Comparisons between Asian-American and Non-Asian students. *Contemporary Educational Psychology* 19: 302–322.

Wigfield, A. (1994). Expectancy-value theory of achievement motivation: A developmental perspective. *Educational Psychology Review* 6 49–78.

Wigfield, A., and Eccles, J. (1989). Test anxiety in elementary and secondary school students. *Educational Psychologist* 24: 159–183.

Wigfield, A., and Eccles, J. (1992). The development of achievement task values: A theoretical analysis. *Developmental Review* 12: 265–310.

Wigfield, A., Eccles, J., MacIver, D., Reuman, D., and Midgley, C. (1991). Transitions during early adolescence: Changes in children's domain-specific self-perceptions and general self-esteem across the transition to junior high school. *Developmental Psychology* 27: 552–565.

Wlodkowski, R. (1988). *Enhancing Adult Motivation to Learn.* San Francisco: Jossey-Bass.

Wolters, C. (1998). Self-regulated learning and college students' regulation of motivation. *Journal of Educational Psychology* 90:224–235.

Wolters, C., Yu, S., and Pintrich, P.R. (1996). The relation between goal orientation and students' motivational beliefs and self-regulated learning. *Learning and Individual Differences* 8: 211–238.

Zeidner, M. (1998). *Test Anxiety: The State of the Art.* New York: Plenum.

809

Zimmerman, B.J. (1986). Development of self-regulated learning: Which are the key sub-processes? *Contemporary Educational Psychology 16*: 307–313.

Zimmerman, B.J. (1989). A social cognitive view of self-regulated learning and academic learning. *Journal of Educational Psychology* 81(3): 329–339.

Zimmerman, B.J. (1990). Self-regulated learning and academic achievement: An over-view. *Educational Psychologist 25*: 3–17.

Zimmerman, B.J. (1994). Dimensions of academic self-regulation: A conceptual frame-work for education. In D.H. Schunk and B.J. Zimmerman (eds.), *Self-regulation of Learning and Performance: Issues and Educational Applications* (pp. 3–21). Hillsdale, NJ: Lawrence Erlbaum Associates.

Zimmerman, B.J. (1998a). Academic studying and the development of personal skill: A self-regulatory perspective. *Educational Psychologist 33*: 73–86.

Zimmerman, B.J. (1998b). Developing self-fulfilling cycles of academic regulation: An analysis of exemplary instructional models. In D.H. Schunk and B.J. Zimmerman (eds.), *Self-regulated Learning: From Teaching to Self-reflective Practice* (pp. 1–19). New York: Guilford Press.

Zimmerman, B.J. (2000). Attaining self-regulation: A social cognitive perspective. In M. Boekaerts, P.R. Pintrich, and M. Zeidner (eds.), *Handbook of Self-regulation: Theory, Research, and Applications* (pp. 13–39). San Diego, CA: Academic Press.

Zimmerman, B.J., and Kitsantas, A. (1997). Developmental phases in self-regulation: Shifting from process to outcome goals. *Journal of Educational Psychology 89*: 29–36.

Zimmerman, B.J., and Martinez-Pons, M. (1986). Development of a structured interview for assessing student use of self-regulated learning strategies. *American Educational Research Journal 23*: 614–628.

Zimmerman, B.J., and Martinez-Pons, M. (1988). Construct validation of a strategy model of student self-regulated learning. *Journal of Educational Psychology 80*(3): 284–290.

Zimmerman, B.J., and Martinez-Pons, M. (1990). Student differences in self-regulated learning: Relating grade, sex, and giftedness to self-efficacy and strategy use. *Journal of Educational Psychology 82*: 51–59.

Zimmerman, B.J., and Schunk, D. (1989). *Self-regulated Learning and Academic Achievement: Theory, Research, and Practice.* New York: Springer-Verlag.

Zukier, H. (1986). The paradigmatic and narrative modes in goal-guided inference. In R. M. Sorrentino and E.T. Higgins (eds.), *Handbook of Motivation and Cognition: Foundations of Social Behavior* (pp. 465–502). New York: The Guilford Press.

INDEX